theinclusiveclassroom

STRATEGIES FOR EFFECTIVE DIFFERENTIATED INSTRUCTION

theinclusiveclassroom

STRATEGIES FOR EFFECTIVE DIFFERENTIATED INSTRUCTION

fourth edition

Margo A. Mastropieri
George Mason University

Thomas E. Scruggs
George Mason University

Merrill
Upper Saddle River, New Jersey
Columbus, Ohio

Library of Congress Cataloging-in-Publication Data

Mastropieri, Margo A.

  The inclusive classroom: strategies for effective differentiated instruction / Margo A. Mastropieri, Thomas E. Scruggs.—
4th ed.

    p. cm.

  Includes bibliographical references and index.

  ISBN 978-0-13-500170-7 (alk. paper)

  1. Inclusive education—United States. 2. Mainstreaming in education—United States. 3. Classroom management—United
States. I. Scruggs, Thomas E. II. Title.

  LC1201.M37 2010

  371.9'046—dc22   2008052702

Vice President and Editor in Chief: Jeffery W. Johnston
Executive Editor: Ann Castel Davis
Senior Development Editor: Heather Doyle Fraser
Editorial Assistant: Penny Burleson
Senior Managing Editor: Pamela D. Bennett
Senior Project Manager: Linda Hillis Bayma
Project Coordinator: Norine Strang, S4Carlisle Publishing Services
Art Director: Candace Rowley
Photo Coordinator: Shea Davis
Text and Cover Design: Anne DeMarinis
Cover Photo: Chris Castle
Media Producer: Autumn Benson
Media Project Manager: Rebecca Norsic
Senior Operations Specialist: Matthew Ottenweller
Operations Specialist: Laura Messerly
Video President, Director of Sales and Marketing: Quinn Perkson
Marketing Manager: Erica DeLuca
Marketing Coordinator: Brian Mounts

This book was set in AGaramond by S4Carlisle Publishing Services. It was printed and bound by Hamilton Printing Company. The cover was printed by Lehigh Phoenix.

Photo Credits: Tony Freeman/PhotoEdit Inc., pp. 5, 118; Anthony Magnacca/Merrill, pp. 7, 43, 72, 87, 139, 143, 156, 158, 194, 205, 214, 227, 231, 262, 334, 404; Scott Cunningham/Merrill, pp. 8, 55, 165, 202, 213, 304, 313, 327, 332, 340; Jonathan Nourok/PhotoEdit Inc., p. 18 (top); Elizabeth Crews/Elizabeth Crews Photography, pp. 18 (bottom), 29, 40, 185, 189, 268; AP Wide World Photos, p. 21; Carl D. Walsh/Aurora Photos, Inc., p. 31; Cindy Charles/PhotoEdit Inc., p. 41; Mary Kate Denny/PhotoEdit Inc., pp. 47, 66, 161; Brian Vikander/The Stock Connection, p. 52; David Young-Wolff/PhotoEdit Inc., pp. 56, 135, 210, 233, 277, 350, 357; Paul Conklin/PhotoEdit Inc., pp. 59, 64; Doug Martin/Merrill, p. 61; Myrleen Ferguson/PhotoEdit Inc., p. 79; Streissguth, A.P., Landesman-Dwyer, S., Martin, J.C., & Smith, D.W. (1980). Teratogenic effects of alcohol in humans and laboratory animals. "Science, 209", 353-361, p. 82; Courtesy of Compusult, p. 86; Michael Newman/PhotoEdit Inc., pp. 93, 203, 301; Larry Hamill/Merrill, p. 96; Photo courtesy of FrontRow sound systems, p. 98; Robin L. Sachs/PhotoEdit Inc., pp. 100, 252; Dennis MacDonald/PhotoEdit Inc., p. 104; Bob Daemmrich Photography, Inc., pp. 111, 283; Cynthia Cassidy/Merrill, p. 130; Will Hart/PhotoEdit Inc., pp. 131, 377; Todd Yarrington/Merrill, pp. 132, 326, 393; T. Lindfors/Lindfors Photography, p. 141; T. Hubbard/Merrill, p. 146; Patrick White/Merrill, p. 152; PhotoEdit Inc., p. 170; Brian Smith/Brian Smith, Photographer, p. 178; Kevin Radford/SuperStock, Inc., p. 181; Bill Bachmann/PhotoEdit Inc., p. 224; Richard Hutchings/PhotoEdit Inc., p. 234; Rhoda Sidney/PhotoEdit Inc., p. 371; © The Stock Market/Charles Gupton, p. 380.

Pearson® is a registered trademark of Pearson plc
Merrill® is a registered trademark of Pearson Education, Inc.

Pearson Education Ltd., London
Pearson Education Singapore, Pte. Ltd.
Pearson Education Canada, Inc.
Pearson Education—Japan
Pearson Education Australia PTY, Limited

Pearson Education North Asia, Ltd., Hong Kong
Pearson Educacíon de Mexico, S.A. de C.V.
Pearson Education Malaysia, Pte. Ltd.
Pearson Education Upper Saddle River, New Jersey

Merrill
is an imprint of

www.pearsonhighered.com

10 9 8 7 6 5 4 3 2 1
ISBN-13:   978-0-13-500170-7
ISBN-10:   0-13-500170-6

about the authors

MARGO A. MASTROPIERI, PH.D., is University Professor, Professor of Special Education, and past Coordinator of the Special Education Program, College of Education and Human Development, George Mason University. She has served as a Diagnostic-Remediator for the Learning Center at Mount Holyoke College, and as a classroom teacher for students with special needs, from preschool to secondary levels, in Massachusetts and Arizona. Prior to her present position, she served as Professor of Special Education at Purdue University, and Assistant Professor of Special Education at Utah State University, where she also worked as a researcher at the Early Intervention Research Institute. She earned her Ph.D. from Arizona State University. She has co-directed federally funded research projects in mnemonic strategy instruction, and inclusive science and social studies education, at the elementary, middle school, and high school levels, in addition to directing undergraduate, masters, and doctoral level training grants. From 1991 to 1997 she served as Co-Editor of *Learning Disabilities Research & Practice,* the journal of the Division for Learning Disabilities of the Council for Exceptional Children. She presently serves as Co-Editor of the research annual *Advances in Learning and Behavioral Disabilities* (Emerald). Among her publications are over 180 journal articles, 42 chapters in books, and 27 co-authored or co-edited books.

THOMAS E. SCRUGGS, PH.D., is University Professor, Professor of Special Education, and Director of the Ph.D. in Education Program, College of Education and Human Development, George Mason University. He served as a classroom teacher for students with special needs, including gifted students, from preschool to secondary levels in Massachusetts and Arizona. Prior to his present position, he served as Professor of Special Education at Purdue University, where he also had served as Director of the Purdue Achievement Center; and as a Research/Evaluation Specialist at Utah State University. He earned his Ph.D. from Arizona State University. He has directed or co-directed externally funded research projects in peer tutoring, test-taking skills, mnemonic strategy instruction, and inclusive science and social studies education, at the elementary, middle school, and high school levels. From 1991 to 1997 he served as Co-Editor of *Learning Disabilities Research & Practice,* the journal of the Division for Learning Disabilities of the Council for Exceptional Children. Since 1992, he has served as Co-Editor of the research annual *Advances in Learning and Behavioral Disabilities* (Emerald). Among his publications (mostly in collaboration with Margo Mastropieri) are over 190 journal articles, 44 chapters in books, and 28 co-authored or co-edited books.

Both authors are the recipients of the 2006 "CEC Special Education Research Award" for their efforts in working with and advocating on behalf of individuals with exceptionalities.

One of the major features that characterizes our classrooms today is student diversity. Not only have classrooms become more diverse with respect to race, religion, language, and ethnicity, but also more students with disabilities than ever are being included in general education classrooms. Data reported by the U.S. Department of Education indicate that nearly three-fourths of students with disabilities are now being served primarily within the general education classroom setting.

Unfortunately, today's teachers consistently report that they do not feel prepared to teach students with disabilities in their general education classrooms. Only about one-fourth believe that they possess skills necessary for effective inclusive teaching. We have written this book in order to place before teachers a wide variety of effective, research-based strategies that can be effectively applied in today's inclusive classrooms.

Text Philosophy

There are a number of high-quality textbooks on inclusive education available today. This in itself is a notable advance from just a few years ago, and indicates an increasing awareness of the important role of inclusive education in today's schools. We wrote *The Inclusive Classroom: Strategies for Effective Differentiated Instruction* to add our own perspective on inclusive education. We believe that teachers certainly should be provided with necessary information regarding legal issues and the characteristics of students with disabilities and other special needs. In addition, we describe a variety of practical teaching and learning strategies that are directly relevant to the tasks and academic demands required of teachers in inclusive classrooms in today's schools.

However, we do not believe that "inclusion strategies" can be effectively implemented in the absence of overall effective teaching skills. That is, we believe that effective overall teaching and classroom management skills are necessary prerequisites for working with students with disabilities who attend inclusive classrooms. Therefore, we have described inclusion strategies within the overall framework of effective instruction and management of general education classrooms. The organization of this book reflects our perspective.

TEXT ORGANIZATION

PART I: THE FUNDAMENTALS The first section of this book presents the fundamentals of inclusive teaching, including information on the history of special education, the legal and political background of legislation for individuals with disabilities, and relevant, practical information on the Individualized Education Program (IEP) and the changes brought about by the Individuals with Disabilities Education Improvement Act of 2004 (IDEA) and No Child Left Behind (NCLB). Chapter 2 provides specific information on strategies for consultation and collaboration with students, parents, and other school personnel, including special education teachers, paraprofessionals, and other specialized school personnel. Chapters 3 and 4 provide information on the various characteristics of specific disability areas identified in IDEA (as well as Attention Deficit Hyperactivity Disorder), the federal special education law, and general adaptations that can be made for each of these disability areas. Chapter 5 describes other special needs areas not specifically covered under IDEA, including students at-risk and students with special "gifts" and talents.

PART II: DEVELOPING EFFECTIVE TEACHING SKILLS The second section of this book describes a range of strategies that can be applied across curriculum areas and grade levels to address special needs and particular problems. Chapter 6 describes effective strategies for the general education teacher that have been demonstrated to be very helpful in promoting learning in inclusive settings. This chapter covers the variables most closely associated with student achievement, including engaged time-on-task, teacher questioning and feedback, and the most effective uses of praise, with specific reference to students with special needs. Chapter 7 describes behavior management strategies for entire classrooms as well as for individual students, and also describes strategies for improving social skills. Chapter 8 provides strategies for the effective uses of peers to help accommodate diversity in classroom learning and behavior, including peer assistance, peer tutoring, and cooperative learning. These strategies can be used to transform classrooms into effective collaborative learning environments.

Chapter 9 describes strategies for promoting motivation and affect—two very critical components of successful classrooms, and a very common cause of concern for classroom teachers. Chapter 10 describes strategies for enhancing attention and memory, for entire classrooms as well as for individual students with special needs. Chapter 11 discusses strategies for teaching study skills, including organizational strategies, highlighting and outlining skills, listening and note-taking skills, and research and reference skills. Finally, Chapter 12 describes assessment, and how adaptations can be made to accommodate the special needs of individual students as well as the classroom in general.

PART III: TEACHING IN THE CONTENT AREAS The third part of this book describes specific academic areas and strategies that can promote learning in these areas for a wide variety of students. Chapter 13 describes learning in basic literacy areas, including reading, writing, and spelling, and how special problems in learning in these areas can best be addressed. Chapter 14 presents effective strategies for promoting learning in mathematics. Chapter 15 covers science and social studies and provides specific strategies to enhance learning for a variety of special needs areas. Finally, Chapter 16 describes strategies to improve learning and address special problems in career and technical education, and for facilitating transitions to a number of different settings, including post-secondary, vocational, or community environments.

Changes to the Fourth Edition

For the fourth edition, we made a number of changes as a result of helpful suggestions from editors and reviewers that we believe have greatly improved the text. We have reorganized material, particularly in chapters 3, 6, and 16, to make the text more understandable and useful. We have also included more information relevant to secondary students, students with autism, response-to-intervention strategies, and communicating with families of students with disabilities. We have revised and refocused the Inclusion Checklists at the end of the chapters, to improve their utility. Specific strategies for improving classroom learning and behavior are systematically highlighted throughout the text. We updated Technology Highlights and other features throughout the text (see pages ix–xi). In addition, we have provided additional coverage and updated references to each chapter, to reflect the latest research and the changes brought about by recent legislation and the Individuals with Disabilities Education Improvement Act of 2004 (IDEA).

Practical and effective teaching and learning strategies

In writing the fourth edition, we wanted to emphasize the practical, research-based teaching and learning strategies essential in inclusive environments. For this reason, we focus on the basic tools educators need and directly relate this content to the academic and professional demands of teachers in inclusive settings.

Strategies Featured in the Text

Chapters 2 through 16 contain strategies that teachers can use in their inclusive classrooms with all students. The strategy sections are designated with a special design treatment to make them easy to find for the reader. Additionally, almost all of the strategy sections throughout the book are connected to MyEducationLab Activities and Application exercises or Building Teaching Skills and Dispositions assignments.

STRATEGIES FOR
COLLABORATING WITH PARAPROFESSIONALS

CLARIFY ROLES AND RESPONSIBILITIES Paraprofessionals may be aides to special education teachers, specialized aides for students with disabilities, or general aides for teachers within a school. Within those roles, paraprofessionals assume a variety of responsibilities, including recordkeeping, supervising, monitoring seatwork and classroom behavior, feeding

In the Classroom features offer tips, strategies, and resources that address very specific need areas, and may be used directly in classroom situations. These features include effective resource materials that can be practically applied in inclusive classrooms.

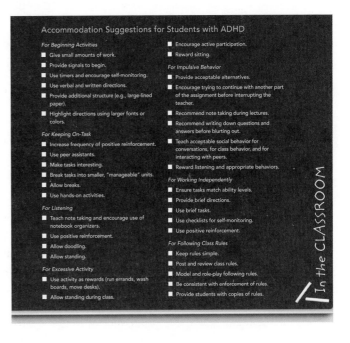

Classroom Scenarios provide context for the specific teaching strategies featured in the text. These cases model how to identify students who should be referred for special services or who would benefit from specific teaching strategies.

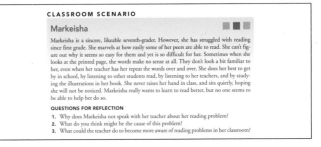

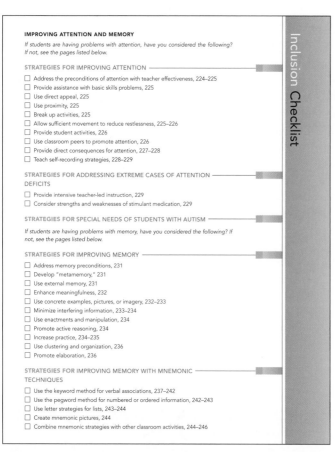

Inclusion Checklist

IMPROVING ATTENTION AND MEMORY

If students are having problems with attention, have you considered the following? If not, see the pages listed below.

STRATEGIES FOR IMPROVING ATTENTION

☐ Address the preconditions of attention with teacher effectiveness, 224–225
☐ Provide assistance with basic skills problems, 225
☐ Use direct appeal, 225
☐ Use proximity, 225
☐ Break up activities, 225
☐ Allow sufficient movement to reduce restlessness, 225–226
☐ Provide student activities, 226
☐ Use classroom peers to promote attention, 226
☐ Provide direct consequences for attention, 227–228
☐ Teach self-recording strategies, 228–229

STRATEGIES FOR ADDRESSING EXTREME CASES OF ATTENTION DEFICITS

☐ Provide intensive teacher-led instruction, 229
☐ Consider strengths and weaknesses of stimulant medication, 229

STRATEGIES FOR SPECIAL NEEDS OF STUDENTS WITH AUTISM

If students are having problems with memory, have you considered the following? If not, see the pages listed below.

STRATEGIES FOR IMPROVING MEMORY

☐ Address memory preconditions, 231
☐ Develop "metamemory," 231
☐ Use external memory, 231
☐ Enhance meaningfulness, 232
☐ Use concrete examples, pictures, or imagery, 232–233
☐ Minimize interfering information, 233–234
☐ Use enactments and manipulation, 234
☐ Promote active reasoning, 234
☐ Increase practice, 234–235
☐ Use clustering and organization, 236
☐ Promote elaboration, 236

STRATEGIES FOR IMPROVING MEMORY WITH MNEMONIC TECHNIQUES

☐ Use the keyword method for verbal associations, 237–242
☐ Use the pegword method for numbered or ordered information, 242–243
☐ Use letter strategies for lists, 243–244
☐ Create mnemonic pictures, 244
☐ Combine mnemonic strategies with other classroom activities, 244–246

Inclusion Checklists at the end of each chapter summarize the strategies described in the chapter and are helpful for finding immediate reference for specific strategies, pinpointing difficulties teachers might be having, or planning prereferral interventions. Teachers may wish to consider the suggestions contained in the appropriate checklists prior to referring students for special education services. For example, if a teacher is considering referring a student for special education based on observed problems with attention or memory, she could first consult the *Inclusion Checklist* in Chapter 10 for a list of possible interventions in these areas. In the fourth edition, the *Inclusion Checklists* are linked to specific page references in each chapter and many of the strategies referenced on the checklists are tied to MyEducationLab course content.

PEARSON myeducationlab

Go to MyEducationLab, select the topic *Autism Spectrum Disorders* and go to the Building Teaching Skills and Dispositions section. As you complete the activity entitled "Instructional Software," reflect on the direct instruction that is happening while using technology for instruction.

MyEducationLab Margin Notes Within every strategies section in chapters 2 through 16 you will find MyEducationLab margin notes that connect the content in the book with Activities and Application exercises or Building Teaching Skills and Dispositions assignments on the MyEducationLab course. Each activity or assignment features videos, simulations, case studies, or strategies that are explicitly tied to topics covered in the text.

Research and resources that support practice and professionalism

Research Highlights explain the research behind certain teaching strategies developed for use with students with special needs, provide resources for further information and explanation, and tie chapter content to the research with reflection questions. The descriptive nature of the *Research Highlights* allows readers to see the need to verify strategies teachers use to appropriately account for their use. In the fourth edition, each *Research Highlight* contains Questions for Reflection.

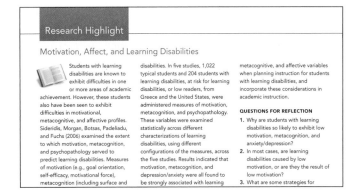

Diversity in the Classroom addresses the fact that classrooms are more diverse not only in respect to students with disabilities, but also with respect to race, gender, religion, language, and ethnicity.

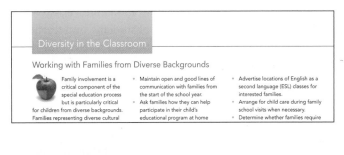

Technology Highlights provide information on technological applications relevant to the content of the chapter. These features provide up-to-date information on new technologies and how they can be employed to improve the academic or social functioning of students with special needs.

Professional Standards (including CEC, INTASC, and PRAXIS II™) are listed at the end of each chapter where relevant.

A Feature for Special Mention

The cover photo and the chapter-opening photos deserve special mention. They were taken by individuals who have disabilities and an abiding love for photography. The photos were obtained from the Disabled Photographers' Society, an organization that provides access to specialized equipment and technical support and assists with other aspects of amateur and professional photography. The cover photo, by Chris Castle, is titled *Oilseed Rape Field*.

The fourth edition has an enhanced instructor support package which includes MyEducationLab, an Online Instructor's Manual with Test Items, Online TestGen assessment software, and Online PowerPoint presentations.

PEARSON
myeducationlab

"Teacher educators who are developing pedagogies for the analysis of teaching and learning contend that analyzing teaching artifacts has three advantages: it enables new teachers time for reflection while still using the real materials of practice; it provides new teachers with experience thinking about and approaching the complexity of the classroom; and in some cases, it can help new teachers and teacher educators develop a shared understanding and common language about teaching . . . ."[1]

As Linda Darling-Hammond and her colleagues point out, grounding teacher education in real classrooms—among real teachers and students and among actual examples of students' and teachers' work—is an important, and perhaps even an essential, part of training teachers for the complexities of teaching today's students in today's classrooms. We have created a website that provides you and your students with the context of real classrooms and artifacts that research on teacher education tells us is so important. Through authentic in-class video footage, interactive skill-building exercises and more, MyEducationLab offers you and your students a uniquely valuable teacher education tool.

In *The Inclusive Classroom: Strategies for Effective Differentiated Instruction*, Fourth Edition, look for the MyEducationLab logo and directive within the margins in the strategies sections. Follow the directive and the simple navigation instructions to access the multimedia ***Activities and Applications*** exercises and ***Building Teaching Skills and Dispositions*** assignments in MyEducationLab that correspond with the chapter topics.

- **Activities and Applications:** These exercises offer opportunities to understand content more deeply and are explicitly connected to chapter topics. These exercises present thought-provoking questions that probe the students' understanding of the concept or strategy that is presented in the text through classroom video footage, simulations, strategies, or teacher and student artifacts.
- **Building Teaching Skills and Dispositions:** These application assignments help students practice and strengthen skills that are essential to quality teaching. Students watch authentic classroom video footage or interact with thought-provoking simulations and critically analyze how they can learn these skills and strategies and then hopefully incorporate them into their teaching repertoire or portfolio.

The rich, authentic, and interactive elements that support the Activities and Applications and the Building Teaching Skills and Dispositions assignments you will encounter throughout MyEducationLab include:

- **Video:** The authentic classroom videos in MyEducationLab show how real teachers handle actual classroom situations. Viewing videos and discussing and analyzing them not only deepens understanding of concepts presented in the

[1]Darling-Hammond, l., & Bransford, J.,Eds. (2005). *Preparing Teachers for a Changing World.* San Francisco: John Wiley & Sons.

book, but also builds skills in observing and analyzing children and class-rooms. Many of the students featured in the text are also featured in the video on MyEducationLab.

- **Simulations:** Created by the IRIS Center at Vanderbilt University, these interactive simulations give you hands-on practice at adapting instruction for a full spectrum of learners.
- **Student & Teacher Artifacts:** Authentic preK–12 student and teacher classroom artifacts are tied to course topics and offer you practice in working with the different materials you will encounter daily as teachers.
- **Case Studies:** A diverse set of robust cases illustrate the realities of teaching and offer valuable perspectives on common issues and challenges in education.
- **Strategies:** These teacher-tested, research-based strategies span grade levels pre-K–12 and all content areas.
- **Lesson & Portfolio Builders:** With this effective and easy-to-use tool, you can create, update, and share standards-based lesson plans and portfolios.

Visit www.myeducationlab.com *for a demonstration of this exciting new online teaching resource.*

ONLINE INSTRUCTOR'S MANUAL WITH TEST ITEMS AND TESTGEN SOFTWARE

All of the instructor supplements are available at the Instructor Resource Center. To access the manual, the PowerPoint lecture presentations, and the test bank and TestGen software (see below) go to the Instructor Resource Center at www.pearsonhighered.com and click on the "Educators" link. Here you will be able to login or complete a one-time registration for a user name and password.

The online Instructor's Manual includes numerous recommendations for presenting and extending text content. It is organized by chapter and contains chapter objectives, chapter summaries, key terms, presentation outlines, discussion questions, application and MyEducationLab activities, suggested readings and test items. The test item bank contains more than 800 questions. These multiple-choice, short answer, and essay questions can be used to assess students' recognition, recall, and synthesis of factual content and conceptual issues from each chapter.

The online TestGen is available in both Windows and Macintosh format, along with assessment software allowing professors to create and customize exams and track student progress.

ONLINE POWERPOINT LECTURE PRESENTATIONS

The transparencies—available in PowerPoint slide format on the Instructor Resources Center—highlight key concepts, summarize content, and provide a presentations outline for each chapter of the text.

Acknowledgments

There are many individuals who contributed to the production of this book and to whom we are indebted. For the fourth edition, we would like to thank our editor Ann Davis for her continuous support for the project, and Heather Doyle Fraser, Development Editor. We feel the fourth edition of this text has been greatly improved by their imaginative and helpful ideas, suggestions, and support. We also thank the technical editors and production staff at Pearson/Merrill and S4Carlisle Publishing Services.

The external reviewers also delivered much useful feedback and provided commentary on earlier versions of this book that were thoughtful, thorough, and professionally delivered. For the fourth edition, we would also like to thank Genevieve Howe Hay, *College of Charleston;* Kimberly King-Jupiter, *Auburn University;* Gary D. Jacobs, *Walsh University;* Kaye Ragland, *Pacific Oaks College;* and Laura Reissner, *Northern Michigan University* for their helpful feedback.

Most of all, we thank the numerous individuals with whom we have had contact throughout our lives who have taught us about individuals with disabilities and teaching. Also included in our thanks are numerous special education professionals, whose research and publications form the core of substance for this book, and without whose contributions this book would not be possible. Finally, we would like to thank our mothers, Dorothy Mastropieri and Janet Hunt Scruggs, who have provided us with a continual source of support; and the memory of our fathers, Francis Mastropieri and Edward Scruggs.

M. A. M.
T. E. S.

PART 1   THE FUNDAMENTALS

CHAPTER 1

Introduction to Inclusive Teaching 3

CHAPTER 2

Collaboration: Partnerships and Procedures 25

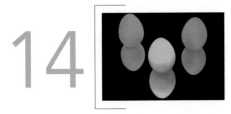

15

CHAPTER 15

Science and Social Studies 361

16

CHAPTER 16

Career and Technical Education, and Transitions 391

Note: Every effort has been made to provide accurate and current Internet information in this book. However, the Internet and information posted on it are constantly changing, so it is inevitable that some of the Internet addresses listed in this textbook will change.

1

Introduction to Inclusive Teaching

2

Collaboration: Partnerships and Procedures

3

Teaching Students with Higher-Incidence Disabilities

4

Teaching Students with Lower-Incidence Disabilities

5

Teaching Students with Other Special Learning Needs

Oilseed Rape Field

CHRIS CASTLE   Chris Castle, who has systemic lupus erythematosus (SLE), has been involved in photography for many years. SLE affects his mobility, requiring him to use a mobility scooter and also causes illness, weakness, and exhaustion, so it affects his photography a great deal. While he can no longer do the studio close-up floral work he once specialized in, he now is more diversified and finds much enjoyment in looking for new subjects for his photographs. He says, "There are a great many things in my life, not just photographically, that I would probably never have done if I didn't have SLE."

1

Introduction to Inclusive Teaching

OBJECTIVES

After studying this chapter, you should be able to:

- Understand federal laws protecting the educational services for students with disabilities.
- Analyze several important court cases relating to students with disabilities, presenting a progression of increasing rights for students with disabilities.
- Identify the disability categories served under IDEA (Individuals with Disabilities Education Act).
- Summarize and describe the legal foundations, litigation, and legislation concerning students with disabilities, such as IDEA, Section 504 (Vocational Rehabilitation Act), and ADA (Americans with Disabilities Act).
- Describe the continuum of services available to students with special needs and the "least-restrictive environment" concept.
- Compare and contrast the issues surrounding inclusive instruction for students with disabilities.

In 1975, Congress passed a law that would change the face of public education in the United States. This law, the Education for All Handicapped Children Act (now known as the Individuals with Disabilities Education Act, or IDEA) specified that all children—including those with disabilities formerly excluded from school—were entitled to a free, appropriate public education. This law went far beyond any previous legislation in specifying that, to the greatest extent possible, this "special" education was to be provided in the least restrictive environment. In other words, students with disabilities were to be educated to the greatest extent possible in the general education classroom. This book is dedicated to describing the means by which this "least restrictive environment" can become a reality.

The passage of IDEA, and its subsequent amendments, has largely achieved its purpose. More than ever, students with disabilities now receive free, appropriate public education. Furthermore, this education is being provided more often in the general education classroom.

Before the passage of IDEA, students with disabilities were often denied access to public education (Knowlton, 2004). In some cases, they were placed in institutions. In other cases, the parents were forced to pay for private schools, often in inappropriate settings. Today, all students with disabilities are legally entitled to a free, appropriate education suited to their needs. The following scenarios compare a case from many years ago with a similar case from today. As a result of IDEA and related legislation, society has an increased understanding of individuals with disabilities and is much better able to accommodate individual differences in schools, in workplaces, and in social settings.

Mr. and Mrs. Patterson

■ ■ ■

In 1960, Mr. and Mrs. Patterson had a brand-new baby girl, Hope. The initial excitement about the successful pregnancy and delivery was soon shrouded by a dark cloud. They were informed by the doctors that their precious infant was retarded. Mrs. Patterson tells their story:

"We felt horrible when the physician informed us that our beautiful baby girl was retarded. I can still hear his words: 'You probably don't want to keep her. The state institution is the best place for infants like her. The staff at the institution will be able to take care of her better than you.' I immediately hated the doctor. How could he be saying this to me about my brand-new baby girl? I felt as if I was having a nightmare and that at any moment I would awake and find that everything was okay.

"At first we were so angry and couldn't help thinking thoughts like: Why did this happen to us? We didn't do anything wrong; this is unfair! We looked for someone to blame. We blamed the doctors and the staff at the hospital. It must be their fault—it couldn't be ours! Then, gradually, we both felt so guilty. We racked our brains for things that we might have done incorrectly during pregnancy. Did I fall? Was I exposed to any harmful substances? We didn't know who to turn to for help. We felt overwhelmed and lost. The only individuals we knew we could speak with were the doctors and staff at the hospital, who had already expressed their opinions to us.

"We loved our baby and decided to keep her. She was very slow at developing. We were always searching for effective ways to help her. Everything was so hard. Each little thing we did seemed like an enormous journey. When Hope reached kindergarten age she had passed some important developmental milestones. We knew she wasn't developmentally the same as other children her age, but we hoped that she might begin to catch up once she was in school.

"Unfortunately, however, within the first week of kindergarten we were contacted by the school and asked to remove Hope from the school. We were told that she wasn't ready for school and that she took too much time away from the other children in the class. If we wanted Hope exposed to any educational program, the only solution available to us was to place Hope in the state institution's school.

"We were again devastated with this horrible decision. We felt as if we had no educational option. We went through the same grieving process as we did when Hope was born. We were angry and felt guilty for sending her away, but we sincerely believed we had no other options available to us. Although we made the best decision for us at the time, we still feel guilty."

Mr. and Mrs. Baxter

Now imagine a family in circumstances similar to the Pattersons over 50 years later. Mr. and Mrs. Baxter have a brand-new baby girl, Holly. The excitement turns to dismay when they are informed by the doctors that their precious infant is severely developmentally delayed. This time, however, the Baxters have additional legal guarantees in place that will provide a free and appropriate education for their child in the least restrictive environment, beginning with early intervention services and continuing through supported employment options into adulthood. Some early intervention programs are available in their own community. Some of the program options are center-based, in which the intervention occurs at the school, some are home-based, in which the intervention takes place in the home, and others are a combination of center- and home-based programs. This means that Holly can participate daily in relevant educational programs in a variety of setting options.

Additionally, established networks of organizations provide support to parents and families of children with disabilities. Although the Baxters will still have some of the same painful experiences that the Pattersons had, at least the federal government has mandated services for families with children with severe special needs. Mrs. Baxter tells her story:

"We felt horrible when the physician informed us that our beautiful baby girl would always be severely developmentally delayed. Her words still ring in my ears. 'Your baby is not normal!' We barely heard the rest of her statement: 'We have a staff of early childhood specialists and nurses who will be in contact with you later today.' We couldn't believe our ears. The doctor must have us mixed up with someone else. There must be a horrible mistake. How could anything be wrong with our brand-new baby girl? I felt as if I was having a nightmare and that at any moment I would wake up and find that everything was okay."

The Baxters, like the Pattersons, went through the same questions of "Why us?" and "What happened?" and the associated feelings of denial, anger, guilt, and aloneness. Later on the same day, however, the Baxters felt the support from an early childhood specialist and a nurse. As Mrs. Baxter reported:

"They explained the types of intervention services that were available for our baby and for us. At first everything seemed like a blur, but then as reality sank in we realized that we had hope for Holly again. Specialized services were available, she would receive assistance, and we would receive educational support. Although we still felt the anger and wanted to blame someone, we began to realize there were individuals and support services that would help us begin to adapt and provide appropriate services for our baby with special needs."

QUESTIONS FOR REFLECTION

1. Describe the various feelings experienced by the Pattersons. In what way were they similar to the feelings expressed by the Baxters? How do you think you would feel as a parent facing these issues?
2. Which of the Baxters' program options do you think you would have chosen? Why?

What Are the Educational Rights for Individuals with Disabilities?

Before the passage of federal legislation mandating services for students with disabilities, these individuals were routinely and legally excluded from school. Johnson (1986, pp. 1–2) documented several instances across the United States, including the following examples:

- In Massachusetts in 1893, a child with disabilities was excluded by a school committee because "he was so weak in mind as to not derive any marked benefit from instruction and further, that he is troublesome to other children. . . ." (*Watson v. City of Cambridge,* 1893).

- In Wisconsin in 1919, a 13-year-old with normal intelligence but physical disabilities was excluded for the following reasons:

  His physical condition and ailment produces a depressing and nauseating effect upon the teachers and school children; . . . he takes up an undue proportion of the teacher's time and attention, distracts attention of other pupils, and interferes generally with discipline and progress of the school. (*Beattie v. Board of Education of City of Antigo,* 1919)

- In 1963, Nevada excluded any student whose "physical or mental conditions or attitude is such as to prevent or render inadvisable his attendance at school or his application to study" (Nevada Revised Statutes, 1963).

- In 1971, Alaska excluded students with "bodily or mental conditions rendering attendance inadvisable" from school (Alaska Statutes, 1971).

Parents of children with disabilities face awesome responsibilities and challenges, including the need to advocate for the rights of their children.

- Virginia law in 1973 allowed school exclusion for "children physically or mentally incapacitated for school work" (Code of Virginia, 1973).

Today, these laws are no longer applicable. According to federal law, all students, regardless of disability, are entitled to a free and appropriate public education, including access to the general education curriculum. Since 1975, public education has truly become "education for all."

Along with increased rights of individuals with disabilities from legislation such as IDEA come increased responsibilities for teachers. General education teachers today have more students with disabilities in their classrooms than ever. In fact, only a small proportion of students with disabilities currently receives more than 60% of their education outside the general education classroom (see Table 1.1). Today, therefore, teachers must be especially aware of their responsibilities in providing appropriate instruction for students with disabilities.

Although more responsibilities are placed on the general education teacher, they should not be considered a burden. On the contrary, classroom diversity—whether in the form of gender, race, ethnicity, or ability—is something to be valued in its own right. Diversity provides a more exciting, dynamic classroom and the opportunity for students to learn that all people are not the same. Diversity provides opportunities for students to understand, respect, and value others for their differences. Finally, diversity provides the opportunity for you to use all of your imagination, skills, and resources, to be the best teacher you can be. In the end, effective inclusive teaching is about being the most effective teacher possible and supporting all students to learn in the least restrictive environment.

Table 1.1 Percentage of Students Ages 6 Through 21 with Disabilities Receiving Services in Different Educational Environments

Disabilities	Served Outside the Regular Class			Separate Environments (e.g., Residential, Separate Facilities, and Home-Bound/ Hospital Environments)
	<21% of the Day	21–60% of the Day	>60% of the Day	
Specific learning disabilities	44.8	37.3	13.0	1.0
Speech or language impairments	88.2	6.8	4.6	0.9
Mental retardation	11.7	30.2	51.8	6.1
Emotional disturbance	30.3	22.6	30.2	18.1
Multiple disabilities	12.1	17.2	45.8	26.4
Hearing impairments	44.9	19.2	22.2	15.3
Orthopedic impairments	46.7	20.9	26.2	6.0
Other health impairments	51.1	30.5	15.0	4.4
Visual impairments	54.6	16.9	15.6	13.4
Autism	26.8	17.7	43.9	14.0
Deaf-blindness	22.2	13.9	33.6	37.8
Traumatic brain injury	34.6	29.9	27.1	10.4
Developmental delay	51.2	28.2	18.6	1.3
All disabilities	**49.9**	**27.7**	**18.5**	**3.9**

Source: Twenty-seventh Annual Report to Congress on the Implementation of Individuals with Disabilities Act (Vol. I, p. 44), 2007, Washington, DC: U.S. Department of Education.

The Least Restrictive Environment

WHERE ARE STUDENTS WITH DISABILITIES SERVED?

Critical to IDEA legislation is the concept of *least restrictive environment.* This phrase means that students with disabilities must be educated in the setting least removed from the general education classroom. To the greatest extent possible, students with disabilities are not to be restricted to education in special schools or special classrooms but rather should have access to the same settings to which students without disabilities have access. When students with disabilities are educated, to any extent, in a different setting, there must be a compelling reason that this setting is in the student's best interest.

MAINSTREAMING AND INCLUSION

Mainstreaming was the first movement devoted to placement of students with disabilities within the general education classroom. Advocates of **mainstreaming** three or four decades ago did not want to see students with disabilities placed in special classes for the entire school day and argued that more exposure to the general classroom would be in everyone's best interest. Often, mainstreaming was thought to be something individual special education students could "earn" by demonstrating their skills were adequate to function independently in general education settings. Since then, the term **inclusion** has been used to describe the education of students with disabilities in general education settings. Although many definitions have been used to describe *inclusion*, the term is generally taken to mean that students with disabilities are served primarily in the general education classroom, under the responsibility of the general classroom teacher. When necessary and justifiable, students with disabilities may also receive some of their instruction in another setting, such as a resource room. Additional support can also be provided within the general education classroom by paraprofessionals or special education teachers. Although this is a similar concept to mainstreaming, a critical difference of inclusion is the view of the general classroom as the primary placement for the student with disabilities, with other special services regarded as ancillary.

Effective inclusive teaching is about being the most effective teacher possible.

In addition to mainstreaming and inclusion, the term *full inclusion* is also used, referring to the practice of serving students with disabilities and other special needs entirely within the general classroom. In full-inclusion settings, all students with disabilities are served the entire day in the general classroom, although special education teachers and other personnel may also be present in the general classroom at times (Knowlton, 2004).

WHO IS SERVED UNDER IDEA?

IDEA is intended to provide necessary support services to students with disabilities. To accomplish this goal, students with disabilities are categorized in particular disability groups. It is important to remember, however, that all students served by IDEA are first human beings and individuals, capable of achievement, accomplishment, friendship, affection, and all other attributes of any other individual. Disability status may not be a permanent characteristic of all individuals; in fact, most people can expect to be considered "disabled" at one time or another in their lives. This in no way detracts from their fundamental worth as human beings. In fact, it is this principle of individual worth that has inspired much of today's special education legislation.

In short, although students served under IDEA have been given a disability "label," it is important to consider the individual first, and then consider the label as a secondary factor, along with other characteristics that help identify the unique aspects of the individual. For this reason, it has been recommended that "person-first" language be adopted (Blaska, 1993). For

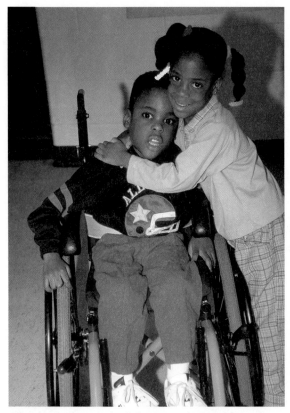
All individuals with disabilities are, first and foremost, individuals.

example, we speak of "students with hearing impairments," rather than "hearing-impaired students." It is also important to remember that we use these descriptions only when it is directly relevant to a situation. When it is not relevant to list hearing impairment as a characteristic, for example, we speak simply of "Amy," or "Richard," or "Ana." For example, Margo, as a high school student, was best friends with Carol, a student one year older. They played on the basketball team together and spent much of their after-school time together. After several years of close friendship, Margo expressed surprise that Carol had not gotten her driver's license, even a year after her 16th birthday. Further, Carol went to a separate setting to take the SAT. When she asked Carol about these things, Carol revealed that she was legally blind. Margo was astonished to hear this—and this situation demonstrated clearly to her that many characteristics of individuals, such as warmth, caring, sincerity, and understanding, can be much more important than disability status. It also demonstrated that important relationships can be developed and maintained that have little or nothing to do with disability status.

GENERAL CHARACTERISTICS   Students served by IDEA are distributed among 13 disability categories. Following is a brief description of each category (see IDEA, 2004; U.S. Department of Education, 2007, pp. 46756–46757). Individual states may use different terminology. These categories are described in more detail in Chapters 3 and 4.

• *Autism:* Autism is a developmental disability generally manifested within the first 3 years of life. Major characteristics can include impairments in communication and reciprocal social interaction, resistance to change, engagement in repetitive activities, and unusual responses to sensory stimuli.

• *Deaf-blindness:* Individuals in this category have moderate to severe impairments in both vision and hearing, causing such severe communication and educational needs that programming solely for children with deafness or children with blindness is not appropriate.

• *Deafness:* Individuals with deafness have hearing impairments so severe that processing linguistic information through hearing is severely limited, with or without amplification, and educational performance is negatively impacted.

• *Emotional disturbance (or serious emotional disturbance):* This category includes individuals with a condition in one or more of the following areas during an extended period of time: (a) inability to learn, not due to intellectual, sensory, or health problems; (b) inability to build and maintain social relationships with peers and teachers; (c) inappropriate behavior and affect; (d) general pervasive depression or unhappiness; (e) tendency to develop fears or physical symptoms associated with school and personal problems; and (f) schizophrenia (a disorder in perception of reality). According to the federal definition, emotional disturbance is not intended to apply to socially maladjusted children unless they are also characterized as having serious emotional disturbance.

• *Hearing impairments:* Hearing impairments, with or without amplification, affect educational performance and developmental progress. The impairment may be permanent or fluctuating, mild to profound, unilateral or bilateral, but includes impairments not included under the definition of deafness.

• *Mental retardation:* Mental retardation or intellectual disability describes significantly below-average intellectual functioning, as well as concurrent deficits in "adaptive behavior" (age-appropriate personal independence and social responsibility). It is manifested between birth and age 18 and negatively affects educational performance.

• *Multiple disabilities:* This category includes any individuals with two or more disabling conditions. However, this category often includes mental retardation/intellectual disability as one of the categories and is usually used when disorders are serious and interrelated to such an extent that it is difficult to identify the primary area of disability. It does not include deaf-blindness.

- *Orthopedic impairments:* Orthopedic impairments are associated with physical conditions that seriously impair mobility or motor activity. This category includes individuals with cerebral palsy, diseases of the skeleton or muscles (such as poliomyelitis), and accident victims.

- *Other health impairments:* This category includes chronic or acute health-related difficulties that adversely affect educational performance and are manifested by limited strength, vitality, or alertness. It can include such health problems as heart conditions, sickle-cell anemia, lead poisoning, diabetes, and epilepsy.

- *Specific learning disabilities:* This category refers to a disorder in one or more of the basic psychological processes involved in understanding or using spoken or written language, which can result in difficulties in reading, writing, listening, speaking, thinking, spelling, or mathematics. The term *learning disabilities* does not apply to children with learning problems that are primarily the result of visual, hearing, or physical disabilities; mental retardation/intellectual disability; emotional disturbance; or environmental, cultural, or economic disadvantage.

- *Speech or language impairments:* A disorder of articulation, fluency, voice, or language that adversely affects educational performance.

- *Traumatic brain injury:* Traumatic brain injury is an acquired injury to the brain due to external force resulting in a total or partial disability or psychosocial impairment, or both, which negatively affects educational performance (does not apply to congenital or degenerative injuries, or to brain injuries acquired during birth).

- *Visual impairments including blindness:* A visual impairment is a loss of vision that, even when corrected, affects educational performance. It may be mild to moderate to severe in nature. Students who are blind are unable to read print and usually learn to read and write using Braille. Students with low vision can usually read when the print is enlarged sufficiently.

In addition, children aged 3 to 9 can be classified as experiencing developmental delay if they have developmental delays in one or more of the following areas: physical, cognitive, communication, social or emotional, or adaptive development; such children may need special education and related services (IDEA, 2004).

OTHER INSTANCES OF CLASSROOM DIVERSITY

IDEA provides service to most of the recognized disability areas. However, there are other sources of classroom diversity, not associated with disabilities, that you need to consider when planning and implementing classroom instruction. These areas include the following:

- *Culturally and linguistically diverse groups:* These students are culturally or linguistically different from the majority U.S. culture or different from the teacher. Teachers should plan and implement instruction that is considerate of and sensitive to students' linguistic or cultural differences (Gollnick & Chinn, 2009).

- *At-risk:* Students characterized as "at-risk" exhibit characteristics, live in an environment, or have experiences that make them more likely to fail in school, drop out, or experience lack of success in future life. These factors are many and varied, but they include "slow learners" not served by IDEA categories and individuals who have sociocultural disadvantages, are at risk for suicide, or come from dysfunctional home environments (e.g., marred by drug or alcohol abuse, domestic violence, or child abuse). Such learners may require any of a variety of adaptations to help them succeed in school and later life (Frieman, 2001).

- *Gifted and talented:* These students exhibit skills or abilities substantially above those of their age in areas such as academic achievement in one or more subject areas, visual or performing arts, or athletics. If the abilities of such students greatly exceed

[handwritten margin notes: ADD; disgraphia; dislexia; discalcula; ELL—be cognizant of potential for mislabelling or not diagnosing]

classroom standards or curriculum, special adaptations or accommodations may be appropriate. Although many states have passed laws providing for the identification and education of gifted and talented students, in many cases funding for gifted programs is not provided (Davis & Rimm, 2004).

Legal Foundations

In the years following World War II, political change, litigation, and resulting legislation began to emerge that increased the inclusion of all groups of people in U.S. society. Most significant was the civil rights movement, which primarily addressed the rights of African Americans in U.S. society. This movement influenced the ideas on which much litigation and legislation involving individuals with disabilities are based. In the *Brown v. Board of Education* (1954) decision, the Supreme Court ruled that it was unlawful to discriminate against any group of people. With respect to school children, the Court ruled that the concept of "separate-but-equal" educational facilities for children of different races was inherently unequal. The justification for this ruling was found in the 14th Amendment to the U.S. Constitution, which states that individuals cannot be deprived of life, liberty, or property without due process of law.

LEGAL PROCEEDINGS AND LEGISLATION

People with disabilities also began to be identified as a group whose rights had been denied. In the years following *Brown v. Board of Education*, court cases were decided that underlined the rights of individuals with disabilities to a free, appropriate education. Other cases supported nondiscriminatory special education placement of individuals from minority groups in the United States. Some of the important court cases relating to individuals with disabilities demonstrate a progression of increasing rights for individuals with disabilities (see also Murdick, Gartin, & Crabtree, 2002; Wright & Wright, 2007; Yell, 2006):

- *1954: Brown v. Board of Education* (Kansas). The Supreme Court determined that "separate-but-equal" education is illegal.
- *1970: Diana v. State Board of Education* (California). The court ruled that children cannot be placed in special education based on culturally biased tests.
- *1972: Pennsylvania Association for Retarded Children (PARC) v. Commonwealth of Pennsylvania* and *Mills v. Board of Education* (District of Columbia) established the right to education for students with disabilities and found that denial of education violates the 14th Amendment.
- *1977: Larry P. v. Riles* (California). A court ruled that the use of standardized IQ tests for placement into special education classes for students with educable mental retardation was discriminatory.
- *1988: Honig v. Doe* (California). This decision was concerned with extensive suspensions of students with emotional disturbances from school for aggressive behavior that the court determined was disability related. The court ruled that a suspension of longer than 10 days was effectively a change in placement, requiring all the necessary procedures governing a change in placement.
- *1992: Oberti v. Board of Education of the Borough of Clementon School District* (New Jersey). A federal district court ruled that a self-contained special education class was not the least restrictive environment for a student with Down syndrome. The court ruled that school districts were obligated to first consider regular class placement, with supplementary aids and services, before considering alternative placements.

Along with this litigation, laws began to be passed that provided further support for the rights of students with disabilities. Some of these laws are summarized in Figure 1.1. In the following text, some of the most significant legislation involving individuals with disabilities is described (see also Murdick et al., 2006; Rothstein, 1999; Yell, 2006). This legislation includes Section 504 of the Vocational Rehabilitation Act, the Americans with Disabilities Act, and the most significant law for special education, the Individuals with Disabilities Education Act (PL 94-142).

1973	Section 504–Rehabilitation Act of 1973, U.S.C. Section 794: Recipients of federal funds cannot discriminate on the basis of disability.
1975	Education for All Handicapped Children Act (PL 94-142), 20 U.S.C. Sections 1400–1461: This law requires, and provides support to, states to implement a plan to provide free education and appropriate related services (on an individualized basis) to students with disabilities, including due-process provisions. It requires Individualized Education Programs (IEPs) for each student served under this law. This law was amended in 1983, 1986, 1990, 1997, and 2004. The 1990 amendments also renamed this law the Individuals with Disabilities Education Act (IDEA).
1977	Final regulations of Education for All Handicapped Children Act are passed.
1978	Gifted and Talented Children's Education Act: This act provides financial incentives for state and local educational agencies to develop programs for gifted and talented students.
1983	Amendments to the Education of the Handicapped Act (PL 98-199): These amendments mandate states to collect data on students with disabilities exiting systems and to address transition needs of secondary students with disabilities. In addition, they provide incentives to states to provide services to infants and preschoolers with disabilities.
1984	Developmental Disabilities Assistance and Bill of Rights Acts (PL 98-527): These acts provide for the development of employment-related training activities for adults with disabilities.
1984	Perkins Act, 20 U.S.C. 2301, 233–234: This act mandates that 10% of all vocational education funding must be for students with disabilities. Vocational education should be provided in the least-restrictive environment; secondary support is provided for students with disabilities.
1986	Education for All Handicapped Children Act Amendments (PL 99-457): These amendments encourage states to develop comprehensive services for infants and toddlers (birth through age 2) with disabilities and to expand services for preschool children (ages 3–5). After the 1990–91 school year, all states must provide free and appropriate education to all 3- to 5-year-olds with disabilities or forfeit federal assistance for preschool funding.
1986	Rehabilitation Act Amendments (PL 99-506): These amendments provide for the development of supported employment programs for adults with disabilities.

Figure 1.1   History of Relevant Legislation

SECTION 504

Section 504 of the Vocational Rehabilitation Act of 1973 (reauthorized as the Carl D. Perkins Career and Technical Education Act of 2006; U.S. Department of Education, 2006) is a civil rights law that prevents discrimination against individuals with disabilities by any institution that receives federal funds and provides for a free, appropriate public education (FAPE). Some private schools that do not receive federal funding may be exempt from Section 504. This law applies both to schools and to the workforce. Section 504 provides for equal opportunities in all aspects of education. Students may not be classified as disabled according to the IDEA guidelines, but they must demonstrate a significant learning problem that affects their ability to function in school. Under Section 504, disability is considered to be an impairment, physical or mental, that substantially limits a major life activity (Smith, 2001; U.S. Department of Education, 2006a). Some students who may not be served under IDEA, because they do not meet the definitional requirements of one of the IDEA disability categories, can still obtain services under Section 504 (deBettencourt, 2002). For example, some students with attention deficit hyperactivity disorder (ADHD), as well as some students who require modifications for their severe allergies or asthma, may be covered under this law. Other types of disabilities likely covered under Section 504, but not IDEA, might include the following (Smith, 2001):

- Students who had been placed in special education programs but have transitioned out;
- Students thought to be socially maladjusted, or who have a history of alcohol or drug abuse;
- Students who carry infectious diseases such as AIDS.

Students can be referred for Section 504 services by anyone but are usually referred by teachers or parents. If a group of knowledgeable school personnel believes the child is eligible, the school must then conduct an evaluation to determine eligibility and the nature of services needed to ensure a free, appropriate public education. The decision is based on professional judgment rather than test scores and numerical indicators. If a student is considered eligible, the law does not provide funding; however, it does require that school personnel create a written plan that will help accommodate these special needs and provide an accessible environment. Accommodation plans can include a statement of student strengths and weaknesses, a list of accommodations to be implemented, and designation of the person(s) responsible for implementation. Accommodations are usually inexpensive, commonsense modifications intended to provide nondiscrimination and free, appropriate public education (Smith, 2001).

AMERICANS WITH DISABILITIES ACT

The Americans with Disabilities Act (ADA) was signed into law in 1990, and mandated that individuals with disabilities should be provided with "reasonable accommodations" in the workplace, and that such individuals could not be discriminated against. ADA also included protections for individuals enrolled in colleges and universities. Adults with disabilities attending universities are also entitled to appropriate modifications in classes. These modifications, in many ways, parallel those made in public schools in compliance with IDEA. Major components of the ADA are given in Figure 1.2.

The Americans with Disabilities Act is of particular significance because of its aim to maximize the employment potential of millions of Americans with disabilities. It can be considered an important extension of IDEA, in that it provides for reasonable accommodations and nondiscriminatory treatment of individuals with disabilities beyond the high school years.

INDIVIDUALS WITH DISABILITIES EDUCATION ACT (IDEA)

This act is the major special education law. Originally signed in 1975 as the Education for All Handicapped Children Act, IDEA has been amended several times since then, most recently in 2004 (IDEA, 2004), as summarized in Figure 1.3. The most important provision in IDEA is that all children, from 3 through 21 years of age, regardless of type or severity of disability, are entitled to a free, appropriate public education. Discretionary assistance is also

- Employers may not discriminate on the basis of disability.
- Employers may not ask if applicant has a disability.
- "Reasonable accommodations" must be provided in the workplace.
- New buses must be made accessible.
- Most communities must provide transportation.
- Rail service must accommodate individuals with disabilities within 20 years.
- Public locations—hotels, stores, and restaurants—are accessible.
- State and local governments may not discriminate.
- Telephone companies must provide adapted communication options for the deaf.

Figure 1.2 Major Components of ADA

Note: From *Americans with Disabilities Act Requirements: Fact Sheet*, 1990, Washington, DC: U.S. Department of Justice.

Content of IEPs
- Present level of performance must include the "child's academic achievement and functional performance."
- Annual goals must be measurable.
- Short-term objectives are required only for children who take alternative assessments.
- IEPs must describe how progress will be measured and when reports will be issued.

Research-based practice
- Statements supporting special education services must be based on peer-reviewed research.

Accommodations and alternative assessments
- Statements indicating the need for individual accommodations for testing and alternative state-wide assessments must be provided.
- Justification for participation in alternative assessments must be provided.

IEP meetings
- The teacher's attendance may be waived (1) if the teacher's curriculum area is not addressed, or (2) if a report based on the curriculum area is submitted prior to the meeting and is approved by the student's parents and the local education agency (LEA).
- Fifteen states may apply for an optional multi-year IEP pilot program. This means that, in some cases, annual IEP meetings may not be required and may be conducted no less than every 3 years.

Discipline
- If students violate a code of conduct at school, they may be suspended for up to 10 days.
- If the behavior was related to the disability, a functional behavior assessment and behavior intervention plan must be completed for the child.
- If the behavior was unrelated to the disability, students may be suspended for more than 10 days, like any other student in the school.
- If students are suspended for more than 10 days, they must be provided with a free and appropriate education, and the IEP team must identify alternative placements.

Identification of learning disabilities
- Schools can use a *Response to Intervention* (see Chapter 3) model to determine eligibility for learning disabilities.

Early intervention funding
- LEAs may apply some of its special education funding to develop coordinated early intervention services, which may include students not identified for special education, but in need of academic or behavioral support.

Special education teacher licensure
- A highly qualified teacher is one who holds full teaching credentials required by state in conformance with *No Child Left Behind Act*. Special education teachers who teach in core subject areas must also hold the full teaching credentials in those subject areas.

Figure 1.3 IDEA 2004 Amendments
Sources: IDEA 2004 (2005), Mandlawitz (2006), and Wright and Wright (2005).

provided to develop interagency programs for all young children with disabilities, from birth to 3 years of age. This provision overrides previous legislation and decisions that limit the attendance of students with disabilities in public schools. Overall, six major principles have remained in the law throughout its amendments (Murdick et al., 2006). These principles are as follows:

1. *Zero reject.* This principle requires that no child with a disability can be excluded from public education.

2. *Nondiscriminatory testing.* Schools are required to use a variety of nondiscriminatory methods to determine whether a student has a disability, and, if so, whether special education is required. Testing must not discriminate on the basis of race, culture, or ethnicity, and must be administered in the student's native language. A variety of measures is required so that placement decisions are not

made on the basis of a single test score. Further, the law is intended to address multicultural issues, as described in the *Diversity in the Classroom* feature.

3. *Free and appropriate education.* Students who have been referred to special education must have an individualized education program (IEP) that details their special learning needs and mandates appropriate services. Short- and long-term goals and objectives for students are listed explicitly on IEPs.

4. *least restrictive environment.* Students with disabilities are entitled to be educated with their nondisabled peers to the greatest extent possible.

5. *Due process.* Due process must be followed in all placement decisions and changes in placement. Records are to be kept confidential, and parents are to be involved in all aspects of the planning and placement process.

6. *Parent participation.* Schools must collaborate with parents in the design and implementation of special education services (see also Hayden, Takemoto, Anderson, & Chitwood, 2008).

Along with these six common principles, several additions have been made to the original law:

1. *Transition services.* All 16-year-old students with disabilities must be provided with a statement of transition service needs on their IEP. These services, which must be included in the IEP by age 16, are intended to facilitate the student's transition from school to community, vocational programs, college, or employment. The transition plan can involve professionals from other agencies, such as social or vocational services. Transition planning conferences are also specified for transition from infant and toddler programs to preschool programs.

2. *Early childhood education.* Amendments to the Education for All Handicapped Children Act (now IDEA) in 1986 and 1990 provided for services to infants, toddlers, and preschoolers with disabilities. Very young children (younger than 3) are entitled to an individualized family service plan (IFSP, which replaces the IEP), which takes family needs and responsibilities into account. Necessary components of the IFSP include (a) current statement of child's functioning levels; (b) current statement of the family's needs and strengths in relation to the child with special needs; (c) statement of the major expected outcomes, including a timeline; (d) statement of the specific services to be provided to meet the special needs of the child and the family; (e) initiation and anticipated duration dates for services; (f) designation of a case manager; and (g) statement of transition steps from infant early intervention services to preschool services. States are required to take action to locate as many young children as possible who may require special education services.

3. *Assessments.* Students with disabilities must participate in general state- and district-wide assessment programs. If students cannot participate in state- and district-wide assessments, justification must be provided, and they must participate in alternative assessments.

4. *Early intervening services.* The 2004 amendments to IDEA specify that not more than 15% of the funding the local education authority receives from the federal government can be allocated to programming for students (K–12, with an emphasis on K–3) not currently identified for special education, but who need additional academic and behavioral support to succeed in the general education environment (U.S. Department of Education, 2006b). These services can include those referred to as response-to-intervention (RTI) tiered services, which are described in more detail in subsequent chapters.

NO CHILD LEFT BEHIND ACT OF 2001

The No Child Left Behind Act (NCLB) is a reauthorization of the Elementary and Secondary Education Act and was not written specifically for students with disabilities. However, many

Multicultural Considerations for the Identification of Individuals with Disabilities

Legal Assistance
Federal legislation has provided protections and guidance for the proper identification of individuals with disabilities. These assurances are to guarantee that only the correct individuals become identified as having disabilities. It is especially important that individuals from culturally and linguistically diverse backgrounds are not overrepresented in special education programs. The following protections are part of the Individuals with Disabilities Education Act (IDEA):

- *Disproportionality requirement:* States must devise plans to prevent overidentification and provide data to document whether disproportionality by race is happening with respect to identification and placement of individuals with disabilities.
- *Development, review, and revisions of IEPs:* Consider the language needs as related to the IEP for individuals with limited English proficiency.
- *Evaluation procedures:*
  - Test materials are not to be discriminatory against races or cultures.
  - Tests must be administered in the individual's native language.
  - Test materials for individuals with limited English proficiency must be used to measure a disability and not the individual's English skills.
  - Tests must be valid and reliable and administered by trained professionals.
  - No single procedure can be used as a sole criterion for determining whether a disability exists.
- *Eligibility determination:* An individual may not be eligible if the only difficulty appears to be limited English proficiency.

The U.S. Office of Civil Rights also provides guidance and protections and is the compliance monitor for prereferral practices that may also influence overrepresentation of individuals from culturally and linguistically diverse backgrounds. These laws include the following:

- *Section 504 of the Rehabilitation Act of 1973 and Title II of the Americans with Disabilities Act:* Provide protection against discrimination for individuals with disabilities and those perceived as having disabilities or those who have been misclassified.
- *Title VI of the Civil Rights Act:* Provides protection from discrimination based on national origin, color, or race.

When districts are out of compliance with these federal laws and have an overrepresentation of individuals from culturally or linguistically diverse backgrounds, they may become involved in legal actions and asked to provide a plan to correct the problems.

---

aspects of the legislation have important implications for students with disabilities (Simpson, LaCava, & Graner, 2004).

The law requires that all children be tested in grades 3 through 8, in reading and math, by tests developed by the states. Schools must demonstrate adequate yearly progress (AYP) toward the goal of 100% proficiency in reading, math, and science for all students within 12 years. Schools must demonstrate that students make progress in equal increments toward this goal, that is, that they are making steady, equivalent gains from year to year. Schools that fail to make AYP for two consecutive years must offer parents of the students the option to transfer to another public school, and the districts must pay the cost of transportation (if allowed under state law). The school district must provide technical assistance to the school. If schools fail to make AYP for more than two consecutive years, more corrective measures must be taken, including replacing staff, implementing different curricula, or, ultimately, a state take-over, hiring a private management contractor, or converting to a charter school (Council for Exceptional Children, 2002). Other aspects of the law include compensatory education grants (Title I), bilingual and immigrant education programs, and standards and provisions for teacher training and recruitment (Wright, Wright, & Heath, 2004).

The NCLB Act has several important implications for special education. If students with disabilities fail to meet adequate yearly progress toward reaching 100% proficiency in reading and math by 2012, the entire school will face a host of accountability measures, as described

Federal Government Updates

One way to keep abreast of the changes in federal legislation is to check regularly the U.S. Department of Education Website (*www.ed.gov*). This Website contains a wealth of frequently updated information as well as links to relevant research and legislation sites. For example, a link to No Child Left Behind (*www.ed.gov/nclb/landing.jhtml*) provides an overview of the act that was signed in January 2002, as well as commonly asked questions and answers that are presented in an easy-to-understand format, links to specific state-level contacts, links for parents and for educators and policymakers, newsletters, and even slide presentations that emphasize key points.

Additional helpful Websites linked to the U.S. Department of Education (U.S. DOE) page are directly relevant to special education initiatives. These sites are the Office of Special Education and Rehabilitative Services Website (*www.ed.gov/about/offices/list/OSERS/index.html*) and the office of Special Education Programs (*www.ed.gov/about/offices/list/osers/osep/index.html*). These sites contain information such as current special education initiatives, including the recent IDEA legislation, possible changes in the identification of learning disabilities, recent research findings from projects funded by the U.S. DOE, model programs and personnel preparation, and the annual reports to Congress indicating the status of special education programs across the country with respect to numbers of children served, aged birth through 21. Information about sponsored special education research can also be found on the Web Links to the Institute of Education Sciences.

Finally, the Council for Exceptional Children (CEC) has numerous updates and interpretations of federal legislation relevant to special education. Check the CEC Website for updates to this information.

previously. Further, if students with disabilities receive accommodations for statewide tests, and those accommodations result in the scores being deemed unreliable or invalid, the students will not be considered to have participated in the assessment. If the overall participation rate does not meet the minimum requirement (possibly as high as 95%), the state can be considered out of compliance and subject to sanctions (Council for Exceptional Children, 2002). Finally, NCLB requires that all teachers hold full state certification or licensure as of 2005. In light of the personnel shortages in special education, meeting these requirements represents a major undertaking (Nougaret, Scruggs, & Mastropieri, 2004; Sindelar, McCray, Kiely, & Kamman, 2008).

One important feature of federal legislation is that it is constantly changing. Some technological approaches for keeping abreast of federal legislation are described in the *Technology Highlight* feature.

Models of Service Delivery

THE CONTINUUM OF SERVICES

The initial emphasis of legal actions was to provide access to educational services for students with disabilities. Once access was obtained, the focus shifted to the setting and placement of students with disabilities during education. Most placement guidelines emphasized availability of a range of services and programs, commonly referred to as a **continuum of services**, within the least restrictive environment for students with disabilities (Knowlton, 2004). *Least restrictive environment* is defined in IDEA as meaning that students with disabilities should be educated in a setting that as closely as possible resembles the general education program while simultaneously meeting the unique special needs for each individual with disabilities. The basic model of a continuum of services ranges from full-time placement in the general education classroom to full-time placement in a nonpublic school facility, on a day or residential basis, based on student need. As the needs of the individual

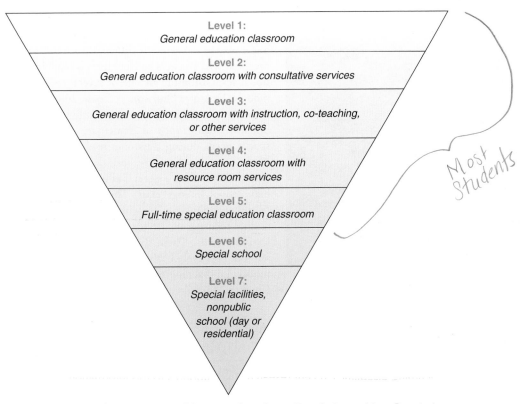

Level 1:
General education classroom

Level 2:
General education classroom with consultative services

Level 3:
General education classroom with instruction, co-teaching, or other services

Level 4:
General education classroom with resource room services

Level 5:
Full-time special education classroom

Level 6:
Special school

Level 7:
Special facilities, nonpublic school (day or residential)

Most Students

Figure 1.4 Sample Continuum of Services, from Least Restrictive to Most Restrictive

with disability increase, the least restrictive environment may be further removed from the general education class on the continuum of services. Figure 1.4 presents a sample of the range of placement options.

WHERE ARE MOST STUDENTS WITH DISABILITIES SERVED?

Most students with disabilities are served in the public school with their nondisabled peers in Levels 1 through 5. In other words, these students receive their education in their local public school. Most students with mild disabilities, including those with learning disabilities, mild mental retardation/intellectual disability, speech and language disabilities, and serious emotional disturbance, are currently served in Levels 1 through 4. That is, these students spend some, if not all, of their day in the general education classroom along with students without disabilities. The general education teacher is responsible for their education for some, if not all, of the day, depending on the amount of time spent in that general education class. Table 1.1 on page 6 provides a listing of disability categories and the proportion currently served outside general education classrooms.

WHAT ARE GENERAL EDUCATION CLASSROOM AND CONSULTATION SERVICES?

In some cases, students may be served in general education classes by general education teachers. Some special services may be provided by a **consultant** who works with individuals as needed. Special education teachers frequently provide consultative services to general education teachers. This consultation is intended to provide assistance and ideas for how to teach and work with the students with disabilities who are placed in general education classes. Although special education teachers may not work directly with identified students, they may meet regularly with general education teachers, review assessment and progress data, and make specific recommendations for addressing special learning needs. These students would be receiving services at Levels 1 or 2 of the continuum of services model.

In other cases, special education teachers and classroom assistants (or paraprofessionals) may deliver instruction to students with special needs in the general education classroom. In

Levels 1 & 2 → Consultant Services.

these cases, students with disabilities still receive all their instruction in the general education classroom, but it may be delivered by different teachers or paraprofessionals. Teachers collaborate and share instructional responsibilities in one of several **co-teaching** models (Dettmer, Thurston, & Dyck, 2005). For example, a special education teacher may lead instruction for small groups of elementary students with special needs during classroom reading instruction. At the secondary level, the special education teacher may co-teach with a general education teacher in a high school biology class. The two teachers share teaching responsibilities, with the special education teacher focusing on strategies for addressing special learning needs. These students would be receiving services at Level 3 of the continuum of services model. Co-teaching models are described further in Chapter 2.

Originally called the Education for All Handicapped Children Act (PL 94-142), the Individuals with Disabilities Education Act (IDEA) mandates that all the children between the ages of 3 and 21, regardless of disability, are entitled to a free, appropriate public education.

resource – leave for support

Self-Contained – Stay

WHAT ARE RESOURCE AND SELF-CONTAINED SERVICES?

Special education teachers also provide instruction in resource and self-contained classrooms within the public schools. In a resource room model, students with disabilities leave the general education class for a designated time period to visit the resource room and receive specialized instruction in areas such as language, reading, and math. For example, Kathi is a sixth-grader who has been classified as having learning disabilities. Kathi is functioning intellectually within the average ability range, but she has reading, spelling, and written language skills at an upper third-grade level. The multidisciplinary team recommended that Kathi receive specialized instruction in reading, written communication, and spelling with a special education teacher 1.5 hours per day in her school's resource room. This means that Kathi would be receiving services at Level 4 of the continuum of services model.

Most of her school day will be spent in the least restrictive environment of her general education class with Mrs. Gomez. Mrs. Gomez will be responsible for Kathi's instruction for the entire time that she is in the general education class. This might even include making some adaptations in instructional procedures and assignments to accommodate Kathi's special learning needs in the general education sixth-grade classroom. For example, during content-area classes, Mrs. Gomez will need to provide adapted reading and study materials appropriate to Kathi's skill levels. During her 1.5 hours in the resource room, Kathi will receive instruction with Mr. Halleran, the special education teacher in the same school. This resource room arrangement represents the least restrictive environment to meet Kathi's special needs in reading, written communication, and mathematics, while maintaining her placement in her general education class for the majority of the school day.

The resource model is often referred to as a *pull-out* model, indicating that students with disabilities are pulled out of the general education class for special education instruction. In a self-contained model of instruction (Level 5 of the continuum of services model), students with disabilities receive all or most of their classroom instruction from special education teachers. Even in these models, however, students with disabilities usually have opportunities to interact with their nondisabled peers during such activities as art, music, physical education, recess, lunch, and assemblies.

Special educators working in resource rooms often provide individualized or small-group instruction for some students with disabilities.

SPECIAL SCHOOLS AND SPECIAL FACILITIES

In some cases, the need for specialized instruction is considered so significant that a special school or other facility is considered necessary. In some cases, special public schools are established to focus specifically on the special needs of the students. In other cases, students are sent to nonpublic schools, either as special day schools or as residential schools. These students would be receiving services at Level 6 or 7 of the continuum of services model. The numbers of special schools or other facilities have declined since the early years of IDEA, as traditional public schools have accommodated more students with disabilities and other special needs within their educational programs.

WHAT OTHER RELATED SERVICES ARE AVAILABLE?

Students with disabilities are also eligible to receive related services, if it is determined that the students require these services to benefit from special education. According to IDEA, related ser-vices may include parent counseling and training, physical therapy, occupational therapy, school health services, or special transportation. This means that in addition to receiving special services along the continuum of services for a primary disability area, some students may also be eligible to receive additional related services. Related services may be delivered to individuals with disabilities in any of the setting options. Although described as "related" services, in many cases these services may be of critical importance in attending to the special needs of individual students (Downing, 2004). For example, Michael, a student with intellectual disabilities, receives physical therapy in addition to his educational program to meet his special needs. Janice requires special transportation services to accommodate her wheelchair, and these are provided as related services.

The continuum of services and related services have been effectively applied throughout the history of IDEA. However, over this same time period, there have been recommendations regarding how all or most students with disabilities could be more easily served entirely within the general education classroom. These movements have been referred to as the Regular Education Initiative and the full-inclusion movement.

THE FULL-INCLUSION MOVEMENT

Over the past decades, the full-inclusion movement came to the forefront (Kauffman & Hallahan, 1995). Full inclusion has been referred to as placing and serving all students with disabilities, regardless of severity or type of disability, entirely within the general education classroom for the entire school day.

Consider the case of Kathi, our sixth-grader with learning disabilities. If Kathi were placed in a full-inclusion classroom, Mrs. Gomez, her general education teacher, would have Kathi in her room all day, every day with all of the other sixth-grade students. Mrs. Gomez would be primarily responsible for all of Kathi's instruction and for making adaptations appropriate for addressing Kathi's learning disabilities. In some full-inclusion models, Mr. Halleran, the special education teacher, would consult with Mrs. Gomez and provide ideas for her to use in teaching Kathi in her IEP need areas. In other full-inclusion models, Mr. Halleran might go into Mrs. Gomez's room and teach Kathi reading, spelling, and writing in that room. In this model, instruction with Mr. Halleran and Kathi may occur at a small table, perhaps with other students with special needs, while other groups of students meet for literacy activities. In still other full-inclusion models, Mr. Halleran may co-teach with Mrs. Gomez for part or all of the school day. During co-teaching, Mr. Halleran and Mrs. Gomez would work collaboratively on planning and implementing instruction for the entire class. In any of these full-inclusion models, however, Kathi remains in the general education class with her nondisabled peers all day, and delivery of services outside the general education class, for any length of time, would not be an option.

As might be expected, considerable debate surrounds the issue of full inclusion. It is important to remember that virtually all educational professionals recommend placement in general education classes for students with disabilities and other special needs; the disagreement usually centers on the extent to which students should be placed in general education settings. Both proponents of full inclusion and proponents of a continuum of services have articulated their positions, which are summarized in Figure 1.5 (see also Fuchs & Fuchs, 1994; Kauffman, 1995; Kauffman & Hallahan, 1995; Lipsky & Gartner, 1997; Scruggs & Mastropieri, 2005; Stainback & Stainback, 1996).

Proponents of Full Inclusion	Proponents of a Continuum of Services
1. *Full inclusion is a civil right.* Students with disabilities have a right to be educated alongside their nondisabled peers. Separate educational settings are inherently not equal.	1. *A continuum of service options is necessary.* Many services needed by students with disabilities are not usually available in the general education classroom. Court decisions have usually placed more emphasis on "appropriate education" than "least-restrictive" components.
2. *Full inclusion reduces stigma.* Harmful stigmatizing effects may be associated with students attending special schools or special classrooms.	2. *The regular classrooms may also be stigmatizing.* Special services, such as speech therapy, physical therapy, or specialized reading instruction may be stigmatizing when undertaken in the company of general education peers.
3. *Full inclusion is beneficial.* Students in full-inclusion classrooms improve their interactions with others, learn to communicate better, develop better social skills, and increase their friendships.	3. *General education teachers are not prepared for full inclusion.* Many general education teachers lack the necessary time and training to make full inclusion a success.
4. *Full inclusion is more efficient.* Fully included students avoid the disruptive and time-consuming effects of being "pulled out" of the general education class to receive special services. Full inclusion guarantees access to the general education curriculum.	4. *General education classrooms may lack appropriate resources.* Students with special needs may require materials at lower reading levels, braillers, speech synthesizers, specialized computers, or specialized training materials that general education classrooms lack.
5. *Full inclusion promotes equality.* Including all students in the same classroom is simply the most fair and equitable solution to the problem of placement. Including all students in the same classroom actively promotes the idea of equality.	5. *Research evidence does not support the superiority of full inclusion.* Although research data are to some extent equivocal, clear evidence of the superiority of full-inclusion placements is presently lacking.

Figure 1.5   Arguments of Proponents of Full Inclusion and Proponents of a Continuum of Services

Controversial

As can be seen, the issue of full inclusion versus a continuum of services is far from settled. Professional organizations and advocates do not always agree on the best service options (e.g., Lane, 1995; Rimland, 1993). Parents also seem to be divided between those who favor specialized placement and services and those who favor integration in the general education class (Palmer, Fuller, Arora, & Nelson, 2001). The *Research Highlight* feature (see p. 22) describes the diversity of opinion that exists among parents of children with severe disabilities.

WHAT DOES THIS DEBATE MEAN FOR TEACHERS?

Teachers need to be aware of the arguments for and against full inclusion. As the controversy continues, it is important to keep abreast of recent research documenting the efficacy of such procedures. You also must become familiar with your own legal responsibilities as a teacher. For example, what are general education classroom teachers' legal responsibilities with respect to the IEP when all instruction is implemented in the general education classroom? Other questions, although not necessarily legal in nature, may be relevant to the spirit of the law.

Teachers should approach the issue in a practical way, with respect to their own school and district. Specific questions to ask about full inclusion include the following:

- What are the school- and districtwide policies and procedures regarding full inclusion?
- What are my obligations as a general educator with respect to the IEP, IEP meetings, case conferences, assessment procedures, annual review meetings, and meetings with parents?

- What types of modifications are expected, and is there a "reasonableness" standard associated with the number and types of modifications expected?

- Is this the best placement option for the student with special needs?

- How will we evaluate whether or not this placement and this set of accommodations are successful?

- What resources are available to assist me in working with the student with special needs?

- How can I receive necessary training for working with students in specific disability areas?

- What kinds of records and documentation should I maintain?

Answers to questions such as these can help determine the best placement options for students with disabilities and other special needs.

TEACHER ATTITUDES

One of the most important determinants of inclusion success is the attitude of the general education teacher toward accommodating students with disabilities. Although most teachers are positive about inclusion, general education teachers report a need for additional planning time, additional training for inclusive teaching, and additional resources, in the form of personnel and specialized instructional materials (Cook, Tankersley, Cook, & Landrum, 2000; Scruggs & Mastropieri, 1996a; 1996b). Teacher and administrator support for collaborative efforts in schools can also affect attitudes. The two scenarios that follow help illustrate the initial implementation of inclusion in two different schools under very different circumstances.

In full-inclusion classrooms, students with disabilities may spend the entire school day in regular classroom settings.

CLASSROOM SCENARIOS

Volunteerism

In a small rural school, Mrs. Ghardisi, the fourth-grade teacher, volunteered to take all the fourth-grade students with disabilities into her classroom. Because she worked well with Mrs. Rana, the special education teacher, she went to her principal and said, "Next year, I would like to have all five of the fourth-graders who have disabilities in my room. They can still go to the resource room for part of the day, but during science class and other content classes, I would like to have all of them. Also, Mrs. Rana and I would like to team-teach during science class when all five children are included."

That summer, Mrs. Ghardisi and Mrs. Rana met and discussed curriculum and planning issues for their science class. Mrs. Ghardisi was considered the "content expert," while Mrs. Rana was the "adaptation expert." When the school year began, they met at least one day a week after school to co-plan the activities for each science class. Mrs. Ghardisi and Mrs. Rana had a good working relationship that enabled them to solve problems as they arose. Because they planned together, they took turns presenting information and monitoring students during class. They were both enthusiastic and worked hard to design adaptations so the five students with disabilities could be active participants. They viewed science as an opportunity to have fun, and their students appeared to really enjoy science.

Mandated Inclusion

In a suburban middle school, Ms. McDuffie, the special education teacher, was told by her building principal 2 days before school began that she was going to implement inclusive instruction for one period per day during the coming year. She was told she would be going into Mrs. Toro's sixth-period, seventh-grade history class on a daily basis. She was informed that three students with learning disabilities were in that social studies class.

Parent Views on Inclusion

Given the debate on issues of inclusion, researchers have been interested in parents' perceptions of inclusion. Palmer et al. (2001) surveyed parents of children with severe disabilities regarding their perceptions toward inclusion. They administered a 62-item survey to 140 parents of children with severe disabilities, including intellectual disabilities, who were being served in traditional school settings. Part of the survey included a scenario describing a supportive inclusive environment that included key components of inclusive environments for students with severe disabilities. These components included: (a) services delivered through collaboration of general and special educators, (b) chronological age-appropriate placement, and (c) no students excluded from placements. For example, one of the statements in the scenario stated: "These students do not spend any time in a special education classroom with other students with disabilities. Instead, a special education teacher and other adults who work at the school help the teacher in the regular class make the materials and lessons more understandable and useful for students with severe disabilities" (p. 470). Parents were then asked to rate whether the program would be a good idea for most or all students and for their own child. Results were mixed, in that some parents of children with severe disabilities indicated that the model of full inclusion would be a good idea for students and for their own child and others did not. For example, statements supporting inclusion included: (a) higher expectations and academic, functional skill, and social skill improvements; (b) home-school placements; (c) all students benefit; and (d) philosophical position. Conversely, statements not supporting inclusion included: (a) type and severity of disability; (b) acceptance of child; (c) negative influence on others in class; (d) inappropriate curriculum; (e) lack of appropriate services and personnel; and (f) size and age of child. The authors concluded that variability exists in parents' attitudes toward inclusion, in that some favored full inclusion while others favored special class placements. They further acknowledged that these findings might not be the same for all parents of children with different disabilities, but that understanding parents' viewpoints is an important consideration in the education of their children.

QUESTIONS FOR REFLECTION

1. Why do you think there were different opinions from parents of children with severe disabilities with respect to their ideas on inclusion?
2. How might the age level and severity of disability of the child influence parental considerations?
3. How might the school's curriculum and the child's grade level interact with parents' decision making?

Unfortunately, Mrs. Toro, the history teacher, had not been informed by the principal that Ms. McDuffie was going to be team-teaching with her. When Ms. McDuffie went to see Mrs. Toro, and explained the situation, Mrs. Toro appeared visibly shaken.

Now both teachers, who had never discussed the possibility of working together, felt awkward. Neither had previously thought about team-teaching, although neither was particularly opposed to the idea. Perhaps more important, the teachers did not have the same preparation periods free, which meant that any co-planning would have to take place before or after school. This would mean that Ms. McDuffie and Mrs. Toro now had additional responsibilities they had not requested.

Neither teacher had a good understanding of the principal's expectations. They were also unsure how to execute the co-teaching. Ms. McDuffie had expertise in special education and in making accommodations, and Mrs. Toro had content expertise in history, but now they had to figure out a way to blend their strengths during one period of instruction per day.

Although both teachers tried to be optimistic, there were so many ambiguities regarding their roles and expectations that they both initially experienced some discomfort with the situation. Mrs. Toro said she would continue to prepare and present information from the social studies textbook to the class and requested that Ms. McDuffie circulate around the room during independent activities to provide assistance to anyone who needed it. Ms. McDuffie agreed to this arrangement but felt uncomfortable during class presentations, as she was unsure of what to do with herself. Both teachers tried to meet and plan, but something else always seemed to take a priority.

QUESTIONS FOR REFLECTION

1. Compare and contrast the two teaching situations. What differences seem most likely to affect the success of inclusive instruction? What changes can you recommend?

2. In the second case, neither teacher had been given adequate notice, nor had they volunteered for team-teaching. What options are available to Ms. McDuffie and Mrs. Toro? How can they begin to monitor and evaluate their team-teaching? How can they overcome the barriers and make the experience successful for them and the students?

It is clear that many aspects must be considered in order for inclusive placements to be successful. These involve careful planning and attention to the multiple perspectives of general education teachers, special education teachers, parents of students with and without disabilities, and, of course, the students themselves. However, with careful planning and appropriate programming, inclusive instruction can prove to be a successful and rewarding experience for everyone.

1 Summary

- In 1975, Public Law 94-142 (IDEA) was passed. This law, and its subsequent amendments, established the rights of students with disabilities to a free, appropriate public education. It further provided that this education would take place, to the maximum extent possible, in the least restrictive environment. Before the passage of this law, students with special needs were routinely excluded from public school.

- IDEA provides for special services for disability areas including autism, deafness, hearing impairments, mental retardation/intellectual disability, multiple disabilities, orthopedic impairments, other health impairments, emotional disturbance, specific learning disabilities, speech or language impairments, traumatic brain injury, visual impairments, and deaf-blindness. However, other groups of students may also require special adaptations by general education teachers, including students who are culturally or linguistically diverse, students at-risk for school failure, and students with gifts or talents.

- Other court rulings and federal laws, such as Section 504 and the Americans with Disabilities Act, have provided for nondiscriminatory treatment of individuals with disabilities.

- Six important principles in IDEA are (1) zero reject, (2) nondiscriminatory testing, (3) free and appropriate education, (4) least restrictive environment, (5) due process, and (6) parent participation.

- Current educational practice provides for a continuum of services for students with disabilities, from full-time placement in the regular education classroom to special residential schools. Currently, most students with disabilities are served in regular education classrooms.

- Some controversy exists over the concept of "full inclusion," the full-time placement of students with disabilities in regular classrooms. Important points have been raised by concerned individuals on both sides of this issue.

- Most teachers favor some form of inclusion for their own classes. However, teachers report a need for sufficient time, training, and resources to teach effectively in inclusive classrooms. When these supports are provided, attitudes toward inclusive teaching also improve.

PROFESSIONAL STANDARDS LINK:
Introduction to Inclusive Teaching

Information in this chapter links most directly to:

- CEC Standards: 1 (Foundations), 2 (Development and Characteristics of Learners), 3 (Individual Learning Differences)

- INTASC Standard: Principle 1 (understands central concept of the discipline)

- PRAXIS II™ Content Categories (Knowledge): 1 (Understanding Exceptionalities), 2 (Issues)

- PRAXIS II™ Content Categories (Application): 5 (Professional Roles)

Note: **CEC** is the Council for Exceptional Children, an organization dedicated to improving educational outcomes for students with disabilities and gifted students. **INTASC** is the Interstate New Teacher Assessment and Support Consortium, which created standards for licensing new teachers to be compatible with the National Board for Professional Teaching Standards. The **PRAXIS** Series™ assessments provide tests for states to use as part of their teacher licensure process. The PRAXIS II® assessments for special education measure core knowledge or principles (Knowledge: 0351 and 0353) and application of core principles (Application: 0352) across disability categories.

Father of Orchidology Impression

MIKE BIRBECK   Mike Birbeck suffered multiple injuries, including a broken back, in a military flying accident in 1982, and is confined to a wheelchair. Since then, photography has been his passion. His pictures have won many international awards, and he is a Fellow of the Royal Photographic Society (FRPS), the British Professional Photographers Associates (FBPPA), and the Disabled Photographers' Society (FDPS), of which he is also President. He was awarded the Royal Photographic Society "Hood Medal" in 2005 for services to photography. He also serves on the Licentiate Distinction Panel at the RPS, and is on their advisory board.

Collaboration: Partnerships and Procedures

OBJECTIVES

After studying this chapter, you should be able to:

- List and describe six major steps involved in effective interpersonal communication.
- Describe the general education prereferral process—including establishing timelines, intervention strategies, and consultation—and applications to response-to-intervention (RTI) models.
- Identify the key components comprising the case conference committee and IEP program, including educational evaluation or assessment steps.
- Gain understanding of the importance of establishing partnerships between special and general educators.
- Identify the benefits of co-teaching, potential barriers to successful co-teaching, and describe strategies for facilitating collaboration among educators.
- Understand the roles and responsibilities of paraprofessionals, and the importance of communicating effectively with paraprofessionals.
- Describe the importance of positive communication and collaboration with parents and families.

IDEA provides the legal right for individuals with disabilities to receive free, appropriate public education. However, for the law to be effective, constructive and collaborative partnerships must be established among parents, teachers, school specialists, school administrators, and community agencies. The school and parents must accept certain basic responsibilities for the system to work effectively. Table 2.1 lists some of these responsibilities. To meet these responsibilities, parents and school personnel must engage in problem-solving strategies, working together to devise procedures necessary for identification, referral, assessment, and placement processes to accommodate students with exceptionalities and other at-risk students.

Collaboration—involving cooperation, effective communication, shared problem solving, planning, and finding solutions—is the process for ensuring that all students receive the free, appropriate public education mandated by IDEA. The establishment of excellent partnerships among all involved in working with students with disabilities is essential for constructive collaboration.

Table 2.1 School and Parent Responsibilities

School's Responsibilities	Parents' Responsibilities
Provide free and appropriate education through age 21.	Provide consent for educational evaluation and placement.
Provide an individualized education program (IEP) for each student who requires special education and related services.	Participate in case conference committee, including development of IEP.
Assure testing, evaluation materials, procedures, and interpretations are nonbiased.	Cooperate with school and teachers.
Educate students with disabilities in the least restrictive environment.	Attend case reviews to ensure IEP remains appropriate.
Assure confidentiality of records for individuals with disabilities.	Reinforce procedures and policies (e.g., help with homework routines).
Conduct searches to identify and evaluate students with disabilities from birth through age 21.	Assist with any home–school behavioral contracting efforts.
Provide procedural due-process rights for students and parents.	Help maintain open communication with school and teachers.

CLASSROOM SCENARIO

Debbie

Debbie is a 10th-grader with physical disabilities and communication difficulties who has been experiencing problems completing her work within a typical school day. This morning, six of Debbie's teachers—her math teacher, Ms. Juarez; her English teacher, Mr. Mantizi; her science teacher, Mr. Stubbs; her history teacher, Ms. Blackman; her speech and language therapist, Ms. Ramirez; and her special education teacher, Mr. Graetz—are meeting with Ms. Meyer, Debbie's paraprofessional, in the small conference room near the front office. They are trying to determine what they can do to help Debbie be more successful in high school. Everyone at the meeting is sincere in their desire to brainstorm ways to arrange the school day so Debbie can learn successfully.

Mr. Graetz, the special education teacher, began the conversation by saying, "Thanks for agreeing to meet this morning to look at what's been happening with Debbie and try to come up with some solutions together. Recently, Debbie appears to be having a hard time keeping up with all of her work. Her grades have started slipping. Maybe if we share some ideas we might be able to help her."

Ms. Blackman, the history teacher, says, "I know that Debbie is interested in the topics we are studying because her eyes become animated during class. But I'm not sure how I can tap into that enthusiasm. Maybe if I could get her to participate more actively she would feel better about school."

The speech therapist, Ms. Ramirez, suggests, "Have you tried allowing Debbie to type out responses to questions on her notebook computer and then asking Ms. Meyer to read her answers to the class?"

"Hey, that's a good idea. I have time to do that while students are completing their lab work in science class," says the science teacher, Mr. Stubbs.

Ms. Juarez, the math teacher, adds, "I sometimes stop the discussion and allow extra time for Debbie to type her responses, and have found that this provides additional thinking time for everyone in my math class. . . ."

And so the discussion continues. These teachers are collaborating by sharing suggestions in instructional modifications with the intention of trying something that will promote school success for Debbie.

QUESTIONS FOR REFLECTION

1. How could any disagreements that arise be handled in this meeting?
2. If you were Mr. Graetz, how could you determine that the suggestions made in this meeting would be carried out?
3. What do you think would be some of the challenges in arranging a meeting such as this?

Collaboration to Meet Students' Needs

Collaboration to decide how to best meet students' needs can occur among teachers and other school specialists during informal meetings, co-teaching, and formal meetings of professionals to recommend interventions or consider the appropriateness of special education services. Collaboration also takes place with parents, siblings, guardians, and families—during parent conferences as well as during day-to-day communication with parents regarding the progress of their children.

SHARED GOALS

Collaboration means working jointly with others, willingly cooperating with others, and sharing in goal setting, problem solving, and goal achievement. For example, a special education teacher might have Marilyn, who is classified as having mild intellectual disabilities, for three periods a day, while the general education seventh-grade content-area teachers have her the remainder of the school day. General and special education teachers must collaborate effectively to implement the goals and objectives on Marilyn's IEP. For example, Marilyn's IEP specifies that general education teachers prioritize objectives, use positive reinforcement, adapt learning activities to reduce the amount of reading and writing required, adapt testing situations, and provide Marilyn with additional support as necessary. For these goals to be implemented consistently throughout the day for Marilyn, this team of teachers must work collaboratively and share ideas for best meeting Marilyn's needs. For effective collaboration to happen, teachers must communicate effectively. This is most possible when collaborators hone their interpersonal skills and interject a positive attitude into the collaboration efforts.

Effective Communication

Interpersonal interactions revolve around communication. When communication is effective, several common elements are in place: active listening, depersonalizing situations, identifying common goals and solutions, and monitoring progress to achieve those goals (Gordon, 2003; see also Ginott, 1995; Ginott, Ginott, & Goddard, 2003).

STRATEGIES FOR COMMUNICATING EFFECTIVELY

USE ACTIVE LISTENING TECHNIQUES   Active listening is demonstrated through both nonverbal and verbal actions. Nonverbally, you demonstrate active listening by maintaining direct eye contact, leaning toward the speaker, nodding your head in agreement or understanding, and demonstrating that you are devoting all of your attention to the speaker. Verbal components of active listening involve responding with affirmative words such as: "Yes," "Yes, I see," "I understand," and, "Can you tell me more?" An active listener is able to restate or summarize the major points of the conversation, and may do this during the course of the conversation with statements such as, "So, what you are telling me is. . . ." Teachers who use active listening techniques are more likely to maintain open communication and to avoid misunderstandings. Active listening is a way of informing the speaker that his or her views are important to you and can be helpful in keeping interactions positive.

DEPERSONALIZE SITUATIONS   Depersonalized conversations avoid negative comments that may hurt an individual's character, and instead emphasize a goal. For example, if a student, Lisa, has been remiss at turning in homework assignments, a "depersonalized" statement is, "Lisa, 7 out of the last 10 homework assignments are missing; what can we do to improve that?" A negative statement that might hinder finding a solution is, "Lisa, you obviously do not care enough about science to turn in your homework."

Depersonalized conversations are beneficial when communicating with everyone, including students, other teachers, school specialists, administrators, parents, and professionals from community organizations.

FIND COMMON GOALS   It is important to restate and summarize conversations to identify common goals. Once common goals are found, conversations can be more positive and productive. Questions such as "Lisa, what do you want to do in science?" and "What are the

PEARSON
myeducationlab

Go to MyEducationLab, select the topic *Collaboration, Consultation, and Co-Teaching,* and go to the Activities and Applications section. As you read and analyze the strategy entitled "Interactive Teaming," think about how you might combine some of the effective communication strategies discussed here with this strategy.

Communication Summary Sheet

For: _____   On: _____
(Student's Name)   (Date)

Conversation Among (list participants):

_____   _____

_____   _____

_____   _____

Goals Identified:

1.

2.

3.

Solution Steps to Be Implemented (and by whom):

Solution Step   *Person Responsible*

1.

2.

3.

Progress Toward Goals Will Be Reviewed On:

_____   _____
(Date)   (By Whom)

barriers currently preventing Lisa from turning in her homework?" can help direct the conversations toward the identification of common goals. A positive and productive common goal among all teachers, the parents, and Lisa could be the following:

> We all want Lisa to succeed, and one way to help her succeed is to find ways to assist her in turning in her homework.

Once common goals are stated positively, it is easier to turn the entire conversation into productive problem solving toward goal attainment.

BRAINSTORM POSSIBLE SOLUTIONS   Effective communicators can use brainstorming techniques during meetings to help identify ways to achieve any common goals. During brainstorming, suggestions for solutions are compiled by participants, without passing judgment on any of them. The list of possible solutions can then be prioritized from those offering the most potential for success to the least. When all participants join in the creation of possible alternatives for helping Lisa succeed, they are more invested in reaching their goal. In Lisa's case, a brainstormed list created by her, her teachers, and her parents might include the following: serving detention for a month; quitting her job; keeping an assignment notebook; eliminating or restricting her television-watching; staying after school once a week for homework assistance; and rewarding Lisa if she meets a certain criterion by the end of the quarter.

SUMMARIZE GOALS AND SOLUTIONS   Summarizing the statement of goals and proposed solutions verbally (and perhaps in writing), before the end of the meeting, is beneficial for all participants. This prevents any misunderstandings and provides an opportunity for clarification. In our example, the teacher summarizes the meeting by stating, "Let me summarize what we all agreed on. We all want Lisa to succeed in science. One way to have Lisa be more successful is to help her turn in all of her homework assignments. One thing Lisa will do is keep an assignment notebook in which she records her assignments and due dates, which she will show daily to her parents and teachers. Another step will be for Lisa and her parents to find a place at home for her to complete her homework. Her parents will assist her by asking regularly if she has completed her homework assignments. Finally, Lisa will attend after-school help sessions if she does not understand what to do to complete the assignments. We will meet and review Lisa's progress toward her goals within one month, at which time we will determine whether we need to modify any of the possible solutions."

FOLLOW UP TO MONITOR PROGRESS Summarization makes the entire conversation positive and concrete. A goal statement is made, possible solutions are listed, one is selected for implementation and evaluation, and follow-up target dates are set for monitoring progress toward goal attainment.

All steps promote communication with everyone involved in educating students with disabilities. Review the *In the Classroom* feature, which can be used to ensure decisions made by the group during problem solving are more easily executed. Whatever model of communication you use, note that practicing good communication skills enables you to be effective in the many roles associated with collaboration.

Collaboration and Communication for Intervention

Many types of collaboration occur in larger groups or "teams" within schools. One type of schoolwide team is the general education **prereferral intervention team.** In many states the general education prereferral team meets before an actual referral for special education services. Depending on the school district, these teams may also be referred to as multidisciplinary teams, child study teams, general education assistance teams, prereferral assistance teams, or teacher assistance teams. No matter what the team is called, its function is to determine the need for educational interventions to assist individual students who are struggling to succeed at school. In addition, the teams' intervention strategies assist teachers who, after careful observation, are unsure whether a student needs special education services. Hence, the team's first purpose is to see if intervention strategies can make a difference for the student. The team convenes after a formal request is made to the building principal or other designated individual within a school.

GENERAL EDUCATION PREREFERRAL REQUEST

A formal prereferral request can be made by a teacher, school specialist, parent, school administrator, or the student. For example, a request might be made by a general education teacher who has worked with a student for a period of time and finds that all her efforts have not made the differences they should have in that child's educational success.

Documentation of observations, student work samples, test scores, and other relevant data often is submitted with a formal intervention request. It is important to reiterate that before Mrs. Mayer requested help from the intervention team, she had taken a number of steps to address the problem. Often, these steps are sequential, in that each item checked should be undertaken before the next concern. Mrs. Mayer

Effective collaboration depends on cooperation, shared goals, and shared problem solving.

first reviewed Omar's records to verify that vision and hearing screenings had taken place. Parent conferences and student interviews were conducted to discuss the problem areas and consider possible solutions. She collected, analyzed, and filed samples of Omar's recent academic class work and evidence of disciplinary actions. She informally asked for advice from other teachers, school counselors, special education teachers, and mainstream assistance teams. Mrs. Mayer made documentation available to the intervention team of specific intervention strategies she had tried before asking the team for help. All of this information was useful to team members in deciding what other modifications, adaptations, or interventions might be tried to find the best educational program for Omar. For an illustration of all the steps in the referral process, see Figure 2.1.

Figure 2.1 Steps in the Referral Process

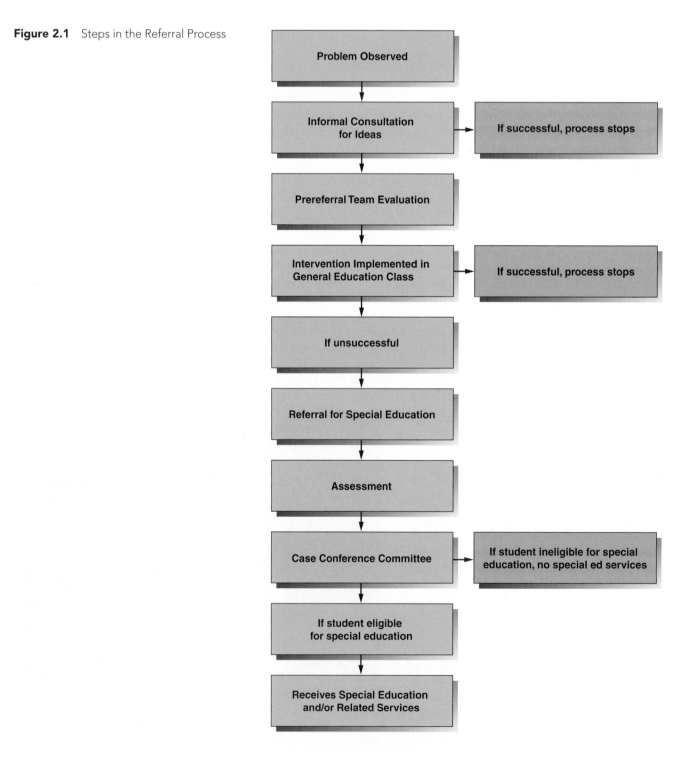

Omar

Mrs. Mayer is a second-grade teacher. In November, she began to worry about one of her students, Omar. At the beginning of the school year, Mrs. Mayer noticed that Omar seemed to be behind his classmates academically. In spite of additional review of first-grade material, Omar continued to have problems with reading and writing tasks and had a hard time maintaining attention to tasks.

When November arrived and Omar was still struggling, Mrs. Mayer decided that she and Omar needed some assistance. She contacted her school's general education prereferral intervention assistance team. The team members included a first-, third-, fourth-, and fifth-grade teacher, a school psychologist, the principal, and a special education teacher. The team scheduled a meeting to discuss the nature and severity of Omar's difficulties and designed intervention strategies that Mrs. Mayer could implement and review within a specified timeline.

QUESTIONS FOR REFLECTION

1. How would you determine whether a problem was serious enough to contact the prereferral intervention assistance team?
2. How would you determine whether your assessment of Omar's problem was objective and unbiased?

THE INTERVENTION PROCESS

The strategies addressed in the intervention process are designed, implemented, and evaluated before any formal referral for special education services. These are not special education procedures but are part of the general education system required by some state special education legislation (see, for example, guidelines for "General Education Intervention" on the Website of the Indiana State Department of Education). The *In the Classroom* feature on page 32 identifies a checklist of steps in a prereferral process.

Prereferral procedures are preventative in nature, intended to reduce inappropriate referrals and decrease the likelihood of future problems. These procedures provide general education teachers and students with immediate assistance with classroom-related problems, including disciplinary issues. To determine whether the general education intervention is appropriate, team members may observe the student before the prereferral intervention takes place. It is wise to try to involve the parents whenever possible; however, before any general education intervention plan is implemented, parents must be notified in writing of the team's recommendation for intervention strategies and the rationale behind implementing them. Finally, the intervention is implemented.

ESTABLISHING TIMELINES   Once intervention strategies are developed, timelines are set to accompany the implementation and review of those strategies. In Mrs. Mayer's case, a strategy was designed to be implemented with Omar. A 1-month timeline was established for her to implement, monitor, and evaluate Omar's progress. If adequate improvement is observed, the intervention will continue (or discontinue if it appears no longer necessary). However, if inadequate progress is noted, one of two steps may occur. First, the strategies may be redesigned along with new timelines, which Mrs. Mayer would then implement. Second, if the problem seems more severe or persistent than general classroom interventions can address, the team may decide to begin the referral process for special education

The prereferral process often begins when a classroom teacher recognizes that a student's classwork is well behind that of expected or typical performance.

services. At that point, Omar's parents will be contacted and asked to give permission for an educational evaluation for possible special education services. Omar's parents can request an educational evaluation for special education at any time during this process, and their request will be honored and not delayed due to the implementation of the general education intervention.

INTERVENTION STRATEGIES   Intervention strategies vary depending on the specific needs of the student, but may include modifications in (a) the curriculum, (b) instructional procedures, (c) classroom management, or (d) classroom environment. Curriculum modifications involve altering the curriculum or adapting the curriculum currently used, such as using materials at a lower reading level. Modifications in instructional procedures include providing additional instruction or using different presentation formats, varying the types of practice activities, modifying task demands or testing procedures, or regrouping students within instructional activities. Modifying classroom management procedures involves intensifying behavioral monitoring for increasing attention to task, providing individual student behavioral contracts, or increasing reinforcement. Environmental modifications consist of rearranging the classroom desks, making the classroom more accessible, or changing seating positions. Finally, other resources available within the school and community may be used to assist in making general education interventions.

RESEARCH ON PREREFERRAL INTERVENTIONS   Buck, Polloway, Smith-Thomas, and Cook (2003) surveyed 50 state departments of education and the District of Columbia regarding their prereferral intervention practices, and found that there was considerable variability from state to state, in whether prereferral interventions were required, the terminology used to describe them, and how they were carried out. Although prereferral intervention practices are not always successful (Rock & Zigmond, 2001), they are often effective in preventing special education placement (Burns & Symington, 2002).

RESPONSE-TO-INTERVENTION (RTI) PROCEDURES   Since the passage of the 2004 amendments of IDEA, schools have been allowed to use federal funds to provide *early intervening services* for students experiencing difficulty in school but not yet referred for special education (see Chapters 3 and 13). These services may be delivered in *tiers* of increasing intensity, where, for example, Tier 1 interventions may be research-validated teaching practices, with targeted adaptations implemented when needed. Tier 2 interventions can be planned for students who fail to respond to Tier 1 interventions (Division for Learning Disabilities, 2007). These second-tier interventions can take place with small groups of students who have not responded well to Tier 1 interventions, and may in the future become a very commonly applied type of prereferral intervention. Tier 2 interventions may include, for example, 20 or 30 minutes of intensive small-group instruction in reading. The goal is to help students acquire needed class-room skills, within a specific time period (e.g., 10–20 weeks; Vaughn & Roberts, 2007). If students still do not make acceptable progress, students may be provided with even more intensive (Tier 3) services, including referral for evaluation for special education placement. Research suggests that Tier 2 interventions in reading can help many students gain important skills (Kamps et al., 2008), and may lead to a reduced rate of referral for special education services.

Collaboration for Referrals and Placements

The special education referral process can be initiated by almost anyone, including the student, although the student's teachers or parents usually make the referral. Each school has written referral procedures, designated staff for the various positions within the referral process, and accompanying forms.

Once the prereferral team determined that the strategies Mrs. Mayer had implemented on her own were insufficient to help Omar successfully perform in second grade, the referral process for educational evaluation began. Mrs. Mayer completed a "Referral Evaluation Form" from the school (see Figure 2.2 for a sample referral form). Once the referral form was completed, Omar's parents were contacted and asked to meet with school personnel. They were told that their son had been referred for an educational evaluation. They were told why he was referred and were asked to provide written permission to proceed. Omar's parents were informed about the evaluation procedures, and told that a case conference committee meeting would be scheduled within 65 school days of the parents' signing the permission for testing. They were also told about how the school had already attempted to help Omar through the general education prereferral intervention.

Date Received _____

Student's Name _____ Sex _____ Birthdate _____

School _____ Grade _____ Teacher _____

Parent/Guardian _____ Primary Language _____

Address _____ Home Phone _____ Work Phone _____

Current Educational Program _____

Referring Person _____
                    (signature)   (title)   (date)

Principal/Designee _____
                         (signature)   (date)

1. Please describe briefly the reason(s) for this referral.

2. Documentation of the general education intervention (attach copy of the GEI plan): What are effects of intervention?

   Comments from the remedial reading instructor, if applicable:

Figure 2.2 Sample Referral Form   (continued)

3. Documentation of support services such as counseling or psychological (nontesting) services provided by school or other agency.

   Comments and observations from the school counselor:

   Has a previous psychological evaluation been conducted?

   Yes _____   No _____   Date _____   Agency _____

4. Documentation of conferences, or attempts to conference, with the parent and appropriate school personnel concerning the student's specific problem(s).

5. Which of the disabilities/handicaps do you suspect?

   _____ Autism   _____ Communication disorders   _____ Emotional disability

   _____ Hearing impairment   _____ Learning disability   _____ Mental disability

   _____ Orthopedic impairment   _____ Other health impairment

   _____ Traumatic brain injury   _____ Visual impairment

6. In what subjects are the student's problems most apparent?

7. List schools previously attended and dates:

8. Comments from school nurse:

   Current general health _____

   Previous medical problems _____

   Is the student taking medication? ____ If yes, specify _____

   Vision: L _____ R _____ Correction _____

   Date of vision screening _____ (must be done within a year)

9. Comments from speech, hearing, and language clinician:

   Hearing: L _____ R _____ Correction _____

   Date of hearing screening _____ (must be done within a year)

   Is the student receiving speech and language therapy? In the past?

10. Copy and attach information from the student's education record:
    1. Previous achievement test results
    2. Grades earned since school entry
    3. Attendance record
    4. Summary of disciplinary actions

Complete and send all referral information to Special Services.

Figure 2.2   *(Continued)*

All information should be presented verbally and in writing for the parents, and in the parents' native language. If parents speak Spanish, then school personnel must communicate with the parents using Spanish. Some school districts have developed handouts describing parents' rights. Figure 2.3 contains a handout used by the Crawfordsville Community School Corporation based on Indiana state special education law.

I. Educational evaluations and placement in special education programs cannot be done without written parental consent.

II. Parents have the right to inspect school records within a reasonable period of time of their request.

III. Parents have the right to have educational records explained to them by school personnel.

IV. Parents have the right to receive copies of the student's educational record.

V. Parents have the right to ask that records be amended if they believe that the information therein is incorrect.

VI. Tests during the evaluation should be valid, fair, and in the child's native language.

VII. The parent has the right to an independent educational evaluation at the school's expense if the parent disagrees with the findings of the evaluation completed by the school personnel.

VIII. The case conference committee must consider the results of independent evaluations obtained by parents.

IX. The parents must be notified in writing of an upcoming case conference. The conference should be set at a mutually agreeable time and place. The notice should be in the parents' native language and should include a list of those expected to participate in the conference.

X. The parent may bring any other individual to the conference including an advocate.

XI. The case conference committee must receive written parental consent before a child can be placed into any special education program. Parents must receive a copy of the educational evaluation, their parental rights, and the case conference summary.

XII. The public agency (school) must ensure that a child is placed with nondisabled peers to the maximum extent of his/her abilities.

XIII. A case conference must be scheduled at least once a year to review a child's educational program and placement.

XIV. A number of educational placements should be discussed at case conferences to ensure that children are placed in the least-restrictive environment.

XV. A parent, public agency (school), or state agency may initiate a due-process hearing whenever any of these parties is concerned or dissatisfied with the educational evaluation, placement, or program of a student. This request must be made in writing.

XVI. Parents may bring legal counsel and individuals with training and knowledge in special education to a hearing.

XVII. Mediation may be sought when the parent and the school cannot through the case conference committee process agree on the student's identification, evaluation or educational placement.

XVIII. Complaints alleging the violations of these rights and the laws pertaining to special education may be submitted to the state Department of Education.

XIX. The public agency must appoint a surrogate parent whenever a child with a suspected disability is a ward of the state or whenever no parent is identified or can be located.

Figure 2.3 Summary of Parental Rights
Note: From "Parental Rights: Crawfordsville Community School Corporation." Reprinted with permission.

THE EDUCATIONAL EVALUATION OR ASSESSMENT STEP The educational evaluation for a referral to special education is much more comprehensive than the evaluation described for prereferrals by the general education teams. This evaluation provides extensive information on how the student learns best and the student's level of performance, and identifies strengths and potential need areas. The evaluation team includes a school psychologist and

General Education Teachers teach any grade level, any subject area, K–12; may be responsible for implementing part or all of a student's IEP.

Special Education Teachers teach any grade level, any disability area K–12; may teach in any of settings described for general education teachers; usually have primary responsibility for the implementation of the IEP.

School Psychologists or Diagnosticians take the lead on the educational evaluations, have major responsibilities in administering, scoring, and interpreting tests; sometimes serve as behavioral consultant to teachers.

Counselors advise students; may conduct some social and emotional assessment; may deliver counseling sessions or advise teachers on how to deal with social-emotional needs for their students.

Speech/Language Therapists work with students who require assistance with any speech and or language needs.

Physical Therapists provide assessment and interventions in gross motor areas.

Occupational Therapists provide assessment and interventions for students in the fine motor areas.

School Nurses often provide medical histories, distribute medications to students; provide a link between families and other school personnel.

School Administrators provide administrative assistance among all involved; may include school principals, vice principals, directors of special education, directors of special services, and special education coordinators.

Social Workers provide the link between families and schools; have similar roles to that of counselors.

Paraprofessionals provide assistance to teachers, special education teachers, and students with disabilities.

Other school specialists provide assistance in specialized ways, including adaptive physical education; sign language interpreting; bilingual special education; mobility specialists, psychometrists (complete educational testing), probation officers, and other consultants as necessary.

Figure 2.4 School Personnel as Team Members and Their Roles

other school specialists as needed (see Figure 2.4). For example, if a child is suspected of having a problem involving speech or language, then a speech and language therapist would be a member of that evaluation team. In the case of Omar, who is suspected of having reading and writing problems that may be associated with learning disabilities, a teacher of students with learning disabilities will be a member of that team.

The education evaluation includes various activities, procedures, and tests. A physical examination, developmental history, and vision and hearing tests may be required. A battery of academic, intellectual, adaptive, and social-emotional tests are administered, depending on the specific referral reason. Observations of the student throughout the school day may be completed. The classroom teacher is asked to evaluate the student's classroom strengths and need areas.

All testing must be culturally unbiased, completed in the student's native language, and must consider cultural background and presumed disability, to provide the most accurate picture of the student's current level of functioning. This means, for example, that if a student's native language is Spanish, then it may be important to administer tests in Spanish; otherwise, an inaccurate picture of the student's abilities may be obtained. Parents, teachers, or other school personnel can request a reevaluation whenever one is deemed necessary.

THE CASE CONFERENCE COMMITTEE A case conference committee or multidisciplinary team is composed of all individuals concerned with a particular student. The amendments to IDEA require that general education teachers participate in the development, review, and revision of IEPs. Moreover, the amendments require that parents be included as members of any group that makes educational decisions about their child. The members include the parents and their child; general and special education teachers; the school psychologist; school administrators, such as the building principal or special education director; and any other related personnel, such as the school nurse, counselor, and social worker, or specialists such as speech and language, physical, or occupational therapists.

A case conference committee meeting is convened after the educational evaluation is finished. The meeting is intended to determine whether the student is eligible for special education and related services. If so, then the IEP is developed and appropriate educational services decisions are made. Case conference committee meetings also take place during each annual review.

EASE THE CONCERN OF PARENTS AND STUDENTS During these meetings, all members of the committee should be made to feel welcome and comfortable. Parents and students may feel overwhelmed, intimidated, or frightened by attending a meeting with so many school personnel. Prepare for meetings by thinking about how to present information in comprehensible ways for parents and students. It may be beneficial to practice with another teacher when describing classroom routines. For example, parents may be unfamiliar with terminology that is used so commonly among teachers (e.g., *decoding* is a term frequently used by teachers but not necessarily by parents and children). Try to describe class activities, student performance, and behaviors using concrete, simple, direct language. Teachers frequently use abbreviations or acronyms when speaking with each other (e.g., saying "LD" instead of "learning disabilities"), and should avoid doing so when speaking at case conference committees, so that parents do not become lost in the "educational jargon." Secure brochures describing common disabilities in ways suitable for parents and for students. Brochures, important phone numbers, e-mail addresses, and Websites can be printed on handouts for parents.

When parents feel comfortable at the meeting, they will be more likely to share important information about their child. Parental input at the meeting can be invaluable. Parents have insight into their child's behaviors that no one at the school may have considered. They can provide input regarding the student's study habits at home and any difficulties encountered during homework. During the case conference committee, one member records the information on the case conference summary form. A copy of this is distributed to the parents at the end of the meeting. Figure 2.5 displays a sample case conference summary form. If the student does not qualify for special education, the student may still qualify for services under Section 504 of the Vocational Rehabilitation Act (see Chapter 1). Figure 2.6 presents a flowchart of student needs considered under IDEA and under Section 504.

RELATED SERVICES Related services are other services that are necessary to help students with disabilities benefit from special education services. Related services may include physical therapy, occupational therapy, audiological services, counseling, rehabilitation counseling, social work services, parent counseling, psychological services, school health services, medical services, early identification, transportation, recreation services, or other services identified by the case conference committee. If a situation requires substantial mobility adaptations, the case conference committee might recommend bus routes with special or adapted vehicles, assign an aide as an assistant, or acquire special equipment such as oxygen, ramps, or lifts.

THE INDIVIDUALIZED EDUCATION PROGRAM (IEP) An IEP is written by the case conference committee when it is determined that a student is eligible for special education services. The IEP has several major components, including the following:

- Student's current level of academic achievement and functional performance
- Statement of measurable annual goals, including academic and functional goals
- Statement of short-term objectives for children who take alternative assessments
- Statement of special and related services, based on peer-reviewed research and any program modifications to be provided for support for the child
- Statement of any individual modifications in state- or districtwide assessment procedures
- Statement of why a child cannot participate in state- or districtwide assessment procedures if an alternative assessment is recommended
- Initiation dates of service delivery and the duration and frequency of services
- Statement of transition services for all students 16 years of age and older, including appropriate post-secondary goals and transition services needed to meet goals
- Statement of how annual goals will be measured, how parents will be informed, and how progress will be monitored

CASE REVIEW CONFERENCE SUMMARY

Student's Name _____ DOB _____ School _____

Parents/Guardian _____ Address _____

Phone _____ Surrogate Parent _____

Committee Meeting: _____
            (date)   (time)   (location)

The Case Review Committee was composed of the following:

_____

Chairperson   Administrator

_____

Teacher   Teacher   Teacher

_____

Evaluation Team Member(s)

_____

Parent(s)   Student

_____

Others

The eligibility decision has been _____

Least restrictive placement has been _____

Purpose of conference   _____ initial evaluation   _____ re-evaluation   _____ review of IEP

                              _____ transition planning   _____ new to district

Multidisciplinary report of present level of performance:

_____

_____

_____

_____

Based on the data presented, the following eligibility decision was made:
The student is

_____

Placement recommendation:

_____

    Harmful effect considered: _____ yes

Options considered: _____

Reasons options were rejected: _____

Other factors relevant to the proposed placement _____

_____

Signatures of committee members with dissenting opinions:

      _____

      _____

      _____

Figure 2.5 Summary from Case Conference Committee Meeting

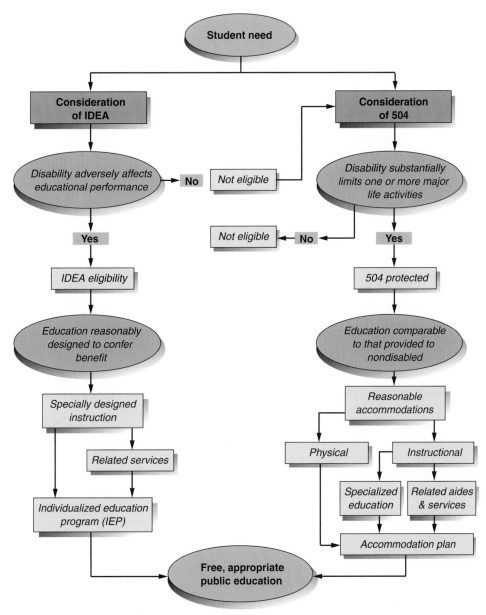

Figure 2.6 IDEA/504 Flowchart

Note: Reprinted with permission from "Student Access: A Resource Guide for Educators," by Council of Administrators of Special Education, 1992, Council for Exceptional Children.

Moreover, when a special education student is placed in a general education setting, the IEP will contain modifications needed, including curriculum, instructional procedures, staffing, classroom organization, and special equipment, materials, or aides.

Although IEP formats used by school districts vary across the country, all must contain the required components. Some computerized IEP programs are available commercially and are used to assist in developing the basic format of the IEPs (see the *Technology Highlight* feature).

School districts provide the parents with a written summary of the case conference committee meeting (see Figure 2.5), a copy of the IEP, and a copy of the parental rights (see Figure 2.3), and parents must provide written consent agreeing to the IEP before any services can begin.

WRITING GOALS AND OBJECTIVES A critical component of the IEP is the specification of the long-term annual goals and short-term objectives. Short-term objectives are required only for students who take alternative assessments. Long-term annual goals are based upon the case conference committee's judgment of what the individual student should accomplish within a year. Annual goals can refer to academic functioning, such as reading grade-level textbooks at specific skill levels, or social behavior, such as exhibiting appropriate behavior in

IEP Software

Special education paperwork can be reduced by using efficient systems for recording data, maintaining records, and for communications. Advances in technology can help teachers save valuable time. For example, teachers can use basic templates with school stationery for communications in a word processing program, and databases containing frequently used names and addresses. Such timesaving programs are common features on most computers.

There are also a number of software programs commercially available to assist with writing IEPs. Many of these programs share common features in that they work easily on both PC and Mac computer platforms. Many contain general templates of information that is required by law to be included in the IEPs. Some also contain banks of possible IEP objectives. Some of the available programs include: *Goalview, Edupoint, IEP Planner, IEP Plus, IEP Ware, IEP Online, Welligent, IEP Team Software,* and *Tera Systems IEP Manager*. A simple search using one of the widely available search engines such as google.com on the Web will provide numerous commercially available programs.

Commercially available programs are usually advertised as highly relevant, timesaving devices that help teachers produce high-quality IEPs. Although this may be true in many cases, teachers should use caution to ensure that students' IEP objectives are not limited simply to what is available within individual software programs.

the cafeteria. In some cases, annual goals can refer to adaptive behavior or life skills, such as ordering independently in a restaurant or managing a personal bank account.

Annual goals are measurable, positive, student-oriented, and relevant (Polloway, Patton, & Serna, 2001). Goals that are measurable can be more easily evaluated later. For example, "[Student] will read and comprehend grade-level reading materials," is much easier to measure at the end of the year than, "[Student] will improve reading." Positively written goals (e.g., "[Student] will use appropriate language in the classroom at all times") provide better implications for instruction than negatively written goals (e.g., "[Student] will stop swearing"). Student-oriented goals describe what the student will do (as in the previous examples), rather than what others will do (e.g., "[Student] will be given spelling worksheets"). Finally, relevant goals are not always limited to academic goals, but provide for the student's current and future needs, including social-emotional functioning, communication, and career-vocational areas, when appropriate (Polloway et al., 2001).

Short-term objectives are more limited and precise, and specify the steps to be taken to achieve long-term annual goals. For example, short-term objectives relevant to a long-term annual goal in reading should specify the subskills (e.g., letter identification, word recognition) that students will acquire on the way to meeting the long-term goal. Short-term objectives should also be measurable, positive, student-oriented, and relevant. In addition, short-term objectives are usually best when they specify conditions, behavior, and criteria. As an example, consider the following objective: "In the lunchroom, [student] will use appropriate tone of voice at all times." In this case, "lunchroom" specifies the conditions, "appropriate tone of voice" specifies the behavior, and "at all times" (i.e., 100% of the time) specifies the criteria. When objectives are specified in this way, they can be easily evaluated on the way toward meeting long-term goals.

TRANSITION SERVICES Transition services are required to be written into IEPs when students turn 16 but, in fact, may be appropriate at younger ages (Pierangelo & Giuliani, 2004). IDEA and its amendments also require transitioning for preschoolers.

Parent input can be invaluable because of their insight about their children's behavior, habits, interests, and attitudes away from school.

Often, transition services can be implemented the year before students begin to accumulate credits toward high school graduation. At the annual review meeting, when the student is 16, the case conference committee may determine student educational, vocational, or employment training needs. Specific interagency linkages and responsibilities must be explicated in the individualized transition plan (ITP), which is a supplement to the IEP. The committee also determines whether students may require continual adult services upon completion of high school.

MONITORING IEPS   Legal safeguards are provided to ensure IEPs are monitored to reflect accurately the needs of individuals with disabilities. Regular reviews and evaluations of progress are required. Due-process procedures are always available to resolve any disputes between the parents and the school district regarding the student's education.

Due Process   Due process is how conflicts are resolved between parents and schools regarding the student's education. Disagreements can arise in several areas: whether a student is eligible for special education, the outcome of an educational evaluation, the educational placement, the IEP, or some aspect of the "free, appropriate public education" (FAPE) guaranteed by IDEA.

Several alternatives exist for resolving these disagreements, some of which take place before a formal due-process hearing. The simplest procedure for resolving conflicts is through informal meetings with parents and school personnel.

If conflicts remain unresolved during informal meetings, mediation can be used to try to resolve the dispute. Mediation is a voluntary process that must be requested by both parties. After a formal mediation request is signed by both parties, the state selects a mediator and schedules a hearing within 10 working days. Mediators should be trained in special education and mediation, possess excellent interpersonal skills, and serve as neutral facilitators. If mediation is successful, a written agreement is completed and forwarded to the case conference committee for its approval. Many conflicts can be resolved through mediation (Murdick, Gartin, & Crabtree, 2006).

A request for a due-process hearing is a formal request by either the parents or the school district to have the dispute arbitrated by an independent hearing officer. This process is more formal than mediation and must take place within timelines as specified in the law. The case is presented to the independent hearing officer, who makes a decision based on evidence presented by both parties. Both parents and school district may be represented by legal counsel, present information pertaining to the case, bring forth relevant witnesses, and are entitled to see, at least 5 days before the hearing, any evidence the other party plans to introduce. Due-process hearings can be open or closed to the public, and the student may or may not be present. After listening to all the evidence, hearing officers produce a written decision. After the hearing decision, but within a specified number of days, the decision must be either executed or appealed to the appropriate state board of special education by either party.

The appeal of the due-process-hearing decision must describe the parts of the decision that are objectionable and the associated rationale. The state board of special education is required to schedule another impartial review of the hearing and report on its decision. Its decision is considered final, unless either party appeals to the civil court within 30 calendar days. Throughout this process, the students remain in their current placement unless both parties agree to something else.

Special education departments in each school district have policies and procedures outlining teachers' roles and responsibilities should they become involved in these processes. The intent of the law is to best serve the student with disabilities, and these safeguards are in place to ensure that both parents and school district personnel are afforded due-process rights.

Reviews of student IEPs need to be done regularly to assess student progress and create new goals as dictated by that progress.

Co-Teaching

 Scruggs, Mastropieri, and McDuffie (2007) conducted a "meta-synthesis" of qualitative research on co-teaching. These authors identified 32 studies that employed interviews, observations, and examination of classroom products to describe the practice of co-teaching in inclusive classrooms. Using research integration procedures, they combined information from these studies to draw more general conclusions about how co-teaching is being implemented in schools. The final sample of participants in all of these studies included 454 co-teachers, 42 administrators, 142 students, 26 parents, and 5 support personnel.

One widely reported finding was the overall positive acceptance of co-teaching by teachers and students. Teachers felt that co-teaching in inclusive classes was beneficial for teachers, as well as for students with and without disabilities. For example, one general education co-teacher from a study by Frisk (2004) remarked, "'I learned so much this year from my partner. I learned how to adapt lessons for each student; she really taught me

so much'" (p. 98). In another study, a special education teacher spoke about a student with special needs who "'was truly amazed to find that he could do OK in here. . . . When he realized all of this, he was willing to work harder than he ever had in the self-contained classes'" (Walther-Thomas, 1997, p. 399). A student with a hearing impairment in an investigation by Luckner (1999) reported, "'It's a good class for me because I learn more stuff'" (p. 27). These findings are consistent with a recent study by McCann (2008), who reported that general education teachers' attitudes toward inclusion of students with disabilities increased substantially when asked about co-taught classrooms.

However, several concerns were also raised about the implementation of co-teaching. Many teachers emphasized the need for more administrative support, more time to plan for co-teaching, and for additional training. Many teachers also felt that the personal compatibility of the co-teachers was important. Although many models of co-teaching have been proposed, the most commonly observed model was "one teach, one

assist," with the special education teacher often playing a subordinate role. Sometimes this diminished role was associated with the more limited content knowledge of the special education teacher. Finally, many observed classrooms provided a whole-class instruction model, with little specific individualization for special needs. Nevertheless, a number of co-taught classrooms were exemplary, and demonstrated the high degree of success that can be realized when teachers work collaboratively for the benefit of both the whole class and the special needs of individual students.

QUESTIONS FOR REFLECTION

1. What factors might influence the success of co-teaching arrangements?
2. How might teachers better plan for co-teaching?
3. Should teachers be allowed to volunteer for co-teaching, and choose their own partners, or should administrators make these decisions?
4. Should co-teaching practices in elementary schools differ from those in high schools?

Annual Reviews   Annual review meetings are conducted to monitor progress. During these meetings, teachers, parents, and other team members discuss the student's progress and make recommendations to amend, modify, or adjust the IEP as necessary. Changes in a student's educational placement to a more or less restrictive environment might be made based on the review.

Collaboration as Partnerships

Relationships develop among the many individuals working together to design optimal educational programs for students with disabilities. Relationships of special education and general education teachers may develop into collaborative consultation for shared decision making and planning, and co-teaching relationships. Collaborative partnerships can also develop with paraprofessionals and with parents and families. These partnerships can substantially improve the school and life functioning of students with disabilities. The *Research Highlight* feature describes collaborative practices of schools achieving excellence for students with and without disabilities.

CONSULTATION BETWEEN SPECIAL AND REGULAR EDUCATORS

Consultation exists when two individuals, such as special and general educators, work together to decide on intervention strategies for a specific student. During these meetings, which can be formal or informal, and verbal or in writing, effective communication procedures are critical.

For example, special education teachers may send weekly notes or e-mails to general education teachers to ask about the progress of specific students with disabilities. Teachers then describe any potentially difficult assignments with which they expect students with disabilities will require additional assistance, as in the following examples:

- A biology teacher indicates that a science fair project is being assigned next week. It will be due in a month, and students with disabilities may benefit from extra assistance.
- A history teacher indicates an important unit test is approaching, and students with disabilities may require additional studying assistance.

This information alerts special education teachers who can then help decide whether additional assistance is needed and then work with teachers in developing appropriate interventions as needed for students with disabilities.

In other cases, teachers may ask for specific input from the special education teacher, for example, on how to deal with behavior problems. Kampwirth (2006) described how a special education teacher partnered with a general education teacher. After discussion, the general education teacher focused on two specific concerns: teasing and not turning in homework. The two teachers worked out specific plans for conferencing with the student, home-school notes with the parent, and peer mediation in class. These interventions were monitored and found to be effective in improving the student's behavior.

CO-TEACHING

Different models of collaboration and co-teaching are used to meet the needs of diverse learners within a single classroom setting. During co-teaching, two teachers are present in the inclusive classroom during instructional periods (Friend & Cook, 2007).

There are several different ways co-teaching can be carried out (Correa, Jones, Thomas, & Morsink, 2005; Friend & Cook, 2007). In **interactive teaching** (or **team teaching**), teachers take turns presenting and leading classroom activities, and share responsibilities equally. In other cases, one teacher assumes more responsibility for delivering instruction, and the other teacher assists individual students (**one teach, one drift**), or observes individual students to improve instructional decision making (**one teach, one observe**). In **station teaching**, smaller groups of students move through several independent workstations for new information, review, or practice, while the teachers monitor different stations. In **parallel teaching**, the class is divided into skill or ability groups, and each teacher leads one group. In **alternative teaching**, one teacher leads the larger group, while the other teacher (often, the special education teacher) provides additional practice or strategies to students who may require additional support. In practice, however, roles of the two teachers can deviate from these (Weiss & Lloyd, 2003).

Co-teaching at the secondary level can present some unique challenges, because of such factors as increased emphasis on content knowledge, the pace of instruction, scheduling constraints, the expectation for independent study skills, and high-stakes testing (Mastropieri & Scruggs, 2001). Murray (2004) suggested that general education teachers develop "dream lists" of what they would like most from special education teachers with whom they would be collaborating. These teachers then meet with special education teachers to revise and discuss the lists, and reflect on the outcome of the meetings. Similarly, Murawski

Team teaching is one model of co-teaching in which two teachers share the responsibility of one classroom, often with a great number of students or multiple students with special needs.

and Dieker (2004) recommended systematically sharing hopes, attitudes, responsibilities, and expectations before proceeding with co-teaching. They provided a chart of teacher activities to help organize tasks. For example, if one teacher is lecturing, the other teacher could be modeling effective note-taking procedures or managing classroom behavior. While one teacher is passing out papers, the other teacher could be reviewing directions and demonstrating the first problem. As one teacher prepares lesson plans, the other teacher could provide suggestions for accommodations and adaptations for diverse learners. Establishing a chart such as this could help maximize efficiency during co-teaching. Murawski (2006) underlined the importance of common planning for inclusive teaching, parity in teacher roles, and the use of varied instructional models.

Sufficient planning time for the two teachers to work cooperatively to develop lessons to co-teach is very important (Murray, 2004). Ask for assistance from school administrators to include as much co-planning time as possible. Consider using the following guidelines when establishing co-teaching:

- Decide goals and objectives for co-teaching.
- Inform parents and request their support and permission, especially if co-teaching alters any IEP placement decisions that were made with parental consent.
- Determine student and teacher attitudes toward the co-teaching.
- Determine how instructional responsibilities will be shared during co-teaching, what co-teaching models will be implemented, how parity of co-teaching roles will be established, what instructional adaptations will be made for students with disabilities, and how the effectiveness of co-teaching arrangements will be evaluated.

RESEARCH SUPPORT   Generally, teachers and students have reported positive attitudes toward co-teaching (Weiss & Brigham, 2000). Reported benefits of co-teaching include improved instruction, increased enthusiasm for teaching, more communication, and more opportunities to generalize learned skills to the general education class environment (Scruggs et al., 2007; see *Research Highlight*).

Challenges to effective co-teaching have also been described (Murray, 2004; Weiss & Lloyd, 2003) that include budgetary constraints, lack of sufficient planning time, lack of cooperation, personality conflicts, and increased teacher workloads. Other concerns include maintaining the full continuum of services for students, fear of losing necessary services, confronting negative attitudes, and confidentiality issues. Finally, the diminished role of the special education teacher and the frequent use of a whole-class approach to instruction has sometimes been a concern (see *Research Highlight*). Use of effective communication strategies discussed earlier, and effective teaching strategies described throughout this book, can help ensure that the co-teaching experience is pleasant and productive.

Conners (2008) observed and interviewed 30 special education middle school teachers during co-taught and self-contained classes. All teachers were previously identified as expert special education teachers by district personnel. Based on these observations and interviews, Conners concluded that these expert special education teachers demonstrated excellent co-teaching behaviors. These behaviors included those described in Table 2.2.

Although Conners (2008) and others have described the characteristics of effective co-teachers, little empirical research has documented the overall effectiveness of co-teaching, or supported the use of one model of co-teaching over another (Murawski & Swanson, 2001). More recently, however, research supporting the practice of co-teaching has emerged (e.g., Castro, 2007; McDuffie, Mastropieri, & Scruggs, in press). Teachers implementing co-teaching should collect evidence in their own classrooms to support the effectiveness of their practices.

STRATEGIES FOR
COLLABORATING WITH PARAPROFESSIONALS

CLARIFY ROLES AND RESPONSIBILITIES   Paraprofessionals may be aides to special education teachers, specialized aides for students with disabilities, or general aides for teachers within a school. Within those roles, paraprofessionals assume a variety of responsibilities, including recordkeeping, supervising, monitoring seatwork and classroom behavior, feeding

Table 2.2 Expert Co-Teaching Characteristics and Behaviors

Collaborative Co-Teachers

- *Capitalize* on each other's strengths
- *Complement* each other's teaching styles
- *Negotiate* all practice
- *Respect* what each "brings to the table"
- *Exhibit* comfort and trust with each other's teaching style
- *Make* their personalities and teaching styles complement one another, and work to establish good rapport
- *Demonstrate* evidence of co-planning and personal commitment to the co-teaching relationship

Both Teachers Viewed as a "Teacher"

- *Share and value* all students and have high expectations for everyone
- *Share roles and all responsibilities* in an equal partnership
- *Demonstrate flexibility* within roles
- *Exhibit* smooth transitions between teachers during instruction
- *Alternate* roles continuously during instruction, while both teachers exhibit a teaching mode at all times

Note: From *An In-depth Study of Expert Middle School Special Educators* (Table 6, p. 129), by N.A. Conners, 2008, unpublished doctoral dissertation, Fairfax, VA: George Mason University. Adapted with permission from the author.

and toileting, and providing instruction. It is important that paraprofessionals are viewed as part of a team and that they receive appropriate role clarification, training, and supervision (Giangreco, Edelman, Broer, & Doyle, 2001; Riggs, 2004). In many cases, paraprofessionals have not been informed specifically what their duties are, a situation that can lead to communication problems (Trautman, 2004).

Develop schedules for paraprofessionals that include the person responsible and the date for completion of specific tasks. Schedule also where all people will be at different times of the day or week (Pickett & Gerlach, 2003).

Very specialized responsibilities may be assigned to a paraprofessional. In the case of Jamal, a third-grader who uses a motorized wheelchair and has difficulties communicating and using his hands, a paraprofessional accompanies him throughout the school day. The paraprofessional functions as Jamal's assistant and accompanies him before, during, and after school in any activities, including helping him eat at lunch and dress appropriately for physical education and recess. It may be a new experience for general education teachers to have another adult in their classrooms during instruction, but once teachers become familiar with the activities Jamal can accomplish independently, they will gain a better understanding of how to maximize the role of the paraprofessional. For example, activities the paraprofessional can help Jamal with include handling his class materials, reading tests out loud to him, writing down his responses, and assisting with mobility.

Paraprofessionals assist students in their tasks throughout the school day. However, it is possible for paraprofessionals to spend too much time in close proximity with their students. This can lead to more limited sense of ownership by and less interaction with the teacher, separation from classmates and peer interaction, overdependence on adults, and a loss of personal control (Giangreco et al., 2001; Giangreco & Broer, 2007). Students should receive all the assistance they need, but not more than they require.

COMMUNICATE EFFECTIVELY WITH PARAPROFESSIONALS On occasion, teachers may feel overwhelmed with their responsibilities and find it difficult to know what to do with paraprofessionals. This may be especially true if paraprofessionals have strong personalities, are older, or have worked in schools longer than the teacher. If a touchy situation arises, such as disagreeing on the amount of assistance necessary for a student, relations may become strained. To defuse these situations, use effective communication and problem-solving strategies to identify the problem and brainstorm potential solutions. If you do not think you can handle the situation alone, seek the assistance of a more established teacher within your school. Often, simply discussing the situation makes everyone feel more comfortable.

PEARSON
myeducationlab

Go to MyEducationLab, select the topic *Collaboration, Consultation, and Co-Teaching,* and go to the Activities and Applications section. Then watch the two videos "Collaboration and Communication with Teachers, Paraprofessionals, and Parents" and "Fluency Building: Social Studies Flashcards." As you answer the accompanying questions, reflect on how this teacher collaborates with paraprofessionals.

COLLABORATING WITH PARENTS AND FAMILIES

Building positive partnerships with parents yields important benefits to your students' education. Establish positive communication early in the school year and aim toward strengthening home–school cooperation. You will learn a great deal about your students from the parents' perspective of how they learn and interact in the home and outside of school (Overton, 2005).

BE SENSITIVE TO VARIABILITY IN BACKGROUNDS AND FAMILY STRUCTURES

Parents represent the continuum of educational backgrounds, as well as racial or ethnic and socioeconomic status. Be sensitive to all individual parental needs and make all parents welcome in your classroom. Many parents feel intimidated by teachers, so be sure to let them know you share their goal of wanting the best for their child.

State information in such a way that non-educators can understand what you are saying. If parents do not read or speak English, make the communications available in formats that are comprehensible to them. This may mean having native-language notes available for parents who do not read or speak English, or having interpreters available for those with hearing impairments or who speak another language. Remember to have information read to parents who may not have prerequisite literacy skills themselves.

Families of today represent a wide array of configurations. Chances are, the stereotypical family, consisting of a mother who stays at home taking care of children and a father who works outside of the home, may not be representative of many of your students' families. You may be working more closely with an individual who is not a parent but rather is the legal guardian of your student. Be sensitive to all family configurations. The *Diversity in the Classroom* feature provides some suggestions for interacting with diverse families.

Go to MyEducationLab, select the topic *Collaboration, Consultation, and Co-Teaching,* and go to the Activities and Applications section. As you watch the video entitled "Home/School Communication," and answer the accompanying questions, think about how you could adapt or use these strategies in your classroom.

MAINTAIN POSITIVE COMMUNICATION
A good way to initiate positive communication with parents is to send introductory notes home at the beginning of the school year. For example, Ms. Susan Chung, an eighth-grade English teacher, sends home a short note introducing herself and describing her class.

A positive first communication is especially important if a problem arises later and contact with home is necessary. Parents may be more likely to feel comfortable discussing sensitive issues concerning their child if you have contacted them earlier. If you only communicate when there is a problem, parents get the understandable impression that you only want to see them when something bad has happened, and they may become more reluctant to maintain communication with the school.

Many teachers also request parents' assistance regularly in their classes. This happens more frequently at elementary levels but also occurs at the secondary levels. For example, letters may be sent home asking if any parents could volunteer in the class. Sometimes teachers specify what types of volunteer activity would be beneficial (e.g., making photocopies, cutting out pictures from magazines, or baking cookies for class parties). At other times, teachers might ask for help in obtaining specialized materials needed during specific units of instruction. But no matter what the request, it is important to emphasize that you realize it may be impossible for some parents to volunteer in class due to other responsibilities or to contribute financially to class activities. Be sure parents understand that neither of these limitations undermine the value of their roles in supporting the education of their children.

Sending home "happy notes" is another way to maintain positive communication with parents. Happy notes communicate positive things from school that day, week, or month. School-to-home notebooks also can be effective means of maintaining communication with parents. Balance affirming messages with areas of concern, ask parents how they wish to communicate, and determine what information is most important for them (Davern, 2004).

COMMUNICATE ABOUT HOMEWORK
Establish a "homework communication line" with parents. Some teachers have students maintain assignment notebooks in which daily homework assignments are recorded, including a listing of the materials necessary to complete assignments. When Mrs. Hesser, a fifth-grade teacher, assigned problem numbers 2 through 8 on page 27 in the math book, due Thursday, the students wrote down that information, along with the notation that they need to take home their math books to complete the assignment. If there is no assignment, students are required to write "No homework tonight" in the assignment book. Parents are shown

Working with Families from Diverse Backgrounds

 Family involvement is a critical component of the special education process but is particularly critical for children from diverse backgrounds. Families representing diverse cultural and linguistic backgrounds can provide important information on their child's culture, language spoken at home, beliefs, customs, and other relevant background information. Schools need to be sensitive to all cultural values, beliefs, and needs when working with families from culturally and linguistically diverse backgrounds. Some of the following can help build strong trust and collaboration with families:

- Maintain open and good lines of communication with families from the start of the school year.
- Ask families how they can help participate in their child's educational program at home and school.
- When families speak a language other than English, have interpreters present for parent conferences and other school events such as open house, school plays, concerts, and athletic events.
- Translate home announcements and other school-related documents that go home so parents can access the content.

- Advertise locations of English as a second language (ESL) classes for interested families.
- Arrange for child care during family school visits when necessary.
- Determine whether families require transportation assistance to attend school functions.
- Arrange tutoring programs to assist both students and families who may require additional assistance with understanding school assignments.
- Schedule multicultural events during which individuals from different backgrounds have opportunities to share information about their respective backgrounds, food, clothing, and culture.

---

assignment books nightly, and are asked to check and initial the book. This extra supervision keeps parents informed of assignments and provides opportunities for monitoring homework. In some schools, "homework hotlines" have been established, in which parents can call a phone number, or check a Website, that informs them of their child's homework assignments.

RESOLVE DISAGREEMENTS On occasion, some parents may appear hostile toward teachers. In these cases, it is recommended that teachers obtain district assistance immediately. Some districts may recommend that specific documentation procedures be implemented; others may recommend that parent conferences be scheduled and attended by several teachers, including the building administrators. Understand that parent hostility might be due to a number of reasons, and assistance is available to help improve parental relations and ensure the best possible education for the student.

Maintaining a homework assignment notebook is one way to establish a line of communication between parents and teachers.

PARTNER WITH PARENT ADVISORY GROUPS Set up a parent advisory group in your school to meet every month or two. This group can function as a liaison between parents and the school regarding class projects, special curriculum areas, or regular school functions, and as a disseminator of information. Teachers can share information about special class projects with all parents at regular parent advisory group meetings. For example, these meetings might be a nice time for Mrs. Hesser to let parents know about the assignment notebooks. Mrs. Hesser could make sure that all the parents knew that during the upcoming parent advisory meeting she would be presenting that information and that she welcomed their comments regarding how they thought the process was working.

Other suitable topics include discussing the upcoming co-teaching planned by the sixth-grade and special education teachers or discussing special education referral information. Again, these meetings afford extra opportunities for positive communication and collaboration efforts among family members and school personnel. Finally, teachers can ask the group to assist in identifying topics of interest to parents and specific presentations could be tailored to their needs.

HELP PARENTS AND FAMILIES COPE WITH DISABILITY ISSUES   It may be difficult for some parents to understand and accept that their child has a disability. In these cases, request assistance from the school social worker, counselor, or special education teacher. Parents may be frightened or feel overwhelmed when trying to understand why their child has a disability, what needs to be done, and how they can help. It may be beneficial for parents to attend support groups for parents of children with specific disabilities. Use the expertise of the specialists within your school district to gather as much information as possible for the parents.

Most schools have brochures and reference lists of sources suitable for parents to read concerning specific disability areas. Many parents appreciate knowing names of books or articles that describe additional information on their child's disability. Reference lists can identify where the materials can be located (e.g., the town library, the school library, the special parents' library). Professional organizations also maintain reference lists on specific disability areas. For example, the Council for Exceptional Children is a major special education organization that not only maintains reference lists, but also has divisions specific to disability areas, such as the Division for Learning Disabilities and the Council for Children with Behavioral Disorders. Each division provides information pertaining to specific disability areas, including journals, newsletters, and Websites.

2 Summary

- Collaboration—involving cooperation, effective communication, shared problem solving, planning, and finding solutions—is the process for ensuring that all students receive the free, appropriate public education mandated by IDEA.

- Both schools and parents have responsibilities under IDEA. Partnerships can involve parents and professionals representing a variety of areas, including general and special education teachers, administrators, school psychologists, counselors, social workers, and community mental health agencies.

- Effective communication is critical for successful collaboration. Effective communication involves active listening, depersonalizing situations, finding common goals, brainstorming steps for achieving common goals, identifying possible solutions, and summarizing the conversation. These steps can be very helpful in solving problems.

- General education prereferral interventions are steps taken by schools to promote success in the regular classroom before deciding on referral for special education. These actions can involve general and special education teachers, specialists, administrators, parents, and students.

- Effective communication and collaboration is particularly important in the referral and placement process. For case conference committees to perform successfully, effective communication is essential.

- Building effective collaborative partnerships is one of the most significant tasks of a successful inclusive teacher. With effective teamwork, solutions can be found to any number of problems.

- Collaboration can take the form of consultation, in which teachers work together to decide on intervention strategies for a specific student. Communication can take the form of notes, informal conversations, or scheduled meetings.

- Collaboration can also take the form of co-teaching, in which a general education and special education teacher teach together in an inclusive classroom setting. Some models are (a) interactive teaching (one teach, one drift; or one teach, one observe), (b) station teaching, (c) parallel teaching, and (d) alternative teaching.

- Effective collaboration with paraprofessionals can improve communication and clarification of roles and responsibilities.

- Effective collaboration with parents is a key to effective inclusive teaching. Teachers should consider variability in family backgrounds and family structures, and maintain close, positive contacts with parents.

PROFESSIONAL STANDARDS LINK:
Collaboration: Partnerships and Procedures

Information in this chapter links most directly to:

- CEC Standards: 5 (Learning Environments and Social Interactions), 7 (Instructional Planning), 9 (Professional and Ethical Practice), 10 (Collaboration)

- INTASC Standards: Principles 1 (understands central concepts of the discipline), 2 (provides appropriate learning opportunities), 9 (relationships with school personnel, families, agencies), 10 (reflects on practice)

- PRAXIS II™ Content Categories (Knowledge): 1 (Understanding Exceptionalities), 2 (Issues)

- PRAXIS II™ Content Categories (Application): 1 (Curriculum), 4 (Managing the Learning Environment), 5 (Professional Roles)

COLLABORATION: PARTNERSHIPS AND PROCEDURES

If you would like to improve your communication and collaboration skills, have you employed effective communication strategies, including the following? If not, see the pages listed below.

STRATEGIES FOR COMMUNICATING EFFECTIVELY

STRATEGIES FOR COLLABORATING WITH PARAPROFESSIONALS

STRATEGIES FOR COLLABORATING EFFECTIVELY WITH PARENTS AND FAMILIES

Daisies in the Wind

CHRIS CASTLE Information about the photographer appears on page 2.

3

Teaching Students with Higher-Incidence Disabilities

OBJECTIVES

After studying this chapter, you should be able to:

- Describe and discuss the prevalence and characteristics of students with communication disorders.
- Describe and discuss the prevalence and characteristics of students with learning disabilities.
- Describe and discuss the prevalence and characteristics of students with intellectual disabilities.
- Describe and discuss the prevalence and characteristics of students with behavioral disorders and emotional disturbance.
- Describe and discuss the prevalence and characteristics of students with attention deficit disorder (ADD) and attention deficit hyperactivity disorder (ADHD).
- List, describe, and recommend adaptations and modifications to promote inclusion of students with higher-incidence disabilities.

Individuals who have higher-incidence disabilities—the disabilities that are most commonly seen in schools—include a wide range of abilities and disabilities, from mild to severe in intensity. Some higher-incidence disabilities are temporary, whereas others are lifelong conditions. Higher-incidence disability areas include speech or language impairments, learning disabilities, mild or moderate intellectual disabilities, and emotional disturbance. Together these disability areas make up over 80% of the total population of students ages 6 to 21 with disabilities served under IDEA (U.S. Department of Education, 2007), and about 8% of the school-age population. The percentages of students in each category in the United States are as follows:

> Speech or language impairment—18.7%
>
> Learning disabilities—47.3%
>
> Mental retardation/intellectual disabilities—9.6%
>
> Emotional disturbance—8.1%

Although the mental retardation figure includes those with severe intellectual disabilities, about 85% of the individuals in that group would be characterized as having mild or moderate intellectual disabilities, as described in this chapter.

In addition to the higher-incidence special education categories identified under IDEA, approximately 3% to 5% of all students may have attention deficit hyperactivity disorder (Kauffman & Landrum, 2009). Most of these students are served full time in general education classrooms, and about half of them qualify for special education services under IDEA (Council for Exceptional Children [CEC], 1992).

confused.

Speech or Language Impairments

PREVALENCE, DEFINITIONS, AND CHARACTERISTICS

Individuals classified with speech or language impairments make up 18.7% of all students ages 6 to 21 served under IDEA, and represent 1.7% of the school-age population. **Speech** is the system of forming and producing the sounds that are the basis of language, and **language** is considered the system of communicating ideas. Most students receiving speech and language therapy work individually or in small groups with a specialist for brief sessions several times a week and usually spend the remainder of their day in general education classes. In some schools, speech and language teachers may conduct therapy sessions in the general education classroom (Owens, Metz, & Haas, 2006).

Some students with speech and language disorders may have another primary disability area, such as a learning disability, cerebral palsy, traumatic brain injury, or other severe disabilities. The latter groups are more likely to be using **Alternative and Augmentative Communication** (AAC) devices to help them communicate.

Speech (sounds)
* voice
* articulation
* fluency

EXAMPLES AND CHARACTERISTICS OF SPEECH DISORDERS   Speech disorders may exist as voice, articulation, or fluency disorders. Voice disorders involve volume, pitch, flexibility, and quality of voice and affect about 3% to 6% of school-age children (Owens et al., 2006). Examples of voice disorders include speech that is chronically strained, hoarse, breathy, or nasal. In the most severe instances, voice is not present at all.

Articulation disorders represent the largest subgroup of communication disorders (about 75%), and include difficulty pronouncing words, including omissions ("libary" for "library"), additions ("terribubble" for "terrible"), distortions (such as lisping), and substitutions (e.g., "tram" for "clam"). A child with articulation problems might say, "wabbits aw fuwwy animals."

Fluency disorders are interruptions in the natural flow or rhythm of speech. A common fluency disorder is **stuttering**, "an involuntary repetition, prolongation or blockage of a word or part of a word that a person is trying to say" (Curlee, 1989, p. 8). Most people who stutter begin stuttering before age 5, but only after they have begun to speak in sentences.

Expressive
Receptive

EXAMPLES AND CHARACTERISTICS OF LANGUAGE DISORDERS   Language disorders are problems in using or comprehending language, either expressive (using language) or receptive (understanding language of others). Language disorders may involve difficulties with phonology, morphology, syntax, semantics, or pragmatics. **Phonology** involves the ability to

blend and segment the sounds that individual letters or groups of letters make to form words. For example, it may be difficult for students to identify the final sound in the words *cap* and *cat* if they have a phonological problem. **Morphology** involves the meaningful structure of words, as expressed in **morphemes,** the smallest units of language that carry meaning or function. For example, the word *swimmer* contains two morphemes: a **free morpheme** (can stand alone as a word; *swim*), and a **bound morpheme** (depends on other words; *-er*). **Syntax** is the grammatical structure of language and is concerned with such things as word order and noun–verb agreement. **Semantics** refers to the meanings of words used in language. For example, the sentence, "Walk can I take?" may convey a semantic meaning but is not syntactically correct. **Pragmatics** refers to the use of language in the context of social situations. For example, students typically speak to teachers in a different manner than they would speak to classmates (Owens et al., 2006).

One of the most severe language disorders is **aphasia,** which refers to difficulties speaking (expressive aphasia) or comprehending (receptive aphasia) language. Aphasia often accompanies brain injuries, and individuals may experience difficulty retrieving words that they knew before the injury (Owens et al., 2006).

Parents are often the first to recognize problems young children have with articulation or fluency of speech.

In the most severe communication disorders, individuals cannot speak and must learn to rely on ACC devices (Beukelman, & Mirenda, 2006).

CAUSES OF SPEECH OR LANGUAGE IMPAIRMENTS

In most cases, specific causes of speech and language disorders are unknown. Some children have severe language delays during early childhood development, but reasons for the delay are unknown. Voice disorders can be caused by growths, infections, or trauma to the **larynx** (structure containing the vocal cords); infections of the tonsils, adenoid glands, or sinuses; or physical disorders such as **cleft palate,** in which the upper part of the oral cavity is split. The cause of stuttering is presently unknown (Owens et al., 2006).

IDENTIFICATION AND ASSESSMENT OF COMMUNICATION DISORDERS

Parents are usually the first to identify a potential speech or language problem, when, for example, their 2-year-old has not begun to develop language. Primary school teachers may be the first to refer a child for a speech and language evaluation when they notice problems with speech or language. Frequently administered tests include articulation tests, auditory discrimination tests, language development tests, vocabulary tests, and language samples taken from a variety of social contexts.

STRATEGIES FOR
MAKING ADAPTATIONS FOR STUDENTS WITH SPEECH OR LANGUAGE IMPAIRMENTS

It is important to provide an open, accepting classroom environment to promote acceptance, decrease anxiety, and minimize opportunities for ridicule.

ADAPT THE PHYSICAL ENVIRONMENT   Place students with communication disorders near the front of the room for easier listening. This will also enable easier access if they need help or if you have devised a special cueing system with them for responding orally in class. The following *In the Classroom* feature provides a checklist for considerations for adaptations in the physical environment.

ADAPT MATERIALS   Allow students to use any technology that may help them with their disability area. A variety of alternative methods are now available to improve classroom communication.

Use Alternative or Augmentative Communication   Adaptive communication methods are referred to as Alternative and Augmentative Communication (AAC) techniques. AAC symbols and techniques fall into two broad categories—aided and unaided. Aided communication involves the use of some external device, such as simple handmade materials, a picture board, or more sophisticated computer-assisted devices. Unaided communication does not involve any apparatus other than the individual's own body. Examples include manual signing, making physical gestures, miming, pointing, and moving the eyes (Lloyd, Fuller, & Arvidson, 1997).

Alternative communication techniques involve the use of communication boards to assist communication. Communication boards contain pictures or words of commonly asked questions and responses to questions. When asking or responding to questions, students can point to the picture that communicates what they mean. Pointing devices that attach to the head can be used for students who have difficulty pointing with their hands or fingers. When the AAC user is unable to point, a communication partner can help identify the correct symbol. Some commercially available boards, such as the *Vanguard Plus* or *SpringBoard Lite* available from the Prentke Romich Company, produce speech output when the corresponding symbol or picture is touched.

More recent advances in technology have also incorporated the use of synthesized speech sounds when using some alternative communication devices, such as the *ECO-14* by Prentke Romich. Students can type information into computers, and computers will produce the speech output for them using a variety of tones.

ADAPT INSTRUCTION   Effective teaching practices, including clear, well-organized presentations and activities, will help meet the needs of students with speech and language disorders in your classroom. Appropriate pace of instruction and maximized student engagement—including frequent questioning and feedback—can help ensure academic success.

Sample Environmental Adaptation Considerations

Seating Position

_____ near teacher

_____ near peer assistant

_____ near paraprofessional

_____ near board

_____ near front of room

_____ alone

_____ quiet space

_____ other

Seating Planned for

_____ lunchroom

_____ assemblies

_____ bus

_____ all classes

_____ other

Rearrange Physical Space

_____ move desks

_____ move class displays

_____ other

Reduce Distractions

_____ visual

_____ auditory

_____ movement

_____ other

Provide Daily Structure

_____ first thing to do when entering class

_____ second thing

_____ third thing

_____ being prepared

_____ other

Provide Designated Places

_____ in-boxes

_____ out-boxes

_____ other

Provide Orderly Models

_____ organized desks

_____ organized lockers

_____ other

PEARSON myeducationlab

Go to MyEducationLab, select the topic Communication Disorders, and go to the Activities and Applications section. As you read and analyze the strategy entitled "Teaching Students with Expressive Language Disorders," compare and contrast this strategy with the ones we discuss here in the book.

Facilitate Verbal Responding   Allow sufficient time for students with communication disorders to speak when responding. Do not impose time pressures on oral responses, and resist the temptation to finish words or talk for the student who stutters. When a student finishes, repeat the response for the entire class to hear when needed. For example, Mr. Lee allowed Natalie, a student with a speech and language disorder, sufficient time to respond, and then said, "Natalie, that was a good answer. Natalie said, 'The numbers 11 and 23 are both prime numbers.'" When referring to stuttering, talk about it like any other matter; do not make it something to be ashamed of.

A high school history teacher, Mrs. Stobey, met at the beginning of the school year with Micky, a student who stuttered. Together they decided that if Micky raised his hand, it indicated he felt comfortable trying to participate in the discussions, and only then would Mrs. Stobey call on him to talk.

Initially, ask a student who stutters questions that can be answered in just a few words. Talk with the student about a preferred time to be called on. If you are going to call on many students in class to answer questions, the student who stutters may prefer to be called on relatively early, to allow less time for anxiety to develop (Stuttering Foundation of America, 2007).

Monitor your pace of instruction, especially when introducing new vocabulary to students with receptive language disorders. Use language cards containing representational pictures and illustrations depicting the definitions. Whenever possible, use concrete examples, rather than lengthy verbal descriptions, to illustrate new concepts.

Practice Oral Presentations   If oral presentations are mandatory, practice alone with students first and provide feedback. Consider allowing students to present with partners or in small groups, such that each group member has a different role during oral presentations.

Enlist Peer Assistance   Sometimes students who stutter are teased by their peers. Speak privately to the student about teasing and brainstorm ways to respond. Speak to peers (particularly those suspected of teasing) and enlist their support in ensuring that all students are treated fairly (Stuttering Foundation of America, 2007).

ADAPT EVALUATION Some students may require extended time periods to complete class tests. Others may require the assistance of readers, scribes, or communication boards and communication partners while taking tests. If your testing parallels your classroom instruction, students should be able to use the same materials and procedures they normally do in class when taking tests.

Learning Disabilities

PREVALENCE AND DEFINITIONS

Learning disabilities (LD) is a general term describing a group of learning problems. Students with LD are highly represented in general education classes, as LD is the largest single disability area. Approximately 4.3% of all school-age children are classified as having learning disabilities (U.S. Department of Education, 2007), or 47.3% of the children requiring special education services in the schools. About twice as many males as females are identified as having learning disabilities (Oswald, Best, Coutinho, & Nagle, 2003).

Communication boards can greatly improve learning and classroom interactions.

CLASSROOM SCENARIO

Maria

Maria is a 12-year-old girl of average intelligence and has a pleasant, cooperative disposition. She tries hard to succeed in school but has great difficulty reading independently. She writes slowly, using simple statements and words that are easy for her to spell. Her writing is labored and does not accurately reflect her thinking.

Maria receives assistance with her reading and writing in the resource room 4 days a week. Mr. Harrison, Maria's teacher, has prioritized Maria's class assignments. Mr. Harrison does not require that she read or write independently to participate in class activities. In social studies, for example, when the class is given an assignment to read parts of the textbook, Maria is allowed to read together with a classmate. The classmate reads questions from the assignments aloud, and Maria is allowed to write simple answers to the questions or to dictate longer answers to her partner. Mr. Harrison uses clear, structured presentations to maximize Maria's understanding of the lessons. Finally, Maria's performance is systematically monitored to ensure that she is learning adequately and that the need for further adaptations is examined. By the second semester, Maria's reading and writing skills have improved enough that she is encouraged to independently complete reading and writing assignments when possible but to ask a classmate or teacher for specific assistance when required.

QUESTIONS FOR REFLECTION

1. What else could be done to help improve Maria's reading and writing skills?
2. What other adaptations could be provided to help Maria show what she knows?

Learning disabilities is used as an umbrella term to refer to a group of individuals with average or above-average intelligence who nonetheless have difficulties with academic tasks. The federal definition is given as follows:

> "Specific learning disability" means a disorder in one or more of the basic psychological processes involved in understanding or using language, spoken or written, which may manifest itself in an imperfect ability to listen, think, speak, read, write, spell, or to do mathematical calculations. The term includes such conditions as perceptual handicaps, brain injury, minimal brain dysfunction, dyslexia, and developmental

Unexpected learning problems may suggest the presence of a learning disability.

aphasia. The term does not include children who have learning problems that are primarily the result of visual, hearing, or motor handicaps, of mental retardation, of emotional disturbance, or of environmental, cultural, or economic disadvantage. (*Federal Register*, 1977, p. 65083)

The standard that learning problems are not the result of sensory, motor, intellectual, emotional, or sociocultural influences is sometimes referred to as an **exclusionary** clause.

Over the years, many definitions of *learning disability* have been proposed by various task groups and professional organizations (Hallahan & Mock, 2003). Most definitions share components with the federal definition.

Most states previously required the presence of a *discrepancy* between ability and achievement to support identification of a learning disability. For example, Edward had a Full-Scale IQ (Intelligence Quotient) score of 101 and a standard score of 85 on a test of reading achievement. This amounts to a discrepancy of 16 standard score points between ability (the IQ test) and achievement (the reading achievement test), where the Full-Scale IQ is average (about the 50th percentile), and the reading achievement score is substantially lower (about the 16th percentile). Other evidence in support of the presence of learning disabilities was also usually required (Mercer & Pullen, 2009). According to the most recent IDEA amendments, states may no longer require schools to use discrepancy criteria. Instead, schools are encouraged to determine whether students respond to research-based interventions, as described in a following section (Division for Learning Disabilities, 2007; Wright & Wright, 2005).

CAUSES OF LEARNING DISABILITIES

The specific causes of learning disabilities remain unknown but are generally believed to be associated with brain function. Three major factors—organic, genetic, and environmental—have been hypothesized as possible causes. Organic factors include indications of brain differences in size or functioning perhaps due to differences during the development of the brain. Medical research in detecting brain dysfunctions has yielded evidence for a neurological basis that may be linked to possible causes of LD (Fletcher et al., 2002). Possible genetic factors include heredity, in that students with reading problems often have other family members with similar problems, and that identical twins are more likely than fraternal twins to share learning disabilities (Astrom, Wadsworth, & DeFries, 2007; Thomson & Raskind, 2003). Finally, environmental factors such as poor diet and nutrition and exposure to toxins such as alcohol, smoke, and cocaine, either prenatally or postnatally, may contribute to learning disabilities (Mercer & Pullen, 2009).

ISSUES IN IDENTIFICATION AND ASSESSMENT OF LEARNING DISABILITIES

One controversial issue involves whether students classified as learning disabled represent a truly specific category—that is, that they are distinguishable from students who are simply low achievers (e.g., the bottom 25% in achievement). Some researchers have maintained that there are few meaningful differences between the two groups of students (Fletcher et al., 2002). However, Fuchs, Fuchs, Mathes, Lipsey, and Roberts (2002) conducted a **meta-analysis** (research synthesis) of 86 studies comparing students with LD and low-achieving students in reading and found that students with LD generally scored considerably lower than low-achieving students. Debate on this issue continues.

Another related issue is the use of IQ–achievement discrepancy criteria. Lyon et al. (2001) argued that discrepancy criteria are not conceptually sound, are vulnerable to measurement error, and inhibit early identification of learning disabilities. In addition, MacMillan and Siperstein (2002) suggested that schools may not always apply discrepancy criteria correctly in identifying students with LD. Nevertheless, students with learning disabilities are generally thought to experience serious academic problems in spite of average or above-average general ability, and therefore could be expected to demonstrate some type of discrepancy (Mastropieri & Scruggs, 2002b). Schools are not required to use IQ–achievement discrepancy criteria for identification.

RESPONSE TO INTERVENTION   As an alternative to discrepancy criteria, schools are now encouraged to employ a response-to-intervention (RTI) approach, where general education teachers implement scientifically based practices and use curriculum-based measurement (see Chapter 12) to document student progress on a regular basis. Students who prove to be "treatment-resisters" (do not show adequate progress in spite of extra attention) may be eligible for more intensive interventions or referral to special education (Division for Learning Disabilities, 2007; Gresham, 2002). These criteria are now specifically encouraged in the most recent IDEA amendments (Wright & Wright, 2005).

RTI is intended to prevent academic failure through early intervention, frequent progress monitoring, and a system of increasingly intensive research-based interventions (implemented in multiple levels, or *tiers*) for children who fail to respond sufficiently. Increasing intensity is usually associated with (a) more systematic and explicit instruction, (b) more frequently implemented instruction, (c) instruction of longer duration, (d) smaller and more homogeneous student groups, and (e) instructors with greater expertise (Fuchs & Fuchs, 2006). Students who do not respond sufficiently to multiple tiers of intervention are considered *treatment-resisters,* and are eligible for special education referral.

Different versions of RTI include from two to fours tiers. In addition, RTI varies with respect to the approach employed. Most present RTI models employ either a *problem-solving* approach, or a *standard-treatment-protocol* approach. For example, one educational agency employs a four-tiered problem-solving approach. At Tier 1, the teacher confers with the student's parents to help resolve the learning or behavioral problem. If the problem is not resolved, at Tier 2, the teacher meets with the school's assistance team to identify the problem and plan an intervention. If the student does not succeed at this level, the agency staff are called in to redesign and coordinate the implementation of the Tier 3 intervention. If the student does not succeed at this level, special education assistance may be requested (Fuchs & Fuchs, 2006).

For an example of a standard-treatment-protocol approach, Tier 1 could include some specific, evidence-based reading practice in the general education classroom, perhaps including classwide peer tutoring in reading, explicit instruction in reading skills and subskills where needed (see Chapter 13), and monitoring of student progress. For students who do not succeed in this program, Tier 2 might include standard small-group (four or five students) instruction in reading, perhaps for 30 minutes per day, 4 days per week, for 10 to 12 weeks. For students who do not succeed on this level, Tier 3 might include highly intensive, individualized instruction based upon the student's individual needs. If Tier 3 procedures are not successful, the student may be referred to special education placement. In some cases, special education referral and placement is the Tier 3 intervention. Special education referral can also be initiated by parents at any time. As with the problem-solving approach, there are presently many different versions of the standard-treatment-protocol approach.

RTI procedures are also associated with some controversy. Standard implementation procedures have not yet been developed, the degree to which RTI discriminates between learning disabilities and other disabilities such as intellectual disabilities is not known, and procedures for identification are less clear in areas other than early reading (e.g., math, writing, secondary content areas). Further, presently there are many different versions of RTI, and procedures for determining "success" in a given tier also vary widely (Berkeley, Bender, Peaster, & Saunders, in press; Fuchs & Fuchs, 2006; Fuchs, Mock, Morgan, & Young, 2003; Gerber, 2005; Mastropieri & Scruggs, 2005; Scruggs & Mastropieri, 2002). However, these issues may be addressed more satisfactorily in the future, as schools develop more experience with RTI.

CHARACTERISTICS OF LEARNING DISABILITIES

Individuals with learning disabilities possess a variety of characteristics that distinguish them from other students. However, not all individuals with learning disabilities have all the characteristics described in this section.

LANGUAGE AND LITERACY   Many students with learning disabilities experience difficulties with both expressive and receptive language, including the following:

- Discriminating between sounds (e.g., mistakes *cat* for *cap*)
- Misunderstanding grammar (including use of certain pronouns and prepositions)
- Understanding subtleties in language
- "Word-finding" abilities or retrieving appropriate words when needed (Faust, Dimitrovsky, & Shacht, 2003)

Most students with learning disabilities have significant reading problems (Mercer & Pullen, 2009). Many students with learning disabilities lack **phonemic awareness**—the awareness that words are made up of individual speech sounds (Mann, 2003). Reading problems result when such students are unsuccessful at learning the sound codes represented by the letters in the alphabet and at applying those codes for successful reading ("decoding"). These individuals often have slow and labored oral reading abilities, are not inclined to read for pleasure, and lack any effective strategies for fluent reading. Reading comprehension difficulties frequently accompany decoding problems (Fletcher, Lyon, Fuchs, & Barnes, 2007). Other literacy problems encountered by students with learning disabilities include handwriting, spelling, and written composition (e.g., Graham, 2004; Gregg & Mather, 2002).

MATHEMATICS   It is estimated that two-thirds of students with learning disabilities have mathematics disabilities (Fuchs & Fuchs, 2003; Mastropieri, Scruggs, Davidson, & Rana, 2004). Students may exhibit difficulties in learning math facts, rules, procedures, or concepts, and in personal math such as managing money (Geary, 2003).

ATTENTION AND MEMORY   Many students with learning disabilities experience difficulties with sustaining attention to tasks. Some have more serious problems referred to as **attention deficit hyperactivity disorder** (ADHD; American Psychiatric Association, 2000). Many students who have a primary disability area such as learning disabilities, emotional disabilities, or intellectual disabilities may also have ADHD (Cutting & Denckla, 2003).

Many students with learning disabilities have deficits in both long- and short-term memory, and working memory for verbal information (**semantic memory**), the ability to hold information while simultaneously processing the same or other information (Swanson, Cooney, & McNamara, 2004). Memory problems can impede successful school performance unless students are provided with effective mnemonic (memory-enhancing) strategies to help compensate for such difficulties.

THINKING AND REASONING   Thinking and reasoning difficulties are apparent in many individuals with learning disabilities. Abstract reasoning may be especially problematic (Mastropieri, Scruggs, Boon, & Carter, 2001; Woodward, 1994). Such individuals may take longer than others to learn new tasks and information. Other problems may include difficulties organizing thinking, drawing conclusions, over-rigidity in thinking, and general lack of effective strategies for solving problems.

METACOGNITIVE ABILITIES, INCLUDING STUDY SKILLS, LEARNING STRATEGIES, AND ORGANIZATIONAL STRATEGIES   **Metacognition** refers to the knowledge about one's own learning and understanding. Students with well-developed metacognitive skills know how to study effectively, monitor their own understanding (**self-monitoring**), and wisely plan and budget their time. They are familiar with cognitive strategies that help them learn and remember more efficiently, and regulate their own strategy use (**self-regulation**; Gaskins & Pressley, 2007). In contrast, many students with learning disabilities lack these metacognitive skills necessary to become successful, self-sufficient learners (Harris, Reid, & Graham, 2004). They may appear disorganized and lack an understanding of what to do or how to proceed with academic tasks or assignments.

SOCIAL-EMOTIONAL FUNCTIONING   As many as one-third to one-half of students with learning disabilities may also exhibit problems with social or emotional functioning. Social-emotional problems include social skill difficulties, low self-esteem, low self-awareness and self-perception, low self-concept, weak self-confidence, anxiety, or depression (Elbaum & Vaughn,

2003; Hutchinson, Freemen, & Berg, 2004). Individuals with learning disabilities are more susceptible to adjudication than the population as a whole (Vaughn, Sinagub, & Kim, 2004).

GENERALIZATION AND APPLICATION   Most students with learning disabilities—as well as other high-incidence disability areas—have difficulty generalizing learned information to novel situations. Some students may master content-area material in special education settings but fail to apply that information to the general education classroom or real-life settings (Mercer & Pullen, 2009).

STRATEGIES FOR
MAKING CLASSROOM ADAPTATIONS
FOR STUDENTS WITH LEARNING DISABILITIES

ADAPT THE PHYSICAL ENVIRONMENT   Rearrange seating positions near students or personnel who can help students in the classroom and during school functions, and who can help them focus their attention. Arrange desks so they face away from any obvious distraction. When needed, arrange for a special quiet space within your classroom. Model organization of the physical environment by designating specific locations for books, coats, lunch boxes, and other personal materials. In addition, demonstrate how desks, lockers, and notebooks should be organized. Structure daily routines and schedules: clearly identify the first, second, and third thing to be done when entering the class, and provide clear schedules for students to follow (see Chapter 11).

ADAPT INSTRUCTIONAL MATERIALS   For students with literacy problems, adapt materials to reduce literacy requirements whenever possible; for example, use hands-on learning activities, videotaped or DVD presentations, computer simulations, and partner reading (see Chapters 15 and 16). Some assistive technology applications to reduce literacy requirements are described in the *Technology Highlight* feature. Teach students to adapt their own materials and study skills for classroom learning. These adaptations could include keeping assignment notebooks, scheduling time, and using prompts for employing cognitive strategies when studying, as discussed in Chapter 11.

ADAPT INSTRUCTION   Instructional procedures can be modified to facilitate successful inclusion of students with learning disabilities (Mastropieri & Scruggs, 2002a). The use of the teacher effectiveness variables (see Chapter 6), including maximizing student engagement, providing structured and clearly presented lessons, and monitoring student progress toward goals, can help students with learning disabilities learn more effectively. For example, provide clear organization to your presentations, and make your expectations very explicit. Question students frequently (with a high probability of successful answers), and ask students to rephrase information in their own words to monitor their understanding; use their answers to monitor and adjust your instruction. Periodically review previously learned material to promote long-term learning, and use specific strategies to enhance memory (see Chapter 10). Use peer tutors when needed to support learning, as described in Chapter 9. Provide clear directions and frequent reminders for assignments. Use research-based literacy practices, as described in Chapter 13, and use explicit instruction of study skills, as described in Chapter 11.

ADAPT EVALUATION PROCEDURES   Adapt test formats (e.g., multiple choice, matching) so that they are easy to understand. Practice taking tests with students and teach test-taking skills. Read test items to students with learning disabilities when this practice does not violate test standardization and reading is not being tested. Consider alternatives such as

Go to MyEducationLab, select the topic *Learning Disabilities*, and go to the Activities and Applications section. As you read and analyze the case entitled "Effective Room Arrangement," consider how this adaptation can be helpful to students of all ages.

Careful attention to seating arrangements can help promote attention and interest.

Assistive Technology Ranges from Low Tech to High Tech

Assistive technology (AT) refers to supports that help individuals maintain, increase, or improve their capabilities. AT, a critical component of IEPs for students with disabilities, is written into IDEA 2004. AT consists of devices and services. *AT devices* refers to any tools that range from low tech to high tech, or represent the range of simple adaptations to more complex technological solutions. *AT services* refers to the supports and training an individual might require to learn and use the AT devices. The following table presents examples of low- and high-tech solutions.

Area	Low Technology	High Technology
Writing	Pencil grip; scribes take notes for individual	Notebook computer and audio tape recorder used to take notes
Reading	Picture cards to enhance meaning	Software such as *Boardmaker*, *Boardmaker Plus*, or use of text readers
Mobility	Canes	Walkers or wheelchairs
Math	Lined or graph paper and pencil	Activities and tools available on Websites (e.g., http://illuminations.nctm.org) Tools with Web-based activities using interactive Web-based components

portfolio assessment and performance assessment, rather than relying entirely on traditional test formats. Use frequent formative evaluation so that you can evaluate regular progress toward meeting objectives. These adaptations will help ensure that you are obtaining a fair and accurate picture of what students with learning disabilities know and whether they are meeting their objectives (see Chapter 12).

These examples are illustrations of how AT solutions can range from simple low-tech to higher-tech adaptations. Many low-tech solutions are inexpensive and represent modifications to existing tools. The pencil grip is an example of a low-cost, low-tech AT device that can assist a child with proper pencil grasping. If the pencil grip successfully assists the student in improving in writing, other higher-tech options may be unnecessary.

In making recommendations for AT, evaluate the individual and the situation to determine the optimal AT device. Train the individual to use the AT device and then evaluate again to determine whether the device is effective. AT devices and training can be important home-based components as well. Show or describe to parents the range of AT devices from low to high tech that are available and explain how such devices can help facilitate their child's growth at home. Since it has been observed that many potentially valuable high-tech solutions go unused due to inadequate training, be sure to implement and evaluate, and follow up any AT training.

Intellectual Disability

PREVALENCE AND DEFINITIONS

Individuals classified as having mental retardation/intellectual disability represent 9.6% of the students ages 6 to 21 served under IDEA (U.S. Department of Education, 2007), or about .9% of the school population in general. Although this number includes all individuals with mental retardation served under IDEA, as many as 85% have mild or moderate intellectual disability, as opposed to severe disabilities, which are discussed in Chapter 4 (Drew & Hardman, 2007).

Although *mental retardation* is commonly used, other terms also are used to describe this condition, including *intellectual disability, cognitive disability, mental deficiency, mental subnormality, mentally handicapped,* or *intellectually challenged.* Mental retardation is also referred to as one type of the more general term *developmental disability* (Beirne-Smith, Patton, & Kim, 2006). The American Association on Mental Retardation (AAMR) has recently changed its name to the American Association on Intellectual and Developmental Disabilities (AAIDD; Schalock et al., 2007). The definition of the AAIDD (2008) states that:

> Intellectual disability is a disability characterized by significant limitations both in intellectual functioning and in **adaptive behavior** as expressed in conceptual, social, and practical adaptive skills. This disability originates before age 18. (p. 1)

This definition also includes five assumptions to be used in applying the definition: (1) consideration of the context of community, peers, and culture; (2) consideration of cultural and linguistic diversity; (3) consideration of strengths as well as weaknesses; (4) the necessity of developing a profile of needed supports; (5) the expectation that the individual's functioning will improve over time with appropriate supports.

According to the American Psychological Association (APA), mild mental retardation represents the upper range of functioning within the mental retardation classification, with IQ scores between 55 to 70. Scores between 35 and 54 are considered moderate mental retardation, scores of 20 to 34 are severe, and scores below 20 are associated with profound mental retardation (Jacobson & Mulick, 1996). The American Association on Intellectual and Developmental Disabilities (AAMR, 2002) does not employ a classification system based on IQ level. Rather, the AAIDD definition suggests that individuals could be evaluated relative to a system of services and supports. These include support areas (e.g., human development, teaching and education, home and community living), relevant support activities (e.g., individual's interest, activities and settings for participation), and levels and intensity of supports (intermittent, limited, extensive or pervasive). These levels were intended to replace previous classification systems of mild to severe mental retardation, although these latter terms are still widely used (Berine-Smith et al., 2006).

CAUSES OF INTELLECTUAL DISABILITY

The vast majority of causes of intellectual disability is unknown, and some speculate that known causes account for only 10% to 15% of the cases of retardation (Beirne-Smith et al., 2006). The causes of mild mental retardation are more difficult to determine than causes for severe and profound mental retardation. Known causes can be classified into genetic factors, brain factors, and environmental factors.

GENETIC FACTORS Genetic disorders or damage to genetic matter can cause intellectual disability. Disorders can include chromosomal abnormalities and genetic transmission of traits through families. **Down syndrome** is an example of a genetic disorder. It is sometimes referred to as trisomy 21, because the 21st pair of chromosomes divides into three (trisomy) instead of a single pair of chromosomes. Down syndrome represents 5% to 6% of individuals with intellectual disability, and is associated with some specific characteristics, including intellectual functioning in the mild to moderate ranges, short stature, upward slanting of the eyes, and a susceptibility to heart defects or upper respiratory infections (Beirne-Smith et al., 2006).

Recent research into the heritability of different traits, and other types of chromosomal abnormalities, has added to the knowledge base surrounding causes of some types of intellectual disability. Medical tests can detect the presence of some genetic abnormalities, including Down syndrome, during early pregnancy.

BRAIN FACTORS Brain factors refer to defects in the brain or central nervous system. These can occur during prenatal development, perinatally (during the birth process), or postnatally (after the baby is born). Brain factors may be congenital (present at birth) or may appear later in life. Prenatal factors include exposure to rubella (German measles) and syphilis (Beirne-Smith et al., 2006). Exposure to alcohol during prenatal development can lead to fetal alcohol syndrome (FAS), which may result in retardation (Connor, Sampson, Bookstein, Barr, & Streissguth, 2001).

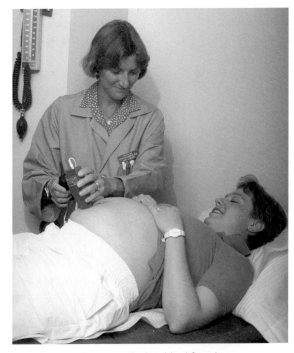

Good prenatal care and a healthy lifestyle are important during pregnancy.

Infections such as meningitis and encephalitis, which cause inflammations to the brain, may result in brain damage. Some forms of retardation are associated with cranial malformations that result in microcephaly or hydrocephaly. **Microcephaly** is associated with a very small skull, whereas **hydrocephaly** is often characterized by an enlarged head due to an interference in the flow of cerebral spinal fluid in the head. Finally, it is known that **anoxia**, or lack of oxygen to the brain, any time including during birth causes brain damage and may result in intellectual disability, depending upon the extent of the damage (Beirne-Smith et al., 2006).

ENVIRONMENTAL INFLUENCES Environmental influences refer to factors such as poor nutrition during prenatal development that can influence the development of the brain and result in retardation (Cohen, 2000). Many premature and low-birth-weight babies may have intellectual disabilities. The ingestion of lead, often through lead-based paint, can also cause retardation. Although factors such as poverty and lack of early sensory stimulation are associated with retardation, it is more difficult to prove that such environmental factors always lead to mental retardation. Future research may uncover additional important factors related to causes and prevention of intellectual disability (Beirne-Smith et al., 2006).

ISSUES IN IDENTIFICATION AND ASSESSMENT OF INTELLECTUAL DISABILITY

Both intellectual functioning and adaptive behavior are assessed in making determinations regarding mental retardation/intellectual disability. Individually administered intelligence tests are used in most states to assess intellectual functioning, and usually contain, for example, measures of vocabulary, common knowledge, short-term memory, and ability to solve mazes and jigsaw puzzles. Adaptive behavior scales assess how well individuals are able to perform daily living skills, self-help care, communication skills, and social skills. Although there is variability across states, in most states an individual should be functioning at least two standard deviations below average (approximately the second percentile) on both measures to be classified as having intellectual disabilities. (Jacobson & Mulick, 1996).

CHARACTERISTICS OF INTELLECTUAL DISABILITY

The most common features associated with intellectual disability include slower pace of learning, lack of age-appropriate adaptive behavior and social skills, and below-average language and academic skills. Many individuals with intellectual disabilities exhibit poor motor coordination, which can be improved by working with occupational therapists, physical therapists, or adaptive physical educators (Mohan, Singh, & Mandal, 2001). However, most students with mild and moderate intellectual disability have the ability to learn to read, write, and do mathematics, up to the sixth-grade level, or higher in some cases. Following is an autobiographical statement written by Kirstin Palson, an individual with mental retardation who was institutionalized as a child. The statement was included in a book of poetry she wrote.

> **From "About the Author":**
>
> My name is Kirstin Ann Palson. I was born in Boston, Massachusetts, in 1952 with complications. My diagnosis was mental retardation plus cerebral palsy, due to brain damage at birth. It was difficult those early years. Because of my behavior problems, I was sent to the Wrentham State School when I was seven years old. Those were horrendous times. At the age of fourteen I came out of Wrentham. I have overcome my handicaps, graduated from High School at twenty-two, and worked as a volunteer library aid in two elementary schools. For two years after graduation, I had a struggle getting employment. Finally I got a full time job in a company and worked five years. The company moved out of town and I struggled with unemployment and job search for six and a half months. I have gained employment in another company full time. I got both jobs on my own.
>
> I have a great love for words. When I was growing up, it was the reading of children's stories by Mom at bedtime which gave me the ability for reading and loving books. During the past years I have given books of my poetry to family members as gifts, especially at Christmas. My love for poetry is still with me and will remain forever more. K. A. P. (1986)

- Prepare general education students for the arrival of students with disabilities by asking a special educator to talk about disabilities and explain strengths and limitations of individuals with disabilities.

- Encourage students to ask questions, and set a model of open acceptance.

- Tell students about their roles as possible peer tutors and helpers. Provide models of how peers can assist, but make it clear that they should also encourage independent

functioning. They should not try to do everything for students with disabilities.

- Explain that all classmates, even if they are not peer tutors or helpers, can encourage students with disabilities to be active participants and members of the class.

In the CLASSROOM

INTELLECTUAL AND COGNITIVE FUNCTIONING   Individuals with intellectual disability exhibit deficits in intellectual functioning. In addition, these individuals usually function substantially below their age peers in related areas, including metacognitive abilities, memory, attention, thinking, and problem-solving abilities. Like students with learning disabilities, individuals with mental retardation often have difficulty generalizing learned information to novel situations (Mastropieri, Scruggs, & Carter, 1997).

SOCIAL AND ADAPTIVE BEHAVIOR   By most definitions, individuals with mild intellectual disability have less-well-developed adaptive behavior than their peer counterparts, including such behavior as using the telephone or dressing appropriately. They may appear socially immature, exhibit inappropriate social behavior, or have difficulty making and maintaining friendships. Some individuals may become easily frustrated when they experience difficulty and then may act inappropriately, drawing negative attention to themselves. On the other hand, some individuals with intellectual disability have particularly amiable dispositions and are well liked by others (Drew & Hardman, 2007).

Some individuals with intellectual disability tend to have an *external locus of control*, meaning they see their lives as being controlled and influenced by factors outside of themselves (e.g., fate, chance, other people; Ezell & Klein, 2003). This external locus of control may hinder their development of self-reliance. A related problem is *outerdirectness*—that is, looking to external cues or modeling behavior of others rather than relying on their own judgments (Zigler, Bennett-Gates, Hodapp, & Henrich, 2002).

LANGUAGE   Both receptive and expressive language are problem areas for individuals with intellectual disabilities. There is usually a direct relationship with severity of retardation and all aspects of language development (Vicari, Caselli, Gagliardi, Tonucci, & Volterra, 2002). Communication skills are typically less well-developed and can result in misunderstandings of directions (Cascella, 2004). Students may exhibit difficulties with comprehension of abstract vocabulary and concepts (Vicari et al., 2002).

ACADEMIC SKILLS   Individuals with intellectual disability may have difficulty learning basic skills of reading, writing, and mathematics (Young, Moni, Jobling, & van Kraayenoord, 2004). The rate of learning new information may be very slow, and students may require repetition and concrete, meaningful examples for all learning activities.

MAKING CLASSROOM ADAPTATIONS
FOR STUDENTS WITH INTELLECTUAL DISABILITY

Peers should be trained to avoid doing too much—or too little—for students with intellectual disability.

MAKE PREPARATIONS   Careful preparation can greatly enhance the successful inclusion of students with intellectual disability. First, have an open, accepting classroom environment so that students feel welcome as genuine class members. Provide students with the same materials—desks, lockers, mailboxes—as the other students. Involve students in daily activities. Meet with them privately and preteach the daily routine. Show them where materials are kept and how things in the class proceed. This will help build their confidence before they come in for the first time in company with their general education peers. More information for preparing classmates is given in the *In the Classroom* feature.

MONITOR PEER RELATIONSHIPS   Although peers can be good friends and strong supporters of students with mental retardation, teachers also should be aware that some students may try to take advantage of students with intellectual disabilities. For example, in one sixth-grade class, several boys bullied a boy with intellectual disabilities and consistently took away part of his lunch. In another example, high school students who had been smoking cigarettes in the girls' restroom handed their cigarettes to a girl with intellectual disabilities when a teacher entered the restroom. Careful monitoring can decrease the likelihood of such negative situations occurring and increase the likelihood that peer relations will be positive and productive.

MODIFY INSTRUCTION   Many of the modifications described in the learning disabilities section may also be helpful for students with intellectual disabilities. However, additional modifications probably will be required if the general education experience is to be successful.

- *Prioritize objectives* for students with intellectual disabilities in general education classes, and teach directly to these prioritized objectives.

- *Adapt materials* to the needs of students by reducing reading, writing, and language requirements and simplifying worksheets (see Chapters 15 and 16).

- *Adapt instruction* by employing clear, organized presentations, providing concrete, meaningful examples and activities, providing frequent reviews, and encouraging independent thinking (see Chapter 6).

- *Communicate with families* to further your understanding and obtain additional information on how students work best. The *Diversity in the Classroom* feature describes a model of "Person-Centered Planning" for working with Asian American families.

- *Adapt evaluation* using individual testing, portfolio assessments, tape or video recordings, or others as described in Chapter 12.

- *Use specialized curriculum* when necessary. Some students with intellectual disabilities may require an alternative, more functional curriculum. Such a curriculum may include communication, community living, domestic skills, socialization, self-help, and vocational and leisure skills. Additionally, some students may benefit from a life-skills curriculum, which emphasizes transition to adulthood. This curriculum could include education in home and family, community involvement, employment, emotional-physical health, and personal responsibility and relationships (see Cronin, Patton, & Wood, 2007; see also Chapter 16).

**PEARSON
myeducationlab**

Go to MyEducationLab, select the topic *Intellectual Disabilities*, and go to the Activities and Applications section. As you watch the video entitled "Functional Curriculum: Integrated Lesson," and answer the accompanying questions, reflect on how this teacher integrated both academic and functional skills into this lesson.

Person-Centered Planning: Multicultural Considerations for Working with Asian American Families

Bui and Turnbull (2003) synthesized the literature on Asian American families with children with disabilities and person-centered planning. Since *Asian American* refers to a broad range of individuals from a variety of countries (e.g., China, Japan, Korea, Vietnam, Thailand, Cambodia, Malaysia, Indonesia), they cautioned educators about making any generalizations across Asian American cultures.

Person-centered planning relies on a family approach to make decisions about individuals with disabilities. This approach attempts to reflect individual desires of the person with disabilities, involves those who care about that individual in planning, and highlights community resources rather than availability of services (see also Blue-Blanning, Turnbull, & Pereira, 2000). They concluded that with specific modifications, person-centered planning might be effective for working with Asian American families and made the following recommendations:

- Establish a relationship with the family.
  - Determine the level of acculturation (e.g., length of time in the United States).
  - Obtain formal introductions to the family, including the main authority person.
  - Learn about the cultural beliefs of the family.
- Preconference planning
  - Arrange for interpreters to be present.
  - Arrange meeting times that are convenient for families.
  - Organize transportation and child care when necessary.
- During the conference
  - Attend to verbal and nonverbal cues.
  - Allow sufficient time for processing information.
  - Allow family decision making in private.

Emotional Disturbance

PREVALENCE AND DEFINITIONS

Individuals classified as having emotional disturbance (or behavioral disorders) represent 8.1% of all students ages 6 to 21 served under IDEA, or .7% of the school population (U.S. Department of Education, 2007). However, prevalence studies have suggested that the actual percentage may be much higher. Boys outnumber girls in this category by about 3.5 to 1 (Oswald et al., 2003).

Emotional disturbance refers to a number of different, but related, social-emotional disabilities. Individuals classified as emotionally disturbed meet at least one of several characteristics that persist over time and that impact on school functioning, including the following:

a. An inability to learn that cannot be explained by intellectual, sensory, or health factors.

b. An inability to build or maintain satisfactory interpersonal relationships with peers and teachers.

c. Inappropriate types of behavior or feelings under normal circumstances.

d. A general pervasive mood of unhappiness or depression.

e. A tendency to develop physical symptoms or fears associated with personal or school problems. (Code of Federal Regulations, Title 34, Section 300.7[c][4][i])

Individuals classified as emotionally disturbed represent a range of severity, and the disability itself may be temporary or permanent. Specific emotional disturbance areas include childhood **schizophrenia; selective mutism** (failure to speak in selected circumstances); seriously aggressive or acting-out behavior; conduct disorders; inappropriate affective disorders such as depression, social withdrawal, psychosomatic disorders, anxiety disorders, and self-mutilating behaviors; and excessive fears (or phobias). Individuals characterized as socially maladjusted (e.g., juvenile delinquency) are not considered emotionally disturbed according to IDEA, unless they also exhibit other evidence of emotional disturbance (Kauffman & Landrum, 2009).

CAUSES OF EMOTIONAL DISTURBANCE

Most behavioral disorders or emotional disturbances have no known cause. However, possible causes include biological, family, school, and cultural factors (e.g., Kauffman & Landrum, 2009).

Biological factors are genetic, biochemical, and neurological influences that interact and result in emotional disabilities. Schizophrenia, autism (see Chapter 4), and **Tourette syndrome**—a tic disorder characterized by involuntary muscular movements, vocalizations, and/or inappropriate verbal outbursts—all appear to have biological bases that interact with other factors and may contribute to emotional disturbances. However, Tourette syndrome is not necessarily associated with emotional disturbance. Family factors (such as domestic violence) are also considered to be strong contributing factors to emotional disturbance. School factors (such as failure to accommodate for individual needs, inappropriate expectations, or inconsistency) can also contribute to an emotional disability. Finally, certain cultural environmental factors (including peer group, urbanization, and neighborhood factors) interact with the individual, the home, and the school and may also contribute to emotional disabilities (Kauffman & Landrum, 2009).

ISSUES IN IDENTIFICATION AND ASSESSMENT OF EMOTIONAL DISTURBANCE

Individuals with emotional disabilities are difficult to objectively identify and classify. Moreover, there appears to be a reluctance on the part of school personnel to label a child "emotionally disturbed" (Kauffman & Landrum, 2009). Traditional measures to identify emotional or behavioral disabilities include teacher checklists, parental checklists, classroom behavioral observations, and tests of intelligence, achievement, and psychological status. Checklists are listings of frequently observed behaviors. Teachers and parents complete checklists by indicating the types and severity of problem behaviors. Direct observations are conducted during classes, on the playground, at lunch, and in other parts of the school.

CHARACTERISTICS OF EMOTIONAL DISTURBANCE

As with most categories of exceptionality, not all individuals with emotional disturbance will exhibit all the characteristics described in this section.

SOCIAL BEHAVIOR   Most students with emotional disturbance have problems with their social behavior, often manifested as less mature or inappropriate social skills (Kauffman & Landrum, 2009). Some students may be particularly aggressive with peers and adults and cause harm when playing or interacting with others. These students act out in class, do not appear to respond appropriately to discipline from teachers, and may seem oblivious to class and school rules (Furlong, Morrison, & Jimerson, 2004). Students with behavioral disorders are at higher risk for substance abuse (Steele, Forehand, Armistead, & Brody, 1995).

Other students may exhibit social behavior similar to that of younger children and act socially immature. Some students may withdraw from others and appear socially isolated. Although withdrawn students may not call as much attention to themselves as conduct-disordered students, they nonetheless may require intensive interventions (Gresham & Kern, 2004). These students may exhibit symptoms of depression. Social isolates do not interact with any peers or adults, and in the most severe cases may exhibit selective (or elective) mutism. Individuals with selective

To succeed, teachers working with students who have emotional and behavioral disorders need to provide positive comments, be patient and tolerant, and initiate behavior modification strategies.

mutism have the physical ability to talk but nevertheless do not speak in appropriate situations (Brigham & Cole, 1999). All of these emotional or behavioral disorders share the characteristic of an inability to interact appropriately with others, including peers, teachers, siblings, and parents, which negatively affects school performance (Cullinan, 2004).

Students with emotional disturbance may also inappropriately attribute their behavioral or social problems to causes outside themselves, saying things such as, "Teachers are out to get me," or "Other kids always get me into trouble." By doing this, these students are able to avoid acknowledging or evaluating their own behavior and their own role in behavior problems.

AFFECTIVE CHARACTERISTICS   Some students with emotional disturbances have serious affective disorders. Affective disorders can take many forms, but the most commonly recognized forms include depression, severe anxiety disorders, phobias, and psychosomatic disorders (Kauffman & Landrum, 2009). Individuals with many of these disorders may be treated with different medications.

ACADEMIC CHARACTERISTICS   Research has indicated that students may function two or more years below grade level in reading, math, writing, and spelling (Lane, 2004; Reid, Gonzalez, Nordness, Trout, & Epstein, 2004; see the *Research Highlight* feature). These deficiencies may be related to the emotional disabilities. For example, if students have severe anxieties, they may be unable to attend, listen, and learn in school. Some students lack social skills that are necessary for school success (Kavale, Mathur, & Mostert, 2004). Others may exhibit severe deficiencies in metacognitive skills, memory skills, and attention, which may in turn lead to academic underachievement (e.g., Osborn & Meador, 1990). Students with emotional disturbance are at risk for dropping out of school, hindering their future life possibilities. Nevertheless, some students with emotional or behavioral disabilities attain average, or even above-average, academic achievement.

STRATEGIES FOR
MAKING CLASSROOM ADAPTATIONS
FOR STUDENTS WITH EMOTIONAL DISABILITIES

General adaptations can facilitate the inclusion of students with emotional and behavioral disorders into general education classes. The *In the Classroom* feature on page 69 lists some examples. Some specific adaptations to promote successful inclusion are presented next.

PREPARE THE CLASS   Prepare your class for students with emotional disabilities. Set up models for tolerance and acceptance. Provide opportunities for students with emotional disabilities to assume class responsibilities, such as distributing papers. Give examples of ways general education peers can help students with emotional disabilities, such as how to ignore inappropriate behaviors. Some students may be able to serve as peer tutors or assistants to help support and reinforce appropriate behaviors from students with emotional disabilities. However, select peers carefully; not all peers would be good choices. Remember that sometimes emotionally disturbed students will do better working alone even when the rest of the class is working in small groups. Chapter 8 provides additional information on using classroom peers.

ADAPT YOUR TEACHING STYLE   Illustrate the rules with clear examples and specify rewards for following rules as well as consequences when rules are disobeyed. Be consistent when enforcing rules, but make sure the overall classroom atmosphere is positive, not punitive. Provide models of acceptable behaviors to avoid confusion or misinterpretation on the part of students:

> "Here's one thing you can say if you think another student is sitting too close to you. . . . ?" "Here is something you should *not* say. . . ."

Maintain a positive relationship with students with emotional disabilities. Use positive comments frequently to reinforce good behavior when you see it. Say things like the following:

- "Jeff, I appreciate the way you tried hard in class today. I know that math is not your favorite subject."
- "Leslie, I am glad that you volunteered an answer in class today. Thank you for doing that."

PEARSON
myeducationlab

Go to MyEducationLab, select the topic *Emotional and Behavioral Disorders*, and go to the Activities and Applications section. As you watch the video entitled "Social Skills Lesson," consider how this lesson could be helpful for all students in a classroom.

Academic Status of Students with Emotional/Behavioral Disabilities

Reid and colleagues (2004) synthesized the results of 25 studies examining the academic status of students with emotional/behavioral disabilities (EBD) from 1961 to 2000. The final sample of students across all studies included 2,486 students with EBD, with an average age of 11.22 years and an average IQ of 94.89. From the studies reporting demographic data, 80% of the sample were boys, 69% Caucasian, 27% African American, 3% Hispanic, and 1% mixed racial and ethnic backgrounds. These studies yielded 101 effect sizes with a mean effect size of −.69 (SD = .40). This means that, on average, students with EBD were performing significantly lower than their same-aged peers without disabilities on all reported academic measures.

Findings were examined across a number of possible mediating variables, including academic subject area, setting, age, and method of identification. These variables were examined to determine whether one or more might account for the lower

performance of students with EBD. Students with EBD performed significantly lower than their peers across reading, math, spelling, and written expression, with the relatively lowest areas in math and spelling. These academic performance differences are similar to those that have been reported previously in research syntheses for students with learning disabilities.

When students with EBD were classified into younger (less than 12 years) and older (greater than 12) groups, it was found that both age groups performed significantly lower than normally achieving peers. Students in residential and self-contained settings performed significantly lower in academic areas than students in other settings. This is not surprising, since those settings are more restrictive in nature and students placed there would most likely have more serious difficulties. It was also reported that the method of identification of emotional disturbance did not appear to account for the lower performance of students with EBD.

The authors concluded that students with emotional/behavioral disabilities, as a group, exhibit significant and general academic deficits. However, additional research is needed to further our understanding of the academic performance differences of students with EBD. In addition, it was recommended that future researchers more carefully define their samples of students with EBD, to help provide a better understanding of this population.

QUESTIONS FOR REFLECTION

1. Why do you think students with EBD perform significantly lower than average in all academic areas?

2. Why do you think students in residential and self-contained settings might present more difficulties?

3. What might this lower performance in academics mean for placement and instruction for students with EBD?

4. Why is it important to have additional information or demographic data, such as age, ethnicity/race, and gender, on students with EBD?

Positive comments can be varied so they are suitable for either elementary-, middle-, or secondary-level students.

Before reprimanding negative social behavior, say, "Stop and think about what you just did. What should you have done? Now, try to do it more appropriately."

Be tolerant, and use judgment in allocating times for enforcing compliance, times for cooling off, and times for allowing divergent responding. For example, one fifth-grade teacher, Mrs. Bahs, allowed a student with emotional disabilities to remain at his desk even though she had asked all students to move to the floor in the front of the room to view a new class iguana. In this way, she was able to prevent a confrontation, and allow the student to participate in his own way.

Some students may have specific fears and anxieties, such as the dark, water, or getting dirty. Be aware of those fears by communicating with special education teachers, parents, and the students themselves. If class activities seem to bring out those fears in some students, have alternative activities available that they can work on independently.

Many students in your classes, especially students with emotional disturbance, can benefit from general social skills instruction. For example, review more acceptable ways of asking and answering questions and more suitable ways of resolving conflicts at appropriate times.

General Accommodations for Students with Emotional Disabilities

- Establish an open, accepting environment.
- Clearly state class rules and consequences.
- Emphasize positive behaviors and program for success.
- Reinforce positive behavior.
- Supply extra opportunities for success.
- Be tolerant.
- Use good judgment.
- Teach social skills.
- Teach self-control, self-monitoring, and conflict resolution.

- Teach academic survival skills.
- Teach positive attributions.
- Carefully select partners.
- Have alternative activities available.
- Design activity checklists.
- Use carefully selected peers as assistants.
- Have groups of "one."
- Use behavioral contracts.

Teach students to monitor their own behavior and to make positive attributions. Teach students how to attribute their successes to positive strategies and effort on their part, rather than to luck or other external forces. Teach them likewise to attribute their failures to things under their control, like their own behavior, and not to external factors, such as, "The teacher hates me." Model effective positive attributions by saying, for example: "I used the 'stop and think' strategy before acting, so I stayed out of trouble!" (see Polsgrove & Smith, 2004).

Use behavioral contracts with students with emotional disabilities. Behavioral contracts are individually negotiated contracts between the teacher and student. Specific behaviors students are expected to complete are listed along with designated rewards for the positively accomplished goals and are described in more detail in Chapter 7.

ADAPT OTHER CLASSROOM FEATURES   Consider additional classroom adaptations, including the following:

- *Adapt the physical environment* by considering seating arrangements and by keeping potentially harmful objects or substances away from easy access. Consider the degree of proximity to teachers, aides, and students with whom the target student interacts negatively.

- *Adapt materials,* when needed, using the suggestions listed for students with learning disabilities and intellectual disability. Devise self-monitoring checklists that students can use to check off activities as they complete them. Break assignments into short segments to avoid overwhelming students.

- *Adapt instruction,* using the teacher effectiveness variables and teacher presentation variables to ensure that content is covered adequately. Teach the classroom social skills necessary for success.

- *Help students focus* by teaching clearly and enthusiastically, providing additional review, and teaching self-monitoring for attention, as discussed in Chapter 10.

- *Adapt evaluation* by providing distraction-free environments for exams, providing extended time allocations during testing periods, and ensuring that students have the skills to take tests efficiently (Scruggs & Marsing, 1988; Shriner & Wehby, 2004), as described in Chapter 12.

Attention Deficit Hyperactivity Disorder

DEFINITIONS, PREVALENCE, AND CHARACTERISTICS

Robert has an attention deficit hyperactivity disorder; his family and teacher could benefit from suggestions as to how to best work with him. Robert's disruptive behaviors and his inability to sustain attention could put Robert at risk for failing in school (Brown, 2005). Attention deficit hyperactivity disorder (ADHD) refers to a "persistent pattern of inattention and/or hyperactivity-impulsivity that is more frequently displayed and more severe than is typically observed in individuals at a comparable level of development" (American Psychiatric Association, 2000, p. 85). Observations made in the classroom will identify these students as those who often say "Huh, what?" immediately following directions; often appear to be daydreaming; act before they think; blurt out answers; interrupt; and constantly fidget, wiggle, and move around. Table 3.1 highlights the sharp contrast between commonly noted behaviors on elementary school report cards and the behaviors of students with ADHD.

CLASSROOM SCENARIO

Robert Black

Robert Black had so much energy that he drove everyone around him crazy, including his parents; his teacher, Ms. Moore; and his classmates. When he arrived at school everything around him appeared to get caught in a whirlwind of activity: Papers flew to the floor, books were dropped, toys were broken, classmates were annoyed, and teachers threw their hands up in dismay. Robert was a nice 8-year-old boy, but he could not focus on one thing at a time. He seemed mesmerized by everything, moving from activity to activity with limitless energy. When someone spoke, he would interrupt and start talking about something that popped into his head. If he saw something that interested him, he would immediately take it in his hands. His feet, hands, and eyes seemed to be moving constantly. He seemed unable to sit still. Ms. Moore was frustrated and unsure of how to handle Robert in the class, so she called Mr. and Mrs. Black and asked them to come in for a conference. What became immediately evident at the parent conference was that Mr. and Mrs. Black were experiencing similar problems and frustrations at home with Robert—and had been since he was 2 years old.

QUESTIONS FOR REFLECTION

1. Why do you think Mr. and Mrs. Black were experiencing similar challenges with Robert at home?
2. What types of strategies might be helpful for Robert and his parents to use at home?
3. What behavioral and instructional supports are available for working with Robert in school?

Table 3.1 Elementary School Report Cards and Commonly Observed Statements Describing Students with ADHD		
	Typical Behaviors on Report Cards	**Observed Statements Describing ADHD Students**
Compliance	• Follows directions • Obeys rules	• Frequently ignores directions • Talks continuously
Self-Control	• Waits turn • Tolerates frustration	• Impatient • Gives up easily
Social	• Polite, courteous	• Often interrupts
Development	• Keeps hands to self	• Touches everything
Attention	• Stays on task • Makes efficient use of time	• Rarely finishes work • Frequently fidgeting

Note: Adapted from *Rethinking Attention Deficit Disorders* (p. 126), by M. Cherkes-Julkowski, S. Sharp, and J. Stolzenberg, 1997, Cambridge, MA: Brookline Books. Copyright 1997 by Brookline Books. Adapted with permission.

From 3% to 5% or more of all school-age children may have ADHD (Kauffman & Landrum, 2009). Most students with ADHD are served full time in general education classrooms, with only about half of them qualifying for special education services under IDEA (CEC, 1992).

The *Diagnostic and Statistical Manual-IV—Text Revision* (DSM-IV-TR) of the American Psychiatric Association (APA, 2000) describes criteria for classification as ADHD. The symptomatic behaviors must be maladaptive and must be present for a minimum of 6 months to warrant a classification as either inattentive ADHD or hyperactivity-impulsivity ADHD. Some symptoms should have been present before 7 years of age. Furthermore, a child must display a minimum number of identifying characteristics before ADHD is diagnosed. For example, students must meet six of nine characteristics under Inattention, or six of nine characteristics under Hyperactivity/Impulsivity. Figure 3.1 presents these criteria. There also must be evidence of impairment in social, occupational, or academic functioning, and some impairment from the symptoms must be present in at least two settings.

Any inattentiveness, impulsivity, and hyperactivity must be observed across settings (APA, 2000). Or, as in the case of Robert, the teacher and parents must observe similar behavior patterns at school and at home. Although some symptoms change over time, ADHD is now considered potentially a lifelong disorder (APA, 2000). Males outnumber females about 3 to 1 in the disorder (Barkley, 1998; Bender, 1997).

Students with ADHD are thought to be more likely to have a learning disability than other children. In a sample of students with ADHD, Barkley (1990) identified 21% with disabilities in reading, 26% in spelling, and 28% in math (see also Barkley, 1998).

Inattention:

1. Often fails to pay attention to details or makes careless mistakes in schoolwork, work, or other activities.
2. Often has difficulty sustaining attention in tasks or play activities.
3. Often does not seem to listen when spoken to directly.
4. Often does not follow through on instructions and fails to finish schoolwork, chores, or duties in the workplace (not due to oppositional behavior).
5. Often has difficulty organizing tasks and activities.
6. Often avoids, dislikes, or is reluctant to engage in tasks that require sustained mental effort.
7. Often loses things necessary for tasks and activities.
8. Is often easily distracted by extraneous stimuli.
9. Is often forgetful in daily activities.

Hyperactivity:

1. Often fidgets with hands or feet or squirms in seat.
2. Often leaves seat in classroom or in other situations in which remaining seated is expected.
3. Often runs about or climbs excessively in situations in which it is inappropriate.
4. Often has difficulty playing or engaging in leisure activities quietly.
5. Often on the go or acts as if driven by a motor.
6. Often talks excessively.

Impulsivity:

1. Often blurts out answers before questions have been completed.
2. Often has difficulty waiting for a turn.
3. Often interrupts or intrudes on others.

Figure 3.1 DSM-IV Diagnostic Criteria for ADHD

Note: From *Diagnostic and Statistical Manual of Mental Disorders*, Fourth Edition, Text Revision. Copyright 2000 American Psychiatric Association. Reprinted by permission.

A student who displays maladaptive, inattentive behavior for a period of 6 months or more may have attention deficit hyperactivity disorder (ADHD) and be served under Section 504 of the Vocational Rehabilitation Act of 1973.

CAUSES OF ADHD

Precise causes of ADHD are unknown; however, it is thought that many factors contribute to it (Kauffman & Landrum, 2009). These factors include genetic, nongenetic, psychosocial, and neurobiological bases. Genetic evidence is based on research with families whose members have ADHD. Some researchers estimate that as many as 32% of children with ADHD have parents or siblings with ADHD (Biederman et al., 1992), and concordance of ADHD has been seen to be much higher in identical (monozygotic) twins than in fraternal (dizygotic) twins, suggesting a genetic component (Barkley, 1998). Many children with ADHD exhibit attention and self-control difficulties at a very early age (Kauffman & Landrum, 2009). Nongenetic factors include prenatal and perinatal factors, allergies, and thyroid disorders (Riccio, Hynd, & Cohen, 1997). Although both food additives (Feingold, 1975) and sugar (Smith, 1975) have been proposed as causes of ADHD, research has not substantiated these as plausible causes of ADHD (Barkley, 2000; Wolraich, Milich, Stumbo, & Schultz, 1985), although they may play a role in some individual cases. Other research has investigated the psychosocial and neurological correlates associated with ADHD, with evidence growing in support of neurological indicators (Riccio et al., 1997). To date, however, as with many disorders, no definitive single etiological factor has been uncovered. At present, it seems that ADHD appears to be more influenced by neurological and genetic factors than by social or environmental factors (Barkley, 1998).

ISSUES IN IDENTIFICATION AND ASSESSMENT OF ADHD

Many experts recommend a two-step approach to the assessment of ADHD. The first step is to determine whether ADHD exists, and the second step is to determine whether the student's educational progress is adversely affected by it (CEC, 1992). During the first step, information is collected on observations of the individual's behavior throughout the day, medical history, family information, school information, social-emotional functioning, and cognitive-academic functioning. A medical exam, clinical interview, and rating scales of the individual's behavior completed by parents and teachers can be part of this evaluation process (Kauffman & Landrum, 2009; Schwanz & Kamphaus, 1997).

There is no IDEA category representing ADHD, so identified students do not necessarily qualify for services. To qualify for special education services in the "other health impairment" category of IDEA, it must be documented that the ADHD has an adverse effect on educational performance. To qualify for special services under Section 504 of the Vocational Rehabilitation Act, it must be documented that the ADHD substantially limits learning. If either of these requirements is met, an intervention plan is designed and implemented as either part of the IEP in compliance with IDEA or the accommodation plan for compliance with Section 504. In the event that students with ADHD do not meet criteria for either IDEA or Section 504, no special accommodations are designed as part of any legally mandated system. However, these students with ADHD also frequently benefit from some of the general classroom adaptations described in this text and listed in the following section.

STRATEGIES FOR
MAKING CLASSROOM ADAPTATIONS
FOR STUDENTS WITH ADHD

Many adaptations described for students with higher-incidence disabilities are appropriate for students with ADHD, as are strategies for improving attention as described in Chapter 10. The following *In the Classroom* feature provides some suggestions for accommodations that can add to classroom success (see also Barkley, 2000; Bender, 1997; Markel & Greenbaum, 1996).

Accommodation Suggestions for Students with ADHD

For Beginning Activities

- Give small amounts of work.
- Provide signals to begin.
- Use timers and encourage self-monitoring.
- Use verbal and written directions.
- Provide additional structure (e.g., large-lined paper).
- Highlight directions using larger fonts or colors.

For Keeping On-Task

- Increase frequency of positive reinforcement.
- Use peer assistants.
- Make tasks interesting.
- Break tasks into smaller, "manageable" units.
- Allow breaks.
- Use hands-on activities.

For Listening

- Teach note taking and encourage use of notebook organizers.
- Use positive reinforcement.
- Allow doodling.
- Allow standing.

For Excessive Activity

- Use activity as rewards (run errands, wash boards, move desks).
- Allow standing during class.

- Encourage active participation.
- Reward sitting.

For Impulsive Behavior

- Provide acceptable alternatives.
- Encourage trying to continue with another part of the assignment before interrupting the teacher.
- Recommend note taking during lectures.
- Recommend writing down questions and answers before blurting out.
- Teach acceptable social behavior for conversations, for class behavior, and for interacting with peers.
- Reward listening and appropriate behaviors.

For Working Independently

- Ensure tasks match ability levels.
- Provide brief directions.
- Use brief tasks.
- Use checklists for self-monitoring.
- Use positive reinforcement.

For Following Class Rules

- Keep rules simple.
- Post and review class rules.
- Model and role-play following rules.
- Be consistent with enforcement of rules.
- Provide students with copies of rules.

In the CLASSROOM

IMPLEMENT BEHAVIORAL INTERVENTIONS Behavioral interventions are strategies that use the principles of consistent behavior management (see Chapter 7 for additional information). Students' behaviors are first analyzed with respect to **antecedent** and **consequent** events (that is, what happened before and after the undesirable behavior occurred). Strategies are then implemented systematically based on that analysis (Duhaney, 2003). For example, a teacher observed that every time a worksheet was distributed in class, Max got out of his seat to sharpen his pencils and get a drink of water, bothering several classmates in the process. After this, the teacher would reprimand Max, which would make Max feel sullen and resentful. After analyzing this behavior, it seemed likely that Max was reacting to the difficulty or interest level of the task, and his own predisposition toward physical activity. The teacher decided to have Max sharpen his pencils and get a drink of water before class every day. In addition, the teacher would praise Max for remaining in his seat and leaving classmates alone after the worksheets were passed out. The teacher also monitored the content of the academic activities, to make sure they were of the appropriate difficulty level and held some interest for Max. She provided alternative opportunities for Max to leave his

Analysis → Strategies

Go to MyEducationLab, select the topic *Attention-Deficit/Hyperactivity Disorder*, and go to the Building Teaching Skills and Dispositions section. As you complete the activity entitled "Self-Monitoring," consider how Max, the example here in the text, could be helped by the interventions in place for Brandon.

seat under teacher supervision, so he could engage in some physical movement when needed. Such strategies can be effective when they are designed to meet the specific needs of problem behaviors.

IMPLEMENT COGNITIVE-BEHAVIORAL INTERVENTIONS Cognitive-behavioral interventions use the same principles of behavior management just described, but in addition add a **self-instruction and self-monitoring** component to the intervention. For example, Max could be taught to keep daily records of (1) how often he remembered to sharpen his pencils and get a drink of water before class, and (2) whether he was able to stay in his seat once the worksheet was handed out. Specific rewards might even be paired with how well he monitored his own behavior. Other commonly used cognitive-behavioral interventions involve the use of self-monitoring for on-task behavior and task completion. Strategies such as these have been particularly successful with students with ADHD. More specific details on implementing cognitive-behavioral strategies are provided in Chapters 7 and 9.

MONITOR USE OF MEDICATIONS As many as 2 million students with ADHD take psychostimulant medications, such as Ritalin (methylphenidate) or Cylert (dextroamphetamine), to help control their attention and hyperactivity (Austin, 2003). The number of children taking medications for ADHD has risen significantly in recent years. If students are taking medications, teachers must keep thorough records of behavior to help monitor the effects of medications. Reviews of research on the effects of stimulant medication generally indicate positive benefits, in that attention to task increases and hyperactivity decreases (Kauffman & Landrum, 2009). However, the practice of administering medications has remained controversial. Some educators and physicians argue that the side effects of medications can be harmful and that no students should be given medications to control their classroom behavior. Barkley (1998) suggested that some organizations have overstated the dangers of medications in an attempt to influence public opinion. When medication is prescribed, however, concomitant behavior therapy, such as the cognitive and behavioral interventions described previously, is generally also recommended.

3 Summary

- About 90% of the population of students with disabilities has learning disabilities, mental retardation/intellectual disability, emotional disabilities, or communication disorders. Most students with higher-incidence disabilities are served in the general education classroom.

- In many cases, causes of these high-incidence disabilities are unknown, although many biological and environmental explanations have been proposed.

- Students with communication disorders may exhibit problems with speech or language. Speech disorders may involve voice, articulation, or fluency; language disorders may involve difficulties with phonology, morphology, syntax, semantics, or pragmatics of language use.

- Students with learning disabilities make up about half of students with higher-incidence disabilities. These students may exhibit specific problems in basic academic skill areas, as well as areas such as language, attention, memory, and metacognition.

- Students with intellectual disabilities exhibit deficiencies in intellectual functioning, and corresponding levels of adaptive behavior. These students also may exhibit learning problems related to language, social behavior, attention, reasoning, and problem solving.

- Students with behavioral disorders or serious emotional disturbance may exhibit problems in classroom behavior and social relations, or may exhibit disorders of affect, such as anxiety or depression.

- A variety of adaptations in the physical environment, instructional materials, instructional procedures, and evaluation procedures can make the general education classroom a positive learning experience for students with higher-incidence disabilities.

- Students with attention deficit disorder and attention deficit hyperactivity disorder may be served under Section 504 or IDEA. Adaptations for this group of individuals may include behavioral approaches, cognitive-behavioral training, medication, or a combination of the three.

PROFESSIONAL STANDARDS LINK:
Teaching Students with Higher-Incidence Disabilities

Information in this chapter links most directly to:

- CEC Standards: 2 (Development and Characteristics of Learners), 3 (Individual Learning Differences), 4 (Instructional Strategies), 6 (Language)

- INTASC Standards: Principles 1 (understands central concepts of the discipline), 3 (understands learning differences, adapts instructional opportunities), 4 (instructional strategies), 5 (creates learning environments)

- PRAXIS II™ Content Categories (Knowledge): 1 (Understanding Exceptionalities), 2 (Issues)

- PRAXIS II™ Content Categories (Application): 1 (Curriculum), 2 (Instruction)

TEACHING STUDENTS WITH HIGHER-INCIDENCE DISABILITIES

If a student with higher-incidence disabilities is having difficulties in your classroom, have you tried the following general modifications? If not, see the pages listed below.

STRATEGIES FOR STUDENTS WITH SPEECH OR LANGUAGE IMPAIRMENTS

☐ Adapt the physical environment, 53
☐ Adapt materials, 53
☐ Adapt instruction, 53–55
☐ Adapt evaluation, 55

STRATEGIES FOR STUDENTS WITH LEARNING DISABILITIES

☐ Adapt the physical environment, 59
☐ Adapt instructional materials, 59
☐ Adapt instructional procedures, 59
☐ Adapt evaluation procedures, 59–60

STRATEGIES FOR STUDENTS WITH INTELLECTUAL DISABILITY

☐ Make preparations, 64
☐ Monitor peer relationships, 64
☐ Modify instruction, 64

STRATEGIES FOR STUDENTS WITH EMOTIONAL DISTURBANCE

☐ Prepare the class, 67
☐ Adapt your teaching style, 67–69
☐ Adapt other classroom features, 69

STRATEGIES FOR STUDENTS WITH ATTENTION DEFICIT HYPERACTIVITY DISORDER

☐ Implement behavioral interventions, 73–74
☐ Implement cognitive-behavioral interventions, 74
☐ Monitor use of medications, 74

Inclusion Checklist

Osteospermum

CHRIS CASTLE   Information about the photographer appears on page 2.

4

Teaching Students with Lower-Incidence Disabilities

OBJECTIVES

After studying this chapter, you should be able to:

- Describe and discuss the prevalence and characteristics of students with physical disabilities and other health impairments.
- Describe and discuss the prevalence and characteristics of students with autism.
- Describe and discuss the prevalence and characteristics of students with severe and multiple disabilities.
- Describe and discuss the prevalence and characteristics of students with visual impairments.
- Describe and discuss the prevalence and characteristics of students with hearing impairments.
- List, describe, and be able to recommend adaptations and modifications to promote inclusion of students with lower-incidence disabilities.

Individuals who have lower-incidence disabilities are far less commonly represented in schools than individuals with higher-incidence disabilities. Lower-incidence disabilities cover a wide range of disabilities, which can be present at birth (**congenital**) or acquired later in life (**adventitious**). Some lower-incidence disabilities are associated with very severe impairments; others involve only mild impairments. Some lower-incidence disabilities are temporary; others are permanent or even life-threatening. Lower-incidence disabilities include physical and other health impairments, autism, severe and multiple disabilities, visual impairments, and, hearing impairments. It is exciting to see some of the creative adaptations that have been developed to help students with lower-incidence disabilities become more successful in inclusive classes.

Physical Disabilities and Other Health Impairments

PREVALENCE, DEFINITIONS, AND CHARACTERISTICS

Physical disabilities (or orthopedic impairments, according to IDEA) and other health impairments include many types of disabilities that range from mild to moderate to severe, and from temporary to permanent or life-threatening. Approximately .78% of the school-age population has a physical (.10%) or other health-related disability (.68%), or 8.7% of the students served under IDEA (U.S. Department of Education, 2007). Physical disabilities are often described as either orthopedic or neuromotor impairments, and IDEA considers neuromotor impairments part of the orthopedic impairments category. **Orthopedic impairments** involve damage to the skeletal system, and **neuromotor impairments** involve damage to the nervous system (Best, 2005c). Frequently physical disabilities are referred to by the affected parts of the body.

For example, **quadriplegia** means both arms and legs are impaired, **paraplegia** means the legs are impaired, **hemiplegia** means either the left or right side of the body is involved, and **diplegia** means both legs are involved more than the arms (Best & Bigge, 2005). Common physical disabilities include cerebral palsy, epilepsy, spina bifida, muscular dystrophy, rheumatoid arthritis, scoliosis, osteogenesis imperfecta, and athrogyrposis (Best, 2005c).

Other health impairments include physical or medical conditions resulting from diseases or illnesses (Haslam & Valletutti, 2004). Great variability exists in severity level of impairment. Some health impairments improve over time while others do not (Valletutti, 2004). Major health conditions include cancer, acquired immune deficiency syndrome (AIDS), allergies, asthma, and fetal alcohol syndrome (Haslam & Valletutti, 2004) and are discussed next. Other conditions are presented in Figure 4.1. School-related difficulties due to physical disabilities and other health impairments are covered by the provision of "special education services" under IDEA 2004. Sometimes physical disabilities or other health impairments do not lead to difficulties in academic or intellectual functioning. Some students with other health impairments, including asthma, AIDS, tuberculosis, diabetes, drug or alcohol addiction, or behavioral problems, might not qualify for services under IDEA, but may qualify for services under Section 504 of the Vocational Rehabilitation Act (Smith, 2002).

PHYSICAL AND HEALTH-RELATED DISABILITIES

CEREBRAL PALSY   Cerebral palsy is the most common physical disability, with about 1 to 2.4 occurrences in every 1,000 births, and about 15% of premature infants (Heller & Garrett, 2008). It is a neurological disorder that causes permanent disorders of movement and positions. Cerebral palsy is not progressive in nature, which means it does not worsen over time. It does, however, range in impairment levels from mild to moderate to severe. Individuals with cerebral palsy may or may not have coexisting difficulties in language, communication, vision, hearing, psychosocial, self-help, and intellectual development (Blasco & Blasco, 2004). Between 25% and 50% of individuals with cerebral palsy may be subject to seizure disorders (Best & Bigge, 2005).

Cystic Fibrosis. Cystic fibrosis is an inherited disease in which upper respiratory and digestive problems are chronic due to the inability of the pancreas to produce digestive enzymes (Kelly, 2004). Glands in the bronchial tubes also malfunction and produce thick mucous that stagnates in the bronchial tubes. Treatments include special diets and intensive respiratory therapy (Kelly, 2004). Work closely with medical staff to monitor the condition.

Hemophilia. Hemophilia is an inherited sex-linked disorder in which the blood does not clot properly and excessive bleeding may occur with minor cuts or injuries (Kelly, 2004). Know relevant first aid information. Internal bleeding is very serious. Watch for falls at recess or during physical education classes. Avoid dangerous situations in which cuts are possible. Follow safety guidelines when using sharp objects or cutting tools.

Rheumatic fever. Rheumatic fever usually begins with a throat infection that may lead to painful swelling in the joints that can spread to the heart or brain and result in severe damage. Consult with medical personnel and your student's family to design optimal interventions.

Cancer. Cancer is a group of diseases in which the normal process of cell production malfunctions. Cell growth is uncontrolled, becomes malignant, and damages healthy tissues. Individuals with cancer may require special supports for both social-emotional well-being and for accommodating less energy and pain during school activities. Radiation treatments have been associated with learning disabilities, so additional instructional accommodations may be needed (Best, 2005).

Tuberculosis. Tuberculosis is a disease in which bacteria infect the lungs, and may spread to the brain, kidneys, or bones.

Nephrosis and nephritis. Nephrosis and nephritis are disorders of the kidneys. These disorders, if left untreated, can result in kidney failure.

Sickle-cell anemia. Sickle-cell anemia is an inherited disease in which an abnormal red hemoglobin is formed (Kelly, 2004). This results in less oxygen in the body, and the malformed cells may move improperly through the bloodstream, resulting in additional complications. Students with sickle-cell anemia may tire more easily and may need accommodations such as reduced assignments commensurate with their energy-ability levels.

Figure 4.1   Other Health-Related Disorders

The most common forms of cerebral palsy are spastic (characterized by increased muscle tone), athetosis (characterized by involuntary nonpurposeful movements), ataxic (characterized by lack of coordination in balance and equilibrium), and mixed (Best & Bigge, 2005). Many individuals with cerebral palsy use wheelchairs or other motorized vehicles to assist with mobility, or use other adaptive devices to assist with fine motor control and speech and language difficulties (Blasco & Blasco, 2004). **Alternative and Augmentative Communication** (AAC) techniques used with some individuals with cerebral palsy and other disabilities include communication boards containing pictures or words of commonly asked questions and responses to questions, and computerized devices using synthesized speech. The *Technology Highlight* feature describes uses of technology to improve communication, *News-2-You* and *Boardmaker*.

SPINA BIFIDA   Spina bifida is caused during fetal development when the vertebrae do not properly enclose the spinal cord, causing the nerves that control muscles in the lower body to develop incorrectly. Spina bifida occurs in 1 in about 2,000 births. Resulting motor impairment can range from mild to severe and include loss of sensation to paralysis in the lower body. Spina bifida is often associated with hydrocephalus, a condition in which cerebrospinal fluid collects in the brain tissues. If left untreated, swelling can cause severe brain damage and result in intellectual disability and attention and learning problems (Heller, 2008). Shunts, or one-way valves, are inserted surgically to drain the fluid from the brain to reduce the risk of pressure on the brain and possible resulting brain damage. Shunts need to be replaced as children grow. Be aware of warning signs or changes in a student's behavior, as sudden changes may indicate shunt blockage or infections. Alert parents immediately of any changes.

Individuals with spina bifida—and other physical disabilities—may lack bladder and bowel movement control due to paralysis of the lower body. Most children use a catheter, or bag to collect their urine. Many children are taught to use a procedure called "clean intermittent catheterization" (CIC; Heller, Bigge, & Allgood, 2005). Request guidance from school nurses or other educational team members to learn how to assist a child with this procedure. Plan rest-room breaks to accommodate these students' specialized toileting needs.

Many children with spina bifida walk with braces or crutches, relying on wheelchairs for longer distances. In these cases, maintain classroom space to ensure clear, wide, and open walkways for students with mobility difficulties. Arrange storage for crutches or removable braces near students for easy access.

MUSCULAR DYSTROPHY   Muscular dystrophy refers to a group of diseases that weaken and progressively destroy muscle tissue. Muscular dystrophy occurs in about 1 in 3,500 births. No known cure exists. Some forms of muscular dystrophy are fatal, but other forms are not life-threatening (American Medical Association, 2004). At birth children appear normal; however, between the ages of 2 and 6 they may begin to experience motor difficulties, which increase with age. Often by the ages of 10 to 14 children lose the ability to walk. Children with muscular dystrophy should be lifted only by those with explicit training, as their limbs are easily dislocated. Because the disease is often progressive, it is important to learn what types of muscular difficulties may be expected throughout an academic year (Kelly, 2004).

TRAUMATIC BRAIN INJURY   Traumatic brain injury (TBI), although now a separate category of exceptionality under IDEA, represents a type of physical and cognitive disability. Traumatic brain injury is the result of an external injury that impedes learning along the continuum from mild to severe disabilities, and may result in physical, cognitive, attention, memory, problem-solving, sensory, and psychosocial difficulties. The resulting disabilities may be temporary or permanent. Often traumatic brain injuries are caused from falls or motor vehicle accidents. Child abuse also can be a cause of brain injury (Grandinette & Best, 2008).

About 4% of boys and 2.5% of girls will sustain some type of traumatic head injury before reaching the age of 16 (Schoenbrodt, 2001).

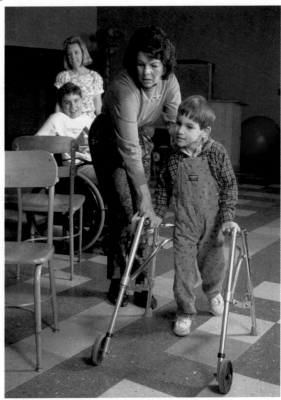

Some physical or health impairments—such as muscular dystrophy—present obvious physical limitations; other conditions—such as asthma, diabetes, and epilepsy—are not as obvious.

Alternative and Augmentative Communication, *News-2-You* and *Boardmaker*

Many students with low-incidence disabilities require some adaptations in literacy materials that will aid their ability to communicate. Several examples of Alternative and Augmentative Communication (ACC) devices are widely available and range from high-tech to low-tech options. This means that some use very little technology, whereas others are reliant on more complex technological systems for delivery. One alternative and augmentative version of a newspaper that is available is *News-2-You (http://www.news-2-you.com)*. *News-2-You* is published weekly during the school year and is available for a subscription fee. The newspaper features relevant newsworthy stories printed using visual symbols that represent words. Each paper includes four to five pages of weekly current-event news stories, a recipe, a joke, a game page, a sports story, and a weekly quiz based on the paper. The paper also includes sample communication boards as downloads that can be used as part of *Boardmaker*, a software program that contains graphics that can be used to develop and design communication displays or Microsoft Word documents (for those who do not have access to *Boardmaker*). The newspaper provides an excellent vehicle for access to news for many students who might otherwise be unable to read a paper. Since the paper is available online on a weekly basis, a teacher can select to have students read it online, from a saved online version on a computer, or in a printed hard-copy format. There is also a speaking version, which reads

text material. The newspaper provides an excellent tool for working on reading comprehension skills with the short quizzes that accompany the weekly papers. Teachers can also decide to make their own versions of newspapers and reading materials using similar formats.

For example, teachers who like the format of *News-2-You* will most likely want to obtain the software *Boardmaker,* which can be used to develop a wide range of displays using the over 3,000 graphic picture communication symbols and over 100 templates for calendars, schedules, and other formats. Pictures can be sized to meet your needs, and *Boardmaker* for Windows comes with

19 languages, including English, Spanish, German, Portuguese, Vietnamese, Russian, and Turkish, but has space for over 150 languages. The software is available from Mayer-Johnson *(http://www.mayer-johnson.com)*. *Boardmaker* can also be combined with *Speaking Dynamically Pro* to include the speech capabilities. This way, the symbols can be used as overlays and can be heard aloud for students who require hearing the symbols in addition to looking at them. *Boardmaker Plus* adds sound, voice, animation, and video capabilities to the software.

A sample page from *News-2-You* showing a restaurant review questionnaire is presented.

Source: Reprinted with permission from Dave and Jackie Clark, *News-2-You, Inc.*

Head injuries occur most often in the warmer spring and summer months, on weekends and afternoons, when children are most likely to be playing outside or riding in cars (Michaud, Duhaime, & Lazar, 1997). Special education services often are provided for the resulting difficulties in school learning. Teachers can play an important preventative role by encouraging students to take safety precautions, such as wearing helmets when riding bicycles.

A significant role of the classroom teacher is in assisting successfully with the reintegration and transitions the individual has to make from the hospital to rehabilitation to the classroom. Successful transition planning includes preparing peers for the changes in the behavior of the affected classmate. IEPs may need to be adjusted and modified more frequently due to changing conditions in students with a traumatic brain injury.

Students with TBI who recover adequate intellectual functioning but who continue to exhibit difficulties in learning may resemble students with learning disabilities in some respects. Students may continue to change neurologically, even months after their readmission to school. Achievement test scores may be misleading because they may reflect knowledge or skills acquired prior to the injury. Further, psychosocial problems may emerge as a consequence of coping with challenges associated with TBI. Unpredictable difficulty could occur even years after the injury, if parts of the brain were injured that are needed for later maturation (Ylvisaker & Feeney, 1998).

EPILEPSY A seizure is caused when abnormal electrical energy is released in the brain that can cause a loss of consciousness and lack of motor control (Haslam, 2004). The effects can be minimal or severe, depending on the amount of energy released and the number of brain cells affected. The precise cause of epilepsy is not well understood (Heller & Cohen, 2008), but some cases are due to brain damage from physical trauma or infections.

Any child may have a seizure. Individuals may experience a single seizure associated with a head injury or high fever, and never have one again. About half of those with seizure disorders also have intellectual disabilities. Repeated seizures are indicative of epilepsy. No matter what the physical condition that leads to a seizure, be aware that seizures vary in duration, frequency, onset, movements, causes, associated disabilities, and control.

Seizure disorders can be treated with antiepileptic medications, special diets, vagus nerve stimulation, and surgery (Heller & Cohen, 2008). Because of the chance of body injury or brain damage, it is wise to learn about the correct handling of seizures and to educate all students about seizures and their treatment. Some suggestions are provided later in the chapter.

ARTHRITIS Arthritis is a disease in which the muscles and joints are affected. Juvenile rheumatoid arthritis is chronic arthritis present in an individual before the age of 16. Arthritis can be painful and can severely impede mobility. Treatments are directed toward relieving pain, increasing function, and avoiding further deterioration, and include heat–cold therapy, massage, electrical stimulation, and exercise such as aquatic movement, under the supervision of a physical or occupational therapist. However, at present, no known cause or cure exists (Heller & Avant, 2008). Because mobility may be hindered, some children with severe arthritis use canes or braces while walking. Be aware that these students will have good days and bad days, and build in extra rest periods during more painful days. Students may experience great difficulty trying to grip a pencil. Writing may be extremely tedious and painful. Reduce writing demands by allowing students to use tape recorders or other students as scribes. Provide extended time for written assignments.

ASTHMA AND ALLERGIES Asthma is associated with breathing difficulties due to sensitivity to airborne particles, and can be exacerbated during exercise. Children with severe asthma often require restricted athletic activities and may need to be reminded to take appropriate medication (Shouldice, 2004). Physicians can provide relevant information on particular adaptations for individual cases.

Allergies are conditions in which elements in the environment cause allergic reactions in some individuals. Exposure to pollens, molds, dusts, animal dander, and carpet fibers can cause reactions such as congestion in the nose, chest, and eyes. Allergic reactions to certain foods, such as milk, fish, or nuts, can cause skin rashes and more serious mouth and throat reactions. Still other reactions are caused from insect bites such as honey bee stings, and can result in anaphylactic shock, a condition that can be fatal if not treated immediately (Shouldice, 2004). Many individuals who know they have these conditions carry emergency kits with them. Be sure to have plans in place for dealing with such medical emergencies, including the quickest ways to seek medical assistance.

Know which of your students have asthma and allergies, the associated allergens, the preventative medications, first aid, and the specific nature of the allergic reactions. In some cases, it may be necessary to maintain a dust- and animal-dander-free environment to avoid allergic reactions. In other cases, teachers or other school staff can monitor food consumption during lunchtime and class parties (Valletutti, 2004).

DIABETES   Diabetes is an inherited condition in which sugar is not metabolized correctly due to insufficient production of insulin in the pancreas (American Medical Association, 2004). Individuals with diabetes have strict diets and special schedules for administering medication that need close monitoring. Learn the warning signs of diabetic shock and be ready to administer first aid (Daneman & Frank, 2004). The school nurse can usually provide relevant information for classroom teachers, who can share information with all students. Monitor dietary needs during the school day for students with diabetes (or create a plan for an aide to do so), especially if extra food or physical activities are added to the regular schedule. Careful planning with the family and other health-care providers is necessary to ensure safety during daily class activities, and especially for special events such as field trips or overnight trips.

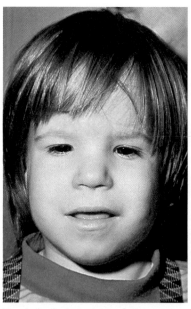

Fetal alcohol syndrome places a child at risk for a variety of developmental disabilities.

FETAL ALCOHOL SYNDROME   Fetal alcohol syndrome (FAS) results when pregnant mothers consume alcohol that damages the developing fetus (Jones, Smith, Ulleland, & Streissguth, 1973). This places a child at risk for a variety of developmental disabilities, including intellectual disability, learning disabilities, and physical disabilities, in addition to problems with attention and impulsivity (Streissguth, 1997). Exposure to substances during the first trimester is likely to cause neurological and structural damage to the developing fetus (Briggs, 2001). Effective service delivery for infants born under these conditions comes from personnel from health, social services, mental health, children's services, education, and drug and alcohol programs, who must collaborate to work effectively with the family.

ACQUIRED IMMUNE DEFICIENCY SYNDROME   Acquired immune deficiency syndrome (AIDS) is caused by the human immunodeficiency virus (HIV), which destroys a form of white blood cells, weakening the immune system. HIV can be transmitted to an unborn fetus during pregnancy, or during childbirth to an infant, or through infected breast milk during nursing (Byrom & Katz, 1991). Other sources of transmission include sexual activity and blood exposure, through, for example, shared needles in intravenous drug use or transfusions of contaminated blood (although this occurred most frequently prior to 1984, when blood screening was initiated). HIV is not spread by casual contact. Children with AIDS may have coexisting characteristics such as developmental delay, cognitive disabilities, and any of a number of physical or health conditions, including problems with respiratory, cardiovascular, motor, or kidney functioning (Best & Heller, 2008).

Recently developed combination therapies, known as highly active antiretroviral therapy (HAART), have proven very effective in reducing HIV/AIDS symptoms, and have even restored functioning of the immune system. However, HAART does not eliminate the infection. Improved preventative treatments have also reduced significantly the transmission of HIV from mother to child (Best & Heller, 2008).

STRATEGIES FOR
MAKING CLASSROOM ADAPTATIONS FOR STUDENTS WITH PHYSICAL DISABILITIES AND OTHER HEALTH IMPAIRMENTS

Although each individual and disability area may require specific adaptations, the following guidelines can help you develop adaptations for accommodating individuals with physical and other health impairments (see also Best, Heller, & Bigge, 2005; Haslam, 2004).

PREPARE THE CLASS   Prepare the class for students with disabilities who are about to enter the class. Describe the students' special needs, and the roles of classroom peers in supporting the inclusive classroom. One way to enhance disability awareness in students is by using classroom simulation activities and demonstrations using adaptive devices (e.g., Hallenbeck & McMaster, 1991). Simulations can be designed for almost any disability area. For example, having students keep one of their hands behind their backs while attempting to perform regular class activities lets them experience the challenges encountered daily by other students. Similarly, allowing students to try out wheelchairs or use walkers, braces, or canes will enable them to appreciate the challenges encountered in simple tasks such as getting a drink from a water fountain or getting to and from the playground. Simulations for cognitive impairments can also be designed, such as having students try to read a foreign language, or write with their eyes closed. Discussions with all students following simulation activities can help increase their awareness of the frustrations that may be encountered by students with disabilities. Although disability simulations may not significantly improve attitudes (Flower, Burns, & Bottesford-Miller, 2007), the activities may provide students with some insights into the challenges faced by individuals with disabilities, and the need for adaptations.

MONITOR MEDICAL GUIDELINES   Medical needs are of primary concern. Devise checklists containing reminder steps for general class and emergency procedures specific to the medical conditions of students. For example, a medical checklist could include items such as: check medication schedule, monitor medication effects and side effects, monitor first aid and emergency procedures, and communicate with parents. Maintain careful records of student behavior (such as lethargy or fatigue) and communicate clearly any changes in your students' behavior.

Be aware of medications. An awareness of the types of medications, specific uses, and potential side effects is also necessary. Careful monitoring of students' behaviors while on and off medication (for example, with observational records) can provide valuable educational insights, for teachers and for prescribing physicians.

A school nurse or other designated school official distributes medications to students from a centralized location in the school, usually the nurse's office. Be sure that students obtain their medication at the scheduled times and that they ingest the medication when administered. Some students feign taking their medication and attempt to give or sell it to others. This is a serious problem that can become troublesome or dangerous if not monitored closely.

Plan for Fatigue   Students with physical disabilities or other health impairments, such as traumatic brain injury and muscular dystrophy, may tire more easily than other students. If so, schedule frequent rest breaks throughout a day, prioritize daily schedules, and schedule break periods in the nurse's office if needed. If students lack the strength to carry necessary materials from class to class and to and from school, obtain duplicate sets of books and materials. Some students may require a shortened school day while they recuperate from illnesses. Reduce assignments, prioritize to ensure that students receive the most critical information, and assign peers to share class notes and materials.

Establish Emergency Procedures   All classes containing students with physical and other health impairments may require specialized classroom procedures for emergencies such as fire or tornadoes. For example, assistance may be required to move adaptive equipment along with the student. Also, depending on the position of the individual in the class when the emergency alarm sounds, students may need assistance into their wheelchairs, braces, or other adaptive mobility devices. During fire drills, students often proceed to an athletic field adjacent to the school, and mobility across the uneven grass may be especially difficult for some students with physical disabilities. Others tire easily and cannot walk quickly enough to maintain the speed of evacuation with the rest of the class.

Pair students with and without disabilities for evacuation efforts during emergencies. It may be helpful to have more than one student assigned to assist each student with disabilities. You can add the names of peer assistants to the overall listing of procedures on your "emergency chart." Be prepared: outline emergency procedures in advance and practice them many times so that if an actual emergency situation occurs, all students are well prepared for any evacuation procedures.

Plan for Seizures   Know which of your students are likely to have seizures and what first aid treatment is appropriate. Since seizures range in severity from very minor to very intense and severe, consult your student's family and physician for precise medical treatment. If a

myeducationlab

Go to MyEducationLab, select the topic *Physical Disabilities and Health Impairments*, and go to the Activities and Applications section. As you complete the simulation entitled "Working with Your School Nurse," reflect on the importance of implementing and following a medical plan for students who need it.

seizure does occur, stay calm. You are a model for your students and if you stay calm, so will they. Help the student to the floor. Gently tilt the head to the side so the child does not choke. In any seizure, do not attempt to restrain movements of the individual or place anything in between the teeth or in the mouth of the affected person. Clear all harmful objects out of the way, and place a blanket or pillow under the student's head to minimize the potential for injury.

Try to remember all of the distinctive features associated with the seizure to record on monitoring sheets and share with parents and attending physicians later. Record the date and time of the seizure as well as the behavior exhibited before, during, and after the seizure. Note the student's and peer reactions to the seizure, and any other information that seems relevant (Michael, 1992). If it is the student's first seizure, contact a physician immediately. Moreover, if seizures persist for more than 5 minutes, immediate medical attention should be sought. Notify parents when seizures have occurred (Spiegel, Cutler, & Yetter, 1996).

Learn how to handle a student who has just recovered from a seizure. Some students may feel tired and disoriented after a seizure and may want to lie down and rest. Others may feel fine and simply want to continue with the class activity. Still others may feel embarrassed and may need time outside of the class to regain self-control and self-respect. It is also important to redirect the attention of peers away from the students with the seizure. The individual having seizures should not be made to feel self-conscious. Do anything necessary to make the student feel comfortable. Provide all students with relevant information about seizures and proper ways of handling situations emotionally during and after seizures (Spiegel et al., 1996).

Moving and Positioning Students   Determine what special procedures are required for moving, lifting, or transferring body positions of students with special needs. Some students—for example, those with "brittle bone disease" (osteogenesis imperfecta)—should be lifted only by people with specialized knowledge about how to lift and position the individual. Physical therapists, who often work directly with these students, can provide valuable information to you and your students.

Find out whether students feel more comfortable in some positions than others. Periodically check their positions throughout the school day. Some types of positioning devices, such as braces and wedges, help improve personal comfort, control muscle movements, and position students to more easily communicate or complete schoolwork. Figure 4.2 shows examples of positioning devices.

Adapt for Chronic Medical Conditions   If students in your class have chronic medical conditions, you should know how to accommodate them. Consult with medical personnel to learn to recognize the signs and symptoms of relevant medical problems, and any modifications you can make. Limiting physical activity, administering medications, providing diet and fluid supplements as needed, and providing easy access to bathrooms are among the modifications you can make, depending on the condition.

1.   2.   3.

Figure 4.2   Alternatives to Allow Change of Position Throughout the Day: (1) Sidelyer, (2) Wedge, (3) Tricycle with Built-up Back and Pedals. Adult Three-Wheeled Bikes Are Available for Older Children.

Note: From *Teaching Individuals with Physical or Multiple Disabilities* (p. 198), by S. J. Best, K. W. Heller, and J. L. Bigge, 2005, Upper Saddle River, NJ: Merrill/Prentice Hall. Reprinted by permission.

Dealing with Terminal Illness Health-care and mental-health professionals are good sources of information about dealing with terminally ill students, as are the students' parents. Ask how you should interact with the terminally ill student and the student's classmates (Obiakor, Mehring, & Schwenn, 1997). Mental-health professionals sometimes provide extra guidance and counseling sessions to small groups of students to address their questions about interacting with a terminally ill student. If the student dies, request assistance from the school's crisis intervention team and mental-health professionals. Some professionals speculate that different age-related reactions result when a death occurs (Petersen & Straub, 1992). For example, children ages 6 to 10 may have reduced attention spans, display out-of-character behavior, and lose trust in adults. Children ages 10 to 14 may show anger or psychosomatic illnesses. Adolescents may be suspicious, develop sleeping or eating disorders, lose impulse control, or turn to alcohol and drug abuse (Obiakor et al., 1997).

ADAPT THE PHYSICAL ENVIRONMENT Arrange the classroom to meet the mobility requirements of students with physical disabilities. Provide sufficiently wide aisles to accommodate wheelchairs, walkers, three-wheel motorized wheelchairs, crutches, canes, braces, or other adaptive devices. Most wheelchairs require passages at least 32 inches wide for one wheelchair to pass. Keep aisles clear of debris and monitor regularly to ensure that no books, book bags, backpacks, toys, or other objects impede mobility. Verify that the height of door knobs, water fountains, sinks, and cabinets is accessible for students with physical disabilities. If not, perhaps minor adaptations can be made to ensure equal accessibility.

Examine the type of floor in your classroom, with respect to whether carpeting or tile is used, and the extent to which surfaces either facilitate or impede mobility of individuals with physical disabilities. For example, carpeted floors can decrease slippage, but may also impede mobility of some adaptive devices. Conversely, tile surfaces may be dangerously slippery, especially after washing and waxing.

ADAPT INSTRUCTIONAL MATERIALS Commercially available materials include communication boards, computers to assist with voice synthesizer production, specially designed hand grippers, head pointers, keyboards, touch screens to assist with computer usage, and speech-reading or word-prediction software to minimize difficulty producing output for assignments. Other adaptive devices including flap switches and reaches that can be added to pencils or dowels to extend the grasp of individuals are available from suppliers such as the Prentke Romich Company.

Some teachers assist students with fine motor difficulties in turning book pages by placing double-sided foam tape or cardboard between the pages. Tongue depressors can also serve as handles for turning pages. A book stand can be designed to hold instructional materials at an appropriate height and distance for easy viewing for students with restricted mobility. Choose books that are larger and easier to manipulate. Anchor materials in place by using clipboards or magnets to help stabilize papers (see Best, Reed, & Bigge, 2005).

Enlarge the gripping area of pencils by attaching spongelike material, plastic tubing, or plastic golf balls around pencils and pens. Use felt-tip pens, which require less pressure than some other writing tools. Specialized rubber stamps with large handles that contain commonly written items, such as names, *yes, no, rest room,* and *hungry* also can help students communicate.

Larger paper with extra space between lines helps accommodate writing needs for some students. When class activities involve charting or graphing, provide larger graphs, stickers, or magnets for students to place on graphs rather than using smaller paper-and-pencil versions. Felt boards and pieces of felt are easier for some students to manipulate. Place vocabulary words or other content inside clear picture photograph cubes. Put clear plastic folders or sheet protectors on paper handouts. These are easier to grip than a single sheet of paper and can be held together with a clip. The coating also protects the papers from spills. Use calculators with large numbers that are easier to touch and read.

Stabilize instructional materials with Velcro. Slatted trays or trays with built-in dividers can be used to hold small objects that need to be manipulated during activities. Place a detachable bag or backpack onto the wheelchair for carrying books and other materials. Notes or tape-recorded messages to parents can be placed in the bag before students leave school. Often, simple modifications such as these can allow students with physical disabilities to participate more independently (Best, Reed, & Bigge, 2005).

Specially designed adaptive devices give some students the ability to be more independent.

Some students with physical disabilities may also have the assistance of an animal, such as a specially trained dog, that accompanies them throughout the school day (Heward, 2009). Teachers need to know how they and their students in the class and throughout the school should interact with the animal. Usually, no one is allowed to pet or interact with the animal other than the individual with disabilities. The student's family can provide detailed information on how to interact appropriately with these animals.

ADAPT INSTRUCTION   Schedule extra reading, studying, and instructional support time when needed. Students who have difficulty speaking require extra time to respond to teacher questions. When calling on an individual during class discussions, provide sufficient wait time and make students feel comfortable and not rushed while responding.

Instruction can be adapted, with respect to individual needs, in all academic areas, including literacy, math, and academic content areas, as well as vocational education. Refer to the relevant chapters throughout this text when planning instruction for students with physical disabilities and other health impairments.

Consider assigning a peer assistant to work with individuals with physical disabilities or health impairments. Peer assistants can enable the student to be a more active participant during class activities. In some cases, paraprofessionals are assigned to accompany students throughout the school day. Work closely with paraprofessionals to design effective modifications.

ADAPT EVALUATION   Testing and assessment modifications are necessary for students with physical disabilities and other health impairments. Because many of these students have difficulty reading and writing independently, schedule their tests when a special education teacher, paraprofessional, aide, peer assistant, or tutor can read the test items and record responses. These individualized sessions may require more time than the regularly scheduled exam time slots. Use communication boards during testing situations and record responses as students point to answers on response sheets.

Autism

PREVALENCE, DEFINITIONS, AND CHARACTERISTICS

Autism is a disorder characterized by severe impairments of social, emotional, and intellectual functioning. Children with autism are often described as having great difficulty communicating and interacting with and responding to other people. Many individuals with autism also exhibit stereotypic behavior such as self-stimulating behaviors (e.g., rocking, hand flapping); bizarre speech patterns, such as repeating the words of other people over and over again (echolalia); and disruptive behavior, sometimes including self-injury (Hall, 2009; Simpson & Zionts, 2000). Children with autism are typically identified before the age of 3, although symptoms may appear later in some disorders related to autism (e.g., childhood disintegrative disorder). Frequently, parents are the first ones to become concerned when their infants do not respond positively to being touched and held closely, and when language does not develop along the common developmental milestones.

The causes of autism are unknown, although a number of genetic, neurological, and environmental factors have been proposed (Hall, 2009). Individuals with autism make up approximately .21% of the school-age population, or 2.3% of the students served under IDEA (U.S. Department of Education, 2007). The prevalence of autism appears to be increasing in recent years, although the reasons for this are not completely clear (Hallahan, Kauffman, & Pullen, 2009). One possibility is that changes in diagnostic criteria, along with more public awareness of autism, have led to increased rates of identification (Bishop, Whitehouse, Watt, & Line, 2008).

Related diagnostic categories include autistic disorder, Rett's disorder, childhood disintegrative disorder, Asperger syndrome, and pervasive developmental disorder (American Psychiatric Association, 2000). These categories are now collected under a broader term, **autistic spectrum disorders.** The current diagnoses indicate that individuals with autism may function along a continuum of severe to mild disabilities, and that educational accommodations vary according to an individual's functioning level. Individuals with severe autism may have limited to no expressive and receptive language, while individuals with milder forms of autism may have developed more sophisticated communication, as in the case of those with Asperger syndrome. Although symptoms and severity level vary among individuals with autism, communication and social competence are typically the two greatest challenges. Most individuals with autism have cognitive deficits similar to those of individuals with intellectual disabilities. Individuals with Asperger syndrome, however, can be very intelligent (Hallahan et al., 2009).

Students with autism often withdraw from any kind of physical contact with others.

STRATEGIES FOR
MAKING CLASSROOM ADAPTATIONS FOR STUDENTS WITH AUTISM

Classroom adaptations for individuals with autism can be classified into adaptations for those with severe autism and for those with mild autism. Individuals with severe forms of autism may function similarly to those individuals with severe disabilities, and it is recommended that you employ the suggested adaptations for individuals with severe disabilities. Conversely, for individuals with milder forms of autism, you may wish to consider using modifications recommended for students with mild disabilities, including learning disabilities and behavior disorders. In both cases, work closely with special education teachers and parents. This collaboration ensures that IEP goals and objectives are being addressed, and that you have assistance in interacting with students. The following adaptations are also helpful for including students with autism in general education classes.

ESTABLISH EFFECTIVE COMMUNICATION   Discuss optimal communication patterns and design communication strategies with special education teachers, parents, and peers. Strategies might include sign language or Augmentative and Alternative Communication (AAC) methods. For example, in the following scenario, Tony is a young boy with autism who does not have language, but does communicate with an AAC procedure referred to as the Picture Exchange Communication System (PECS). PECS teaches students to use pictures and symbols to initiate and respond to communication from others (Bondy & Frost, 2002).

CLASSROOM SCENARIO

Tony

Tony had a difficult first day in his inclusive kindergarten. His teachers saw his crying, tantrum-throwing, and acts of aggression, and, fortunately, realized that much of his behavior reflected not simply the fact that he had autism, but rather his inability to communicate in a new environment. His teachers used the Picture Exchange Communication System (PECS) to train him in socially appropriate ways to obtain what he wanted, using the six phases of the training program (Scott, Clark, & Brady, 2000). In the first phases, they determined that Tony enjoyed playing with a particular toy truck. When he reached for it, they placed the picture

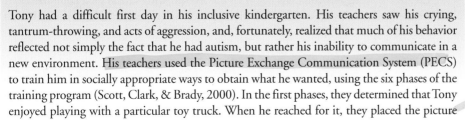

card of a truck in his hand, then guided him to give the picture to his teacher. The teacher immediately gave him the truck. In later phases, Tony was encouraged to go to a touch board for the picture, then discriminate the truck from other pictures, and then build sentence structure by choosing first the "I want" card, followed by the picture of the desired object. In the fifth phase, Tony responds to "What do you want?" questions, and in the sixth phase, Tony uses the PECS cards to answer teacher questions, such as "What do you have?" or "What do you see?"

As Tony learns the PECS program, his tantrum-throwing and inappropriate behavior diminishes, and he learns socially appropriate ways of interacting with others. Other students use the PECS materials to interact with Tony. The PECS training continues to include additional language concepts, such as adjectives, verbs, and yes-no responses. Tony is learning important lessons for communicating and socializing with teachers and classmates.

QUESTIONS FOR REFLECTION

1. Why do you think using the PECS system is easier for Tony than using spoken language?
2. Why would a language training program help to improve Tony's social behavior?
3. How could Tony's classroom peers assist in developing Tony's communication skills?

Figure 4.3 presents examples of commonly used symbols in different communication systems.

USE DIRECT INSTRUCTION AND APPLIED BEHAVIOR ANALYSIS Many students with autism (and many other students as well) benefit from direct instruction, including small-group or one-to-one structured, teacher-directed lessons, with lots of direct questioning, student responding, teacher feedback and praise, and careful recording and monitoring of progress toward predetermined objectives, as described in Chapter 6. Instruction is carefully sequenced according to student needs (e.g., Polloway, Miller, & Smith, 2004). For example, if a student had no expressive language, training might begin with the teacher providing reinforcement for imitating sounds, such as "aaa," followed by imitating words (e.g., "hat"), followed by responding to simple directions, ("Point to the hat"), followed by word production ("What is this?" [teacher points to a hat]). Throughout this progression, the teacher would provide explicit feedback and reinforcement for attending and for correct responding.

Applied behavior analysis involves the use of reinforcement (e.g., praise, tokens, edible reinforcements) for displaying appropriate behaviors (e.g., sitting, attending, responding), and carefully recording student behaviors on charts that are used in decision making (Hall, 2009). These practices may also employ functional behavioral assessments and Positive Behavior Supports, as described in Chapter 7. Teachers may document the antecedents as well as observed consequences of specific behaviors (e.g., screaming, tantrum-throwing), and then arrange the environment and environmental consequences to minimize inappropriate behaviors.

DEVELOP SOCIAL COMPETENCE Unless you design behavior plans with the student's IEP team and implement these plans systematically, you may find it easy to become overwhelmed by the student's challenging behaviors (Ruble & Dalrymple, 1996). Teach students to wait their turn, share materials, and to know when they need to be quiet and when they can talk. Teach them to use socially appropriate behaviors throughout the school day to help promote generalization of appropriate social behavior. Reward successive approximations (as students come closer to their goals), and work toward having students become more independent. Develop behavior management plans based on an analysis of student preferences and classroom dynamics. Direct instruction and applied behavior analysis techniques can be helpful in these areas.

Create a learning environment in which the student with autism feels comfortable, including a predictable schedule of daily activities, a pattern of events, and class routines. Use pictures to list the sequence of activities if the student is a nonreader, and allow the student to order the sequence if possible. If you change the class routine, prepare the student in advance to avoid undue stress.

One promising technique for improving social behavior is the use of social stories (Barry & Burlew, 2004; Gray & Garand, 1993). Social stories use simple sentences and pic-

PEARSON myeducationlab

Go to MyEducationLab, select the topic *Autism Spectrum Disorders* and go to the Building Teaching Skills and Dispositions section. As you complete the activity entitled "Instructional Software," reflect on the direct instruction that is happening while using technology for instruction.

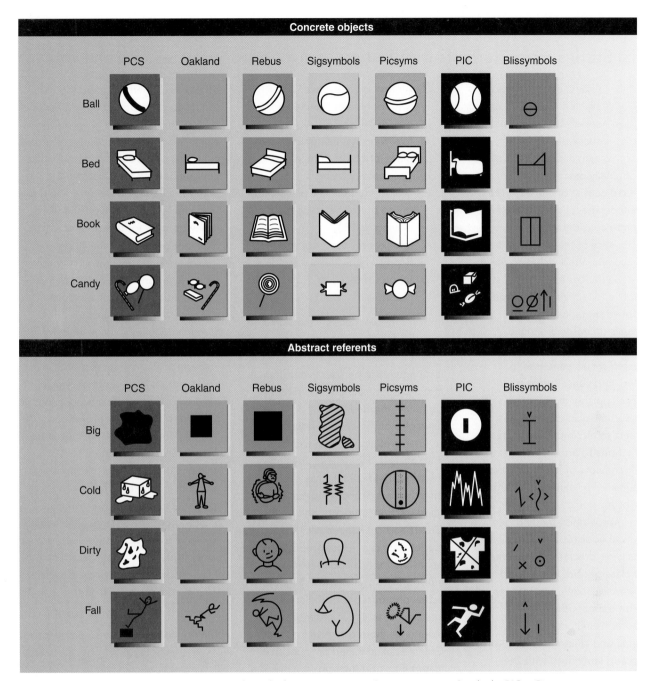

Figure 4.3 Sample Communication Board Symbols (PCS = Picture Communication Symbols; PIC = Pictogram Ideogram Communication)

Note: Reprinted with permission from "Non-speech Modes and Systems," by G. C. Vanderheiden and L. L. Lloyd, 1986, in S.W. Blackstone (Ed.), *Augmentative Communication* (pp. 48–161), Rockville, MD: American Speech–Language Hearing Association.

tures to demonstrate the desired social behavior and the feelings and reactions of others, such as, "When I return my tray after I have finished eating, my teacher is happy." The *Research Highlight* feature demonstrates an application of social stories to improve the social functioning of students with autism in a middle school setting (Graetz, Mastropieri, & Scruggs, in press).

Enlist the help of peers to reinforce socially appropriate behavior. Group students with autism with higher-functioning students. Students with autism can be included successfully in cooperative learning groups when paired with partners who have been taught to communicate effectively with them (Kamps, Leonard, Potucek, & Garrison-Harrell, 1995).

Social Stories Help Students with Autism Learn Appropriate Social Behaviors

 Graetz et al. (in press) studied the effects of social stories in improving social behaviors of adolescents with autism. Social stories were originally described by Gray (1994) and consist of stories written from the perspective of the student, taking into consideration the characteristics of the target student. Gray recommended including three types of sentences in the social story: descriptive, directive, and perspective. Descriptive sentences tell what individuals do in social situations, whereas directive sentences indicate suggested social responses to targeted situations. Perspective sentences portray the responses of others to the social situation.

Graetz et al. (in press) created social stories to improve target social behaviors of five adolescents with autism. For example, a targeted behavior for one student, Ronnie, was to improve his standing behavior in physical education classes since he was lying down for almost the entire class period. Ronnie's social story was six pages in length, printed on white paper with colored photographs including himself, his teachers, and classmates, and was bound and laminated with the following pages:

1. Ronnie Learns to Stand and Play (with photo of Ronnie standing).
2. My name is Ronnie and I go to Lawrence Middle School (with a photo of the school).
3. Almost every day we have P.E. (with photos of Ronnie and classmates at P.E.).
4. Everyone stands up. Everyone plays (photo of Ronnie and classmates playing in P.E.).
5. I will stand up. I will play (with photo of Ronnie standing and playing in P.E.).
6. It makes my teachers and friends happy when I stand up and play (photo of teachers, Ronnie, and classmates).

In this example, pages 1 through 3 are the descriptive sentences. Pages 4 and 5 are the directive sentences, and the last page is the perspective sentence. In the Graetz example, the directive sentence emphasizes only positive examples of the desired behavior.

Graetz et al. (in press) used a multiple baseline research design (Martin & Pear, 2003) to assess the effectiveness of social stories for middle school students with autism. Graetz and colleagues designed social stories to improve inappropriate behaviors for five adolescents with autism. The social stories included actual photographs of the students and their teachers in order to make the stories more concrete for students. Graetz et al. included only positive statements of the targeted behaviors.

Stories targeting inappropriate behaviors were written for Ronnie (as noted) and the other four participants. One story was written to improve proper speaking tone of voice. Another was written to decrease hand-wringing behaviors. Others targeted the reduction of mouthing objects for one student and reduction of use of the word "what" while speaking. All stories consisted of the same general format but emphasized the targeted behaviors. Stories were introduced to students by their teachers and were reviewed daily for the duration of the intervention phase of the study.

Results indicated that the targeted social behaviors improved for four of the five students almost immediately and appeared to maintain over time. Students all loved to have their own social story booklets. Teachers reported enjoying seeing the success and improvement in student behaviors. Unfortunately, excessive hand-wringing behavior did not decrease for one student. This may have been because this student had exhibited hand-wringing behavior since he was 3 years old, and, in this case, the behavior was too well established to be eliminated by a social story. Nevertheless, the overall results of this investigation suggest that social stories may be an important intervention for improving the social skills of adolescents with autism.

QUESTIONS FOR REFLECTION

1. Why do you think the social stories were effective?
2. Why do you think the social story was ineffective at reducing inappropriate behaviors for one of the participants?
3. Describe other types of behaviors that might respond well to social stories.

Watch for signs that the student is becoming stressed. Students with autism may react aggressively or withdraw completely under novel or stressful situations. Try to predict when the class demands might become stressful and attempt to eliminate the sources of stress.

Finally, establish and maintain effective communication with all individuals who are in contact with students with autism. Communicate regularly with parents. Send home weekly or daily notes, short audiotaped messages, or a journal that travels back and forth from you to parents.

Severe and Multiple Disabilities

PREVALENCE, DEFINITIONS, AND CHARACTERISTICS

Many individuals with severe disabilities have severe and profound mental retardation/ intellectual disability. Some individuals with moderate mental retardation may also be included in this group (Beirne-Smith, Patton, & Kim, 2006). Individuals with severe impairments may have several coexisting disabilities (for example, sensory or physical disabilities). Moderate mental retardation is classified according to an IQ test score continuum of 35 to 54; severe retardation is represented by scores between 20 and 34, while profound retardation is classified as any score less than 20 (Jacobson & Mulick, 1996). The American Association on Intellectual and Developmental Disabilities (AAIDD; formerly American Association on Mental Retardation, or AAMR) proposed a classification system for intellectual disability based upon level of support needed, with severe and profound retardation requiring more extensive and pervasive support (AAMR, 2002). Individuals with moderate, severe, and profound mental retardation represent about 15% of all individuals with mental retardation/intellectual disability, or about .02% of the school-age population and .14% of the students served under IDEA (Beirne-Smith et al., 2006).

Multiple disabilities refers to the presence of two or more impairments that significantly influence an individual's ability to learn and function without adaptations, and that cannot be accomodated in special education programs devoted to only one of the impairments. A major disability with minor impairments or secondary conditions is not considered multiple disabilities; at least two separate categories of impairment must be present (Best, 2005a). The only exception to this is deaf-blindness, which is a separate category of disability under IDEA. Students with multiple disabilities represent about .20% of the school-age population, and about 2.2% of the students served under IDEA (U.S. Department of Education, 2007).

EDUCATIONAL PLACEMENT CONSIDERATIONS   The optimal educational placement and the design of effective instruction for students with severe and multiple disabilities are usually determined by the case conference team. The priorities vary depending on the age, severity level, and needs of the individual. Priorities come from family, medical, school, leisure, transitional, vocational, and peer-support concern areas and are designed to match each student's needs and strengths.

Students with severe and multiple disabilities generally have severe cognitive and adaptive behavior difficulties and require instruction in self-help skills, communication skills, functional academic skills, daily living skills, community awareness, and recreation, social, and vocational education skills. These students benefit greatly from positive social interactions with their general education peers. The creation of peer-support networks, friendship circles, social circles, and participation in after-school activities is strongly advocated for individuals with severe disabilities (Westling & Fox, 2004). The *Diversity in the Classroom* feature describes the Comprehensive Support Model for working and planning with families from culturally diverse backgrounds.

STRATEGIES FOR
MAKING CLASSROOM ADAPTATIONS
FOR STUDENTS WITH SEVERE AND MULTIPLE DISABILITIES

Because of the nature of severe and multiple disabilities, most students require special education and related services from many educational team members, including physical therapists, occupational therapists, speech and language therapists, adaptive physical education specialists, special educators, and paraprofessionals. Establish good working relationships with these partners and arrange the classroom for easy access by these specialists. Specialists may include their activities along with general education instruction. For example, specialists can assist with positioning and grasping techniques during classes involving art activities or computer applications. Arrange a special place in the classroom for specialists to work with the students with severe disabilities within the general education classroom. This should be done in a way that neither draws unnecessary attention to students with severe disabilities nor distracts the rest of the class.

Supporting Diverse Families: The Comprehensive Support Model

Students with disabilities and their families from diverse cultures are confronted with numerous challenges. The Comprehensive Support Model (CSM) is intended to provide a model for better serving students with exceptionalities and their diverse families (Obiakor, Utley, Smith, & Harris-Obiakor, 2002). CSM is based on the model educational services used in the African village, which values all parts of society. That is, the student, family, school, community, and government work together to solve educational problems. Five interacting components are important for effective implementation of CSM.

First, CSM assumes students will have active roles in the planning, self-responsibility, and implementation of their educational programs. Students are encouraged to be motivated and active participants in school. Second, CSM acknowledges that families are important members who provide critical linkages between home and school. Families are encouraged to participate in activities during and after school hours. Third, CSM recognizes that school personnel are important, as they can provide understanding and valuing of diverse cultures and help to infuse culturally responsive instruction in classes. Schools can be catalysts for organizing programs for all teachers on culturally responsive practices. Programs can provide assistance on using culturally appropriate assessments and promotion of self-concept for students from all cultures. Fourth, CSM acknowledges that the community contains numerous untapped resources to enhance the education of all students. Some of these resources from the entire community include clergy from all religions, community leaders, and members of all the various neighborhoods. Community members can serve as mentors and role models for students. Finally, local, state, and federal governments play important roles in CSM. Governments provide funding for school programs and provide guidance to assure protection of rights for all students with disabilities from diverse cultures. When all components of CSM are working together, students with disabilities from diverse cultures and their families will have greater opportunities for success.

myeducationlab

Go to MyEducationLab, select the topic *Physical Disabilities and Health Impairments*, and go to the Activities and Applications section. Watch the video entitled "Physical Disabilities." This student has severe physical disabilities; consider the role his paraeducator must assume every day to ensure academic success.

ESTABLISH GOOD WORKING RELATIONSHIPS WITH PARAPROFESSIONALS
Paraprofessionals (or paraeducators) are often assigned to accompany students with severe disabilities for the entire school day. This means general education teachers would have another adult in the classroom whenever the student with severe disabilities is present. Because many teachers are used to being alone in their classrooms, having another adult in their room while teaching may require some adjustment (Downing, Ryndak, & Clark, 2000). The benefits can far outweigh the disadvantages because paraprofessionals can assist in many instructional and administrative responsibilities, as well as self-help care (Carroll, 2001; Giangreco, Broer, & Edelman, 1999). These might include the following:

- Adapting materials under the direction of the teacher or special education teacher
- Administering tests individually to students with severe disabilities
- Reviewing and practicing materials already covered in class
- Presenting adapted materials to students
- Taking notes for students
- Assisting teachers during a class presentation
- Promoting peer cooperation during class
- Helping to arrange the classroom environment to accommodate activity needs
- Grading papers and assisting with recordkeeping
- Assisting with duplicating or laminating class materials
- Attending case conferences or team meetings as necessary
- Assisting with feeding and toileting
- Assisting with dressing before and after recess

- Supervising during recess
- Assisting with mobility during class-changing time periods, including going to lunch and before and after school

Use strategies discussed in Chapter 2 to promote positive interactions with paraprofessionals. Also, be careful that paraprofessionals assist students with disabilities without preventing their access to other students or teachers (Giangreco & Broer, 2007).

INCREASE DISABILITY AWARENESS Prepare your students for the arrival of a student with severe or multiple disabilities. Information regarding the strengths and needs of the individuals can be conveyed using a variety of formats, to promote students' awareness of disability-related issues (Sapon-Shevin, 1992). One method of presenting information is to have guest speakers present information on specific disability-related issues pertaining to the student who

Paraprofessionals assist teachers with many administrative and instructional responsibilities.

will be included within the class. Special education teachers, parents of students with disabilities, speech–language therapists, physicians, school psychologists, or local disability organizations such as the Council for Exceptional Children (CEC) or the Association for Retarded Citizens (ARC) can present relevant information (see Plumb & Brown, 1990).

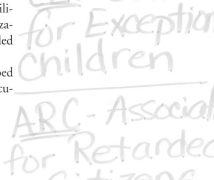

Paula Billingsley, a first-grade teacher at Strong Elementary School (Texas), described how her students began to express their natural curiosity about "Lisa," and she used their curiosity to provide a teaching moment:

> One of the advantages of teaching first grade is that the children are totally honest. After about a week of having Lisa with us and watching her communicate with sign language, and using her book with symbols, the children began to ask questions about how Lisa was learning. We seized the moment and began answering questions about Lisa. They were so concerned and interested in their fellow classmate. How did she learn, can she see them (she tends to hold her head sideways and be involved in her own world), would she ever go to college, could they help her learn, could they learn to talk with her, and where did she go when she was not with us? I listened to their questions with tears in my eyes as I realized they had a genuine interest in her and wanted to be a part of her learning experience. Aren't children wonderful with their nonjudgmental behavior!

CONCEPTUALIZE INCLUSIVE INSTRUCTION Several authors have suggested a variety of ways to begin to conceptualize the inclusion of students with severe disabilities into general education classes (Snell & Brown, 2005; Westling & Fox, 2004). These include the following:

- Focus on activities that can be engaged in by all students, without modification, such as homeroom or music class.
- Use *multilevel curriculum instruction*, or **differentiated instruction**, such as having a student in a wheelchair work on control of different muscles while the rest of the class does exercises on floor mats during physical education class.
- Engage in *curriculum overlapping*, for example, having the student work on communication skills in the context of working on another academic area, such as mathematics (Snell & Brown, 2005).

MONITOR SPECIAL HEALTH-CARE NEEDS Many students with severe disabilities have coexisting medical needs and require special health-care adaptations and accommodations. Some students may be medically fragile, have infectious diseases, or simply have coexisting severe medical needs.

Consider writing daily health-care plans for individuals with severe medical needs. Health plans, written with input from the student's health-care provider, can detail information pertaining to the condition itself, restrictions in activities or precautions to be considered, the independence of the student in health care, medication schedules, whether students can recognize signs or symptoms of their own disorders, toileting schedules, and emergency plans for medical or other emergency situations (such as procedures for contacting medical assistance and parental notification).

Some students need assistance from medical technology, such as respirator support, intravenous or nutritional support, alternative bowel and bladder assistance, breathing support with the use of ventilators, suctioning to remove mucous—especially for those with tracheostomies, and continuous feedings provided by pumps. The establishment of good, open lines of communication with health-care professionals and parents will enable general education teachers to better accommodate individuals requiring such assistance in their classes (Best, Heller, & Bigge, 2005).

MAKE CLASSROOM ADAPTATIONS   Students with severe disabilities may have coexisting physical disabilities. In these cases, adaptations to the physical environment and instructional materials—such as those detailed in the students with physical disabilities section described earlier—will be required.

In addition, many of the adaptations described for students with intellectual disabilities in Chapter 3 may be beneficial. Prioritize the educational and social objectives for the time spent in the general education class. Once the goals are prioritized, you will be in a better position to design and implement any necessary adaptations.

Primary adaptations for students with severe and multiple disabilities may involve devising procedures for communication systems (including alternative and augmentative communication), handling instructional materials, allowing additional time to complete activities, and devising activities that appear instructionally relevant and meaningful for students.

Work closely with the special education teacher to develop an appropriate and effective manner of interacting with students with severe disabilities. Because many students with severe disabilities have limited language skills, make certain that all your communications are clear and understandable.

Students with severe disabilities may be learning different things than other students in the classroom, and therefore will have different learning objectives. Make certain that you are familiar with all the IEP objectives for students with severe (or any other) disabilities. All objectives should be stated in a way that progress can be directly observed and recorded. For example, if one of a student's objectives involves interacting more positively with other students, be certain you know exactly what is meant by *positive interaction* (e.g., more direct eye contact, friendly expression, positive statements or gestures), and monitor progress on this objective.

Visual Impairments

PREVALENCE, DEFINITIONS, AND CHARACTERISTICS

Individuals with visual impairments make up one of the smallest disability areas, or about .04% of the school-age population and .4% of the students served under IDEA (U.S. Department of Education, 2007). Visual impairments range from mild to moderate to severe, and both legal and educational definitions exist. The legal definition includes acuity assessment information, and the educational definition is linked to learning to read. Individuals are classified as legally blind if their **visual acuity** is 20/200 or less even with corrective lenses, and partially sighted if their visual acuity is 20/70. This means a person who is legally blind can see something at 20 feet that a person with normal vision can see at 200 feet, and a person who is partially sighted can see something at 20 feet that a person with normal vision can see at 70 feet. Legal classification qualifies individuals for tax advantages and some other legal benefits (Heward, 2009).

Educational definitions are based more on the method necessary for learning to read. For example, many individuals classified as legally blind have some vision and can learn to read using enlarged print. These students are often referred to as students with low vision. Other individuals have such limited vision that they are referred to as totally blind and learn to read using the **Braille** system (raised dots that are read with fingertips), or by ear using audiotapes. The federal definition is "an impairment in vision that even with correction, adversely affects a child's educational performance. The term includes both partial sight and blindness" (20 U.S.C. 1401(3); 1401(30); U.S. Department of Education, 2008).

Visual impairments can be present at birth or acquired later in life. Common causes of visual impairments include **glaucoma** (excessive pressure on the eyeball), **cataracts** (clouding of the lens), **diabetic retinopathy** (lack of blood to the retina), **coloboma** (parts of the retina improperly formed), **retinitis pigmentosa** (degeneration of the retina), and **retinopathy of prematurity** (excessive oxygen to premature infants). Muscle functioning disorders of the eye, such as strabismus (crossed eyes) and nystagmus (rapid involuntary eye movements), also may result in visual impairments.

Individuals with visual impairments can have one or more of a wide range of disabilities, from mild to severe. A common characteristic includes delayed language development due to the restriction of visual experiences (Warren, 1984). Students with severe visual impairments may rely on the tactile and auditory senses rather than the visual sense (Hull, 1990). These students need to hold and feel three-dimensional objects to obtain a sense of the phenomena. If entire objects are held at once, students obtain a complete **synthetic touch** of the article. If objects are too large to be held, however, different segments of the object must be touched sequentially. Using this **analytic touch**, the segmented touches must be recombined mentally to form "the whole." These skills are referred to as tactile learning, and some research indicates that strategies can be used to teach students with visual impairments how to use and improve their tactile sense of learning (Berla, 1981; Griffin & Gerber, 1982). Because these students may miss opportunities for learning incidentally from seeing everything in their environment, it is necessary to present this information in alternative formats.

Some students with visual impairments engage in such repetitive behavior as head weaving or body rocking. These are known as stereotypic behaviors and are not harmful, except they can attract unwanted or negative attention. Stereotypic behaviors are sometimes addressed by reinforcement, self-monitoring, or physical prompts (Heward, 2009; Ross & Koening, 1991).

Mobility skills vary among individuals with visual impairments depending on the age of onset, degree of severity, and the individual's spatial ability. Spatial ability appears to affect the mobility access of individuals with visual impairments (Bigelow, 1991). Some individuals with visual impairments learn to walk with canes, although the training can be lengthy and difficult. Some canes have light sensors near the tip that emit sounds when the amount of light changes, indicating shadows or objects in the path ahead. Some individuals learn to walk with human guides and Seeing Eye dogs, although the latter are not usually seen with children (Davis, 2003).

STRATEGIES FOR
MAKING CLASSROOM ADAPTATIONS FOR STUDENTS WITH VISUAL IMPAIRMENTS

First, ensure that your classroom has clear, open walkways. Devise and teach classroom procedures for responding to emergency situations, including fire and tornado drills. Assign peers to assist students with visual impairments during emergency evacuations. Develop safety guidelines for using objects that are potentially harmful to students with visual impairments.

The following list offers strategies you can use to make your classroom more inclusive for students with visual impairments.

ADAPT THE PHYSICAL ENVIRONMENT   Keep aisles clear, wide, and open. Familiarize students with the physical arrangement of the room and notify students if any changes are made. Extra space will be necessary to accommodate equipment for braille and reading enlarged-print materials.

ADAPT INSTRUCTIONAL MATERIALS   Enlarge and enhance printed materials, including dramatically increasing the size of fonts. Increase visibility of materials, which might include bold-lined paper, special lighting, and magnification lenses. Certain technology may

PEARSON
myeducationlab

Go to MyEducationLab, select the topic *Visual Impairments*, and go to the Activities and Applications section. As you complete the simulation entitled "Instructional Accommodations," consider how you would adapt instruction for two students with visual impairments.

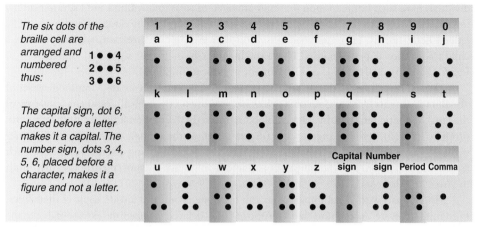

The six dots of the braille cell are arranged and numbered thus:

1 ● ● 4
2 ● ● 5
3 ● ● 6

The capital sign, dot 6, placed before a letter makes it a capital. The number sign, dots 3, 4, 5, 6, placed before a character, makes it a figure and not a letter.

| 1 | 2 | 3 | 4 | 5 | 6 | 7 | 8 | 9 | 0 |
| a | b | c | d | e | f | g | h | i | j |

| k | l | m | n | o | p | q | r | s | t |

| u | v | w | x | y | z | Capital sign | Number sign | Period | Comma |

Figure 4.4 Samples of Braille

Note: Reprinted with permission from the Division for the Blind and Physically Handicapped, Library of Congress, Washington, DC.

Print can be enlarged for individuals with low vision.

be used, such as projection microscopes, closed-circuit television, scanners, and equipment to convert print to tactile formats (Best, Reed, & Bigge, 2005). Convert print to braille formats, using the Perkins Brailler or specialized computer programs such as *Duxbury.* Figure 4.4 shows examples of braille. Use oral output devices, which produce speech, to enable students with visual impairments to participate in the same activities as their peers. These include the *Jaws* software program, the *Kurzweil 1000,* and the *Braille and Speak.* Use Descriptive Video Services, provided on many public television broadcasts, to provide additional verbal descriptions of visual events (Cronin & King, 1990). Use tactile and three-dimensional models to enhance conceptual understanding.

ADAPT INSTRUCTION   Be explicit when giving oral presentations. Avoid vague phrases such as *over here, almost, this,* and *that,* and use specific language such as *above your head, on your right,* and *the beaker in my hand.* Use time orientations such as "The model is on my desk at 2 o'-clock." When walking with students, describe upcoming barriers by saying, for example, "We are approaching an uphill ramp." When addressing students with visual impairments, always state their name first, so they know you are speaking to them, and speak in a normal tone of voice.

However you modify your instruction, provide sufficient time for students with visual impairments to complete class activities. Remember that reading enlarged print and braille takes longer than reading regular print. Check with students to determine the optimal pace at which they are capable of working.

When assessing students with visual impairments, allocate sufficient time for students to complete tests. Extra time is required to transcribe responses from braille to print formats or to use peer assistants.

Hearing Impairments

PREVALENCE, DEFINITIONS, AND CHARACTERISTICS

Individuals with hearing impairments make up .11% of the school-age population, and 1.2% of the students served under IDEA (U.S. Department of Education, 2007). Hearing impairments range in severity from mild to moderate to severe to profound, with the greatest educational distinctions occurring between hard of hearing and deaf. Individuals classified as hard of hearing can hear speech tones when wearing hearing aids, whereas persons who are deaf cannot hear even with hearing aids.

The age that a child loses hearing affects the degree of language delay and development. Children who are born with deafness have congenital hearing losses (**prelingual**) and more difficulty with language development than those who acquire deafness after age 2 (**postlingual**).

Pure tone audiometers are used to assess hearing ability. Tones with different pitches (or frequency measured in Hertz [Hz]) and volume (measured in decibels [dB]) are presented via headphones, and individuals raise their hand when they hear a sound. Levels of hearing impairment are classified along a continuum, with reference to zero dB indicating the quietest sound a person with normal hearing can detect. Individuals with slight hearing losses (27–40 dB) may not have difficulty in most school situations. Individuals with mild losses (41–55) may miss up to 50% of classroom discussion if voices are faint or faces cannot be seen. Individuals with moderate losses (56–70 dB) can understand only loud speech, and may have limited vocabularies. Individuals with severe losses (71–90 dB) may be able to hear loud voices within 1 foot from the ear, and speech is likely to be impaired. Individuals with profound losses (> 90 dB) may hear some loud sounds, but are more likely to sense vibrations, and may rely on vision rather than hearing as a primary vehicle for communication (Heward, 2009). Specialized tests are needed to accurately assess the cognitive and academic functioning of individuals with hearing impairments (Owens, Metz, & Haas, 2006).

Causes of hearing impairments include heredity, prenatal infections such as maternal rubella, ear infections, meningitis, head trauma, prematurity, and oxygen deprivation during birth. Impairments can be **conductive**, meaning the outer or middle ear along the passageway is damaged; **sensorineural**, referring to inner-ear damage; or they can be a combination of the two (Owens et al., 2006).

Many children with hearing impairments have academic and cognitive deficiencies or developmental lags due to difficulties processing language (Meadow-Orlans, 1990). For example, the average 18-year-old with a hearing impairment can comprehend text at only the fourth-grade level (although many exceptions exist). In many inclusive classes, there may be very little interaction between students who are deaf and students who hear normally, perhaps increasing feelings of isolation and loneliness (Hallahan, Kauffman, & Pullen, 2009).

EDUCATIONAL PROGRAMMING

An ongoing debate exists over what should be considered the best approach for teaching individuals with severe hearing impairments. Some advocate **total communication** (Owens et al., 2006), which involves using speech (lip) reading, gestures, and sign language, or both oral and manual methods. Teachers using total communication rely on the structure of the English language, and speak while signing during communications with students who are deaf. Some advocate the use of only oral approaches, eliminating any manual components used in total communication. Teachers using only oral approaches rely heavily on parental and family involvement as well as auditory, visual, and tactile methods of presentation. Finally, others advocate using only sign language or manual approaches. These individuals advocate the exclusive use of sign language because they maintain that a unique "culture of the deaf" exists among those who communicate with sign language. They believe that when individuals with hearing impairments are taught only to speech-read or use oral techniques, they are denied full participation in the culture of the deaf (Owens et al., 2006; Reagan, 1990). Individuals from this position say they are not disabled, but that they are part of another cultural group composed of individuals who are deaf.

Several signing systems are in use today, including American Sign Language (ASL), Finger-spelling, and Signing Exact English. All systems use manual signs made with the hands and fingers to represent words, concepts, and ideas. However, they are based on different systems. **American Sign Language** (ASL) is a visual-spatial language, and is not phonologically based, like English. Each sign has three parts: hand shape, location, and movement. ASL has its own rules of semantics, syntax, and pragmatics, and its own vocabulary (Owens et al., 2003). Fingerspelling is a manual alphabet of 26 distinct hand positions used to represent each letter in the English alphabet. Fingerspelling is especially appropriate for unfamiliar words such as proper names. The following *In the Classroom* feature (p. 99) displays sample sign language positions and Finger-spellings. Some teachers use Fingerspelling while speaking to students with hearing impairments. Signing Exact English is a system that employs components of ASL, but attempts to use correct English usage for facilitating the learning of reading and writing literacy skills in English for students who are deaf. No clear research evidence exists to promote one approach over the other in teaching students who are deaf. Therefore, it is likely that this debate will continue into the future.

STRATEGIES FOR
MAKING CLASSROOM ADAPTATIONS FOR STUDENTS WITH HEARING IMPAIRMENTS

myeducationlab

Go to MyEducationLab, select the topic *Hearing Loss and Deafness*, and go to the Activities and Applications section. Watch the two videos entitled "The Inclusion of Students with Hearing Impairments" and "Hearing Impairment." As you answer the accompanying questions, reflect on the similarities and differences between these two situations.

Students with hearing impairments can benefit from instruction in general education classes if specific adaptations are made. Specific accommodations vary depending upon the degree of hearing impairment and whether students have interpreters to accompany them throughout the school day. If you have a student with hearing impairments in your class, establish classroom emergency procedures for use during fire and tornado drills. Many fire alarms can be equipped with a light that flashes while the bell rings, alerting students with hearing impairments. Consider assigning a peer assistant who can pass along information that comes from the announcement system and who can be a buddy during any emergency situations. In addition to these guidelines, consider the following strategies (see also Pakulski & Kaderavek, 2002; Stewart & Kluwin, 2001).

ADAPT THE PHYSICAL ENVIRONMENT   Seat students close enough to the front of the class to maximize their hearing and enable them to read speech. They should also be able to turn to face other students while they are speaking. Because hearing aids are especially sound-sensitive, loud or irritating noises should be avoided. Consider choosing a room with carpeting and located away from noisy school areas, such as the cafeteria and gym.

ADAPT INSTRUCTIONAL MATERIALS   Use technology, including hearing aids, television captioning, adapted telephone equipment (TTY), computer-assisted instruction, and the Internet. When appropriate, use FM sound systems, which include cordless microphones for teachers and receivers that attach to hearing aids for students. Pass your microphone to classmates who are speaking in a class discussion so they can also be heard. Audio enhancement systems using infrared microphones have also been installed in classrooms. Some teachers report that these devices improve the volume and clarity of their speech, for the benefit of all students (Mathews, 2008). Use visuals such as illustrations, diagrams, pictures, and three-dimensional models to introduce vocabulary and concepts and enhance comprehension. Use language cards that contain vocabulary and illustrations of concepts and definitions that can accompany verbal presentations and be used to preteach. Encourage students to maintain personal dictionaries of their language cards.

ADAPT INSTRUCTION   Create authentic experiences by connecting new language and knowledge to real-world experiences in a context relevant to the student's linguistic and experiential background. As you teach, reiterate major points, write out assignments, or write down questions on overhead transparencies or the chalkboard. Give students outlines or closing summaries as handouts. Repeat questions or answers that other students contribute, to enable students with hearing impairments to fully participate in class. Sequence steps or procedures on written cards and place them in clear view.

FM sound systems can help teachers communicate with students who have hearing impairments.

Use hand signals or devise a signaling system to denote transitions, and allow students with hearing impairments or interpreters to review questions, answers, and concepts. Alert students as to when to look or listen, and position yourself so that students with hearing impairments can clearly see your face, without shadowing from backlighting or the reflection of glaring light.

Use a "listen, then look, then listen" sequence of instruction, so students can focus on your face as you speak, then focus on the other aspects of the lesson separately, then focus on your face again. Say, for example, "Now, I'm going to pour the oil in with this water" (listen); then pour the oil (look), then say, "I poured the

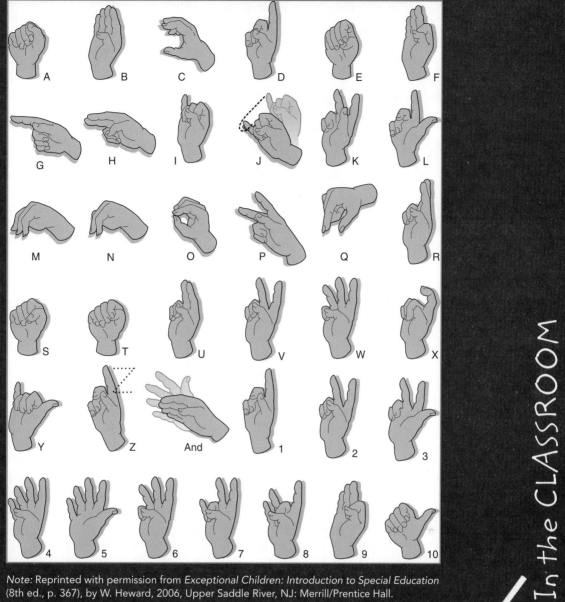

Note: Reprinted with permission from *Exceptional Children: Introduction to Special Education* (8th ed., p. 367), by W. Heward, 2006, Upper Saddle River, NJ: Merrill/Prentice Hall.

In the CLASSROOM

oil into the water. Who can tell me what happened?" (listen). Repeat information from the school public address system to ensure students have understood the announcements.

Be sure to plan for interpreters. Interpreters often assist students who are deaf, by translating lecture information, tutoring, and assisting special and regular education teachers (Salend & Longo, 1994). Extra space, including chairs or desks, may be required for interpreters to be near students with hearing impairments. Since interpreters are typically adults and taller than your students, check to see that all children have a clear view of important classroom information. Prepare your students for the interpreter and clearly explain the roles and functions the interpreter will have while in your classroom. Schedule time alone with the interpreter to discuss your typical classroom procedures, materials, and routines. Remember that an interpreter cannot proceed at the same pace as your verbal presentation, and you need to slow your rate of presentation accordingly.

Many students with hearing impairments communicate with sign language systems that employ their own unique rules of grammar.

Work with family members to maximize the educational experience of students. Parents and other family members have an important influence on students with hearing impairments, with respect to such activities as going out and interacting with people, joining sports and other recreational activities, and monitoring and assisting homework (Stewart & Kluwin, 2001). Work with family members to help them prioritize and encourage important activities.

ADAPT EVALUATION Testing and evaluation modifications for students with hearing impairments might include providing individual testing times in separate rooms and extending the time limit as necessary. Remember to allow sufficient time for interpreters during oral testing situations. Allow students to draw illustrations of concepts. Use performance-based testing measures and identification formats whenever possible (see Chapter 12).

4 Summary

- Lower-incidence disabilities occur less frequently in the general population than other disability areas. Lower-incidence disabilities include physical disabilities, other health impairments, autism, severe and multiple disabilities, visual impairments, and hearing impairments.

- Students with physical disabilities may exhibit difficulties using their arms, legs, or both arms and legs. Some of these students may exhibit problems with communication. Specific adaptations for increasing mobility, assisting with fine motor control, and improving communication skills help students become more independent and successful.

- Students with other health impairments may have serious medical needs that require special attention and that restrict their learning in school. Coordination with medical professionals while monitoring health and educational needs helps these students with school success.

- Students with autism may have mild to severe difficulties, but usually have serious difficulties with social behavior. Students with more severe autism have difficulties with language, communication, cognitive tasks, attention, memory, and basic skills.

- Some students with severe disabilities have severe mental retardation/intellectual disability and exhibit difficulties in cognition, adaptive behavior, academic, social, self-help, problem-solving, attention, and memory areas.

- Individuals with visual impairments represent the smallest category of exceptionality. Students may have very low vision to no vision. These students may have difficulty learning unless adaptations are made, such as arranging the physical environment for easy accessibility, enhancing printed materials, using braille and oral formats, and using concrete tactile and three-dimensional examples.

- Students with hearing impairments have mild to severe hearing losses. Individuals with mild to moderate hearing impairments usually wear hearing aids, while individuals who are deaf use sign language, total communication, or some aural techniques for communication. Students may require specific language, communication, and social skills instruction.

- Arrange special classroom procedures for emergency situations for classrooms containing individuals with lower-incidence disabilities. Some of these individuals may miss the usual safety alert systems, tire more easily, or have special medical or mobility needs that require special preparation.

- A variety of adaptations in the physical environment, instructional materials, instructional procedures, and evaluation procedures can make the general education classroom a positive learning experience for students with lower-incidence disabilities.

PROFESSIONAL STANDARDS LINK:
Teaching Students with Lower-Incidence Disabilities

Information in this chapter links most directly to:

- CEC Standards: 2 (Development and Characteristics of Learners), 3 (Individual Learning Differences), 4 (Instructional Strategies), 6 (Language)
- INTASC Standards: Principles 1 (understands central concepts of the discipline), 3 (understands learning differences, adapts instructional opportunities), 4 (instructional strategies), 5 (creates learning environments)
- PRAXIS II™ Content Categories (Knowledge): 1 (Understanding Exceptionalities), 2 (Issues), 3 (Delivery of Services)
- PRAXIS II™ Content Categories (Application): 1 (Curriculum), 2 (Instruction)

TEACHING STUDENTS WITH LOWER-INCIDENCE DISABILITIES

If a student with lower-incidence disabilities is having difficulties in your classroom, have you tried the following? If not, see the pages listed below.

Inclusion Checklist

STRATEGIES FOR MAKING CLASSROOM ADAPTATIONS FOR STUDENTS WITH PHYSICAL DISABILITIES AND OTHER HEALTH IMPAIRMENTS

Prepare the class, 82–83
☐ Monitor medical guidelines, 83–85
☐ Adapt the physical environment, 85
☐ Adapt instructional materials, 85–86
☐ Adapt instruction, 86
☐ Adapt evaluation, 86

STRATEGIES FOR MAKING CLASSROOM ADAPTATIONS FOR STUDENTS WITH AUTISM

☐ Establish effective communication, 87–88
☐ Use direct instruction and applied behavior analysis, 88
☐ Develop social competence, 88–90

STRATEGIES FOR MAKING CLASSROOM ADAPTATIONS FOR STUDENTS WITH SEVERE AND MULTIPLE DISABILITIES

☐ Establish good working relationships with paraprofessionals, 92–93
☐ Increase disability awareness, 93
☐ Conceptualize inclusive instruction, 93
☐ Monitor special health-care needs, 93–94
☐ Make classroom adaptations, 94

STRATEGIES FOR MAKING CLASSROOM ADAPTATIONS FOR STUDENTS WITH VISUAL IMPAIRMENTS

☐ Adapt the physical environment, 95
☐ Adapt instructional materials, 95–96
☐ Adapt instruction, 96

STRATEGIES FOR MAKING CLASSROOM ADAPTATIONS FOR STUDENTS WITH HEARING IMPAIRMENTS

☐ Adapt the physical environment, 98
☐ Adapt instructional materials, 98
☐ Adapt instruction, 98–100
☐ Adapt evaluation, 100

Purple Flower

DARREN SMITH   Darren Smith, an I.T. manager and photographer, was introduced to photography by his grandfather who was a cameraman for the BBC News for 28 years. Darren has rheumatoid arthritis; he struggles with his camera due to limited movement in his elbows and can only use the camera in his left hand. He explains his passion for photography: "Photography justifies the pain I go through. It's like a drug to me."

5

Teaching Students with Other Special Learning Needs

OBJECTIVES

After studying this chapter, you should be able to:

- Describe and discuss the prevalence and characteristics of students who are gifted, creative, or talented.
- Describe and discuss the prevalence and characteristics of students from culturally and linguistically diverse backgrounds.
- Describe and discuss the prevalence and characteristics of students at risk for school failure.
- List, describe, and be able to recommend adaptations and modifications to promote inclusion of students with other diverse learning needs.

Not all individuals with diverse or special learning needs are classified as having disabilities. Students with other special learning needs represent a wide range of abilities and include (1) students who are gifted and talented, (2) students from different cultural and linguistic backgrounds, and (3) students who may be considered at risk for school failure. These students belong to an increasing population in schools and are served in general education classes.

Gifted, Creative, and Talented

DEFINITIONS, PREVALENCE, AND CHARACTERISTICS OF GIFTED, CREATIVE, AND TALENTED

Individuals with special gifts and talents may be extraordinary in intellectual ability, specialized academic areas, music, or the arts (Clark, 2008). Although gifted, creative, and talented individuals are not included in IDEA, these students have unique needs that require special attention and accommodations for them to succeed in school. Various definitions of *gifted, creative,* and *talented* exist in the literature, and there is little agreement on the best definition. Earlier definitions relied heavily on the use of IQ scores for identifying gifted individuals. The Gifted and Talented Act, passed in 1978 (PL 95-561, Title IX, sec. 902) and reauthorized in 1994, included creative capabilities or high performance in the performing arts:

> Children and youth with outstanding talent perform or show the potential for performing at remarkably high levels of accomplishment when compared with others their age, experience, or environment. These children and youth exhibit high performance capability in intellectual, creative, and/or artistic areas, possess an unusual leadership capacity, or excel in specific academic fields. They require services or activities not ordinarily provided in the schools. Outstanding talents are present in children and youth from all cultural groups, across all economic strata, and in all areas of human endeavor. (PL 100-297, sec. 4130)

These federal definitions highlight the areas of giftedness, talent, and creativity, and are more representative of recent trends in gifted education. Other conceptualizations of giftedness continue to broaden the single-intelligence notion (National Association for Gifted Children, 2008). The following are examples of broadened definitions for gifted, creative, and talented youth: (1) three-trait definition, including above-average ability, task commitment, and creativity (Renzulli, 1978); (2) especially high aptitude, potential, or ability (Feldhusen & Moon, 1995); (3) synthetic, analytic, and practical intelligence (Sternberg, 2005); and (4) multiple intelligences (Gardner, 2006). All proposed models include more than a single intelligence quotient as criteria, most include talents as critical components, and many recommend advice on counseling gifted and talented youth. While general intelligence is the most widely accepted consideration by state definitions of giftedness and talent, specific academic ability, creative thinking, talent in the visual or performing arts, and leadership are also considered by many states (Education Commission of the States, 2004).

Given the variety of definitions, it is not surprising that little consensus exists on the actual number of gifted and talented youth. Many reports indicate that 3% to 5% of the population is gifted and talented (Hallahan & Kauffman, 2009); others believe the figures are much higher. Great variability also exists in how individual states identify students with gifts and talents, with some states identifying fewer than 3% of students, and other states identifying more than 10% (Heward, 2009).

INTELLECTUALLY GIFTED Intellectually gifted students are those who have scored very high on standardized tests and usually excel in school. They are frequently very highly skilled verbally and have outstanding memories and literacy abilities—especially in reading and writing—compared with their typical age peers. They also tend to have outstanding critical thinking and problem-solving abilities and insatiable curiosities (Bireley, 1995). Intellectually gifted youth acquire, retain, and manipulate large amounts of information and may appear to learn in intuitive leaps (Davis & Rimm, 2004; Silverman, 1995).

CREATIVE AND TALENTED The definitions of *creative* and *talented* are widely varied, but consensus usually converges on the identification of individuals with exceptional talents in particular areas (Clark, 2008). Creatively gifted and talented youth often excel in the visual or performing arts. These students typically show outstanding abilities at young ages in particular areas. Davis (1995) listed the following 12 categories as representative of creative individuals: original, independent, risk taking, aware of creativeness, energetic, curious, sense of humor, attracted to complexity, artistic, open-minded, need for time alone, and intuitive.

HIDDEN GIFTED, CREATIVE, AND TALENTED
Many students who are gifted and talented remain unidentified or hidden. This may be due to a number of factors. First, they might be underachievers and consequently their scores fall below the cutoff scores for classifying gifted students. Second, intelligence tests and standardized tests may underidentify some students due to cultural or linguistic diversity (Davis & Rimm, 2004; Patton, 1997). Third, girls who may be gifted and talented may be underidentified (Navan, 2008), although precise reasons for this are unknown. Finally, some students may not be identified due to existing disabilities in other areas (learning or physical disabilities). Special attention during classification and screening efforts at identifying gifted and talented youth can help eliminate underidentification of these individuals. Gregory, Starnes, and Blaylock (1988) and Patton (1997) provide some specific suggestions for finding and nurturing potential giftedness among Hispanic and African American students (see also Castellano, 2003). Their suggestions include the following:

Students who are gifted and talented might be easily identified from the products they create or might remain unidentified because they are underachieving.

- Develop a "belief system" in school that culturally and linguistically diverse students can be and are gifted and talented.
- Develop an identification process that reflects appreciation of the culture, language, values, and worldviews of culturally and linguistically diverse students and their families.
- Employ a multidimensional assessment process that includes qualitative as well as quantitative measures.
- Develop programs to educate the public in ways giftedness may be manifested (and sometimes concealed) in different cultures. Collaborate with people knowledgeable in the particular culture for assistance and support.
- Ensure that insights gained in the identification and assessment process are incorporated into the instructional program.

ISSUES IN IDENTIFICATION AND ASSESSMENT OF GIFTED, CREATIVE, AND TALENTED

Several approaches exist for identifying gifted and talented children and youth. Common approaches include nomination methods, standardized test scores, talent pool searches, and a multiple measures/multiple criteria approach. Nomination approaches consist of distributing nomination forms to teachers and parents. Schools often implement an approach by which parents, teachers, peers, and students are provided nomination forms in which they detail reasons for nominating a student (or self) for the gifted and talented program.

Standardized test score approaches include the use of intelligence and achievement test scores. These may be individually or group-administered tests. Cutoff scores to qualify students as gifted and talented are often designated to identify which students score in the top 8% (Renzulli & Reiss, 1991). This approach is usually combined with some other approach, in that standardized test scores are seldom the only criteria considered.

A multiple measures/multiple criteria approach is implemented in many schools (Davis & Rimm, 2004). This approach combines many of the pieces of evidence collected in the approaches discussed previously, but may also include detailed family histories, student work samples and inventories of interests, and discussion of all evidence by a gifted-and-talented screening committee.

STRATEGIES FOR
MAKING ADAPTATIONS FOR STUDENTS WHO ARE GIFTED, CREATIVE, AND TALENTED

Several educational approaches exist for programming curriculum and classes for gifted and talented youth. These include acceleration and enrichment, and are provided in regular classes, resource classes, self-contained classes, university classes, and through mentoring programs (Davis & Rimm, 2004). Careful pretesting identifies skills and information that gifted students have and can be used to place them in more appropriate curriculum.

IMPLEMENT ACCELERATION OR ENRICHMENT PROGRAMS Acceleration refers to moving students through the curriculum at a faster pace than general education students (Davis & Rimm, 2004). Acceleration can mean admitting a child to school early, skipping grades, providing level-appropriate curriculum, or testing out of classes. Advancing students places them in grades that match their achievement levels. For example, a fourth-grader who is working at a sixth-grade level academically might be advanced to the sixth-grade class. Another example is maintaining students in the age-appropriate class, but providing them with the appropriate-level curriculum (sixth-grade level, in this example). It might also mean advancing students several grade levels only in specific academic classes. For example, if seventh-grade students were gifted mathematically, they might be placed with juniors in the Algebra II class, but remain with their age peers for other subjects. Universities also may allow students who are gifted or talented to enroll in college-level courses when prerequisite criteria are met. Students who are gifted or talented frequently take advanced placement tests for college, which enables them to skip college-level courses. Finally, many students are admitted early to colleges and universities.

Acceleration is controversial, with proponents arguing strenuously for and opponents arguing strenuously against acceleration programs. Proponents claim students need acceleration to maintain interest in school and to be challenged adequately. Opponents claim that acceleration harms the social-emotional development of gifted students. Unfortunately, research results are ambiguous and yield no clear definitive answers (Davis & Rimm, 2004).

Numerous models of enrichment exist (Clark, 2008). The common element across enrichment programs is expansion upon the existing curriculum. Students are allowed and encouraged to study topics in depth that extend beyond the scope of the general education curriculum. The goals behind enrichment activities are to allow opportunities for critical thinking and problem solving through in-depth analyses of specific content areas. This is often accomplished by having students work independently on projects within general education classes. However, enrichment may also take place in off-campus settings. For example, students may be assigned to work with mentors in business and industry, or in university settings. In either case, general education teachers can facilitate coordination of programming for students who are gifted or talented.

ADAPT INSTRUCTIONAL MATERIALS   In the case of either acceleration or enrichment, it may be necessary for general educators to adapt curriculum materials to better meet the needs of students who are gifted or talented. When students have demonstrated mastery of content, be prepared to move them ahead in the curriculum or design suitable enrichment activities that enable them to study more in depth in that area. Survey student interests to help provide directions for instructional enhancements. Seek assistance from teachers who work with students who are gifted or talented, experts from specific content areas, and guidance counselors, as well as from the families of the students.

ADAPT INSTRUCTIONAL AND EVALUATION PROCEDURES   Be prepared to adapt your instructional procedures for students who are gifted or talented. They may not require intensive or explicit instruction on new content. You may be able to meet with them independently and briefly explain new concepts and content, thus allowing more time for either acceleration or enrichment activities. Students who are gifted or talented may also be able to provide tutorial assistance to age peers. Be aware that some gifted and talented youth may also require explicit instruction in study and organizational skills when work demands increase for them, as described in Chapter 11. Finally, evaluation methods can be modified to allow for assessment of enrichment and acceleration activities. More performance-based measures (see Chapter 12) may need to be devised to obtain true indicators of students' abilities on such tasks.

Students Who Are Culturally and Linguistically Diverse

PREVALENCE, DEFINITIONS, AND CHARACTERISTICS OF CULTURAL AND LINGUISTIC DIVERSITY

Evidence exists that many students from culturally and linguistically diverse backgrounds are at a higher risk for school failure than students from European American backgrounds (Gollnick & Chinn, 2009). Furthermore, the prevalence rates for students with disabilities are different from those expected in some culturally and linguistically diverse groups. Table 5.1 presents risk ratios provided by the U.S. Department of Education (2007) for each racial/ethnic group in each category of disability. This means, for example, that during the 2003–2004 school year, Black or African American students were 2.3 times as likely to receive services for emotional disturbance as were their age peers from all the other racial/ethnic groups combined, and that Asian/Pacific Islander students were 0.4 times as likely to receive services for learning disabilities as students in other racial/ethnic groups. Table 5.2 presents the percentage of students within each racial/ethnic group who receive services for each category of disability. For example, during the same school year, 2% of Black or African American students received services for mental retardation/intellectual disability, and 1.73% of Asian/Pacific Islander students received services for learning disabilities.

Similar findings have been presented in the past (Chinn & Hughes, 1987; Harry, 1992, 1994). This indicates that little has changed with respect to over- and underrepresentation issues by racial or ethnic group in past decades. Disproportional representation by race/ethnicity has also been reported in a number of other countries (Harry, Arnaiz, Klingner, & Sturges, 2008; Kalyanpur, 2008).

Although exact reasons for observed overrepresentation of some racial/ethnic backgrounds are unknown, several reasons have been hypothesized (see Harry & Klingner, 2006). Some specu-

Table 5.1 Risk Ratios for 6- to 21-Year-Old Students with Disabilities, by Race/Ethnicity and Disability Category

	American Indian/ Alaskan	Asian/ Pacific Islander	Black	Hispanic	White
Learning disabilities	1.8	0.4	1.4	1.1	0.8
Speech or language impairment	1.3	0.7	1.1	0.9	1.1
Mental retardation	1.2	0.5	3.0	0.7	0.6
Emotional disturbance	1.5	0.3	2.3	0.5	0.8
Multiple disabilities	1.4	0.6	1.4	0.7	1.0
Hearing impairment	1.3	1.2	1.1	1.2	0.8
Orthopedic impairment	0.9	0.8	1.0	1.0	1.1
Other health impairment	1.2	0.4	1.1	0.4	1.6
Visual impairment	1.3	1.0	1.2	0.9	0.9
Autism	0.7	1.2	1.1	0.5	1.3
Deaf-blindness	2.5	1.2	0.9	1.0	0.9
Traumatic brain injury	1.4	0.6	1.2	0.6	1.2
Developmental delay	3.6	0.6	1.6	0.5	1.0
All disabilities	1.5	0.5	1.5	0.9	0.9

Source: Data from U.S. Department of Education (2007).

Table 5.2 Students Ages 6 Through 21 Served by IDEA by Racial/Ethnic Group as a Percentage of Population

	American Indian/ Alaskan	Asian/ Pacific Islander	Black	Hispanic	White
Learning disabilities	7.51	1.73	5.57	4.69	3.98
Speech or language impairment	2.21	1.20	1.78	1.52	1.75
Mental retardation	1.04	.41	2.00	.61	.69
Emotional disturbance	1.11	.21	1.39	.42	.69
Multiple disabilities	.28	.12	.27	.15	.20
Hearing impairment	.14	.13	.12	.13	.10
Orthopedic impairment	.10	.08	.10	.10	.11
Other health impairment	.79	.25	.73	.34	.79
Visual impairment	.05	.04	.05	.04	.04
Autism	.15	.26	.22	.12	.23
Deaf-blindness	.01	.00	.00	.00	.00
Traumatic brain injury	.05	.02	.04	.02	.04
Developmental delay	.35	.07	.15	.05	.10
All disabilities	13.78	4.52	12.42	8.21	8.71

Source: Data from U.S. Department of Education (2007).

late that there are insufficient successful role models in schools and society for students from culturally and linguistically diverse backgrounds. Others suggest that cultural and linguistic differences often are inaccurately perceived as detriments (Gollnick & Chinn, 2009; Harry & Klingner, 2006), while others suggest that students from these underrepresented groups are discriminated against because educational methods, traditional assessments, and grading procedures do not accommodate students from various cultural and linguistic groups (Baca, Baca, & de Valenzuela, 2004a; Patton, 1998). It has also been suggested that percentages of some minority populations in special education are relatively higher due in part to low income and resulting disabilities associated with poverty, such as higher rates of exposure to harmful toxins (such as lead, alcohol, and tobacco), low birth weight, poorer nutrition, and less effective schools (Donovan & Cross, 2002; Gollnick & Chinn, 2009). It has also been suggested that representation in special education reflects the larger issue of representation in other remedial or compensatory programs such as Title 1 (MacMillan & Reschly, 1998).

Whatever the theory, however, the fact of overrepresentation of students who are culturally and linguistically diverse in special education is evidence that schools must pay greater attention to issues of cultural diversity. It is of critical importance that assessment instruments and procedures be nondiscriminatory and free of bias, and administered in the student's native language (de Valenzuela & Baca, 2004). The National Research Council has suggested that students be considered eligible for special education only when a student differs markedly from typical performance in specific academic or social-emotional domains, and with evidence that the student has not responded to high-quality interventions in these specific domains of functioning (Donovan & Cross, 2002).

Salend and Duhaney (2005) listed a number of suggestions for reducing overrepresentation of culturally and linguistically diverse students, including the following:

- Help create a diverse and culturally sensitive multidisciplinary planning team for making educational decisions.

- Provide effective prereferral and other ancillary services that can make culturally sensitive recommendations for interventions.

- Use alternatives to standardized testing, such as portfolio assessment, curriculum-based measurement, rubrics, and performance-based assessment (see Chapter 12).

- Look for any cultural factors that might contribute to learning problems, and include these in intervention plans.

- Employ culturally sensitive curriculum of interest to diverse learners.

- Use behavior management strategies that are sensitive to cultural differences in social behavior and include such strategies as culturally relevant reinforcers and group-oriented behavior management techniques.

- Employ culturally responsive teaching strategies, such as, for example, verbal interactions, cooperative learning, divergent thinking, small-group instruction, real-world tasks, and positive teacher–student interactions.

- Encourage family involvement by using positive and respectful language, encouraging face-to-face meetings, and planning creatively to interact with family members in a manner convenient to them.

CULTURAL DIVERSITY Assimilation and cultural pluralism are two prevalent philosophical approaches toward education of culturally diverse populations. Assimilation refers to having students from diverse ethnic and cultural groups assimilate into the dominant cultural group and essentially leave their own culture behind. Conversely, cultural pluralism refers to encouraging students from diverse ethnic and cultural groups to retain their own culture while succeeding in school (Gollnick & Chinn, 2009).

The concept of cultural pluralism becomes increasingly important as the number of individuals from diverse cultural and ethnic groups increases. This means that greater attention is needed to increase respect for all cultural and ethnic diversity in U.S. schools. Many proactive approaches can be implemented in schools to increase appreciation and awareness of cultural and ethnic differences. This approach is sometimes referred to as **multicultural education** because cultural pluralism is endorsed, which means appreciation of all cultures is taught and fostered (Gollnick & Chinn, 2009).

It is difficult to increase respect of all cultural groups without having some knowledge about differences among groups. However, it must be remembered that it is dangerous to generalize from cultural groups to individuals. As Lynch (1992) stated:

> Culture is only one of the characteristics that determines individuals' and families' attitudes, values, beliefs, and ways of behaving. . . . Assuming that culture-specific information . . . applies to all individuals from the cultural group is not only inaccurate

but also dangerous—it can lead to stereotyping that diminishes rather than enhances cross-cultural competence. When applying cultural-specific information to an individual or family, it is wise to proceed with caution. (p. 44)

Just as students with a particular disability may lack all of the characteristics associated with a disability area, the same is true of someone from a particular culture. An individual representing a particular ethnic or cultural group may not be "representative" of that cultural group. However, when teaching and learning about cultures, some general characteristics can serve as guidelines for learning about the various cultural groups. Suggestions for teaching toward a more proactive culturally pluralistic approach and away from a biased, monocultural approach are described in the following list.

- *Reduce teacher bias.*   Increase awareness of prejudices and decrease prejudices and stereotypes. Record yourself teaching (video or audio), and analyze the recording for instances of language or behaviors that do not promote culturally responsive teaching.
- *Eliminate curriculum bias.*   Select curriculum to reflect diversity of all cultural groups; avoid stereotyping and overgeneralizations of cultural groups.
- *Teach about prejudice.*   Discuss racism and discrimination; have students examine news for instances of racism; invite guest speakers; eliminate stereotypes.
- *Improve group relations and help resolve conflicts.*   Use case studies and teach problem-solving strategies.

RECOGNIZE THE NEEDS OF STUDENTS FROM MULTIRACIAL FAMILIES   There is also an increasing number of multiracial and multicultural families in the United States. In the 2000 census, 2.4% of the population identified themselves as being from more than one race (Jones & Smith, 2001). Moreover, multiracial marriages have resulted in more than a million multiracial children being born in the United States. Many of these children cannot be classified by only one part of their heritage. For example, Dorothy Adams, a 36-year-old whose father is African American and mother is Japanese American, stated:

I'm for the multiracial category. When I was a kid, the first time I paid attention to the race box was on a Social Security form. It was a problem to check one box, so I checked black and Japanese. The teacher said to check only one box, so I checked "Other," then wrote in "black and Japanese." I've never gone back to see how I'm listed with Social Security. (Grossman, 1997, p. 13)

Be aware that many people represent a variety of racial and ethnic backgrounds and wish to be treated with sensitivity with respect to their particular heritage.

DEVELOP A PLAN TO ADDRESS LINGUISTIC DIVERSITY   Linguistic diversity is also an increasing issue within public schools in the United States. Currently, as many as four million children in the United States have limited proficiency in English, over 9% of all students in public schools. The 2000 census revealed that 18% of respondents reported speaking a language different from English at home (Shin & Bruno, 2003). Further, this number is increasing at more than four times the rate of total student enrollment (Baca & Cervantes, 2004). Spanish is currently the second most commonly spoken language in the schools (Brice, 2002), but a recent survey of large urban school districts in the United States revealed that at least 42 languages may be spoken in these districts (Antunez, 2003). The *Technology Highlight* feature describes the use of multilingual translators.

These data indicate that difficulties with learning are likely because students may not have acquired the necessary English-language skills for success in English-speaking schools. In addition, it is more challenging to establish effective communication between families and the school when common languages are unknown. It is necessary to enlist the assistance of interpreters who can translate communications, schoolwork, notes, papers, and materials between school and home settings (de Valenzuela, Baca, & Baca, 2004).

Several approaches are available for teaching students with limited English proficiency, and some controversy exists regarding the best approach. It is a matter of debate whether children should be "immersed" in English-speaking classrooms (with English instruction also provided by teachers of English as a second language), or whether English and non-English languages should be combined within classroom instruction. Furthermore, even if different languages are used during

Multilingual Pocket Translators

Students for whom English is a second language may benefit from the use of a multilingual pocket translator. Multilingual translators can be small, pocket-sized electronic devices that contain a keyboard and a small screen. Students can enter text in one language, press a key, and have the text translated into another language. The devices are small enough to be carried from class to class in an unobtrusive fashion. They can provide valuable assistance and allow students to participate in class more frequently and to perform more optimally on class assignments and tests. In some schools students are allowed to use these during the school day and even during statewide competency testing situations. Such devices would also be beneficial for teachers to have to enhance their communication with students and families of individuals for whom English is a second language.

The functions of the various devices range from that of a dictionary, to phrases and idioms, to calculator, to data storage functions, to speech output. Some devices, such as the Language Teacher Pocket Translator, have built in synthesizers that produce a voice output as well. Many models have software available that can be loaded onto notebook computers or other handheld devices including palm pilots. More information on these devices can be obtained from *http://www.translation.net* (Language Teacher Pocket Translator) and *http://www.franklin.com* (Franklin Electronic Publishers, who also produce the Franklin Language Masters and Spell Checkers).

---

instruction, there is disagreement concerning how this can best be done to optimize performance and learning of all students. It has been suggested that students may acquire practical, conversational skills in English much sooner than more formal English for academic areas, and that it may be useful to support students in academic learning in their native language for several years until English skills are maximized (Ovando & Collier, 1998). It is important to note that virtually all concerned professionals agree that some level of support is needed for students who are not fluent in English.

Linguistic diversity is not limited to different languages. Some students may speak a dialect of English, rather than a different language. For example, many African American students may speak a Black dialect or Black English rather than standard English. Using a dialect in school may present some communication difficulties, especially with respect to written language assignments (Gollnick & Chinn, 2009), if teachers are not familiar with the dialect.

BILINGUAL SPECIAL EDUCATION   Bilingual special education refers to services provided for students with limited English proficiency who also have a disability. It is estimated that 14% of students with disabilities do not primarily use English in their homes. These students must accommodate two languages and two cultures, as well as face the challenges posed by their disabilities (U.S. Department of Education, 2003). Students who are bilingual who are also referred to special education are in need of both types of services and may be particularly at risk for inappropriate classification due to difficulties communicating in English (de Valenzuela & Baca, 2004). Bilingual special education teachers deliver services to those students who require bilingual education and special education services (Yates & Ortiz, 2004).

ISSUES IN IDENTIFICATION AND ASSESSMENT

IDEA provides stipulations for evaluations and assessments that are free of cultural and linguistic bias. It is especially important to monitor testing and assessment procedures to ensure this right for students from culturally and linguistically diverse backgrounds. Special precautions should be taken to ensure that ethnicity or cultural differences are not misinterpreted. For example, students in some cultures may tend to avoid direct eye contact with adults, a practice that may be misinterpreted by some teachers unfamiliar with cultural differences.

Overrepresentation in large part may be attributed to inappropriate identification and assessment procedures (Artiles & Zamora-Durán, 1997; Gollnick & Chinn, 2009). For example, African American students may be mistakenly referred for classification as having emotional or behavioral disabilities, because of cultural misunderstandings (Anderson & Webb-Johnson, 1995; Taylor & Whittaker, 2008). Likewise, research has suggested that some students who are bilingual exhibit behaviors that may be interpreted as behaviors similar to students with learning disabilities or behavioral disabilities (Yates & Ortiz, 2004). When students cannot understand the spoken language in class, they may appear uninterested or confused, or act inappropriately. Because these are some of the distinguishing characteristics of students with higher-incidence disabilities, general education teachers may misinterpret those behaviors and overrefer these students for special education services. Baca, Baca, and de Valenzuela (2004b) described the use of prereferral intervention for preventing inappropriate referrals for students who are bilingual, including assessing students in their dominant language. See the *Diversity in the Classroom* feature for a discussion of the response-to-intervention (RTI) model as a multiculturally responsive prereferral intervention strategy.

Evaluation procedures need to be closely monitored to ensure appropriate tests, testing situations, and familiar examiners are provided for such individuals. For example, students who do not speak and understand English fluently should not be placed into special education classes based on their performance on tests administered in English. Because many parents of students from diverse cultural and linguistic backgrounds speak only their native language fluently, have translators available to help facilitate communication efforts between families and schools when language barriers exist (de Valenzuela, et al., 2004).

Assess the special needs of students from culturally and linguistically different backgrounds using test instruments that avoid cultural bias.

English as second language (ESL) teachers who are bilingual specialists can provide valuable information on students who are beginning to learn English as a second language. They can provide suggestions to facilitate comprehension during classes. Bilingual teachers may provide academic instruction in students' native language (Baca, Baca, & de Valenzuela, 2004a). They may also work with special education teachers to ensure that instruction is sufficiently adapted to meet any specific disability needs. Use these specialists to help understand how to better serve students from different linguistic backgrounds. Bilingual special education teachers assume responsibility for the implementation of IEPs and provide ESL and special education instruction for students with both needs (Yates & Ortiz, 2004). These specialists work closely with general educators in inclusive models and coordinate instruction and instructional approaches to ensure IEP goals are met. Finally, consider the following:

- Test scores are only a single indicator of performance.
- Include multiple observations of students' behaviors.
- Testing by itself is insufficient for special education classification.
- Obtain assistance from bilingual and cultural diversity experts.
- Work closely with the families of students who are culturally and linguistically diverse, to obtain the most valid and relevant information. (Baca & Cervantes, 2004; Harry, 1995; Obiakor & Ford, 2003)

STRATEGIES FOR
MAKING ADAPTATIONS FOR STUDENTS FROM CULTURALLY AND LINGUISTICALLY DIVERSE BACKGROUNDS

Many of the adaptations described for students with disabilities may be beneficial for accommodating students from diverse cultural and linguistic backgrounds.

CREATE A CULTURALLY RESPONSIVE ENVIRONMENT Create an open, accepting classroom environment to ensure that students from all cultural and linguistic backgrounds feel comfortable in classes. Make all students and their families feel welcome in your class. Model acceptance and tolerance of individual differences. Teach students that we are all alike and different, and that immigrants from all parts of the world have historically settled in the United States and contributed to its development (de Melendez & Ostertag, 1997). Keep expectations high: Expect the best from all students, and be sure your students are aware of your expectations.

Diversity in the Classroom

Culturally Responsive Prereferral Strategies

Concerns about the overrepresentation of individuals from minority groups in special education have increased in recent years (see Hosp & Reschly, 2002). Prereferral intervention strategies were designed to reduce inappropriate referrals to special education, by differentiating between students who really appeared to need referral to special education and students who did not. Previous models have yielded an overrepresentation of students from minority backgrounds.

A promising, newer prereferral intervention strategy is response to intervention (RTI, see Klingner & Edwards, 2006; Vaughn & Fuchs,

2003). RTI is a model designed to provide the very best research-based instruction to students and to identify those students who do not respond appropriately to that instruction. Typically, there are several levels of RTI, ranging from large- to smaller-group instruction. However, no single model has yet gained national acceptance. Ideally, an RTI model is implemented on several levels, each of which contains high-quality instruction. Students who do not respond (nonresponders) to this sequence of research-based instruction would then be referred to special education (see Gerber, Jimenez, Leafstedt, Villaruz, Richards, & English, 2004).

If RTI also includes culturally responsive instruction and principles of universal design (see Burstahler, 2005; Culturally Responsive Instruction, 2008), this may prove to be a valuable step in reducing inappropriate referrals of culturally and linguistically different individuals. Garcia and Ortiz (2005) indicated that teachers can be trained to use culturally responsive instructional strategies that lead to an increased awareness of the sociocultural background of their students. When this occurs, teachers are better able to distinguish between students who may really require referral to special education and students who simply may be culturally and linguistically different.

Complete a needs assessment to determine the ethnic, cultural, and linguistic background of the school, students, and community. Learn how school knowledge is perceived in students' cultures, and the types of knowledge and skills that are valued (Gollnick & Chinn, 2009). Assess students' prior knowledge of and experience with academic content. The *In the Classroom* feature (p. 117) presents a needs assessment suggested by de Melendez and Ostertag (1997). Information obtained can be used to plan activities that address all cultural and linguistic backgrounds.

Accommodate culturally diverse families. Culturally diverse families may (or may not) differ from the majority culture in areas such as discipline practices, home–school communication, and school involvement (Taylor & Whittaker, 2008). Learn to avoid preconceptions, and to recognize and respect differences as you develop appropriate interactions with families (Harry, Klingner, & Hart, 2005).

Include books and stories in your curriculum to enhance understanding of other cultures. East and Thomas (2007) have developed annotated bibliographies of over 450 titles in recent multicultural literature (see also Norton, 2008; Taylor & Whittaker, 2008). Some recommended books are presented in Figure 5.1 (see also National Education Association, 2005).

ADAPT INSTRUCTION Teach about sensitivity and acceptance issues. Role-play scenarios that are concrete and meaningful to students. Examine curriculum materials to ensure they eliminate stereotypes. Examine your teaching style and practices to ensure all students are treated equally and offered chances of success. Figure 5.2 provides suggestions to increase appreciation of others.

Monitor the pace of instruction to ensure students with limited English proficiency are succeeding. Use concrete and familiar examples as frequently as possible when describing new concepts. Provide hands-on activities to ensure active involvement and active learning for all students (Baca & Almanza, 1991). By using many modalities when teaching, you will help clarify language and provide multiple examples for developing new vocabulary words. Help students relate any prior knowledge to new concepts you present (Gollnick & Chinn, 2009). Incorporate feedback from assessments and from solicited student opinions to maximize the effectiveness of your classroom and to make your classroom motivating, enjoyable, and productive (see Chapter 9).

Go to MyEducationLab, select the topic *Cultural and Linguistic Diversity*, and go to the Activities and Applications section. Complete the simulation entitled "Teachers at the Loom," and reflect on how these activities can help you create an open classroom environment.

Title	Subject (estimated reading level)
Who Are You? Voices of Mixed Race Young People (P. F. Gaskins, Holt, 1999)	Stories about multiracial children (8–12).
Teaching with Folk Stories of the Hmong (D. Cha & N. J. Livo, Libraries Unlimited, 2000)	Teaching resource on Hmong cultural traditions. Companion to *Folk Stories of the Hmong* by the same authors (9–12).
Arab American Enciclopedia (A. Ameri & D. Ramey, Eds., Gale Group, 2000)	Information about Arab Americans (5–12).
Happy Birthday, Mr. Kang (S. Roth, National Geographic Society, 2001)	Americanization and cultural traditions (2–5).
Harvesting Hope: The Story of Cesar Chavez (K. Krull, Harcourt, 2003)	Biography of the Mexican American labor leader (6–12).
Ellis Island: New Hope in a New Land (W. Jacobs, Scribner's, 1990)	Describes the role of Ellis Island in immigration to America (3–5).
The Flute Player: An Apache Folktale (J. Lacapa, Northland, 1990)	Folktale of an Apache boy who learns to play the flute for a girl who has captured his heart (3–5).
Children of Promise: African-American Literature and Art for Young People (C. Sullivan, Ed., Harry N. Abrams, 1991)	Stories, poems, plays, speeches, and documents that describe the African American experience (6–8).
Look What We've Brought You from Mexico: Crafts, Games, Recipes, Stories, and Other Cultural Activities from Mexican-Americans (P. Shalant, Julian Messner, 1992)	Describes the many contributions to the United States from Mexican culture (6–8).

Figure 5.1 Books to Promote Multicultural Awareness

For Younger Students	For Older Students
Share children's literature and stories about many cultures.	Complete a class, school, and community cultural and linguistic diversity profile.
Make a classroom "quilt."	Teach about inequity and individuals who have fought to combat inequitable practices.
Develop a class family cookbook.	
Discuss foods eaten at meals by different cultural groups.	Teach about cultural contributions: The arts, folk art, music, dances, literature, and crafts
Prepare, cook, and eat ethnic foods.	Traditions, holidays, festivals, myths
Dress in ethnic clothing.	Distinguished individuals and their accomplishments
Wear ethnic jewelry and accessories.	
Play ethnic music.	Prepare, cook, and eat ethnic foods.
Teach ethnic dances.	Dress in ethnic clothing.
Teach words and phrases from different languages.	Play ethnic music.
Invite parents in to share family traditions.	Teach ethnic dances.
Make illustrated family histories and post them in the classroom.	Teach words and phrases from different languages.
	Bring in international newspapers or newspapers written in a language other than English.

Figure 5.2 Classroom Practices to Increase Appreciation for Others

- Children with poor academic performance
- Children who are born exposed to alcohol and other narcotic substances
- Children who abuse alcohol and drugs
- Abused and neglected children
- Children living in poverty conditions
- Children suffering from depression and suicidal tendencies
- Students who are pregnant or parents
- Homeless children and children who move excessively
- Children with excessive absenteeism
- Students who have been suspended two times within a year
- Students who drop out of school
- Children who are slow learners
- Students who have experienced traumatic events such as death of someone close to them
- Children whose parents are alcoholics or drug abusers
- Students who are older than their grade-level peers due to retention
- Children who may be from urban, suburban, or rural settings
- Children who are angry or socially alienated

Figure 5.3 Major At-Risk Factors

Students at Risk

DEFINITIONS, PREVALENCE, AND CHARACTERISTICS OF STUDENTS AT RISK

Students at risk for school failure come from diverse environments and represent all racial, ethnic, and linguistic backgrounds. They also span all socioeconomic classes, although students coming from severe poverty may tend to be at a higher risk than others. At-risk students may ultimately fail or drop out of school and experience difficulties later in life. These students are usually found in general education classes, may require additional assistance from teachers, and may benefit from classroom modifications similar to those suggested for students with higher-incidence disabilities. Many educators have identified factors associated with at-risk students (Frieman, 2001; Gardner, 1983). These factors are listed in Figure 5.3, and describe a variety of situations.

ABUSED AND NEGLECTED CHILDREN   Child abuse and neglect can have devastating emotional, physical, cognitive, social, and intellectual effects on children; reported cases have been increasing in the United States (Crosson-Tower, 2007). Federal legislation, the Child Abuse Prevention and Treatment Act of 1974 and its subsequent amendments, defined child abuse and neglect as maltreatment, sexual abuse or exploitation, mental or physical injury, withholding medical treatment for life-threatening conditions, or negligent treatment of children younger than 18 by persons responsible for the child (Warger, Tewey, & Megivern, 1991). In some cases, child abuse has been linked to causing disabilities in children. For example, severe shaking of infants has been linked to brain injury (Klein & Stern, 1971); some cases of abuse have been related to cerebral palsy (Diamond & Jaudes, 1983); other cases have been linked to intellectual disabilities and learning disabilities (Caplan & Dinardo, 1986). The best overall predictor of child abuse and neglect is poverty (Children's Defense Fund, 2005). Table 5.3 presents behavioral and physical indicators of child abuse and neglect.

Schools and teachers have the responsibility to report any signs of child abuse or neglect as per state and local definitions and guidelines. A sample reporting form is shown in Figure 5.4. Determine state definitions and local procedures for reporting any cases and adhere to those policies and procedures upon noticing any cases of child abuse or neglect (Crosson-Tower, 2007; Garbarino, Brookhouser, & Authier, 1987).

Table 5.3 Some Physical and Behavioral Indicators of Child Abuse and Neglect

Type of Abuse or Neglect, Definition	Physical Indicators	Behavioral Indicators
Physical Abuse: Any act which, regardless of intent, results in a nonaccidental physical injury to a child	Questionable injuries, such as: • Bruises, welts, or other injuries • Burns • Fractures • Lacerations or abrasions	• Being uncomfortable with physical contact • Being wary of adult contacts • Showing behavioral extremes, either aggression or withdrawal • Not wanting to go home • Reporting an injury by a parent • Complaining of soreness or moving uncomfortably • Wearing excessive clothing to cover the body • Chronically running away from home (adolescents) • Reluctance to change clothes for gym activities (attempt to hide physical injuries)
Neglect: A caregiver's failure to provide something that a child needs	• Undernourished appearance • Lethargic • Signs of inadequate food or sleep • Untreated injuries • Evidence of unattended illness	• Begging for or stealing food because of persistent hunger • Poor hygiene • Inappropriate dress for the weather • Accidents and injuries • Risky adolescent behavior • Promiscuity, drugs, and delinquency • Being shunned by peers • Clinging behavior
Sexual Abuse: The misuse of adult authority by involving children in sexual activities	• Most physical indicators would be found during a physical exam by a medical practitioner	• Expressions of age-inappropriate knowledge of sex and sexually "pseudomature" behaviors • Sexually explicit drawings • Highly sexualized play • Statements of unexplained fear of a person or place • Stated desire to avoid a familiar adult • Expressions of excessive concern about gender identity (boys) • Nightmares • Sleep interruptions • Withdrawal • A child's statement of sexual abuse

Source: Child Abuse and Neglect: Recognition, Reporting, and Responding, resource packet, 2003, Virginia Department of Social Services, Virginia Commonwealth University, Virginia Institute for Social Services Training Activities, and Virginia Department of Education, Richmond, VA: Author.

HOMELESS CHILDREN The term *homeless* refers to individuals who lack a nighttime home, cannot afford housing, or live in provided public or private shelters, cars, or elsewhere (Heflin & Rudy, 1991). The number of homeless individuals in the United States is rapidly growing, and includes an increasing number of families with children from infants to teenagers (Children's Defense Fund, 2005). Some estimates indicate that 90% of the homeless families are single mothers with an average of two to three children (Bassuk & Rubin, 1987; Stronge & Tenhouse, 1990). The U.S. Department of Education (USDOE) has estimated the number of homeless children and youth to be 1.35 million, a number that has been increasing (National Coalition for the Homeless, 2007). Approximately 87% of homeless school-age children are enrolled in school, and about 77% attend school regularly (USDOE, 2003). Homeless children are twice as likely to receive services for learning disabilities, and are three times as likely to receive services for emotional disturbance (Children's Defense Fund, 2005).

Child Abuse–Neglect Reporting Form

Oral report made to principal or designee: Date: _____ Time: _____

Child's name _____ / _____ / _____
                     Last name (legal)   First   Middle

Age _____ Birthday _____

Child's address _____

Names and addresses of parents or other person(s) responsible for the child's care.

Father _____ Mother_____

Guardian or caretaker _____

Address _____ Telephone _____

Observations leading to the suspicion that the child is a victim of abuse or neglect. Supply time and date of observation(s).

Additional information. Interview with the child and name of other school employees involved.

Written report made to principal or designee: Date: _____ Time: _____

Signature _____   Signature _____
            Initiator of the report   Observer of the Interview

To be filled out by the principal or designee:

Oral report made to: Written report made to:

Local City Police   _____   Local City Police   _____
County Sheriff   _____   County Sheriff   _____
Division of Family Services _____   Division of Family Services _____

Date: _____ Time: _____   Date: _____ Time: _____

Principal's signature _____

_____

Distribute copies: 1. Mail to agency receiving the oral report.
                                2. Mail to the district's pupil personnel office.
                                3. Place in principal's child abuse–neglect file.
                                   (Not to be placed in child's personal file.)

Figure 5.4   Sample Child Abuse and Neglect Reporting Form

Note: From *Child Abuse and Neglect: A Primer for School Personnel* (p. 34), by D. F. Kline, 1977, Reston, VA: Council for Exceptional Children. Copyright 1977 by CEC. Reprinted with permission.

It is important to realize that homeless children have to confront many barriers to succeed in school and in life. Issues for homeless children include transportation problems; social barriers due to transience; lack of money for food, clothing, and shelter; appearance; acceptance by peers; legal barriers; family problems; and excessive absenteeism. Even more important are issues surrounding their self-esteem, security, safety, and trust (Frieman, 2001). Some schools with high rates of homeless children have modeled examples of safe, comfortable environments by:

- assessing students' abilities and strengths directly, and not assuming they will be slow learners.

- arranging for toys and play time for younger children.

- adjusting expectations for homework for students who must live in homeless shelters, which typically do not provide a place to do homework.

A Needs Assessment for an Educational Setting

Sample Questionnaire

A. The Community
1. What is the cultural and ethnic makeup of the community?
2. What languages are spoken?
3. What are the immediate priorities of the community?
4. What are the main community issues?
5. How do the community members feel toward the school, toward my classroom?

B. The School
1. What is the cultural and ethnic makeup of the school?
2. What is the diversity profile of the school?
3. What attitudes do teachers and staff have toward diversity?
4. Is anyone engaged in a multicultural program? What approaches are they following?
5. Are multicultural programs among the school's priorities?
6. Would the faculty, administrators, and staff support my efforts?

C. Children and Families
1. What are the families like? Socioeconomically, how are they defined?
2. What elements of diversity are reflected in these families?
3. What are some of the essential needs of families?

4. What are their religious affiliations?
5. Can I address those needs in my classroom?
6. What are the traits that, ethnically and culturally, characterize children in my classroom?
7. What diversity issues are unclear to my students (e.g., language differences, equality, interracial relations)?
8. How do children see me?

D. The Classroom
1. What are the ethnic and cultural origins of the children in this classroom?
2. What opportunities do they have for dealing with diversity at the school?
3. Generally, how do children interact in this classroom?
4. Have there been any incidents because of racial or cultural differences?
5. Are there children who tend to use racial slurs or pejorative terms against others?
6. How do students respond when a person with given cultural characteristics comes into the classroom?

Note: From *Teaching Young Children in Multicultural Classrooms: Issues, Concepts, and Strategies* (p. 217), by W. R. de Melendez and V. Ostertag, 1997, New York: Delmar. Copyright 1997 by Delmar. Reprinted with permission.

In the CLASSROOM

- helping to identify funds for supplies and trips.
- maintaining an emphasis on building self-esteem. (Frieman, 2001)

ALCOHOL AND SUBSTANCE ABUSE   Students who use alcohol and other narcotics illegally are at a higher risk for failing in school and in life. Reports indicate that although overall drug use has been declining somewhat, 39% of all high school seniors have reported using illegal drugs (Johnston, O'Malley, Bachman, & Schulenberg, 2004). This figure is distressing, but even more alarming are the reports that indicate that children in elementary schools are using drugs. These students are at a greater risk for failing. Students may become more withdrawn and act irrationally. Moreover, many may become involved in stealing and other illegal activities to maintain their drug habits.

Miksic (1987; see also Kauffman & Landrum, 2009) described elements of a successful substance abuse education program. These elements include a clear, well-defined school policy regarding how teachers and administrators will deal with drug use and possession; a basic drug education classroom curriculum; increasing teacher awareness; a supportive atmosphere for teacher training in dealing with drug abuse problems; involving families as well as students; teacher self-evaluation;

Homelessness and poverty can create social, financial, and other barriers that preclude student success at school.

use of peer-group approaches; and promoting understanding that emotional concerns, such as self-esteem, are often associated with substance abuse.

Drug abuse is not appropriately treated in the classroom (Frieman, 2001); however, teachers should know whom to contact if a drug-related emergency occurs. Watch out for unusual behavior or sudden changes in mood or behavior. It is appropriate to make referrals when drug use has been identified, particularly when it is associated with disruptive classroom behavior or problems in academic functioning (Kerr & Nelson, 2006).

FAMILY POVERTY It has been well documented that children living in poverty are at high risk for failing in school and life (Frieman, 2001; Tornquist, Mastropieri, Scruggs, Berry, & Halloran, in press). Poverty complicates life success and places children at risk for failure for a variety of complex reasons. First, prenatal care may be inadequate or nonexistent for those in low-income families. This alone may result in low-birth-weight infants who are at higher risk for ill health and disabilities. Second, children born of substance abusers are at a greater risk for health-related problems (Frieman, 2001; Vincent, Poulsen, Cole, Woodruff, & Griffith, 1991). Third, children born of teenage mothers are more likely to be impoverished. Fourth, continued poor nutrition, lack of health care, and the low educational achievement of parents are factors associated with poverty that can perpetuate failure in school. In addition, families in poverty are less able to provide the educational materials, computers, or travel experiences that can enrich students' backgrounds and provide support for school learning. Children from families in poverty are more likely to be obligated to work to contribute to family income; these responsibilities may detract from schoolwork. Vincent et al. (1991) provide suggestions for educators in dealing with some of these high-risk factors. These include developing trust and planning predictable, secure, and stable environments. The *Research Highlight* feature on the following page describes an investigation of the relation between poverty and special education placement.

YOUNG, PREGNANT, AND PARENTS Teenagers who are pregnant or become parents are at risk for failing in school, and present a high at-risk factor for their unborn child (Muccigrosso, Scavarda, Simpson-Brown, & Thalacker, 1991). Teenage pregnancy is found across all racial, ethnic, and socioeconomic strata. Many teenagers lack appropriate educational backgrounds, have poor prenatal care, and have babies that are also at very high risk for failing in school and life. Educational programs providing information about pregnancy, abstinence, sexually transmitted diseases, and AIDS are needed on a widespread basis to inform youth about the consequences of teenage pregnancy. More programs are needed to provide child care for teenagers with babies to help them complete their high school requirements and pursue advanced-degree training.

WARNING SIGNS FOR SUICIDE OR VIOLENCE Many students in today's schools are at risk for suicide or violence, so it is important to be alert for warning signs. Five children or teens commit suicide every day on average, and eight children or teens are killed by firearms each day (Children's Defense Fund, 2005). According to Guetzloe (1991), suicide warning signs include: (1) an inability to recover from loss, such as a death in the family or loss of a friendship; (2) obvious changes in sleeping patterns, weight, or personality; (3) dramatic changes in school behavior including academic performance; (4) neglect of personal appearance; and (5) an increase in use of drugs or alcohol. In addition, students may give away prized personal possessions or make overt threats of suicide.

If you encounter a student who is threatening suicide, stay with the student, and speak in a calm and nonthreatening manner. Introduce yourself if you do not know the student, and let the student know you are there to help. Try to get the student to talk, and acknowledge the student's feelings. Try to reinforce statements that describe alternatives to suicide, and ask the student to discard potentially harmful objects or substances. Remind the student that others care and would like to help (Guetzloe, 1991). Teachers should take all threats of violence, to self or others, seriously, and report them promptly to parents, co-teachers, counselors, and building administrators.

Poverty and Disability

 For many years, concerns have been expressed over increases in special education enrollment, and disproportionate representation of minority students in special education (Hosp & Reschly, 2002). More recently, researchers have begun to examine the relationship between poverty and disability. Tornquist et al., (in press) reanalyzed a subset of the large, nationally representative Special Education Elementary Longitudinal Study (SEELS) data set (Wagner, Marder, Blackorby, & Cardosa, 2004) to examine the relationship between poverty and disability. Poverty figures are based on a ratio of family income and number living in the household. Since the federal poverty measure has limitations and may underestimate poverty, Tornquist et al. used four categories of poverty and one nonpoverty category in completing their analyses. The poverty classifications included 50% of the federal income measure (extreme poverty), the federal measure, 1.5 times the federal measure, and twice the federal measure. One and one half times the federal measure represented eligibility for free and reduced lunches, while twice the

federal measure represented eligibility for Children's Health Insurance Programs. Incomes higher than twice the federal measure were included in the nonpoverty category.

Descriptive analyses yielded some findings similar to what is already widely known, as well as some surprising findings. Across all poverty categories there were more boys than girls, with over 90% reporting speaking English at home, who are more likely to live with two parents as income increases, and who represented a range of ethnicities. Learning disabilities, speech impairments, and intellectual disabilities were the most frequently reported primary disabilities across all categories. Lower-income levels were associated with more individuals living in a household, less education of parents or guardians, and greater likelihood of having parents who had never married.

In the extreme poverty category several different patterns emerged, especially with respect to the nonpoverty group. For example, in extreme poverty the number of males and females was more equivalent (56.5% versus 43.5%, respectively), whereas the distribution across all other categories appeared to be less

equivalent, with approximately 68% males and 31% females. African Americans in extreme poverty comprised 60.2% of the sample, compared with only 6.2% in the nonpoverty category. In the extreme poverty category, 20% of the sample was classified as having intellectual disabilities compared to only 4.9% in the nonpoverty group. Fifty-nine percent of the children in extreme poverty lived with a single parent, compared with 11.1% in the nonpoverty group. Thirty percent reported more than seven individuals sharing a single dwelling in the extreme poverty category, compared with 4.2% in nonpoverty. Finally, poverty, more than ethnicity, was a significant predictor of achievement. These findings shed some light on the relationship between disability and poverty, a topic which will no doubt be explored further in the future.

QUESTIONS FOR REFLECTION

1. Why might different patterns emerge for individuals living in extreme poverty?
2. What are the educational implications of these findings?
3. Why might poverty influence the occurrence of disabilities?

COORDINATING INSTRUCTION WITH COMPENSATORY EDUCATION PROGRAMS

Schools may qualify for federal funding for compensatory education under Title I of the No Child Left Behind Act if they have concentrations of students from low-income and/or immigrant families. Funds may be provided for additional teachers, paraprofessionals, and supplies, so that additional remedial instruction can be applied. If students are receiving additional assistance in basic skills from Title I, it is important that these programs are well coordinated with other types of instruction the student may be receiving. Information on effective collaboration strategies is provided in Chapter 2.

STRATEGIES FOR
MAKING ADAPTATIONS FOR STUDENTS WITH SPECIAL AT-RISK FACTORS

Students at risk for failure represent a wide and varied range of problems and potential difficulties. Most important is to maintain an open, accepting classroom environment and let your students

Go to MyEducationLab, select the topic *Emotional and Behavioral Disorders*, and go to the Activities and Applications section. As you read the case entitled "Eric's Last Stand," and answer the accompanying questions, think about all of the factors that may be affecting this child's behavior.

know they are welcome in your room. Seek assistance from other school support personnel and students' families. Be considerate of students' needs, maintain realistic but high expectations, and encourage them to succeed in class. Provide additional opportunities for them to be successful in school. Model enthusiasm toward learning, encourage active participation, make students feel comfortable, and be ready to provide for additional supports and adapt instruction, as described next.

PROVIDE FOR ADDITIONAL SUPPORTS   Help to coordinate services among community social services agencies, school, and parents to maximize the effectiveness of service delivery. Find out about and inform parents of all available services, including free meals, education, health-care services, and mental-health services. Many parents may be unaware of services available to them. Provide assistance in obtaining support services of counseling and social work, when needed. Help arrange before- and after-school care and activities for students who may lack supervision outside of school hours. Arrange for awareness training for personnel in your school for children at risk and at-risk factors (Heflin & Rudy, 1991).

ADAPT INSTRUCTION   Remediate basic skills when needed, by providing for additional instruction with paraprofessionals or tutors, so that students can apply themselves on higher-order academic tasks. Consider using the instructional adaptations suggested for students with higher- and lower-incidence disabilities with students considered at risk for school failure (see Chapters 3 and 4). These include adapting the physical environment, instructional materials, instructional procedures, and evaluation procedures, with respect to specific special needs. Many students at risk may have a more limited experiential background, so be sure that prerequisite knowledge is understood by all students. Make sure that your classroom environment is seen as welcoming and supportive to all students, and that all students feel safe in your classroom. Do not hesitate to seek assistance from school administrators or other personnel when uncertain.

Students at risk for school failure present some unique and special challenges for educators. Nevertheless, successfully adapting instructional practices to help a student succeed, who might otherwise have failed, can be one of the most rewarding experiences you can have as a teacher.

5 Summary

- Students with diverse learning needs other than specific disability areas also are found in general education classes and can benefit greatly from teacher assistance and attention.

- Students with diverse learning needs include those who are gifted, talented, and creative; those from cultural and linguistically diverse backgrounds; and those at risk due to factors such as poverty, drug use, homelessness, teenage pregnancy, and child abuse and neglect.

- Students who are gifted, talented, or creative may be identified by a variety of methods, including test scores, behavioral descriptions, and qualitative/descriptive methods. Students who are gifted, talented, or creative may be served by acceleration programs, enrichment programs, or a combination of approaches.

- Students who are culturally or linguistically diverse may also present some special learning needs. Teachers should adopt a culturally sensitive, pluralistic approach that incorporates an awareness of cultural differences, and their implications for learning.

- Because students who are culturally or linguistically diverse are often overrepresented in special education placements, teachers should be particularly careful when considering referral for special education. Unbiased testing, culturally sensitive behavioral expectations, and prereferral intervention strategies can help address this important issue.

- Factors that may place students at risk for school failure include poverty, drug use, homelessness, teenage pregnancy, and child abuse and neglect. Contact and communication with students in question, their families, relevant school personnel, and community agencies can help address risk factors.

PROFESSIONAL STANDARDS LINK:
Teaching Students with Other Special Learning Needs

Information in this chapter links most directly to:

- CEC Standards: 2 (Development and Characteristics of Learners), 3 (Individual Learning Differences), 4 (Instructional Strategies), 5 (Learning Environments and Social Interactions), 6 (Language), 8 (Assessment), 9 (Professional and Ethical Practice)

- INTASC Standards: Principles 1 (understands central concepts of the discipline), 3 (understands learning differences, adapts instructional opportunities), 4 (instructional strategies), 5 (creates learning environments), 9 (relationships with school personnel, families, agencies), 10 (reflects on practice)

- PRAXIS II™ Content Categories (Knowledge): 1 (Understanding Exceptionalities), 2 (Issues), 3 (Delivery of Services)

- PRAXIS II™ Content Categories (Application): 1 (Curriculum), 2 (Instruction), 3 (Assessment)

TEACHING STUDENTS WITH OTHER SPECIAL LEARNING NEEDS

If a student with other diverse learning needs is having difficulties in your classroom, have you tried the following? If not, see the pages listed below.

STRATEGIES FOR MAKING ADAPTATIONS FOR STUDENTS WHO ARE GIFTED, CREATIVE, AND TALENTED

- [ ] Implement acceleration or enrichment programs, 105–106
- [ ] Adapt instructional materials, 106
- [ ] Adapt instructional and evaluation procedures, 106

STRATEGIES FOR MAKING ADAPTATIONS FOR STUDENTS FROM CULTURALY AND LINGUISTICALLY DIVERSE BACKGROUNDS

- [ ] Create a culturally responsive environment, 111–112
- [ ] Adapt instruction, 112

STRATEGIES FOR MAKING ADAPTATIONS FOR STUDENTS WITH SPECIAL AT-RISK FACTORS

- [ ] Provide for additional supports, 120
- [ ] Adapt instruction, 120

Inclusion Checklist

PART 2 Developing Effective Teaching Skills

The Cullin Hills

MARGARET MEARS   Margaret Mears's interest in photography began when she visited a photographic equipment exhibit and was astounded at the quality of the work shown from the Disabled Photographers' Society. Margaret has limited mobility due to osteoarthritis and asthma, which makes traveling difficult. However, some of the best photographs come out of the most difficult situations. Margaret endured an 18-hour bus ride through a severe snowstorm to photograph the image "The Cullin Hills" on the Isle of Skye in Scotland.

6

Effective Differentiated Instruction for All Students

OBJECTIVES

After studying this chapter, you should be able to:

- Describe the PASS variables and their application to effective instruction in inclusive settings:
- Describe how to **P**rioritize instruction.
  —Describe planning for content coverage and curriculum decisions.
- Describe how to **A**dapt instruction.
  —Identify the different types and levels of learning to be considered in instruction.
- Describe how to **S**ystematically teach in inclusive settings.
  —Describe the teacher presentation (SCREAM) variables.
  —Identify strategies for maximizing academic engagement (time-on-task).
  —Compare and contrast higher-level and lower-level questioning.
- Describe how to **S**ystematically evaluate the outcomes of inclusive instruction.
  —Describe the use of practice activities to reinforce recall and comprehension.

To be an effective inclusive classroom teacher, you must first be an effective teacher. You must employ the skills that enable you to expect, and receive, the very best in learning and achievement from your students. This chapter describes the variables most important for maximizing student learning, and ways you can implement these variables in your classroom. As you learn to apply these strategies consistently and systematically, you will see the learning, achievement, and attitudes of all of your students increase dramatically.

Research over the past several decades, known as *teacher effectiveness research,* has identified the variables most strongly associated with student achievement (e.g., Good & Brophy, 2007; Mastropieri & Scruggs, 2004; Wittrock, 1986). Some of this research also has shown that teachers who are most effective at including students with disabilities and other diverse learning needs are also generally effective classroom teachers (Larrivee, 1985; Scruggs & Mastropieri, 1994b). Overall, this research has been critically important in identifying the things teachers should do and not do to maximize learning for all students. In this chapter, we summarize much of what has been learned from this research.

Promoting Effective Differentiated Instruction: The PASS Variables

To maximize the success of students with special needs in inclusive settings, we recommend using the **PASS** variables (Mastropieri & Scruggs, 2002; Scruggs & Mastropieri, 1995). PASS represents a way of thinking and approaching differentiated, inclusive instruction. PASS stands for:

1. **P**rioritize instruction.
2. **A**dapt instruction, materials, or the environment.
3. **S**ystematically teach with the "SCREAM" variables.
4. **S**ystematically evaluate the outcomes of your instruction.

The PASS variables can be used as a guideline for planning, delivering, and evaluating effective inclusive instruction for specific students with special needs. The *In the Classroom* feature provides a sample working adaptation sheet that can be used to modify instruction using the PASS variables. Using these variables and other information from this chapter, you can deliver effective instruction to all your students.

P: Prioritize Instruction

When planning instruction, it is very important that you determine the relative importance of what you will teach. There are elements of your instruction that are very important for every student to learn; others are of less importance. For example, a teacher found that some students spent a lot of time staining slides of onion cells; there was a lot of mess to clean up, and poorly stained slides could not be viewed easily. She determined that understanding cell structure was the most important element of this unit, and that staining slides was less important, and adjusted her instruction accordingly to spend the most time on the content with the highest priority.

Prioritizing instruction should not be thought of as something teachers can only apply to individual lessons; you should prioritize all of your instruction, by planning for content coverage, basing your instruction on prioritized objectives, considering scope and sequence, selecting appropriate curriculum, and pacing instruction to maximize coverage of your prioritized objectives.

STRATEGIES FOR
PLANNING FOR CONTENT COVERAGE

The importance of content coverage is obvious, in that students almost certainly will not learn content that has not been covered. However, the amount of content covered must be appropriate to the skills and abilities of the students learning the content, and must reflect your instructional priorities. Careful planning of content coverage can help ensure that learning will be maximized for all students. Several important considerations to make when planning content coverage include objectives, scope and sequence, curriculum, and pacing.

BASE INSTRUCTION ON SPECIFIC PRIORITIZED OBJECTIVES   All content to be covered should be based on specific instructional objectives. Objectives state the outcomes of instruction in ways that allow you to find out whether your instruction was successful. Objectives specify (1) the content of the objective (what is being taught), (2) the conditions under which a student's performance will be assessed (e.g., in writing, oral responding), and (3) the criteria for acceptable performance (level of achievement). For example, consider the following objective: "The student will write five precipitating causes of the Civil War with 100% accuracy." The content of the objective is the causes of the Civil War; the conditions specify that students will write; and the criterion for acceptable performance is 100% accuracy. Another example of an objective is as follows: "The student will read 3 pages from the grade-level reading materials at a rate of 120 words per minute with 95% of words read correctly." This objective also specifies the content, the conditions, and the criteria to be achieved. Another objective could state, "After silent reading of a grade-level narrative reading assignment, the student will verbally restate the setting, main characters, problem, and resolution with 100% accuracy."

Because the content of instruction is based on objectives, it is important to include as many objectives as necessary to maximize content coverage. This is particularly important for students who receive special education services, because their IEPs (see Chapter 2) are based on

**myeducationlab**

Go to MyEducationLab, select the topic *Collaboration, Consultation, and Co-Teaching,* and go to the Activities and Applications section. As you read and analyze the case entitled "A Broken Arm," reflect on how these two teachers differ in their ideas about instructional objectives for students.

objectives. An effective inclusive teacher specifies objectives and translates IEP objectives into relevant methods and materials, with the assistance of the special education teacher.

In order to ensure that all students are learning and engaged with the curriculum, teachers may need to select and prioritize objectives for some students with disabilities. This means examining all instructional objectives, determining which are the most important for students with disabilities who are included in general education classes, and eliminating objectives that are unnecessary for those students. For an example, Cliff has severe arthritis and has a great deal of difficulty using a pencil and completing tasks that require much fine motor control. He uses canes to assist with mobility. His fifth-grade teacher, Mr. Masoodi, employs a hands-on approach to science instruction. To accommodate Cliff's needs, Mr. Masoodi prioritized his class objectives. He examined the content and selected the most important objectives for Cliff. He determined that understanding of critical scientific concepts and a positive attitude toward science had the highest priority as objectives. Handwriting and physical manipulation of instructional materials had a lower priority, and were not always required in Cliff's case. By first examining all the class objectives and then reviewing Cliff's instructional needs, Mr. Masoodi was able to prioritize objectives for Cliff.

PLAN INSTRUCTION BASED ON SCOPE AND SEQUENCE   Scope and sequence refer to the breadth and depth of content that will be presented in school (scope) and the order in which the content will be presented (sequence). All areas of instruction should be presented with respect to an overriding scope and sequence of prioritized instructional objectives. Scope and sequence allow for long-term planning and evaluation of instruction, provide implications for time allocations, and set the overall pace of instruction. Most states have published their curriculum guidelines that contain scope and sequence for all subject areas across grade levels. Prioritized content should receive substantial attention within the scope and sequence of instruction.

SELECT APPROPRIATE CURRICULUM   The curriculum not only includes the instructional materials used for learning, but also refers to the course of study for each discipline and the scope and sequence within each grade level necessary to build conceptual understanding. Curriculum serves as an interface between the student and the learning objectives, and has been described as the overall experience provided to a student by the school (Gartin, Murdick, Imbeau, & Perner, 2002). Specific curriculum issues are discussed in detail in Part III, Chapters 13 through 15.

Curriculum decisions can play an important role in inclusive schooling. The accompanying *In the Classroom* feature shows a checklist of curriculum materials being considered to maximize learning for all students. When serving on curriculum adoption committees, or making a choice from existing school materials, be certain to consider the points noted to maximize learning for all students. Curriculum materials that feature many of these characteristics should be given a higher priority than those with fewer of these characteristics.

Curriculum need not be the same for every student. In fact, curriculum can be carefully selected to address specific learner needs, and important individual curriculum decisions are a very important component of differentiated instruction.

PACE INSTRUCTION EFFECTIVELY   Pacing refers to the rate at which teachers and students proceed through the curriculum, and is another way of prioritizing instruction. For example, Mr. Isaac teaches American history, but has only gotten to World War II by the end of the school year. He has determined (intentionally or not) that events in American history from 1945 to the present have a lower priority, since he did not cover this content. Unless the content at the beginning of the text has a higher priority, and content at the end of the text is judged to be of less value, however, more efficient planning would have produced a pace of instruction that better reflected instructional priorities.

One of the most significant problems teachers encounter in inclusive settings is adjusting the pace of instruction to diverse learning needs. While some students appear to master new content almost as soon as they are exposed to it, other students require substantially more instructional time to learn the same content. Students who have learned certain concepts should not be held back, but could be engaged in learning more in-depth knowledge about a concept, or learning about related concepts, while other students receive additional practice.

Checklist for Curriculum Materials for Inclusive Environments

- Do the materials provide sufficient opportunity for active student involvement, or do they simply provide verbal information to be recalled?

- Are the materials written on a level that is most comprehensible to all students, or do they include unnecessary complexity or an overabundance of unnecessary vocabulary?

- Do the materials lend themselves to use by cooperative learning groups or other peer-interactive activities?

- Do the materials allow for sufficient practice of key concepts before moving on to other content?

- Do the materials provide simple means for frequent evaluation of learner progress toward prespecified goals and objectives?

- Do the materials include examples of individuals from culturally diverse backgrounds, and people of diverse learning abilities?

- Do the materials provide recommendations for modifications for students with disabilities or other special needs?

- Do the materials provide validity data that demonstrate that positive learning gains can be realized from use of the materials?

A: Adapt Instruction, Materials, or the Environment

Once the instructional objectives have been prioritized, the instruction, materials, and/or the environment can be adapted to accommodate more completely the needs of the students with disabilities. These adaptations carefully link the characteristics of the curriculum with the characteristics of the learner, and are at the heart of differentiated instruction. For example, students in Cliff's group often recorded Cliff's notes for him or carried out experiments according to Cliff's directions, when needed. Mr. Masoodi provided extra time for Cliff to work on the science activities when needed. Mr. Masoodi also adapted materials, for example, by acquiring hand-lenses that were larger and easier to handle. Mr. Masoodi also adapted the environment by rearranging desks to create more aisle space for Cliff and his two canes. Similar adaptations for differentiated instruction, for a wide variety of objectives, are described throughout this text.

Appropriately developed adaptations allow students of different abilities to succeed within the same curriculum, and are at the heart of differentiated instruction. Adaptations intended to address special learning needs are described in detail throughout this text. When planning adaptations to improve student learning, consider specifically *what* will be taught, and to *what level of proficiency*. These considerations have been referred to as **types** and **levels of learning** (Mastropieri & Scruggs, 2002). Knowing what types and levels of learning are desired provides guidelines for planning instructional adaptations.

STRATEGIES FOR
MAKING ADAPTATIONS

BASE ADAPTATIONS ON STUDENT CHARACTERISTICS   All instruction is concerned with the interaction of characteristics of the learner with the characteristics of the instructional methods, materials, and/or environment. Appropriately adapted methods or materials take this interaction into account. Specific adaptations in a variety of academic and behavioral skills and content areas are described in detail throughout this text, and were described previously in Chapters 3, 4, and 5. Table 6.1 lists some examples of possible adaptations based on specific learning characteristics.

Table 6.1 Adaptations Based on Student Characteristics

Learner Characteristics	Possible Adaptations
Physical	• Optimal location of student in classroom • Rearrange classroom layout to promote mobility, accessibility for wheelchairs or braces • Adaptations to promote grasping (e.g., pencil grips, alligator clips, Velcro) • Peer assistance to support physical manipulation • Technological adaptations for computer use
Sensory	• Physical adaptations to accommodate low vision (e.g., clear routes through the classroom) or hearing ability (e.g., carpets to reduce extraneous noise) • Adaptations to promote access to text (e.g., braillers, Kurzweil readers) • Peer assistance to support access to visual or auditory stimuli • Sign language support for hearing impairments • FM systems to promote hearing
Language	• Language cards for specific vocabulary • Boardmaker or teacher-made communication boards • Targeted language instruction • Hands-on/activity-oriented instruction • Peer models/peer assistance • Peer tutoring/cooperative learning • Sign language instruction • Performance assessment
Literacy	• Direct teaching of literacy skills • Literacy strategy instruction • Books on tape • Kurzweil readers • Software for reading computer screens • Peer reading/writing assistance • Adapted worksheets to reduce literacy demands • Hands-on/activity-oriented instruction • Peer tutoring/cooperative learning
Emotional/ Behavioral	• "Safe" areas of classroom for target student to use when needed • Reduced interaction with peers if needed • Recording chart for monitoring target behaviors with token systems • Post positive behaviors • Peer support • Class rewards for target student behavior • Self-monitoring systems • Parent involvement for social behavior

BASE INSTRUCTIONAL ADAPTATIONS ON TYPES OF LEARNING Different types of learning occur in school, across all different subject areas. These types include learning of discriminations, facts, rules, procedures, concepts, and problem solving/critical thinking. Although there can be much overlap on school tasks, it is helpful to examine some of the distinctions among the categories. Teachers who understand the different types of learning required of students are more able to plan effective instruction. They are also more able to plan effective instructional adaptations, focused specifically on the nature of the learning task. That is, when a student is demonstrating difficulty with a learning task, it is helpful to determine the type of learning the task represents (e.g., factual learning rather than math or social studies or English) when planning adaptations.

Discrimination Learning Discrimination often occurs early in learning and involves determining how one stimulus is either the same or different from another stimulus. In learning the alphabet, numbers, colors, shapes, or math concepts, for example, learning to discriminate between, for example, a triangle and a square, may be difficult at first for students with disabilities. Careful attention to the relevant and irrelevant distinctions between various stimuli can help improve **discrimination learning** for students with disabilities. For example, the critical feature that distinguishes "p" from "q" is the relative placement of the round part of the letter. The critical feature that distinguishes squares from triangles is the number of sides (and not, for example, size). For students exhibiting difficulty in discrimination learning tasks, additional repeated practice that emphasizes comprehension of the critical distinctions can be beneficial.

Factual Learning **Factual learning** is a common aspect of school learning and includes vocabulary words and their definitions, names of famous people and their accomplishments, dates and causes of historical events, addition facts, and names of rivers. Some factual learning is in the form of **paired associates,** where one thing is paired with another (e.g., Ulan Bator = Capital of Mongolia; or the Italian word *mela* = "apple"). Other factual learning is in the form of a **serial list** (e.g., "a–b–c–d–e–f–g…"; or, "2–4–6–8–10…"), where information is learned with respect to a specific sequence. Appropriate strategies include redundancy, drill and practice, enhancing meaningfulness, and use of elaborations or other memory-enhancing techniques (see Chapter 10); all of these strategies can be useful in adapting instruction for special needs.

Rule Learning Rules are also pervasive in school, and many students with disabilities and other special needs have difficulties learning these rules. Examples of **rule learning** include social behavior rules (e.g., "Always raise your hand before speaking in class.") and math rules (e.g., "When dividing fractions, invert the divisor and multiply."). Rules often include discriminations and facts, and appropriate circumstances for use of those rules. For example, students might need to know that the rules for speaking in class are different in Mr. Halleran's class than they are in Ms. Butcher's class, and that they need to learn to apply the rules appropriately in each class. Some individual students may have more difficulty assimilating these differences.

Procedural Learning **Procedural learning** involves the sequential execution of multiple steps, and is found frequently in school tasks. Remembering and executing the steps involved in going through the cafeteria lunch line (e.g., take your place at the end of the line, take your tray, pick up your silverware) is one example of procedural learning. Academic examples include reading comprehension strategies (for example, determine the purpose, survey the material, read, recite, review), math algorithms (for example, learning to execute the steps in solving long division problems), and study strategies. This can involve describing or listing the steps in the procedure, modeling or demonstrating the application of the procedure, or prompting students to execute the steps of the procedure. Procedural learning requires that students (1) recognize when a specific procedure is called for (for example, a strategy for learning a list of spelling words), (2) retrieve the steps in the procedure (C–C–C, or Cover, Copy, and Compare), and (3) correctly execute the procedure (use the strategy correctly to learn the list). When students exhibit difficulty with procedural learning tasks, consider which of these three steps they have not mastered.

Learning factual information can be difficult for some students with disabilities.

Conceptual Learning Most tasks involve some conceptual learning, which can be taught using procedures similar to discrimination, factual, and rule-learning paradigms. **Concepts** are completely learned only when the concept can be applied to a new instance. For example, students do not know the concept of "dog" if they can only identify their own household pet as a dog—they must be able to identify dogs they have never seen before.

Concepts can range from simple ("red") to more complex ("radial symmetry," "nonpolar covalent bonding"). Conceptual learning can be enhanced by the use of examples (e.g., of radial symmetry, or of the color red), provision of noninstances ("this is not an example of a carnivore"), and statement and application of rules ("insects have six legs; how many legs does this specimen have?"). These enhancements can be helpful for any students who do not immediately master relevant concepts.

Concrete experiences can help students develop an understanding of concepts.

Problem Solving/Critical Thinking **Problem solving** refers to determining solutions when no specific strategy for solving the problem is known. Similarly, **critical-thinking** skills refers using active reasoning to acquire novel concepts, ideas, or solutions, or to evaluate or analyze information to reach a justifiable conclusion. These types of learning are commonly found in science and mathematics curriculum (e.g., geometric proofs), but could also be found in any other area (e.g., understanding or solving a social problem in social studies). Problem solving and critical thinking are important goals in education, but also present some of the greatest challenges for students with disabilities. They can be enhanced by the use of teacher "think-alouds" ("Here's how I think as I try to solve this problem…"), and careful questioning or coaching techniques, described elsewhere in this chapter, as well as in Chapters 14 and 15.

BASE INSTRUCTIONAL ADAPTATIONS ON THE APPROPRIATE LEVEL OF LEARNING Another important consideration for teachers when planning instructional adaptations is the level of proficiency to be attained by the student for any of the previously described types of learning. Levels of learning address *how well* something will be learned, and it may be possible to isolate learning problems within these parameters. For example, if we say that a student "has not learned" something, it may be that the student *has* learned at one level (e.g., initial acquisition), but not on the level necessary for success (e.g., fluency or application). These levels include—in order of complexity—initial acquisition, fluency, application, and generalization. Consideration of the appropriate level of learning can help when planning adaptations.

Acquisition and Fluency **Acquisition** refers to a simple accuracy level criteria, such as 9 out of 10 correct responses to listing 10 letters of the alphabet. Accuracy criteria are important in the initial stages of learning. **Fluency** combines the accuracy criteria with a specified amount of time. For example, 90% accuracy within 2 minutes, or 90 out of 100 letters correct in 5 minutes. Fluency is particularly important when tasks need to become automatic, such as in basic literacy, math, and letter-formation skills. Many students, for example, have acquired the skills needed to read individual words, but are not sufficiently fluent to comprehend what they are reading. Such students would benefit from fluency instruction.

Application and Generalization **Application** refers to applying learned skills or content to relevant contexts, and **generalization** is the ability to transfer previous learning to novel situations. For example, applying a social skill learned in a lesson in the special education setting to a role-play activity is an example of the application level. An example of generalization could be employing appropriately, in an inclusive classroom setting, a social skill previously learned in the special education classroom.

Application and generalization levels of learning can be difficult for some students with disabilities to attain (Sabornie & deBettencourt, 2004). Simply because a student has learned a particular skill (e.g., telling time, or a social skill for greeting new people) in one situation, you

Go to MyEducationLab, select the topic *Instructional Practices and Learning Strategies,* and go to the Building Teaching Skills and Dispositions section. As you complete the activity entitled "Fluency Building," compare and contrast the strategies depicted in these videos.

Students who thoroughly understand new concepts are more likely to apply them to new situations.

should not assume the student will now apply or generalize that skill to every appropriate situation. In many cases, specific strategies to promote application and generalization are needed.

Application and generalization levels of learning can be promoted by training "loosely" and allowing flexibility in responding; by using "indiscriminable contingencies" (rewarding students when they do not know they are being observed); by using modeling and role play; by employing classroom peers; by encouraging self-monitoring, where students evaluate their own performance; and by retraining the desired behavior in a variety of different circumstances (see also Alberto & Troutman, 2009; Scruggs & Mastropieri, 1994a).

Identification Versus Production   For any of the levels of learning, students can be asked to identify or produce relevant responses. **Identification** includes such responses as pointing to the correct answer (for example, on a communication board) and responding to matching, multiple-choice, or true/false test formats, and is usually learned more readily. **Production** is more difficult and includes such responses as writing, saying, computing, orally spelling, and exhibiting appropriate behavior. When planning instruction, consider whether students will be required to identify or produce correct responses. For example, if students are required to produce correct responses (such as spelling words), it is important that they practice producing, rather than simply identifying, correctly spelled words during instruction.

Consider Types and Levels of Learning to Address Specific Learning Problems   To best address special learning needs, first determine where the problems lie. For example, Janine cannot remember the correct sequence of steps in multiplying an algebraic expression. Mario can identify but not produce correctly spelled words from his weekly list. Shawna can control her impulsivity in the classroom but not the cafeteria. Once these are identified as problems of procedural learning, identification/production, and generalization, respectively, they can be specifically addressed. As such, your instruction can be much more precise (and much more effective) than if these problems are simply considered to be problems with math, spelling, or social behavior. Tables 6.2 and 6.3 present some suggested instructional strategies to accompany specific levels and types of learning. Remember that many different strategies may be successful, and that in teaching, identification and production formats can be considered with any of the other levels and types of learning.

USE PRINCIPLES OF UNIVERSAL DESIGN   Universal design (UD) principles involve developing materials or the environment to improve accessibility for all learners (e.g., Burstahler, 2005). Major principles for development proposed by the Center for Universal Design at North Carolina State University (Principles of Universal Design, n.d.) include the following: (a) equitable use to provide identical or highly similar access for all; (b) flexibility in use to include range of user preferences; (c) simple and intuitive use; (d) design communicates necessary information to users; (e) minimizes errors; (f) minimizes physical effort; and (g) appropriate size and space. The Center for Applied Special Education Technology (CAST) provides specific guidelines for the development of new materials to promote accessibility for diverse learners, rather than adapting existing materials. Those guidelines provide options for the representation (e.g., options that vary the size of font or amplitude of sound), the expression (e.g., options for interacting with hand, switch, or adapted keyboard), and the engagement (e.g., options in level of perceived challenge, type of rewards or recognition, level of novelty) of materials. CAST's guidelines (CAST, 2008) involve using multiple options for language, symbols, and expression, and options for comprehension and self-regulation. One example of a curriculum material designed with UD principles is WiggleWorks (produced and distributed by Scholastic), which provides a blend of technology, literature, and teacher support to help students develop reading and writing skills.

Table 6.2 Instructional Strategies for Specific Types of Learning

Type of Learning	Instructional Strategies
Discrimination	Present examples and nonexamples; use models, prompts, and feedback; provide instruction on the relevant dimensions; use mnemonics (e.g., "This is purple. This is not purple. Is this purple?"; "This is the letter 'b.' Notice that the bubble at the bottom faces toward the right.").
Factual	Repetition, rehearsal, and practice using drill procedures (e.g., "*Dorado* means fish. What does *dorado* mean?"); chunking pieces of information together; elaborating on information to enhance meaningfulness (e.g., with labeled pictures of fish); using mnemonic strategies ("*Dorado* means fish. *Dorado* sounds like *door*. Think of a fish on a door").
Rule	Practice using the rules; repetition; making up meaningful "sayings" using the rules; drill and practice with the rules; modeling applications of the rules (e.g., "Remember, 'i before e except after c' is the rule to use to check your spelling." "Everyone, repeat the rule for recess: 'stay on the grass.'").
Procedure	Model use of procedures; cue cards with steps of procedures written out as reminders; drill and practice; practice with applications using the procedures; mnemonics involving acronyms; feedback on recall of steps and accurate use of steps (e.g., "First we get our materials. Second, we write our names on the papers. And third, we complete the task." "Remember that SQ3R stands for Survey, Question, Read, Recite, and Review.").
Concept	Use procedures for teaching rules and discriminations; use examples and nonexamples; model; prompt; give feedback; use "if–then" scenarios to demonstrate instances and noninstances of concepts; use coaching questioning procedures, application activities, and elaborations to enhance meaningfulness (e.g., "if an insect has six legs and three body parts, then is this [show picture] an insect?").
Problem solving	Use modeling, coaching, and prompting; demonstrate examples of successful problem solving; show how to activate prior knowledge and use that to solve problems (e.g., "Why do anteaters have long front claws? I don't know, but what else do I know about anteaters? What do they eat? Where do they live? Now do I know why they might have long front claws?").

However, since many materials were developed without the principles of UD, those existing materials may be adapted or differentiated more successfully by using the UD guidelines.

S: Systematically Teach with the SCREAM Variables

Systematic teaching is the third component of the PASS variables and builds on the previous ones; indeed, in order to systematically teach you need to incorporate planning for content and prioritizing objectives as well as adapting instruction, materials, or the environment. Systematic teaching refers to the use of effective teaching techniques for content coverage and teacher presentations, known as the SCREAM variables: **s**tructure, **c**larity, **r**edundancy, **e**nthusiasm, **a**ppropriate rate, and **m**aximized engagement through questioning and feedback (Mastropieri & Scruggs, 2002, 2004; Scruggs & Mastropieri, 1995). If you implement these techniques and consider the specific needs of students with disabilities, all students may be more successfully included, and overall classroom achievement will improve.

STRATEGIES FOR
IMPLEMENTING THE SCREAM VARIABLES

STRUCTURE YOUR LESSONS   Structure refers to the organization of the components of the lesson. Structure does not necessarily mean that the content of your lesson will be teacher-driven

PEARSON myeducationlab

Go to MyEducationLab, select the topic *Intellectual Disabilities*, and go to the Activities and Application section. As you watch the video entitled "Guided Notes Study Cards," reflect on how this lesson meets the description of the SCREAM variables discussed here.

Table 6.3 Instructional Strategies for Specific Levels of Learning

Levels of Learning	Instructional Strategies
Acquisition	Slower pace of instruction, modeling, demonstrations, lots of reinforcement for accurate responding, examples and nonexamples, direct questions (both lower-level and higher-level questions depending upon the nature of the content: e.g., "An ecosystem is a place where living and nonliving things affect and depend on each other. Look at our terrarium, here are some examples of living and nonliving things.... How do they affect and depend upon each other? ... So what is the definition of an *ecosystem?*").
Fluency	Faster pace of instruction; reinforce more rapid, accurate responding; graphing performance and goal-setting; vary schedules of reinforcement; vary types of reinforcers (e.g., "Let's see how quickly and accurately we can complete our math problem solving today ... I'll set the clock ... ready ... go.").
Application	Provide several instances and application problems; model procedures and directions; provide demonstrations; make examples concrete and meaningful; use active coaching with questioning to prompt correct responding (e.g., "Remember how we did ..., This is just like it, only now....?").
Generalization	Ensure students have mastered relevant skills; train and retrain in "realworld" settings and situations; train loosely, using multiple examples of stimuli; use peer assistance; use indiscriminable contingencies; train self-monitoring; use modeling and role play; reinforce generalization; practice skills ("When we go to the store, we are going to use the *polite behaviors* that we practiced in class. What are we going to do? If you need help, how will you ask? Is this a good way?").

or that your students sit in rows doing worksheets. Rather, lessons are structured when you (1) communicate to students the overall organization and purpose of the lesson, (2) display outlines of the lesson and indicate transition points, (3) emphasize the critical points of the lesson, and (4) summarize and review throughout the lesson. Following is an example of structure in teacher dialogue, taken from a fourth-grade science lesson on ecosystems:

> The first thing—and Mrs. (name of special education teacher), if you would like to write this on the board—the first thing you're going to do is get your supplies and aquarium.... The second thing that I want you to do is put your gravel in, which is step number 2 ... [repeats].... The third thing that's going to happen is that you are going to fill out parts of your activity sheet.... (Mastropieri et al., 1998, p. 18)

Structure is particularly helpful for students who have difficulty sustaining attention, or who exhibit difficulties in language comprehension. Structure refers not only to providing an overall organizational framework for the lesson, but also to ensuring that students understand this organization.

Communicate Lesson Structure to Your Students   Carefully design your lessons with a clear idea of the structure, including stating the purpose, reviewing the main ideas, and making clear transitions between lesson elements (Good & Brophy, 2007). You will communicate structure best to your students if you yourself are very familiar with the structure and organization of your lessons.

Tell students the structure of the lesson. This can be done by announcing the components of the lesson directly, by writing the outline on the board or on an overhead projector, and by using illustrations or handouts to indicate the lesson's sequence.

Remind students about the structure throughout the lesson. Say, for example, "Remember, when you finish your group work, we are going to meet again as a class to review what we have learned about bird migration."

PROMOTE CLARITY IN YOUR PRESENTA-TIONS A teacher exhibits clarity when he or she speaks clearly and directly to the point of the objective, avoids unclear or vague language or terminology, and provides concrete, explicit examples of the content being covered. Clear presentations address only one objective at a time, and are directed explicitly to the lesson objective.

Some lesson activities take place in groups.

Select Vocabulary and Syntax That Are Familiar to All Students in the Class If you use words that are unfamiliar to all students, take a minute to practice the word meaning. If English language learners are included in the class, use illustrations, physical modeling, or hand gestures to support verbally provided directions. These procedures are also beneficial for communicating with students with hearing impairments who have language difficulties, and students with learning disabilities who have language comprehension difficulties. When employing co-teaching, as described in Chapter 2, the special education teacher can assume the role of promoting clarity and understanding where needed.

Eliminate Vague Language in Your Presentations Smith and Land (1981) reported that vague terms added to teacher presentations consistently lowered achievement. These terms are highlighted in the following teacher presentation:

> This mathematics lesson *might* enable you to understand *a little more* about *some things* we *usually call* number patterns. *Maybe* before we get to *probably* the main idea of the lesson, you should review *a few* prerequisite concepts. *Actually,* the first concept you need to review is positive integers. *As you know,* a positive integer is any whole number greater than zero. (Smith & Land, 1981, p. 38)

Clarity is also impeded by *mazes,* which include confusing word patterns ("we don't know it can't be done without…"), false starts ("facilit…I mean, make it better to…"), and unnecessary or irrelevant repetition ("This is, this is…it's true that this is the most important…"). Smith (1977) reported that lower student achievement was found in classrooms where teachers said "uh" frequently. Avoid also vague language such as "kind of," "you know," "sort of," and "pretty much." Avoid *negated intensifiers* ("not a lot," "not much," "not very"), *indeterminate quantification* ("a number," "a few of," "several"), and *ambiguous designation* ("some kind of," "somewhere"). Instead, use clear, direct, and precise language (Good & Brophy, 2007; Smith & Land, 1981). Clarity can be particularly important when restating comments made by individual students, so that they will be more understandable to all students.

EMPLOY REDUNDANCY EFFECTIVELY Redundancy increases learning by emphasizing and reinforcing the most important aspects of lessons. Unlike unnecessary and irrelevant repetition of words, continued re-emphasis of key concepts, procedures, and rules is critical to the success of the lesson. Many students with disabilities require additional opportunities to hear, see, and practice lessons before mastering the objectives. It is unnecessary for components of the lesson to be identical to provide redundancy for students.

Embed redundancy in your presentations. Discuss the main points of the lesson, and then be sure to refer to the key concepts throughout the lesson. Question students directly on these key concepts to enforce their learning.

Create opportunities for extra practice to help provide redundancy for selected students. For example, supplemental practice times can be arranged for students either before or after school, or during lunch and study hall periods. Peers who have mastered the topics can be asked to provide assistance during these additional practice periods. Focus on the most important content and provide many opportunities for responding.

Create opportunities to apply and generalize learned information to novel situations. For example, prompt students to use newly learned arithmetic to compute the cost of a single slice of a whole pizza, or to use a reading comprehension strategy to study a social studies book.

TEACH WITH ENTHUSIASM!   Students consistently learn more and appreciate the content more when teachers display enthusiasm in their teaching. Enthusiasm also creates higher levels of student engagement with the lesson, increasing academic learning time. Enthusiastic teachers create exciting learning environments, in which students perceive that learning is fun, challenges are great, curiosity is enhanced, and thinking is encouraged (Good & Brophy, 2007). Enthusiastic teaching can be especially helpful for students who have histories of academic failure and are poorly motivated to succeed in school. For example, some students with disabilities are used to performing poorly in classes and have little motivation to attempt to succeed; however, an enthusiastic teaching style can provide the necessary excitement and encouragement to motivate such students to be successful (Brigham, Scruggs, & Mastropieri, 1992; Mastropieri, Scruggs, & Cicciarelli, 2007). More detailed information about the use of teacher enthusiasm is provided in Chapter 9.

Speak enthusiastically, using an upbeat tone of voice, a rapid (but not too fast) presentation rate, and a varied inflection. Use some variation in choice of words. Be physically enthusiastic: use physical gestures and movement to emphasize your points and convey interest in the topic. Use eye movements and facial gestures to animate your presentations. Openly accept student contributions, and demonstrate a high overall interest and energy level.

USE AN APPROPRIATE RATE OF PRESENTATION   Effective teachers deliver instruction at the optimal rate. Generally, a brisk rate of presentation throughout the lesson, and a brisk rate of interacting with students, works well with enthusiasm variables and helps keep lessons interesting and motivating. During basic skills instruction, a fast pace may be important in increasing learning (Carnine, 1976; Gleason, Carnine, & Vala, 1991). However, an excessively rapid rate of presentation may not be related to increased learning. When learning outcomes are not being met, changing the overall rate of presentation may allow information to be better understood by all students.

Begin with a brisk presentation rate, and frequently question students. Students' answers to your questions will tell you whether you are proceeding too rapidly. Tape record yourself, and evaluate your rate of presentation. Perhaps your rate of presentation is good, but other presentation elements (speaking directly and clearly, and with sufficient volume) are inhibiting understanding and need to be modified.

Some teachers begin lessons with a brisk rate of presentation, but later slow down, and lose student attention by overly focusing on minor issues, or by questioning some students repetitively while the rest of the class waits. If some individual students, but not others, need additional practice, work with them individually, in small groups, or with peer tutors (Brophy & Good, 2007).

MAXIMIZE ACADEMIC ENGAGEMENT   Research has consistently supported the idea that the more time students devote to a particular subject or skill, the more likely they are to master it. This is true whether the area is reading, science, creative writing, archery, music, or debate: More time effectively engaged in learning leads to more (and better) learning outcomes. Maximizing student engagement and time-on-task is the best single way of increasing your students' learning. Research has shown that teachers who maximize student engagement are also effective in many other ways, as described in the *Research Highlight*.

It seems clear that Jimmy's learning will not improve until he can increase the amount of time spent on his work. Although most teachers **allocate** appropriate time for learning a certain subject (by, for example, scheduling a specific amount of time per day to reading instruction), a far smaller number of teachers ensure that students are actually **engaged** in learning, to the greatest extent possible, during this allocated time. This distinction between allocated and engaged academic time is critical for student learning. In some cases, teachers may be able to greatly increase classroom learning simply by increasing student engagement rates.

Characteristics of Highly Engaging Teachers

 Seo, Brownell, Bishop, and Dingel (2008) studied the classroom reading practices of beginning special education teachers, with particular reference to their ability to promote student engagement. Although academic engagement is often thought of as time spent on-task, it is better conceptualized as a broader construct, referring to "the intensity and emotional quality of children's involvement in initiating and carrying out learning activities" (Skinner & Belmont, 1993, p. 572). Viewed this way, academic engagement includes classroom behaviors and emotional responses, such as active participation in learning activities, volunteering to read aloud, asking or answering questions, asking for assistance when needed, volunteering, using specific learning strategies, and demonstrating interest and enthusiasm in learning (see also Greenwood, Horton, & Utley, 2002). Teachers who are able to elicit these behaviors can be considered highly skilled in engaging students.

These researchers used a rating scale to identify 14 beginning special education teachers as most engaging, highly engaging, moderately engaging, or low engaging. They then observed these teachers over a 6-month period. Using qualitative data analysis techniques, Seo et al. (2008) identified four themes related to instructional engagement that differentiated these teachers: (a) instructional quality, (b) responsiveness to student needs, (c) socio-emotional climate of the classroom, and (d) student autonomy. The most highly engaging teachers were relatively consistent in demonstrating these themes; however, most other teachers were not. For example, the most engaging teacher, "Kayla," also used high-quality and well-integrated reading instruction (see Chapter 13). She was consistently responsive to student needs—immediately correcting errors and providing feedback, anticipating academic and behavioral problems, and dealing with them proactively. She created an open,

accepting, and positive classroom environment, providing frequent positive comments and encouraging positive interactions among students. Finally, she promoted student autonomy by encouraging student choice and self-regulated learning. In contrast, teachers who were not rated as high in student engagement were found to be less effective in other areas of instruction. These findings suggest that teachers who promote high rates of engagement in their students are also found to be highly skilled in many other areas of teaching.

QUESTIONS FOR REFLECTION

1. Why do you think a teacher's ability to promote student engagement would play such an important role in other areas of instruction?
2. What could teachers do to become better at promoting student engagement?
3. Would strategies for promoting engagement differ between elementary and secondary grade levels?

CLASSROOM SCENARIO

Jimmy

Jimmy is a 10-year-old fifth-grader who was having trouble succeeding academically in school. His teacher, Ms. Marshak, believed that Jimmy had the overall ability to succeed in her classroom, but he rarely completed his work. As a result, he was falling far behind the other students in the class.

Ms. Marshak began to pay more attention to how Jimmy was spending his time. She found that he was often the last student to take his books, paper, and pencil from his desk and begin working. During this period, he also spent more time than other students going to the pencil sharpener, asking to get a drink of water, daydreaming, or playing with pencils or rulers in his desk. When Ms. Marshak recorded his behavior at the end of every minute over a 30-minute period, she found that Jimmy was actually working on his assignment only 10 of the 30 times she sampled his behavior. Clearly, Jimmy needed to increase the amount of time he put into his schoolwork.

QUESTIONS FOR REFLECTION

1. Why is Jimmy off-task so often? How could you find out?
2. Why doesn't concern about poor grades motivate Jimmy to work harder?
3. What are some simple things Ms. Marshak could do to help Jimmy?

But what are the specific techniques you can use to maximize academic engaged time? In a broad sense, teachers need to maximize student learning by maximizing student engagement with instruction and instructional materials. Selecting materials that are at the correct level of difficulty and that are motivating and interesting for students will help with this. Additionally, teachers need to carefully plan, monitor, and reward high rates of engagement, such as in the scenario about Jimmy, and carefully implement questioning, praise, and feedback. However, the first step is to understand what is meant by academic engaged time, or "on-task" behavior.

On-task behaviors of students vary depending on the grade level of the students, the curriculum, the type of lesson, the learning activities, and the behavior of the teacher. However, in general, students are considered on-task when they are doing such things as actively looking at or otherwise attending to the teacher, instructional materials, or other students who are actively engaged. Giving direct answers to relevant teacher questions or asking relevant questions are also considered on-task behaviors. During teacher presentations, examples of on-task student behavior include actively listening, taking notes, outlining, and asking for clarification. Likewise, being appropriately engaged in science experiments or math manipulatives and engaging in relevant debate in social studies can also be considered on-task behaviors. Overall, student behavior is usually considered on-task if it is logically related to instructional activities.

Some students with disabilities may be engaged in different ways. For example, some students, including students with visual impairments, with emotional handicaps, or with autism, may not be actively watching the teacher, but nonetheless provide other signs that they are attending. Students with physical disabilities may interact differently with educational materials, but nonetheless can be observed to be interacting. Students with hearing disabilities may need to watch the interpreter rather than the teacher. Some students with learning disabilities are unable to listen and take notes simultaneously, but may be on-task. Careful consideration of the special needs and abilities of different learners will reveal how different students may display appropriate on-task behavior.

On the other hand, off-task behavior is not logically related to academic learning. Off-task behavior can include tardiness, daydreaming, attending to inappropriate material, asking irrelevant questions or making irrelevant statements, or interacting inappropriately with peers or instructional materials. These activities are negatively related to learning; in other words, the more off-task behavior that occurs in a classroom, the less learning takes place.

STRATEGIES FOR
MAXIMIZING ON-TASK BEHAVIOR

Your on-task behaviors as a teacher influence how much students learn. These include statements directly relevant to the lesson, questioning and feedback directly relevant to the lesson, and demonstrations and modeling relevant to the lesson.

USE EFFECTIVE QUESTIONING TECHNIQUES   Teachers must be effective at questioning students. Generally, the more questions asked that are directly relevant to the lesson, the more students learn from the lesson. Questioning has several purposes. First, questioning allows teachers to monitor students' understanding of the content being presented. In inclusive classrooms, questioning can be particularly helpful in determining whether all students understand the content being presented. When breakdowns in understanding are revealed through questioning, teachers can modify and adjust their instruction (considering such things as rate of presentation, choice of vocabulary, and use of examples) to address students' learning needs more effectively.

Second, questioning allows students to actively practice the information being covered. In this way, repeated questioning related to the same concept can provide the redundancy necessary for information to be learned and remembered:

TEACHER: In Boston, in 1770, what was one of the major concerns of the colonists, Marcia?

MARCIA: Taxation without representation.

TEACHER: Taxation without representation. What's another way of saying that, Dan?

DAN: That, uh, you have to pay taxes, but you don't have someone to represent you in the government.

TEACHER: You pay taxes, but don't have a representative, good!

Questioning can be delivered to individuals or groups. When addressed to individuals, state the question first, before calling on a particular student. If you give a student's name first, other students may be less likely to carefully consider an answer. For example, ask, "Why do you think Germany would strengthen its relation to Mexico during the first years of World War I? Frederick, why do you think this happened?" Rather than, "Frederick, why do you think Germany….?"

Be certain the question is clearly stated, so that students will know what type of response is expected, and that instructional time will not be lost in subsequent clarification. For example, referring to a passage in a text, a teacher might ask, "What problem do you see with this statement?" While the teacher may be expecting an answer regarding verb tense, students might not know what the teacher means by "problem." Instead, she might ask, "Is there a problem with

Effective questioning in inclusive classrooms means providing students with extra time to answer.

verb tense in this statement?", or, more generally, "Is there a grammatical problem in this sentence?" (Good & Brophy, 2007).

When addressing the question to groups, it may be possible to promote "covert" responding on the part of all students, which will maximize student engagement. For example, "Now I want everyone to think about this problem, and make a prediction: If I add weight to this pendulum, will it swing more rapidly? Everyone think (pause), now, thumbs up for yes, thumbs down for no." Alternatively, ask students to write down answers to questions individually, to be read back later. For example, "Everybody, write down a definition of *metonomy*, and give an example. When you're done, we'll compare answers."

There are also different types of questioning, including lower-level questioning and higher-level questioning. Lower-level questioning usually involves repetition or restatement of previously covered information, and is often used in basic skills instruction or in early stages of learning. For basic skills and basic facts, questioning should be fast-paced and require simple, direct answers (examples: "What is the silent *e* rule?" "What is the Pythagorean theorem?" "What are the three branches of government?"). For this type of questioning, teachers should aim for 80% to 100% correct responding. This type of questioning is frequently used when building fluency with responding, such as when practicing math facts or vocabulary definitions using flashcards.

Higher-level questioning requires more in-depth thinking. For higher-level responses requiring thinking and reflection, questioning should proceed at a slower rate and may not require simple, direct answers. For example, "Why do you think a type of mossy algae is usually found on the north side of trees? Would this be true all over the world?" In this example, students could consider the general position of the sun in the northern hemisphere, and conclude that the south side of trees may often be drier. Considering the characteristics of mossy algae, students may conclude that it may more frequently—but not always—grow on the north side of trees. This, of course, would not be generally true in the southern hemisphere. With such questioning, you should consider that students will need more time for reflection, and may need additional questioning to direct their thinking (e.g., "What conditions are favorable for mossy algae?").

Research has documented that when students with mild disabilities have been "coached" to answer higher-level questions, they can be successful (Scruggs, Mastropieri, & Sullivan, 1994; Sullivan, Mastropieri, & Scruggs, 1995). For example, consider the coaching dialogue in Figure 6.1 used with students with learning disabilities and mild intellectual disabilities to promote thinking about animals. This type of explicit coaching provides the structure and support students need to promote reasoning, but still allows them to come up with their own answers.

Some questions—some may say the most important questions—do not have simple answers with which everyone would agree. These include such questions as, "Who was the United States' most important president?", "Should the Ten Commandments be displayed in schools?", and "Does life exist on other planets?" Some students may have difficulty answering questions like this.

Figure 6.1 Coaching Dialogue

Note: From "L'instruzione Mnemonica e L'interrogazione Elaborativa: Strategie per Ricordarsie per Pensare," by M. A. Mastropieri, 1995, In C. Cornoldi & R. Vianello (Eds.), *Handicap e Apprendimento: Ricerche e Proposte di Intervento* (pp. 117–124), Bergamo, Italy: Juvenilia. Copyright 1995 by Juvenilia. Reprinted with permission.

> *Experimenter:* Anteaters have long claws on their front feet. Why does this make sense?
>
> *Student:* I don't know.
>
> *Experimenter:* Well, let's think. What do you know about anteaters? For example, what do they eat?
>
> *Student:* Anteaters eat ants.
>
> *Experimenter:* Good. And where do ants live?
>
> *Student:* They live in holes in the ground.
>
> *Experimenter:* Now, if anteaters eat ants, and ants live in holes in the ground, why do you think that anteaters have long claws on their front feet?
>
> *Student:* To dig for ants.
>
> *Experimenter:* Good. To dig for ants.

When presenting this type of question, inform students that a specific answer is not required, but rather an answer that reflects both knowledge of the subject and careful thought about the answer. Give students models of good possible answers. Ask students to consider subquestions, such as, "What qualities are considered important in a president?", "What is the relevance of the 'establishment of a religion' clause in the 1st Amendment?" or, "What conditions appear necessary for life to develop? What is the likelihood that these conditions exist elsewhere in the universe?"

Good and Brophy (2007) suggested that teachers generally should avoid four types of questions:

1. questions that require yes or no answers;
2. "tugging" questions ("What else?" "Yes. . ." Tell me more. . .");
3. "guessing" questions, that is, asking students to guess when students do not have relevant information; and
4. leading questions ("Isn't that so?").

Overall, the best questions are clear, purposeful, brief, phrased in simple language, sequenced, and thought-provoking (see also Groisser, 1964).

PROVIDE HELPFUL FEEDBACK   How teachers respond to student answers is as important as how the questions are asked. Appropriate feedback can be helpful in informing students of their level of understanding, providing redundancy, and encouraging students to continue to learn (Burnett, 2003). Feedback should be clear and overt, so that there is no ambiguity about the teacher's evaluation of the answer. When appropriate, it should provide the entire class with information on the correctness of the response of an individual student.

During rapid questioning, drill and practice of skills, or review of previously learned material, feedback may be simple and brief. In some cases, the fact that the teacher has continued with the lesson imparts the information that the previous answer was correct (e.g., multiplication facts prompted by flashcards). At other times, feedback may be more substantive.

The type of feedback delivered depends to some extent on the response that has been given. If a student does not respond right away, you should try to elicit some type of response to determine the level of student understanding. It is important to consider whether the question is a lower-level question that should require only a short "wait time" (the amount of time the teacher waits for a response) or a higher-level question that may require a longer wait time for the student to develop a more thoughtful answer. Research has shown that longer wait times (when appropriate to the question) are associated with better and longer student responses, and an increase in voluntary student contributions (Good & Brophy, 2007).

When students do not respond correctly, it is important to determine whether the answer is unknown, the question was unclear, or whether the student simply did not hear the question. You should also determine whether students can answer the question with additional coaching or prompting. Teachers should not appear to "badger" students who clearly do not know how to respond. However, it is important to retest students later in the lesson.

For completely incorrect responses, a simple, tactful statement that the answer was incorrect may be sufficient. Simply state the correct answer, provide the student with a prompt or additional information and restate the question, or call on another student for the answer.

If an answer is partially correct, first acknowledge the part of the answer that was correct, then provide additional prompts or restate the question to elicit the rest of the answer, or call on another student. For any answer that was incorrectly answered, partially or completely, teachers should make an effort to return to the question with individual students later in the lesson to ensure that the material was learned.

If the question was correctly answered, acknowledge the correctness of the answer and move on in the lesson:

TEACHER: Now, which astronomer first determined that the planets travel in an elliptical pattern? Juanita?

JUANITA: Kepler.

TEACHER: Kepler, correct.

PRAISE STUDENTS FREQUENTLY   Praise can be an important motivator for students. When the situation warrants it, actively praise your students for paying attention to the lesson, carefully considering teacher questions, and providing answers that are correct, or at least reasonable and thoughtful. Effusive or overelaborate praise may not be helpful in many instances, because it may interrupt the flow of the lesson or embarrass students (particularly students at the secondary level). However, most teachers deliver too little praise to students. Praise may be particularly important to help students with disabilities or special learning needs persist in their efforts to learn. Chapter 9 provides more discussion of the best uses of praise.

STRATEGIES FOR
MAXIMIZING TIME FOR LEARNING

MAXIMIZE ON-TASK TEACHER BEHAVIOR   Teachers also may be off-task, and this behavior can impede student achievement. One example of off-task behavior is making unnecessary digressions, such as talking about personal experiences or current events that are irrelevant to the lesson. Students with special learning needs may find it especially difficult to follow teachers when they are making irrelevant digressions. During practice activities, teachers can be off-task by being unprepared with student materials, or by speaking loudly to an individual student and disrupting other students. Teachers can also be off-task by not returning promptly after breaks, allowing longer-than-necessary transition times, and by being unprepared for teacher presentations. The Technology Highlight describes a helpful timer for class use.

Class composition may also influence classroom interactions. The *Diversity in the Classroom* feature describes the differences in attitudes and classroom interactions between same- and mixed-gender classes.

Research suggests that much **academic engaged time** is lost for a number of reasons, including inefficient transition activities, inappropriate verbalizations, and inappropriate social behavior.

STREAMLINE TRANSITION ACTIVITIES   Transition activities involve students moving from one location, subject, or group to another. Academic engaged time can be lost during transitions through such activities as going to the restroom, sharpening

Effective teaching means that no matter what teaching strategy you use, you consciously think about your goals for the lesson and stay on-task with those goals.

Managing Time with the Time Timer™

Many students have difficulties with understanding the concept of time, especially when told they need to keep working for a specified amount of time. Other students have difficulties with transition periods and changing from one activity to the next. A technological device called the Time Timer may help students visually see the amount of time left as they work and help them comprehend in a more concrete fashion the amount of time left for work or the amount of time left for one activity before moving to the next activity. The visual timer is a clock that comes in various sizes. One standard version is approximately 8 inches square and has a 60-minute timer. A smaller, 3-inch-square version is also available that can be clipped to a student's belt. When setting a specified amount of time, say 15 minutes, that amount of time appears in red. A red disk actually shows on the timer when a time is set. As the time passes, the red disk disappears, such that when time is up, the red disk is gone. When this happens, students can visually see the red disk disappearing as time passes and

Time Timer LLC. Reprinted with permission.

obtain a better picture of the amount of time left. Such a device may help students feel more comfortable with the concept of time because it makes the concept more concrete for them.

pencils, and unnecessary socializing. Students with disabilities can lose time going between the regular classroom and the resource room.

One way to maximize transition efficiency is to set time limits and reinforce adherence to those limits. For example, if classes begin at the sound of a bell, let students know exactly what is expected of them when the bell rings. Typically, students should be in their places and prepared with their materials at this time. Any time lost after the bell—for example, sharpening pencils or finding workbooks or other materials—takes away from instructional time. Likewise, at the end of the class, if materials are not put away before students leave, time may be lost at some other point in the day. If your students are transitioning to a resource room, you should document the time they left the classroom and report the time to the resource teacher. Similarly, the resource teacher should inform you when students have left the resource room to return to your class.

One obvious way to promote efficient transitions is to inform students that time lost in transition will be made up during free time, in after-school detention, or during other student activities. However, teachers can also reinforce prompt transitioning more positively by awarding points, stickers, or tokens (see Chapter 7), or simply by responding positively to students when they make smooth transitions.

You can make efficient transitions by being prepared ahead of time with materials for the next activity, and not losing time looking for instructional materials, organizing supplies, or inefficiently passing out student materials. By setting a good model for transitions, you can promote good transitions in your students.

REDUCE INAPPROPRIATE VERBALIZATIONS   Academic engaged time is lost when class discussions drift away from the point of the lesson. Teachers may find themselves wandering, and students may also wander by raising irrelevant issues. Some students deliberately attempt to keep teachers off-task to avoid getting to homework, tests, or other undesired activities. Monitor inappropriate verbalizations by audiotaping or videotaping individual lessons, and review them in reference to the purpose of the lesson and the appropriateness of teacher and student verbalizations.

At times, however, digressions may reflect genuine curiosity or interest on the part of students, or a developing understanding of the concepts. When this happens, acknowledge that

Student Interactions and Attitudes in Single-Gender Versus Mixed-Gender Classrooms

Researchers have speculated whether differences between same-gender and mixed-gender school settings influence students' education. Some findings indicate that females are less likely to be called on and less likely to volunteer in mixed-gender settings (American Association of University Women [AAUW], 1998). Special education research has not typically addressed this issue. It is well known that males outnumber females in special education settings. However, little is known about interactions and attitudes of students in same- versus mixed-gender special education settings. Madigan (2003) addressed this issue by conducting an observation and interview study with females with learning disabilities who were either Latino or African American. All students either attended a same-gender or mixed-gender special education class in the same high school.

Students were observed during classes and interviewed in small groups and alone. The mixed-gender class was taught by a male teacher with 15 years of experience and the all-female class was taught by a female teacher with 2 years of experience. Behaviors measured included independent hand-raising, answering teacher questions, interacting in class discussions, on-task behavior, and assignment completion. Overall, females in the single-gender class exhibited more of these behaviors, with the exception of hand-raising. This difference, however, was attributed to the fact that the teacher of the mixed-gender class required hand-raising, while the teacher of the single-gender class did not.

Overall patterns from interviews supported observational findings, in that students in single-gender classes participated more during class and felt more comfortable. Females in mixed-gender classes reported feeling frustrated frequently with the male students. Furthermore, interview data revealed that while all females found special education settings supportive, irregardless of single- or mixed-gender setting, they also felt some stigma associated with special education. These feelings emerged when they were asked about the views of general education students. Results provided some interesting information for gender and classroom configurations for students with disabilities. Although the results cannot be considered evidence that same-gender classes are generally superior, they do provide some interesting information for teachers to consider when teaching mixed-gender classes.

---

the lesson objective has changed, and evaluate it with respect to the changes that were made. Alternatively, you can inform students that they will talk about those other important ideas after the class finishes the present activity.

REDUCE INAPPROPRIATE SOCIAL BEHAVIOR Inappropriate social behavior, including passing notes, teasing, arguing, and fighting, is one of the greatest threats to academic engaged time. Handle inappropriate social behavior quickly and efficiently, so that as little instructional time as possible is lost. Punitive classroom environments that include long-winded lectures on social behavior are not as effective (or as time-efficient) as positive learning environments where good behavior is expected and rewarded, and misbehavior is dealt with efficiently. Strategies for reducing inappropriate classroom behavior are discussed in detail in Chapter 7.

USE STRATEGIES FOR INDIVIDUAL CASES
Many classrooms contain one or more students who seem to spend far less time on schoolwork than other

Handling inappropriate social behavior quickly and subtly can keep the class on-task.

students. Frequently, these are the very students who need to spend more time on their schoolwork, such as Jimmy in the earlier scenario. In such cases, try to increase the students' amount of engaged time on task. Following are some procedures that may be helpful:

1. *Be certain the student can do the work.* Many students become off-task if they cannot (or believe they cannot) do the assigned work. If you find the work is too difficult, assign more appropriate work or modify assignments. Also, consider enlisting support from special education teachers, paraprofessionals, or classroom peers.

2. *Try simple strategies, such as direct appeal and proximity.* Tell individual students you would like to see them working harder on schoolwork. Tell them that you will send a signal when they are getting off-task by approaching their desks. When students return to work, walk away.

3. *Provide simple rewards or consequences.* Students can be offered stickers, free time for a preferred activity, or other rewards for completing all work in a specified time period. Alternately, students can be required to make up work they have not completed.

4. *Notify parents or guardians.* Contact parents or guardians to elicit their suggestions or support for increasing on-task behavior. Perhaps arrangements can be made to link home privileges or rewards to assignment completion in school. In some cases, simply communicating the idea that parents and teachers are interested in the student's academic progress can make an important difference.

S: Systematically Evaluate the Outcomes of Your Instruction

The last S in PASS stands for *systematic evaluation*. Systematic evaluation means frequently measuring students' progress toward meeting the instructional objectives of the class, as well as IEP objectives, using the formative evaluation procedures described in Chapter 12. Teachers should continuously monitor and adjust instruction based upon student progress on formative evaluation measures.

FORMATIVE EVALUATION   Formative evaluation refers to the frequent and systematic monitoring of learner progress toward prespecified goals and objectives. It is different from summative evaluation, in which, for example, tests are given at the end of a school year to determine how much was learned during the year. Teachers who use formative evaluation monitor student progress continuously throughout the school year, and do not wait until the end of the year to determine whether learning took place. Formative evaluation techniques, reviewed briefly here, are described in detail in Chapter 12.

Research has suggested that formative evaluation works best when it is used at least twice a week. In some cases, student learning (for example, words read correctly per minute) can be recorded on a chart or graph, so that rate of learning can be assessed. In other cases, student progress may be more difficult to place on a chart, but progress can still be monitored. One example might be handwriting, where weekly samples are collected in student folders.

Systematic evaluation of student performance or products over time can provide teachers with important information regarding the adequacy of students' progress. This information is used, in turn, to make further adaptations in instruction to ensure learning is maximized for all students. When progress for one or more students is not acceptable, teachers can consider how to modify and adapt instruction to help students meet learning goals. For example, using the information from this chapter, a teacher could decide to increase academic engagement, to increase review activities, to improve teacher presentations, or to make further adaptations in instructional materials. The Inclusion Checklist at the end of this chapter, and the other chapters in this book, provide suggestions for improving instruction in specific areas, in response to outcomes of systematic evaluation of student performance.

Formative evaluation can be conducted on a variety of student outcomes, including regular "probes" of student skills and knowledge, evaluations of regularly implemented practice activities, and homework products, as described in the following section.

IMPLEMENT CURRICULUM-BASED MEASUREMENT *Curriculum-based measurement* refers to regular assessment of student progress toward prespecified goals and objectives using frequently administered "probes" of student performance. For example, in reading instruction, Ms. Sánchez assigned Billy regular 1-minute timed readings of grade-appropriate text. For each timed reading, Ms. Sánchez calculated correct and incorrect words read per minute, and placed the results on a chart that demonstrated Billy's progress over time. Teachers can evaluate progress on these measures to determine whether instructional modifications are necessary for the student to meet long-term goals (see also Chapter 12). Curriculum-based measurement can also be conducted on a variety of student activities, as described next.

MONITOR AND EVALUATE PRACTICE ACTIVITIES Practice activities are intended to reinforce memory and comprehension of information that was gained in the lesson. If the lesson involves the teaching of skills, such as how to write the letters "p," "d," and "q" in cursive, practice activities are used to promote application and skill development, and to ensure the skills learned will be remembered. If the lesson involves the acquisition of content information, such as the causes of the War of 1812, practice activities promote recall, comprehension, and application objectives. The products of practice activities can provide teachers with formative evaluation of student understandings of and progress on the curriculum.

Practice activities are particularly helpful for students with special needs, as they provide more engaged time to ensure relevant concepts are fully understood. Often, practice activities are taken from worksheets or workbooks, but practice activities can take other forms as well, such as practice with tutors or classroom peers, flashcards, computer software, group problem solving, or application tasks using relevant materials. Table 6.4 provides examples of appropriate practice activities.

Practice activities can be divided into *guided* and *independent* practice (Mastropieri & Scruggs, 2004; Rosenshine & Stevens, 1986). Guided practice takes place under teacher supervision, and is most appropriate immediately after presentation of the initial concept. Students' rates of correct responding may be lower, and more teacher supervision is needed. Independent practice is done with indirect teacher supervision (some independent practice activities can be done as homework), and is undertaken when students' rates of correct responding are very high, and students can correct themselves by proofreading and checking their work.

Both types of practice are necessary to ensure that concepts are mastered and remembered, and that learning is complete for all students. Request assistance from special educators for devising supplemental practice activities and determine when and where the extra practice can occur—for example, study hall, other school periods, or homeroom. Any successful practice activity must meet several criteria. First, it must be directly relevant to the objective of the lesson. Second, practice activities must be used to enhance learning that occurred during the earlier part of the lesson; practice activities usually are not intended to introduce new information or skills. Students with disabilities or other special learning needs are particularly unlikely to learn new information from worksheet-type activities. Therefore, select practice activities that enhance and augment learning that has already occurred.

myeducationlab

Go to MyEducationLab, select the topic *Assessment*, and go to the Activities and Applications section. As you watch the video entitled "DIBELS: Progress Management," reflect on how this curriculum-based measure can help teachers adjust their instruction to meet the needs of students.

Table 6.4 Appropriate Practice Activities

Lesson	Practice Activity
Writing words in cursive for handwriting practice	*Guided:* Teacher provides dictation, work checked after every sentence.
	Independent: Students write from manuscript models, check each other's work at the end of the period.
Solving quadratic equations from a formula	*Guided:* Students solve problems one at a time, while the teacher monitors their execution of each step.
	Independent: Students solve a set of problems independently, corrected by the teacher at the end of the activity.

Practice activities also must be at an appropriate level of difficulty. If they are too difficult, students will not be able to work on them independently. If they are too easy, student learning will not be enhanced. Finally, it must be remembered that students soon tire of repetitive worksheet-type activities. Keep the pace and enthusiasm level as high as possible during guided practice (e.g., "Everyone who thinks they have the answer, put your thumbs up!"). During independent practice, teachers should reinforce prompt, accurate, and neat responding, and should keep the activity moving at an efficient pace.

Homework can often be considered a type of independent practice activity, undertaken outside the classroom. Because teachers are less likely to be available to answer questions when homework assignments are being completed, it is necessary that students completely understand assignments before taking them home. It may be helpful to complete the first part of the homework assignment in class, as a guided practice activity, to be certain every student knows how to complete the assignment. Homework completion can be facilitated by having students meet in groups at the beginning of class, under the direction of rotating group leaders, to record and provide peer feedback on homework assignments (Jakulski & Mastropieri, 2004).

When using guided and independent practice activities, in the form of classroom and homework activities, evaluate student products carefully, and use this information as formative evaluation to determine whether students are making adequate progress, and if not, how instruction will be modified and adjusted to meet student goals and objectives. For example, satisfactory performance on independent practice and homework activities indicates that students have learned the material and are functioning satisfactorily. Difficulties in independent practice and homework activities suggest that students need further examples, explanation, and guided practice.

FREQUENTLY REVIEW IMPORTANT MATERIAL AND EVALUATE STUDENT PERFORMANCE

Near the end of a lesson, it is important to summarize what has been learned and review this information with students. It is also important to review information weekly and monthly, to ensure that previously learned information is not forgotten and that students understand the relation between previous and current learning. Information gained from regular review can provide formative data on student learning and retention over time, and can provide important information for possible instructional modifications.

Although frequent review is helpful for all students, it is particularly important for students with disabilities, who are more likely to forget or not understand the relevance of previously learned material. This extra review and evaluation may be especially helpful before exams. As discussed in the redundancy section, students with disabilities not only benefit from review, but may require more review to be successful. Additional review of successfully learned content can be helpful in "overlearning" information, which can help promote long-term retention, application, and generalization.

Special education teachers can assist in providing additional review for students with disabilities or brainstorming ideas for review. For example, you could make videotapes of the class engaged in activities during the instructional unit, and then show them to students who may benefit from extra review of the information. Students can make "descriptive video scripts" (narrations describing everything in the video) to accompany the videos either on paper or on tape recorders. Students with visual impairments may benefit from the descriptions. Photographs, student journals (including photo and vocabulary journals), and daily logs can also provide material for review.

Reviewing information—opportunities for overlearning—promotes application and generalization of concepts.

Using a digital camera and scanner, you and your students can create websites that contain their journals and portfolios. Sunburst's school version of Web Workshop, for example, contains many easy-to-use templates to help students create websites. Student performance on these activities can also provide the basis for formative evaluation.

Putting the PASS Variables to Work: Including Model Lesson Components in Instruction

The teacher effectiveness variables most closely related to high achievement have been described. But how do these variables appear in a real lesson? As you review the structure of a model lesson, observe how teacher effectiveness variables fit into a lesson sequence, as indicated in Figure 6.2.

Daily Review
- Begins with a review of previous learning.
- Provides teacher with information on how much was learned and retained from previous lessons.
- An example of daily review:
  "We have been studying ecosystems. Hold up your hand if you can tell me what an ecosystem is [calls on individual students]. Yesterday, we said that ecosystems have nonliving and living parts. We listed several nonliving parts of ecosystems. Write down on your paper three nonliving parts of an ecosystem. [The teacher waits for a minute or two, walking around the classroom to encourage students to think and write answers.] Now, who can tell me what you wrote . . . ."

Statement of Purpose
- State the main objective of the current lesson in language meaningful to students.
- An example stated clearly and simply is the following:
  "Today we are going to learn about the living parts of ecosystems, and how they may interact with the nonliving parts."

Presentation of Information
- Present the content of the lesson using a variety of instructional materials, depending on the purpose and objectives of the lesson.
- Use the teacher presentation or SCREAM variables. That is, deliver content or procedures with structure, clarity, redundancy, enthusiasm, appropriate rate, and maximized engagement using questioning, feedback, and praise.

Guided Practice
- Practice newly acquired content, skills, or concepts with teacher guidance.
- Carefully monitor students and provide corrective feedback, as necessary.

Independent Practice
- Provide opportunities for students to repeat, apply, and extend information from the lesson more independently.

Formative Evaluation
- Evaluate students' independent performance.
- An example could take the form of a brief quiz: "See if you can solve the following problems independently."
- Results provide the basis for decisions about the adequacy of student progress and can be considered in planning future lessons.

Figure 6.2 Putting the Components into a Model Lesson

6 Summary

- The PASS variables stand for: **p**rioritize instruction; **a**dapt instruction, materials, or the environment; **s**ystematically teach; and **s**ystematically evaluate the outcomes of instruction. The PASS variables provide a model for planning and delivering effective differentiated instruction in inclusive settings.

- *Prioritize* instruction to ensure that students are working on the most important objectives, and that objectives reflect the characteristics of the student.

  — Planning for content coverage involves prioritizing instruction, and is a critical component of teacher effectiveness. Teachers must consider carefully the role of prioritized objectives, scope and sequence, curriculum, and pacing of instruction over time.

- *Adapt* instruction, materials, and/or the environment to meet the specific characteristics of the student. Appropriately adapted instruction is a significant component of *differentiated instruction*.

  — Types of learning include discrimination, factual, procedural, rule, conceptual, and problem solving/critical thinking.

  — Levels of learning include acquisition, fluency, application, and generalization. Students can provide either identification or production responses. Consideration of types and levels of learning can be beneficial when planning appropriate differentiated instructional strategies.

- *Systematic teaching* refers to maximizing the effectiveness of your instruction, and includes effective teacher presentations using the SCREAM variables.

  — Effective teaching strategies include maximizing academic time-on-task, making effective teacher presentations, monitoring practice activities, review, and formative evaluation. All are critical components of effective teaching for all students.

  — Effective teacher presentations use the SCREAM variables, including **s**tructure, **c**larity, **r**edundancy, **e**nthusiasm, **a**ppropriate rate, and **m**aximized engagement. Additionally, effectively used questioning, feedback, and praise are all important contributors to student learning.

- *Systematic evaluation* refers to continuous measuring of student progress toward meeting the specific objectives. Teachers should continuously monitor and adjust instruction based on their students' progress on formative evaluation measures.

  — Curriculum-based measurement provides the basis for evaluating student progress in learning and determining whether student goals and objectives are being met.

  — Practice activities provide opportunities for students to solidify and apply their learning, and provide more opportunities for formative evaluation of student progress over time. Practice activities can include guided practice, in which teachers closely monitor student responding, and independent practice, in which students work more independently. Homework can be considered a type of independent practice activity.

  — Frequent review promotes retention and long-term learning, and provides teachers with opportunities to evaluate student learning. Students with disabilities may especially require frequent review of previously learned material.

PROFESSIONAL STANDARDS LINK:
Effective Differentiated Instruction for All Students

Information in this chapter links most directly to CEC Standards:

Standard 4—Instructional Strategies, particularly:
Skills:

- Use strategies to facilitate integration into various settings.

- Select, adapt, and use instructional strategies and materials according to characteristics of the individual with exceptional learning needs.

- Use strategies to facilitate maintenance and generalization of skills across learning environments.

Standard 6—Instructional Planning
Knowledge:

- Theories and research that form the basis of curriculum development and instructional practice.

- Scope and sequences of general and special curricula.

Skills:

- Identify and prioritize areas of the general curriculum and accommodations for individuals with exceptional learning needs.

- Use task analysis.

- Sequence, implement, and evaluate individualized learning objectives.

- Prepare lesson plans.

- Prepare and organize materials to implement daily lesson plans.

- Use instructional time effectively.

- Make responsive adjustments to instruction based on continual observations.

EFFECTIVE DIFFERENTIATED INSTRUCTION FOR ALL STUDENTS

If you are having problems with classroom or individual academic achievement, have you examined the following? If not, see the pages listed below.

STRATEGIES FOR PLANNING FOR CONTENT COVERAGE

STRATEGIES FOR MAKING ADAPTATIONS

STRATEGIES FOR IMPLEMENTING THE **SCREAM** VARIABLES

STRATEGIES FOR MAXIMIZING ON-TASK BEHAVIOR

STRATEGIES FOR MAXIMIZING TIME FOR LEARNING

STRATEGIES FOR PROMOTING SYSTEMATIC EVALUATION OF INSTRUCTION

Lights on the M1

RAYMOND WILLS Raymond Wills has chronic obstructive pulmonary disease; photography and the recent acquisition of an electric wheelchair serve as outlets of independence and freedom for him. A few years ago he drove to a quiet bridge above the M1 motorway in England and set up his camera to take the image "Lights on the M1." (It was just one of a series of slides that he produced that evening.) Raymond is now limited to trips where he can use his electric wheelchair, but he still likes to go out for the day when he can, and he has some photo shoots planned for the near future.

7

Improving Classroom Behavior and Social Skills

OBJECTIVES

After studying this chapter, you should be able to:

- Describe how to observe, record, and manage classroom behaviors.
- Identify effective classroom management strategies.
- Discuss less-intensive classroom behavior strategies as well as more formal management systems, and their implications for classroom management.
- Compare and contrast different methods of assessing social skills.
- Describe interventions to improve social skills.
- Discuss and evaluate important considerations for social skills training.

All students must know how to interact with others appropriately in group learning experiences, how to engage in classroom discussion, and how to distinguish between classroom behavior that promotes learning and classroom behavior that disrupts learning. Classrooms are well managed when students stay on-task academically, but also feel free to participate actively in classroom activities, take risks, and interact positively with others. By attending to two important components of the classroom social environment—classroom behavior and social skills—you can dramatically improve the success of your students.

Managing Classroom Behavior

Student behavior is in many ways a response to the environment, which includes the teacher, peers, other school personnel, and even the physical environment (Kerr & Nelson, 2006). In all cases, an important key to effectively managing classroom behavior—and controlling the negative behaviors of some individual students—lies in establishing positive, caring relationships with all students in your class, implementing and consistently enforcing effective rules for classroom behavior, and helping students learn to make positive choices that increase their level of success in school.

One problem teachers frequently have is precisely describing the problem behavior that they would like the student to change. While it may be true from the teacher's point of view that a student "misbehaves" or "has a bad attitude," such terms do not specify the behavior problem so that strategies for changing the behavior can be easily implemented and evaluated. Before effective interventions can be implemented, you must first carefully define classroom behavior, so it can be easily observed and recorded.

OBSERVING AND RECORDING CLASSROOM BEHAVIOR

DEFINE BEHAVIOR   Before interventions on classroom behavior can be carried out, carefully observe and document those behaviors. This process allows you to determine precisely what behaviors need to be changed, and to evaluate whether progress is occurring after interventions. Several observation systems can be employed to accomplish this.

The first step in observing and recording behavior is to *operationally define* the behavior in question. This means that you describe the behavior so that another person knows exactly what is meant. For example, if you describe a student as "has a bad attitude," it may be difficult to know exactly what you mean. However, if you use specific behavioral descriptions, such as "late to class 70% of the time," or "takes at least 10 minutes after the assignment has been given to become actively engaged, 50% of the time," it is much easier to know what is meant. It is also much easier to specify how the behavior is to change, and to know whether it has changed. For example, if "late to class less than 20% of the time" is specified as a behavioral objective, it will not be difficult to determine whether this objective has been met. Many students with disabilities have behavioral objectives such as these included on their IEPs.

Following is an example of an **operational definition** of "on-task" behavior (other definitions are possible and may be more appropriate in particular situations):

- *On-task.*   Student's eyes are directed toward the teacher (or classmate, if making a relevant contribution) or instructional materials (e.g., books, pencil, paper, laboratory materials), and student is manually engaged with instructional materials when appropriate.

Observing and documenting student behavior is the first step in determining an appropriate intervention strategy to help the student control future behavior.

When you use operationalized behaviors, it is easier to create a behavioral objective (see Chapter 6) specifying (1) the content of the objective, (2) the conditions under which a student's performance will be assessed, and (3) the criteria for acceptable performance. For example, an objective for on-task behavior could be: "The student will exhibit on-task behavior in social studies class, to a criterion of 85%, for four out of five consecutive days." This behavior can then be recorded, in baseline (pre-intervention) or intervention conditions, to determine whether it has improved.

USE OBSERVATION AND RECORDING SYSTEMS   Table 7.1 provides some examples of observation and recording systems. These can be used to record specific behaviors, depending on the type of target behavior and the circumstances under which it is exhibited (see, e.g., Alberto & Troutman, 2009; Martin & Pear, 2007).

Observing and recording behaviors are much more difficult with large numbers of students. Some strategies for observing with large classes include enlisting the assistance of an aide, enlisting peer assistance, observing a small number of students at a time, or videorecording the entire class and recording observations later. When observing the whole class, try using seating charts and time sampling at longer intervals. For example, at the end of every 10-minute interval, make a checkmark on the square representing the desk of every student who is off-task.

DETERMINE THE CONTEXT OF BEHAVIOR   One good strategy for determining the dynamics of classroom behavior is to use an "ABC" chart (Bijou, Peterson, & Ault, 1968; Kerr & Nelson, 2006). The teacher creates a chart with three columns: Antecedent, Behavior, and Consequence (see Figure 7.1 for an example). The target behavior to be observed is noted in the middle column (e.g., pushing, hitting), and the events that occurred immediately before

Table 7.1 Observation and Recording Systems

Name	Description
Event recording	Observer tallies the number of times a particular behavior occurs. This procedure is best when documenting behaviors that are discreet, such as talk-outs, tardiness, or tantruming. If the duration of these behaviors is always similar, or irrelevant, the observer simply records the number of events.
Duration recording	Observer records (e.g., with a stopwatch) the cumulative amount of time during which the behavior occurs. This system is appropriate when the length, or duration, is of concern. For example, a teacher may wish to record the total amount of time a socially withdrawn student engages in solitary play activities during recess. The observer starts the stopwatch when the socially isolate play begins, and stops it when the child begins interacting with others. The recording resumes when the child returns to isolated play.
Interval recording	The observer sets an interval, say, 1 minute, and documents whether a particular behavior has occurred at any time during that interval. For example, if talking to classmates is the target behavior, the observer records for each 1-minute interval whether the behavior has occurred. At the end of the period in question (e.g., a 50-minute class period), the number of intervals in which the behavior has occurred is divided by the number of intervals (e.g., 50). Therefore, if talking to classmates was recorded for 10 intervals, then the amount of talking for the time period could be recorded as 10/50=20%.
Time sampling	At a specific point of time, the observer records whether a behavior is occurring. For example, a recorded "beep" goes off in an observer's headset every minute. At that instant the observer records whether the behavior (e.g., on-task) is being exhibited. At the end of the period, as with interval recording, the observer can divide the number of times a target behavior has occurred with the number of times that were sampled.

the behavior (antecedent) are also noted, as well as the consequence, or what happened following the behavior.

Examining the ABC chart, you can ask, for example, when and where does the target behavior occur, who is present when it occurs, and what activities or events precede the target behavior? It is also important to note what happens after the target behavior occurs, what changes after the target behavior is exhibited, and what the student receives (or avoids) after the target behavior occurs (Barnhill, 2005). For example, you may find that peer attention was almost always a consequence of the behavior (verbal aggression toward teacher), or that independent

Student's name: __Marcie__   Observer: __Mrs. Wilson__

Setting: __Cafeteria__   Date: __April 3, 2008__

Observation time period: __Lunch, 12:15 – 12:45__

Antecedent Events	Behaviors Observed	Consequent Events
12:22: Marcie approaches a table in the lunchroom where several students are seated.	Shawna told Marcie, "You can't sit here!"	Marcie sits at another table.
12:28: Students seated at lunch table.	Shawna calls out to Marcie, "Marcie, you stay over there."	Marcie makes a face at Shawna.
12:45: Students are leaving the lunch area.	Shawna steps in front of Marcie, ostentatiously.	Marcie pushes Shawna, and says, "You get away from me!"

Figure 7.1   Example Record Form for an ABC Analysis

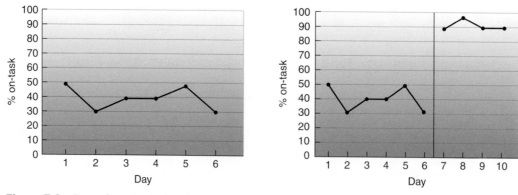

Figure 7.2 Recording On-Task Behavior   **Figure 7.3** Recording an Intervention on On-Task Behavior

work assignments usually were the antecedent. Such analysis can lead to a better understanding of where, when, and why this behavior is occurring (Crone & Horner, 2003).

These insights are helpful in planning interventions. Consider a case in which Sean, a 10th-grade student, typically acts out in socially immature ways when given written assignments in English class. This gains the attention of some students, which appears to reinforce Sean. You may decide to examine the assignments to determine whether they are (or Sean perceives them to be) too difficult or uninteresting. If so, you could reduce the difficulty level of the assignments, increase the interest level, and provide some specific positive support for Sean's assignment completion. Further, you could arrange an intervention in which you support other students for ignoring Sean when he acts out. Although these strategies are likely to work, they may not—to be more certain of their effectiveness, graphically present data on Sean's behavior both before and after intervention.

MAKE GRAPHIC PRESENTATIONS OF STUDENT BEHAVIOR   Behavior is much easier to evaluate over time if it is presented in some type of chart or other graphic display (Martin & Pear, 2007). For example, suppose the percent of time-on-task during math class is recorded for that week. Usually the amount of behavior exhibited is recorded on the vertical axis, and the time (e.g., days) is recorded on the horizontal axis, as shown in Figure 7.2.

In this figure, the vertical axis records the percent of on-task behavior for each day, and the horizontal axis records the days when the behavior was measured. On-task behavior is *stable* (does not appear to be going up or down over time), but is lower than desirable. If an intervention is planned, such as praise for on-task behavior and for task completion, the effectiveness of this intervention can be evaluated, as illustrated in Figure 7.3.

From the data in Figure 7.3, it appears that the intervention is having a positive effect on the behavior, at least initially (for more complex designs for establishing the validity of an intervention, see Martin & Pear, 2007). For the most positive behavioral effects, use effective classroom management strategies.

STRATEGIES FOR
USING EFFECTIVE CLASSROOM MANAGEMENT STRATEGIES

ESTABLISH A POSITIVE CLASSROOM ATMOSPHERE   The first and most important step in effective classroom management is establishing and maintaining a positive, supportive classroom atmosphere. Students are more likely to follow directions, work hard, and exhibit positive classroom behavior when they feel wanted and appreciated by the teacher. This may be especially true of particularly difficult students, who may not trust adults, and who may feel that most teachers are "out to get them."

Project a Feeling, Caring Persona   Convince students that you like them (even though you might not always appreciate their behaviors). Take time to greet students at the door when they first come into the classroom. Address students by name, and express an interest in their activities. Build up a store of positive comments to individual students, so that if later you must deliver negative feedback, it is not the first evaluation you have made of the student. Above all, try to assure all students that you genuinely like them, and you have their best interests in mind. Even though you will have both positive and negative reactions to their specific behaviors, you nevertheless always value them as individuals.

Teach with Sincerity and Enthusiasm Use interesting and motivational activities, and avoid long-winded lectures and lengthy and independent worksheet activities (Brigham, Scruggs, & Mastropieri, 1992). Vary the classroom activities, and avoid a tedious sameness in classroom routines. Prolonged boredom in classrooms promotes alienation, indifference, and ultimately, behavior problems. If students enjoy your class and are interested in the subject, they will be less likely to misbehave.

Try to maintain a very high rate of correct student responses to your questions, to build student confidence. Tape-record yourself during class and review the tape to determine whether you are being as positive as you would like to be.

If you find a student in your class who exhibits hostile or aggressive behaviors, it is particularly important that you establish relations that are as positive as possible. This is true even if the student is rarely or never positive with you. You must enforce rules fairly and consistently, and you must not give in to student attempts to control the classroom agenda; nevertheless, you should always remain calm and polite, reminding difficult students that you simply wish to see them make good decisions.

LESS-INTENSIVE CLASSROOM MANAGEMENT STRATEGIES

As much as possible, keep your management strategies simple, low-key, direct, and practical. Low-intensity behavior management can be more effective for you in the long run, and reduce the danger of behavior escalating in the face of more intensive interventions. Such strategies include rules, praise and ignoring, proximity, direct appeals, and the judicious use of reprimands.

POST AND DISCUSS CLASSROOM RULES An important early consideration for effective classroom management is familiarizing all students with your classroom rules. For younger students, post the classroom rules in a place where all students can observe them. Write them as positively as possible. When rules are first posted, describe them carefully to the class, model the behaviors covered by the rules, and ask students to give their own examples. Discuss instances and noninstances of following the rule. Following is an example from a third-grade class:

> TEACHER: One rule we have says "Respect other people." That means that I don't do anything hurtful or inconsiderate to any other person. For example, if I am a student and I take another student's eraser without asking to borrow it, is that respecting other people?
>
> CLASS: No.
>
> TEACHER: No, it's not. If I tease another student on the playground, is that respecting others?
>
> CLASS: No.
>
> TEACHER: No, teasing isn't respecting others. Who can give me a good example of what you could do to respect others? James?
>
> JAMES: You could move over and make room for them when we do group work.

Refer to these rules often when discussing classroom behavior. Keep the rules simple, and list only a few. Rules for older students could be similar to the rules described previously; however, it may be better to pass them out with other student materials rather than posting them in the classroom—discuss them generally, remind students when needed, and ask students to come to you if they have questions.

While providing rules is an important first step in classroom behavior management, rules that are not enforced will soon lose their effectiveness. Several low-intensity strategies can help enforce your classroom rules.

PEARSON
myeducationlab

Go to MyEducationLab, select the topic *Classroom/Behavior Management*, and go to the Activities and Applications section. As you read the case entitled "Back to Square One," examine how many of the strategies discussed here are implemented in the case.

PRAISE POSITIVE BEHAVIORS AND IGNORE INAPPROPRIATE BEHAVIORS

While potentially dangerous disruptive behavior must be attended to immediately, many inappropriate behaviors can be effectively controlled by ignoring and pointing out positive models (Madsen, Becker, & Thomas, 1968). For example, Sandra's fifth-grade teacher noticed that she was not getting her books and materials ready for a new lesson, so she acknowledged a positive example of a student seated near Sandra and said, "I like the way Melissa has put away her spelling book and taken out her reading book. She has all her materials ready and is ready to start class. Thank you, Melissa."

Such comments show well-behaved students that their efforts are appreciated and provide a model for other students. Ignoring inappropriate behavior and focusing attention on productive behaviors has been found to substantially improve behavior in elementary classrooms (Becker, Madsen, & Arnold, 1967).

CONTROL BEHAVIOR WITH PROXIMITY   Effective teachers do not remain seated at their desks, but establish a more dynamic presence in the classroom, attracting student attention by moving around the classroom. Moving closer to students who are beginning to demonstrate off-task or disruptive behavior can, in many instances, help to minimize classroom behavior problems. Conroy, Asmus, Ladwig, Sellers, and Valcante (2004) found that teacher **proximity** generally increased appropriate behaviors of students with autism in general education settings (although a smaller number of students with autism did not respond positively to adult proximity). Also, be careful that your proximity does not become a reinforcer. Carey and Bourbon (2004) reported that a student with ADHD began to act out more so that he could receive the reward (for him) of more teacher proximity.

MAKE DIRECT APPEALS   Often overlooked as a behavior management strategy, **direct appeals** can be effective. Students can simply be asked personally to follow class rules more carefully; alternately, a more systematic procedure can be used (Beck, Roblee, & Johns, 1982). Mary, an eighth-grader in Ms. Simms's math class, frequently whispered and giggled with her neighboring classmate during whole-class activities. During an independent seatwork activity, Ms. Simms asked to speak to Mary privately:

> Mary, you're a good student, and I appreciate the good work you do in class. But I have a problem. Often, when I try to speak to the whole class, or do an activity with the whole class, I notice you talking to your friend Shawna. This makes it hard for me to concentrate on my teaching when I know you are talking to someone else. Also, I think you and other students are distracted by your talking and don't learn as much as you should. So what I want you to do for me is talk to Shawna during recess, or break, or lunch, but please not during class. Do you think you can do that?

Ms. Simms also related that if she saw Mary talking again, she would prompt her to stop, by moving toward Mary's desk (proximity). After this conversation, Mary's talking decreased substantially, and after a few prompts, remained in control throughout the school year.

USE REPRIMANDS JUDICIOUSLY   Although positive responses to positive behavior are among the best overall methods of classroom management, negative feedback in the form of reprimands is sometimes necessary to help students succeed in your class. Overall, reprimands are best viewed as direct feedback that the student's behavior is inappropriate. If they are provided in a way that indicates concern for the student's well-being, they can be effective in improving behavior. Reprimands are less effective when viewed as punishment—that is, that criticism and scorn, or a negative, aggressive, or hostile tone of voice is expected to prevent the student from repeating the inappropriate behavior.

Kerr and Nelson (2006) have reviewed the research on reprimands, and the accompanying *In the Classroom* feature offers a list of their recommended guidelines for using reprimands. It is also important

For some students, correcting inappropriate behavior can be done with a direct appeal in a one-on-one conversation.

A Summary of Research on Reprimands

- Reprimand students privately, not publicly, to avoid humiliating or embarrassing the student.

- Stand near the student you are reprimanding. This allows you to use a more confidential tone of voice. However, remaining one-leg-length away respects the student's personal space.

- Use a normal tone of voice. Students can become desensitized over time to raised voices, and may be less inclined to respond defensively to a calm tone.

- Look at the student while you are speaking, but do not insist that the student return your eye contact. Forced eye contact can be viewed as hostile and aggressive, and in some cases can violate some cultural norms.

- Do not point your finger at the student you are reprimanding, as this again conveys aggression and hostility.

- Do not insist on having the last word. This may be particularly true when dealing with adolescents. The final goal of your reprimand is increased student compliance with class rules, and if this goal is achieved in the long run (e.g., the student ultimately returns to work, or stops bothering a classmate), a little face-saving posturing may be allowable.

Source: Adapted and reprinted with permission from Kerr, M. M., & Nelson, C. M. (2002). *Strategies for Managing Behavior Problems in the Classroom* (4th ed., pp. 209–210). Upper Saddle River, NJ: Merrill/Prentice Hall.

In the CLASSROOM

that teachers link reprimands directly to class rules, and avoid warnings, threats, sarcasm, or ridicule that may further alienate the student. On the other hand, avoid allowing students to argue with you, by saying, for example:

- "For what? What'd I do?"
- "I didn't do anything!"
- "You let Fredericka do it!"
- "James started it!"

In some instances excessive warnings have been known to increase the amount of inappropriate behavior (e.g., Twyman, Johnson, Buie, & Nelson, 1994). If your reprimand is ineffective, and the behavior persists, avoid making additional reprimands. Instead, a more intensive, prearranged contingency should be enforced (e.g., the student loses a privilege, or a call is made to the student's home). If a student repeatedly argues with you, it may be helpful to set "arguing" as a personal target for that student to work on.

VALIDATE THE STUDENT'S FEELINGS   Sometimes when faced with a reprimand, students accuse teachers of unfair treatment: "It doesn't matter what I do, you're always picking on me!" This type of accusation often results in a defensive statement from the teacher: "I am not picking on you," or, "I treat everyone in this class the same."

Instead of making a defensive comment, try validating the student's feelings by asking for specifics: "I really don't want you to think I am always picking on you. If you give me specific examples, maybe we can solve this problem." Such an approach not only avoids a confrontation, it also validates the student's expressed feeling (whether "true" or not), as well as subtly challenging the student to document "always" being picked on. It also openly attempts to keep the lines of communication open (Canter & Canter, 1993).

MORE FORMAL CLASSROOM MANAGEMENT STRATEGIES

Informal management systems can be helpful; however, when problems continue, more formal management systems may be necessary as a supplement to your ongoing informal management strategies.

Go to MyEducationLab, select the topic *Classroom/Behavior Management*, and go to the Building Teaching Skills and Dispositions section. As you complete the activity entitled "Multilevel Motivation Systems," think about how these strategies could be used with a larger group of students.

SYSTEMATICALLY REINFORCE POSITIVE BEHAVIOR   Praise is an effective method of promoting a positive classroom atmosphere and positive social behavior. However, sometimes more tangible reinforcement is required. Tangible reinforcement includes such things as stickers, stars, or **primary reinforcers** such as snacks or drinks. Positive reinforcement can be very effective with students with a variety of special needs in a variety of circumstances (Watling & Schwartz, 2004). Some teachers disapprove of tangible reinforcers because they believe students should learn to work for the satisfaction of doing well in school. However, for some students, more tangible rewards may be necessary to help them succeed in the general education classroom. Survey students or keep personal records to determine what sort of reinforcers appeal to your students. Check out teacher stores that carry stickers, pencils, or other supplies that could be used as rewards. Rewards should be applied consistently, for following specific rules or meeting specific academic or behavioral objectives.

Sometimes a student with special needs may require rewards for doing things for which other students in the classroom do not require rewards. For example, Larry is a student with intellectual disabilities, who is newly enrolled in a general education sixth-grade classroom, and exhibits a great deal of difficulty sustaining attention on academic tasks. Larry does not respond well to reprimands, but he loves animal crackers. His special education teacher, Ms. Mills, told the general education teacher, Ms. Irby, that Larry would work for prolonged periods of time (with prompting) for a reward of a small number of animal crackers. With the approval of Larry's mother, Ms. Irby made an arrangement with Larry that if he continued working on his assignments for 5 minutes he would receive 1 point. After he collected 25 points, he could receive an animal cracker to eat at lunch. She made a point sheet, and let Larry know after every 5-minute period whether he had earned a point.

Sometimes individual rewards can be combined with group rewards. If students feel "left out" that students with special needs are receiving rewards while they do not, allow the class to have some group reward if the students with special needs meet their goals. This allows students to help and encourage the students, rather than feeling left out. Emphasize that some students need to be treated a little differently to succeed in school, and that fairness has more to do with meeting people's needs than with everyone being treated exactly the same.

REWARD STUDENTS WITH TOKEN SYSTEMS   **Token systems**, or token economies, can be used with individual students, small groups of students, or entire classrooms (Kerr & Nelson, 2006). In a token system, students who follow class rules are awarded points at the end of specified time periods, such as class periods. The positive benefits of token systems have long been observed (Jenkins & Gorrafa, 1974; McLaughlin & Malaby, 1976). Remember Larry and how tokens for animal crackers were used as a reward for increased on-task behavior? His tokens were offered in shorter increments of time because this met his special need.

For other situations, however, you may want to award bonus points for unusually hard work or cooperative behavior. A sample chart that can be used to record tokens awarded to individual students is presented in Figure 7.4.

In this figure, students receive a star if they follow a classroom rule throughout a particular time period. In some cases, the period can be the entire school day. For younger students or students with special needs, it may be more appropriate to evaluate behavior after each period. Students can accumulate stars, or points, and exchange these later for small prizes (such as stickers or school supplies) or privileges. Entire classrooms can be awarded points after each period, depending on the behavior of all students, and thus accumulate points toward group rewards, such as a popcorn party or a longer recess break. Teachers can also post a "menu" of prizes or privileges that can be exchanged for tokens, and the corresponding "price" of each. For older students, try

Tokens awarded for good behavior can be accumulated and redeemed for a greater reward or privilege.

Class Rules

1. Always respect other people.
2. Raise your hand before speaking.
3. Remain in your seat.
4. Ask for help when you need it.
5. Complete all assignments.

Rule

Student	1	2	3	4	5
Marybeth	*	*	*	*	*
Bill	*	*	*	*	
Shawna		*	*		*
Michelle	*	*	*	*	*
Arnold	*	*	*	*	
James	*	*	*	*	*
Dustin	*	*	*	*	*
Chico		*	*	*	*
Kelly	*			*	*
Pam	*	*	*	*	*

Figure 7.4 Sample Recording Chart for Token System

holding an "auction" of possible prizes that students can bid on. Students can be surveyed ahead of time on their preferences for prizes.

Like all behavior management systems, token systems are most effective when they are used primarily to reward positive behavior. In many cases, not earning positive points can motivate students to exhibit appropriate behavior. However, when necessary, token systems can also be used as punishment for seriously inappropriate behavior, such as deliberately endangering the safety of classmates. In a procedure also known as **response cost** (Buchard & Barrera, 1972), previously earned points are withdrawn for serious misbehavior. If using response cost, be certain that students have been informed of this possible consequence ahead of time, and that the procedure produces the desired results.

TRAIN POSITIVE ATTRIBUTIONS Many students with problem behaviors make **negative attributions**—that is, they attribute things that happen to them to forces outside of their own control. For example, Nick is an eighth-grader who had been classified as having behavioral disorders because of his oppositional and disruptive behaviors with teachers and peers (*Snapshots 2*, 1997). When asked, however, Nick attributes his behavior problems to, first, a teacher's unexplained prejudice ("*she always picked on me*") and, second, to the unexplained influence of the passage of time ("*It's like, every other year, I'm good or I'm bad*").

In each instance, Nick explained his behavior as being under the control of other people or other events, and not under his own control. The teacher's job is to help Nick learn to attribute social consequences to behavior that he controls. Nevertheless, Nick probably will make more **positive attributions** only after he has internalized the relevance and importance of these attributions, and begins to believe that refocusing attributions is really in his own interest.

Negative attributions can be resistant to change, because they serve both to excuse the individual from blame or criticism and to justify inappropriate behaviors. Retraining in more appropriate attributions usually takes time, and requires frequent review of appropriate attributions for positive outcomes . . .

> *The reason you got to come with us to the zoo today was that you tried very hard to control your talk-outs this week. Good job!*

. . . as well as negative outcomes:

> *The reason you got detention today is that you chose not to do your work and you argued with your teacher. Let's talk about some ways to keep out of detention in the future.*

POST POSITIVE BEHAVIOR Public posting of students' behaviors has also been shown to reduce behavior problems (Kerr & Nelson, 2006). In one instance, public posting of daily quiz scores where behavior had been a problem improved both behavior and quiz scores (Jones & Van Houten, 1985). The daily quiz scores were displayed on laminated pieces of poster board, and were recorded for 5-day periods. In other variations, students' behavior can be evaluated and recorded on a publicly posted chart. Students who follow all class rules can be given a star next to their name for each class period, day, or other appropriate length of time.

USE NEGATIVE CONSEQUENCES JUDICIOUSLY Punishment, in the form of negative consequences for inappropriate behavior, is less effective in the long run than positive reinforcement, and should not be used when more positive alternatives are available (Maag, 2001). However, punishment is sometimes necessary to maintain order and provide a safe environment for all students. Canter and Canter (1993) recommend posting a "discipline hierarchy" so that students are informed about the consequences for violating a rule. Another advantage of posting rules and consequences is that the teacher can assume the role of enforcer or arbiter of class rules, rather than the role of a dictator who administers rewards and punishments at whim. If rules are consistently enforced, the teacher can merely state, "I'm sorry you broke the rules, too, but you were aware of the consequences. I will try to help you follow the rules better in the future."

A sample discipline hierarchy for grades 4 through 6, recommended by Canter and Canter (1993), lists consequences for rule infractions, from "warning" (first time), to brief amounts of time away from the group (second and third time), to calling parents (fourth time), and sending to the principal (fifth time). A "severe" clause refers to any severe breach of class rules, such as vandalism or fighting, and it replaces the routine sequence of the discipline hierarchy. That is, if a student disrupts the entire class or endangers the safety of other students, the student is sent directly to the principal, regardless of whether it is the first, second, or third violation of a rule.

A "think sheet" documents that the student understands the rule that was broken, why the rule was broken, the consequences of breaking the rule, and has a strategy for dealing with the same situation more appropriately in the future.

Other more severe types of punishment are also sometimes used. **Suspension** involves not allowing the student to return to school for a specified time period. Some schools use **in-school suspension**, in which the student must attend a specific suspension room in the school, but is not allowed in the regularly assigned classroom. Removing the student from school usually involves a group decision of teachers and administrators. Many states limit the number of days a student with disabilities may be suspended (e.g., 10 days) until it is considered a change of placement, and require a formal placement decision of the multidisciplinary team. It is also important to consider whether the behavior for which the student is being suspended is a consequence of the disability. If so, suspension may be considered a type of denial of school services because of the student's disability—which, of course, is inappropriate.

Some states also allow teachers or administrators to administer **corporal punishment,** such as paddling or some other method of inflicting physical pain. Such treatment should not be used, as it is almost never more effective than alternatives, and is almost certain to promote resentment and anger in the student (Center for Effective Discipline, 2008; Council for Children with Behavioral Disorders, 1990; Kerr & Nelson, 2006).

USE TIMEOUT FOR SPECIFIC BEHAVIOR PROBLEMS **Timeout** refers to some type of separation of the student from the routine classroom environment, usually for a violation of class rules. It can include **contingent observation timeout,** where the student is seated nearby and can still observe group activities; **exclusionary timeout,** where the student is removed from the instructional activity; and **seclusionary timeout,** where the student is removed from the instructional setting to another setting such as a timeout room.

Timeout can be useful to help students cool down after a volatile situation, or provide them time to quietly reflect on their behavior. In other cases, timeout may serve as tangible feedback about their classroom behavior. Overall, timeout is most effective when the classroom activities the students are excluded from are enjoyable and rewarding, and the students do not feel reinforced for the attention they receive when placed in timeout. It is also important that timeout periods be brief (e.g., 1 to 5 minutes) and that timeout is part of a larger behavior management plan that is mostly positive. Student behavior

A timeout chair or location enables students to observe activities they miss because of inappropriate behavior.

should be monitored while in timeout, and timeout should never be considered a type of incarceration (Kerr & Nelson, 2006). Behaviors that result in timeout, such as specific disruptive events, should be posted and discussed with the class before implementation of the procedure.

Use Debriefing Procedures After Timeout Regardless of the type of timeout, students need to be debriefed before returning to full status in the classroom. This is a form of attribution training and serves to ensure that students are aware of the behavior that resulted in the timeout and how they could handle a similar situation better in the future. Before returning to the classroom, students should be able to state clearly why they were placed in timeout (i.e., for which specific behaviors) and how such events can be avoided in the future. If, for example, a student's misbehavior was the apparent response to the perceived actions of another student ("Billy was teasing me"), the student should discuss how to respond appropriately to such behavior in the future.

PLAY THE GOOD BEHAVIOR GAME Researchers including Harris and Sherman (1973) have described a behavior management technique referred to as the Good Behavior Game. Using this procedure, the teacher divides the class into two or more groups. During an instructional period, each disruptive or noncompliant behavior counts as a point for the team of the offending student. Rules such as the following are set: "(a) raise your hand before talking; (b) sit in your seat properly; (c) pay attention; (d) keep your hands to yourself; and (e) stay in your seat" (Brigham, Bakken, Scruggs, & Mastropieri, 1992, p. 7). At the end of a designated time period, the team with the fewest points is declared the winner, and may be provided with a group reward.

SET UP STUDENT CONTRACTING Behavioral **contracting** involves the establishment of a written agreement that formalizes the behaviors a student agrees to exhibit, and the positive consequences that will result from the fulfillment of the contract. Often, the negative consequences of not fulfilling the contract are also specified. Contracts can be a positive way to provide a role for families in improving classroom behavior. For example, Morris has been erratic in turning in his homework for math class. Sometimes he completes his homework assignments and turns them in promptly; other times he does not turn in his homework and acts defensive and belligerent when questioned about it.

In a written, dated, and signed contract, Morris's parents agreed to take Morris to a popular amusement park for 2 days if he turns in all of his homework assignments in math for the next 2 months, with no more than two lapses. On the other hand, if he misses more than two homework assignments in the next 2 months, he will lose some of his television privileges, according to the severity of his lapses.

Families can be a strong source of support for schools. The *Diversity in the Classroom* feature demonstrates how teachers can sometimes overlook the potential for forming rewarding partnerships with families.

Diversity in the Classroom

Caution: Stereotyping Is Harmful

 Harry, Klingner, and Hart (2005) provided a poignant description of some African American families involved in their ethnographic research. Families in their research represented nontraditional configurations of families, including single parents or single adults or relatives as heads of households consisting of several children living at home. Living conditions for some of the families were well beyond the poverty demarcations established by the federal government. Some heads of households had experienced difficulties with alcohol or drug addictions and some parents of the children had been imprisoned or were deceased.

In spite of these life challenges, however, Harry et al. (2005) demonstrated that these families love and support their children. All families demonstrated caring, loving relationships with their children. Many of these families provided supportive educational environments at home. Furthermore, these families cared about the schooling and educational programs for their children. Unfortunately, however, these researchers also discovered that some school personnel devalued these families, holding their lower-socioeconomic status and racial backgrounds as barriers, and provided unsupportive working relationships. This research demonstrates clearly the need for school personnel to be open and supportive to all families, regardless of the familial configuration and racial or socioeconomic status. By building stronger relationships based upon family strengths, teachers can improve communication and provide a richer and more effective educational experience for all children.

PEARSON myeducationlab

Go to MyEducationLab, select the topic *Classroom/Behavior Management*, and go to the Activities and Applications section. As you watch the two videos entitled "Self-Management: Brandon's MotivAider and Picture Schedule," and "Self-Monitoring: Get 'Em On Task," compare and contrast these two self-monitoring techniques.

PROMOTE SELF-MONITORING **Self-monitoring** strategies involve teaching students to monitor and evaluate their own classroom behavior (Freeman & Dexter-Mazza, 2004; Hughes, Ruhl, & Misra, 1989; Maag, 2004). In some cases, students may be asked to monitor their general on-task behavior. In other cases, students may monitor themselves for a specific behavior, such as teasing. Before implementing self-monitoring interventions, meet individually and discuss with the students the purpose and importance of classroom behavior, and how they will benefit personally from better classroom behavior. The students should be made to understand that the intervention is in their best interest.

To implement a self-monitoring system for a target behavior, such as teasing, provide the student with a self-monitoring sheet for the target behavior. The behavior should be operationalized, so that it is very clear what constitutes teasing and what does not. These definitions will depend on the particular student's behavior. For example, teasing could in some cases include making statements such as, "Cornelius is a stupid jerk." Teasing in other cases could involve making faces at another student, staring at another student, or scratching the head with the middle finger while looking at another student. The student is familiarized with the self-monitoring sheet and how to use it. After each specified time interval (e.g., 5 or 10 minutes), prompt the student, or play a timed and tape-recorded "beep" or ask the student to take responsibility for monitoring the clock. The student then checks the appropriate column for "teasing" or "not teasing" over the time interval. At the end of a class period, or the end of a day, you and the student compare notes. See the *Technology Highlight* feature for some suggestions for self-recording. Students may not only receive rewards or consequences for behavior, but also receive rewards for matching your recording of teasing. The purpose is to make students conscious of their behavior, so they have more control of their actions. Self-monitoring sheets could be used with several students at a time, to record several different target behaviors.

TEACH STUDENTS SELF-INSTRUCTION STRATEGIES **Self-instruction** or **self-regulation** training involves teaching students to employ self-directed statements that guide social problem solving, and may be particularly useful at the upper-elementary or secondary level. Questions can involve defining the situation, thinking through possible solutions, and choosing the best option (see also Finch, Spirito, Imm, & Ott, 1993; Mastropieri & Scruggs, 2002). Following is a possible example:

From Beep Tape to Vibrating Watch to Assist with Self-Monitoring of Attention

 Self-monitoring of attention can be successfully implemented with many students with attention difficulties at many age levels. Several types of self-monitoring procedures have proven effective. Key elements in the self-monitoring system include (a) precisely defined behaviors to be monitored, (b) a recording sheet or system that is easy to use, and (c) a predetermined system for knowing when to monitor the behaviors. Once these elements are established, many students are very successful at improving their attention to school-related tasks.

In defining the appropriate behaviors, work closely with the student to describe exactly what is meant by paying attention or by staying on-task during class. Specific examples of the behaviors using instances and noninstances are usually helpful at first. A simple recording sheet that contains two columns, one for on-task and one for off-task, on which students are taught to place a checkmark if they are on- or off-task is also a good starting place.

Finally, a system for helping students monitor their behaviors must be designed. One way is to make what has been referred to as a *beep tape*. This is an audiotape that teachers or parents can make that contains a "pencil tap" or other distinctive noise at random intervals on the audiotape. Initially, the "taps" should be recorded closely together, giving the students many opportunities at practicing recording the behavior. Each time the tape "taps" or beeps, students are required to check off whether they were on-task or off-task. Initially, teachers want to check students' recording behaviors with their own recording to ensure accuracy by students. As students improve at monitoring their behaviors, the "taps" can occur at larger intervals. Often students can use earphones to listen to the audiotape so that the tape is unheard by classmates.

One criticism of this method has been the lack of portability into the inclusive class due to the potential obtrusive nature of a cassette tape and beeps or taps. Recent technological advances have provided another alternative for students. Watches that provide a vibrating sensation on the wrist have been developed and can be used to self-monitor behaviors as well. These watches will be completely unobtrusive and yet provide students with the feedback they might need to monitor their attention in classes in the form of a small vibration to the wrist. Some watch models can switch from audible to vibrating systems. Additional information on one type of vibrating watch, the *VibraLITE 3*, can be found at *http://dynamic-living.com/vibrating_watch.htm*.

Additional types of vibrating devices have also been developed. The *MotivAider* is a small, pager-size device that can be programmed to vibrate at various intervals, for different duration and intensity levels (see *http://www.habitchange.com/motivaider.php*). Similar devices that can be worn on a belt or in a pocket to produce vibrations or audible sounds include *Polder Digital Timer with Vibrating, Audible, and Illuminated Alarm* (Polder), the *Invisible Clock II Vibrating Reminder* (Time Now Corporation), and the *Multifunction Vibrating Timer* (TN Corporation).

Check each step, and think before you act!

1. What happened?
2. What are all possible solutions?
3. What is my goal for right now?
4. What is the best thing for me to do?
5. Did I make the best choice?

Teachers should model and role-play these thought processes. For example, the teacher should say:

What happened is that Kimberly is making faces at me. The **possible solutions** are that I could make faces back at her, I could tell the teacher, or I could try to ignore her and finish my work. ***My goal for right now*** is just to finish this assignment, so I think the best thing to do is try to ignore her, and see if she stops. If she doesn't, I tell the teacher. Well, she stopped making faces at me (or if she didn't, I didn't notice), so I think I made the best choice.

TRAIN FOR GENERALIZATION   Most positive social behaviors are of limited use unless they can be shown to generalize to appropriate situations outside the training context (Maag, 2004). It is particularly important that students in inclusive settings are able to generalize all the positive social behaviors they have learned in other settings; however, students with special needs often demonstrate problems in generalizing learned behavior (Cowan, 2004; Scruggs & Mastropieri, 1984). As important social behaviors are learned, make a list of all the settings and situations into which the behavior must generalize, and all the individuals who will observe the generalized behavior. Then, create a plan to promote generalization across all these settings and individuals.

Several strategies are available for promoting generalization, some of which have already been described. Self-monitoring and self-instruction are very relevant in promoting generalization, through the use of cognitive routines. Students can use self-monitoring techniques to evaluate and modify their behavior in different contexts, such as the teasing example described previously. In addition, strive to teach behaviors that will be reinforced in natural settings, such as positive social responding. On other occasions, be sure that all relevant teachers and staff are aware of the behavior and reinforce it whenever it occurs. Classroom peers can also be very helpful in ensuring target behavior maintains over time and generalizes by, for example, providing positive attention when students exhibit target behaviors. Train "loosely," so that students are provided with a variety of situations and a number of possible responses. Be ready to reinforce any unprompted generalization of a learned behavior. Finally, when needed, retrain positive behaviors in several appropriate contexts; for example, retrain appropriate sitting in all relevant contexts, such as classroom, resource room, homeroom, assemblies, and school bus. By using a variety of possible strategies and monitoring their effectiveness, students will be much more likely to generalize their positive behaviors (Cowan, 2004; Maag, 2004; Scruggs & Mastropieri, 1994; Stokes & Baer, 1977).

STRATEGIES FOR
HANDLING CLASSROOM CONFRONTATIONS

One of the things that frightens teachers most is direct confrontations by students. Confrontations can constitute direct challenges to the authority of the teacher, and can, depending on how they are handled, have a profound effect on the classroom environment.

The problems of confrontations can be seen in the following dialogue (see also Canter and Canter, 1993):

CLASSROOM SCENARIO

Marcus

Ms. Rothchild, the English teacher, has practiced brainstorming and organizing ideas with the class, and has just directed them to start working on the first draft of their persuasive essays. Several minutes after giving the direction, she notices that Marcus has still not begun to write.

MS. ROTHCHILD: Marcus, time to get started.

MARCUS: I don't feel like it. Leave me alone, okay?

MS. ROTHCHILD: Do you need some help getting started?

MARCUS: I said I don't feel like it. Get out of my face.

MS. ROTHCHILD: I don't appreciate your tone, young man. I gave you a direction and I expect you to follow it.

MARCUS: (*raising his voice*): Back off. I told you I don't feel like it!

MS. ROTHCHILD: (*raising her voice*): Now you listen to me! I've had enough of your attitude. Now get started on your assignment or else!

MARCUS: (*mumbling*). I'll tell you where you can put your assignment. . . (*students laugh*)

MS. ROTHSCHILD: What did you say?

MARCUS: Nothing. Maybe you're hearing things. (*more laughter*)

MS. ROTHSCHILD: That's it, Marcus. I've had enough of your backtalk. Apologize right now or you'll be in detention for the rest of the year.

MARCUS: Yeah? Well I don't care what you think. I'm out of here. (*overturns desk and storms out of the classroom*)

QUESTIONS FOR REFLECTION

1. What factors could have prompted Marcus's strong response to such a reasonable teacher direction?
2. What contributions are made by both Marcus and the teacher that escalate this conflict?
3. What are some alternative responses by the teacher and by Marcus that could have improved this situation?

Marcus has placed himself in a situation where his anger and anxiety can only escalate. The teacher, by also being confrontational, has helped place Marcus in this position. The teacher has reacted emotionally, and this emotional reaction has fed into Marcus's desire to control the situation. A difficult situation has become more difficult, the teacher's relationship with Marcus has deteriorated, and now the entire class is off-task. Some students, such as Marcus, may not believe that teachers can be trusted to act in the students' best interest, and may feel compelled to fight teachers in these situations.

DIFFUSE CONFRONTATIONS WITH A CALM, MEASURED RESPONSE Canter and Canter (1993) recommend several steps for dealing with this type of confrontation. The most important thing to remember is to *remain calm.* Count to 3, 4, 5, or 10 if necessary. Control your breathing by taking long, slow breaths. Take yourself out of the situation by depersonalizing it. In Marcus's case, if you have been doing your job as a teacher, he is probably responding to his own past experiences, lack of trust, and his own needs at the moment. *Don't take it personally.* Remind yourself, "This is not about me!" If you are able to remain calm, you will have more control of the situation. Your calmness and task-orientation in the face of hostility can go far toward resolving the situation.

The most effective approach would be not to escalate the situation in the first place by making loud reprimands and threats. Remain calm, restate your desire privately to Marcus that he return to work, and restate your personal interest in his succeeding in your classroom:

MS. ROTHSCHILD: (*quietly and calmly*) I understand you're upset, Marcus, but I really need you to go back to work just now. I know you can do well on this.

If necessary, move Marcus away from his peers, and speak to him privately—preferably with Marcus seated with his back to the class. Then, if Marcus is still upset, give him a little time and space to make a positive choice.

Speak to the student later if this seems a better solution. Ultimately, of course, your rules must be enforced. However, keep in mind the bigger picture of establishing trust and helping Marcus fit into the classroom environment. Do not behave in such a way that Marcus feels heroic by standing up to your raised voice and threatening manner. Make Marcus believe that you wish him to get started on his work simply because you want him to succeed in school and do not want to see him get a failing grade on the assignment. Do not feel that you must have the last word in the dialogue. As one principal said, "Teenagers need the last word a lot more than I do!" (Kerr & Nelson, 2006, p. 265). If

Confrontations must be handled effectively to maintain a productive classroom atmosphere.

Marcus returns to work, even while grumbling and rolling his eyes, you have achieved your purpose for the moment, and you have prevented an unpleasant situation from escalating.

If a student's behavior seems very much out of character, it may be wise to ignore the behavior for the moment, and then later speak about the problem when the student has calmed down somewhat. It may also be necessary to back off for a certain period of time, if the student's behavior appears particularly volatile or threatening, or if a student refuses to leave the peer group. If you believe that situations such as this are possible in your classroom, find out ahead of time how to call for support (Canter & Canter, 1993).

Kerr and Nelson (2006) provided several additional suggestions for de-escalating verbal confrontations, including the following:

- "Pick your battles," by declining to fight over inconsequential issues.
- Listen to what the student is saying, to reduce hostility, and help find a good solution.
- Avoid sarcasm, which often escalates tension.
- Allow students to save face by avoiding humiliating or embarrassing a student.
- Stay in control of your own emotions.

Kerr and Nelson (2006) emphasize that you should get to know your students, including their personal and cultural backgrounds and beliefs. Better awareness of your students can lead to better communication and better overall classroom management.

STRATEGIES FOR
IMPLEMENTING SCHOOLWIDE DISCIPLINE SYSTEMS

myeducation**lab**

Go to MyEducationLab, select the topic *Classroom/Behavior Management,* and go to the Activities and Applications section. As you watch the video entitled "Schoolwide Positive Behavior Support: Principal's 200 Club," reflect on the success of this schoolwide PBS plan.

An obvious advantage of schoolwide discipline systems is that the same rules are enforced in the same way throughout the school, and the structured consistency can be beneficial to limit-seeking students, as well as to students who have difficulty adjusting to different standards or rules being enforced in different classrooms (Kerr & Nelson, 2006). Some disadvantages to schoolwide discipline systems are that, unless specifically programmed, they may not effectively address the needs of all individual students, and that, if misunderstood or misapplied, they can promote an overall punitive atmosphere throughout the school. Any behavior management system must be as positive and supportive to the needs of students as possible, as schools that are perceived as punitive or oppressive will be resented and may actually encourage noncompliance and vandalism (Mayer, Nafpaktitis, Butterworth, & Hollingsworth, 1987; Rosenberg & Jackman, 2003). These concerns have led to the development and application of Positive Behavior Supports (PBS).

IMPLEMENT POSITIVE BEHAVIOR SUPPORTS Previously, schoolwide discipline has emphasized reacting to specific student misbehavior with the use of punishment-based strategies. Teaching the behavioral expectations and rewarding students for following them, on the other hand, is a much more positive approach than simply waiting for misbehavior to occur before responding. The overall purpose of schoolwide PBS is to establish a positive climate in which appropriate behavior is the expectation for all students (National Technical Assistance Center on Positive Behavioral Interventions and Supports, 2007). As such, PBS employs, on a schoolwide level, principles very similar to those discussed previously in this chapter.

Positive behavior supports rely on behavioral principles to produce socially important outcomes with procedures that are socially and culturally appropriate (Crone & Horner, 2003; Kerr & Nelson, 2006). Behavioral support is not viewed simply as a way of reducing or eliminating inappropriate social behavior through punishment or extinction, but rather as a process of assisting students in being successful within a social or educational context (Lewis-Palmer & Barrett, 2007). It involves a functional behavioral assessment (FBA) to determine the nature of problem behavior, and how it is maintained within a social system (typically including A-B-C charts such as the one in Figure 7.1). Based on the FBA, a behavioral support plan can be developed that focuses on (a) altering the environment so that problem behaviors become irrelevant, (b) teaching new skills to students to supplant previous counterproductive behaviors, and (c) establishing consequences that make inappropriate behaviors less effective, and ultimately irrelevant (Crone & Horner, 2003; Horner & Sugai, 1999).

Nelson and Sugai (1999; see also Crone & Horner, 2003) described the schoolwide application of positive behavior supports as a four-stage process, undertaken by a rotating committee of eight (or fewer) members representative of the entire school staff (behavior support team). During Stage One, the committee defines and identifies the problems to be addressed by the schoolwide PBS program. This can be accomplished by surveys and interviews, direct observations, and archival school data. During Stage Two, the committee undertakes a site analysis to determine that the extent aspects of PBS are in place. In Stage Three, the committee works to develop and implement the PBS programs in four systems: schoolwide, for all staff, students, and settings; specific setting or nonclassroom systems (e.g., restrooms, cafeterias); classroom systems; and systems for support of individual students, usually those with serious and chronic problem behavior. The program is developed and revised through a multistep consensus-building process. As the programs are implemented, progress is monitored in Stage Four with respect to baseline data collected during needs assessment. Findings of the evaluation are shared with all staff members on a regular basis, and the programs are adjusted as needed, based on the results of the evaluation.

For example, office referral data could indicate that inappropriate behavior often occurs outside the music room during transitions. These instances could be further investigated with interviews of the relevant teachers and direct observations of the hallways at this time. It could be determined, for example, that much of the inappropriate behavior is involved with the unstructured milling about of many students in a relatively small area. A potential solution could be to announce that students stay to the right when exiting the music room; to ensure one class has exited the room before others enter; or to have students exit by a different door. The selected interventions are then monitored to determine whether they have addressed the problem (Kerr & Nelson, 2006).

PBS programs have produced positive results. PBS programs try to solve significant behavior problems by examining behavior in the context of the entire social system, and by devising overall positive alternatives to inappropriate behavior (Barnhill, 2005; Safran & Oswald, 2003). Since teachers and schools in many instances choose reactive, negative consequences to disruptive or noncompliant behavior (Crone & Horner, 2003), PBS provides significant positive alternatives to achieving success. For an application of a schoolwide behavior management program based upon the response-to-intervention (RTI) model, see the *Research Highlight*.

STRATEGIES FOR
CONFRONTING BULLYING

IMPLEMENT A BULLYING PREVENTION PROGRAM   Bullying is a fact of life in all schools, and students with disabilities are frequently the targets of bullying (in some cases they may act as the aggressors). Sustained bullying can become a significant problem for schools, and can contribute to an anxious and fearful environment (Davis & Davis, 2007). More recently, **cyberbullying**, in which harassing messages or malicious rumors are sent through computers or cell phones, has been widely reported (Mason, 2008).

Heinrichs (2003) described characteristics of successful bullying prevention programs, including the following:

- Increase the awareness and involvement of adults.
- Survey students about bullying.
- Supervise high-risk areas during breaks.
- Form teacher discussion groups and coordinating groups.
- Display class rules about bullying.
- Have class meetings on bullying with students.
- Talk seriously with bullies and targets.
- Have serious talks with parents of all involved students.

Targets of bullying can be provided with specific strategies, for example, to recognize the signs of bullying, not to display behaviors that invite bullying, and to avoid high-risk areas. Bullies can be provided with appropriate social skills training and consequences for aggressive acts toward others. Communicate with parents or other family members of bullies

RTI for Problem Behaviors

RTI (response-to-intervention) procedures seek to identify and treat learning problems with a multiple-tier system (see Chapter 3). For example, all students are provided with evidence-based instruction in reading (Tier 1). For students who exhibit learning problems, a second tier of small-group, higher-intensity instruction is delivered. For students who fail to show adequate progress in this second tier, a third tier of even more intensive services (perhaps including assessment for special education services) is implemented.

Fairbanks, Sugai, Guardino, and Lathrop (2007) extended this RTI model to classroom behavior problems. That is, the Tier 1 intervention could include a universal schoolwide behavior management system, where behavioral expectations are explicitly stated, consequences are consistently applied, and progress toward meeting schoolwide goals is regularly monitored. The Tier 2 intervention is targeted toward students who do not succeed in the Tier 1 program, and could include "check in, check out" (CICO) interventions including additional structure and feedback, and in some cases daily behavior report cards. If

students still exhibit problem behaviors, a Tier 3 individualized intervention, such as a functional behavior assessment (FBA; see Positive Behavior Supports section in this chapter) and appropriate, intensive individual interventions may be necessary.

In the first study, 10 second-grade students nominated by teachers who did not respond positively to the schoolwide behavior management system (Tier 1) were presented with a uniform CICO intervention with increased structure, additional skill instruction, and increased feedback. All students received CICO cards, on which they were evaluated every 60 minutes on respecting others, managing self, and solving problems responsibly, on a 3-point rating scale (0 = not met; 1 = OK; 2 = great). Other students in the class ("coaches") were encouraged to help the target students ("leaders") stay on task and live up to class expectations. If student points at the end of the day met a specific criterion, the class earned a reward (e.g., a class game, extra recess). The criterion for rewards increased periodically, from 75% of points to 90% of points. Results indicated that 4 of the 10 students made significant behavioral improvements as a result of

the targeted intervention. Two of the remaining students remained in the CICO intervention, and 4 of the remaining students received individually developed function-based supports (Tier 3), with specific individualized target behaviors and associated rewards and consequences as well as frequent monitoring of performance. These four students, whose behavior did not improve during the Tier 2 CICO intervention, exhibited substantial behavior improvement in the Tier 3 intervention. In contrast, the two students who did not succeed in the CICO intervention, and were continued on that intervention, did not improve their behaviors. These results, taken together, demonstrate the potential of a three-tiered system for improving classroom behavior in inclusive classes.

QUESTIONS FOR REFLECTION

1. Why did some students not respond well to the CICO intervention, with student behavior points and class rewards?
2. Could this model be effective in upper-elementary or secondary classes?
3. Why do you think the other students were included in this intervention?

and targets of bullying. Bystanders (almost always present when bullying occurs) can be encouraged not to support or reinforce such behavior. Finally, all parties can be encouraged to contact responsible adults when they see bullying occurring. Effective schoolwide bullying prevention programs have reduced bullying problems by as much as 50%.

Teaching Social Skills

Appropriate behavior from students is often limited because some students lack adequate knowledge of certain **social skills**. Social skills are the behaviors we use to work and socialize with other people. Good, or at least adequate, social skills are necessary for successful functioning in school, in society, and on the job.

Many different types of behaviors or responses can qualify as social skills. In fact, it could be argued that specific social skills are required for any social act a person engages in throughout life. Skills commonly defined as social skills and studied by researchers are listed in Table 7.2.

It may be useful to distinguish among the factors that apparently control particular social skills deficits. For example, Dale is an affectionate boy with intellectual disabilities who is disposed to hug nearly anyone he encounters. Dale continues to hug people even though he receives subtle (and sometimes not so subtle) feedback that his hugging is not always welcome. This behavior also is considered "weird" by Dale's classmates. Dale's behavior is apparently controlled by the social satisfaction he gains from hugging, as well as his seeming inability to distinguish when his hugging is welcome and when it is not.

Table 7.2 Specific Social Skills	
Content Area	**Component Skills**
Conversation skills	Joining a conversation Interrupting a conversation Starting a conversation Maintaining a conversation Ending a conversation Use of appropriate tone of voice Use of appropriate distance and eye contact
Assertiveness skills	Asking for clarifications Making requests Denying requests Negotiating requests Exhibiting politeness
"Play" interaction skills (e.g., making friends)	Sharing with others Inviting others to play Encouraging others Praising others
Problem-solving and coping skills	Staying calm and relaxed Listing possible solutions Choosing the best solution Taking responsibility for self Handling name calling and teasing Staying out of trouble
Self-help skills	Good grooming (clean, neat) Good dressing (wearing clothes that fit) Good table manners Good eating behaviors
Classroom task-related behaviors	On-task behavior Attending to tasks Completing tasks Following directions Trying your best
Self-related behaviors	Giving positive feedback to self Expressing feelings Accepting negative feedback Accepting consequences
Job interview skills	Being prepared (dress, attitude, etc.) Being attentive Listening skills Asking for clarification Thinking prior to speaking

Note: From *Effective Instruction for Special Education* (3rd ed., p. 252), Austin, TX: Pro-Ed. Copyright 2002 by Pro-Ed. Reprinted with permission.

Working collaboratively and sharing are important social skills.

Kyle, on the other hand, is a student with emotional/behavioral disorders who is often verbally abusive to other students and teachers. Kyle is aware that his behavior is not appreciated by others, and he is able to distinguish between socially appropriate and socially inappropriate speech. When Kyle believes it is in his direct interest, his speech is positive and appropriate. Kyle's behavior, however, is apparently controlled by the attention and reinforcement he seems to receive from upsetting others with his speech.

In both cases, students exhibit inappropriate social skills. In both cases, students are unaware that it is in their own long-term interest to improve their social behavior. However, Dale does not seem to be fully aware of the effects of his social behavior, while Kyle does appear to be aware of the social consequences of his behavior. For both Dale and Kyle, social skills training is necessary.

STRATEGIES FOR
ASSESSING SOCIAL SKILLS

USE A VARIETY OF CLASSROOM SOCIAL ACCEPTANCE AND SOCIAL SKILLS

MEASURES Several methods are available for assessing social skills and social acceptance of students in your classroom. One method involves the use of a **sociometric measure**. In this measure, you can ask students to write down their three favorite and three least favorite classmates. Any given student's score is simply the number of "nominations" received by classmates; this could be either the number of positive nominations or the number of negative nominations. For younger students, you need to record shared, confidential verbal responses. Also determine the students who receive neither positive nor negative nominations.

Sociometric ratings can help provide a sense of how well liked individual students are; however, they are not a direct measure of social skills. For students who receive many negative ratings, it may be necessary later to determine exactly what the particular student does that is not positively valued by others, so that these behaviors can be changed.

Teacher rating scales are another method of determining individual strengths and weaknesses in social skills. Some social skills curriculum materials include teacher checklists that can be linked directly to the curriculum. The ACCEPTS program (Walker et al., 1988), for example, has questions, as part of its screening checklist, to determine whether placement in the program is appropriate, as shown in Figure 7.5.

The ACCEPTS program also includes a placement test with items such as, "The student takes initiative to assist others when they need help" (Walker et al., 1988, p. 138). Teachers respond to this item on a 5-point scale, where 1 = not descriptive or true, and 5 = very descriptive or true.

The *Job-Related Social Skills* curriculum (Montague & Lund, 1991) also includes teacher surveys of particular social skills, in which items are rated from 1 (never) to 5 (always). Sample items include "Is the student confident in knowing where to get information?" and "Can the student handle other people's complaints graciously?" (p. 35). Each item is linked to specific lessons in the curriculum.

Probably the best overall method of assessing social skills is by direct observation of social behavior in naturalistic settings, using observational procedures such as event recording, described previously. These observations, based on operationalized behaviors, can determine the specific levels of the behavior being exhibited (or not being exhibited), and can be used later to determine whether any interventions appear to be positively influencing behavior. For example, you could observe a particular student and record the number of positive versus nega-

Figure 7.5 Sample Questions from Social Skills Screening Checklist

Note: From *The Walker Social Skills Curriculum: The ACCEPTS Program* (p. 132), by H. M. Walker, S. McConnell, D. Holmes, B. Todis, J. Walker, & N. Golden, 1988, Austin, TX: Pro-Ed. Copyright 1988 by Pro-Ed. Reprinted with permission.

tive comments made to others during a cooperative learning activity. When an intervention on the student's social skills is implemented, further observations could determine whether the intervention was effective.

STRATEGIES FOR SOCIAL SKILLS TRAINING

Many different interventions to improve social skills have been undertaken. These have included both teacher- or researcher-developed training and commercially available curriculum materials (e.g., *Getting Along with Others*, Jackson, Jackson, & Monroe, 1983; *Teaching Social Competence to Youth and Adults with Developmental Disabilities*, Jackson, Jackson, & Bennett, 1998). However, most social skills training procedures are classified into four categories: (1) modeling, (2) shaping, (3) coaching, and (4) modeling/reinforcement (Mastropieri & Scruggs, 2002; Matson, Matson, & Rivet, 2007). Modeling involves demonstrating the appropriate social behavior and allowing students to observe. Shaping involves the use of positive reinforcement to promote the use of a social skill. Coaching requires the use of verbal cues to improve target behaviors, and modeling/reinforcement employs a combination of observation and shaping techniques.

TRAIN SPECIFIC SOCIAL SKILLS   Social skills training often begins with a definition and discussion of the target social skill. The teacher models positive and negative examples of the social skill (for example, inviting others to play), and asks students to identify these examples. Then the teacher may describe some scenarios for role-playing guided practice activities, and students offer suggestions or demonstrate examples of appropriate behavior. Students may be given independent practice activities, in which they are asked to record their own social behavior in relevant social situations outside of class. Formative evaluation is used to determine whether the purposes of the lessons have been accomplished. In this way, social skills instruction parallels the components of academic instruction described in Chapter 6, including review, statement of objective, presentation of information, guided practice, independent practice, and formative evaluation.

For example, in the ACCEPTS program (Walker et al., 1988), Skill 1 (Using Polite Words) in Area III (Getting Along) involves the teaching of the use of polite words in appropriate circumstances. After the review of the previous day's skill, the teacher defines polite words and gives examples (e.g., "please," "thank you," "I'm sorry"). Students are then provided with opportunities to identify the polite words in teacher-provided examples, and later to produce polite words in appropriate situations. The teacher provides positive and negative examples (e.g., bumping into someone's chair and saying/not saying "excuse me"), and asks students to identify the examples. Students respond to teacher modeling, and then produce their own polite words in response to teacher scenarios (e.g., ". . . you need to borrow

PEARSON
myeducationlab

Go to MyEducationLab, select the topic *Emotional and Behavioral Disorders*, and go to the Activities and Applications section. As you watch the video entitled "Social Skills Lesson," compare and contrast this lesson with our discussion here on social skills training.

Checklist for Social Skills Training Materials

- ■ Does the curriculum's scope and sequence parallel the skills you wish to teach?

- ■ Does the curriculum provide pretests and posttests of social skills?

- ■ Does the material provide sufficient practice activities?

- ■ Does the curriculum provide generalization training activities and strategies?

- ■ Does the curriculum provide validity data—that is, have the materials been successfully implemented with students similar to yours?

- ■ Can the material be easily adapted to special learning needs?

a pencil. What polite word do you use?," p. 65). Similar types of instruction have been employed with students with autism, in social stories that are developed for individual students to work on specific target behaviors (Graetz, Mastropieri, & Scruggs, in press), as described in the *Research Highlight* feature in Chapter 4. Baker (2006) has described procedures for teaching conversation skills, cooperative play skills, and friendship and conflict management skills for individuals with Asperger's syndrome and social communcation problems. Other materials and techniques for social skills training include those described by Baker (2006) and Leber (2002).

CHOOSE CURRICULUM MATERIALS THOUGHTFULLY   Many curriculum materials are available for teaching social skills. In selecting a particular curriculum material, ask yourself several questions to ensure that it will meet your needs. The accompanying *In the Classroom* feature lists these factors (see also the curriculum checklist in Chapter 6). If the material you are considering does not address one or more of these elements, determine whether it can be appropriately adapted or whether you should consider selecting a different program.

CONDUCT ON-THE-SPOT TRAINING   It is also important to monitor appropriate social skills outside of your training situations. If specific social skills have been targeted and practiced with particular students, prompt and reinforce those skills throughout the day. For example, Colin has a habit of taking things that he needs from classmates and teachers without asking permission. Even though he has learned and practiced more appropriate ways of interacting with others, he may still benefit from additional practice whenever this behavior reoccurs. If he takes a pencil without asking during math class, you could correct his behavior by reminding him to "ask politely," as covered in social skills training.

TRAIN FOR GENERALIZATION   In most cases, trained social skills are of limited use if these skills do not generalize to other social situations. Generalization of social skills, like other behaviors described previously, must be specifically programmed (Alberto & Troutman, 2009; Stokes & Baer, 1977). Programming for generalization of social skills could include the following strategies (see also Bellini, Peters, Benner, & Hopf, 2007; Smith & Gilles, 2003):

- Make sure that students have mastered the skills they are to generalize. Students will not generalize behaviors they have not learned adequately in the first place. For example, a conversation skill that is not completely learned is not likely to generalize to other settings.

- Make the training as meaningful and realistic as possible, so students can recognize situations for which generalization is appropriate. For example, when training job interview skills, make the situation as much like a real job interview as possible.

- Teach behaviors that will maximize students' social success and minimize their failures. This will make students want to generalize and maintain their behavior.

- Use real-life homework assignments for application of learned social skills (see Moore, Cartledge, & Heckaman, 1994). For example, have students apply their skills in maintaining a conversation outside of class, and report on their success the next day.

- Enlist the help of peers, parents, and school personnel with prompting and reinforcing the social skills. Teach others what social skills to prompt or watch for, and how they can be appropriately rewarded.

- If necessary, initially accompany the student into the generalization setting or situation and prompt and reinforce there.

- Teach self-management skills, so students learn to recognize appropriate situations for generalizing a social skill, and monitor their success.

- Use periodic retraining and reminders of social skills (e.g., "Remember how we practiced accepting feedback?").

VALIDATE TREATMENTS   Comprehensive reviews of research on social skills training have concluded that, overall, social skills training produces relatively modest effects (Kavale, Mathur, & Mostert, 2004; Kavale & Mostert, 2004; Bellini et al., 2007). Nevertheless, there is no doubt that many students lack important social skills and that many students benefit from social skills training. Carefully document the effectiveness of your training to ensure that social skills instruction is having a maximum impact in improving the social skills of your students.

7 Summary

- Much of student behavior is controlled by the classroom environment.

- Classroom behaviors can be better observed, managed, and evaluated if they are operationalized and monitored by formal observation and recording systems, such as event recording, duration recording, time sampling, and interval recording.

- Establishing a positive classroom atmosphere is an important key to effective behavior management.

- Less-intensive strategies, such as establishing rules, praise and ignoring, proximity, direct appeals, and reprimands, are helpful in maintaining appropriate classroom behavior.

- More formal management systems for effective behavior management include positive reinforcement, punishment, token systems, attribution training, public posting, timeout and level systems, the Good Behavior Game, and contracting.

- Self-monitoring and self-instruction training is helpful in allowing students to become more aware and take more control of their own behavior.

- A variety of strategies can be used to deal effectively with confrontations, and to prevent them from escalating.

- Schoolwide discipline systems have been effective in managing classroom behavior across entire school environments.

- Several methods exist for assessing social skills, including surveys, checklists, role play, and direct observation.

- Social skills are usually taught by modeling, reinforcement, shaping, and modeling/reinforcement. Several strategies can be effective in promoting generalization of social skills.

- The effectiveness of social skills training, like other academic and behavioral interventions, should be monitored and validated in individual cases.

PROFESSIONAL STANDARDS LINK:
Improving Classroom Behavior and Social Skills

Information in this chapter links most directly to:

- CEC Standards: 2 (Development and Characteristics of Learners), 3 (Individual Learning Differences), 4 (Instructional Strategies), 5 (Learning Environments and Social Interactions), 7 (Instructional Planning)

- INTASC Standards: Principles 3 (understands learning differences, adapts instructional opportunities), 5 (creates learning environments)

- PRAXIS II™ Content Categories (Knowledge): 3 (Delivery of Services)

- PRAXIS II™ Content Categories (Application): 4 (Managing the Learning Environment)

IMPROVING CLASSROOM BEHAVIOR AND SOCIAL SKILLS

If you are experiencing classroom behavior problems, have you considered the following? If not, see the pages listed below.

STRATEGIES FOR OBSERVING AND RECORDING CLASSROOM BEHAVIOR

GENERAL STRATEGIES FOR USING EFFECTIVE CLASSROOM MANAGEMENT STRATEGIES

LESS-INTENSIVE CLASSROOM MANAGEMENT STRATEGIES

MORE FORMAL MANAGEMENT STRATEGIES

STRATEGIES FOR HANDLING CLASSROOM CONFRONTATIONS

STRATEGIES FOR IMPLEMENTING SCHOOLWIDE DISCIPLINE SYSTEMS

STRATEGIES FOR CONFRONTING BULLYING

STRATEGIES FOR SOCIAL SKILLS TRAINING

Wiz Kid

SHIRLEY BRITTON did not become a photographer until 2001 when she went back to college for media studies after being diagnosed with severe inflammatory arthritis and fibromyalgia in 1996. Three years after entering the program, she was teaching art, photography, and color therapy at the college. Britton uses an electric wheelchair and must use a tripod or chestpod to hold the camera. With respect to photography and its role in her life, she says, "My viewpoint is obviously different, being a wheelchair user. Photography has given me a purpose again to help others, to inspire others, and to make new friends."

8

Promoting Inclusion with Classroom Peers

OBJECTIVES

After studying this chapter, you should be able to:

- Describe how to use classroom peers to promote social acceptance.
- Describe how students can be employed as peer assistants, and describe different uses of peer assistance.
- Describe and evaluate different types of peer tutoring programs (cross-age, same-age, and classwide).
- Gain understanding of peer tutoring and the benefits for tutors and tutees.
- Describe how to set up and evaluate a peer tutoring program.
- Discuss the benefits and challenges of cooperative learning, and describe types of cooperative group arrangements.
- Compare and contrast the uses and features of cooperative learning and peer tutoring.

Your general education classroom students can play a critically important role in successful inclusion of students with special needs. You and your students can set the stage for celebrating diversity within your class by openly accepting all students as equal members of the class, and building a true community of learners. Within this community, an accepting atmosphere is established in which all students help and encourage one another to reach their own potential. You can assist your students by teaching them several strategies for working more effectively with classmates who have special needs. These strategies help promote acceptance of all students, and teach students how to support one another using peer assistance, peer tutoring, and cooperative learning. All of these strategies can be implemented during academic and nonacademic situations and will help you and your students maintain a helpful, positive class environment.

Peer-Supported Social Acceptance

STRATEGIES FOR PROMOTING SOCIAL ACCEPTANCE

Classroom peers can become involved in accepting students with special needs from their first placement in a general education classroom. Describe the new students before they arrive in class, remind the class what it feels like to enter a new classroom environment, and ask them to brainstorm strategies to help the new students feel more accepted (Stainback & Stainback, 1990). Then select one or more of these strategies that seem promising and ask for volunteers to implement them. For example, some students may volunteer to create a poster welcoming the new students into the classroom. Other students may volunteer to offer personal words of encouragement and support. Still other students may offer to help the new students orient to the new classroom, or offer to telephone them at home. At the same time, introduce the new

Classroom peers can help establish a welcoming environment for students with special needs.

student to the materials, expectations, and tasks of the general education classroom, in a procedure known as "priming" (Myles, 2007).

When you help students with special needs become true members of your class, you will help prevent them from being ostracized or rejected by classroom peers (Manetti, Schneider, & Siperstein, 2001). In many ways, classroom peers are the key to social acceptance, and under the right circumstances can provide necessary assistance for helping students with disabilities be more accepted in the classroom (Frederickson & Furnham, 2004).

BUILD COMMUNITY WITH *CIRCLE OF FRIENDS*
In the **Circle of Friends** activity (Forest & Lusthaus, 1989; Frederickson & Turner, 2002, 2005), you distribute papers with four concentric circles drawn, and a stick figure in the middle. Students are told to write in the first circle the most important people in their lives, such as family members. In the second circle, they are to put their best friends, and in the third circle, they are to put other people they enjoy playing with or interacting with. In the fourth circle are people who are paid to be in their lives, such as doctors and dentists. When students have filled out the circles, ask the class how they would feel if they only had their mother in the first circle and no one in the second and third circles. After students share their feelings (e.g., "I would hate myself," or "I would be unhappy all the time"), inform the class that the new student might not have very many people in the second and third circles. The point of the activity is to demonstrate that everyone needs "circles" of friends, with people in every circle. Not everyone needs to be the student's best friend, but all can be friendly and interact well with the student.

Six to eight students are selected to form the Circle of Friends, and weekly meetings are held, from 6 to 10 weeks, led by an outside facilitator (e.g., the classroom teacher). In these meetings, mutual support is emphasized, and target goals and strategies are developed and discussed. Previous successes are celebrated, and problem-solving strategies for the future are discussed. Role play can be used to practice particular behaviors (e.g., a particular social skill target, and students' suggested responses). Circle of Friends activities have been seen to increase social acceptance (Frederickson & Turner, 2002, 2005).

PROMOTE ACCEPTANCE WITH *SPECIAL FRIENDS*
Cole, Vandercook, and Rynders (1988) described a **Special Friends** program in which upper elementary students were trained to interact with students with severe disabilities. The training sessions, which covered rules, procedures, and disability awareness, are described in Table 8.1. The students then interacted with their Special Friends 2 to 4 times per week, 15 minutes per session, for 8 weeks. Students enrolled in this program enjoyed the interactions with their Special Friends, and maintained their contact with them after the sessions ended (see also Favazza, Phillipsen, & Kumar, 2000).

Another positive classroom activity to promote social acceptance involves dividing all students into pairs based on shared interest areas and asking them to complete a joint project on a subject they are both interested in. Or, divide students into pairs and ask each student to complete a list of positive attributes of the other student (Stainback & Stainback, 1990). These lists can then be read to the class.

Peer Assistance

Peer assistance, or peer support, refers to pairing students for the purpose of having one student available to assist another student when necessary. Peer assistance from a buddy can be helpful in promoting success in inclusive classrooms. However, peers should lend assistance only when help is required. For example, some students may need directions read to them; others may need

Table 8.1 Content of Special Friends Training Sessions

Session	Topic of Session	Activities
1	*Rules and Roles of Special Friends*	Play with your friend with some fun toys and activities.
2	*How Do We Play Together?*	Demonstrate a model play interaction, followed by a discussion about giving your friend a choice, helping only if necessary, taking turns, praising, and being enthusiastic.
3	*How Do We Communicate?*	Discuss nonverbal communication and guidelines for communicating (eye contact, talk, allow time for response, try another way if your friend does not understand you, and don't give up).
4	*What Is a Disability?*	Students experience various simulated disabilities, followed by a discussion of their feelings and perceptions of people with disabilities.
5	*What Is a Prosthesis?*	Discuss the use of tools that people need to do tasks that they would not be able to do or do as well without them. Show examples of prostheses.
6	*How Does a Person with Disabilities Live?*	Invite a person with disabilities to talk with the students. Provide opportunity for the students to ask questions.
7	*What Is a Friend?*	Discuss friendship in general and then ask students to contemplate similarities and differences in their relationships with a Special Friend and with a best friend.
8	*Why Integration?*	Discuss the SF program—what are the benefits for them? Discuss the positive and negative aspects of having a friend in their lunchroom, recess, and classes.

Note: From "Comparison of Two Peer Interaction Programs: Children With and Without Severe Disabilities," by D. A. Cole, T. Vandercook, & J. Rynders, 1988, *American Educational Research Journal, 25*, pp. 415–439. Copyright 1988 by American Educational Research Association. Reprinted with permission.

assistance getting materials to their desks; and others may require help transcribing lecture notes. Peers can support students who might need a door opened or furniture moved to accommodate a wheelchair. But when help is unnecessary, students with disabilities should be encouraged to perform tasks as independently as possible (Cushing & Kennedy, 2003).

Peer assistance need not be arduous or time consuming for the helpers. Many of the activities are tasks the peer assistant is performing anyway, and helping their buddies usually does not take much extra time. Peers can share responsibilities with peer assistants. Overall, however, it is important to consider that peer assistance can be beneficial for the student helper, promoting such positive attributes as awareness of the needs of others and social responsibility.

STRATEGIES FOR ENLISTING PEER ASSISTANCE

TRAIN STUDENTS IN PEER ASSISTANCE Peer assistance programs should be set up in a systematic manner. The following *In the Classroom* feature offers a checklist for implementing peer assistance programs. The first consideration is to determine the precise nature of the situation that requires peer assistance. It is insufficient, for example, to think, "Mario has a visual impairment. I must assign a peer assistant to help Mario." Rather, consider the specific need that you believe peer assistance can address and how it can be addressed. For example, you may think, "Mario has a visual impairment, and sometimes needs someone to read information to him that is written on the blackboard."

Next, identify the student or students who can serve as peer assistants. In selecting peer assistants, teachers must exercise their best judgment based on their knowledge of the students in their class. In the past, teachers usually considered only the most responsible students, those who exhibited qualities of academic responsibility and conscientiousness as peer assistants. However, it may be as beneficial to consider less obvious students, such as those who are shy or who at times have minor difficulties themselves with classroom assignments. These students usually are not only very capable of assuming the responsibilities, but also may flourish when given the opportunity to be a peer assistant.

Provide advanced training to both students before starting the peer assistance. Inform students exactly what the relationship will entail. When the procedures are clear to both participants, role-play a few practice sessions and then implement the peer assistance program. Finally, monitor the program to determine that it is meeting its objective.

TRAIN PEERS TO ASSIST STUDENTS WITH DIFFERENT TYPES OF DISABILITIES

Peers can assume the role of assistant with any student. Table 8.2 provides some tasks and strategies that peer assistants can engage in with students with disabilities. Although some tasks appear very disability-specific, others are more general and extend across disability areas. For example, during emergency situations it is essential that specific students have been designated to assist students with disabilities who may require special assistance. Monitor closely all emergency-related procedures.

Peer assistants also can help address safety issues by assisting with the handling of potentially dangerous materials—such as those that are breakable, sharp, or hot—that may be used in laboratory activities. Peers can describe or assist with the proper handling of materials that may be dangerous for someone with vision or fine motor difficulties.

Table 8.2 Suggestions for Use of Peer Assistants by Specific Disability and Task/Situation Area

Disability Area	Tasks/Situations	Strategies for Peer Assistants
All disabilities	Classroom activities	Answer questions and provide examples.
All disabilities	Emergencies (fire or tornado drills)	Provide assistance in exiting rapidly and safely.
Visual impairments	Mobility in unfamiliar places or rearranged rooms	Describe verbally the layouts of the rooms; guide students around new places.
Visual impairments	Written materials that are not enlarged print or braille	Read orally.
Visual impairments	Videotapes that are not in descriptive video format	Provide additional verbal descriptions.
Hearing impairments	Lectures or films without closed-captioning	Provide supplemental verbal or written information.
Hearing impairments	Abstract materials	Provide concrete models or descriptions.
Physical disabilities	Mobility	Provide assistance as necessary.
Physical disabilities	Fine motor tasks such as writing	Turn book pages, hold objects, take notes, act as scribe, provide copies of own notes.
Attention deficit hyperactivity disabilities	Attending	Reward student for on-task behavior and prompt student to get back to task.
Behavioral disabilities	Social skills	Provide appropriate social model.
Learning and cognitive disabilities	Writing	Act as scribe, take notes, share copies of notes.
Learning and cognitive disabilities	Reading	Read orally and provide summaries of materials.

When classroom activities are to be undertaken, peer assistants can provide concrete visual models to demonstrate what students are to do. When extensive listening is required, such as during teacher presentations, peer assistants can make copies of their notes so that students with hearing impairments or writing difficulties can focus their attention on the speaker or interpreter. Peers can also assist with speaking tasks if students with communication difficulties lack the stamina to complete a classroom presentation. For any kind of oral assignment, a peer assistant could share some of the speaking responsibilities.

Peers can assist with physical mobility by moving obstructions or collecting classroom materials. Peers can also assist students with classroom organization skills, including locker organization, homework assignments, and keeping notebooks organized. In some cases, peers can promote appropriate social behavior by providing explicit models of positive classroom behavior and subtle prompts when appropriate.

Maintaining constant attention to speechread a lesson taught through direct instruction can tire a student with a hearing impairment. Thus, a peer assistant can provide a concrete visual model to demonstrate the concepts or assignments that students are to do.

PROMOTE PEER SOCIAL INITIATION Peer **social initiation** refers to procedures intended to enlist peer assistance in promoting social interaction with withdrawn or "isolate" children, including children with autism (Kamps et al., 2002; Kerr & Nelson, 2006). This is done by such acts as asking the isolate student to play, giving or sharing a desired toy, or assisting the student in using a particular material. This technique has been used successfully with students (often, preschool or primary-grade students) from a variety of disability areas, including nondisabled students who exhibit some social withdrawal (e.g., Odom et al., 2003). These procedures can also be used with any shy child. Very young peer assistants, and even assistants with autism, have been successfully trained in initiating social interactions (Shabani, Katz, & Wilder, 2002).

According to Kerr and Nelson (2006), teachers should choose peer assistants who (1) attend school regularly, (2) consistently exhibit appropriate social skills with peers, (3) follow instructions reliably, and (4) can maintain concentration on the task for at least 10 minutes per session.

myeducationlab

Go to MyEducationLab, select the topic *Autism Spectrum Disorders,* and go to the Activities and Applications section. As you watch the video entitled "Social Skills," reflect on how these two students are offering peer assistance to Allison.

The first step in training is to explain to the peer assistant what will be expected (e.g., "Try to get Chris to play a game with you"). Assistants should be prepared for rejection and teachers can role-play ignoring a positive social gesture from the peer assistant. Tell the student not to give up, but to keep trying. If toys are being used to initiate social interaction, point out the target students' favorite toys, or provide cue cards to prompt the peer assistant. Continue to role-play until the student becomes skilled at persisting to prompt appropriate interaction; this may require at least four 20-minute sessions. Be sure the peer assistant is reinforced and supported for her efforts, and understands the importance of this intervention. The peer-mediated social initiation procedure is then undertaken, as described in the following *In the Classroom* feature.

Overall, classroom peers can be used in many ways to promote social acceptance. By considering the great potential of peer assistance in promoting social acceptance, assisting with academic tasks, and planning strategies, you and your students can create positive and accepting social environments.

Peers can also be employed to increase socialization skills, such as sharing ideas, correcting and praising others, and helping others, with students with autism. The *Research Highlight* feature on page 185 describes a recent investigation into this area.

Peer Tutoring

Peer tutoring is one of the most widely studied interventions in education. Many positive effects of tutoring have been noted, indicating that tutoring can be a powerful tool in improving inclusive classroom performance (Fuchs, Fuchs, & Burish, 2000; Stenhoff & Lignugaris/Kraft, 2007). Figure 8.1 highlights some student and teacher reactions to tutoring programs, and the following scenario discusses an application of peer tutoring.

I enjoy tutoring a lot. I really look forward to it. It's my favorite part of the day. Some mornings I'll wake up and not want to go to school. Then I'll remember, David gets to start a new book today, or something like that, and I'll be excited all day!
Karen Mylerberg, sixth-grade tutor, Franklin School.

Kara, a sixth-grader, tutored Michael, a third-grader, in reading. Kara's parents reported that she commented daily on Michael and his reading lesson. "She talks about her job all the time." Michael must also talk about Kara, for at Christmas, Michael made "candy sundaes" for Kara and his resource room teacher. Expressions of caring such as these are not uncommon.
LMJ, special education resource teacher.

My children like working with their tutors more than anything else! P.E., music, and other activities that are usually favorites with children don't have as much appeal for them as the one-to-one companionship with their tutors.
Mary Davis, second-grade teacher, Audubon School, Redmond, Washington.

Scott, a fourth-grade youngster 2½ years behind in reading, was being tutored by the special education resource room teacher. Due to scheduling problems he had to be tutored during his lunch recess two times a week. Scott was not terribly enthusiastic about missing lunch recess and his teacher had to "find" him on those days. Later, as part of a cross-age tutoring program, Scott was assigned a fifth-grade girl, Kelly. With Kelly as his tutor, Scott always came to the resource room voluntarily. Scott and Kelly formed a good relationship and both gave up more recess time to make a "sticker poster for good work," which was hung in the resource room. In fact, Scott enjoyed being tutored by Kelly more than by the teacher. His own involvement in planning his lesson, and his perception of Kelly's commitment toward his learning to read, made noon recess an acceptable sacrifice.

LMJ.

Figure 8.1 Comments About Tutoring Programs
Note: From *Cross Age and Peer Tutoring: Help for Students with Learning Problems*, by J. R. Jenkins & L. M. Jenkins, 1981, Reston, VA: Council for Exceptional Children. Copyright 1981 by CEC. Reprinted with permission.

1. Set aside at least 8 minutes for each target individual during the play session.
2. Try to use the same free-play area with the play materials suggested each day.
3. Before each intervention session, review with the peer trainer the activities that are most likely to succeed.
4. Remind the peer trainer before each session that the pupils may not respond at first but to keep trying.
5. Remind the peer trainer to play with only one target individual at a time. It helps if the adult in the session reminds the peer trainer when to change to and when to begin play with another student.

6. Reinforce the peer trainer for attempting to play with the withdrawn individuals. If the session is going slowly, you may wish to reinforce the peer trainer during the session. Otherwise, provide the peer trainer with some form of reinforcement at the end of the session.

Note: From *Strategies for Addressing Behavior Problems in the Classroom* (4th ed., p. 266), by M. M. Kerr and C. M. Nelson, 2002, Upper Saddle River, NJ: Merrill/Prentice Hall. Copyright 2002 by Merrill/Prentice Hall. Reprinted with permission.

CLASSROOM SCENARIO

Peer Tutoring in Seventh-Grade History

This year Ms. Conners, the seventh-grade history teacher, found the overall performance of her students with learning disabilities on weekly quizzes to be very poor, and she was beginning to wonder whether some of the students belonged in her class.

"Why should they be in my class if they cannot keep up with the work?" she asked Ms. Cuenca-Sanchez, the seventh-grade special education teacher. Ms. Cuenca-Sanchez knew something had to be done soon. She believed that with additional practice, the students with learning disabilities could master the class content.

After meeting with Ms. Conners and examining the students' schedules, she decided that she could set up a 25-minute peer tutoring program 3 days a week during seventh-period study hall so that most of the students could practice studying and reviewing history with one another. The steps in the program are described as follows:

Step 1: *Determine the Content for Tutoring Material*
Ms. Cuenca-Sanchez met with Ms. Conners weekly and generated a list of the most important information from each social studies chapter. For example, some of the information on the World War I chapter included the following:
- Woodrow Wilson was the president of the United States.
- William Jennings Bryan, a pacifist, was secretary of state.
- Definition of alliance system, and how military alliances contributed to the start of World War I.
- Names of countries in the Central Powers and in the Allied Powers.
- Initial U.S. position was neutrality.
- Incidents leading up to the U.S. involvement in World War I, including the Zimmermann Note and the sinking of the *Lusitania*.
- Famous individuals of the era and their accomplishments, including flying ace Eddie Rickenbacker and songwriter George M. Cohan.

Step 2: *Devise a Tutoring Plan*
Ms. Cuenca-Sanchez designed a plan for tutoring that included specific procedures for students to use while tutoring each other, and rules for appropriate

behavior during tutoring sessions. In her program, students would serve as both tutors and tutees during sessions, because they all needed review and practice in history. She put the questions and answers on index cards, to be used as the tutoring materials. For example, one card read on one side: "Who was Eddie Rickenbacker, and what was he famous for?" The other side held the answer: "Eddie Rickenbacker was a flying 'ace,' who shot down 26 enemy aircraft."

Ms. Cuenca-Sanchez established guidelines for the tutoring session, which she posted on the wall:

1. Be nice to your partner, and sit facing each other.
2. Decide who will be the tutor first. The first tutor will go through the cards, asking each question in order. When the tutee responds, the tutor will verify the answer. If it was answered correctly, the tutor will place it in the "correct" pile. If answered incorrectly, the tutor will correct the tutee, ask the question again, and after it is answered correctly, will place it in the "incorrect" pile. The cards in the "incorrect" pile are asked again after the set of cards is completed. After 10 minutes, a timer rings, and students reverse roles.
3. Speak in a pleasant tone when asking questions and when responding.
4. Encourage your partner by using statements like, "Great job, good answer," or "Can you think of anything else?" For incorrect answers, the tutor can state, "No, the answer is _____. What (who) is _____ ?"
5. At the end of the two tutoring periods, students should quiz each other on the entire list, and record the number of correct answers.

Step 3: *Tutor Roles and Behaviors*

Next, Ms. Cuenca-Sanchez planned a couple of sessions to review the tutoring roles and behaviors. She presented the guidelines and modeled both the tutor and tutee's roles for the students. She then provided them with opportunities to practice both roles and provided feedback. When students had mastered the tutoring behaviors and understood their roles, she began the tutoring sessions.

Step 4: *Monitor Performance*

During the tutoring sessions, Ms. Cuenca-Sanchez collected systematic data on the efficacy of the tutoring. She wanted to know whether tutoring improved students' scores on their weekly quizzes in Ms. Conners's history class and if students enjoyed the tutoring. She began to collect students' weekly quiz scores and charted them. She also devised a questionnaire for students to answer periodically, regarding their opinions of tutoring.

After a month of tutoring and collecting data, Ms. Cuenca-Sanchez found that students' quiz scores had increased an average of 30 points, and that nearly all students reported enjoying being both tutors and tutees. Nearly all students reported that they did better on the weekly quizzes as a result of the tutoring sessions.

Step 5: *Collaborate with the History Teacher*

Ms. Conners also observed that many of the students were doing much better on the weekly quizzes. She considered the tutoring program successful, and believed that there were many other students in her class who could benefit from tutoring sessions. With Ms. Cuenca-Sanchez' help, she began implementing 15-minute sessions in her own class 3 days per week. Under this new tutoring program, all students in her class benefited. Ms. Cuenca-Sanchez was able to reduce the students' tutoring sessions to 1 day per week, arranging for additional tutoring sessions only before major tests.

QUESTIONS FOR REFLECTION

1. Why do you think Ms. Cuenca-Sanchez felt she needed to include directions such as, "be nice," and "speak in a pleasant tone"?
2. If tutoring has been found to be effective by research, why did Ms. Cuenca-Sanchez add Step 4?
3. In what other areas do you think tutoring would be helpful?

Improving Interactive Play for Students with Autism

Students with autism frequently fail to exhibit age-appropriate social skills, rarely interacting with age peers and initiating social interactions even less frequently. Licciardello, Harchik, and Luiselli (2008) evaluated a procedure to train 4 fourth-grade students with autism to initiate social play with their peers.

The social skills intervention included three procedures: preteaching, prompting, and praise/reward. Classroom assistants were trained to implement the interventions during regularly scheduled play periods. At the beginning of this period (preteaching), the assistant asked an autistic student to select a preferred toy and choose general education peers who could be play partners. The student then reviewed with the assistant how to ask

a peer to play with him or her, and practiced initiation behaviors. The assistant then told the participant that he or she could earn a reward for playing appropriately with a peer.

When the play period began, the assistant observed the target student and provided a verbal prompt (e.g., "Mike, remember what we talked about? Go ask Jimmy to play with you"; Licciardello et al., 2008, p. 31) if the student did not initiate a social interaction within 1 minute. The assistant provided acknowledgment and praise when the student initiated social interactions or responded to a peer social initiation (e.g., "Good Wes, you asked Ben to play the game!" p. 31). At the end of the play period, the student was given a favorite toy or sticker, or access to a favorite activity if he or she had demonstrated at least one positive interaction with a peer.

The social behavior of the four autistic students was evaluated using a single-subject research design, and results indicated that all four students made substantial improvement in both initiations and responses to peer initiations during the play period, as a result of training and reinforcement. These results provide a simple way to increase the social interaction between students with autism and their peers.

QUESTIONS FOR REFLECTION

1. Why did the researchers choose a play period to implement the social interaction intervention?
2. How could you implement this intervention in a situation other than play period?
3. After training, what could you do to help students with autism improve their social interactions without prompting and reinforcement?

BENEFITS OF PEER TUTORING

Tutoring can be helpful in addressing diverse learning needs in inclusive classrooms, and can be applied to a number of content and skill areas (Fuchs et al., 2001; Saddler & Graham, 2005). However, tutoring, just like any educational strategy, should not be considered a panacea. When using peer tutoring, monitor the effectiveness of the intervention, and be prepared to adjust the program as needed.

Reviews of research have emphasized the benefits of tutoring (Scruggs & Mastropieri, 2004; Spencer, 2006; Stenhoff & Lignugaris/Kraft, 2007), and described the circumstances in which it is most effective. Overall, peer tutoring has been effective in improving academic skills in the subject tutored, particularly when compared with traditional, whole-class instruction. However, it may not always be more effective than other alternatives; for example, a well-implemented independent study strategy or high-intensity small-group, teacher-led instruction may be as effective as peer tutoring (Higgins, 1982; Sindelar, 1982). However, tutoring is likely to be very useful when individual teacher assistance is not available, and when students lack effective independent study skills.

Peer tutoring can mutually improve the academic performance of the tutee and tutor.

Students serving as tutors also usually benefit from tutoring, where tutors serve as "experts" in the content being tutored. However, the benefits are not as reliable as those for tutees. Tutors usually benefit academically from tutoring in areas in which they have gained some initial competence, but still need some fluency building and comprehension development. Although it is often reported that students can improve in overall self-esteem from tutoring, these benefits are less reliable. Nevertheless, appropriately trained tutors frequently benefit in attitude toward their tutoring partner, attitude toward the content being tutored, and, in some cases, attitude toward school (Scruggs & Mastropieri, 1998). Students with disabilities in tutoring programs often report making new friends, and may enjoy higher levels of social acceptance (Fuchs, Fuchs, Mathes, & Martinez, 2002).

STRATEGIES FOR
IMPLEMENTING A TUTORING PROGRAM

Tutoring programs must be carefully planned and systematically implemented. The following *In the Classroom* feature presents some suggestions for planning and implementing tutoring programs. Remember also that students serving as tutors often model their teacher's behavior—so be sure that your own teaching style is a good model for your classroom tutors.

WORK ACROSS GRADE LEVELS TO IMPLEMENT CROSS-AGE TUTORING In **cross-age tutoring,** older students serve as tutors for younger, lower-functioning students. The roles of tutor and tutee are clearly established, and do not alternate. An example of cross-age tutoring would be students from a nearby high school volunteering to tutor elementary school students who are having difficulty in school. The volunteers can schedule their time with the classroom tutor, be assigned a tutee, and be given explicit directions on their roles and responsibilities. It is also a good idea to have the tutors keep a notebook that details the dates and times of each session, the material tutored, and a report of the student's progress. Tutees can learn much from such partnerships, and volunteer tutors can gain valuable experiences, especially if they are considering a career in education or child care.

IMPLEMENT SAME-AGE TUTORING WITHIN YOUR CLASS   Students can also tutor students of the same age. In some cases of **same-age tutoring,** students who are more skilled in a particular area can tutor less-skilled students. In other cases, pairs of students can alternate roles. This alternating-role tutoring can work particularly well when students drill one another with flashcards. In this way, the tutor does not need to know the correct answer because it is printed on the back of the card, as in the scenario with Ms. Cuenca-Sanchez.

STRATEGIES FOR
PROMOTING LEARNING WITH CLASSWIDE PEER TUTORING

One of the most highly recommended strategies for promoting achievement among diverse groups of learners is **classwide peer tutoring** (Greenwood, Arreaga-Mayer, Utley, Gavin, & Terry, 2001). All students in the class are divided into pairs of students, who then alternate roles of tutor and tutee to master basic academic skills. The most significant feature of classwide peer tutoring is the dramatic increase in engaged time-on-task and opportunities to respond. For example, consider a 45-minute, fifth-grade reading class of 30, in which one student is called on to read aloud at a time. In this class, each student will read aloud for an average of no more than 1.5 minutes per class. In a classwide peer tutoring program, however, students in this same class could read aloud for an average of as much as 22.5 minutes per class, an increase of 1,500%! As described in Chapter 6, increasing engaged time-on-task—or "maximizing engagement"—is closely linked to academic success. Although not successful in every case, research has documented the overall positive benefits of classwide peer tutoring (Fuchs et al., 2001; McMaster, Fuchs, & Fuchs, 2006). Successful classwide peer tutoring programs have been established in reading (McMaster et al., 2006), elementary and secondary math (Calhoon & Fuchs, 2003; Fuchs, Fuchs, Hamlett, & Appleton, 2002), and spelling (Maheady, Mallette, & Harper, 2006), as well as secondary content areas such as social studies (Mastropieri, Scruggs, & Marshak, 2008). It has also been found to be successful as a strategy for English language learners with learning disabilities (Sáenz, Fuchs, & Fuchs, 2005), and has been recommended as a "Tier 1" Response to Intervention (RTI) approach (McMaster, Kung, Han, &

myeducationlab

Go to MyEducationLab, select the topic *Learning Disabilities,* and go to the Activities and Applications section. As you watch the video entitled "Extra Tutoring," consider the benefits of cross-age tutoring for all involved.

myeducationlab

Go to MyEducationLab, select the topic *Learning Disabilities,* and go to the Building Teaching Skills section. As you complete the activity entitled "Classwide Peer Tutoring," compare and contrast the different methods of peer tutoring depicted in these video clips.

Planning and Implementing a Tutoring Program

1. Clarify the specific objectives of the tutoring program, including both academic and social objectives when appropriate.

2. List objectives in a form that can be easily measured. For example:

   "Students serving as tutees will improve reading fluency by 30% on classroom reading materials in the next 12 weeks."

   "Performance of all students on weekly spelling tests will improve to an average of 85%; no student will score lower than 60%."

   "Within 8 weeks, students involved in tutoring will report that math is at least their third-favorite class."

3. Choose tutoring partners carefully. No firm conclusions can be drawn to direct tutoring choices; nevertheless, several considerations should be taken into account. Some teachers have recommended choosing students as tutors who are conscientious in class, and who generally have to work for their grades. These teachers have believed that the brightest students may have less empathy for students who do not learn easily (Jenkins & Jenkins, 1981), although exceptions to this

are commonly found. Other considerations include the compatibility of the tutoring pair. Teachers should find pairs who will work together well; however, they should also encourage pairing students who are different in gender, race, or socioeconomic status whenever possible, and not exclusively support established social groupings.

4. Establish rules and procedures for the tutoring program. These rules should cover how students are to interact with each other, and specify the type of interactions that are not acceptable. Procedures should specify the times and dates of tutoring, the materials to be used, and the specific activities to be undertaken.

5. Implement the tutoring program, monitor it carefully, and be consistent in enforcing the rules and procedures. Modify rules and procedures as necessary.

6. Evaluate the program frequently, and do not wait for the end of the program to determine whether it was effective. Collect information throughout the program, and predict whether it will be successful. If progress is not being made, modify the program.

Cao, 2008). Following are procedures for implementing classwide peer tutoring in reading (see Fuchs & Fuchs, 2005; Fuchs, Fuchs, & Burish, 2000).

IMPLEMENT CLASSWIDE PEER TUTORING IN READING   To use the Peer-Assisted Learning Strategies (PALS) program (McMaster et al., 2006), first pair each student with a partner. After the teacher announces the reading selection and tells the class to start, the stronger reader reads the passage aloud to the partner for 5 minutes. The roles are then reversed, and the weaker reader reads for 5 minutes. During oral reading, the partner follows along and corrects reading errors. After the 10-minute total reading session is a 2-minute "Retell" session, in which the weaker reader is prompted to answer:

- What did you learn first?
- What did you learn next?

The partner provides feedback on the answers. In the third segment, "Paragraph Shrinking," the weaker student is asked by the partner to provide the following information for each paragraph:

- Name the "who" or "what."
- State the most important thing about the "who" or "what."
- Say the main idea in 10 words or less.

When an error is made, tell partners to say, "No, that's not quite correct," and encourage the student to skim the passage for the answer. The last segment is the "Prediction Relay," and is composed of four segments:

Predict	_____	What do you predict will happen next?
Read	_____	Read half a page.
Check	_____	Did the prediction come true?
Summarize	_____	Name the who or what.
	_____	Tell the most important thing about the who or what.
	_____	Say the main idea in 10 words or less. (Mathes, Fuchs, Fuchs, Henley, & Sanders, 1994, p. 46)

Give students prompt cards that contain this information to assist them in questioning their partners.

Every 4 weeks, rearrange the tutoring pairs, and divide the entire class into two teams (e.g., a "Red" team and a "Blue" team). During classwide peer tutoring sessions, give students a score card, on which points are tallied for good reading and good tutoring skills. At the end of a 4-week session, tally all individual score cards, and encourage the entire class to congratulate the winning team. The second team is also congratulated. Then, two new teams are formed and students again begin earning and accumulating points.

IMPLEMENT THE ELEMENTS OF CLASSWIDE PEER TUTORING SYSTEMATICALLY   Mathes et al. (1994) and Fuchs, Fuchs, and Burish (2000) have made several recommendations for implementing classwide peer tutoring, based on several years' experience in research and practice. These recommendations include the following:

Tutoring Materials   You can use a variety of reading materials in classwide peer tutoring programs, including basal readers, novels, library books, and content-area textbooks. It is not necessary for all pairs to read from the same book; both members of a tutoring pair are encouraged to read from the less-capable reader's book to ensure that both students receive practice in reading. If a weaker reader is compelled to read from a text that is too difficult, the tutoring experience may become ineffective and frustrating.

Other helpful materials include a timer or stopwatch for timing sessions, and a calculator for adding up team points. Student materials include, in addition to the reading materials, a prompt card, a score card, and pencils.

Scheduling   Schedule regular tutoring sessions, for example 3 days per week, 35 minutes per day, for 15 weeks. Be sure to schedule the reading class when all members of the class are present (i.e., none, or as few as possible, are attending resource programs or other special services).

Training   Devote one 45-minute session to teaching students how to use the materials correctly and how to be a helpful partner. Further, spend about two sessions for teaching each of the three reading activities, and teach only one activity at a time. That is, you could train and practice Retelling for the first week. The second week, train Paragraph Shrinking, and the third week, practice Retelling and Paragraph Shrinking together. The fourth week, add Prediction Relay, and begin to practice all three activities together.

Students need time and practice acquiring the skills of sequencing, skimming, summarizing, main idea, and predicting. Main idea and summarizing may be the most difficult concepts to teach; it may be helpful to use pictures to promote the idea of the most important "who or what" before transferring the concept to reading.

Interpersonal Skills   Along with other researchers, Mathes et al. (1994) found that "many students left to their own devices may become bossy, impatient, or disrespectful toward their tutoring partner. . . . Giving positive feedback and rewards is not a natural behavior for most children" (p. 47). Teach students specific words and gestures for reinforcing partners, and emphasize good sportspersonship and cooperative behavior. Close monitoring of interpersonal skills is recommended in order to keep students positive toward one another.

USE CLASSWIDE PEER TUTORING ON THE SECONDARY LEVEL   Classwide peer tutoring has also been successfully implemented in middle school and high school settings, in areas such as reading (Fuchs et al., 2001), social studies (Maheady, Sacca, & Harper, 1988;

Spencer, Scruggs, & Mastropieri, 2003), English (Mastropieri, Scruggs, Mohler, et al., 2001), and chemistry (Mastropieri, Scruggs, & Graetz, 2005). In these investigations, students with a number of different types of disabilities were able to function effectively as tutors and tutees, and improved in academics and classroom behavior when they did so.

Mastropieri, Scruggs, Spencer, and Fontana (2003) employed classwide peer tutoring in inclusive high school world history classes with students with learning disabilities, emotional disturbance, or mild intellectual disabilities. Students were divided into tutoring pairs, each including a stronger and a weaker reader. At the beginning of tutoring, "admirals" read one paragraph of the history text while "generals" listened and then students reversed roles, reading the same paragraph a second time. Immediately after oral reading, students employed summarization strategies to promote reading comprehension. Students asked each other after reading each paragraph, "What is the most important what or who in the text?", followed by "What is the most important thing about the what or who in the text?", and "What is the summary sentence?", similar to previous applications (e.g., Fuchs et al., 2001). After the tutoring session, the teacher provided whole-class review. Compared to students receiving more traditional instruction, students who participated in classwide peer tutoring scored much higher on chapter tests, unit tests, and an end-of-year cumulative exam.

Peer tutoring has also been employed in inclusive high school chemistry classes (Mastropieri et al., 2005). Student tutoring pairs used materials with which they questioned each other on important target content (e.g., "What is nonpolar covalent bonding?") as well as broader elaborations of that content ("What else is important to know about nonpolar covalent bonding?"). Tutoring was used as a supplement to regular instruction (about 15–20 minutes of a 90-minute class) to help ensure that students mastered basic facts and concepts in chemistry. Students who participated in classwide peer tutoring in chemistry outperformed students who did not use peer tutoring, and the learning gains were particularly strong for students with learning disabilities. In seventh-grade history classes, teachers divided students into tutoring pairs, and had them question each other using teacher-made "fact sheets," consisting of the most important content from the unit. Students—particularly those with special needs—scored higher on unit tests when classwide peer tutoring was implemented (Mastropieri et al., 2008).

Cooperative Learning

Cooperative learning has been widely recommended as a technique to promote inclusive education of diverse learners (Johnson & Johnson, 1986). It has been seen to result in increased achievement (Johnson, Maruyama, Johnson, Nelson, & Skon, 1981), improved attitude toward the subject matter (Slavin & Karweit, 1985), and increased cooperation among students from different ethnic backgrounds (Oortwijn, Boekaerts, & Vedder, 2008). In cooperative learning, students are assigned to small groups and work collaboratively to complete group activities. Cooperative learning programs can be configured in many ways. Johnson and Johnson (1986) have described some important overall elements in implementing cooperative learning programs, as described next.

Cooperative learning improves classroom learning while enhancing socialization among diverse learners.

STRATEGIES FOR
IMPLEMENTING COOPERATIVE LEARNING

CREATE OBJECTIVES Carefully specify the academic objectives to be accomplished, as well as the collaborative skills objective, which includes the interpersonal skills and small-group skills that will be addressed. Whenever you implement a cooperative learning activity, you should specify the collaborative skills that will be necessary to complete the activity successfully.

Go to MyEducationLab, select the topic *Instructional Practices and Learning Strategies*, and go to the Activities and Applications section. As you watch the video entitled "Cooperative Learning" (in the cooperative learning subsection), reflect on all of the different components of the STAD model.

According to Johnson and Johnson (1986), "These collaborative skills have to be taught just as purposefully and precisely as academic skills" (p. 555).

DETERMINE GROUP PARAMETERS   Cooperative learning groups usually range from two to six students. The groups should be larger when materials are scarce, or when limited time is available to complete the activities. If students are younger or inexperienced with cooperative learning activities, the group size should be smaller. Students should not work in groups of four or more if they have not mastered the preskills of group work.

It is also important to plan carefully whether students should be in homogeneous or heterogeneous groupings. While it is helpful to have groups that work well together, it is also important to mix groups by gender, race/ethnicity, and ability level. Sometimes random assignment to groups is effective. Teachers should also consider how long they want groups to operate together. For example, for a longer project in plant growth and development, it may be necessary for groups to remain intact throughout the activity. For other projects, groups can be changed more frequently. When absenteeism is a problem in the school, group assignments may need to be made daily.

Also consider the physical arrangement of the groups. Ideally, groups sit around a circular table that is small enough to provide close proximity, and large enough to accommodate relevant materials. However, teachers usually must cope with the best furniture available. Just be sure that groups are arranged so you can easily move from one to another. When distributing materials, try to arrange for cooperation. One way to do this is to only provide one set of materials that must be shared efficiently for the task to be completed.

It is also important to consider the roles that students will assume during the cooperative learning activity. Usually it is helpful to assign specific duties to individual students to promote teamwork and cooperation. These roles might include a summarizer (who restates the conclusions, consensus, or final products of the group), a checker (who ensures that all students have understanding of the activity objectives), an accuracy coach (who corrects or verifies other students' responses), and an elaboration seeker (who attempts to relate learning of the present activity to other situations; Johnson & Johnson, 1986). Of course, individual students are also responsible for all other aspects of the assigned tasks. Another, more procedural set of roles, involving groups of four students, is recommended in the *Full Option Science System* materials (Lawrence Hall of Science, available through Delta Education), and is described in Table 8.3.

Peers can also work cooperatively on computer activities, as described in the *Technology Highlight* feature. Use of peers in these activities is particularly useful when there are more students than computers in a classroom, but the use of peers can also serve important learning objectives.

EXPLAIN GOALS, RULES, AND PROCEDURES   Before group activities begin, be sure that all students understand both the assignment and the purpose of the activity. Group goals and rewards should be carefully explained to all group members, for example, bonus points for

Table 8.3	Student Cooperative Learning Roles in the Full Option Science System	
Role	**Responsibility**
Reader	**Reader** reads all print instructions, ensures that all students in the group understand the task, and summarizes the activity.
Recorder	**Recorder** is responsible for recording all the data, including observations, predictions, and estimations. This involves using pens, pencils, and the appropriate chart and graph paper.
Getter	**Getter** is responsible for getting all the necessary materials and for returning them at the end of the activity. This involves walking and carrying equipment, such as trays, microscopes, water, slides, pans, and eye droppers.
Starter	**Starter** begins the manipulations of the materials, supervises the assembly of materials, and ensures that all group members have equal opportunity to use the hands-on materials.

Note: From *A Practical Guide for Teaching Science to Students with Special Needs in Inclusive Settings* (p. 78), by M. A. Mastropieri & T. E. Scruggs, 1993, Austin, TX: Pro-Ed. Reprinted with permission.

Working with Peers on Computers

 Computers provide ideal opportunities for peers to work collaboratively. Students enjoy the motivating aspects of working with computers, and working collaboratively on projects involving computers can be a rewarding experience for all students. For example, students who are working on developing multimedia projects can assist one another in activities including finding appropriate sources from the Internet, downloading multimedia files, developing podcasts, and editing pictures and other multimedia to include in their projects. One student can be designated as the official computer operator and the other as a co-navigator. Roles can be reversed during the project after specified amounts of time. Before assigning partners, students can be ranked according to their computer expertise along a continuum of expert to novice. This information can be used to pair students so that computer experts are paired with novices. The models suggested for implementing peer tutoring and cooperative learning in other subject areas can be applied to computer use during either peer tutoring or cooperative learning scenarios.

Several researchers have successfully involved collaborative group work using multimedia projects and using computers to write essays. In an investigation by Ferretti, MacArthur, and Okolo (2001), students with learning disabilities and typically achieving partners worked collaboratively in small groups on developing multimedia technology-based projects in social studies. Students worked collaboratively and all students gained in the social studies content being studied, although students with learning disabilities learned less than their typically achieving peers.

Consider pairing students to prepare presentations made on the computer. For example, many teachers have successfully taught students to use PowerPoint™ software to develop multimedia presentations. Some of the presentations can be simple, using only text, while more complex presentations can involve pictures, graphs, animation, and sounds. Pairing students to develop these projects can help all students gain the technological expertise necessary to function independently. See also Ferretti et al. (2005) for additional information.

---

completing the task within a certain time period. Overall, students should be aware that they are responsible for (a) their own learning, (b) the learning of the group, and (c) the learning of the entire class, in that order. The criteria for success should be explained to the students. Individual accountability within the group structure is necessary (Stevens & Slavin, 1991), and should be clearly specified. Also, when appropriate, students could be informed that they can assist other groups if they have finished their own assignment first. Students trained appropriately in cooperative learning behaviors generally outperform students in less-structured cooperative learning activities (Gillies & Ashman, 2003).

Because cooperative learning activities are different from many other classroom activities, particularly independent seatwork, students need to be informed of what is and is not appropriate in cooperative learning exercises. One method of conveying expectations is by use of a **T-Chart** (Johnson, Johnson, & Holubec, 1991), which employs two columns in the shape of a T. The T-Chart specifies what the room will look like (e.g., "All students participating") and sound like (e.g., "Low voices from students in groups") if the rule is being followed. Other classroom rules for cooperative learning that could be displayed on a T-Chart include "Everyone shares with others" or "Students encourage each other."

MONITOR GROUP ACTIVITIES When cooperative groups begin working, your role differs dramatically from more traditional instruction. Many teachers begin by presenting information to the class as a whole and then break students into their groups. Instead of directly presenting information or demonstrating procedures to the whole class for the entire period, the teacher's role involves moving around and monitoring group activities. Ensure that students remain on-task and interact appropriately. When necessary, you may assist with the task or demonstrate procedures. When students are interacting inappropriately, intervene to model, demonstrate, and teach the collaborative skills necessary for the task to be accomplished. Finally, when the activities are completed (or allocated time expires), you must provide closure to the lesson by restating the objectives, summarizing the major points, having students provide

Evaluation Checklist for Cooperative Learning

Process Evaluation Component

- Is the student working with the group members?

- Does the student appear to understand what to do?

- Is the student capable of doing the assigned tasks?

- Do the group members encourage independent work when appropriate?

- Are all group members actively engaged in the activity?

- Do the group members appear to be getting along?

- Do the students exhibit appropriate social behavior?

- Do the group members share materials appropriately?

- Do the group members speak in a pleasant, quiet tone of voice?

- Does the group start and finish activities on time?

Product Evaluation Component

- Did the student complete the activity?

- Does it appear that the work completed meets the objective for the learning component of cooperative learning?

- When given a performance-based assessment covering the objectives, do students demonstrate mastery of their prioritized objectives?

- When questioned, can students with disabilities explain what they did or show you what they learned?

---

ideas or examples, and answering any final questions. Because cooperative learning activities are less formally structured than more traditional methods, summarizing and providing closure are critically important. Group activities can easily overrun the allotted time, so plan carefully to ensure that enough time remains for closure and summaries at the end of the activity.

EVALUATE INDIVIDUAL AND GROUP EFFORTS   Evaluation needs to occur throughout the cooperative learning process and include any individual and group products. You can evaluate the process for students with special needs by observing them while they are working in their groups. The *In the Classroom* feature lists some ideas for evaluating the process. Group efforts should be considered, and students should be individually evaluated for their own learning and their contributions to the group process. Finally, teachers and students should both evaluate how well the groups functioned and consider how the group could function better in the future (Mastropieri & Scruggs, 1993).

INTEGRATE STUDENTS WITH SPECIAL NEEDS INTO COOPERATIVE LEARNING GROUPS   Students with special needs can benefit academically and socially from participating in cooperative learning. However, these benefits are not automatic. Take steps to ensure that students with special needs benefit as much as possible as well as interact positively and effectively with peers.

Prepare Students with Special Needs   Cooperative learning is frequently described as an important inclusion strategy because it enables students with special needs to receive additional attention and assistance from peers, while making their own contributions to the group (Johnson & Johnson, 1986). Nevertheless, students with disabilities may be fearful or anxious about joining a cooperative learning group, and some may actually prefer to work independently (Jenkins & O'Connor, 2003). It is important to explain procedures and roles carefully, so students will understand the expectations. It may be helpful to role-play the role the students will assume before the activity. Present them with a role in the group that is appropriate for their skill levels. For example, if a student does not read at the appropriate grade level, provide a role of organizing, summarizing, or restating what others have reported. If the student lacks some specific social or academic skill that is important for group functioning, see if the special education teacher can teach some of these skills before the student joins the group.

Prepare Students Without Disabilities   As stated earlier, classroom peers play an integral role in the integration of students with disabilities and other special needs into the general education classroom. However, students must be taught how to interact appropriately and how to accept individual differences in learning (Jenkins & O'Connor, 2003). Positive peer interactions should be prompted and carefully monitored. As an example of unproductive interactions on a group learning task, O'Connor and Jenkins (1996) provided the following observation:

> Toby, a fifth-grade boy with [learning disabilities], rarely received productive help from his partners, although he frequently requested it. By this point in our observation, Toby's partner had long since ceased to follow Toby's reading or correct his errors. Toby stopped reading and announced, "I need help." The partner supplied a word, but it was not the word in the text. Toby used it anyway, and they both laughed. This game escalated until each time Toby needed decoding help, his partner said, "I'm a dumbo," which Toby inserted into the sentence.... Eventually, Toby tired of the game. "I need help," he said again, but from this partner he would not receive it. (p. 36)

Some students may need particular types of assistance in cooperative group situations, such as help turning pages or understanding directions. The special education teacher may be able to meet with relevant cooperative groups and explain how best to interact with the student with special needs.

When students are working to earn group points or rewards, sometimes they are concerned that having a student with special needs will impair the group's chances to succeed. In these cases, consider varying the group criteria for different members, or the amount of material each student is expected to master. For example, in a group spelling activity, an individual with learning disabilities may be expected to learn only certain targeted spelling words from the list. These students can also be evaluated with respect to how much they improved over the previous time period, rather than how much they learned in a particular activity. Individual students can be given different assignments, lists, or problems appropriate to their abilities, and can be evaluated on the percent correctly completed. Finally, consider awarding bonus points for groups that include students with disabilities. This may make group members more receptive to including students with special needs.

CREATE DIFFERENT TYPES OF COOPERATIVE GROUP ARRANGEMENTS

Cooperative learning activities can be arranged in many ways, and many types of tasks can be adapted for cooperative learning. Johnson, Johnson, and Holubec (1991) listed several, including the following intended to help teachers get started with cooperative group activities:

1. Discuss a lesson with your neighbor for 3 to 5 minutes, asking questions and clarifying.
2. Form reading groups, in which three students serve as reader, recorder, and checker, in reading material and answering questions.
3. Have students meet in small groups and check homework assignments, discussing and resolving any questions that were answered differently.
4. Students meet in groups to proofread and critique each other's papers, and meet again to respond to revisions.
5. Students work in small groups to prepare for specific tests.

Slavin (1991) described several types of more formal cooperative learning arrangements and activities. These groups included the following:

1. *Student Teams-Achievement Divisions (STAD):* After the teacher has presented a lesson, students meet in heterogeneous groups to study the material. After the study session, students take a quiz and are graded with respect to how much improvement was made over the previous test. The winning group is recognized in a class newsletter.

2. *Team-Assisted Individualization (TAI):* In this procedure, students are given pretests on an academic area, and placed in a structured curriculum based on their score. Students are then placed in heterogeneous groups and help each other complete their assignments. Rewards are based on the number of activities completed and on percentage correct.

3. *Cooperative Integrated Reading and Composition (CIRC):* Students work in cooperative groups on reading and writing assignments. For part of the instruction, teachers lead the instruction. Then students work cooperatively on decoding, vocabulary, writing, spelling, and comprehension activities, and prepare each other for tests.

4. *Jigsaw:* This is a popular cooperative learning strategy, in which each student learns a particular piece of information and then contributes it to the group. Students are tested individually on their learning of all the material. In another version of jigsaw, each student contributes a particular component of a larger task and then the larger task is presented to the entire class. For instance, one group could be preparing a presentation on Dr. Martin Luther King. One student could prepare information on King's early life; another could prepare information on King and the civil rights movement; another could gather material from King's speeches; and a fourth could collect information about King's assassination. The group then meets and cooperatively compiles the entire presentation, with each student informing the group what she has learned. Souvignier and Kronenberge (2007) reported successful applications of jigsaw activities in math and science with students as young as third grade; however, overall learning was not always more effective than teacher-directed instruction.

5. *Group investigation:* Group investigation requires the most independence on the part of cooperative groups. In this method, students decide how they will learn the material, how they will go about organizing the group to best facilitate learning, and how they will communicate their results to the other students in the class.

While some activities are intended to be undertaken throughout the year, for example, in science or mathematics, other cooperative group activities can be designed for a single lesson. Teachers should consider their own classroom needs to design the best arrangement for cooperative group learning.

USE PEER MEDIATION STRATEGIES TO RESOLVE CONFLICTS In some cases, peer mediation strategies have been used to manage conflict situations that occur among peers. Johnson, Johnson, Dudley, Ward, and Magnuson (1995) trained students in how to identify conflicts, how to negotiate, and how to mediate, to better resolve peer conflicts. The negotiation procedure had five parts:

1. Jointly define the conflict (that is, both parties agree on the nature of the conflict).

2. Exchange positions and interests (each party describes his or her own position on the conflict).

3. Reverse perspectives (each party states the other party's point of view).

4. Invent at least three optional agreements for mutual gain (that is, solutions that benefit all parties).

5. Reach an integrative agreement (the optional agreement that seems best to all parties).

Peer mediators trained in resolution strategies can help manage peer conflicts.

After twelve 45-minute training sessions, Johnson et al. (1995) reported that the training had a significant effect on the strategies students used and the resulting resolutions of conflicts (see also Stevahn, Johnson, Johnson, & Schultz, 2002).

ADVANTAGES AND CHALLENGES
OF COOPERATIVE LEARNING

ADVANTAGES It has been reported that cooperative learning is an effective strategy for improving achievement, group interactions, social learning, and improving the learning of students with disabilities and other special learning needs (Johnson et al., 1991; Slavin, 1991). With cooperative learning, students with disabilities can be included in—and contribute to—activities that they otherwise may not be able to participate in individually (Mastropieri et al., 1998). Johnson and Johnson (1986) concluded the following:

> In both competitive and individualistic learning situations teachers try to keep students away from each other. "Do not copy," "Move your desks apart," and "I want to see how well you can do, not your neighbor" are all phrases that teachers commonly use in their classrooms. Students are repeatedly told, "Do not care about the other students in this class. Take care of yourself!"... Cooperative learning, however, should be used whenever teachers want students to learn more, like school better, like each other better, have higher self-esteem, and learn more effective social skills. (p. 554)

CHALLENGES In spite of the benefits of cooperative learning, some potential limitations also exist that teachers should consider. Tateyama-Sniezek (1990) reviewed literature on cooperative learning in research in which students with disabilities were participants, and in which their achievement was examined separately from students without disabilities. She concluded that students with disabilities often did not learn significantly more than if they participated in alternative learning conditions. Stevens and Slavin (1991) responded that the effects for students with disabilities were generally positive, even if they were not always statistically significant. McMaster and Fuchs (2002) conducted a review of more recent research, and concluded that outcomes were variable for students with learning disabilities, and overall not stronger than those of other types of peer mediation. However, cooperative learning programs appeared to be more successful when they combined individual accountability and group rewards. Jenkins and O'Connor (2003) concluded that teacher classroom behavior and student social skills were important to the success of cooperative learning. It should be noted that positive effects for students with disabilities are often, but not always, realized in cooperative learning interventions, and that teachers should plan and monitor the interventions carefully to ensure they are having the desired effect (see also McMaster & Fuchs, 2005).

Overall, cooperative learning has been popular with teachers. Nevertheless, teachers have made several suggestions regarding cooperative learning, including the following: plan for increased teacher preparation and transition time, increase allocated time for lessons, and work to reduce any student anxieties about working together and teaching one another. Additionally, take care to ensure all students are working appropriately (and collaboratively) on the activities, ensure that assignments are at the appropriate level for all students, enforce individual accountability systems, and be prepared for higher noise levels (Jenkins & O'Connor, 2003).

Many of these potential concerns, however, may occur with other instructional arrangements, and strategies for dealing with several of these challenges have been presented earlier in the chapter. As with any educational intervention, teachers must ensure that they have maximized the positive benefits while addressing possible limitations.

Overall, cooperative learning can be an effective strategy for promoting inclusive instruction. For example, Mastropieri et al. (1998) employed cooperative learning to promote learning in a hands-on elementary science class, which included five students with disabilities, including learning disabilities, emotional disturbance, mild intellectual disabilities, and physical disabilities. Not only did students in this class greatly outperform students in comparison classes, which employed traditional textbook-based instruction, the students with disabilities overall achieved at about the middle level of their own class! Small cooperative group work has also been promising with English language learners, as described in the *Diversity in the Classroom* feature (Norland, 2005). Appropriately employed, cooperative learning can be an important strategy for many classroom situations.

Collaborative Activities with English Language Learners

Many students prefer to work with peers during school for some activities. Most students who have participated in peer tutoring have reported enjoying working with partners. Sometimes students with disabilities have reported they have felt more comfortable reading with a single partner during peer tutoring than reading aloud in front of an entire class (see Mastropieri et al., 2001). Not surprisingly, similar findings have been seen when students who are English language learners have been working in peer tutoring and small cooperative group learning situations. Norland (2005) reported that English language learners preferred working with partners during science activities. Her observations revealed that middle school students with lower English proficiency apparently felt more comfortable asking peers, rather than teachers, for assistance during science classes. During these activities, students interacted appropriately with class materials, but when they encountered difficulties in comprehension, they readily asked peers for assistance and rarely raised their hands for teacher assistance.

These findings indicate that use of peers and small-group activities may be more advantageous when working with English language learners who have varying degrees of English proficiency. Consider the level of English proficiency and be sensitive to whether students feel more comfortable asking assistance from peers.

8 Summary

- Peers can be taught a variety of strategies that involve students helping each other during classroom and school activities.

- Peer assistance can be used to promote inclusion of students with a variety of special needs.

- Circle of Friends and Special Friends are training programs that can promote classroom acceptance of students with disabilities or other special needs.

- Peer assistance refers to pairing students for the purpose of having one student available to assist another student when necessary.

- It is important to identify the situations that require peer assistance, appropriately train students, match peer assistants and buddies carefully, and monitor progress and modify as necessary.

- Tutoring is a powerful tool in improving classroom performance, and can also be very helpful in addressing diverse learning needs in inclusive classrooms.

- Tutors and tutees both can gain academically and socially from tutoring interventions, although the procedures and outcomes should be carefully monitored.

- Classwide peer tutoring is one of the most highly recommended strategies for promoting achievement among diverse groups of learners.

- Cooperative learning is another strategy that can improve achievement and social integration of diverse learners.

- Cooperative learning interventions require specifying objectives, making placement decisions, explaining the task, monitoring effectiveness, and evaluating student achievement.

- A variety of formal and informal procedures for cooperative learning can be employed, to address a variety of classroom situations.

PROFESSIONAL STANDARDS LINK:
Promoting Inclusion with Classroom Peers

Information in this chapter links most directly to:

- CEC Standards: 4 (Instructional Strategies), 5 (Learning Environments and Social Interactions), 7 (Instructional Planning)

- INTASC Standards: Principles 3 (understands learning differences, adapts instructional opportunities), 4 (instructional strategies), 5 (creates learning environments), 6 (fosters inquiry, collaboration, interaction)

- PRAXIS II™ Content Categories (Knowledge): 3 (Delivery of Services)

- PRAXIS II™ Content Categories (Application): 2 (Instruction), 4 (Managing the Learning Environment)

PROMOTING INCLUSION WITH CLASSROOM PEERS

If you wish to increase cooperation and collaboration in your inclusive classroom, have you considered the following? If not, see the pages listed below.

STRATEGIES FOR PROMOTING SOCIAL ACCEPTANCE

☐ Build community with Circle of Friends, 178

☐ Promote acceptance with Special Friends, 178–179

STRATEGIES FOR ENLISTING PEER ASSISTANCE

☐ Train students in peer assistance, 179

☐ Train peers to assist students with different types of disabilities, 179–180

☐ Promote peer social initiation, 180–181

STRATEGIES FOR IMPLEMENTING A TUTORING PROGRAM

☐ Work across grade levels to implement cross-age tutoring, 186

☐ Implement same-age tutoring within your class, 186

STRATEGIES FOR PROMOTING LEARNING WITH CLASSWIDE PEER TUTORING

☐ Implement classwide peer tutoring in reading, 187–188

☐ Implement the elements of classwide peer tutoring systematically, 188

☐ Use classwide peer tutoring at the secondary level, 188–189

STRATEGIES FOR IMPLEMENTING COOPERATIVE LEARNING

☐ Create objectives, 189–190

☐ Determine group parameters, 190

☐ Explain goals, rules, and procedures, 190–191

☐ Monitor group activities, 191–192

☐ Evaluate individual and group efforts, 192

☐ Integrate students with special needs into cooperative learning groups, 192–193

☐ Create different types of cooperative group arrangements, 193–194

☐ Use peer mediation strategies to resolve conflicts, 194

Steel Wool

ALAN RAYMOND   A local charity gave Alan Raymond a camera while he was recovering in the hospital from a road accident in which he lost both legs. But it wasn't until he was 21 years old that he took photography up more seriously after purchasing his own camera. "I have enjoyed it ever since, from 35mm film (including processing and printing in my own darkroom) — and now working with digital. I work from a wheelchair."

9

Enhancing Motivation and Affect

OBJECTIVES

After studying this chapter, you should be able to:

- Describe the preconditions to improving motivation and affect in the classroom.
- Identify techniques for improving and enhancing student motivation and affect.
- Describe strategies for increasing self-efficacy.
- Demonstrate the uses of goal setting and attribution training.
- Discuss strategies for increasing students' personal investment in shared decision making in the classroom.
- Identify and implement strategies to make learning more fun, exciting, and meaningful.
- Describe the uses of praise and reward to reinforce students' success in the classroom.
- Compare and contrast tangible and intangible rewards.

Setting the Stage for Academic Success

Because of their combined effect on student learning, motivation and affect may be the most important topics in this book. While motivation and affect overlap to some extent, they are used to represent important, separate aspects of school functioning. **Motivation** refers to the degree to which students desire to succeed in school, while **affect** refers to the students' emotional mood and personal feelings. **Intrinsic motivation** refers to participation in an activity purely out of curiosity, desire to succeed, or desire to contribute. **Extrinsic motivation**, on the other hand, refers to participation in an activity in anticipation of an external reward (Dev, 1997). Martin Ford (1995) has argued that motivation "is the single most important factor in long-term competence development" (p. 72).

Given that instruction is adequate, high levels of motivation and positive affect provide students opportunities to master the learning tasks set before them. However, at one time or other, students—particularly those with disabilities and other special needs—can lack motivation and positive affect (e.g., Carlson, Booth, Shin, & Canu, 2002). Students who lack a life history of success may be more likely to quit working on a task because they believe they have little chance of succeeding (Licht, 1992).

Some students with disabilities may be more likely to fail at academic tasks, and to attribute such failure to personal inadequacies rather than to lack of effort. Finally, students with disabilities and other special needs may be more at risk for affective problems such as depression and low self-esteem (Harter, Whitesell, & Junkin, 1998; Sideridis, 2007), as in the case of Danny, described in the following scenario.

CLASSROOM SCENARIO

Danny

Danny is enrolled in a ninth-grade mathematics class. In fifth grade, he was classified as learning disabled in reading, and he attends the resource room for four 50-minute periods per week for help with his reading. He is interested in basketball and has many friends. In math class (pre-algebra), however, his manner is anything but cheerful. He received a failing grade the first semester, and seems to be headed for another at the end of the next grading period. During lecture or class discussion, Danny seems to simply stare off into space. When given classroom assignments, he makes a modest effort to complete them, but it is clear from his manner that he is just waiting for the bell to ring. He turns in only about half of his homework assignments—and most of these are either incomplete or incorrect. Clearly, mathematics is neither an academic strength nor an interest area for Danny; nevertheless, it seems likely that he could produce much-higher-quality work if he applied himself more and developed a more positive attitude toward math. However, when his math teacher Mr. Hamilton spoke with him about his attitude, Danny seemed to believe his problem was hopeless. "What's the use?" he said. "You know I'll just fail anyway."

QUESTIONS FOR REFLECTION

1. Why do you think Danny feels this way about math?
2. When do you think simple statements of encouragement by his teacher would be likely to help? What kinds of statements would be best?
3. What are some ways his friends could help?

The best way to handle motivational and affective problems of all students, including those with disabilities, is to start by making the classroom a positive and motivating experience for all students.

Henry Winkler is a star of television and film, yet he struggled with learning disabilities throughout his school years. As a consequence, he began to doubt his own ability to succeed. Nevertheless, he persevered, and discovered he loved and excelled at acting. Today he is a very highly respected, Golden Globe Award–winning actor, director, producer, and author, who gives motivational speeches to students with learning challenges, as well as to their teachers (Winkler, 2008). A letter Mr. Winkler wrote to encourage and motivate students with learning disabilities is presented in Figure 9.1.

STRATEGIES FOR
ADDRESSING PRECONDITIONS FOR POSITIVE MOTIVATION AND AFFECT

Before any attempt to improve motivation and affect will succeed, several preconditions must exist (Brophy, 1987). These are not motivational strategies in themselves, but they set the stage for the development of motivation and positive classroom affect. These preconditions include the following:

- A supportive, organized classroom environment
- Instructional materials that are at an appropriate difficulty level
- Meaningful and relevant instructional tasks
- Task-oriented classrooms

Making decisions to create the most ideal conditions for motivating students, and increasing positive affect, is within your control as a teacher, and can make an enormous difference in the classroom atmosphere and student achievement.

CREATE A SUPPORTIVE, ORGANIZED CLASSROOM ENVIRONMENT A classroom that is managed and structured well, that has clear expectations, and that provides a sense

Go to MyEducationLab, select the topic *Classroom Behavior/Management*, and go to the Activities and Applications section. As you watch the video entitled "Classroom Climate," reflect on the positive peer support depicted in the clip.

Henry Winkler

Dear Students,

Yes, I'm learning challenged and now that I'm older my memory seems to have fallen down a dark hole, so I'm really, really, really challenged.

On the other hand my life is good. I'm acting, directing, producing. I have a wonderful wife, three great kids and 2 dogs - a Labrador retriever named "Tootsie" and a King Charles Cavalier named "Monty".

When I was in school, a lot of subjects were very hard for me. I couldn't get math, I still can't spell and when I read, the words started doing the monster mash on the page. It was very hard to focus.

It is very important to know what it is you want to do and it is also very important to know that there is greatness in everyone of you - all the members of your class.

Just because we are learning challenged does not mean we are stupid. A learning challenge is not a disease, you can't catch it, and it is certainly not caused by lack of intelligence. As a matter of fact, we just have to figure out how to solve problems in other very creative ways.

I wish you all luck. I want you to be very proud of ourselves and remember that hard work, and knowing what you want, will always put you in good stead.

Self respect is cool so are all of you

Warmly,
Henry Winkler

Figure 9.1 Copy of Letter Written by Henry Winkler to Students with Learning Disabilities

Note: Henry Winkler is best known for playing Arthur Fonzarelli (the "Fonz") on *Happy Days*. Winkler has also continued to produce and direct movies (*Cop and a Half*, *Memories of Me*) and has starred in *Scream*, *The Waterboy*, and *Click*. Reprinted with permission of Fairdinkum Productions.

of safety and support to every student creates an ideal environment for the use of motivation strategies and positive affective learning. On the other hand, a disorganized or punitive classroom is unlikely to promote motivation and affect. A positive and motivating classroom can contribute greatly to success for all students, including those with special needs.

Elicit Positive Peer Support   Teachers can encourage peers to help create supportive, accepting classroom environments. In one such activity, a student from the class sits in the

An effective teacher provides a classroom environment that is supportive and safe for all students.

"hot seat," which may be a special chair designed for that activity. All other classmates take turns contributing only positive comments about the student in the hot seat. One fourth-grade teacher, Mrs. Ramirez, uses this activity regularly (about twice a week). Initially, the teacher sat in the hot seat and modeled types of comments that students should make. She said, for example, "Everyone has to think of nice things to say about me. Would this be a nice comment? 'Ms. Ramirez has a nice smile.' Would this be a nice statement? 'Ms. Ramirez is wearing an ugly dress.'" After the students appeared to understand the rules and types of appropriate comments for the activity, Ms. Ramirez selected a student to sit in the hot seat. She monitored the comments students made, and determined how long to continue the activity.

If you use this activity as a teacher, randomly select students or devise a systematic schedule to ensure that all students have opportunities to sit in the hot seat. Throughout the remainder of the day, week, month, and school year, use the positive comments that are said about students to reinforce the concept of an open, accepting environment for all students.

Use Statements That Promote Acceptance   Another important way for teachers to create supportive classrooms is through the use of statements that demonstrate that all students are accepted. Any statements you make carry a lot of weight with your students, so emphasize statements that indicate how each student in your class is an important contributing member. This attitude helps your students not only to accept the divergent responses of others, but also encourages other students to make positive contributions to the class. For example, one teacher said the following to her class on the value of diversity to her class:

> We're all different in some ways. Even [name] wears glasses. And the twins, they are different, aren't they, even from one another? You have to expect that kind of difference; it's sometimes fun and happy to work with someone who is a little different. You don't always have to work with the same kinds of people, do you? It makes life more exciting to work with different kinds of people. (Scruggs & Mastropieri, 1994, p. 796)

Consider surveying students' feelings about being in the classroom. A classroom survey can provide important feedback on how the classroom environment is perceived. You can use this feedback to improve the atmosphere in your classroom.

Another important consideration for creating a supportive atmosphere is ensuring your classroom is culturally responsive, that is, supportive of students' diverse cultural identities and building upon the strengths of your students and their families. The *Diversity in the Classroom* feature provides some suggestions.

ENSURE THAT MATERIALS ARE OF AN APPROPRIATE DIFFICULTY LEVEL   The second precondition for improving motivation and affect is to ensure that curriculum content is taught at the appropriate difficulty level. If students consistently are provided with tasks that are too easy, they quickly lose interest and take little satisfaction in doing well. On the other hand, if the content is too difficult, students are less likely to persist in their efforts to master it and may begin to display negative attitudes toward the content. The content must be at the difficulty level at which students are likely to succeed if they apply a reasonable amount of effort. Questioning students and frequently monitoring their progress should help you determine the appropriateness of the difficulty level. In inclusive settings, devote extra attention to students with special needs to ensure that activities are the correct level for the class as a whole, but are not too difficult for them. Conversely, gifted students may need more challenging tasks than those provided to other students.

Creating a Culturally Responsive Classroom

Culture influences all aspects of life and school. Students' culture shapes their own language, behavior, emotions, customs, and traditions. Because of the importance of culture, students feel more motivated to learn if the classroom is responsive to their own culture. Gollnick and Chinn (2009) referred to students' cultures as microcultures consisting of interactions of race, ethnicity, language, gender, class, religion, age, geography, and disability. All of these characteristics merge to form an individual's culture, which in turn interacts with the dominant culture.

Gaining an understanding and an appreciation of these cultural influences will assist in developing culturally responsive education, which, in turn, should increase student investment in learning. For example, learn how education is viewed from the perspectives of your students and families. Find out how students and families perceive school visits, homework, school authority figures, and school activities. Learn about the cultural identities and strengths of your students and families. Design instruction and strategies to encourage involvement for members of all cultures in relevant school activities. Emphasize cooperation and motivation while relating educational goals to students and their families in culturally meaningful ways.

Set up or expand a literacy center at your school that emphasizes literacy for all and represents all cultural and linguistic groups. For example, King Middle School's literacy center began providing literacy assistance to adults and families in the evenings while supporting students during the school day (Ginsberg, 2005). Attendance at the center was encouraged for anyone requiring assistance with English. Community members from similar linguistic backgrounds might be available to help individuals feel more comfortable. The literacy center became a focal point for the community, holding events such as book discussions and folk art festivals sponsored by the local parent organization.

Demonstrate a sincere, caring, accepting attitude toward all individuals. Help students and families know that everyone, regardless of cultural or linguistic background, is an important member of your school's community.

ENSURE THAT TASKS ARE MEANINGFUL   A third precondition for improving motivation and affect is that the learning tasks are seen by students as meaningful and worth learning. Students must consider the information or skills they are learning to be personally interesting, relevant, helpful in their lives, or likely to prove useful in their future. This is accomplished, first, by you as a teacher assessing the content for importance. Second, take time to point out to students the importance and worth of the information being learned.

Third, behave as though the content being learned is important by modeling enthusiasm and interest in the content. Students will more likely see the value of the lesson if the instructional materials and student-assigned tasks reflect the worth of the content. Countless worksheets, or lists of uninteresting material to be memorized, are likely to have a negative effect on motivation. The choice of instructional materials and the meaningful presentation of them—making them explicitly or implicitly relevant to your students' lives—will promote motivation. For example, students who participate in classroom activities on democracy are more likely to appreciate relevant concepts than students who simply read about democracy.

Keep in mind that many students with special needs may not immediately understand the worth of an academic activity, so monitoring students' understanding of the relevance of schoolwork is important. When students begin to think that learning is meaningful to

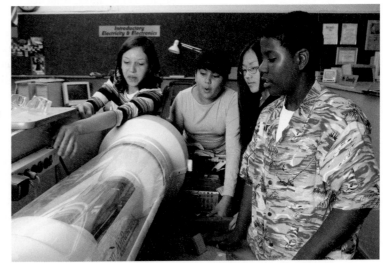

Planning meaningful learning tasks is one important way to motivate students.

them, motivation will increase. Ways to make learning more worthwhile and meaningful to students include the following:

- Select topics that reflect students' interests.
- Relate the content being studied to local issues or problems that are familiar and important to students.
- Allow students to select their assignment from a list of options; for example, students may choose to write a paper or draw and label illustrations to complete a task demonstrating their knowledge of the migration patterns of birds.
- Begin and conclude classes with statements such as: "This is an important topic because . . . ," and, "Why was this an important topic for us to learn about?"

CREATE TASK-ORIENTED, NOT EGO-ORIENTED, CLASSROOMS The overall orientation of the classroom environment is also an important condition for enhancing motivation and affect. Nicholls (1989) described important differences between what he characterized as **ego-oriented** and **task-oriented classrooms.** In ego-oriented classrooms, students function in an overall competitive environment with each other. Success for individual students is defined with respect to the performance of other students and is associated with high academic capacity (e.g., that successful students are "smart," outperforming other students). Failure, or doing worse than other students, is associated with low capacity (e.g., that unsuccessful students are "dumb," and perform more poorly than other students). In such classrooms, students are graded on the "curve" (i.e., relative to each other), percentile ranks on standardized achievement tests are emphasized, and all grades may be publicly posted. Ego-oriented classrooms may be viewed positively by the top few students who think they are likely to achieve at the highest level. However, such classrooms may actually decrease motivation for the majority of students who think they are not "smart" and therefore have little chance of achieving at the highest level. If students think they have low (or not sufficiently high) capacity for learning, they will be less likely to try their best in the future.

Task-oriented classrooms provide a very different atmosphere. Students are led to believe that success is not defined as their "capacity" but rather is determined by a combination of factors that they can control. These factors include interest and a sincere effort to learn. Students are evaluated with respect to their previous performance and not against the performance of others. They are acknowledged for persistence of effort and a positive attitude toward learning. With student permission, products are publicly posted when they demonstrate an impressive display of effort. Even top students can benefit from the task-oriented classroom, because they learn that only substantial efforts are rewarded. Sample teacher comments characteristic of ego-oriented and task-oriented classrooms are given in Table 9.1.

Students with special needs can benefit greatly from the atmosphere provided by task-oriented classrooms. Most students with disabilities are very much aware that they perform academically below most students without disabilities. Thus, in ego-oriented, competitive classrooms, many students with disabilities soon realize they cannot effectively compete with other students, and stop trying. However, in task-oriented classrooms, even though students may perform at different levels of competence, all students have an equal chance at making an effort to learn. When best efforts are rewarded, rather than supposedly "fixed" abilities such as intelligence, leadership, or creativity, all students can benefit.

Table 9.1 Ego-Oriented Versus Task-Oriented Classrooms

Classroom Orientation	Representative Teacher Comments
Ego-Oriented	"Marcy, you're the smartest student in the class!" "Class, look at how smart Fredrica is, to have figured this out!" "Richard, why can't you be more like Bernie?"
Task-Oriented	"Marcy, this is your best work yet!" "Fredrica must have worked very hard to have figured this out!" "Richard, I know you can do much better on this assignment if you use the strategies we practiced and put more effort into it."

Improving Student Motivation and Affect

STRATEGIES FOR
IMPROVING MOTIVATION AND AFFECT

Once the important preconditions have been met to create a positive classroom atmosphere, you can turn to several general categories of techniques to enhance motivation and affect both in individual students and in your class as a whole: improving **self-esteem** and **self-efficacy**, increasing a personal investment in learning, making learning fun and enjoyable, and using praise and rewards.

RAISE STUDENTS' SELF-ESTEEM   *Self-esteem* is a general term for the regard in which individuals hold themselves. Generally, students who feel good about who they are and what they can do are more successful than students who do not feel good about themselves (Harter, 2001). Self-esteem has been found to differ among boys and girls, Caucasian and minority students, and students with and without disabilities (e.g., Harter et al., 1998; Scruggs & Mastropieri, 1983). However, self-esteem has also been seen to be quite variable within all these groups. That is, some students with disabilities exhibit very high self-esteem and some high-achieving students exhibit low self-esteem.

Students with disabilities may be particularly vulnerable to beliefs that they do not compare favorably with their classmates. This suggests that students with disabilities should be carefully monitored for such affective characteristics as self-esteem, and that the student's sense of worth and efficacy be promoted wherever possible. This can be accomplished by providing students with tasks at which they can succeed, and providing positive feedback and rewards for their success. Be sure that students with special needs know that they have an important role to play in the classroom by providing roles in which they can assume responsibility and ownership, such as care of classroom pets, distributing materials, or collecting papers. Such assignments, as well as public statements of support, can convince students with special needs that their presence is valued. Classroom peers can also assist in helping other students feel better about themselves (see Chapter 8).

PROMOTE SELF-EFFICACY   Students are motivated to persist on tasks at which they believe they will succeed. They are more apt to think they will succeed on future tasks if they have succeeded on similar previous tasks. In this situation, students believe they have the knowledge and the skills to ensure their attainment of the goal. This confidence in one's own abilities has been referred to as *self-efficacy* (Zimmerman & Kitsantas, 2007). You can improve self-efficacy by structuring academic tasks that can be accomplished with a reasonable effort and high rate of success. Classroom activities benefit all students—especially students with disabilities—when they provide additional practice, continually assess understanding, make connections to prior learning, organize learning in advance of instruction, recognize good social models, and offer support for learning.

Provide Additional Practice to Reinforce Prior Knowledge   Learning is more likely to occur when previous learning was successful. The time you spend making sure that previous material has been completely learned is valuable. Initiate regular reviews and **overlearning** (additional practice after goals have been achieved) to reinforce any knowledge previously presented. This is especially important for students with special needs. Additional practice could be provided by the special education teacher or by a parent, volunteer, or aide.

Motivating students to persist on tasks in which they can succeed can increase their self-efficacy.

Use Ongoing Assessment Strategies   First, be sure your instructional presentations are clear and effective. As you go through the lesson, monitor students' comprehension by asking frequent questions. Carefully supervise guided practice activities, so students do not undertake activities they do not fully understand. Finally, provide independent practice only after you are certain students can be successful independently. If independent practice is not successful, go back immediately to guided practice or review the lesson concepts in a new way. If this structure is carefully followed and necessary adjustments are made in the curriculum materials, students will learn to expect success in the classroom.

Point Out Appropriate Social Models   Social models also can increase self-efficacy. Students may believe they can be successful—even if they have no experience with a task—if they observe students like themselves succeeding at the task. When using this strategy, try pointing out appropriate social models and offering assurances that students can do what the social models have done. Say, for example, "Hey, James couldn't do this either last week. James worked hard and learned to do this, so I'm sure you can learn to do it, too!"

Provide Positive Support   Direct encouragement from teachers can help students' self-efficacy. Saying, "I really believe you will be able to do this if you give it a try!" provides positive support for effort, rather than criticism for failure, and can demonstrate your confidence in individual students. It will also provide evidence that success is possible. On the other hand, such statements are unlikely to be effective if the student mistrusts you or doubts your sincerity.

Demonstration of genuine teacher interest at appropriate times can also improve student motivation and attitude toward schoolwork, as shown in the continuation of Danny's scenario.

CLASSROOM SCENARIO

Danny

Mr. Hamilton arranged for a meeting with Danny. During this meeting, Mr. Hamilton expressed his concern about Danny's progress in math, and his hope that he could improve. Danny seemed pleased with the extra attention from Mr. Hamilton, but indicated his overall pessimistic attitude: "I appreciate you trying to help me, Mr. Hamilton, but it's no use. I'll never learn this math." Mr. Hamilton replied, "Danny, I think you're just not giving yourself a chance."

Mr. Hamilton arranged to edit Danny's homework assignments so that he could spend more time on a smaller number of problems within Danny's current skill level. He would discuss the problems briefly with Danny in the few minutes before the class started; he would also arrange for a peer to help Danny during class exercises. Mr. Hamilton also began to privately praise Danny when he made an effort and completed his assignments: "You see? I told you, you would begin to catch on if you made this kind of effort!" When Danny's assignments were not completed, Mr. Hamilton acted disappointed, but hopeful that the next assignment would be done correctly: "Danny, we both know from before that you can do better than this—I hope to see something really impressive on your next assignment!"

By the end of the second quarter, Danny's grades had improved from an F to a D+. On the last test of the semester, Danny earned a C+. Mr. Hamilton wrote a note to Danny's parents stating that he was the most improved student in his class. With additional prompting, Danny continued to perform successfully throughout the second semester. Danny concluded, "At first I thought I could never do it. But math's really not that bad, if you put your mind to it!"

QUESTIONS FOR REFLECTION

1. Why do you think Mr. Hamilton was frustrated with Danny's performance in math?
2. What types of additional strategies might be helpful for Danny to use at home?
3. How can a monitoring system be established to determine whether the instructional interventions are working effectively?

Avoid Counterproductive Statements   One well-meaning strategy that is often counterproductive is characterizing a particular task as "easy," saying, for example:

- "You can do this. It's easy!"
- "Anybody should be able to do this!"

Such statements are often intended to convince students that a task is doable and within their reach, but the effects of such statements can be very different. Because teachers rarely need to encourage a student to accomplish truly "easy" tasks, the use of this strategy has often been used with tasks that the student considers difficult. However, the strategy can undermine motivation: little satisfaction is gained from accomplishing an "easy" task; shame and embarrassment result from failing at a task that is considered "easy."

Also, remember that if students express satisfaction in their performance by stating that a particular task was easy, use prudence in agreeing completely with the student. As discussed later in this chapter, students need to learn to attribute their success on academic tasks to effort, rather than the ease of the task. You could say something like, "It may have been easy for you because you worked hard to learn it, but I don't think it was really that easy!"

TEACH STUDENTS TO SET GOALS   Once students believe they are capable of accomplishing a task, involving them in goal setting can increase their motivation to complete that task. Research has found that students often increase their achievement when they help set their own goals (Fuchs et al., 2003; Konrad, Fowler, & Walker, 2007). Students involved in setting their own goals and in monitoring their own progress will be more likely to see learning goals as meaningful and personal—more so than if they are simply imposed by the teacher. Motivation can be maximized when goals meet the standard of "optimal challenge"—that is, the goal is difficult for the student to attain, but can be achieved with vigorous or persistent effort (Ford, 1995).

Establish Goals and Monitor Progress   Realistic, but high, goals should be set and progress toward goal attainment monitored on graphs or charts (Fuchs, Fuchs, & Deno, 1985). Daily goals can be established and progress can be charted. For example, students can select goals for solving a certain number of math problems, reading a specific number of pages in the social studies text daily, for getting 90% correct on weekly spelling tests, or for getting 80% or higher on biology unit tests. Goals also can be set for a specific amount of time-on-task. For instance, 30 minutes can be established as a daily goal for working on math problem solving, reading assignments, or practicing spelling words. The charts and graphs can track progress toward attaining those goals. A sample goal sheet is depicted in Figure 9.2.

GOAL SHEET

Student name _____

Dates _____

Class _____

# of daily math problems	Monday	Tuesday	Wednesday	Thursday	Friday
Daily Goal:	20	20	20	25	25
Accuracy Goal:	18	19	20	20	22
Number Completed	16	19			
Number Correct	16	19			
Teacher Comment	Good work; try working faster	Super job!			

Figure 9.2   Sample Goal-Setting Sheet

Teachers can combine aspects of goal setting with self-efficacy and have students predict the amount of time they will work successfully. Self-monitoring charts can be developed to monitor progress toward goal attainment. For example, have students complete the statement goal, such as, "I will work hard by trying my best and not getting out of my seat for 5-minute segments. When the bell rings, if I have been working hard, I can place a checkmark in the YES column. If I have not been working hard when the bell rings, I will place a checkmark in the NO column."

Encourage Parent/Family Involvement   Parents are usually the primary advocates for their children and can be an invaluable source for promoting self-efficacy and supporting the continued efforts of students. This is particularly true for students with special needs. Communicate frequently with parents to share your expectations for the student and ask for parents' help in meeting these goals. Parents often will agree to participate in a reinforcement system, through which the student is rewarded at home for positive effort made during school. Parents can also be a positive source of support in reaffirming the value of school learning.

TRAIN STUDENTS TO USE POSITIVE ATTRIBUTIONS   **Attribution training** is another important strategy teachers can use to increase motivation and positive affect, and raise self-esteem. With this technique, students are taught to attribute success to their own efforts and academic strategies and to attribute failure to their lack of effort or failure to use appropriate strategies. Students who learn to attribute success and failure to things they control are more likely to try hard and succeed in the future than those who do not (Berkeley, Mastropieri, & Scruggs, 2007).

Attributions that correctly attribute success or failure to student behavior—things a student does or could do—are called positive attributions. Negative attributions, on the other hand, attribute success or failure to such things as inherent ability or teacher prejudices. Examples of positive and negative attributions are given in Table 9.2.

All students should be made aware that blaming their failures on others or on their own personal traits is not acceptable. When students fail, they should be reminded of choices they made themselves that contributed to that failure. When students are successful, they should be reminded of the positive things they did that brought on that success (Fulk & Montgomery-Grimes, 1994).

As a teacher, you should be alert to the development of negative attributions, particularly for students with special needs. To counter these kinds of attributions, first make certain that all assignments are within the ability of the student. Then simply do not accept negative statements such as "I'm stupid" or "I'm handicapped." These declarations should not be allowed to justify failure. You can reply to such attributions with statements such as, "No, the reason you

---

Table 9.2   Student Attributions for Success or Failure

Positive Attributions	Negative Attributions
Success	**Success**
"I succeeded on the spelling test because I used the spelling strategy I learned."	"I succeeded on the spelling test because I got lucky."
"I got an 'A' on my science project because I started early and used my time effectively."	"I got an 'A' on my science project because my teacher likes me."
Failure	**Failure**
"I failed the math test because I put off studying until the last minute, and then I fell asleep. Next time I'll start earlier."	"I failed the math test because I'm stupid at math."
"I didn't do as well as I could have on the test because I didn't study for an essay test. Next time I'll practice writing essay answers when I study."	"I didn't do well on the test because the teacher doesn't grade fairly."

failed is that you gave up too soon," or "No, the reason you failed is that you didn't use the strategies you practiced for that test."

Students with disabilities, perhaps more than other students, need to be reminded of the important role of personal commitment and effort. Reinforcing positive efforts students make can be voiced by saying something like, "That was difficult, but you worked hard and finished it anyway!"

The combination of attribution and strategy training (i.e., training in a specific academic strategy, such as a summarization strategy for reading comprehension) is a powerful tool for success. For example, Borkowski, Weyhing, and Carr (1988) taught students with learning disabilities to use specific summarization strategies and specific attribution strategies. Some of the important attribution statements were, "I need to try to use the [e.g., summarization strategy]," while actually using the strategy. In addition, students were shown a cartoon character saying, "I tried hard, used the strategy, and did well," to emphasize the role of effort (p. 49).

Although students with disabilities often do not exhibit positive attributions, it would be a mistake to assume that all students with disabilities have problems in these areas (Mamlin, Harris, & Case, 2001). Before initiating attribution training, be certain that students have a specific need for such training. Nevertheless, it may always be useful in classroom instruction to remind students of the relationship between effort or strategy use and academic success.

ARRANGE COUNSELING INTERVENTIONS WHEN NEEDED Counseling interventions have been designed to address self-esteem and other affective problems of students and may involve a number of techniques (Thurneck, Warner, & Cobb, 2007). School counselors frequently work with students with disabilities, using individual and group counseling (e.g., Mishna, 1996), by providing feedback for multidisciplinary teams, self-esteem activities, and social skills training. Counselors also often report that advocacy and problem solving for students with disabilities are important features of their work (Dunn & Baker, 2002; Milsom, 2002), and they may assist students with disabilities in transitioning to college (Milsom & Hartley, 2005). Research on counseling interventions for students with disabilities have yielded positive findings on measures of increased relaxation, decreased school truancy, increased self-esteem, and general well-being. Positive benefits were reported after relatively short interventions consisting of weekly sessions for 6 to 10 weeks (Omizo & Omizo, 1987; Mastropieri, Scruggs, & Butcher, 1997). Such information indicates that after a relatively small number of group counseling sessions, some students with difficulties may experience positive benefits in social-emotional functioning. Although the training and activities of counselors may vary from school to school (Milsom & Akos, 2003), counselors should be considered potentially important participants in the lives of students with disabilities, and should be consulted as appropriate in individual situations.

Exercise Care When Handling Serious Affective Disorders Some disorders of affect are very serious and may not be substantially improved with the application of the strategies described in this chapter. If you encounter students with serious affective problems, obtain outside professional assistance and contact the parents. Special education teachers, counselors, or school psychologists may help or refer you to other professionals if you have a student who appears to exhibit signs of severe depression, anxiety, or suicidal behavior.

INCREASE STUDENTS' PERSONAL INVESTMENT IN THE CLASSROOM Students who believe they have some ownership in what is happening in your classroom are also more likely to make an effort to help the classroom be successful. If they have had some input in classroom decision making, students are also more likely to identify positively with classroom activities. Conversely, students who think they have no influence in how classroom business is conducted are more likely to lose motivation and interest. In some extreme cases, such perceived disenfranchisement can lead to more serious antisocial acts.

Share Decision Making for Classroom Procedures Students may feel more involved with the classroom if they play some role in the decisions that affect how the classroom functions. For example, we have observed teachers who allow students to decide what the seating arrangement of the class would be even when this arrangement was different from traditional seating arrangements

Getting students involved in decision making can allow students to see their role in carrying out fair and acceptable classroom procedures.

(Scruggs & Mastropieri, 1994). If modifications were necessary, as in improving access for students with physical disabilities, students were understanding when the situation was explained to them.

Students can also be involved in decisions such as the sequence in which daily lessons are presented. For example, elementary students may have opinions about what activities they would like to do first thing in the morning, or immediately after recess periods. You also can solicit students' input in developing academic grading standards and rules for classroom behavior. Of course, as the teacher, you would have the final word on standards, but students will appreciate the opportunity to provide input. Provided that at least some of the student input is acceptable to you, standards can be said to be collective decisions, rather than edicts imposed by you on your students. Where differences of opinion between you and your students exist, identify the differences and the reasons you have to enact different standards or choose not to enact certain standards students put forth. Such actions demonstrate to students that their ideas are important, even if they are not always implemented.

Solicit Student Feedback Finally, you may wish to provide students an opportunity to give input anonymously. One way of doing this is by providing a survey of student opinions about things they think are fair or unfair in your class. Students might feel more comfortable providing information about their opinions and attitudes on a questionnaire. Sometimes, teachers are surprised to discover that policies they thought were popular are in fact unpopular with students. Other teachers have a suggestion box in which students can place anonymous comments and feedback. These techniques may also uncover information that students would not volunteer for fear of being accused of "tattling." If you are able to modify the way you manage the classroom in response to student opinion, students are likely to appreciate the consideration they receive. In addition, they are more likely to feel that they are an important part of the classroom.

When soliciting student feedback, be certain to consider minority opinion. Some rules may affect different students in different ways. For example, a cooperative learning feature may not be positively received by some students with special needs, because they may think they are not being treated fairly or respectfully by other students when you are unavailable to supervise the group. You could use this feedback to find better ways to teach students how to behave in groups and better ways to monitor student interactions. Use all survey feedback to enhance learning for all students and to make students feel important as classroom decision makers.

MAKE LEARNING MORE FUN AND ENJOYABLE Techniques that increase self-esteem and self-efficacy encourage positive attributions, and sharing classroom decision making should indicate to students that effective learning requires effort and persistence (Brophy, 2004). However, the classroom should not focus solely on work; teachers should do what they can to make learning experiences as fun and enjoyable as possible. Motivation and positive affect will improve when students have more than a day of drudgery to look forward to each morning. The classroom can be made much more enjoyable if students catch the enthusiasm of teachers and the interest level of tasks is heightened.

Computers can also contribute to a motivating and enjoyable atmosphere. For suggestions, see the *Technology Highlight* feature.

Make Tasks More Interesting A number of strategies are at your disposal to utilize to make learning more interesting and fun (Mastropieri, Scruggs, & Ciccerelli, 2007), such as the following.

PEARSON
myeducationlab

Go to MyEducationLab, select the topic *Content Area Teaching*, and go to the Activities and Applications section. As you watch the two videos entitled "Middle School Science: Think-Pair-Share" and "Middle School Science: Response Cards" (in the Science subsection), reflect on the different ways this teacher engages her students.

Motivation, Affect, and Learning Disabilities

Students with learning disabilities are known to exhibit difficulties in one or more areas of academic achievement. However, these students also have been seen to exhibit difficulties in motivational, metacognitive, and affective profiles. Sideridis, Morgan, Botsas, Padeliadu, and Fuchs (2006) examined the extent to which motivation, metacognition, and psychopathology served to predict learning disabilities. Measures of motivation (e.g., goal orientation, self-efficacy, motivational force), metacognition (including surface and deep processing strategies), and psychopathology (including depression and anxiety) were employed to determine their relation to learning

disabilities. In five studies, 1,022 typical students and 204 students with learning disabilities, at risk for learning disabilities, or low readers, from Greece and the United States, were administered measures of motivation, metacognition, and psychopathology. These variables were examined statistically across different characterizations of learning disabilities, using different configurations of the measures, across the five studies. Results indicated that motivation, metacognition, and depression/anxiety were all found to be strongly associated with learning disabilities, classifying students accurately between 77% and 96% of the time. These findings suggest that teachers should consider motivational,

metacognitive, and affective variables when planning instruction for students with learning disabilities, and incorporate these considerations in academic instruction.

QUESTIONS FOR REFLECTION

1. Why are students with learning disabilities so likely to exhibit low motivation, metacognition, and anxiety/depression?

2. In most cases, are learning disabilities caused by low motivation, or are they the result of low motivation?

3. What are some strategies for including motivational, metacognitive, and affective considerations in instruction of students with learning disabilities?

---

1. *Prepare more concrete, meaningful lessons.* Students are more motivated to learn information that is concrete and personally meaningful. Include as many examples as possible of how the concepts being learned are relevant to the students' personal lives. For example, when presenting information on the branches of government, you can discuss executive, legislative, and judicial actions that are undertaken in school, on the athletic field, and in the home, and the reasons these actions are necessary. For secondary students, if the level of concepts goes beyond what they encounter in daily life, provide examples of how the skills being taught can be used in their jobs, careers, or independent living.

Concreteness and meaningfulness can also be enhanced by classroom exhibits and demonstrations. Hands-on science curriculum materials provide students concrete experiences to help them better form science conceptions. Hands-on activities illustrate the nature of science more easily than written words only. Such materials are particularly helpful for students with special needs, because they lessen the need to study abstractions from the text. If science curriculum materials are not available, consider bringing interesting classroom demonstrations to class. For example, one teacher greatly increased classroom excitement by bringing her pet iguana to class!

Illustrations can bring concreteness and greater meaning for some students who are visually oriented. The construction of murals, posters, bulletin boards, or three-dimensional projects all can promote learning. Creating portfolios of students' work, rather than consistently relying on paper-and-pencil tests, also can make the content more meaningful for learners.

2. *Create cognitive conflict.* Interest in learning can be aroused by discussion or demonstration of situations that promote **cognitive conflict**, situations that are not easily predictable or explainable at first. The presentation of discrepant events can create cognitive conflict in students. A discrepant event is an event (often in science) whereby things behave differently than expected (Gable, 2003). Some examples of discrepant events include "dancing" raisins, where raisins appear to move up and down independently in a soft drink. Further observation and deduction reveals that the raisins raise and lower because of the carbon dioxide in the soft drink.

Advancing Technologies Are Motivating!

Advancing technologies are especially motivating tools for students with disabilities. Classrooms containing computers with or without Internet access can be used as motivation and rewards (although Internet access is ideal, many of the technological advances can be used without accessing the Internet). Skills requiring drill and practice are more motivating when completed using game-like activities on computers. Students will have more ownership of their learning during instruction when they are encouraged to use computers to find answers to questions that arise in the classroom.

Encourage students to find answers using electronic multimedia encyclopedias available on CD-ROM. Entries may not only have photographs and illustrations, but also interactive media with video and audio components that add to the excitement of finding answers to

classroom discussions. Many encyclopedia programs are relatively inexpensive, including *World Book*, *Britannica*, and *Encarta*, and many encyclopedia programs can now be accessed online.

Online access broadens the amount of information available and includes the use of the various Internet search engines such as Yahoo! and Google and others directed more specifically to your students' age group. Surfing using these search engines opens the world to students. Technology enables students to access more information in less time than ever before. Some Websites encourage students to submit homework questions! Educationally relevant podcasts can be downloaded and used to supplement textbook content. The Website http://schoolcomputing.wikia.com/wiki/Podcasts provides information on how to use and develop podcasts in schools. Students can produce their own podcasts that contain summaries

of what they have learned and then share those summaries with peers. For example, Willowdale Elementary School in Omaha, Nebraska, has a Website containing radio podcasts developed by students (http://www.mpsomaha.org/willow/radio/). Schools could create daily podcasts of future school events to help increase home–school communication.

Arrange pen pals via e-mail for your students to share their school experiences with other students from across the country and the world. Websites exist that help arrange pen pals and contain bulletin boards for student resources as well as resources for teachers.

Encourage students to search and find answers to their questions! Allowing these activities demonstrates that students have active roles in their own learning and will help to increase their ownership in their learning and serve to help motivate them to continue to succeed in school.

Another example is an electric repulsion coil, which dramatically repels, rather than attracts, objects (be sure to ask for assistance and take appropriate safety measures for novel science demonstrations). Discrepant events enhance curiosity and interest and increase motivation to learn (Wright & Govindarajan, 1995).

Additional activities presented in other subject areas can have the same effect. Discussion of equivocal moral or political issues—such as whether carrying concealed weapons should be prohibited, or the idea that overpopulation of protected Canadian geese in a community might ultimately lead to their extermination—may raise students' level of interest as it raises their concern about issues. The more personally relevant the issues are, the more involved students are apt to become.

Before beginning any cognitive conflict activities, students need to be reassured that any guesses they make to explain discrepant events or opinions they may have on moral or social issues will be accepted with tolerance and respect. If you establish a safe risk-taking environment within the class, more students will be encouraged to participate.

3. Use novel ways to engage students. Sometimes students begin to lose motivation simply because instruction has become stale and predictable. In this case, interest may be restored by incorporating novel ways of doing things. Changing the order of classroom routines, reallocating classroom responsibilities, and rearranging classroom seating are all ways to increase novelty.

You also can provide variety in the way instruction is delivered. Here are some suggestions:

- Use different media, such as tape recordings, songs, videos, and newspaper articles.

- Invite guest speakers known to be knowledgeable or "expert" on a specific topic.

- Direct students to prepare their own presentations on topics, either individually or in small groups.

- Use computer applications to allow students to review or practice, using tutorial or simulation activities that reinforce content.

- Pose questions such as, "Does gum weigh more or less after chewing? How could we find out?"

- Modify the way you ask for assignments to be done, creatively alter homework routines, and alternate the use of group and individual assignments when appropriate.

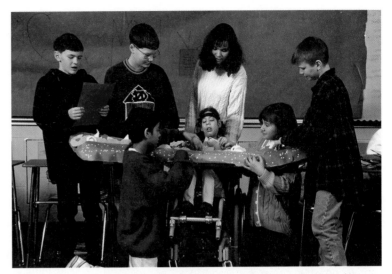

Challenging students cognitively or engaging them in novel activities can create a motivating classroom environment.

Although novelty alone may not consistently improve motivation and affect, it can be useful when combined with other techniques described in this chapter.

One concern should be mentioned with the use of novelty in classrooms that include students from some disability areas. Some students with autism, or some forms of intellectual disabilities or other disabilities, may find it very difficult to deviate from established classroom routines. Sometimes, simply being included in a "regular" classroom may constitute as much novelty as some students can easily accommodate. If students who prefer "sameness" in their environments are placed in your inclusive class, school psychologists and special educators can provide specific information for dealing with novelty situations.

4. *Develop competitive and gamelike activities.* Competition that pits students against one another, and for which students may not perceive an equal chance of winning, may be detrimental to a motivating classroom; such competition is more characteristic of ego-oriented classrooms. However, when students believe they have a fair chance of winning, and when the same small group of students does not always win, competition and gamelike activities can provide a high degree of motivation and interest in the class.

The following is an example of small-group competition in a practice activity: First, divide students randomly into several small groups. Then direct one individual student from each group to take turns answering questions about the topic being studied. Allow the selected students to accept suggestions from other students in their group but let them know that they must decide on the answer individually. When an answer is correct, the group receives a point. At the end of the activity, the group with the most points is the "winner." In some cases the winning group may be given a reward or privileges of some kind, but students may find it sufficiently rewarding simply to be on the winning team. Each time the game is played, assign students to different groups.

Students with special needs can be easily included in activities such as the one described, because they are able to contribute fully to the activity. This cooperative aspect makes such activities more fair and increases chances of success for students with disabilities.

5. *Make use of cooperative learning.* Cooperative learning strategies can also be used to enhance student interest, affect, and motivation (see Chapter 8). Students often enjoy working together on projects, and these opportunities may make learning more enjoyable for them. Group projects, group participation in science activities, group studying, guided-practice activities, and group competition in gamelike activities described in the previous section are helpful in enhancing student interest. However, monitor group activity carefully to ensure that all students are

Your enthusiasm in teaching a lesson will be contagious.

being treated fairly and that all students are participating equally and learning adequately from the activities (McMaster & Fuchs, 2002).

6. *Don't overdo motivational attempts.* As in many other areas of promoting student motivation and positive affect, teachers can appear to be trying too hard to make activities interesting and enjoyable. If students see such efforts as contrived and artificial, your efforts may fail. Ongoing feedback from students, surveys of student interest in different activities, and direct questioning and prompting when needed can provide important information on whether teacher attempts to make the class more interesting are actually succeeding.

7. *Be enthusiastic!* As described in Chapter 6, enthusiasm is one of the teacher presentation variables that helps to develop student interest and make learning more fun. Enthusiastic teachers enhance motivation by modeling interest in the subject being learned and the amount of enjoyment that can be attained when learning occurs. Enthusiastic teachers also are more interesting presenters, so students are more likely to pay attention to what is being presented.

Teaching with enthusiasm involves the use of several techniques, described by researchers (Bettencourt, Gillett, Gall, & Hull, 1983; Brigham, Scruggs, & Mastropieri, 1992; Patrick, Hisley, & Kempler, 2000) and listed in the following *In the Classroom* feature. These techniques demonstrate that enthusiasm is something that teachers *do,* not something that teachers *are.* It is clear that teachers can change the amount of enthusiasm they display and improve student motivation and affect when they do so.

Enthusiasm is an attribute that you can vary within your own teaching (Brigham et al., 1992). And although it may make you a little self-conscious at first, you can practice being enthusiastic simply by raising and lowering the intonation of your voice and by using your hands and arms when you talk to students to explain or elaborate on a point. Statements made enthusiastically can gain students' attention. For example, one fourth-grade teacher used the following statement to gain attention and to control transitions within her classroom during an ecosystems science activity: "Class, when I say 'Ecosystems are a blast,' everyone go to your science groups!"

Enthusiastic teaching also involves open acceptance of student contributions. This is of critical importance for students with special needs, who may believe their contributions are not welcome. In the case of disabilities such as communication disorders or hearing impairments, it may take longer for students to communicate ideas to the class. In other cases, the ideas, answers, or suggestions may seem less sophisticated than those of some other students. In these instances, it is particularly important for teachers to demonstrate enthusiastically that ideas and input from all students are welcome. One fourth-grade teacher noted:

> I have a difficult time saying any of my "kids" have behavior problems. I view each child in my class as a challenge and rarely do they have problems I can't "get at" through my teaching approach. My main focus at *all* times is to be upbeat, fast-paced, and in a great mood!! This alleviates many "problems." (Mastropieri, Scruggs, & Bohs, 1994, p. 142)

Can enthusiasm be overdone? Possibly. But one essential element of enthusiasm is that it must be (or appear to be) sincere. If students regard teachers' enthusiasm as genuine, they will probably welcome and appreciate very high levels of enthusiasm. On the other hand, if the enthusiasm seems forced or insincere, students will be less likely to appreciate it. Overall, however, our experiences (and research evidence) have convinced us that teacher enthusiasm promotes motivation and positive affect, and that enthusiasm is often underused but rarely overused.

PRAISE STUDENTS AND REWARD THEIR EFFORTS Praise and concrete rewards are often the first things people think of when considering ways to increase motivation and affect. Naturally, most people (including teachers!) feel more valued and more motivated when they are praised and positively rewarded for their achievements.

Go to MyEducationLab, select the topic *Classroom Behavior/Management,* and go to the Activities and Applications section. As you read and analyze the case study entitled "Encouraging Appropriate Behavior," focus on the strategies for specific praise and incorporating criterion-specific rewards.

Teacher Enthusiasm Variables

- *Rapid speaking rate, varied inflection, uplifting vocal delivery.* This prevents teacher dialogue from sounding redundant, monotonous, or boring.

- *Animated, wide-open eyes.* Animated eyes model a state of alertness and interest in the classroom activity.

- *Physical gestures that emphasize what is being said.* Teachers can help emphasize the interest level and importance of what is being covered with demonstrative physical gestures.

- *Dramatic and varied body movements.* Dramatic body movements attract student visual attention, which in turn can lead to more positive attending.

- *Facial expressions that are animated and emotive.* Facial expressiveness conveys positive attitude toward and interest in the subject.

- *A varied choice of words.* Variation in language usage prevents dialogue from sounding boring and predictable.

- *Active and open acceptance of ideas or suggestions made by students.* Open acceptance of student ideas, input, and thinking conveys that teachers are secure with their own knowledge and anxious to hear other ideas.

- *General demonstration of a high energy level.* This variable suggests that enthusiasm is not simply the sum of several individual components. Enthusiasm is conveyed through the entirety of teachers' overall manner.

Note: From "Effects of Teacher Enthusiasm Training on Student On-task Behavior and Achievement," by E. M. Bettencourt, M. H. Gillett, M. D. Gall, & R. E. Hull, 1983, in *American Educational Research Journal*, *20*, pp. 435–450. Copyright 1983 by American Educational Research Journal. Adapted with permission.

In the CLASSROOM

Praise Student Effort The effective use of praise is of paramount importance to enhancing motivation and affect, and, appropriately employed, closely conforms to the idea of a task-oriented classroom. Praise is highly motivating to students because it provides encouraging feedback for student efforts and demonstrates that their work is being appreciated.

Jere Brophy (1981, 2004) has investigated the appropriate uses of teacher praise, based upon research evidence. A summary of his conclusions is presented in Figure 9.3. Henderlong and Lepper (2002) reviewed more recent research literature, and generally supported Brophy's conclusions while pointing out some areas where praise is not effective. Overall, praise that is vague or that describes general traits of students has not been successful in promoting motivation and positive affect. This includes praise that conveys to students that they have some "trait" that the teacher considers valuable (e.g., "You are very bright."). Praise such as this—comments that give students the message that they are praiseworthy without making any particular effort—usually does not motivate students.

Conversely, effective praise is given contingent upon truly meritorious work, positive student efforts to meet specific criteria, and tangible improvement from previous work. This kind of praise clearly links accomplishment with effort, and suggests strongly that similar efforts in the future also will be praiseworthy. In this way, students receive the message that hard work, effective study strategies, and persistence of effort—variables under student control—are truly valuable. The most effective praise, then, is contingent, specific, and sincere—criteria not always met in the classroom (Henderlong & Lepper, 2002).

Explanations for giving praise can be combined with praise statements. For example, "That's great! I like how neat your work is!" combines a praise statement with the action that deserves the praise. This combination of statements informs students why they are being praised, and works well with students with and without disabilities. It might be particularly important to point out to students with disabilities the reason that praise is being given. Students usually enjoy being praised and will often work harder to obtain more praise from

- Praise should be used to reinforce **specific student behaviors.** It should specify exactly what the student did to warrant praise. It should not be random or vague (e.g., "You are a good student.").
- Praise should sound **sincere and genuine.** It should not sound unconvincing or mechanical.
- Praise should **specify the criteria** being met (e.g., "You had no spelling errors") and **relate the achievement to previous work** (e.g., "This is one of your best papers yet!").
- Praise should be delivered when the student has made a **noteworthy effort** (that is, noteworthy for that student; e.g., "You really worked hard to complete this assignment so well!"). It should not be given for indifferent or routine efforts.
- Praise should indicate the **relation between student effort and achievement** (e.g., "You worked really hard to earn this grade!"). It should not suggest that the student was "lucky" or the task was easy.
- Praise should **promote personal satisfaction** on the part of the student (e.g., "You should be very proud of the job you did on this!"). It should imply that the student enjoyed accomplishing the task, or that the student wanted to accomplish the outcome that was praised.
- Praise should suggest that **similar efforts will be met with success in the future** (e.g., "If you keep working this well, you will get an A on all your assignments!").

Figure 9.3 Effective Uses of Praise

Note: From "Teacher Praise: A Functional Analysis," by J. Brophy, 1981, in *Review of Educational Research, 51,* pp. 5–32. Copyright 1981 by American Educational Research Journal. Adapted with permission. See also Henderlong and Lepper (2002).

teachers. Although praise works well with all grade levels of students, consider the appropriateness of particular statements selected for targeted grade levels. Table 9.3 presents sample praise statements with corresponding explanations for both elementary- and secondary-level students.

Students at all age and grade levels desire praise from their teachers, and many statements can be used successfully with all age levels. Remember to vary the praise statements. For example, when one phrase or word is used repeatedly (e.g., "Good"), it may lose its effect. The *In the Classroom* feature provides some adjectives that can be used for praising students, and corresponding behaviors that can be combined with them to create many alternatives to "Good!"

Students usually enjoy public praise. Comments that praise students' persistence of effort can be publicly announced or posted on a banner or sign in the classroom. Some schools have

Table 9.3 Praise Statements and Explanations for Praise

Elementary-Level Examples	Secondary-Level Examples
• That's wonderful! You showed me how to write your name! • Super! I can tell you are trying your very best! • I like the way you are working! • Exactly right! You completed all the problems! • Good job! You seem to understand how to answer those questions. • Great work! I like the way you tried to read all the words! • Super duper! You showed me that you can proof your paper! • Great! You did a nice job in math class today! • I'm proud of you! You completed all of the writing assignment!	• That's a great observation! You understand how a pendulum works! • Terrific paper! Your writing has really improved. • Keep up the hard work! Your compositions are really improving! • Good work—I know you worked very hard to complete the project! • Great sentences! Will you share your paper with the class? • Nice going! Can you repeat the phrase in Spanish again? • That's definitely A+ work! I liked the way you drew an illustration to explain your answer! • Much better! Your history test grade is improved!

Note: In reality, many statements could be used with either elementary or secondary students.

weekly assemblies during which "Student of the Day," "Student of the Week," or "Class of the Week" awards are distributed in front of the entire student body. This action rewards individuals publicly and promotes the idea that the school is appreciative of motivation and effort.

Good work, effort, and behavior can also be praised by sending positive notes home regularly. This communication with parents helps maintain a good relationship between school and home. Notes can be designed for elementary, middle, or secondary school levels and for any subject area.

USE REWARDS TO REINFORCE STUDENT SUCCESS In previous decades, when behavioral models of teaching were more widespread, motivation was sometimes referred to as little more than the strength of the reinforcer being used (e.g., Martin & Pear, 1978). We chose to include a discussion of rewards later, rather than earlier, in this chapter because we wanted to emphasize the idea that enhancing motivation and positive affect can involve much more than simply providing rewards for desired behavior. Nevertheless, we do not wish to understate the powerful effects of rewards in promoting learning and positive social behavior.

Avoid the Overjustification Effect Some researchers have suggested that rewards—as extrinsic, or external, motivation—can undermine intrinsic motivation, the internal desire to achieve. Lepper and Hodell (1989) cited research suggesting that (1) when interest in the activity is already high, and (2) when the reward is so tangible that it can be considered a "bribe," rewarded students can feel less satisfied with their performance and less likely to undertake the same activity than students who do not receive rewards. This outcome is referred to as the **overjustification effect**. Therefore, if you have applied strategies described previously in this chapter, and find that students are already very interested in the activity, it may be prudent to avoid direct, tangible rewards. In these cases, however, praise for positive effort and task completion may still be appropriate.

Distinguish Between Rewards and "Bribes" Rewards may often be condemned as "bribes," and irresponsible use of rewards may indeed have such an effect. However, since you as a teacher expect to be rewarded by receiving your paycheck, it does not seem surprising that often students also work toward rewards! In our pragmatic view, rewards should be considered as a potent tool when used under the right conditions. Another consideration in the rewards-versus-bribes argument was voiced by a special education professional in Indiana, who said, "Bribes, to me, are payments made for illegal actions, and I never do this with students. I reward my students for honest, hard work."

Set up Conditions for Rewards   For some less interesting tasks, such as memorizing spelling words or mathematical formulae, rewards can provide students with reasons to persevere on tasks that will be helpful to them at a later date. Because the learning of many basic skills areas, such as spelling, fall into this category, and students with disabilities typically exhibit difficulties mastering basic skills, rewards may play an important role in inclusive settings. It should also be noted that reinforcement frequently has been demonstrated to be effective with students with special needs (Maag, 2001).

Set up Performance Criteria   Rewards should be given in response to previously stated performance criteria. Rewards should reflect perseverance and hard work, and generally all students should have an equal opportunity to receive rewards. The relation between the reward and the behaviors that led to the reward should be made clear. Also note that if the effort exhibited is praiseworthy, future efforts could result in further rewards.

Develop Appropriate Performance Criteria for Students with Special Needs
Several techniques help low-achieving students to perceive an equal opportunity for rewards. One way is to set performance standards that reflect improvement over previous efforts, rather than standards that compare students with other students. Rewards can be provided for aspects of tasks at which all students have an opportunity to succeed. For example, in small reading groups, individual students could be directed at random intervals to begin reading (e.g., using a spinner). Students could be awarded one point for knowing where to begin reading when they are called on. Such a system rewards paying close attention to the reading task, something at which all students have a reasonable chance of succeeding.

Use Tangible and Intangible Rewards   Tangible rewards include prizes (such as stickers, pencils, erasers, decals, or bookmarks) or consumables (such as crackers, cookies, or juice). In a "token system," tokens such as chips, stars, or checkmarks in a book are awarded for specific positive academic or social behaviors. Specific numbers of these tokens are later exchanged for desirable rewards or classroom privileges.

Intangible rewards can also promote motivation and positive affect. Besides teacher praise, which has been described, you can reward students by publicly posting their name as, for example, "Student of the Week." You may also try providing desired free-time activities, such as a favorite game—or privileges, such as the right to be out of seat without permission. Intangible rewards are less costly and appear less like bribes. The following *In the Classroom* feature provides possible tangible and intangible rewards for a token system.

You can also provide group rewards to promote positive social and academic performance of the entire class. If, for example, the class is completing an activity in small groups (and the groups are equally constituted), a group reward such as a desired activity can be awarded to the first group that finishes or to the group that provides the best product. Alternatively, the reward could be presented to the class as a whole, if the class meets a specific standard over a period of time. For example, provide bonus free time to the class if all assignments are turned in on time for that week. Such rewards allow students to help or encourage other students to meet class criteria. However, they may also encourage group sanction of individual students whose behavior may have cost rewards for the entire class, so monitor the consequences carefully.

At several times throughout the school year, survey students to determine their preferences for rewards. Their responses can be used in developing any possible reward systems.

Justify Fairness When Necessary   The final consideration for rewards is that some students with disabilities may have a greater need for reinforcement than other students do, to ensure continued persistence of effort. Although it may be necessary for some students to receive rewards to exhibit the same efforts that other students give without rewards, it is sometimes difficult to explain this to the class. If one student is rewarded for working hard on a particular

A Token System

Tokens are received by:
1. Being in seat and prepared for class when the bell rings (1 token).
2. Turning in class assignments on time (1 token).
3. Improving over previous quiz (1 token).
4. Working hard on class activities, decided by teacher (1 token).

Tokens can be redeemed for:
1. Pencils (5 tokens).
2. Stickers (10 tokens).
3. Free time (20 tokens).
4. Release from one homework assignment (20 tokens).
5. Eat lunch with teacher (25 tokens).
6. Caretaker of class pets for a week (30 tokens).

task, should not all other students who work hard be similarly rewarded? Not always. One possibility in such cases (as appropriate) is to provide rewards discreetly, such as after class or during visits with the special education teacher. Another possibility is simply to explain the situation to the class in a business-like fashion and make little ceremony about it. Another possibility is to reward all students in some fashion for continued efforts on tasks, but to award more substantial rewards to students who seem to require this, and to offer more intangible rewards to others.

One final possibility is to explain to the class how "fairness" in life may mean different things for different individuals. The excellent illustration by Richard Lavoie in the videotape *How Difficult Can This Be: The F.A.T. (Frustration, Anxiety, Tension) City Workshop* (Lavoie, 1996) could be shown to the class as an example. In the videotape, Lavoie explains how, if a member of the class had a heart attack and needed CPR, it would be absurd to say, "I cannot give [student's name] CPR, because if I did I would have to give CPR to everybody!" The belief that *fairness* means *sameness for everyone* is disputed. *Fairness* is then described as meaning that each individual receives what he or she needs, and not that each individual receives the same (see also Lavoie, 2007).

9 Summary

- Motivation and affect are extremely important variables that can make the difference between success and failure in the classroom. Many students with special needs may benefit particularly from strategies to enhance motivation and affect.

- Before implementing specific strategies to enhance motivation and affect, ensure that the necessary preconditions have been met. These preconditions include creating a supportive, well-organized classroom environment; assigning tasks that

are meaningful, concrete, relevant, and of the appropriate difficulty level; and creating task-oriented, rather than ego-oriented, classes.

- Motivation and affect can be improved by engaging in practices to improve students' self-esteem, such as providing positive statements, assigning classroom responsibilities, and use of classroom peers.

- Self-efficacy is an important determiner of positive motivation and affect. Students succeed, and believe they will be successful, when provided with additional practice, advance organizers, appropriate social models, and positive support.

- Students' motivation and affect improve when they participate in setting goals for themselves and assist in monitoring their progress toward meeting these goals.

- Students feel more in control when they learn to attribute their classroom successes or failures to their own behaviors, such as appropriate effort, attitude, or use of academic/behavioral strategies.

- Students feel more ownership in the classroom when they participate in decision making involving classroom rules and procedures.

- Students are more motivated to learn when learning is fun and interesting. Use a variety of approaches, media, gamelike activities, and peer interactions to prevent classroom learning from becoming monotonous and routine. Express personal enthusiasm in the subjects being covered, and teach with enthusiasm!

- Students are motivated to learn when their accomplishments are acknowledged and rewarded. Use positive feedback and praise frequently to demonstrate your positive regard for students' accomplishments. Use rewards, in the form of prizes, privileges, or tokens, when needed to acknowledge achievement and maintain persistence of effort.

PROFESSIONAL STANDARDS LINK:
Enhancing Motivation and Affect

Information in this chapter links most directly to:

- CEC Standards: 2 (Development and Characteristics of Learners), 3 (Individual Learning Differences), 4 (Instructional Strategies), 10 (Collaboration)

- INTASC Standards: Principles 3 (understands learning differences, adapts instructional opportunities), 4 (instructional strategies), 5 (creates learning environments), 6 (fosters inquiry, collaboration, interaction)

- PRAXIS II™ Content Categories (Knowledge): 3 (Delivery of Services)

- PRAXIS II™ Content Categories (Application): 2 (Instruction)

ENHANCING MOTIVATION AND AFFECT

If you are having problems with student motivation or affect, have you considered the following? If not, see the pages listed below.

STRATEGIES FOR ADDRESSING PRECONDITIONS FOR POSITIVE MOTIVATION AND AFFECT

☐ Create a supportive, organized classroom environment, 200–202
☐ Ensure materials are of an appropriate difficulty level, 202
☐ Ensure that tasks are meaningful, 203–204
☐ Create task-oriented, not ego-oriented, classrooms, 204

STRATEGIES FOR IMPROVING MOTIVATION AND AFFECT

☐ Raise students' self-esteem, 205
☐ Promote self-efficacy, 205–207
☐ Teach students to set goals, 207–208
☐ Train students to use positive attributions, 208–209
☐ Arrange counseling interventions when needed, 209
☐ Increase students' personal investment in the classroom, 209–210
☐ Make learning more fun and enjoyable, 210–214
☐ Praise students and reward their efforts, 214–217
☐ Use rewards to reinforce student success, 217–219

Clock and Pendulum

M WOODNOTT Mary Woodnott has inflammatory arthritis, fibromyalgia, and chronic fatigue syndrome. Although she cannot carry a lot of kit around due to her disabilities and often relies on help with her equipment, she still gets out on her "good days" to take photographs with a fresh perspective.

10

Improving Attention and Memory

OBJECTIVES

After studying this chapter, you should be able to:

- Understand the importance of attention and memory for the school success of students with special needs.
- Describe preconditions for improving attention in the classroom.
- Design and implement strategies for improving attention.
- Describe extreme cases of attention deficits and the effects of stimulant medications.
- Describe preconditions for improving memory for students with special needs.
- Design and implement strategies to enhance memory.
- Describe, create, and apply mnemonic strategies (keyword, pegword, and letter strategies) to improve and enhance memory.

Attention and memory are two fundamental psychological processes necessary for learning to occur. It is easy to understand that instruction, however well presented, is of little value if it is not remembered. Conversely, it is possible to remember only those things to which we have paid attention in the first place!

In this chapter, we describe the problems students may have with attention and memory, and describe a number of strategies you can use to improve the attention and memory of your students. Given the significance of these important psychological processes to classroom learning, it is likely that careful application of the principles and strategies described in this chapter can make an important difference in the school success of all students, including those with special needs.

Attention

ATTENTION AND STUDENTS WITH SPECIAL NEEDS

All students exhibit occasional lapses in attention, either because of a lack of interest in a subject, boredom, fatigue, or from being distracted by temporary anxieties or concerns. However, many students with special needs exhibit difficulties with attention. For example, poor attention and concentration are commonly reported characteristics of students with learning disabilities (Lerner & Kline, 2006). Students with intellectual disabilities may fail to sustain attention in class, and may exhibit difficulties attending to the appropriate stimulus in a lesson, such as focusing on the shape or color of the hands of a clock rather than the position

Teaching effectively requires maintaining students' attention.

of the hands in a lesson on telling time (Beirne-Smith, Patton, & Kim, 2006).

Some students with physical or sensory impairments also have difficulty sustaining attention when attending to particular tasks that interact with disability areas. For example, some students with cerebral palsy have difficulty keeping their heads aligned and eyes focused on a class demonstration; some students with hearing impairments may tire from lengthy intervals of speechreading (Heward, 2009). For some students with attention deficit disorder (ADD) and attention deficit disorder with hyperactivity (ADHD), attending is a significant problem. Some students with ADD or ADHD may qualify for services under IDEA or Section 504 (see Chapter 3).

Serious problems with attention can severely impede learning (Barkley, 2005). Fortunately, many strategies are available for improving student attention, as described in the following section.

CLASSROOM SCENARIO

Ana

Ana is a fifth-grader with average academic abilities and a positive disposition. However, she has difficulty sustaining her attention to school tasks for more than about 3 minutes at a time. When prompted, she returns to task, but within a few minutes, she is again off-task, looking out the window, playing with her pencils, or doodling on her paper. This happens during teacher presentations, seatwork activities, and sometimes during group activities. As a consequence, her grades have been falling, especially in math.

QUESTIONS FOR REFLECTION

1. Why do you think Ana is having problems sustaining attention?
2. What adaptations to the classroom environment might help Ana?
3. How could peers help Ana pay better attention?

STRATEGIES FOR
IMPROVING ATTENTION

ADDRESS THE PRECONDITIONS OF ATTENTION WITH TEACHER EFFECTIVENESS
It is inappropriate for teachers to implement special interventions to improve attention without first making their classrooms as interesting and engaging as possible. For example, if you lecture day after day using the same presentation style, it would not be surprising if the attention of many of your students began to wander.

If getting and holding students' attention is a problem, first consider whether you are using effective teacher planning and presentation variables consistently (see Chapter 6). If each lesson does not contain elements such as structure, clarity, redundancy, and enthusiasm, it is unlikely to sustain student attention. Determine, for example, whether you have done as much as you can to teach enthusiastically (Salend, Elhoweris, & Van Garderen, 2003).

A huge part of teaching effectively—and thus maintaining student attention—is using interesting and motivating examples to enhance lessons. These examples allow teachers to personalize instruction and make the subject more meaningful and useful to students.

Finally, consider whether you are using attention-getting demonstrations. Demonstrations can include use of "real" objects in teaching mathematical operations; showing artifacts in lessons on the Civil War; demonstrating, rather than describing, the effects of certain chemical interactions; or dressing in historical clothing and acting out life from different geographic regions and time periods. Pictures and illustrations can also be helpful when actual demonstrations are not possible.

However, if some students continue to have difficulty sustaining attention, try the following strategies. For a meta-analysis of interventions for ADHD, see the *Research Highlight* feature.

PROVIDE ASSISTANCE WITH BASIC SKILLS PROBLEMS Many students with special needs do not read or write as well as other students in the class. These students may appear less attentive because paying attention requires reading from a text or writing notes that are beyond their skill level. For these students, find other means for them to acquire relevant information. Strategies for addressing these problems are provided in Chapters 11 and 13.

Some students do not complete assignments appropriately because they were not paying attention to directions. When giving directions, prompt student attending ("Listen carefully to what I'm going to say"), speak in a clear voice, and limit classroom distractions. Write the steps of the assignment so students can read as well as listen. Directions should include information about the content and format of the assignment, the reason it is being assigned, how students may receive assistance from others (e.g., adults, peers, and technology), how much time it should take to complete, and how it will be evaluated. Clear and specific directions can improve the performance of poor attenders (Salend et al., 2003).

In other cases, students may lose focus because they do not process oral language as fast as it is spoken. When this happens, try to find ways to reduce the rate of speaking, increase redundancy, provide "advance organizers," or find other means to present information. Mr. Davis, an eighth-grade social studies teacher, displayed charts containing the organizational framework of units during the entire month-long units. Students said the charts helped them refer back to major points during classes and helped promote a better understanding of everything in the unit. Mrs. Fluke, a fourth-grade teacher, placed language cards containing pictures illustrating the concepts of new vocabulary on a bulletin board. She encouraged her students to make versions of the cards for their personal picture dictionaries.

USE DIRECT APPEAL Direct appeal is a simple, sometimes overlooked strategy for improving attention and behavior problems (Beck, Roblee, & Johns, 1982; Redl, 1952; see also Chapter 7). To use direct appeal, find a quiet time and place to speak to students individually. Explain the problem as explicitly as possible, including the effect of the problem on you and other students as well as the target students. Then make a direct request to the students to improve their behavior. This strategy is likely to be effective when students recognize they are not paying attention and would like to succeed in school. An example of direct appeal is given in Figure 10.1.

USE PROXIMITY Proximity is another simple strategy that can be effective in promoting attention (Conroy, Asmus, Ladwig, Sellers, & Valcante, 2004). Simply move physically toward or stand near a student who is beginning to lose attention. This can prompt the student to refocus attention. Once this strategy has been established, it may be possible in time to fade it to a direct glance or a gesture that the student can easily interpret as a prompt to refocus attention. It also may be helpful to move the student or rearrange the classroom to accommodate teacher proximity.

BREAK UP ACTIVITIES Some students may be able to sit still and concentrate on a task for a certain number of minutes. Attention spans vary with age and maturity of students. In general, however, rather than giving a student the full length of time to complete a relatively lengthy assignment, divide the task into 10 subtasks of, say, 3 minutes each. At the end of each subtask, the student's progress could be checked, recorded, and praised by you or an assigned classroom peer. Dividing tasks into smaller segments is a great strategy for helping students with limited abilities to stay focused.

ALLOW SUFFICIENT MOVEMENT TO REDUCE RESTLESSNESS In some cases, especially in the elementary grades, students begin to lose concentration if they have been made to sit still for a long time. Recording when student attention begins to fade is a way to determine when periods of student inactivity are too long. If students regularly begin to lose attention after extended periods of sitting, consider rearranging the classroom schedule (e.g., recess periods) to allow for more movement (Kerr & Nelson, 2006). Adjust the amount of time spent

Teacher: Christine, may I speak with you privately for a minute?

Christine: OK.

Teacher: I think you're having a problem in my class. Do you know what I think it is?

Christine: No.

Teacher: Sometimes in class, I think you are having problems paying attention.

Christine: Oh.

Teacher: I think that because sometimes I see you just looking out the window, or doodling with your pencil, or wearing a blank expression on your face, as if you're daydreaming. Do you think that happens sometimes?

Christine: Yeah, I guess so. I guess I'm just not that interested in history.

Teacher: Well, I'm afraid that when that happens, it makes class harder for me, because I think I'm not getting through to you. Also, I think other students notice you and it makes them more likely to not pay attention.

Christine: Oh.

Teacher: But here's what I'd like to suggest. You daydream in class because you aren't interested in history. But if you think about what we're discussing a little more, and you raise your hand in class more often, I guarantee that you will begin to find class more interesting. You will also find that the time passes much more quickly. And most important—and this is what I want—you will find that you will get a much better grade in my class. So what do you say? Will you give it a try?

Christine: OK, I'll try.

Figure 10.1   Example of Direct Appeal

on each discipline and consider alternating between quiet sit-down activities and more actively involved learning activities. If your schedule cannot be easily changed, try giving students a minute to "stand, stretch, reach up to the ceiling, take a deep breath and let it out slowly, and march in place." Brief movement intervals are helpful in promoting student attention. Also, including student movement in lessons can be helpful.

PROVIDE STUDENT ACTIVITIES   Students are much more likely to pay attention when they are asked to complete activities than when they are asked to listen to someone talk. Providing relevant activities can be an excellent way of promoting attention. For example, instead of asking students to listen to a verbal presentation on how a telegraph works, students could work in small groups to construct their own telegraphs, and then send and decode messages to one another. Such activities help to focus student attention and make learning concepts more meaningful.

USE CLASSROOM PEERS TO PROMOTE ATTENTION   Classroom peers also can be effective in working with students who have attention problems (Plumber & Stoner, 2005). Flood, Wilder, and Flood (2005) demonstrated that unsupervised peer attention can help maintain off-task behavior in students with ADHD. However, peers can be trained to prompt and reinforce attending behavior. Peer interventions can be set up through group activities or working one on one. Peers could be asked to work in pairs with students who have some difficulty sustaining attention. Such collaborative sharing of activities can help students with attention problems by providing ongoing prompts for students to attend only to relevant tasks.

Peers seated near target students can also prompt attention. Peers can be trained to provide subtle cues to students (e.g., lightly touching the student's back) when lapses in attention are observed; they can be asked to report inattention to you only when these more subtle prompts are disregarded. Before you use this kind of strategy, be sure everyone involved is amenable to trying to use peer intervention strategies. Be sensitive to the needs of the students you are trying to help. Choose peer assistants wisely, perhaps using those students who appear to have strong interpersonal skills.

Interventions for Students with ADHD

Purdie, Hattie, and Carroll (2002) synthesized the results of 74 studies examining interventions with 2,193 individuals with attention deficit hyperactivity disorder (ADHD) published from 1990 to 1998. Interventions consisted of pharmacological, behavioral, educational, or combinations of treatments. More studies were conducted using pharmacological than educational treatments, and more studies measured behavior over other outcome measures. The average treatment length was 58 days. The overall effect size across all interventions and outcome measures was .48, which indicates a moderately positive effect for the interventions.

The strongest effects were reported for studies evaluating medications (.45

effect size), followed by school-based and non-school-based interventions, each of which obtained effect sizes of .39. Cognitive behavioral interventions, including self-regulation components, in both school and non-school-based treatments obtained the highest effects, of .49 and .58, respectively. Negative physical side effects from medications ranged from −.01 to −4.08, indicating that individuals may experience unpleasant side effects from taking medications, including nausea and insomnia.

Effects on behavior, such as on-task and attention, were .56, slightly greater than social (.38) and cognitive (.28) outcomes. Unfortunately, fewer studies examined the effects of the treatments on academic achievement, and few studies assessed the long-

term impact of these interventions. It is encouraging that behavior of individuals with ADHD was substantially improved across these studies when cognitive behavioral interventions using self-regulation were implemented. For additional information on ADHD, see Barkley (2005).

QUESTIONS FOR REFLECTION

1. What other factors might influence treatments to reduce ADHD?
2. What additional outcome measures would you like to see evaluated during interventions to assist students with ADHD?
3. How could you help monitor any long-term effects or negative side effects of medications for students with ADHD?

PROVIDE DIRECT CONSEQUENCES FOR ATTENTION You can increase attention in individual students by measuring and reinforcing it (Crossairt, Hall, & Hopkins, 1973; Walker & Buckley, 1968). Set an egg timer, alarm clock, wristwatch alarm, vibrating watch, or tape recorder to sound at random intervals (the length of the interval depends on the frequency of prompts the student needs). Whenever the alarm sounds, determine whether the target students were paying attention at that instant. If so, they can be rewarded with verbal praise, points on a check sheet, or tokens that can be accumulated and exchanged at a later date for desired objects, privileges, or activities. For example, a student who earns 90% of possible tokens over a 2-week period might be entitled to take an extra recess with another class, go out for an ice cream, or have a special break with you. If other students appear to resent this arrangement, consider including the rest of the class in some reward scheme for good behavior, such as a pizza party or game time. Allow the target student to work for a class reward or privilege, such as bonus recess time, or a favored activity. In this way, the class can share responsibility for the target student's success or failure, as in the continuation of Ana's scenario.

Record any student's success at paying attention over a period of time and reinforce that behavior with positive recognition or rewards.

Ana

■ ■ ■

Ana's teacher, Mrs. Lawson, asked a responsible student to sit behind Ana and prompt Ana when her attention wandered for more than a few seconds. This seemed to help, but Ana still seemed to need frequent reminders to maintain her concentration. Mrs. Lawson determined from talking to Ana and other students that Ana liked to please her classmates. Mrs. Lawson told Ana that she could help do something nice for the class. The peer that was monitoring Ana's inattention would tally each time Ana was prompted. If the number of prompts declined by half by the end of the week, Mrs. Lawson would allow her to distribute animal crackers to everyone in the class. Almost immediately, Ana began to pay more attention. After 3 weeks, Ana only required minimal prompting to stay attentive.

QUESTIONS FOR REFLECTION

1. Why do you think these strategies were successful for Ana?
2. What might be another way to use peers to assist?
3. How could a parent adapt these strategies for home use?

Mild corrections or reprimands have also been found effective for students with attention problems (Abramowitz, O'Leary, & Futtersak, 1988; Abramowitz, O'Leary, & Rosen, 1987). Generally, short reprimands have been found to be more effective than long reprimands, and immediate reprimands have been found to be more effective than delayed reprimands (Montague, Fiore, Hocutt, McKinney, & Harris, 1996). Saying something like, "When you pay attention in class, the teacher is very happy with you. When you don't pay attention, your grades will suffer," reminds students of the rule, their responsibilities, and the consequences, without placing too much emphasis on the reprimand component. Remember that reprimands lose their effectiveness if they are used too often (see Chapter 7).

TEACH SELF-RECORDING STRATEGIES **Self-recording** and self-regulation strategies are useful in teaching students how to monitor and evaluate their own attention (Harris, Friedlander, & Saddler, 2005; Harris, Graham, Reid, McElroy, & Hamby, 1994). Special educators often teach self-monitoring strategies in their classrooms, and therefore many students with special needs may have already learned how to use self-recording strategies. Self-monitoring skills learned in a resource setting have been observed to improve student attention in the regular classroom (Rooney, Hallahan, & Lloyd, 1984). With systematic communication between the regular and special education teachers, problems with attention can be improved.

To start a self-recording system, set up a procedure for delivering randomly spaced beeps, as described in the previous section. (If the sounds are distracting to other students, use a vibrating watch, or prerecord randomly spaced beeps on a tape recorder and have the target student listen with earphones.) The cueing interval can be set at random between 10 and 90 seconds (average about 45 seconds) at first and expanded as attention improves. This procedure could be used with several students at a time. If students have hearing impairments that prevent them from hearing an auditory cue, pair the sound with a light stimulus, or provide the signal to a peer who then provides a visual or tactual cue to the target student.

When the cue sounds, the target students should indicate whether they were paying attention by placing a checkmark on a self-monitoring sheet. The self-monitoring sheet should have two columns. At the head of the first column is, "Was I paying attention?", including examples such as "Looking at teacher," and "Reading textbook." At the head of the second column is, "Was I **not** paying attention?", including examples such as "Looking out the window," and "Daydreaming." Under each column is a numbered underline (or box) where students can record their level of attending ("yes" or "no") after each cue.

At first, you should also make your own record of student attending, and compare the two records at the end of the period. Students can be reinforced for recording at all appropriate times, and for approximating the results obtained by you. For example, if you record 70% paying attention, the student should be rewarded for recording something between 60% and 80%. As the recording becomes reliable, create a graph of student attending, and look for progress over time. Some investigators have demonstrated that it may not be necessary for teachers to verify accuracy of attending for the procedure to be effective.

Before beginning a self-recording intervention, meet individually with the students and discuss why paying attention in class is important and how the students will benefit from attending better. The students need to understand that the self-recording is in their best interest and that they will benefit as a result. It might be helpful to involve parents to support this intervention.

As students improve in monitoring their attention, you can set timers so that they sound less frequently. However, serious attending problems are unlikely to disappear in a short time. Consistency on your part is helpful in effecting long-term improvements in attention. Continue to give frequent and regular feedback to students on their ability to attend, and on their consistent self-monitoring of their own attention.

As an alternative, students can be trained to record their performance—for example, the number of times a weekly spelling list was practiced correctly (Harris et al., 2005). This method has also been shown to be effective, although not always more effective than self-recording of attention, and students may prefer this method.

STRATEGIES FOR
ADDRESSING EXTREME CASES OF ATTENTION DEFICITS

Some extreme cases of attention problems are challenging to address in a general education classroom without intensive assistance from special educators. These students may appear so distractible that they can not reasonably be expected to attend appropriately for more than a few minutes at a time. In these cases, some special techniques may be helpful.

PROVIDE INTENSIVE TEACHER-LED INSTRUCTION For students with extreme attention problems, brief, intensive teacher-led instructional sessions may be the most realistic teaching strategy. These sessions can be delivered either one to one or in small groups with a great deal of teacher–student interaction; novel, interesting, age-appropriate tasks; and frequent reinforcement including preferred activities (Kerr & Nelson, 2006). Because your time for one-to-one instruction may be limited, this kind of intensive instruction may have to be accomplished by a closely supervised aide, an appropriate tier in an RTI program, or the special education teacher.

CONSIDER STRENGTHS AND WEAKNESSES OF STIMULANT MEDICATION Another alternative used more frequently in recent years is the administration (under medical supervision) of stimulant drugs to help students focus attention more appropriately. Although medication has certainly been helpful in many cases, often reducing the symptoms of ADHD, concern has been expressed that it has been overprescribed in recent years (Snider, Busch, & Arrowood, 2003). Stimulant medication generally affects behavior and attention more than higher-order skills, learning, or achievement (Montague et al., 1996). Side effects can include insomnia, decreased appetite, irritability, mood changes, weight loss, abdominal pain, and headaches (Hallahan & Cottone, 1997). High doses have infrequently been associated with compulsive behaviors, movement disorders, or tics (Snider et al., 2003). If relevant and qualified professionals agree that stimulant medication is indicated for a specific student, your job as a teacher should be to collect formative data that identifies how the medication affects the student's behavior both positively and negatively. It is also important for all participants to be aware that the long-term effects of stimulant medication have yet to be fully determined (Austin, 2003).

In some cases, stimulant medication used in conjunction with cognitive/behavioral training can be effective (Austin, 2003; Montague et al., 1996). In addition, parent training in cognitive/behavioral interventions and communication strategies has sometimes been effective in managing noncompliant behavior, reducing stress, and improving the quality of family relationships (Hallahan & Cottone, 1997). Families can also be enlisted to provide consistency and support for school-based interventions (Duhaney, 2003).

Go to MyEducationLab, select the topic *Autism Spectrum Disorders*, and go to the Activities and Applications section. As you watch the video entitled "Reading/ Language Arts Lesson," pay close attention to all of the strategies the teacher is using to keep her student engaged.

Some students with autism have severe attention problems. Autistic students may attend little or not at all to teachers, even though they can be demonstrated to have adequate hearing (Simpson & Zionts, 2000). Students with such severe attention deficits may benefit from one-to-one instruction, direct provision of tangible or edible reinforcers for attending and responding appropriately, and ongoing supervision. Parents and special educators may be able to provide more specific information on the needs of individual students. Educational placement in the general education classroom is possible if special educators or highly trained aides are available to provide individual attention.

Rocha, Schreibman, and Stahmer (2007) described the problems of children with autism in the area of **joint attention,** which is the ability of an individual to coordinate attention between a desired object and a person in a social context, for example, to follow an adult's eye gaze directed to a specific object. Rocha et al. reported that students with autism improved joint attention with intensive trial-based instruction, prompting, and reinforcement. Parents directed their gaze to a particular object (a desired toy); if the child followed the gaze, he or she was given a reinforcement (time to play with the toy). If not, the child was prompted and then reinforced for a shorter period.

Developmentally appropriate interventions may also increase the attending of students with autism. For example, social stories (Scott, Clark, & Brady, 2000) may improve attending because of their focus on the student and his or her specific needs (see Research Highlight, Chapter 4). Other approaches that focus instruction on the student's own specific interests may also improve attending (Greenspan, Wieder, & Simons, 1998).

CLASSROOM SCENARIO

James

James was classified as having learning disabilities. With extra practice and resource room assistance, he was able to cope with the reading demands of his seventh-grade class; however, he continued to have difficulty remembering information for tests. A major concern of his was a test of states and capitals that was coming up in 4 weeks, and was considered a test that all seventh-graders must pass. He had studied on his own and even with classmates, but he had a difficult time remembering more than a few states and capitals at a time. He asked his resource teacher, Mr. Pearl, for help.

QUESTIONS FOR REFLECTION

1. What are some reasons James may be having trouble remembering states and capitals?
2. What are some other common facts that students may have difficulty remembering?
3. What would you recommend that Mr. Pearl do to help James?

Memory

Memory is a psychological process that is critically important for school learning. The great majority of items on classroom tests as well as statewide high-stakes tests require students to remember specific facts and concepts relevant to the content area (Frase-Blunt, 2000; Putnam, 1992). Even when teachers devote more of their test questions to such higher-order tasks as analysis, synthesis, and evaluation, students must first *remember* relevant information before they can reason effectively with this information. Effective memory therefore is a necessary requirement for school success.

Many different types of memory have been described (Baddeley, 2004). These include **semantic memory** (for facts and concepts about the world), **episodic memory** (of previous personal experience), and **everyday memory** (for information encountered in everyday experience). Memory researchers also frequently distinguish between relatively limitless **long-term memory** and **short-term memory,** that holds information only briefly (e.g., a telephone number) while it is used, placed in long-term memory (e.g., by rehearsal), or forgotten. Information actively processed in short-term memory (for example, in solving a two-part math problem) is referred to as **working memory** (Van Daal, Verhoeven, & Van Leeuwe, 2008). Many students with special needs exhibit difficulties in one or more of these areas of memory (Beirne-Smith et al., 2006; Van der Molen, Van Luit, & Jongmans, 2007). Specific strategies, however, have been seen to be effective in enhancing memory for all students, and are described in the remainder of this chapter.

Some knowledge that students need requires memorization.

STRATEGIES FOR IMPROVING MEMORY

ADDRESS MEMORY PRECONDITIONS   Before describing memory strategies that may prove to be extremely effective in helping your students remember important school content, consider the preconditions that must be in place for learning and memory to occur. One critical precondition is ensuring that all students are attending appropriately to instruction. Increase attention by maintaining a well-organized and distraction-free classroom (see Chapter 7) and by trying the strategies discussed in the first part of this chapter.

Next, keep students motivated to learn. Even if they are paying attention, students will learn and recall little if they are not interested in or do not see the value of the content, or do not believe they can succeed. Similarly, students are unlikely to remember information if they do not have a positive affective response to the content presented; that is, if they have indifferent or negative feelings toward the subject, or if their morale is low. Finally, learning will be minimized if lessons appear boring and monotonous. Once the preconditions for good memory have been met, the following suggestions should improve students' memory.

DEVELOP "METAMEMORY"   **Metamemory** is the metacognitive process of knowing about memory. Specifically, metamemory is the process of knowing when, where, and how to remember (Brown, 1978). Many students, especially in the elementary grades, are unaware of the nature of memory, and how they can learn to remember better. Activities and class discussions on memory and how it functions could help many students learn how to remember more efficiently. For example, help students understand that we may forget because of fatigue, interference, passing of time, lack of effort, or because the content was unfamiliar or difficult. Likewise, memory improves with age, experience, prior knowledge, and use of memory strategies. Training aspects of metamemory, through stories, examples, and activities, can help improve students' ability to remember (Lucangeli, Galderisi, & Cornoldi, 1995).

USE EXTERNAL MEMORY   External memory refers to the use of devices to increase memory (Baddeley, 2004). In schools, external memory can be used to remember homework assignments, locker numbers, important school dates, and to bring relevant materials home (or back to school). External memory examples include writing things down in notebooks, appointment books, or language cards; placing things to be remembered in places where they will be seen (e.g., putting homework by the outside door); and physical prompts (e.g., attaching a note to clothing or backpack). Although external memory is not permissible in all situations (e.g., most written tests), students can be informed about appropriate times to use external memory to improve school functioning. The *Technology Highlight* feature provides an example of a device for enhancing external memory.

PEARSON
myeducationlab

Go to MyEducationLab, select the topic *Instructional Practices and Learning Strategies*, and go to the Activities and Applications section. As you complete the simulation entitled "Using Learning Strategies," reflect on how the LINCS strategy helps students with memory.

Personal Digital Assistants Improve Independence

Students must remember many things to be successful in school, such as dates when projects are due and tests will be given, communications to be brought home for parents to read and sign, dates for field trips or special events, and class schedules. Remembering all these things may be particularly difficult for students who have difficulty with memory or organizational skills. To help these and other students, personal digital assistants may be useful.

Personal digital assistants (PDAs) are small handheld devices that perform a multitude of tasks, from calendar functions, to-do lists, address books, and gaming, to word processing, spreadsheets, and more. PDAs range in size from very small handheld devices (Palm Pilot size) to somewhat larger sizes. The screens also range from smaller black-and-white to larger color screens. Memory capacity also ranges from small to large. All PDAs connect to larger computers to download and upload data, and many also have wireless capabilities. Newer PDAs may contain cameras, cell phones, and, when enabled with wireless capabilities, have the capacity to send pictures via e-mail.

PDAs have enormous potential for assisting students with disabilities with organizational skills. To-do lists can be homework assignments or tasks associated with before- and after-school activities. Ferguson, Myles, and Hagiwara (2005) successfully taught an adolescent with autism spectrum disorder to use a PDA at home and school to monitor task-completion activities. For example, this boy experienced difficulties getting ready to leave for school in the mornings.

Activities included getting dressed, washing up, taking medications, eating breakfast, getting school materials together, and leaving for school on time. Each task was associated with a time for completion, columns to indicate completed independently or with prompts, and the time. All recording sheets were entered into a Hewlett-Packard Jornado 560 PDA. Alarms were initially programmed into the PDA to alert the boy to do an upcoming task. School-related tasks and evening home tasks were also eventually loaded into the PDA. Either the boy's mother or school personnel checked his task completion during the intervention. Results indicated that this boy with autism learned to complete required tasks on time with the assistance of his PDA reminders. Future applications of PDAs with school-aged students with disabilities appear limitless.

ENHANCE MEANINGFULNESS   We remember meaningful information better than non-meaningful information (Underwood, 1983). You can make learning more meaningful by providing specific examples that are directly relevant to your students' experiences. For example, in a presentation about how each of the three branches of government—legislative, executive, and judiciary—functions, use examples that are directly relevant to schools and show how these examples affect students. That is, legislative bodies establish specific laws for the establishment and operation of schools, the executive branch is responsible for enforcing these laws, and the judicial branch adjudicates and interprets these laws. Students can study and discuss how the actions of each of these branches affect their own lives personally with respect to school policy.

USE CONCRETE EXAMPLES, PICTURES, OR IMAGERY   Concrete information is better remembered than abstract information (Baddeley, 2004). You can enhance the concreteness of relevant content by bringing in examples of the topics being studied. For example, the study of trilobites (prehistoric marine animals) can be made more concrete by bringing in fossil specimens of trilobites, and can be used in discussions of the characteristics of trilobites. Such enriched thought, activity, and discussion can greatly improve memory of the content.

Video Presentations   When specific examples cannot be brought to class, for example, because of their size, cost, or limited availability, consider enhancing visual images through CDs, videotapes, or pictures. For example, videotapes or DVDs provide excellent recordings of things students might not ordinarily have an opportunity to see, such as tornadoes, and can provide interesting visual coverage of such things as Mayan architecture, insect life, or microorganisms. When selecting video presentations, be certain that they assist directly in enhancing the concreteness of specific information to be remembered. View the presentation selectively, to focus specifically on instructional objectives (example: focusing on architecture—an instructional objective—in a videotape on ancient Greece). Finally, do not be afraid to provide redundancy in viewing, to help enhance the specific facts or concepts to be remembered. For students with visual impairments, descriptive video may be available or can be created (see Chapter 4).

Illustrations Using pictures, illustrations, or graphics enhances the concreteness and memorability of information (Mayer, Hegarty, & Mayer, 2005). Pictures are frequently provided in student textbooks, or in overhead transparencies included in instructors' materials. Try to locate pictures that are directly relevant to instructional objectives—for example, illustrations that document clearly the physical characteristics of insects or the living conditions of American pioneers. The World Wide Web is an excellent place to find all types of pictures. Ask your students to pay attention to specific aspects of the picture that are directly relevant to your instructional objectives (e.g., "Jackie, point out the thorax of the insect in the picture" or "Bill, show me on the picture the things that make you know that it is a picture of a beetle"). Reading through diagrams carefully with students, and questioning them frequently, helps ensure that diagrams are understood (e.g., "Darryl, show me where the switch is in this electrical diagram"). After pictures and diagrams have been studied, question your students about the illustrations with their books closed, or the projector turned off, so they continue to practice studying the mental image of the illustration. Peers may assist students with visual impairments with the careful description of pictures, diagrams, or illustrations. Additionally, tactual representations of pictures can be created, as described in Chapter 4. Remember, however, that pictures may not promote learning if they distract students from the specific content to be learned (Uberti, Scruggs, & Mastropieri, 2003).

A visual presentation of information can facilitate learning and remembering over a long period of time.

Imagery If you cannot locate relevant pictures, and if you feel unable to draw pictures yourself, you can encourage students to use their mental imagery to create pictures. For example, to help understand that whales are the largest animals on Earth, encourage students to imagine an enormous whale next to a much smaller elephant. Students should be encouraged to create details of the image, and discuss them with the class for accuracy. For example, you could suggest that students imagine a very large whale, and an elephant standing next to the whale that is only about as large as the whale is from its eye to the tip of its mouth. Students could then be asked other questions (example: "Which way is the elephant facing?") to make the image more permanent. Later, when students are asked this information ("What is the largest animal?"), they can also be asked to report how they remembered that fact. With practice, students can improve their ability to use imagery.

Another way to improve the concreteness of a subject is through field trips to relevant zoos, museums, or nature areas. As with videotape presentations, focus your students' attention on the specific objectives to be met during field trips, and monitor that students are meeting these objectives. When appropriate, call ahead so that necessary preparations for specific students with disabilities can be made.

MINIMIZE INTERFERING INFORMATION Interference, in the form of competing or distracting stimuli, can inhibit memory (Baddeley, 2004). Sometimes students forget information because interference was present, or the emphasis on the targeted content was insufficient to promote good memory. Be sure your presentation focuses directly on the content to be remembered, and avoid interfering or distracting information that is not directly relevant.

Teachers can inadvertently provide interfering information if they digress from the presentation, provide unnecessary elaboration or examples that are not directly relevant, or frequently interrupt presentations and lectures with behavior management issues. In general,

Students can benefit from role-play activities, as in this mock trial preparation activity.

consider that information is more likely to be remembered when it is presented clearly, directly, and without unnecessary embellishment.

USE ENACTMENTS AND MANIPULATION

We remember things we do better than things we hear and recite (Cohen, 1989). This may explain some of the positive effects typically found for hands-on science activities (Scruggs & Mastropieri, 2003). For example, students who have studied firsthand the effects of weak acid on the mineral calcite are more likely to remember these effects (the calcite begins to deteriorate) than if they simply read about the subject. Similarly, students are more likely to remember electric circuits they have constructed than electric circuits they have read about.

PROMOTE ACTIVE REASONING Information is better remembered if students actively participate in the learning process, particularly by actively reasoning through the content (Craik & Lockhart, 1972). Answering any type of relevant question usually promotes better memory than passive listening to teacher lectures. Answering factual questions helps focus attention on the significant components of the content (e.g., "Who were the major U.S. novelists of the first half of the 19th century—Jeff?"). Answering questions that require reasoning can also help improve memory (e.g., "What do you think Hawthorne is trying to say about medical science in *Rappacini's Daughter*—Marie?").

Provide additional coaching to assist students with disabilities when support is needed in thinking through information systematically and arriving at their own conclusions. Coach students to provide their own explanations about factual information, as in the following example:

TEACHER: The camel has a double row of eyelashes for each eye. Why does this make sense?

STUDENT: I don't know.

TEACHER: Well, let's think. What do you know about camels? For example, where do they live?

STUDENT: In the desert.

TEACHER: In the desert, good. And what is it like in the desert?

STUDENT: Hot and dry.

TEACHER: Good, what else can you think of about deserts?

STUDENT: Um, it's sandy. And windy.

TEACHER: Good, sandy and windy. So why would it make sense that camels would have two rows of eyelashes?

STUDENT: Oh! To keep the sand from blowing in their eyes.

TEACHER: To keep the sand out of their eyes, good!

Sullivan, Mastropieri, and Scruggs (1995) demonstrated that students taught with these questioning strategies remembered and understood more information than students who had been directly provided with the same information (e.g., "The camel has a double row of eyelashes for each eye, to keep out the blowing sand").

INCREASE PRACTICE Information is better remembered if it is practiced or rehearsed (Burns, 2005). Rehearsal or repetition has frequently been demonstrated to improve recall among students of all ages and ability groups. This is an important component of the "redundancy" variable discussed in Chapter 6. To increase the effects of practice, you should first target the information that is most important to be remembered. Then provide as much practice as possible in individual lessons by questioning. Questioning and practice after learning has

Boundaries in Family and Professional Relationships

Regular practice at home is a key factor in memory of academic content. Parent and school relationships that improve communication and foster support for practice at home thus are critical to school success, and may be of particular importance when working with culturally diverse families. In order to support school–family communication most effectively, it is important to be aware of boundaries. "Boundary" refers to the rules associated with the ways in which relationships function.

Nelson, Summers, and Turnbull (2004) examined the boundaries in family and professional relationships in special education. They held focus groups with parents and professionals in special education to help determine what types of boundaries were seen in their relationships.

Parents, professionals, and administrators from three states participated in individual interviews and focus groups to determine their opinions about optimal family and professional relationships. Participants represented culturally diverse groups, including 41% African American, 17% Hispanic, and 30% White, and represented a range of socioeconomic status from lower to higher. Parents

had children with a variety of disabilities of all ages, from preschool to high school and post-secondary. The participating professionals were mostly White and female (70% and 91%, respectively), most of whom (70%) were direct service providers.

During the first of two focus group interviews, participants were provided with guided questions to solicit information on successful and unsuccessful relationships between parents and professionals. In the second interview, participants were provided with a list of major themes from the first round and asked to respond, elaborate, or expand. Follow-up individual interviews were also held.

Findings revealed three major boundary themes: availability and accessibility, breadth of responsibility, and dual relationships. Parent responses included interest in the following:

- Flexibility for meeting times, including before and after school hours and weekends;
- Defining responsibilities broadly to include home visits, evening phone calls, and assuming additional tasks;
- Going beyond the job description to do things (e.g., visit child in hospital); and

- Maintaining contact even after the child moves on to new teachers.

Responses of professionals included:

- Belief that flexibility for meeting times was important, but identified the challenges of meeting all needs with flexibility;
- Support for going beyond the job description and increasing their breadth of responsibilities. Professionals reported participating in weddings, funerals, and birthday parties, but also acknowledged the challenges of "bringing the job home with them and going too far"; and
- Expression of a need for setting limits with assistance or "friendships."

Both parents and professionals acknowledged the need for flexibility in meeting times and the desire to go beyond the simple job description to assist children and families. Professionals were cautiously aware of boundaries and some expressed setting limits for specific topics, including discussing religion and marital relationships with families. Teachers should consider the results of this study when discussing ways for improving parent–professional relationships.

been achieved is referred to as **overlearning**, and can be an effective strategy for promoting long-term memory. Independent study skills can also promote recall and retention, after content has been introduced and practiced. Review at home with family members is also an excellent way to increase recall of academic content. The *Diversity in the Classroom* feature describes involvement with families to help promote academic learning.

Increased practice can also be given as a classwide tutoring activity. You might be surprised to discover how much more information your students can learn in brief (e.g., 10–15 minutes), fast-paced daily sessions in which pairs of students question each other on the significant parts of lessons to be remembered, such as multiplication facts, spelling words, key facts and concepts in a geography unit, or parts of speech. You can feel even more confident about student success if you pair students with special needs with students who have demonstrated that they can be effective partners.

USE CLUSTERING AND ORGANIZATION   Information is better remembered if it is organized in some meaningful way (Baddeley, 2004). For example, products produced and exported by a country could be grouped as agricultural, industrial, and mining products before students practice remembering the list.

Another strategy is to incorporate content within a type of graphic organizer, including organizational charts, visual displays, **semantic maps,** or **relationship charts** (Gustashaw & Brigham, 2006). These displays present a spatially organized, as well as semantically organized, representation of the topic. For example, in a unit on Argentina, a visual display can be created that organizes the different areas of study in the unit, such as land features, natural resources, climate, history, and culture (see Figure 10.2).

PROMOTE ELABORATION   Information is better remembered if it is elaborated (Rohwer, Raines, Eoff, & Wagner, 1977). You can provide simple elaborations to help students remember new words. For example, "To remember the meaning of *precipitation,* think of the 'sip' sound in 'precipitation': Animals can 'sip' from puddles left from precipitation." To promote elaboration, ask students to think of everything they can about a topic (e.g., "What else does buoyancy remind you of?" "How does a *buoy* remind you of *buoyancy?*"). Asking students simply to think about what a new word sounds like, and how that links to its meaning, improves recall of the information. More formal forms of elaboration are known as mnemonics.

STRATEGIES FOR
IMPROVING MEMORY WITH MNEMONIC TECHNIQUES

Everyone remembers using specific mnemonic techniques to remember information. For example, most people remember using the word-acronym *HOMES* to remember the names of the Great Lakes. Many also remember the traditional rhyme "In fourteen hundred ninety-two, Columbus sailed the ocean blue" to remember the year that Columbus first sailed to America. What many people do not know is that mnemonic strategies are versatile and can be used in hundreds, even thousands, of situations to improve memory.

Another interesting research finding is that mnemonic strategies are powerful. Learning gains of as much as 2-to-1, or even 3-to-1, are common in mnemonic strategy research with a variety of students, including those with intellectual disabilities, learning disabilities, behavioral disorders or emotional disturbance, and even gifted and normally achieving students (Scruggs & Mastropieri, 2005; Wolgemuth, Cobb, & Alwell, 2008). Students with visual impairments may benefit less from mnemonic pictures, and more from the verbal elaborations (Paivio & Okovita, 1971).

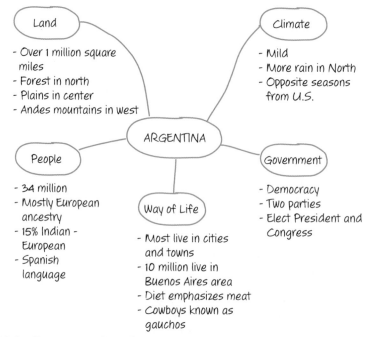

Figure 10.2   Organizational Display

Nevertheless, mnemonic strategies, like any other teaching or learning strategies, have their limitations. Mnemonic techniques are most effective when they are:

- used to reinforce objectives to remember specific content,
- directly taught and practiced,
- combined with comprehension instruction,
- included with application activities.

Three specific types of mnemonic strategies—the **keyword method,** the **pegword method,** and **letter strategies**—have been successful in enhancing memory for students with memory difficulties (Mastropieri & Scruggs, 1991).

USE THE KEYWORD METHOD FOR VERBAL ASSOCIATIONS

The keyword method is used to strengthen the connection between a new word and its associated information. For example, the Italian word *strada* means *road* (Figure 10.3). To strengthen this association, the learner is first provided a "keyword" for the new word, *strada.* A keyword is a word that is familiar to the learner, but that *sounds like* the new word and is easily pictured. In the case of strada, a good keyword is *straw,* because it sounds like *strada* and is easy to picture. Next, a picture (or image) is created of the associates interacting together. Again in the case of *strada,* the interactive picture could be a picture of straw lying on a road. This picture then is shown to the student, while the teacher says the dialogue in Figure 10.3.

Keyword strategies have been successfully used to teach the following:

- Foreign language vocabulary
- Scientific terms such as *ranidae* (Figure 10.4)

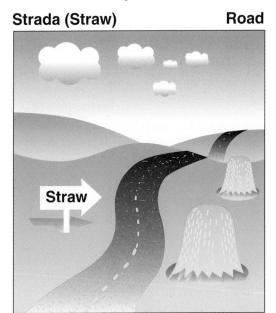

Strada (Straw)   **Road**

Straw

The Italian word *strada* means road. The keyword for strada is *straw* [show picture]. Remember this picture of straw lying on a road. Remember this picture of what? Good, straw lying on a road. Now, when I ask you for the meaning of *strada,* think first of the keyword, *straw.* Then think back to the picture with the straw in it, remember that the straw was on a road, and then retrieve the answer, *strada* means road. Now, what does *strada* mean? Good, *strada* means road. And, how did you remember that? Good, you thought of the keyword, *straw,* and remembered the picture of the *straw* on the road.

Figure 10.3 Keyword Mnemonic Strategy for Strada = Road

Note: From "Uso Della Mnemotechnica Nell'insegnamento a Studenti con Distubi di Apprendimento," by M.A. Mastropieri, 1993, in R. Vianello & C. Cornoldi (Eds.), *Disturbi di Apprendimento: Proposte di Intervento, Congresso Internazionale CNIS* (pp. 15–32), Bergamo, Italia; Juvenilia. Reprinted with permission.

Ranidae (Rain)   **Frog**

Figure 10.4   Keyword Mnemonic Strategy for Ranidae =
Common Frogs
Note: From "Mnemonic Vocabulary Instruction for Learning Disabled
Students," by M. A. Mastropieri, T. E. Scruggs, J. R. Levin, J. Gaffney, &
B. McLoone, 1985, *Learning Disability Quarterly, 8,* pp. 57–63. Copyright 1985
by Council for Learning Disabilities. Reprinted with permission.

Zimmerman   **Note to Mexico**
(Swimmer)   **to fight U.S.**

Figure 10.5   Keyword Mnemonic Strategy for Zimmerman =
Sent a Coded Note to Mexico
Note: From "Constructing More Meaningful Relationships: Mnemonic
Instruction for Special Populations," by M. A. Mastropieri & T. E. Scruggs,
1989, *Educational Psychology Review, 1*(2), pp. 88–111. Reprinted with
permission.

- English vocabulary (e.g., *barrister* is a lawyer, provide a picture of a bear, keyword for barrister pleading a case in a court room)
- People and their accomplishments, such as Zimmerman, the German foreign minister who sent the coded "Zimmerman Note" to Mexico that precipitated U.S. entry into World War I (Figure 10.5)
- Map locations for Revolutionary War battles
- States and capitals

These strategies can be helpful for students who need assistance remembering long lists of information for school, as seen in the second part of James's scenario.

The *In the Classroom* feature presents mnemonic strategies for learning all of the states and capitals. Figure 10.6 illustrates the strategy for learning that Tallahassee is the capital of Florida.

CLASSROOM SCENARIO

James

Mr. Pearl, James's resource teacher, told James that he thought he had the solution to his problem. He constructed keywords and simple pictures for all the states and capitals information, such as those in the previous list. He spent one period with James, explaining the keyword method and how it could be used to remember states and capitals. He demonstrated by teaching James capitals for six states. First, they practiced state names and their keywords (e.g., Arkansas—ark). Next they practiced capital names and their keywords (e.g., Little Rock—a little rock). Then he went over the six pictures of states and capitals and practiced the strategies, as follows:

MR. PEARL: The capital of Arkansas is Little Rock. The keyword for
             Arkansas is . . . ?

JAMES: Ark.

MR. PEARL: Good, and the keyword for Little Rock is . . . ?

JAMES: A little rock.

MR. PEARL: Good! Now, remember this picture [shows picture] of Noah's Ark
             landing on a little rock. Remember this picture of what?

JAMES: Noah's Ark landing on a little rock.

MR. PEARL: [turns over the picture] And the capital of Arkansas is . . . ?
JAMES: Little Rock.
MR. PEARL: Little Rock, good.

When James was certain he knew how the strategies worked, Mr. Pearl told him to study no more than six pictures at a time, and test himself frequently on the information he had accumulated. Mr. Pearl tested him periodically, and encouraged him to keep studying.

When the time for the states and capitals test came, James received one of the highest scores in the class! The seventh-grade teacher, Mrs. Sullivan, was so impressed that she asked James how he was able to do so well. James showed her the mnemonic pictures, and Mrs. Sullivan asked Mr. Pearl if she could use the strategy with her entire class the following year.

Figure 10.6 Illustration of Mnemonic Strategy to Remember That Tallahassee (Television) Is the Capital of Florida (Flower)

Uberti et al. (2003) used mnemonic keyword strategies to improve learning and recall of new vocabulary words (e.g., *ionosphere, fjords, jettison*) prior to a story-reading activity in inclusive third-grade classes. Although the keyword strategies improved all students' recall of word meanings, students with learning disabilities benefited the most from the keyword method, learning two to three times as many words as students in alternative conditions.

Terrill, Scruggs, and Mastropieri (2004) created keyword mnemonic strategies to help their high school students with learning disabilities learn important vocabulary words in preparation for the SAT. For example, for the vocabulary word *palatable,* the keyword was *table,* and a picture was shown of people sitting at a table enjoying a meal. A sentence under the picture stated, "All the food on the **table** tasted very good." Students learned and remembered 92% of the words they learned mnemonically and only 49% of the words they learned using more traditional activities, such as drill and worksheet activities.

Fontana, Mastropieri, and Scruggs (2007) used mnemonic keyword strategies in inclusive high school world history classes. For example, to learn the meaning of "anarchist," students were shown a picture of *ants* (keyword for anarchist) overturning government buildings to remember that anarchists are against all forms of government. In this investigation, students

Mnemonic Strategies for Remembering the States and Their Capitals

Other strategies are possible; test these to see if they work well with your own students. Use your own artwork, student art, or clip art to create mnemonic pictures. Practice with students (or have students practice with partners) until recall is fluent and automatic. Practice recalling capitals ("What is the capital of Maryland?") as well as states ("Of what state is Bismarck the capital?").

State (keyword)	Capital (keyword)	Mnemonic Picture
Alabama (band)	Montgomery (monkey)	*Monkeys* playing in a *band*.
Alaska ("I'll ask her")	Juneau ("Do you know?")	Students talking: "*Do you know* the capital of Alaska?" "*I'll ask her!*"
Arizona (arid zone)	Phoenix (phone-x)	*Phone-x* (telephone) in an *arid zone* (desert).
Arkansas (ark)	Little Rock (little rock)	Noah's *Ark* landing on a *little rock*.
California (calf horn)	Sacramento (sack of mint)	A *sack of mint* on a *calf's horn*.
Colorado (coloring)	Denver (den)	A child's "*coloring den.*"
Connecticut (convict)	Hartford (heart)	A *convict* in prison, with a broken *heart*.
Delaware (devil)	Dover (dove)	A *dove* on a *devil's* pitchfork.
Florida (flower)	Tallahassee (television)	A *flower* on a *television* set.
Georgia (George Washington)	Atlanta (Atlantic Ocean)	*George* Washington wading in the *Atlantic* Ocean.
Hawaii ("How are ya?")	Honolulu ("Honey, I'm Lou!")	A dialogue between two people: "*How are ya?*" "*Honey, I'm Lou!*"
Idaho ("I don't know")	Boise (boys)	Teacher and students: "What's the answer, *boys*?" "*I don't know!*"
Illinois (ill)	Springfield (spring)	A man who drank from a *spring* is feeling *ill*.
Indiana (Indian)	Indianapolis (Indianapolis 500)	An *Indian* driving a race car in the *Indianapolis* 500.
Iowa ("I owe ya!")	Des Moines (the mines)	A boss of the *mines* telling a worker, "*I owe ya!*" (his paycheck).
Kansas (can)	Topeka (top)	A *top* spinning on a *can*.
Kentucky (kennel)	Frankfort (frankfurter)	Dogs in a *kennel* eating *frankfurters*.
Louisiana (Louise and Anna)	Baton Rouge (batons and rouge)	Louise and Anna wearing *rouge* and twirling *batons*.
Maine (horse's mane)	Augusta (a gust of wind)	A *gust of* wind blowing a horse's *mane*.
Maryland (marry)	Annapolis (apple)	A couple getting *married* eating *apples*.
Massachusetts (mast)	Boston (boxer)	A *boxer* boxing in front of a ship's *mast*.
Michigan (pitch again)	Lansing (lamb)	A *lamb* at bat telling the pitcher, "*Pitch again!*"
Minnesota (mini-soda)	St. Paul (St. Paul)	*St. Paul* drinking a *mini-soda*.

(continued)

Mnemonic Strategies for Remembering the States and Their Capitals—*continued*

State (keyword)	Capital (keyword)	Mnemonic Picture
Mississippi (misses)	Jackson (jacks)	Two girls (*misses*) playing with *jacks*.
Missouri (misery)	Jefferson City (chef)	A *chef* in *misery* because his cake fell.
Montana (mountain)	Helena (Helen of Troy)	*Helen of Troy* standing on a *mountain*.
Nebraska (new brass)	Lincoln (Abe Lincoln)	Abe *Lincoln* polishing *new brass*.
Nevada (new ladder)	Carson City (car city)	A man climbing a *ladder* to get to *Car City*.
New Hampshire (hamster)	Concord (conquer)	A *hamster* as a *conquerer*.
New Jersey (jersey)	Trenton (tent)	A *tent* with a *jersey* on it.
New Mexico (Mexico)	Santa Fe (Santa Claus)	*Santa Claus* going to *Mexico*.
New York (new pork)	Albany (all baloney)	Man at deli counter: "Is this *new pork*?" Butcher: "It's *all baloney!*"
North Carolina (carolers)	Raleigh (trolley)	*Carolers* singing in a *trolley*.
North Dakota (northern coat)	Bismarck (businessman)	A *businessman* dressed in a *northern* (cold weather) *coat*.
Ohio ("Oh, hi!")	Columbus (Christopher Columbus)	A person saying, *"Oh, hi, Columbus!"*
Oklahoma (oak home)	Oklahoma City (Oak Home City)	Building an *oak home* in *Oak Home City*.
Oregon (ore)	Salem (sailboat)	A *sailboat* carrying *ore*.
Pennsylvania (pen)	Harrisburg (hairy)	A *hairy* (furry) *pen*.
Rhode Island (road to an island)	Providence (provide)	A builder says he will *provide a road* to the *island*.
South Carolina (southern carolers)	Columbia (column)	*Carolers* singing in front of a southern mansion with *columns*.
South Dakota (southern coat)	Pierre (pier)	A man wearing a *southern* (warm weather) *coat* standing at a *pier*.
Tennessee (tennis)	Nashville (cash)	Playing *tennis* for *cash*.
Texas (taxes)	Austin (ostrich)	An *ostrich* says, "I'll never be able to pay these *taxes!*"
Utah (you saw)	Salt Lake City (salt lake)	Dialogue: "What was it *you saw*?" "*Salt* in the *lake!*"
Vermont (worm mountain)	Montpelier (mountain pliers)	Removing worms from worm mountain with *mountain pliers*.
Virginia (fur)	Richmond (rich man)	A *rich man* buying a *fur* jacket.
Washington (ton of wash)	Olympia (Olympic)	An *Olympic* event: *Wash a ton* of laundry.
West Virginia (vest fur)	Charleston (King Charles)	King *Charles* wearing a *vest* made of *fur*.
Wisconsin (whisk broom)	Madison (maid)	A *maid* using a *whisk broom*.
Wyoming (Y-home)	Cheyenne (shy Anne)	*Shy Anne* lives in the *Y-home* (home shaped like a "Y").

characterized as English language learners benefited most from the strategies, remembering 30% more information when instructed mnemonically.

Combine Mnemonic Strategies with Reconstructive Elaborations. **Reconstructive elaborations** refers to procedures for reconstructing information into more meaningful and memorable forms. Three types of reconstructions include acoustic (or keyword) reconstructions, symbolic reconstructions, and mimetic reconstructions (Scruggs & Mastropieri, 1989, 1992).

The **keyword** method (or **acoustic reconstructions**) is best used when the information to be learned is unfamiliar. Such terms as *saprophytic, nepenthe,* or *carnelian* are excellent candidates for the keyword method because they are unfamiliar, and similar-sounding keywords (acoustic reconstructions) can be created. Unfamiliar proper names (e.g., *Modigliani, Volga*) also fit into this category.

Some information is familiar to students, but is more *abstract* and difficult to picture. In such cases, teachers can use **symbolic reconstructions,** in which the information is reconstructed into a symbolic picture, rather than a keyword (acoustic) picture. For example, to demonstrate the U.S. policy of neutrality before World War I, a picture could be shown of Uncle Sam (symbol for U.S. policy) watching the war in Europe and exclaiming, "It's not my fight!"

Some information is familiar and concrete, and does not need to be transformed into familiar forms. In these cases **pictorial or mimetic reconstructions** work best. For example, a U.S. history text states that World War I soldiers stationed in unhealthy trenches were more likely to die from disease than from battle wounds. Since students probably are already familiar with "trench" and "disease," it is not necessary to create keywords; rather, simply picture *sick soldiers* in *trenches* to demonstrate the relation. Students can simply think back to the picture and retrieve the answer (Mastropieri & Scruggs, 1989). Similarly, to help students remember that sponges grow on the ocean floor, simply show a picture of sponges growing on the ocean floor.

Reconstructive elaborations refers to a method for classifying important information in terms of familiarity and concreteness, and developing appropriate strategies. This method can be useful in planning and developing mnemonic strategies across larger units of content.

USE THE PEGWORD METHOD FOR NUMBERED OR ORDERED INFORMATION

Pegwords are rhyming words for numbers, and are useful in learning numbered or ordered information. Commonly used pegwords are provided in Figure 10.7 (see also Browning, 1983; Willott, 1982). For example, to remember that insects have six legs, picture an insect crawling on *sticks* (pegword for six). To remember that spiders have eight legs, picture a spider spinning a web on a *gate* (pegword for eight).

Pegwords can be helpful in remembering the three classes of levers (based on the arrangement of fulcrum, load, and force). For example, a rake is an example of a third-class lever (with the ful-

Number	Pegword	Number	Pegword
one	bun, sun, or gun	fourteen	forking
two	shoe	fifteen	fixing
three	tree	sixteen	sitting
four	door or floor	seventeen	severing
five	hive	eighteen	aiding
six	sticks	nineteen	knighting
seven	heaven	twenty	twin
eight	gate	thirty	dirty or thirsty
nine	vine or lion	forty	party
ten	hen	fifty	gifty
eleven	lever	sixty	witchy
twelve	elf	seventy	heavenly
thirteen	thirsting		

Figure 10.7 Pegwords

Figure 10.8 Pegword Mnemonic Strategy for Classes of Levers: Oar = 1st Class, Wheelbarrow = 2nd Class, Rake = 3rd Class

Note: From *A Practical Guide for Teaching Science to Students with Special Needs in Inclusive Settings* (p. 154), by M. A. Mastropieri & T. E. Scruggs, 1993, Austin, TX: Pro-Ed. Copyright 1993 by Purdue Research Foundation. Reprinted with permission.

crum at one end and the force at the middle), so you can provide a picture of a rake leaning against a *tree* (pegword for three). Examples of each of the three classes of levers are shown in Figure 10.8.

Pegwords can also be used to remember lists of information, such as the following:

- possible reasons (ranked by plausibility) that dinosaurs might have become extinct (Veit, Scruggs, & Mastropieri, 1986).
- the hardness levels of minerals (pegwords can also be combined with keywords for this; Scruggs, Mastropieri, Levin, & Gaffney, 1985).
- the order of U.S. presidents (Mastropieri, Scruggs, & Whedon, 1997).
- multiplication tables (pegwords can be used with other pegwords; Greene, 1999; Willott, 1982; see Chapter 14).

USE LETTER STRATEGIES FOR LISTS   Letter strategies can be useful for remembering lists of things. For example, the HOMES strategy prompts recall of the names of the Great Lakes (H—Huron; O—Ontario, etc.). However, this strategy will only be effective if students are familiar enough with the names of the Great Lakes that thinking of a single letter will prompt the entire name. That is, if students are not familiar with the name Ontario, the letter "O" will not be enough to help them remember it. To ensure letter strategies are effective, ask students to rehearse the names represented by the letters.

The HOMES strategy is an example of an **acronym.** An acronym is word formed from the first letters of the words to be remembered. Another example of an acronym is "FARM-B," which is used to remember the names of the classes of vertebrate animals (F—fish, A—amphibian, R—reptile, M—mammal, B—bird). A picture showing vertebrate animals on a farm can help enforce this concept. In this strategy, the "B" serves no particular purpose—it is just left over after "farm" is spelled. Students need to practice this to remember it is FARM-B, and not some other letter.

In spite of their success and popularity, acronyms are not as versatile as other mnemonics. The reason for this is that many lists of things to be remembered do not contain first letters that can easily be combined into words. For example, the first letters of the planets in the solar system (M, V, E, M, J, S, N, U, P), cannot be easily combined into an acronym, mostly because the list contains seven consonants and only two vowels. Also, it seems important to create a mnemonic that preserves the order of the planets from the sun. To accomplish this, an **acrostic** can be used instead. To form an acrostic, a word is created from each first letter, and the words are arranged to make a sentence. To remember the planets, a good acrostic is, "My very educated mother just served us nine pizzas." The first letter of each of the words in this sentence represents the planets in order of their distance from the sun. Another example of an acrostic is "My Dear Aunt Sally," which reminds students to *M*ultiply and *D*ivide before they *A*dd and *S*ubtract in a math sentence (see Chapter 14). Another version is, "Please Excuse My Dear Aunt Sally," which includes *P*arenthetical expressions and *E*xponents, prior to the previously described sequence of operations. The elaborated sentence, "King Philip's Class Ordered a Family of Gentile Spaniels," can promote memory of taxonomic ranks: Kingdom, Phylum, Class, Order, Family, Genus, and Species. Both acronyms and acrostics must be practiced to ensure all aspects of the mnemonic have been mastered.

Finally, letter strategies can be combined with keywords or pegwords. For example, to promote recall of three countries in the Central Powers during World War I, provide a picture of children playing tag in Central Park. *Central Park* is a keyword for Central Powers, and *TAG* is an acronym for Turkey, Austria–Hungary, and Germany (Figure 10.9). To help students remember freedoms guaranteed by the First Amendment to the Constitution, provide a picture of a rap singer who *raps* about *buns*. *Buns* is a pegword for one, or first, amendment, and *RAPS* is an acronym for the freedoms of religion, assembly, press, and speech.

CREATE MNEMONIC PICTURES   Although some mnemonic pictures are available commercially (see Burchers, Burchers, & Burchers, 1997, 2000, for some vocabulary materials), in most cases teachers will have to develop their own materials. Some teachers feel that they cannot use mnemonic strategies because they are not artistically inclined, and feel unable to draw good mnemonic pictures. However, it is not necessary that the pictures be "artistic"; rather, it is only important that they are recognizable. You can use stick figures or cut-outs from magazines to create pictures. Some teachers have enlisted the assistance of an artistic student to help. However, clip art is probably the easiest way to create excellent mnemonic pictures. Software containing literally hundreds of thousands of clip art pictures is available commercially, and clip art is sometimes included on word-processing and office software. As an alternative, a great deal of clip art is available on the Internet, and can be located by typing in "clip art" followed by the picture being sought (e.g., "clip art frog") on a search engine. Mnemonic pictures are not difficult to create and, once created, can be used again and again to improve students' memory of important content. In some cases, materials have already been created. For mnemonic strategies for learning hundreds of secondary-level vocabulary words, for example, see Burchers, Burchers, and Burchers (1997, 2000).

COMBINE MNEMONIC STRATEGIES WITH OTHER CLASSROOM ACTIVITIES
Mnemonic strategies are not only powerful tools for improving memory, they are very versa-

Figure 10.9   Mnemonic Strategy for Central Powers
Note: From *Teaching Students Ways to Remember: Strategies for Learning Mnemonically* (p. 119), by M. A. Mastropieri & T. E. Scruggs, 1991, Cambridge, MA: Brookline Books. Copyright 1991 by Brookline Books. Reprinted with permission.

Central Powers
(Central Park)

Turkey
Austria Hungary
Germany

TAG!

Central Park

tile, and can be incorporated with other means of instruction. For example, the keyword method was used to improve recall of important vocabulary (e.g., predator-prey; parasite-host) for hands-on science learning. Students used the keyword method to help remember important vocabulary, while they engaged in hands-on activities to enhance their understanding of important scientific concepts relevant to ecosystems (Mastropieri et al., 1998).

Mnemonic strategies have also been employed in peer tutoring configurations in high school chemistry classes. Mastropieri, Scruggs, and Graetz (2005) combined mnemonic strategies with peer tutoring to develop recall and comprehension of important science content. For example, to learn that a *mole* is the atomic weight of a substance in grams, students were shown a picture of a mole sitting on a scale, getting its weight in grams. Students tutored each other on their recall of the fact and strategy. However, students also questioned each other on additional information about moles, for instance, what is important to know about moles and examples of moles and how they are calculated (see Figure 10.10).

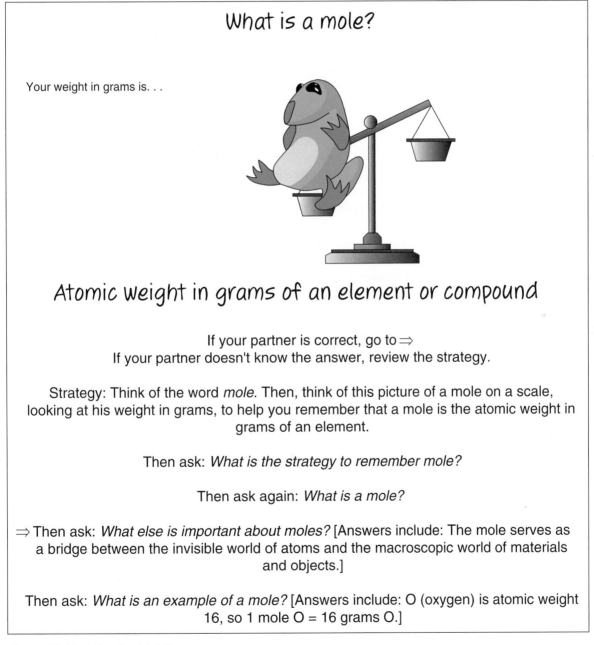

Figure 10.10 What Is a Mole?

Note: From *Teaching Tutorial: Mnemonics Instruction,* by T. E. Scruggs & M. A. Mastropieri, 2002, TeachingLD.org, copyright 2002 by TeachingLD.org, Division for Learning Disabilities. Reprinted with permission.

Although mnemonic strategies have provided very powerful effects in experimental research in special and inclusive settings, they should not be considered a panacea for learning. Attend to all the strategies for improving memory, be sure to provide lots of practice, and monitor comprehension and application of learning to other domains. By using all these strategies, and evaluating progress, you can maximize all your students' memory for school success.

10 Summary

- Attention and memory are two important psychological processes necessary for success in school. Being able to attend to and remember academic content is often a problem for many students with special needs. However, research has uncovered many successful strategies for enhancing attention and memory.

- Effective teaching, including using the teacher planning and presentation variables, can help all students pay more attention in class.

- Simple strategies for increasing attention include asking students directly to try to pay attention better, or moving closer to the student who struggles to attend.

- Breaking activities into smaller segments, alternating among various types of class activities, allowing opportunities for movement, using reinforcement, and teaching self-recording may also help improve attendance.

- Peer assistance can be used to promote attention of students with a variety of special needs. Reinforcement of attention and teaching self-recording strategies can also be effective.

- Meeting the preconditions for improving memory may help many students remember better. These preconditions include promoting attention, motivation, and positive attitudes.

- Teaching students metacognitive awareness strategies ("metamemory") helps promote better memory strategies for all students.

- Using pictures, enhancing meaningfulness, using activities, providing sufficient practice, and promoting active learning all help promote better memory for students with disabilities.

- Using mnemonic strategies such as the keyword method, the pegword method, and letter strategies helps promote learning of unfamiliar content.

PROFESSIONAL STANDARDS LINK:
Improving Attention and Memory

Information in this chapter links most directly to:

- CEC Standards: 3 (Individual Learning Differences), 4 (Instructional Strategies), 5 (Learning Environments and Social Interactions), 6 (Language), 7 (Instructional Planning)

- INTASC Standards: Principles 2 (provides appropriate learning opportunities), 3 (understands learning differences, adapts instructional opportunities), 4 (instructional strategies), 5 (creates learning environments), 6 (fosters inquiry, collaboration, interaction), 7 (plans instruction)

- PRAXIS II™ Content Categories (Knowledge): 3 (Delivery of Services)

- PRAXIS II™ Content Categories (Application): 1 (Curriculum), 2 (Instruction)

IMPROVING ATTENTION AND MEMORY

If students are having problems with attention, have you considered the following?
If not, see the pages listed below.

STRATEGIES FOR IMPROVING ATTENTION ───

- [ ] Address the preconditions of attention with teacher effectiveness, 224–225
- [ ] Provide assistance with basic skills problems, 225
- [ ] Use direct appeal, 225
- [ ] Use proximity, 225
- [ ] Break up activities, 225
- [ ] Allow sufficient movement to reduce restlessness, 225–226
- [ ] Provide student activities, 226
- [ ] Use classroom peers to promote attention, 226
- [ ] Provide direct consequences for attention, 227–228
- [ ] Teach self-recording strategies, 228–229

STRATEGIES FOR ADDRESSING EXTREME CASES OF ATTENTION ─── DEFICITS

- [ ] Provide intensive teacher-led instruction, 229
- [ ] Consider strengths and weaknesses of stimulant medication, 229

STRATEGIES FOR SPECIAL NEEDS OF STUDENTS WITH AUTISM ───

If students are having problems with memory, have you considered the following? If not, see the pages listed below.

STRATEGIES FOR IMPROVING MEMORY ───

- [ ] Address memory preconditions, 231
- [ ] Develop "metamemory," 231
- [ ] Use external memory, 231
- [ ] Enhance meaningfulness, 232
- [ ] Use concrete examples, pictures, or imagery, 232–233
- [ ] Minimize interfering information, 233–234
- [ ] Use enactments and manipulation, 234
- [ ] Promote active reasoning, 234
- [ ] Increase practice, 234–235
- [ ] Use clustering and organization, 236
- [ ] Promote elaboration, 236

STRATEGIES FOR IMPROVING MEMORY WITH MNEMONIC ─── TECHNIQUES

- [ ] Use the keyword method for verbal associations, 237–242
- [ ] Use the pegword method for numbered or ordered information, 242–243
- [ ] Use letter strategies for lists, 243–244
- [ ] Create mnemonic pictures, 244
- [ ] Combine mnemonic strategies with other classroom activities, 244–246

Shadow

PAUL PRIMUS   Paul Primus already had a passion for photography before being diagnosed with ankylosing spondylitis, but it was just a hobby. After the diagnosis, he chose to fully embrace photography and take his life in that direction. "Being disabled has given me a new viewpoint on how I see the world. It has opened many new avenues up for me and inspired me to educate myself further in photography and graphic design. I'm sure that if I had not become disabled, I would not be in the position that I'm in today. I believe 'that with determination you can overcome any barriers that you have to confront in life.' "

11
Teaching Study Skills

OBJECTIVES

After studying this chapter, you should be able to:

- Demonstrate understanding of tools to develop independent learners and personal organizational skills.
- Identify ways to clearly state class expectations for successful completion of homework.
- Define the purpose, requisite skills, and various strategies to practice effective listening skills.
- Identify and demonstrate understanding of various note-taking skills and strategies.
- Demonstrate familiarity with various library resources and reference skills necessary to complete successfully a report or project.
- Describe and apply strategies for assisting students with disabilities to prepare reports and projects.

Good study skills are necessary for success in school. Although some general education students appear to develop excellent organization and study skills independently, most students with disabilities and students at risk for failure in school can benefit from explicit instruction in organizing themselves for studying and completing assignments in a timely fashion. Research has demonstrated that individuals who are trained to use efficient study and organizational strategies perform better and are more likely to succeed in school (Berry, Hall, & Gildroy, 2004).

CLASSROOM SCENARIO

Ravi

When Ravi, a ninth-grader with learning disabilities, entered Mr. Ford's room, he was holding a stack of books with papers sticking out from all angles. Some of the papers were bent, some were folded, some were slightly torn, but all books had been covered with brightly colored paper. As he approached the desks, his glasses were sliding down toward the end of his nose and he slightly bumped the edge of one of the tables. Before you could blink your eyes, everything that had been in his arms was strewn all over the floor. Ravi smiled sheepishly as he began to pick up his belongings.

Somewhere in that pile of books and papers there was evidence of Ravi's attempts at completing his homework. When Mr. Ford asked him about it, Ravi said, "I've done some of the homework, but I can't seem to find it at the moment. . . ." This was a typical day for Ravi. Although he usually attempted his assignments, he either could not find them or he would forget about his homework and appear confused when asked about it—almost as if it were the first time he had heard of the assignment.

Learning strategies help all students study more effectively. This chapter describes how to help your students become more personally organized and efficient at planning for homework, developing effective listening and note-taking skills, and learning to use outlining and guided notes. In addition, strategies are presented for using libraries, writing reports, completing long-term assignments and projects, and studying for later retrieval.

Tools for Developing Independent Learners

Study skills are tools for learning. Several excellent study skills books are available (e.g., Carter, Bishop, Block, & Kravits, 2005; Greene, 2004; Wood, Woloshyn, & Willoughby, 1995). Most study skills textbooks present a number of study skills and strategies with the expectation that students will master all strategies with minimal instruction. Many students with disabilities, however, do not have good study and learning strategies and experience difficulties when trying to use these strategies independently. These students may require extensive explicit instruction in learning strategies, controlled practice, and feedback before they are able to execute them successfully independently. Teaching students to become independent learners and thinkers includes providing "tools for learners" in self-instruction, self-monitoring, self-questioning, and self-reinforcement (Deshler & Schumaker, 2005).

STRATEGIES FOR
DEVELOPING PERSONAL ORGANIZATIONAL SKILLS

myeducationlab

Go to MyEducationLab, select the topic *Inclusive Practices*, and go to the Activities and Applications section. As you read the strategy entitled "Organization is at Hand: PDAs in the Inclusive Classroom," consider how important this technology could be for a student with a disability.

Personal organizational skills include using time schedules; understanding class and school schedules; using a daily, weekly, and monthly planner; and being organized for completing homework assignments. These skills are what some experts call good self-management skills. Other organizational skills include knowing how to analyze tasks required for assignments and optimizing performance and studying time (Guerin & Male, 2006). Provide general information about study skills to your entire class, and arrange small groups of students who need additional instruction in study skills. Special education teachers can work with you and provide instruction in these strategies for those who need it. Finally, you may decide to team-teach groups of students who need to learn these strategies. However you present them, study and organizational skills will reap huge benefits in student performance.

POST AND REVIEW CLASS AND TIME SCHEDULES   All grade levels follow systematic schedules. Present the schedules to students with disabilities in clear, comprehensible language to ensure they are prepared for each segment of the school day.

Many elementary teachers write daily agendas or schedules on the board that contain all daily class activities, such as the one shown in Figure 11.1. The list can include reminders to bring specific materials for various classes and brief descriptions of homework assignments. Future events also can be highlighted. For example, highlighting special classes such as art, music, and physical education can help students remember to bring sneakers and shorts for gym class or instruments for music class. Although many students may not require these reminders, students who do need them will not feel singled out when you make the information available to all.

Secondary schools require students to see many teachers throughout the school day. Some schools have a constant number of daily periods throughout the week, while other schools have rotating schedules—referred to as block scheduling—that alternate daily. Although they allow longer class periods, block systems can be confusing. You may need to review and re-review schedules with some students. Figure 11.2 shows an example of a block schedule.

How to Start   At the beginning of a new year or semester you may need to describe for students how to locate rooms within the school. This is especially important in very large build-

8:00–8:10	Get ready for the school day (sharpen pencils, use restrooms)
8:10–8:15	Complete scrambled sentence activity
8:15–9:15	Reading
9:15–9:40	Recess and restroom breaks
9:40–10:40	Mathematics
10:40–11:15	Writing and Language Arts
11:15–12:15	Lunch and Recess
12:15–1:15	Science
1:15–2:15	Social Studies
2:15–2:45	Physical Education (Tues–Thurs)

BRING SHORTS and SNEAKERS for GYM Tomorrow!!!

Music (Mon)

Art (Wed–Fri)

Figure 11.1 Sample Elementary School Daily Agenda

Black Day Schedule

Daily Order	Period
1. First	1. English, room 204
2. Second	2. Phys. Ed, gym
3. Third	3. Algebra I, room 105
4. Fourth	4. Study Hall, cafeteria

Red Day Schedule

Daily Order	Period
1. First	5. Biology, room 209
2. Second	6. U.S. Government, room 115
3. Third	7. Band, music room
4. Fourth	8. Spanish, room 215

Figure 11.2 Sample Secondary School Schedule

ings, where one floor looks similar to another. One idea might be to make yourself, a peer, or an aide available to meet students before or after school to go over their class schedules and walk it through with them. Follow up by meeting students after each class when needed and walk with them to the next class until students demonstrate confidence about where they are and where they need to be at what time. All students wish to appear as competent as their peers seem to be, and although they might be confused about building layouts and schedules, they may not want to risk embarrassing themselves by asking for help. Your awareness and subtle ways of keying into students' needs can enhance students' self-perceptions.

Don't Forget Lockers   As students move from class to class they may need to visit their lockers for books or materials. This can be particularly challenging for some students with disabilities because the use of lockers requires extra time and mental and physical challenges. If students have trouble remembering the combination, practice with the students, or suggest they write the combination (secretly) on a wallet-size card for easy access until they master the information.

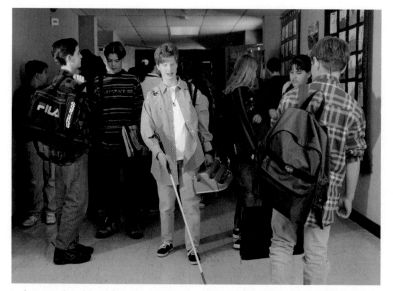

In large school buildings, practice finding the rooms where classes will take place is an essential "beginning-of-the-year" activity for secondary students with disabilities.

Provide extra time and instructions for opening lockers. Some students have been known to carry everything (all books, notebooks, lunch, and coats) around all day simply because they could not open their lockers. Another student pretended she hated physical education and refused to participate in gym, when she actually did not know how to open her locker that contained her gym clothing. Finally, note the accessibility of lockers. Lockers or locks that are placed too high or low can cause unnecessary frustrations.

Clearly Post and Review Schedule Changes
Some students do not handle changes well, but if they are prepared ahead of time, they will be more likely to adjust to the changes. For example, explain what will happen if you are absent from school and a substitute teacher is assigned to take over the class. Believe it or not, some students with emotional disabilities may be very upset when you are absent! These changes may be particularly difficult for some students if you are gone for a long period of time, such as for an extended medical or maternity leave. When students are informed ahead of time, these transitions can be handled more smoothly.

At the middle and secondary levels, it is common for students to have different teachers for each subject. Each teacher may establish different class routines and expectations. Many students with disabilities require extra help learning the routines that are used in each teacher's classroom (Mastropieri & Scruggs, 2002). For example, some teachers may require students to be seated when the class bell rings, while others may require that students only be inside the room when the bell rings. Encourage students to write down any specific expectations and routines for each class and teacher. Take care to show students your own class expectations, schedules, and routines and provide support for them while they are learning all of the new routines simultaneously. A little role-playing or memory game might help. For example, say the name of a teacher to a group of students and ask them to quickly tell you the unique expectations that teacher has.

USE STRATEGIES FOR DAILY, WEEKLY, AND MONTHLY PLANNING   Many adults use daily planner calendars that contain space for weekly and monthly entries. These planners are ideally suited to keeping track of both long-term and short-term school assignments. Show students a variety of planner formats and have them select one that meets their needs. Show them how most effective people in all disciplines use some type of planner to help keep organized. Ask other teachers, the principal, parents, and businesspeople from the community to visit your class and share the way they plan and schedule events.

Explain the differences between long- and short-term planning. Provide examples of how studying time needs to be divided among subject areas and across types of assignments (Rafoth, Leal, & DeFabo, 1993). Provide examples of "to-do" lists and show students how to prioritize them. Some people like to do the easiest thing on the list first; others prefer to get the hardest item out of the way first. Figure 11.3 shows a sample planner and to-do list that might work for individual content areas. Encourage students to discuss optimal ways of proceeding for themselves. Students with disabilities may need specific examples of each step spelled out for them. For example, general education students with good study habits:

1. review their assignment notebooks,
2. prioritize what needs to get accomplished,
3. set goals of finishing tasks for themselves, and
4. work hard to accomplish those goals.

Conversely, students with disabilities may be forgetful and may not deliberately plan their activities. Some may need teachers to complete sample planners for them and take them step by step through the thinking involved in figuring out what to do.

Student _____				_____ Quarter		
Subject	To do	Assigned on	Due date	Turned in on	Parent initials

Figure 11.3 Sample Planner and To-Do List

USE TASK ANALYSIS TO ORGANIZE ASSIGNMENTS **Task analysis** is the process of taking a large task or assignment, breaking it into subcomponent smaller tasks, and estimating task completion time for each subcomponent. Teach students to write out the assignment, decide what must be done, sequence the steps of what must be done, and estimate the amount of time necessary to complete each step. For example, a biology teacher may make an assignment that students read pages 264–277 in the textbook, write a summary paragraph, and answer questions 13–21 at the end of the chapter. A task analysis may reveal that the student must:

- locate the textbook and a quiet area to work;
- find the relevant text pages and read carefully, highlighting or taking notes;
- write a summary paragraph based on reading and notes;
- locate the relevant questions at the end of the chapter;
- answer all questions, referring to text and notes; and
- check all work and be certain all components of the assignment are completed.

Figure 11.4 shows a planning task sequence for preparing a book report.

TEACH STRATEGIES FOR HOMEWORK COMPLETION Homework is assigned at virtually all grade levels, but increases in regularity and complexity with each grade level (Jakulski & Mastropieri, 2004). Homework provides opportunities for students to develop fluency with the information being taught and to develop organizational and self-study skills.

Some homework assignments may need to be reduced in size and scope for students with disabilities, who may need more time to process and complete the same activities. Polloway, Foley, and Epstein (1992), for example, reported that students with learning disabilities had more than 2½ times more difficulties completing homework than their peers did. Because performance on homework is often included in computing semester grades, consider modifying the amount and type of homework or the grading procedures for students with disabilities (Polloway, Epstein, Bursuck, Jayanthi, & Cumblad, 1994). Figure 11.5 lists some assignments and possible adaptations.

Most students with disabilities find it helpful to record their assignments in an assignment notebook. Include spaces for teachers' and parents' signatures to help ensure that your students asked someone to verify whether assignments were completed accurately. This also keeps parents informed so they can monitor homework progress daily. Most parents likely would appreciate a letter requesting their assistance in establishing homework procedures and arranging an environment conducive to studying at home (see Figure 11.6). Myles, Ferguson, and Hagiwara (2007) reported that an adolescent autistic student with Asperger syndrome greatly improved recording homework assignments by using a personal digital assistant (PDA).

When assigning students homework, provide clear instructions, and always explain the purpose of the assignment. Write assignments in the same location daily so that students can find them easily and copy them accurately into their assignment notebooks. Such predictable, consistent practices can help students establish patterns that promote success.

myeducationlab

Go to MyEducationLab, select the topic *Instructional Practices and Learning Strategies*, and go to the Activities and Applications section. As you analyze the strategy entitled "Promoting Generalization," reflect on the aspects of this strategy that you could use to enhance task analysis for assignments.

	Sun	Mon	Tues	Wed	Thurs	Fri	Sat
Week 1							
Week 2							
Week 3							
Week 4							

Assigned Date _____ Due Date _____ Time Available _____ days

1. Go to library and select book. (1 day)
2. Count chapters or pages in book and determine the number of chapters or pages that should be read daily (e.g., 13 chapters or 208 pages). Adjust according to your reading rate and the number of days available. For example, if you can read 1 chapter per day you will need 13 days. If you can read 16 pages a day, you will need 13 days to read the book.
3. Brainstorm book report outline. (1 day)
4. Organize outline from brainstorming activity. (1 day)
5. Fill in details on outline. (1 day)
6. Write draft book report using outline. (2 days)
7. Proof and revise first draft of book report. (2 days)
8. Write final version and proof carefully. (2 days)

Total number of nights necessary to complete assignment—20

	Sun	Mon	Tues	Wed	Thurs	Fri	Sat
Week 1		Go to library and select book	Count pages and chapters and figure out how much to read daily	Read	Read	Read	Read
Week 2		Read	Read	Read	Read	Read	Read
Week 3		Read	Read	Read	Brainstorm book report outline	Organize outline from brainstorming	Fill in outline details
Week 4		Write first draft	Write first draft	Write first draft	Write final draft	Edit and proof final version	Proof final version

Figure 11.4   Task Planning for a Book Report

Several teaching practices can help students complete their homework successfully (see also Jakulski & Mastropieri, 2004):

- Give clear, concise directions for completing assignments; establish due dates that are reasonable and clearly communicated.
- Describe any materials necessary to complete each assignment. For example, will students need to take their textbooks home with them? Will they need to go to the library and sign out materials before they can complete the work? Will they need to bring materials to class?
- If you provide a sample of the homework assignment, complete it together as a class, be specific, and ensure that students understand what they are to do by asking two or three students to repeat or explain the directions.

Subject	Assignment	Adapted Assignment
Spelling	Study 20 words.	Study 10 prioritized words.
Math	Complete 30 word problems.	Complete 15 prioritized word problems.
Reading	Read 2 chapters and write a summary.	Read 1 chapter and tape record a summary of the information; or listen to an audiotape recording of the 2 chapters and tape a summary of both chapters.
Social Studies	Read section 3 in chapter 4 and answer the 20 questions at the end of the section.	Read section 3 in chapter 4 and answer the even-numbered questions at the end of the section (half the questions).
Science	Write a summary of the experiment completed during today's lab.	Tape record a summary of the experiment completed in today's lab.

Figure 11.5 Homework Assignments and Possible Adaptations

- Anticipate any areas of difficulty with an assignment and attempt to provide extra clarification.

- Explain how students can get help if they confront problems. Perhaps some students could be trained as "telephone homework assistants" who could be contacted in the evenings until 8 o'clock. Distribute a list of names and phone numbers of these homework assistants.

- Establish a regular time for collecting and distributing assignments. Establish special locations for dropping off and picking up completed and corrected assignments.

- Consistently collect, grade, and return assigned work. When teachers neglect to collect or return graded assignments, some students take away the message that homework is unimportant to them.

- Coordinate assignments with other teachers. Your students with disabilities will benefit greatly from any shared planning you do with your co-teachers to avoid scheduling several exams on a single day or overlapping longer-term assignments.

- Arrange classroom incentives for completing and turning in homework. Some teachers establish either individual or class rewards to encourage timely completion of homework. For example, Lynch (2006) reported substantial improvement in homework completion of students with disabilities when group rewards (e.g., stickers, extra recess, points toward a pizza party) were provided for homework completion.

- Remember to assign projects that are within the capability levels of all students. Homework is an opportunity to practice previously acquired skills, develop fluency, and practice applying these skills to new contexts.

Clearly State Class Expectations Provide students with specific expectations for completed work. Explain how you intend to evaluate work and provide examples of what you consider to be "model" assignments and insufficiently completed assignments. Is it acceptable, for example, to turn in a page torn from a spiral notebook? May assignments be completed in pencil? Will you accept incomplete assignments or will those be returned with the grade of "F"? Creating a checklist for students to keep in their notebooks would be helpful.

Date _____

Dear Parent,

As we begin this school year I want you to know how delighted I am to have your child, _____, in my class. I am looking forward to meeting you at our first Open House. Please try to come and bring any questions you may have about this school year with you.

I would like to explain to you some of the procedures and requirements of my class so you will have a better understanding of what is expected of your child. I usually assign homework nightly. Most nights the assignments are rather short and can be completed within 20 minutes. A few times throughout the year, however, I assign longer-term projects that will require your child to work a little bit each night over a period of about a month to complete the project. Examples of the longer-term projects include the following:

- Book reports
- Library research projects
- Models of inventions
- Science fair projects
- Interviews with businesspeople from the community

I would like to request some assistance from you to ensure that your child successfully completes his or her assignments. Every afternoon or evening, **please ask your son or daughter to show you the assignment notebook.** Ideally your child should take the initiative and bring the notebook to you. Please initial and date that day's assignments. That will let me know that you have seen the assignment and ensure that it has been successfully completed or that an honest attempt was made to complete it. Some of you may want to see the assignment book and completed assignment, while others of you may wish to see only the assignment notebook.

Second, it would be most helpful if you could establish a **regular space** for your child to complete his or her assignments. That way, when he or she arrives home from school, all necessary school materials can be placed in a specific location and kept all together. Establishing a regular place also helps ensure that the materials are together and will not be forgotten when leaving for school the next morning.

Third, it would be beneficial to **establish a regular time for your child to do his or her homework.** I realize that this can be difficult because of extra-curricular activities. However, establishing regular homework times on Mondays, Tuesdays, Wednesdays, Thursdays, and Saturdays or Sundays can help illustrate the importance of maintaining responsibility for completing homework.

Finally, please feel free to add notes to the assignment notebook if you wish to communicate any information to me. If you have questions concerning your child's performance or understanding of the assignments, I will do my best to help.

If students don't complete or turn in assignments, they will lose points from their grade and be given after-school detention after missing three assignments.

Thanks so much for your help with this important matter. Please feel free to contact me by telephone or e-mail.

Regards,

Figure 11.6 Homework Procedures: Request for Home–School Cooperation

Cooperative Homework Teams O'Melia and Rosenberg (1994) created cooperative homework teams (CHT) to help middle-school students with learning and behavioral disabilities complete their mathematics homework more frequently and more accurately. Students in CHT classes were assigned into three- and four-member heterogeneous cooperative homework teams. During the first period of class, immediately after the opening activity, the teams met, and a "checker" who had been assigned to each team on a rotating basis graded the assignments for the day, using teacher-made answer sheets. The grades are recorded and returned to the students with corrections. Checkers then turned in all the corrected homework. After 8 weeks of this intervention, results indicated that students who had participated in cooperative homework teams had a 74% rate of homework completion, compared to a 55% rate in comparison classes. Further, CHT condition students were 30% more accurate in the assignments they did complete.

Assignment Completion Strategy Hughes, Ruhl, Schumaker, and Deshler (2002) successfully taught middle-school students with learning disabilities an assignment completion strategy that was successfuly used in their inclusive general education classes. See the *Research Highlight* feature for a description of this study.

The Assignment Completion Strategy

Hughes et al. (2002) evaluated the effects of strategic instruction in assignment completion for nine middle-school students with learning disabilities. These students participated in inclusive classes at least three periods per day, and were reported by their teachers as having great difficulty completing and submitting homework assignments, and as being disorganized in their approach to completing assignments.

The strategy was referred to as "PROJECT," and focused on the sequence of skills necessary for assignment completion. As students worked on the strategy, they completed three forms: a monthly planner, a weekly study schedule, and an assignment sheet, all of which were included in an assignment notebook. PROJECT was employed as a first-letter mnemonic device to represent the following steps:

- **P**repare your forms (fill in monthly planners and weekly study sheets).
- **R**ecord and ask (record the assignment on the assignment sheet, using abbreviations and circling appropriate words [e.g., "write"], and ask questions for clarification).
- **O**rganize (break assignment into parts, estimate number of study sessions, schedule sessions, and take materials home).
- **J**ump to it (overcome task avoidance, obtain needed materials).
- **E**ngage in the work (complete assignment and consult parents).
- **C**heck your work (evaluate quality of work and circle a "quality grade," e.g., A, B, C, on the assignment sheet).
- **T**urn in your work.

Students were trained in 30-minute sessions, four times per week, for 4 weeks. At the end of the training, it was observed that eight of the nine students mastered the strategy, and improved significantly in homework completion rates, quality of completed assignments, and quarterly grades. Hughes et al. (2002) acknowledged the success of the strategy, but also highlighted the importance of motivation and the appropriateness of the assignment.

QUESTIONS FOR REFLECTION

1. Would strategy training in one class lead to improvements in other classes? How could you tell?
2. What could you do if you did not have the same amount of time as Hughes et al. to devote to training this strategy?
3. What could you do to increase motivation to complete homework assignments?
4. How could you evaluate the appropriateness of assignments for particular students?

Family involvement can also improve homework completion and improve study skills. See the *Diversity in the Classroom* feature for some suggestions.

STRATEGIES FOR
PROMOTING LISTENING SKILLS

Listening skills are critical for school success (Devine, 1987). Because teachers provide oral directions and instructions continually throughout the school day, students who have good listening skills can follow along, understand what is expected of them, and be successful in school. Many students, however, especially younger elementary-age children and students with disabilities and attention deficit disorders, lack good listening skills. This hinders their ability to succeed in classes (Deshler & Schumaker, 2005).

ADDRESS REQUISITE LISTENING SKILLS   Verify whether students have the appropriate skills for listening by using the teacher checklist in the *In the Classroom* feature on page 259. First, determine if students can hear the speaker adequately. Judge whether the student's position in the classroom interferes with hearing abilities. For example, does the problem exist when information is presented over the loudspeaker, or during audiovisual presentations? Does it exist during teacher presentations in the classroom, in large-group sessions in auditoriums, or outdoors at recess? Difficulties in hearing in any of these environments may indicate a referral is needed for a hearing test. Specific plans can be devised to assist students, providing them with various seating positions to meet their needs. Have students sit near audiovisual equipment or near the front of large auditoriums, or ask peer assistants to help by repeating directions given outdoors.

Increasing Family Involvement

 Communicating effectively with families can help promote use of study skills at home. Create a climate of trust and mutual respect with families to increase the involvement of families representing diverse cultural and linguistic groups (see Garcia & Ortiz, 2005). Ways to build and strengthen this relationship can be established by opening communication lines with all families. When families see that their partnerships and participation are valued in all aspects of school life, they will be more likely to feel that their cultural diversity is respected.

Learn about your students' sociocultural climates at home and in their local communities. Have students share information about their home life to help familiarize you with their families. Create family-life history booklets using multimedia that students can print and share at school and home. Use this information to enhance instructional planning and to prepare for working with families representing diverse cultural backgrounds.

Determine optimal strategies for working with students and families for whom English is a second language. Effective strategies exist for easing communication challenges with individuals who may not use English at home. Use interpreters whenever possible, but also ask students for strategies for communicating with their families. Frequently, students can supply you with additional insights for communicating with their family members. Other strategies can be found in recent research.

Norland (2005) found that English language learners in eighth-grade science classes used a variety of strategies to promote comprehension. Some students learned to take notes and would bring those notes home to study. Other students relied heavily on peers who were also English language learners. As students' confidence and usage of English improved, students began to rely more heavily on teachers for assistance. Norland concluded that language proficiency appeared to be the largest barrier to classroom success. When teachers can implement additional culturally responsive strategies that facilitate English comprehension, students' success will increase.

Teachers can use findings such as these to help improve working relationships with families of English language learners. For example, it may be beneficial to have the students with their family members at parent meetings. Students may be able to help bridge gaps in communication and help build family members' confidence in working with teachers.

Second, determine whether an attention problem exists. To help students come to attention and to encourage active listening from the start, try pairing a visual cue with the beginning of the listening activity. For example, flip the light switch in the room or on the overhead projector to alert students the presentation is about to begin. Pair a teacher movement, such as walking and standing still in the front of the room for a few seconds, with the beginning of new lectures. If sustaining attention is a problem, use strategies for maintaining attention described in Chapter 10. Remember also that attending may be a function of the degree to which you make your presentations interesting. Use the teacher effectiveness variables discussed in Chapter 6, and use interesting and engaging materials. Miller (2003), for example, explained how the listening skills of English language learners can be addressed by using culturally relevant, authentic materials.

Third, determine if students understand the speaker. Unfamiliar accents or dialects can be difficult to understand or the vocabulary and sentence structure may be beyond the lexicon level of students with disabilities. Ask students to repeat what was just said in their own words. You may need to preteach difficult vocabulary and concepts before students can benefit from lecture activities.

Fourth, judge whether students can recognize and select important points from lectures or presentations. Can they follow the sequence of ideas? Do they understand organizational cues used during a lecture, such as *first, second, third, next,* and *then?* Teach students that important points are often introduced at the beginning of lectures and then explained and elaborated on separately after organizational cue statements.

TEACH LISTENING SKILLS   Some students require extra practice in learning how to listen. Use the teacher effectiveness variables discussed in Chapter 6 and design some fun lessons in which students are motivated to learn to listen. Keep the activities short and try the following:

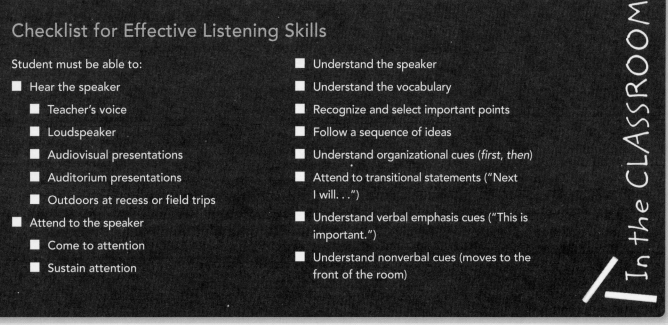

Checklist for Effective Listening Skills

Student must be able to:

- Hear the speaker
  - Teacher's voice
  - Loudspeaker
  - Audiovisual presentations
  - Auditorium presentations
  - Outdoors at recess or field trips
- Attend to the speaker
  - Come to attention
  - Sustain attention

- Understand the speaker
- Understand the vocabulary
- Recognize and select important points
- Follow a sequence of ideas
- Understand organizational cues (*first, then*)
- Attend to transitional statements ("Next I will. . .")
- Understand verbal emphasis cues ("This is important.")
- Understand nonverbal cues (moves to the front of the room)

- Explain the purpose of a listening activity, present information, and then have older students repeat what was presented in their own words. Have younger students act out the sequence of events.

- Model and demonstrate the use of key words and phrases, such as *first, second, third,* and *next.* Give students cards containing cue words and direct them to raise the appropriate cards when they hear them.

- Have students identify important phrases and ask them to tell you when they hear relevant sequences or specific details in the presentations.

- Demonstrate how certain verbal (e.g., "I want you to remember. . .") and nonverbal cues (e.g., extra long pauses) can highlight important information. Have students act out or tell their neighbors the listening cues they hear during a presentation.

- Use topics that are interesting and motivating and include favorite characters from shows, musicians, words from songs, or interviews with famous athletes.

- Give students advance organizers of talks and have them generate questions they would like answered about the upcoming talk.

- Give students several questions before the presentation and have them try to figure out answers to the questions during the talk.

- Ask students to relate the presentation to their own knowledge by asking them what else this talk reminded them of or what else they know about the topic.

- Give outlines or partially completed outlines and study guides to students before listening activities.

- Have students follow along and instruct them to try to listen for "missing" information.

- Segment your presentation into three or four smaller parts. Stop after each segment and have students summarize the major points from each segment and summarize the entire presentation at the conclusion.

When practicing listening skills, emphasize how it is important to try to remember the most important information and the sequence of events. Have students generate questions to use as listening guides. For example, "What is the purpose of this lecture?" "What should I remember from this presentation?" These activities will prepare students for taking notes during lectures. There are, however, some ways you can adjust any lecture or use direct instruction for lower grade levels to effect better listening.

Adjust Lectures   You can include simple techniques during lectures to help facilitate listening and note taking for students (Devine, 1987).

- Begin presentations by stating the overall objectives such as, "Today I will be talking about a, b, and c."
- Include key words and emphasize their use during the presentations, saying in a louder voice, "This is *very* important," or "Here are the three major points," "Listen to this and see if you can _____," "There are five explanations for this event and they are. . . ."
- Write key points on an overhead transparency, chalkboard, or dry erase board while presenting.
- Adjust the pace of the presentation to accommodate students who are taking notes.
- Present schematic diagrams that explain complex concepts or use concrete manipulatives whenever possible to accompany verbal information.
- Stop frequently and encourage students to ask questions about the presented information and have them summarize the content to peers.
- Ask students to predict what a test on the material might include.
- Include "errors" in your talk and ask students to try to find the errors.

Finally, check with any students you suspect might need assistance to see if they obtained the necessary content or if they have any questions. Schedule extra help sessions, office hours, or study sessions when needed.

PLAN FOR SPECIAL LISTENING PROBLEMS   Sometimes there are special problems encountered by students with disabilities during oral presentations. Some of these include the following:

- The pace of the presenter is too rapid.
- Amount of information given is too great.
- Students lack prior knowledge on the presentation topic.
- Language is too difficult.
- Students have difficulties processing and organizing information.

Some presenters speak too rapidly for students with disabilities or students learning English as a second language to comprehend. When this occurs, ask lecturers to slow down and write major points on an overhead projector or chalkboard while speaking. The act of writing while speaking may slow the rate of presentation sufficiently for students. It is appropriate to ask presenters to repeat information to provide an additional opportunity for students to hear the same information. Tape-record important presentations that are presented rapidly, place recorded tapes on reserve or at a listening center, and encourage students to listen again to tapes for review. If variable-speed tape recorders are available, students can play tapes at a comfortable speed for themselves.

The following scenario describes what Mrs. Goodwin does to help her students with disabilities become more familiar with new vocabulary in their general education classes.

CLASSROOM SCENARIO

Mrs. Goodwin

Mrs. Goodwin, a special education teacher, provides all her elementary students with lists of vocabulary that will be covered in future units. She passes the lists out a couple of weeks before the unit is introduced. All students read the words to her and to their parents daily. This familiarizes students with upcoming vocabulary so when they hear the words in general education classes they are familiar with them. Knowing the vocabulary often puts students with special needs one jump ahead of general education students and thus builds self-esteem. The general education teachers tell Mrs. Goodwin that because of this extra practice, students with disabilities are better able to keep up with classwork on the new units. Students also seem to enjoy using the vocabulary lists.

QUESTIONS FOR REFLECTION

1. How would you decide which words should be targeted for practice?
2. What would be the best ways to communicate with parents about the vocabulary learning task?
3. Could you employ a similar technique for material other than vocabulary?

Finally, some students have severe processing and organizing difficulties during listening activities. These students may require oral information to be repeated slowly before they are able to comprehend it. Assistance from special education teachers and speech and language specialists can provide students extra review and practice on the information covered. Also, enlist the help of peer assistants, siblings, and parents to provide additional review and practice at home. Don't forget to use the PASS variables to determine whether all information presented is essential for all students, and that it is appropriately adapted, instructed, and evaluated.

STRATEGIES FOR
TEACHING NOTE-TAKING SKILLS

Note taking provides students with a greater depth of processing of information, and can be used to review information presented orally (Devine, 1987; Gall, Gall, Jacobsen, & Bullock, 1990). Note-taking skills become increasingly important as grade levels increase (Deshler & Schumaker, 2005)—secondary teachers expect students to have good note-taking skills. However, many students are never taught how to take good notes and can benefit from instruction on effective note taking. Several important skills are critical for successful note taking and are listed in the teacher checklist in Figure 11.7. Determine which skills students need help with and ensure that they acquire these skills.

TEACH NOTE-TAKING SKILLS AND STRATEGIES   Teach students that the purpose of notes is to facilitate recall and comprehension of information presented during lectures. Reviewing notes regularly, and particularly just before an exam, can increase a student's chances for success (Carter et al., 2005; Gall et al., 1990).

myeducationlab

Go to MyEducationLab, select the topic *Learning Disabilities*, and go to the Activities and Applications section. As you analyze the strategy entitled "Split-Page Note Taking," reflect on how you could present this strategy to your students and incorporate it into your classroom instruction.

Does the student have:

_____ Listening skills?

_____ Handwriting skills?

_____ Is the student's handwriting legible?

_____ Can the student write rapidly enough?

_____ Keyboarding skills?

_____ Can the student type fast enough?

_____ Are computers and power sources readily available?

Can the student:

_____ Determine the purpose of lectures?

_____ Determine a plan of organization for notes?

_____ Summarize and relate main ideas?

_____ Write down main points?

_____ Use abbreviations?

Does the student:

_____ Read and revise notes?

_____ Study notes?

Figure 11.7   Checklist for Prerequisite Skills for Note Taking

Good note-taking skills are essential for school success.

Be Prepared   Helping students learn how they can be prepared to take notes will promote more self-sufficiency. Be sure they have the right type of paper and pencils or pens to take notes. Encourage students to select the type of paper or pen that is best for them. Allowing students to select their own writing materials may help motivate them during note-taking activities.

Teach How to Write Short Summaries   Showing students how to write summary ideas rather than entire sentences assists them in becoming better note-takers. Demonstrate with examples of good notes and poor notes. Good notes contain major ideas in students' own words and can be used for studying. Poor notes contain lots of unnecessary words such as *the, if, and,* or *but;* or entire verbatim sentences. These practices may make it much more difficult to take notes efficiently.

Ask Questions for Clarification   Encouraging students to ask you to repeat information or clarify the major purpose of lessons helps you monitor whether they know what to write in their notes. A good way to start is to have students ask what the purpose of the lecture is. You can help students with this process by explicitly stating the purpose of the lecture and describing an overall plan of organization before beginning a lecture.

Teach Abbreviations   Using abbreviations reduces the amount of writing and increases the speed of note taking. Teach commonly used abbreviations and have students generate a listing of words and possible abbreviations. For example, "w/" for *with;* "MD" for *doctor;* "<" for *less than;* and "ave." for *average* can be taught and are fairly easy to decipher later. Design practice activities containing common abbreviations and have students practice using and interpreting the abbreviations.

Use Specific Formats for Note Taking   Different note-taking formats are conducive to making notes for certain kinds of topics. Horton, Lovitt, and Christensen (1991) reported that particular column formats helped students perform better in class. Depending on the subject

Class	Date
New Information	Questions or Comments

Figure 11.8   Sample Note-Taking Format

areas in which you teach, you may choose a particular format and encourage students to use it consistently. Distribute blank sheets containing the format, explain how it works, and discuss why you consider it an effective note-taking format. Figure 11.8 displays a note-taking format that you might consider. Show students the importance of leaving spaces in their notes for additions or changes after the lecture, or writing on every other line.

Supplying guided notes to students helps decrease the amount of writing and increase the focus on major ideas. Guided notes are similar to partial outlines, but usually contain more spaces for students to fill in important details during the lectures (Patterson, 2005). Some teachers have students complete guided notes or partial outlines together as a class activity to ensure that students are obtaining critical information from lectures. Guided notes may especially beneficial for topics that contain a great deal of new vocabulary and concepts. Figures 11.9 and 11.10 contain examples of partial outlines and guided notes.

Class: <u>Social Studies</u>   Topic: <u>Products of Indiana</u>   Date: 4/1

Major Ideas	Details	Questions
Agriculture	**Major Crops:** Corn _____ _____ _____	**Where within the state are the various crops grown?**
Industry	**Major Industries** Steel _____ _____ _____	**What are the products of the major industries?** **Where are the major industrial areas located and why?**

Figure 11.9 Guided Notes

Initially, provide many of the elements of the partial outline for your students. As students learn the format you can leave more elements blank.

ARTHROPODS

I. What is an arthropod?
    A. Largest phylum of animals
    B. More than 3/4 of all animals
II. Characteristics of arthropods.
    A. Jointed legs
    B. Exoskeleton
    C. Special heart and blood
III. Types of arthropods
    A. Crustaceans
        1. Crabs
        2. Lobsters
    B. Insects
        1. Beetles
        2.
        3.
    C. Centipedes
    D. Millipedes

Figure 11.10 Partial Outline

Teach Speed and Accuracy Techniques   Start by demonstrating what good note-takers do. Have students share the ways they take notes. For example, some students never take extra time to erase mistakes in their notes, they simply draw a single line through errors. Encouraging students to develop methods and strategies with which they feel comfortable will help them be more effective.

Teach Students How to Study Using Notes   Don't forget to show students what to do with their notes. Many students take notes, close their notebooks after class, and never look at them again. Direct students to review notes after each class and make any corrections or clarifications. They should also jot down questions they may have to clarify later. Show students how they can use "sticky notes" to attach to various pages in their notes to remind them of places for questions.

Finally, teach students how to study using their notes by helping them identify the most important information to study. Then show them how to generate study strategies to facilitate recall and understanding of that important information (Meltzer et al., 1996). Demonstrate strategies to help them remember information in their notes. Explain how they can use their notes to supplement their textbooks when studying for exams.

The LINKS Strategy   The LINKS note-taking strategy stands for **L**isten, **I**dentify verbal cues, **N**ote **K**ey words, and **S**tack information into outline format (Deshler, Schumaker, Alley, Clark, & Warner, 1981). The first two steps encourage students to listen for teacher cues during the lecture. These teacher cues include *organizational cues* (e.g., "Now we will talk about. . ."), *emphasis cues—verbal* (e.g., "Now listen carefully to this. . ."), and *emphasis cues— nonverbal* (e.g., stress, volume, or pace of speaking). When students identify a cue, they are taught to make a circle (a "*link for listening*") on the left margin of their paper. Then they are taught to note *key words* following each cue, writing notes in telegraphic style, including the following:

1. Write words, not complete sentences.
2. Abbreviate words.
3. Do not use any punctuation.
4. Draw a line through an error rather than erase.
5. Allow extra space to add more information.
6. Use synonyms. (Suritsky & Hughes, 1996, pp. 305–306)

The LINKS strategy teaches students to use a two-column format for taking notes. The main ideas go on the left-side column (e.g., names of important people, places, or things) and supporting details (important attributes or characteristics) go on the right-side column.

The AWARE Strategy   The AWARE strategy was developed for college students with learning disabilities, but can be adapted for students in secondary settings (Suritsky & Hughes, 1993). The five steps in AWARE are the following:

1. *A*rrange to take notes
   Arrive early
   Take seat near front/center
   Obtain pen/notebook
   Make note of date
2. *W*rite quickly
   Indent minor points
   Record some words without vowels
   Use common abbreviations
   Note personal examples
3. *A*pply cues
   Attend to accent and organization verbal cues
   Record cued lecture ideas
   Make a checkmark before cued ideas

4. *R*eview notes as soon as possible
5. *E*dit notes
   Add information you forgot to include
   Add personal details (Suritsky & Hughes, 1996, p. 308)

The AWARE strategy can easily be adapted for students in secondary schools. You might try this strategy in your own college courses so you can teach it to students. Provide opportunities to review and offer feedback during the initial phases of instruction.

The Three and Five R's Strategies   Two additional note-taking strategies include three or five steps that all begin with the letter "R" (Alley & Deshler, 1979; Pauk, 1987). Both of these strategies combine ideas for taking and studying notes. The steps in the three-R strategy involve *reviewing, reading,* and *relating:* (1) *review* previous lecture notes and materials before class, (2) *read* the materials for class before class, (3) *relate* the lecture topics to other known information. Teachers can practice with students how to choose and select appropriate materials to review before class, using class materials as examples (e.g., "What would be important to review before the next class?"). Strategies for reading class assignments can also be practiced (e.g., skim the entire reading assignment; read the assignment carefully, highlighting or taking notes; summarize what you have read and ask yourself questions about the material). When the lecture is presented, teachers can practice how students can relate the current material with other known information (e.g., "How does the voyage of Vasco da Gama remind you of Columbus's voyages?").

The five-R strategy is similar but includes more after-lecture studying hints. The first step is *record* important facts and details. The second step is *reduce* the notes to short phrases. The third step is *recite* the important information in your own words. The fourth step is *reflect* on the notes and add any information to them. The final step is *review* all notes and information. One helpful way for students to practice this strategy is in pairs or cooperative groups where students compare notes and recite, reflect on, and review their notes with each other.

Any of these note-taking strategies can help students. Select a strategy, teach it, and monitor its effectiveness. Some students may develop a preference for one strategy over another. Encourage students to use the strategy that maximizes their performance.

ADDRESS SPECIAL NOTE-TAKING PROBLEMS   Some students may experience great difficulties with note taking, in spite of attempts to teach all skills to make students successful. Table 11.1 lists some special problems that may be encountered by students when trying to take notes. These skills may help students overcome some of those problems.

Table 11.1 Special Problems with Note-Taking and Possible Adaptations

Note-Taking Problem	Possible Solutions
Note-taker is too slow	• Provide basic outline as handout • Model outlining on blackboard • Use overhead transparencies during lectures • Copy overhead transparencies for students
Legibility	• Show how illegibility can affect value of notes • Model "shorthand" and abbreviations • Provide a variety of paper and pens
Deciding what to write	• Organize lecture logically • Write key points on board or overhead as you lecture • Provide guided notes as handouts for students
Deciding how to organize	• Provide a note-taking format • Teach a particular note-taking strategy that suits your class
Learning how to use notes	• Show how to review, correct, and elaborate on notes • Model how to use notes for studying • Schedule time for reviewing notes during class

Research and Reference Skills

Although many general education students possess adequate knowledge of library and researching skills, students with special needs benefit from explicit instruction, practice, and feedback on the process (Hoover, 1993). Students need to know how to use reference materials including reference books, indexes (e.g., periodical guides), computer-assisted literature and encyclopedia searches, and use of **search engines** on the **World Wide Web**. You can increase your students' motivation for these activities by always encouraging students to ask questions and to search for the answers. Statements like, "That's an excellent question!" "What is a question we'd like to find the answer for?" "How can we find the answer?" will show your students you value lifelong learning, library, and research skills.

STRATEGIES FOR
TEACHING LIBRARY SKILLS

To get students started, provide maps of the interior of libraries that indicate where various sources are located, including the reference librarians. Arrange meetings with reference librarians so students become familiar with them and feel comfortable asking for assistance. Librarians can schedule special instructional sessions for classes and often will meet with smaller groups of students with special needs to provide extra guidance and practice searching the library. Arrange to have special educators work with librarians to devise specialized training sessions for students with disabilities.

TEACH USE OF REFERENCE BOOKS Familiarizing your students with the reference materials available in the school and public libraries can be made into a motivating activity by challenging teams of students to locate topics within all available sources. Typical materials include dictionaries, encyclopedias, biographical sources, almanacs, and various specific guide books, such as medical guides or natural history guides. Most reference materials are located together in libraries and usually cannot be checked out. Because materials are often shelved in alphabetical order, practice or reference sheets containing the alphabet may be necessary for younger students who have difficulty recalling alphabetical order. Summary guides listing reference books, types of information, and locations can serve as library guides for students. Setting up practice activities during which students are required to locate different pieces of information benefits all students. These activities can be made to be more exciting by arranging practice as part of a scavenger hunt game. Grouping students into scavenger hunt teams will help inspire them, perhaps demonstrating how much fun it is to "find" new information.

TEACH STUDENTS HOW TO USE DATABASES Many students will benefit from instruction on reference databases. Available databases may vary depending on whether the library is housed at an elementary, middle, or secondary school. High schools may have many more databases available than elementary schools. One very useful resource is ProQuest®, which contains periodical abstracts in periodical, scientific (peer-reviewed), and newspaper databases. By clicking on the appropriate source (e.g., children's, humanities, general interest), students can search for relevant articles in a variety of areas. ProQuest will provide the reference information (e.g., magazine title, issue number, date), and an abstract (brief summary) of all articles relevant to the topic entered in by the student. In some cases, the full text of the article is available. Such databases are not difficult to use, although basic familiarity with computer screens and use of the mouse is necessary to use them unassisted. The school librarian can provide specific information on the availability of various databases and how they can be used. Provide explicit practice with students with special needs, when necessary. Students should be able to locate relevant articles, copy down (or print out) identifying information, and know how to use this information to locate the articles. You can create library search activities, where you assign students in pairs or small groups to locate specific articles and identify where they can be found. If students learn to function independently with these skills, they will be able to write more thorough and informative research papers.

TEACH USE OF LIBRARY CATALOGS   Library searches are quick and easy with today's computerized catalogs, but familiarity with particular computer systems is necessary. Searches can be completed by authors, titles, and subject areas, and searches can be completed on books, multimedia materials, and various databases of journals by topical area. Resulting search information is displayed and can be printed out or copied by hand.

Search results contain several important pieces of information. First, Library of Congress or Dewey Decimal System call numbers of books are identified, along with author and publication information of publishers, year, and city of publication. Longer formats are usually available and display abstracts of the materials. Model how reading abstracts and other displayed information helps students decide whether those materials should be included in their search. If materials appear relevant, students can either print the screen information, copy it, or save it to a disk, and then locate the book in the library using the call number. Give your students self-monitoring sheets containing reminders about what information they should keep for looking up materials and for their reference lists.

Searching by author or title can be simpler than searching by topic. A title or author's name will yield all sources containing that title or name. Searching by subject topic is a little more complex and guidance may be necessary to help narrow the descriptors. For example, if students select a broad descriptor like "pollution," several thousand entries might appear. Guide students in narrowing descriptors to focus their search efforts to a more restricted topic that yields a more realistic number of books or articles for them to scan. Divide the topic into smaller subtopics, such as air pollution, groundwater pollution, waste disposal, and agricultural pollution. The resulting search will then be narrower and more focused on the student's interest area.

Making informed decisions about which entries should be examined more closely can be difficult. The selection process requires critical thinking, and students may need assistance focusing their thinking. Teach students to group potential sources into three categories: "Yes, definitely keep," "Maybe, look further and decide," and "No, do not keep." Be sure to review what they do to verify that they understand the process.

The next step is to obtain the "yes" and "maybe" materials and determine if they should be included. If students do not do this component of the task well, they may experience great difficulties completing the remaining steps of the project. Some of your students with disabilities may have difficulty with this component because it relies on reading and thinking skills. Model some samples for the class by speaking aloud the "thinking" you use for inclusion and exclusion of sources. Say, for example, "I will keep this abstract on the hazards of using too much fertilizer because it sounds as if it fits with my topic of agricultural pollution. But I will discard this article on toxic dumps because it doesn't seem to be closely enough related to agricultural pollution." You can divide students into small groups for practicing this task and require students to defend verbally their reasons for including or excluding abstracts.

Although online catalogs have generally replaced the old card catalogs in recent decades, card catalogs can still be found in some schools. These catalogs include a card for each holding in the library, stored in drawers, and can be organized by topic, title, or author. If your school has this system, show students how to decide on the type of search, and then how to search cards alphabetically.

TEACH SKILLS IN COMPUTERIZED LITERATURE SEARCHES   Students need to become proficient at completing literature searches using computers. Similar procedures are used as in searching libraries for materials, but more specialized knowledge of each database is beneficial. Practice selecting descriptors by asking students to write the number of entries appearing for various descriptors. Practice narrowing descriptors is a good way to engage students in gaining the confidence they will need to do successful searches. Require students to practice reading the search results and pinpointing relevant sources. Don't forget to show students how to print, download, and save search results.

Computerized Searches of Encyclopedias   Many schools, in addition to many home computers, have encyclopedias on CD or online encyclopedia access. Model and demonstrate how students can search these encyclopedias using computers. Some entries have oral output accompanying them and are excellent resources for students with reading difficulties. Most

CD-ROM or online encyclopedias are multimedia; contain video, audio, and printed entries; and are ideally suited for students with reading difficulties.

Use of Search Engines on the Internet   So much information can be accessed via the **Internet** that students should have practice in these search procedures as well. Most libraries have online access with numerous search engines to help students locate information on the Web. Become comfortable using computers and searching the Web, so you will feel confident showing your students how to access the wealth of knowledge on the Internet. Since information from the Internet is generally less reliable than information from printed sources, teach students to identify the source of the information and the reliability of that source.

STRATEGIES FOR
PREPARING REPORTS AND PROJECTS

Pearson
myeducationlab

Go to MyEducationLab, select the topic *Content Area Teaching*, and go to the Activities and Applications section. As you watch the video entitled "Pre-Writing in 6th Grade" (in the Language Arts subsection), reflect on how this strategy aligns with the discussions here in the text.

Assignments that involve writing papers are usually very challenging for students with disabilities as well as other students in your classroom (Deshler & Schumaker, 2005). This writing process can be taught directly by practicing some of the subskills involved in writing a report. Gall et al. (1990) list skills of planning, reading, thinking, organizing, and writing as being required for successful report writing.

DEFINE THE WRITING TASK SYSTEMATICALLY   In defining the writing task, Gall et al. (1990) emphasize that it is important to explain the following:

- Purpose of the writing assignment
- Audience for the assignment
- Format for the paper both in terms of substance (book report, poem, short story, newspaper article, research report, other) and style (typewritten, handwritten, paper)
- Required length in pages and in scope and detail
- Date the assignment is due

This is also the time for students to estimate how long each step in the process will take and begin to plan a schedule for completing each step. Some of the steps may require additional subdividing. Have students record steps and due dates in their calendars. Finally, students can begin to work on the project according to their time schedules.

The writing process might begin with the student creating a writing plan. Corrective guidance and feedback for this plan can build the student's confidence and motivation.

PROMOTE TOPIC SELECTION, DEVELOP A WRITING PLAN, AND BRAINSTORM IDEAS Many students have difficulties selecting topics for their papers. Provide examples of topics that appear motivating and interesting to students, but that are manageable in scope.

Provide sample papers that address each purpose as models for students to see how the papers are constructed to answer the intended purpose. Maintain model papers from previous classes and put on reserve in the library. Seeing completed models helps students visualize the final product.

The development of a writing plan is crucial for students. This component requires additional subdividing: Will books be needed from the library? Will reading and taking notes from those books be required? Will students need to interview experts on the topic? Will visits to museums be necessary? This plan will vary depending on the topic and purpose of the assignment.

Show students sample writing plans from different types of written projects. Again model the development of plans during instruction. Have students

Assistive Technology Software for Help with Study Skills

Computer programs to help students with mild disabilities at home and at school with their schoolwork have been developed. For example, KidTools™, KidSkills™, and StrategyTools™ were developed to provide elementary and secondary students with mild disabilities an assistive technological computer program to support self-regulation, learning strategy tools, and research-based tools that students, teachers, and parents can use to support school learning (Fitzgerald & Koury, 2001–2002, 2004–2005; Mitchem, Kight, Fitzgerald, Koury, & Boonseng, 2007). StrategyTools™, which was designed for secondary students, combines 39 computerized research-based tools organized into six major categories containing numerous templates that students, teachers, and parents can personalize. KidTools™ and KidSkills™ were developed for elementary-aged students and then adapted for secondary students into the StrategyTools'™ program. Both the elementary and secondary programs have positive preliminary data to support their use.

StrategyTools'™ categories include: getting organized, learning new information, demonstrating learning, working on projects, solving personal problems, and moving into the future. Each category is located in a difference section of the program. The "Getting Organized" category, which is located in the library section of the program, contains tools for creating to-do lists, week planners, assignment cards, and job aids. The "Learning New Information" category, which is located in the study hall section, contains vocabulary cards, note-taking tools, compare and contrast tools, KWHL cards, and a chunker tool. The "Demonstrating Learning" category, which is located in the classroom section, contains tools such as composer tools, flashcards, memory cards, study guides, planning reports, testing yourself, project review cards, and rubric tools. The "Working on Projects" category, which is located in the computer lab, contains tools including source scanning, big picture card, planning a report, project note cards, project review cards, and getting information tools. The "Solving Personal Problems," which is located in the conference room section, contains tools such as monitoring, making self- and two-party contracts, making choices, solving problems, and commitment cards. The "Moving into the Future" category, which is located in the information center, contains tools including self-awareness, action planners, transition, budgeting, job search, and finding services. *Mitchem et al. (2007) reported that secondary students* and their teachers who used StrategyTools™ over an academic semester were positive in their support of the program. Students further indicated that the tools helped them to be more organized, to recognize possible problematic areas, and to find more appropriate alternative responses.

---

complete partially developed plans before attempting to complete plans independently. During the actual writing of assignments, have students bring in their plans for guidance and corrective feedback from you.

Once the writing topic has been selected, students need to brainstorm ideas of details. Model how during the brainstorming process all ideas are written down, and allow students opportunities to practice the brainstorming component. Then demonstrate how those ideas are evaluated later for relevancy and how determinations are made as to whether to include them within the paper. After that, the relevant ideas are listed in order of importance for the project.

COLLECT AND ORGANIZE IDEAS AND INFORMATION   Lead students to collect and find the necessary information for writing their papers. Students may use the library, World Wide Web, other reference materials, or interviews depending on the paper topic and format required. Demonstrate how to find and collect information.

At this stage, students may write a more detailed outline for their paper. Notes from the obtained information can be included in the outline. Traditional outlines may or may not be used, but be sure to model how use of an organizational framework facilitates the organization of the paper and assists students in completing the written product. Some formats may consist of titles, main ideas, supporting details under each main idea, and summary and conclusion sections. One key factor is to show students how to use the major purpose of the paper to guide the major subheadings for the paper. The *Technology Highlight* feature describes how technology can be used for organization and development of a writing task.

WRITE FIRST DRAFT OF PAPER AND OBTAIN FEEDBACK   After completing the organizational outline or format, have students write the first draft of their paper. It should be relatively easy to write a first draft if note cards containing major points and outlines are used. Each organizational heading becomes a major section of the draft, and students put that information into sentences in their own words. Then elaborations are added to those main ideas and details to complete the rough draft. At this point or earlier, you may need to explain why copying articles is illegal and called plagiarism, and explain how you want your students to cite the information they are using for their papers. This may be especially important if students are downloading complete documents from the Internet.

Encourage students to obtain feedback from someone on their first drafts. The feedback provides them with information about what needs to be revised before completing their final versions. Teachers, parents, siblings, and peers can all be asked for feedback on draft versions.

REVISE AND REWRITE, PROOF, AND EDIT FINAL VERSION   Students should then incorporate the feedback into the revision of their draft. Explain to students how a revision process may involve several changes to their draft. Most revisions employ grammatical, syntactical, semantic, and punctuation changes to improve the paper.

Even though you will probably hear your students groan, explain to them how important it is to edit the paper one more time. It is during this final editing and proofing stage that additional errors are often detected.

Writing papers or completing independent projects is difficult for many students, but critical for success in secondary schools and higher education. Without instruction in the entire process of writing papers and completing independent projects, many students may fail to achieve in this important area. However, by providing extra instruction in the process of writing, students may be better prepared to write papers, and will be more likely to be successful in school.

11 Summary

- Students with disabilities and those at risk for failure in school benefit from explicit instruction and practice in study skills.

- Personal organization skills, such as knowing about class times and schedules, using assignment notebooks and monthly planners, and organizing homework, are important for success in school and can be effectively taught to students with special needs.

- Direct teaching of listening skills helps students with special needs be prepared to learn information presented orally in school.

- Teaching students ways to take notes, including writing short summaries, abbreviations, using specific note-taking formats, and specific note-taking strategies, facilitates learning from lectures and presentations.

- Practice and instruction using the library, including use of reference materials, indices, computerized literature searches, use of the World Wide Web, and use of Internet search engines, assists students with special needs in learning how to search for and locate resources for schoolwork.

- Direct instruction on how to write a research paper, including selecting topics, searching for information, organizing information, writing and editing first drafts, and preparing final versions, is essential for most students with special needs.

PROFESSIONAL STANDARDS LINK:
Teaching Study Skills

Information in this chapter links most directly to:

- CEC Standards: 3 (Individual Learning Differences), 4 (Instructional Strategies), 7 (Instructional Planning)

- INTASC Standards: Principles 2 (provides appropriate learning opportunities), 3 (understands learning differences, adapts instructional opportunities), 4 (instructional strategies), 5 (creates learning environments), 6 (fosters inquiry, collaboration, interaction), 7 (plans instruction)

- PRAXIS II™ Content Categories (Knowledge): 3 (Delivery of Services)

- PRAXIS II™ Content Categories (Application): 1 (Curriculum), 2 (Instruction)

TEACHING STUDY SKILLS

If the student is having difficulty with study skills—including organizational skills, listening skills, note-taking skills, and library skills—have you tried specific strategies for teaching? If not, see the pages listed below.

STRATEGIES FOR DEVELOPING PERSONAL ORGANIZATIONAL SKILLS

STRATEGIES FOR PROMOTING LISTENING SKILLS

STRATEGIES FOR TEACHING NOTE-TAKING SKILLS

STRATEGIES FOR TEACHING LIBRARY SKILLS

STRATEGIES FOR PREPARING REPORTS AND PROJECTS

Inclusion Checklist

Recycle

NORMA BELINI   Norma Belini took up photography 4 years ago as a raw beginner after experiencing a number of physical challenges, including ongoing back injuries, cancer, asthma, and angina. She explains her connection to and passion for photography: "My previous hobbies were 'creative' and photography has enabled me to continue to gain satisfaction from being 'creative'. Photography is my medication and therapy. Photography is what keeps my mind active—and my purse empty!"

12

Assessment

OBJECTIVES

After studying this chapter, you should be able to:

- Describe the use of norm-referenced tests, competency-based assessments, teacher-made tests, and criterion-referenced tests in inclusive settings.
- Identify and implement strategies to modify test formats to meet the needs of students with disabilities.
- Compare and contrast curriculum-based measurement, performance assessment, and portfolio assessment and their applications for students with special needs.
- Describe specific test-taking strategies for taking standardized tests, and how these strategies can be taught.
- Design and implement strategies for taking teacher-made tests such as multiple-choice, true–false, matching, and essay tests.
- Identify procedures and rationales for modifying grading and scoring of tests for students with special needs.

Tests are a significant component of education because they provide information relevant to placement, instruction, and future career decisions. Tests are also being used increasingly to evaluate the performance of schools. Tests, however, must be administered appropriately and interpreted correctly, or they can do more harm than good. It is also important to be able to describe the purposes of different tests to parents, as well as to be able to interpret for parents the information they provide about their child. Teachers should be aware of different types of tests, the purposes they serve, how they can be used, and how they can be interpreted. Skills for maximizing test performance and modifications to accommodate students with special needs are also necessary.

Types of Tests

In education, many different tests address many different, specific needs. One type of test is no "better" than another, because different tests serve different purposes. As a teacher, it is critical to understand what information specific tests provide, and what information they do not provide.

All educational testing serves to compare performance with some type of standard (Howell & Nolet, 2000). One major distinction made in testing is between **norm-referenced** and **criterion-referenced** testing. In norm-referenced testing, student performance is compared with the performance of other students. Students receive scores such as "85th percentile," which means that the student scored higher than 85% of other students on that particular test. In criterion-referenced testing, student performance is compared to specific, specified criteria, usually considered as meeting minimal competency. A written test for a driver's license, in which individuals either pass or fail to meet a certain criterion, is a good example of a criterion-referenced test.

CLASSROOM SCENARIO

Nate ■ ■ ■

Mr. Montoya saw Nate in his middle-school resource room for 45 minutes per day. Although much of the time was devoted to basic skills development, Mr. Montoya also allocated time to helping Nate prepare for upcoming tests. Nate had particular difficulty taking tests in his U.S. Constitution and government class, and Mr. Montoya also was having difficulty helping him. For 2 days before the test he would work with Nate by reviewing the content and creating practice questions for Nate to answer. However, it seemed that no matter how well prepared Nate appeared to be, he did poorly on the test. When Mr. Montoya asked Nate why this was, he just shrugged his shoulders and said the test did not make any sense to him.

Both norm-referenced and criterion-referenced testing can be **standardized,** which means that all students take the test under the same, or standard, conditions. The information that comes from the test results, then, assumes standardized testing conditions were applied (McLoughlin & Lewis, 2008). Standardized administration procedures are published in test manuals and are expected to be closely followed for the test scores to be meaningful.

Another important distinction is whether a test is **summative** or **formative** in nature. Summative testing usually refers to tests given at the end of a particular educational period. Achievement tests given at the end of a school year are good examples of summative evaluation. The results tell how much has been accomplished throughout the educational period, and may provide implications for placement in the next educational period. Many norm-referenced tests are summative in nature, but criterion-referenced tests can also be summative if they are administered at the end of a particular educational experience.

Teachers use formative evaluation when they test at frequent intervals, so that student progress can be evaluated. For example, students who are attempting to learn and remember 100 multiplication facts may take a weekly test on these facts, so that the rate of growth can be evaluated and instructional modifications can be made (e.g., more time-on-task) when growth is unsatisfactory. Formative evaluation is most frequently used in basic skills areas.

Evaluation can also be curriculum-based. This means that the tests are derived directly from the curriculum being taught (Hosp, Hosp, & Howell, 2007). Most teacher-made tests are intended to evaluate student learning of the curriculum, and therefore are types of curriculum-based tests. Distinctions have been made between **curriculum-based assessment**—which could include any procedure that evaluates student performance in relation to the school curriculum, such as weekly spelling tests—and **curriculum-based measurement**—characterized by frequent, direct measurements of critical school behaviors, which could include timed (1- to 5-minute) tests of performance on reading, math, and writing skills (McLoughlin & Lewis, 2008). Curriculum-based measurement is formative in nature, and allows teachers to make instructional decisions about teaching and curriculum while learning is taking place.

Other types of tests include **performance assessments** and **portfolio assessments.** Performance assessments are usually curriculum-based, and require students to construct responses on real-world tasks, usually in ways that allow teachers to evaluate the student's thinking (Fuchs, 1994). Portfolio assessment is also usually curriculum-based, and consists of student products and other relevant information collected over time and displayed in a portfolio. All of these types of tests have relevance to students with special needs. Table 12.1 provides examples of these types of tests applied in the context of reading.

Regardless of the type of test, it must be demonstrated to have **reliability** and **validity** to be of value. All measures of reliability seek to determine that the test is consistent in what it measures. No less important, validity refers to the extent to which a particular test measures what it is intended to measure. Validity is often evaluated by comparing different tests of the same skills or abilities (McLoughlin & Lewis, 2008). For example, students should receive similar scores on different standardized tests of reading achievement, if both tests are valid.

Tests commonly used in special education are listed in Figure 12.1.

Table 12.1 Examples of Reading Tests

Types of Test	Example Reading Test
Standardized, Norm-Referenced	Published reading achievement test administered under standardized conditions. Students may answer test questions on computerized answer sheets or give answers to an examiner in an individual administration. Student's score is compared with scores of a normative sample of students.
Criterion-Referenced	Students' test scores are compared with a certain predetermined criterion level to be considered competent in reading at their grade level.
Curriculum-Based Assessment	Test is based on the reading curriculum materials being used in class.
Curriculum-Based Measurement	Students take brief tests of reading speed, accuracy, and comprehension. These scores are monitored over time to determine whether progress is adequate.
Performance Assessment	Student could be asked to "perform" on a variety of reading-related tasks, such as summarizing a passage, looking up a reference, or identifying a certain printed label in a store.
Portfolio Assessment	A variety of a student's products relevant to reading are collected, for example, list of books read, book reports written, or tape recordings of reading selections.

Intelligence Tests

   Kaufman Assessment Battery for Children II, 2nd ed. (Kaufman & Kaufman, 2006; Pearson/American Guidance Service)

   Stanford-Binet Intelligence Scale, 5th ed. (Roid, 2003; Psychological Corporation)

   Wechsler Intelligence Scale for Children—IV, 4th ed. (Wechsler, 2003; Psychological Corporation)

Achievement Tests

   Kaufman Test of Educational Achievement, 2nd ed. (KTEA – II) (Kaufman & Kaufman, 2004; Pearson/American Guidance Service)

   Key Math—3: Diagnostic Assessment (Pearson/American Guidance Service, 2007)

   Peabody Individual Achievement Test—Revised/Normative Update (PIAT—R) (Markwardt, 1997; Pearson/American Guidance Service)

   Test of Written Language—3 (TOWL) (Hammill & Larsen, 1996; PRO-ED)

   Wide Range Achievement Test—4 (Wilkenson & Robertson, 2006; Western Psychological Services)

   Woodcock-Johnson III: Tests of Achievement (Woodcock, Johnson, & Mather, 2001; Riverside)

   Woodcock Reading Mastery Test—Revised/Normative Update (Woodcock, 1998; Pearson/American Guidance Service)

Figure 12.1 Types of Tests

Adapting Tests for Students with Special Needs

STRATEGIES FOR
ADMINISTERING NORM-REFERENCED TESTS

Some students with special needs exhibit difficulties with norm-referenced tests that may limit the reliability and validity of their test scores. Problems may include language or communication styles (e.g., the need for a sign language interpreter or communication board), the length of the testing, attentional difficulties, or reading difficulties when reading competence is not being tested. Another threat to the validity of individual scores of students with disabilities is that in some cases, individuals with disabilities are not included in the test's standardization sample (Fuchs, Fuchs, Benowitz, & Barringer, 1987). Further, some tests may not be fair for students from some culturally diverse backgrounds (Artiles & Zamora-Durán, 1997; Baca & Cervantes, 2004; Harry & Klingner, 2006). Special considerations including modifications in the testing procedure may be helpful and necessary (see also Chapter 5; Baca & Cervantes, 2004; Ford, Obiakor, & Patton, 1995; Gollnick & Chinn, 2009).

Unfortunately, substantive deviations from standardized administration procedures typically limit the usefulness of the test. If, for example, an individual student is provided with a calculator as a modification to assist with math computation on a problem-solving subtest, the resulting score cannot be fairly compared with students who did not have access to calculators. Even though it can be argued that problem solving, and not computation, is being evaluated, and the student in question has difficulty remembering math facts, it is unknown how the students in the standardization sample would have performed if they also had access to calculators. Therefore, the student's score cannot be easily interpreted with respect to the performance of the norm group (McLoughlin & Lewis, 2008). Nevertheless, there are some instances when modifications in administration of standardized tests may be appropriate, including use of calculators, and some states have published state-approved test accommodations (Johnson, Kimball, Brown, & Anderson, 2001; Massachusetts Department of Education, 2004).

Go to MyEducationLab, select the topic *Assessment*, and go to the Activities and Applications section. As you watch the video entitled "Assessment of Special Needs Students," consider the many ways tests can be modified to meet the needs of all learners.

USE TEST MODIFICATIONS   While performance on modified tests may not always be fairly compared with performance under standardized administration conditions, results still provide relevant information about the skills and abilities of individual students. Test modifications include the following:

- Altering the timing or scheduling of the test
- Extending time limits
- Spreading the test over several shorter time sessions
- Administering the test over several days (Erickson, Ysseldyke, Thurlow, & Elliott, 1998)
- Changing the setting
- Changing to a smaller room
- Moving to a distraction-free room (Elliott, Kratochwill, & Schulte, 1998)
- Testing individually (Massachusetts Department of Education, 2004)
- Altering the presentation of the test
- Simplifying the language
- Providing prompts and feedback (including reinforcement)
- Allowing teachers to read the test and turn the test pages
- Allowing audiotaped, large-print, or braille versions
- Changing the response formats
- Allowing verbal versus written responses
- Allowing circling versus filling in the bubbles (McLoughlin & Lewis, 2008)

If students perform very differently under one or more reasonable modifications, the standardized test may not have provided an accurate depiction of the student's ability. Research to date is somewhat equivocal regarding some of these modifications; for example, extended time sometimes, but not always, has a differential benefit for students with disabilities (Elliott & Marquart, 2004). For a research study investigating the effectiveness of test accommodations, see the *Research Highlight* feature.

USE INDIVIDUALLY ADMINISTERED TESTS   In addition to providing more detailed information about student performance in a particular area, individually administered tests avoid some potential problems associated with group administration, such as reading directions, working independently, and using machine-scored answer sheets. For example, in group-administered tests of reading, students may respond to more complicated formats to assess reading skills, while on an individually administered test, a student's individual reading can be directly assessed through interaction with the examiner. Therefore, it may be appropriate to rely more on individually administered tests for students who have difficulty taking group tests independently.

TEACH TEST-TAKING SKILLS   Some students may know much of the content being tested, but do not understand how to apply that knowledge on the test. In these cases, students can be given specific training in **test-taking skills** appropriate to relevant tests, or administered published practice tests and given feedback on their understanding of test formats (Scruggs & Mastropieri, 1992). Test-taking skills training, appropriate for many different types of tests, is discussed later in this chapter.

INCREASE MOTIVATION In other cases, students may have relevant skills, but not be sufficiently motivated to work their hardest during the test. This may be true for all other types of tests as well as norm-referenced tests. While direct rewarding of test performance may violate standardization, other motivational strategies, such as those suggested in Chapter 9—including goal setting, attribution training, praising students' efforts, promoting self-efficacy and self-esteem, making the classroom atmosphere fun and enjoyable, and increasing students' personal investment—may be helpful in increasing the validity of the test performance of less motivated test-takers.

If a test administrator is someone familiar to a student with special needs, the student might perform better on the test.

IMPROVE EXAMINER FAMILIARITY Some students score better on standardized tests if they are familiar with the examiner than if they are responding to an examiner they have not met before. This may be particularly true of African American and Latino students (Fuchs & Fuchs, 1989), as well as students with learning disabilities (Fuchs, Fuchs, & Power, 1987). Try to arrange for an administrator who is well known by, or acquainted with, the student. If an outside examiner is used, he or she should first establish rapport with the student by introducing himself or herself, engaging the student in personal conversation, explaining the purpose of the testing, describing test activities, and encouraging student questions (McLoughlin & Lewis, 2008). Such established familiarity may improve the validity of test responses.

REQUEST MODIFICATIONS FOR COLLEGE ENTRANCE EXAMS Among the most frequently administered tests for college entrance are the Scholastic Assessment Test (SAT) and the American College Testing (ACT). These are usually administered in a student's junior or senior year of high school. Both of these tests allow special accommodations to be made for students with disabilities (Learning Disabilities Association, 1994).

Students with disabilities may be offered accommodations if they meet eligibility requirements. Accommodations that can be requested include extended time, large type, alternative test form with accommodations required as noted on the student's IEP, a reader or recorder, audiocassette with written form, a magnifying glass, or a four-function calculator.

STRATEGIES FOR
ADAPTING COMPETENCY-BASED AND STATEWIDE ASSESSMENT

Statewide competency testing has helped develop common standards for educational attainment and establish educational accountability. In some states, performance on competency tests has become a requirement for graduation, and other issues of school operation, and has been referred to as "high-stakes" testing. Because of No Child Left Behind legislation, states today have statewide competency tests.

Minimum competency tests share many characteristics with norm-referenced achievement tests. Although competency tests are oriented toward competencies students are expected to attain for promotion or graduation, they are also developed for comparative purposes. Minimum competency tests are also involved with Title I legislation, which requires states to hold all students to the same expectations (Phillips, 1995). Therefore, allowing adaptations for special needs while still maintaining standardization is a concern of competency tests, and can be determined through consultation with test developers or appropriate educational agencies (e.g., school district or state department of education).

Test Accommodations Using Dictation and Speech Recognition

Although testing accommodations are frequently recommended for students with disabilities, it is less certain whether all accommodations result in positive benefits. Accommodations are intended to remove performance barriers while maintaining the integrity and validity of the measure. The number of possible accommodations increases dramatically with the advancement of innovative technologies. MacArthur and Cavalier (2004) examined the effects of dictation using speech-recognition software compared with dictation using a scribe for a written exam with high school students with and without learning disabilities. Dictation with speech-recognition software has potential advantages of allowing students to see and review developing text. All students participated in three testing conditions: handwriting, dictation using a scribe, and dictation using speech software. All

students were trained to use the speech software, *Dragon Naturally Speaking, Version 4* (1998), to write persuasive essays. Students were taught to think of a sentence and dictate it one word at a time when using the software. All students were also taught a strategy to write persuasive essays. Strategic steps, which were consolidated into a graphic organizer, included writing their position, listing evidence points for position statements, noting reasons why some might disagree, and concluding with a strong statement. Students were then given three different essay prompts and required to complete the essays under one of the three conditions.

MacArthur and Cavalier reported that all students successfully learned to use the speech-to-text software, that students with learning disabilities created higher-quality written products when using dictation with a scribe rather than dictation with speech-to-text

software, and that both methods were superior to handwriting. The dictation methods did not result in superior essays for students without disabilities, indicating that use of dictation during essay writing may be a viable and valid test accommodation for students with learning disabilities.

QUESTIONS FOR REFLECTION

1. Why do you think dictation methods might work better for students with learning disabilities than for students without disabilities?
2. Why do you think effects were greater for dictation to a scribe than for speech-recognition software for students with learning disabilities?
3. How could you adapt the writing strategy for a lower-age-level group of students?
4. How could you design practice for learning to use the computer with students with disabilities?

USE TEST MODIFICATIONS OR ACCOMMODATIONS In many cases, testing modifications or accommodations are considered appropriate because they better allow some students to demonstrate what they know. Because many students with disabilities may need accommodations, IDEA requires that individual student IEPs provide testing accommodations for state tests as well as district and teacher-made tests (Salend, 2008). Most states provide standard accommodations that are permissible on statewide competency tests (Johnson et al., 2001, p. 255; Massachusetts Department of Education, 2004). It is important that these accomodations do not change the nature of the test, for example, by reading passages to students on a test of reading comprehension (Salend, 2008).

Thurlow, Lazarus, Thompson, and Morse (2005) obtained policies for accommodations from state departments of all 50 states. They reported that states most commonly allowed accommodations in the areas of:

- *Presentations,* for example, braille, read-aloud, clarification of directions, sign interpretation;
- *Equipment/materials,* for example, amplification, audio-/videocassettes, calculators, magnification;
- *Response mode,* for example, computers, scribes, spell checkers;
- *Scheduling and timing,* for example, extended time, testing over multiple days or at student-preferred times, allowing multiple breaks; and
- *Setting,* for example, individual or small-group administration, separate testing rooms, or testing at student's home. (p. 236)

Salend (2008, p. 17) also described *linguistically based* accommodations, including using familiar language, repeating directions, teaching the language of testing, translating tests, allowing responses in different languages or dialects, providing translators, and use of bilingual materials. Cawthon (2008) surveyed professionals working with students who are deaf or hard of hearing, and reported that accommodations for statewide testing most commonly reported included extra time, small-group administration, and test items and directions read or interpreted.

Some research has been conducted on the effectiveness of accommodations in statewide assessments. To date, the results of this research are somewhat inconsistent and equivocal (Shriner & Ganguly, 2007). Bolt and Thurlow (2004) suggested the effects of accommodations be evaluated for individual students, which can be done by monitoring performance with and without specific accommodations.

USE ALTERNATE ASSESSMENTS Standard statewide assessments may not be appropriate for some students with disabilities. In these cases, it may be possible to arrange for alternate assessment procedures. In the state of Virginia, for example, students for whom the state (Standards of Learning) competency tests are not considered appropriate may participate in the Virginia Alternate Assessment Program. These assessments are administered at ages 8, 10, 13, and 1 year prior to the student's exit year. They consist of a "Collection of Evidence" that measures student performance relevant to IEP objectives that access the state Standards of Learning. The assessment incorporates multiple forms of data collected over time and could include, for example, work samples; student observations; interviews with teachers, parents, or employers; videotapes of social skills or life skills; and journal entries (Training and Technical Assistance Center at the College of William and Mary, 2005). It is understood that students participating in alternate assessment are working on educational goals other than those prescribed for the traditional diplomas (modified standard, standard, or advanced studies), and therefore would not be eligible for those diplomas (Virginia Department of Education, 2007).

REQUEST MODIFICATIONS ON GED TESTS Competency tests also include the Tests of General Educational Development (GED). GED tests are intended to evaluate the knowledge and skills that were intended to have been acquired from a 4-year high school program, but which may have been acquired in a different manner, such as independent study or tutoring. Students with special needs who have not graduated from high school, but believe they have met high school graduation criteria, can take the GED tests. Individuals wishing to take the GED must be a resident of the state in which the test is administered, and usually are older than 18. Also, students must not be enrolled in a public school; so, as a teacher, you may have little direct interaction with students taking the GED. However, you may be able to provide information about the GED to students who are about to leave school without graduating, or to former students who may ask you for assistance in taking the GED.

Students with disabilities may fill out an "Application for Special Testing" and sign a release of information form to have specific medical or psychological records sent to the GED center to be evaluated. Possible modifications that may be obtained include an audiocassette edition of the test (with printed reference copy), large-print version of the test, extended time for taking the test, use of a calculator, frequent breaks, and use of a private testing room (Learning Disabilities Association, 2004).

STRATEGIES FOR
ADAPTING TEACHER-MADE AND CRITERION-REFERENCED TESTS

Putnam (1992) surveyed secondary teachers and concluded that an adolescent with mild disabilities who is enrolled in four content-area classes may be required to take as many as 44 tests during a 45-day grading period! In addition, the use of state high-stakes testing places added demands on students with disabilities. Clearly, helping students be successful in dealing with the challenges of testing is critical to promoting school success. The *Technology Highlight* feature provides suggestions for collecting records and monitoring progress more efficiently.

Teachers can modify their own tests in much the same way that other tests are modified. However, be careful to ensure that your modifications are having the desired effect of accommodating the student's disability. For example, Lewandowski, Lovett, Parolin, Gordon, and Codding (2007) reported that students with ADHD gained less than the students without ADHD from extended time limits on a math computation assessment.

MODIFY TESTS In the earlier scenario, Nate performed well on answering questions on the chapter posed by the resource teacher, but performed poorly on the actual test covering the U.S. Constitution and government. Because he apparently knew much of the required information, it is possible that Nate did not fully understand the format of the teacher-made test. Although training in test-taking skills may be important for Nate in this case, it is also possible that the social studies teacher could be encouraged to make some modifications to the format of the test so that students will better understand what is required of them, as shown in the continuation of the scenario.

CLASSROOM SCENARIO

Nate

Mr. Montoya made an appointment to speak to Nate's social studies teacher, Ms. Leet. She acknowledged that Nate was not doing well on the tests, and expressed a willingness to help solve the problem. Mr. Montoya and Ms. Leet examined the tests together, and Mr. Montoya noted that he believed Nate did know the answer to several of the questions that he had answered incorrectly. It appeared that Nate was more likely to answer questions incorrectly when the items contained double negatives, contained potentially confusing options such as "(e) all of the above except (b)", or when the test called for matching two columns of information. While Mr. Montoya agreed to provide Nate with practice on test-taking skills, and to provide practice tests that more closely resembled Ms. Leet's tests, Ms. Leet agreed to make modifications in her test to make the individual items more understandable. She also asked her class to provide her with some sample items that they thought should be on the test.

With training in test-taking skills and test modifications, Nate's scores increased from an average of D– to an average of C–. In addition, Ms. Leet found that the average score of her entire class seemed to improve.

QUESTIONS FOR REFLECTION

1. If test scores improve, how could you know if your modified tests are more easily understandable, or simply easier?
2. What kind of students would you expect to benefit most from test modifications?
3. How could you determine what aspects of your tests need revision?

Most teachers view reasonable testing modifications favorably (Gajria, Salend, & Hemrick, 1994; Jayanthi, Epstein, Polloway, & Bursuck, 1996). Salend (1995) reviewed the literature on testing modifications, and concluded that "lengthy, poorly designed, messy, or distracting tests can adversely affect student performance" (p. 85). Well-designed tests, on the other hand, can be useful for all students.

Modify Test Formats Format modifications that can be generally employed on teacher-made tests—and which are acceptable to teachers (Gajria et al., 1994)—include the following:

- Prepare typewritten rather than handwritten tests.
- Space items sufficiently to reduce interference.
- Provide space for students to respond on the test itself.
- Provide items in a predictable hierarchy.
- Administer more tests with fewer items, rather than fewer, longer tests.
- When not testing reading, adjust the reading level of the items, or provide assistance with reading when needed.
- Define unfamiliar or abstract words if their meanings are not directly being tested.

Software to Assist with Recordkeeping, Grading, Monitoring Progress, and Response to Intervention

The need to maintain clear, accurate records of student performance and progress is important in education, especially when monitoring progress of students with disabilities who are included in general education classes. Organized systems for creating and maintaining recordkeeping for students' assignments, homework, grades, attendance, portfolio assessment products, and progress monitoring will greatly reduce the amount of noninstructional time for teachers. Fortunately, recent advances in technology have greatly reduced the amount of teacher time needed for many of these tasks. Software is now available that facilitates all recordkeeping and progress-monitoring activities.

Curriculum-based measurement (CBM) is one way to monitor student progress in academic areas. In the future, curriculum-based measurement may be recommended as a way to help identify students with learning disabilities. As described in the text, teachers can develop their own CBM measures; however, some software is available to facilitate the

process of using curriculum-based measurement in basic skills such as reading, math, and spelling. The National Center on Progress Monitoring (NCPM) Website (http://www.studentprogress.org/) provides current sources on progress monitoring, including an analysis of available computer-assisted programs. Progress monitoring can be applied to the implementation of response to intervention (e.g., Fuchs, 2008), and software developed specifically for response to intervention is analyzed on the NCPM site. NCPM standards for evaluating CBM materials include having adequate reliability and validity, alternate forms, sensitivity to student improvement, academic year benchmarks, student learning and/or teacher planning, and specifying rates of improvement. Available materials including software are *RTIm Direct* (available from the Centris Group) and *AIMSweb* (available from http://aimsweb.com).

Software is also available to assist with managing students' assignments, homework, attendance, grades, and reports to both students and parents.

Grade Machine (Misty City Software) contains features that allow teachers to upload student information from existing school database systems. In addition to tailoring systems to include a variety of recordkeeping formats, *Grade Machine* has features such as multilingual report writing (currently in Spanish, French, Russian, German, and English), electronic dissemination of reports to facilitate better home–school communication, and templates or customizing features for maintaining records of attendance, homework, assignments, behavior, and seating plans, as well as grading terms and scales.

Newer software enabling the use of multimedia is available that can assist with the maintenance of portfolio assessment materials. Teachers can manage their own as well as their students' portfolios using available software. Teachers can show their students how to compile their own portfolios using the available technology. With the use of scanners, digital cameras, digital videos, and available software, student products can be collected on a single CD rather than in a huge box.

- Provide models of correctly answered items.
- Change the test setting for students with special needs (e.g., a quiet space where the student can work privately).
- Allow more time for test completion for students who are slower with reading, writing, or processing test requirements.
- Allow students to dictate responses or to use communication boards to indicate their responses. (p. 238)

Specific Formats   Recommendations have also been made for specific types of tests (Salend, 1995):

- For true–false items, write out the words *true* and *false* for clarity, and avoid double negatives or emphasize negatives with bold or underlining. Students may become confused when asked to choose "false" to a negative statement, such as, "The office of president is not described in the Constitution."

- For multiple-choice tests, reduce the number of options, and limit the number of confusing options, such as (a) and (b) but not (c). If possible, have students answer on the test itself rather than a separate answer sheet, particularly at the elementary grades.
- For matching items, reduce the overall number of items. Provide an example of a correctly answered item, and place the entire list on one page.
- For short-answer questions, consider providing a choice of answers for the student to circle, rather than filling in a blank.
- For essay questions, describe what you would like to see included in the essay (without providing too much information), and recommend how the answer should be organized.

MODIFY SCORING PROCEDURES   In addition to format modifications of tests, you can also modify the way you score the tests. If some students have particular difficulty in areas such as spelling and grammar, it probably is unnecessary to penalize these students in every class they take, particularly if they are doing all they can to improve in these areas. If it seems important to grade on spelling, grammar, and neatness, consider grading them separately from actual mastery of the content, and perhaps ascribing these areas less weight. It may also be helpful to reconsider giving partial credit for answers that are incorrect, but nonetheless demonstrate some knowledge of the content covered. It seems reasonable that answers that demonstrate even a little knowledge may be given more credit than answers that reflect no knowledge.

STRATEGIES FOR
USING CURRICULUM-BASED MEASUREMENT

Curriculum-based measurement (CBM) was developed to document student progress through the class curriculum and to assist teachers in creating more effective instructional environments for students (Fuchs, Fuchs, Allinder, & Hamlett, 1992; Hosp, Hosp, & Howell, 2007). Fuchs, Fuchs, Hamlett, Phillips, and Bentz (1994) described two major distinguishing features of CBM.

First, CBM entails a standardized (but probably not norm-referenced) set of procedures for administration. These standardized procedures include sampling test items from classroom curricula, administering the test under the same or similar conditions, summarizing the test information, and using the test information in instructional decision making.

The second distinguishing feature of CBM is its focus on a long-term curricular goal—for example, the goal that you wish students will achieve by the end of the year. To this extent, CBM differs from other types of continuous measurement (or formative evaluation), in which student progress is assessed directly through changing objectives and standards throughout the year. With CBM, the test domain remains constant from the beginning of the school year until the end.

APPLY CBM TO MONITOR LEARNING PROGRESS   For an example of CBM, consider the curriculum area of spelling (Fuchs et al., 1992). The teacher examines the level of the curriculum for an entire domain of words that students are expected to be able to spell by the end of the year. Then the teacher samples from this list, creating, for example, 50 versions of a 20-item spelling test that include words that students will study throughout the year. The teacher administers one of these lists about twice a week under standardized administration procedures (e.g., words are read

PEARSON
myeducationlab

Go to MyEducationLab, select the topic *Assessment,* and go to the Activities and Applications section. As you complete the simulation entitled "Classroom Assessment: Monitoring Academic Achievement in the Classroom," consider the importance of progress monitoring to classroom instruction.

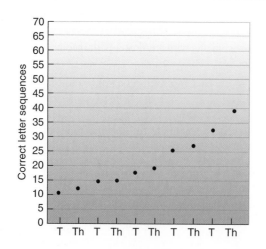

Figure 12.2 Curriculum-Based Measurement in Spelling Chart

once every 7 seconds and students write the words on lined, numbered paper). Student performance can be scored by means of measures that may be more sensitive than number of words spelled correctly, such as number of correct letter sequences (Fuchs & Fuchs, 1994).

Letter sequence scores can then be plotted over time, either for individual students or for the class as a whole (see Figure 12.2). Student progress can be plotted and the teacher can estimate whether students will attain end-of-year goals if they continue to progress at the current rate. If progress seems inadequate, teachers can increase time-on-task or individual work with specific difficult letter patterns (Fuchs et al., 1992).

Curriculum-based measurement is an excellent way to monitor the progress of all students, including those with special needs, toward end-of-year goals. In this way, instructional decisions can be made throughout the year to help ensure that students do meet their goals. CBM has been used in all basic skill areas, including reading, spelling, writing, and mathematics (Stecker, Fuchs, & Fuchs, 2005).

Curriculum-based measurement also has been recommended for use in response-to-intervention (RTI) programs (Hosp et al., 2007). Students' responses to instruction can be measured formatively, based on the curriculum being used, as a guide to evaluation. Using CBM, adequate progress toward long-term objectives can be assessed to aid in placement decisions.

STRATEGIES FOR
USING PERFORMANCE ASSESSMENT

Performance assessment addresses students' ability to interact (perform) appropriately with relevant instructional materials, and the content of instruction. As such, this type of assessment relies much less on direct recall of verbal information than do more typical classroom tests, and more on students' demonstration of understanding (Elliott & Fuchs, 1997). Performance assessment is helpful when testing students who may have word-finding (retrieval) problems, communication disorders, or other skills that limit verbal communication. For example, in an investigation by Scruggs, Mastropieri, Bakken, and Brigham (1993), students with learning disabilities performed relatively poorly on a more traditional test of their recall of vocabulary words after hands-on science instruction. However, they were much more able to demonstrate their knowledge in performance-based tests that required them to determine, for example, which of two minerals is harder, or whether a mineral contains calcite. Performance assessment is an effective way of measuring all students' comprehension of academic content in at least part of virtually all school subjects, including science, math, social studies, music, art, vocational education, and physical education.

Although performance assessments may vary widely, they often have three key elements in common:

1. Students construct their own responses, rather than selecting or identifying correct responses.

2. Teachers can observe student performance on tasks reflecting real-world or authentic requirements.

3. Student responses can reveal patterns in students' thinking and learning, as well as whether the question was correctly answered. (Fuchs, 1994)

IMPLEMENT AND ADAPT PERFORMANCE ASSESSMENT   To set up performance assessment measures, first determine exactly what you want students to be able to do after the instructional unit, and state it as a behavioral objective. The next step is to set up the materials and provide the opportunity for the student to perform on the test. Specific tasks can be placed at several stations around the classroom, and students can move from station to station individually, without observing another student's performance on the test.

A performance test allows students to demonstrate their knowledge.

Scoring is done by using a scoring rubric that lists test items and scoring criteria. For example, consider a performance assessment for a science unit on ecosystems (students had built their own "ecocolumns" using plants, animals, soil, water, and 2-liter bottles), which used the following test item:

- Draw a picture of an ecosystem. Label all parts.

To score this item objectively, a scoring rubric was constructed by which responses could be evaluated. For this item, the scoring criteria included the following:

Scoring Rubric

Score	Scoring Criteria
3	Picture with living and nonliving things appearing to interact in some general way. Living and nonliving things labeled.
2	Picture of living and nonliving things not labeled, or labeled living, or labeled nonliving.
1	One of above or general relevant comment.
0	Nothing of relevance.

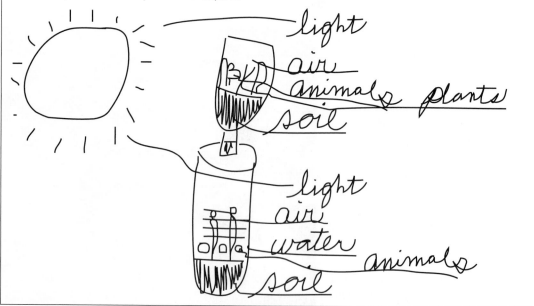

Ecosystems 1

NAME:_____   DATE:_____

SHORT ANSWER:

1. Tell me everything you can about an ecosystem.

an ecosystem
is a place were living an nonliving things
effect and depend on each other.
the living parts of an ecosystem is the plants
animal. the non liv parts are to soil, water,
air, light also and ecosystems

2. Draw a picture of an ecosystem. Label all parts.

light
air
animals plants
soil

light
air
water
animals
soil

Figure 12.3 Student Response on Ecosystem Item of Performance-Based Assessment

Using this key, then, a picture drawn by a student that included both living and nonliving things, but with the items in the picture not labeled, would earn a score of 2 points. An example of a response to this particular item on a performance assessment is given in Figure 12.3. See if you can score number 2 in Figure 12.3.

Schirmer and Bailey (2000) described the development of a rubric for writing assessment that was employed successfully for middle-school students who were deaf. They emphasized that the rubric should be a dynamic tool, capable of accommodating individual differences in student needs, content, assignments, and curriculum. That is, some students may benefit from a rubric that emphasizes word choice as a means for expanding vocabulary, while other students may benefit from a rubric that emphasizes organization of ideas. In creating a writing assessment rubric, teachers should:

- Identify the qualities of writing.

- Create a scale.

- Define each quality by listing the characteristics that describe performance at each point on the scale. (Schirmer & Bailey, 2000, p. 55)

Modified rubrics could include traits and their definitions, and a scale for rating these traits. For example, Schirmer and Bailey (2000) created a rubric for writing assessment, adapted from a published English series, that listed traits, including topic, content, story development, organization, text structure, voice/audience, word choice, sentence structure, and mechanics. Specific definitions were provided for each trait. The *In the Classroom* feature on page 287 includes a math scoring rubric.

Accommodations on performance assessments may also be helpful for students with special needs. Crawford, Helwig, and Tindal (2004) reported some relative benefit from longer time limits on a performance assessment in writing, while Johnson et al. (2001) reported that reading math items to students with learning disabilities provided some benefit to test-takers.

STRATEGIES FOR
USING PORTFOLIO ASSESSMENT

A *portfolio* has been defined as a "systematic and organized collection of evidence used by the teacher and student to monitor growth of the student's knowledge, skills, and attitudes" (Vavrus, 1990, p. 48). Using portfolios for assessment, teachers and students collect and organize relevant products to document performance and progress in different areas of academic and behavioral functioning (Wesson & King, 1996). These products can be collected in accordion folders, or in three-ring notebooks with pocketed dividers. You can refer to portfolios to document current functioning, to determine progress, to share information with parents and other teachers, and to plan appropriate interventions or modifications in the student's educational environment (Salend, 1998). Portfolios can be created in any area of student performance, including literacy, math, and science. Portfolios may also be useful in situations where more traditional, standardized tests may not be appropriate, for example, for some students with autism.

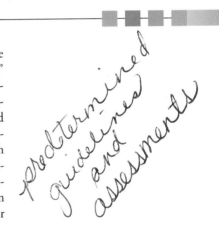

Student portfolios can be tailored to the specific needs of the classroom, the student, or the curriculum, and can therefore be considered quite versatile (Wesson & King, 1996). However, for these same reasons, portfolios may lack standardization and objectivity, and therefore teachers must ensure that judgments based on portfolio products are both reliable and valid. Helpful strategies include using multiple measures of the same skills or products, calculating interrater reliability (where different "experts" independently assess portfolio products), and making comparisons with more traditional measures (e.g., standardized tests or criterion-referenced measurement). Nevertheless, portfolios can provide authentic evidence of actual classroom performance that may be difficult to document by other methods. You can also use the portfolios to reflect on your own teaching. The *Diversity in the Classroom* feature on page 288 describes uses of portfolio assessment for English language learners.

Figure 12.4 provides a list of items that could be included in a literacy portfolio, while Figure 12.5 provides a list of items that could be included in a science portfolio.

- A tape of the student reading from a self-selected piece of literature. The student may reread the same piece periodically, thereby allowing the viewer of the portfolio to clearly see improvement.

- A checklist of skills the student has mastered, such as phonics rules or writing conventions like capitalization and punctuation.

- A log of books read during the year, including dates completed, authors, and student's appreciation ratings of the books.

- Copies of stories the student has written, including in some cases copies of all the draft stages the student has worked through.

- Pictures of a student's project, which shows understanding of a topic. For example, after studying volcanoes, the student may build a volcano and prepare a poster to illustrate how eruptions occur.

- Videotapes of students working cooperatively on language arts projects, such as putting on a skit to show understanding of a story.

- Notes the teacher makes while observing the student at work or conferencing with the student. These notes help the teacher document instructional decisions.

- A chart of progress using curriculum-based measures in reading and written expression.

- Charts the student has developed to track bits of information collected in relation to a nonfiction theme being composed.

- Excerpts from a student's journal and learning log.

Figure 12.4 Potential Items to Include in a Literacy Portfolio

Note: From "Portfolio Assessment and Special Education Students," by C. L. Wesson & R. P. King, 1996, *Teaching Exceptional Children, 28*(2), p. 44. Copyright 1996 by CEC. Reprinted with permission.

- Audiotape of oral reading from science materials collected and added to periodically throughout the year.

- Samples of written work completed throughout the year.

- Samples of laboratory booklets and notes kept throughout the year.

- Samples of formative evaluation measures completed.

- Summaries of performance-based assessments throughout the year.

- Copies of summative evaluation measures (end-of-term exams).

- Teacher observations and anecdotal records regarding performance during general education science class, updated periodically.

- Videotapes taken at various times throughout the year of the student during general education science classes.

Figure 12.5 Sample Portfolio Items for Science

Note: From *A Practical Guide for Teaching Science to Students with Special Needs in Inclusive Settings* (p. 115), by M. A. Mastropieri & T. E. Scruggs, 1993, Austin, TX: Pro-Ed. Copyright 1993 by CEC. Reprinted with permission.

ADAPT PORTFOLIO ASSESSMENT FOR STUDENTS WITH SPECIAL NEEDS In addition to the "traditional" uses of portfolio assessment in education, portfolio assessment can also be used to document the performance of students who have been referred to special education. Swicegood (1994) described how portfolios could be linked with individual student IEPs, by including work products that show growth on IEP objectives and by periodically completing summary sheets that link IEP objectives to documentation in the portfolio.

Wesson and King (1996) provided two case studies of the use of portfolios with students with disabilities. In the first study, a sixth-grade, general education teacher used a portfolio to chronicle the progress of a student, Tom, classified as seriously emotionally/behaviorally disturbed. Tom was described as having difficulties getting along with peers and frequently fighting with

Sample Mathematics Scoring Rubric

4 Exemplary Response
  4.1 Complete, with clear, coherent, unambiguous, and insightful explanation
  4.2 Shows understanding of underlying mathematical concepts, procedures, and structures
  4.3 Examines and satisfies all essential conditions of the problem
  4.4 Presents strong supporting arguments with examples and counterexamples as appropriate
  4.5 Solution and work is efficient and shows evidence of reflection and checking of work
  4.6 Appropriately applies mathematics to the situation

3 Competent Response
  3.1 Gives a fairly complete response with reasonably clear explanations
  3.2 Shows understanding of underlying mathematical concepts, procedures, and structures
  3.3 Examines and satisfies most essential conditions of the problem
  3.4 Presents adequate supporting arguments with examples and counterexamples as appropriate
  3.5 Solution and work show some evidence of reflection and checking of work
  3.6 Appropriately applies mathematics to the situation

2 Minimal Response
  2.1 Gives response, but explanations may be unclear or lack detail
  2.2 Exhibits minor flaws in underlying mathematical concepts, procedures, and structures
  2.3 Examines and satisfies some essential conditions of the problem
  2.4 Draws some accurate conclusions, but reasoning may be faulty or incomplete
  2.5 Shows little evidence of reflection and checking of work
  2.6 Some attempt to apply mathematics to the situation

1 Inadequate Response
  1.1 Response is incomplete and explanation is insufficient or not understandable
  1.2 Exhibits major flaws in underlying mathematical concepts, procedures, and structures
  1.3 Fails to address essential conditions of the problem
  1.4 Uses faulty reasoning and draws incorrect conclusions
  1.5 Shows no evidence of reflection and checking of work
  1.6 Fails to apply mathematics to the situation

0 No attempt
  0.1 Provides irrelevant or no response
  0.2 Copies part of the problem but does not attempt a solution
  0.3 Illegible response

Note: To receive a particular score, a significant number of the associated criteria must be met.

Note: From *Connecting Performance Assessment to Instruction* (p. 24), by L. S. Fuchs, 1994, Reston, VA: Council for Exceptional Children. Copyright 1994 by CEC. Reprinted with permission.

In the CLASSROOM

them, being argumentative and noncompliant with teachers, being socially isolated, and making limited academic progress. Tom's portfolio included a videotape (updated regularly) of Tom's performance during cooperative group lessons, a description of Tom's outside-school social activities, and a list of narrative observations the teacher (or teacher's aide) had made as she watched Tom in social situations, including behavioral observations of Tom's problem behaviors.

In the second case study, a portfolio was created for the vocational experiences of Chris, a 16-year-old student with severe disabilities. This portfolio included a videotape showing Chris working in academic and vocational settings, a transcript of an interview the teacher conducted with Chris, a vocational skill checklist, and a list of Chris's circle of friends (see Chapter 8) and their roles in her life. Chris's teacher hoped the portfolio would be useful when Chris applies for jobs and works in the community (Wesson & King, 1996). Kearns, Burdge, and Clayton (2006)

Assessment Portfolios

With the increased accountability movement and the increased amount of standardized testing in schools, some have advocated the use of assessment portfolios for English language learners (ELLs, Gomez, 2001). Assessment portfolios are defined as the "systematic collection of student work measured against predetermined scoring criteria" (Gomez, 2001, p. 1). Student work includes various types of writing samples, different types of student reports from a variety of subject areas such as social studies and science, samples of math problem solving, and copies of standardized test performance, such as statewide high-stakes tests and other norm-referenced standardized tests. Scoring criteria include scoring rubrics designed specifically for the contained assignments, checklists, and rating scales. Both the types of student work

and the predetermined criteria for evaluating such work need to be established by the school or district.

Advantages of such a system allow for breadth of evaluation of students who are English language learners, and inclusion of those students within the high-stakes testing of districts. In addition, the development of the assessment portfolio provides teachers and administrators opportunities to identify critical components of the curriculum, which can lead to a shared vision of teaching and learning for all students. District personnel can decide to include anything observable, along with its respective scoring criteria, in the portfolio. Such a process may represent a more authentic picture of what ELLs and all students have gained throughout a school year than simply a standardized score on a high-stakes test. The process may also yield information that is easier to communicate with parents. Sharing actual samples of student work and how

it was evaluated during parent conferences might assist parents in understanding their child's level of performance better than a standardized test score.

Challenges associated with assessment portfolios also exist. As with any portfolio, there is a chance of more limited reliability and comparability across classes and grade levels compared with a single standardized test score. It also is a challenge to include standardized administration procedures for all works contained in the portfolio. For example, when including a long-term social studies project, it may be difficult to ensure that the student completed the work entirely independently. Overall, however, assessment portfolios can provide a rich and important complement to more traditional methods of assessment, and may help to reveal relative strengths not documented with standardized tests.

described the use of enhanced portfolio and performance assessments to document adapted grade-level content standards for statewide testing for students with significant cognitive disabilities.

Teach Test-Taking Skills

Tests are given frequently in school to determine how well students have learned various content areas and to determine their overall achievement levels. Many students with disabilities and at risk for failure in school perform poorly on tests because of poor test-taking skills (Deshler & Schumaker, 2006; Scruggs & Mastropieri, 1988, 1992).

Test-taking skills strategies help students with disabilities improve their performance on both standardized and teacher-made tests. Several researchers have described a number of test-taking strategies that have been helpful for all types of learners (Hughes, 1996; Hughes, Schumaker, Deshler, & Mercer, 1988; Kesselman-Turkel & Peterson, 2004; Scruggs & Mastropieri, 1992). This section describes test-taking strategies that are successful in increasing test performance of students with special needs.

STRATEGIES FOR
TEACHING TEST-TAKING SKILLS

TEACH GENERAL TEST-PREPARATION STRATEGIES General preparation strategies refer to things students can do to help when preparing for any exam. Many students, but especially those with disabilities, will benefit from explicit instruction in each of these areas (Wood & Willoughby, 1995).

The first and most important general test strategy is academic preparation. See Chapters 10 and 11 for more information in this area. The next general strategy is physical preparation, and includes getting enough rest and nourishment, particularly before studying and before taking the test. A positive attitude toward tests is also important. Improve test attitudes by helping students set realistic goals, providing practice tests, explaining the purpose of the particular test, rewarding effort, and providing training in test-taking skills.

Anxiety reduction also can help. You can help students reduce anxieties during testing situations by encouraging their use of positive attributions—that is, by helping them focus on effort and strategies, rather than thinking about what their score will be or how others will do (see Chapter 9). Teach students to recognize signs of tension in themselves—such as grinding teeth, biting fingernails, and picking at hair or face—and to respond by consciously relaxing their muscles and controlling their breathing (Erwin & Dunwiddie, 1983; Lucangeli & Scruggs, 2003).

TEACH GENERAL STRATEGIES FOR STANDARDIZED TESTS   You can teach students general strategies that they can apply across a number of standardized tests and testing situations (Pauk, 1987). These strategies include using separate answer sheets, elimination strategies, guessing effectively, and using time wisely.

Separate Answer Sheets   Most standardized tests require students to record their responses by filling a circle or "bubble" on separate answer sheets. Provide students with practice filling in the appropriate answer bubble "quick, dark, and inside the line." If practice tests are provided by the test publisher, provide instruction on the use of separate answer sheets (if not, make simulated answer sheets and test booklets when appropriate).

Use Elimination Strategies   Teach students to eliminate response options they know are incorrect. For example, if there are four answer options and a test-taker can eliminate three of them, then the remaining option must be the correct response.

Guess When Appropriate   Encourage guessing where appropriate, as many students with disabilities and at risk for school failure do not realize that guessing is better than leaving an item blank on most standardized tests.

Use Time Wisely   Teach students to use time efficiently on familiar items, and not to waste time on items they are unlikely to answer correctly. Teach students to monitor their time as they take the test. That is, when the testing period is half over, they should be finished with about half the test.

TEACH SPECIFIC STRATEGIES FOR STANDARDIZED TESTS   Strategies can be employed for specific subtests of standardized tests.

Reading Comprehension Subtests   Most standardized reading comprehension subtests require students to read a specific passage, then answer questions about the passage. Teach students to read as much of the passage as possible, as they can still answer many of the questions even if they have skipped some unfamiliar words. Encourage students to read the entire question and every stem option before selecting responses. Teach students to check back in the passage when possible to verify their answer choice was correct. When reading selections contain information in tables, such as basketball schedules, teach students to quickly skim the information, then look to the questions and refer back to the table to identify answers.

Decoding Subtests   Since students do not respond orally and decode words, decoding subtests on group-administered standardized tests may have unusual formats. For example, students may be asked to match a word that contains the same sound as that underlined in the stem:

1. Which word contains the underlined sound?
   pl<u>ay</u>
   a. plan
   b. yard
   c. afraid
   d. drag

Teach students to say the underlined sound of the word to themselves, and be certain they have found an answer that matches this sound (c. "afraid"), and not the appearance of the stem word (a. "plan").

Mathematics Computation Subtests   Mathematics computation subtests require students to look at test items, compute answers on scratch paper, and select the correct answer from the options provided. Provide students with practice using scratch paper and identifying the correct answer from an array of choices. Teach students to rewrite the problem into the format that they are most comfortable with. Be sure students have sufficient practice with mathematics vocabulary that will be used in word problems. Review words such as *sum, product, difference, quotient,* and other words that may appear on the test.

Mathematics Concepts Subtests   Mathematics concepts subtests cover a range of skills in math and are presented in a variety of formats on standardized tests. Model examples in which you read the question, rephrase it, and then think aloud through to the solution. Some math problems may contain boxes to indicate missing values, as in the following example:

> 2. What number should be in the $\square$?
> $524 - \square = 425 + 75$
>   a. 500
>   b. 75
>   c. 24
>   d. 425

Practice solving problems before the test using those types of boxes or other symbols that may be used on standardized tests. If specific formats that will be used are not known (and this is likely), practice solving problems throughout the year using different answering formats. Be sure students are aware of any specialized vocabulary (e.g., *quotient, subtrahend*) that may be included on the test.

Math Problem-Solving Subtests   Tests of math problem solving require reading the problem, determining what is known, figuring out what operation is called for, generating a plan for a solution, computing the solution, selecting the correct answer from the options, and marking the selected response appropriately on the answer sheet. Provide students with practice using their scratch paper, carefully matching the number of the problem on their scratch paper with the test booklet, along with practice executing all the other necessary steps in the procedure for solving word problems.

Tell students to practice requesting help with the reading if they need it. If test administrators are not allowed to provide assistance in an area, they will simply say, "I cannot help you with that."

Some math problems do not contain all the necessary information to answer the question and students are asked to furnish the missing, but necessary, information. For example:

> 3. Tyler is 66 inches tall. What else do you need to know to figure out how much he grew this year?
>   a. How old he is this year.
>   b. How tall he was last year.
>   c. How tall his father is.
>   d. How much his brother grew last year.

Practice with this type of format is necessary for students with disabilities to ensure successful performance. Model and demonstrate by thinking through the solution aloud. Have students practice using similar procedures.

Science and Social Studies Subtests   The formats for science and social studies exams parallel the formats employed in reading comprehension and mathematics subtests. Many items require students to read expository passages and then answer questions about the passages. Other items require students to examine charts, diagrams, reference materials, or maps and interpret them before selecting correct answers. Provide practice using these various formats with students when teaching throughout the year.

TEACH STRATEGIES FOR TEACHER-MADE TESTS Teachers sometimes use tests developed by textbook publishers to accompany adopted text materials. At other times they develop their own tests. Some items on both teacher-made and publisher-developed tests include objective tests that contain multiple-choice, matching, and true–false items, and written formats that contain short-answer, fill-in-the-blank, essay, and performance-based items. The general preparation strategies, and many of the general strategies described for standardized tests, are also applicable to teacher-made tests. In addition, some specific strategies for teacher-made tests should be learned.

Objective Tests Objective tests contain multiple-choice, true–false, and/or matching items. All strategies described so far may be applicable for helping students prepare for objective tests. However, students should be familiar with the content on teacher-made tests, and they can use this knowledge, or partial knowledge, to improve their test scores.

Written Tests Written tests may contain sentence-completion, short-answer, or essay items. Strategies can help students become better test-takers on these tests.

1. *Sentence Completion Items and Short-Answer Items.* Sentence-completion items are usually short sentences containing blanks that must be filled in correctly ("The longest river in South America is _____"), while short-answer items ask questions requiring a brief response ("What were the causes of the War of 1812?").

Encourage students to provide some answer, even if it is only partially correct. Many teachers give partial credit for some answers, but cannot provide any credit if the items are left blank. Have students guess if they are not completely sure, encourage them to use partial knowledge, and teach them to make the sentence sound logical in sentence-completion items. Sometimes, lists of items are considered acceptable responses for short-answer items. Determine whether sentence fragments or lists will result in the same credit as complete sentences.

2. *Essay Questions.* Essay tests are difficult for students with disabilities, but several strategies exist to facilitate essay test performance. One strategy, referred to as **SNOW**, stands for:

Study the question

Note important points

Organize the information

Write directly to the point of the question (Scruggs & Mastropieri, 1992, p. 89)

Teach students how to implement each step of this strategy and provide corrective feedback on their performance. Have them *study* the questions by underlining the specific words that tell them what to do, such as *describe, define, explain, compare, contrast, list, justify,* or *critique* (see Figure 12.6).

Next, students should *note* important points that come to mind. Then they should *organize* their notes by numbering the main and supporting points in logical order for discussion. Finally, they should *write* concisely and directly to the point of the question.

Performance Tests Performance tests are designed to parallel the exact format of what has been taught and practiced, and are designed to provide better information about instruction (Baron, 1990). A practice test may be helpful for some students in preparing for the test. Teach students to read directions carefully, and not to answer too quickly if something looks familiar. Show them how to talk through the steps of answers before responding.

TEACH OTHER TEST-TAKING STRATEGIES Other test-taking strategies may be helpful in preparing students to take tests. One strategy is called **SCORER** (Carman & Adams, 1972). Each letter in SCORER represents clue words to help students perform better during testing situations: **S**chedule time; **C**lue words (see Figure 12.6); **O**mit hard items; **R**ead carefully; **E**stimate answers; and **R**eview work. This strategy has been successfully used with students of middle-school age (Ritter & Idol-Maestas, 1986).

Another strategy, **PIRATES**, was developed by Hughes, Rule, Deshler, and Schumaker (1993) and Hughes and Schumaker (1991). PIRATES is a seven-step strategy designed to help students perform better on teacher-made tests. Each letter in PIRATES represents a step of the strategy: **P**repare to succeed; **I**nspect the instructions; **R**ead, remember, reduce; **A**nswer or

Command Words on Test Items and Their Implications	
Word	*Possible Implications*
Discuss	Provide reasoning behind; give different points of view.
Describe	Give an overall impression; give examples.
Compare	Show how two or more things are similar; provide examples of common characteristics.
Contrast	Show how two or more things are different; provide examples of differing characteristics.
Explain	Clarify or simplify; describe the rationale behind.
Justify	Argue in favor of; defend.
Critique	Argue in opposition of; find fault with.
List	Give a simple list of elements.
Outline	Give a list of elements organized into a system.

Figure 12.6 Command Words and Their Explanations

Note: From Teaching Test-Taking Skills: Helping Students Show What They Know (p. 90), by T. E. Scruggs & M. A. Mastropieri, 1992, Cambridge, MA: Brookline. Copyright 1992 by Brookline. Reprinted with permission.

abandon; **T**urn back; **E**stimate; **S**urvey. Although generally used with students with learning disabilities and emotional/behavioral disorders, this strategy has also been employed successfully with high-functioning students with autism (Songlee, 2007).

Another strategy is called **ANSWER** (Hughes, 1996). While PIRATES was originally designed for improving performance on objective tests, ANSWER is designed to assist students with essay type exams. The steps in ANSWER can be summarized as:

- **A**nalyze the situation, by reading the item carefully, underlining important words, and estimating time needed;
- **N**otice requirements, by marking different parts of the question and committing to a quality answer;
- **S**et up an outline, including main ideas, and check outline ideas with the question;
- **W**ork in details, remembering previous learning and applying it in appropriate order, using abbreviations;
- **E**ngineer your answer, by writing an introductory paragraph, referring back to your outline, using topic sentences and additional details, and providing examples; and
- **R**eview your work, by checking the entire answer with all components of the question (Hughes, 1996).

Grading

STRATEGIES FOR ADAPTING REPORT CARD GRADING

Report card grading is an essential component of the U.S. educational system (Brookhart, 2004), and the importance of grades in our society cannot be denied. However, across the country, standards for grading appear to be somewhat variable. Polloway et al. (1994) reported that about 39% of the districts surveyed had a specific policy for modifications in grading for students with disabilities (see also Rojewski, Pollard, & Meers, 1992). The most common responses involved modifications reflected in the students' IEPs, decisions made by a committee, and notations of accommodations noted on the report card.

MODIFY GRADING PROCEDURES   There appears to be no one "right" way to proceed when issuing report card grades to students with disabilities. However, following are some considerations that could be helpful in planning grading procedures (Bradley & Calvin, 1998;

Brookhart, 2004; Bursuck et al., 1996; Christiansen & Vogel, 1998; Munk & Bursuck, 1998; Rojewski et al., 1992):

1. *Consult school and district policy.* Some schools have established official policies on issuing report card grades to students with disabilities. Find out whether your school has such a policy, and, if so, follow its guidelines. Make recommendations when needed to appropriate school personnel.

2. *Follow recommendations on the IEP.* IEPs typically state explicit goals and objectives for the academic year. For example, an objective on an IEP may state that the student will score 70% correct on tests given in a general education science class. This goal can be taken into consideration when determining the student's grade in the class.

3. *Make no grading modifications at all.* This approach is adopted by many regular classroom teachers, and there are some advantages to this approach. The grades the students earn reflect directly their success at performing in the regular classroom, and can be a source of pride. However, many students are simply not able to compete successfully in such an environment without any supports, and grading without modifications may doom some students to failure. Carefully consider the effect of adopting such a policy.

4. *Use a pass–fail system.* Consider carefully what the minimum standard for a passing grade would be, considering attendance, effort, and performance. Using the PASS variables, prioritize class objectives so that students with disabilities or other special needs receive as much appropriately adapted instruction on critical objectives as possible. At the end of the grading period, record performance with "pass" or "fail" (or "no pass").

5. *Use a double-standard approach.* With this approach, students with disabilities can be graded using different standards for letter grades. It may not be necessary simply to lower the standards, such that, for example, an "A" on the special education standard is equivalent to a "C" on the general education standard. It is also possible to consider the grade itself differently. For example, a grade on a special education standard could weight more heavily considerations such as effort, persistence, attitude, and progress (see Bursuck et al., 1996). Placing more importance on these areas also demonstrates to students that the grade they receive is more in their control than one that sets unrealistic academic standards and that may lead to resignation or quitting. A special education grading standard could also consider more carefully goals and objectives for the student documented on the student's IEP.

   Often when different grading standards are applied, some notation is included that acknowledges that the standard is different. This could be done by a discreet note on the report card (e.g., "Special grading standard"), or by circling the letter awarded. Use of different grading standards can make goals more realistic and achievable for students. On the other hand, it is important to first determine that usual grading standards are not appropriate for particular students. If it seems that students may be able, with sufficient effort, to meet the same standards as the rest of the class, it may be best not to use a different standard.

6. *Contracting.* In some cases it may be helpful to establish a formal contract with a student regarding report card grades (see Chapter 7). The contract can specify what the student will do to earn a particular grade in the class, with respect to, for example, attendance, punctuality, homework completion, participation, and test scores. Grades are then allocated according to the terms of the contract.

7. *Personal Grading Plans.* Munk and Bursuck (2001) described the development of Personal Grading Plans (PGP) created by teams of general and special education teachers to provide more appropriate grading for individual students. For example, it was determined that science grades of one eighth-grade student with learning disabilities were lower than expected because of the heavy weighting of tests and quiz scores. A PGP was developed that included specific objectives within each thematic unit, with specified criteria and a modified grading scale for each objective. With thoughtful modifications and effective communication such as this, grading can be a useful and productive experience for everyone.

12 Summary

- Many types of tests are used in education; however, all tests must be reliable and valid to be useful.

- Norm-referenced testing compares the score of an individual with the scores of other students in a standardization sample.

- Modifications in standardized tests or administration procedures may detract from the validity of the test. However, such modifications as teaching test-taking skills, enhancing motivation, and enhancing examiner familiarity may improve test validity without compromising standardization.

- Competency-based and statewide testing assesses the skill levels of students and is being used more often in schools. Some modifications in these tests, or alternate assessments, may be appropriate for students with special needs.

- Teacher-made tests can be modified to obtain a clearer picture of student performance, without detracting from the test itself. Modifications can be applied to a variety of test formats.

- Curriculum-based measurement is an excellent means of documenting progress of all students, including students with disabilities or other special needs. Curriculum-based measurement allows the teacher to make instructional decisions as instruction is going on.

- Performance assessment evaluates student competence in particular instructional units. Because it focuses more on doing than writing or speaking, it may be particularly suited for diverse classrooms.

- Portfolio assessment is an ongoing means of obtaining information from student products and other sources. It is a particularly useful form of assessment that also has direct applications to some students with disabilities.

- Explicit instruction on general strategies to improve test performance, such as academic preparation, physical preparation, reducing anxieties, and increasing motivation, can improve the test performance of students with special needs.

- General strategies for improving standardized test performance include using separate answer sheets, using time wisely, elimination, and guessing strategies. Test-taking strategies for specific types of subtests can also improve standardized test performance.

- Test-taking strategies for teacher-made tests include strategies for taking objective tests and written tests, including fill-in-the-blank, short-answer, and essay tests.

- Some other test-taking strategies, such as SNOW, SCORER, PIRATES, and ANSWER, have been successfully taught to students with special needs and have improved their performance.

- Modifications can be made in grading and scoring the work of students with special needs. These modifications can be applied on report card grades, homework, and seatwork.

PROFESSIONAL STANDARDS LINK:
Assessment

Information in this chapter links most directly to:

- CEC Standards: 3 (Individual Learning Differences), 4 (Instructional Strategies), 5 (Learning Environments and Social Interactions), 6 (Language), 7 (Instructional Planning), 8 (Assessment)

- INTASC Standards: Principles 3 (understands learning differences, adapts instructional opportunities), 4 (instructional strategies), 5 (creates learning environments), 8 (assessment strategies), 10 (reflects on practice)

- PRAXIS II™ Content Categories (Knowledge): 3 (Delivery of Services)

- PRAXIS II™ Content Categories (Application): 2 (Instruction), 3 (Assessment)

ASSESSMENT

When assessing students with disabilities, and other special needs, have you considered the following? If not, see the pages listed below.

13
14
15
16

Literacy

Mathematics

Science and Social Studies

Career and Technical
Education, and Transitions

Ironbridge 038

DAVID WORTON   David Worton has polio myletus, which has resulted in atrophied muscles and a curvature of his spine. Progressive weakness and problems holding his camera still provide him with ongoing challenges. However, even with these challenges he receives tremendous enjoyment from his love of photography.

13

Literacy

OBJECTIVES

After studying this chapter, you should be able to:

- Understand considerations and adaptive approaches relevant to basal textbooks, whole-language, reading recovery, direct instruction, and code-emphasis approaches.

- Describe adaptations for promoting word identification, including phonemic awareness, phonics, structural analysis, and basic sight words.

- Understand adaptations and technological advances to promote reading fluency, including repeated readings, curriculum-based measurement, classwide peer tutoring, and various computer programs.

- Design and implement strategies for teaching reading comprehension in inclusive settings.

- Describe and implement instructional and technological adaptations for written expression.

- Implement instructional strategies to enhance and improve spelling for students in inclusive settings.

- Describe and implement effective composition strategies such as self-regulation and self-instruction.

Reading is probably the most important academic skill students will learn in school. Most students acquire this skill with little apparent difficulty; however, for a smaller number, reading can represent a major stumbling block to school success. The process of learning to read begins very early in life and extends well into adulthood.

Skills and understandings important for learning to read begin to develop almost at birth. These include recognizing books by cover, pretending to read, listening to stories, attending to letters, and scribbling. Between the ages of 3 and 4, children begin to understand that it is print that is read in stories and that letters can be individually named. Pre-literate children learn to name some alphabet letters, attend to repeating (e.g., rhyming) sounds in language, and can connect information from a story to life experiences. Clearly, families can play a key role in promoting this important skill development (Snow, Burns, & Griffin, 1998).

In school, children go through a sequence of levels of reading development, beginning with prereading skills such as sound segmentation and continuing through expert reading (Pressley, 2006; Stone, Silliman, Ehren, & Apel, 2004). After the early literacy or prereading stage, learners develop decoding skills (typically, grades 1–2), fluency and automaticity (grades 2–3), uses of reading for learning (grades 4–8), appreciation of multiple viewpoints and levels of comprehension (including literal, inferential, critical, grades 9–12), and construction and reconstruction of reading for one's own purposes (including personal, professional, and civic purposes, college and beyond).

Students with disabilities or other special needs may exhibit difficulties at any, or all, of these levels of learning to read. Some may have specific disabilities in reading, sometimes referred to as **dyslexia** (Chall, 1987; Lerner & Kline, 2006). In other cases, reading problems are a function of more general developmental or language delays, or physical disabilities (Best, Heller, & Bigge, 2005). Students with hearing impairments often acquire reading skills at a slower rate (Stewart & Kluwin, 2001), and students with visual impairments may require specialized materials. Students with emotional or behavioral disorders often read below grade level (Reid, Gonzalez, Nordness, Trout, & Epstein, 2004). However, in all cases, specific adaptations can significantly improve reading ability (Polloway, Smith, & Miller, 2003).

Approaches to Reading

There are several approaches to beginning reading instruction. It is important to understand these different approaches, because they carry different implications for students who are having difficulty learning to read.

CLASSROOM SCENARIO

Markeisha

Markeisha is a sincere, likeable seventh-grader. However, she has struggled with reading since first grade. She marvels at how easily some of her peers are able to read. She can't figure out why it seems so easy for them and yet is so difficult for her. Sometimes when she looks at the printed page, the words make no sense at all. They don't look a bit familiar to her, even when her teacher has her repeat the words over and over. She does her best to get by in school, by listening to other students read, by listening to her teachers, and by studying the illustrations in her book. She never raises her hand in class, and sits quietly, hoping she will not be noticed. Markeisha really wants to learn to read better, but no one seems to be able to help her do so.

QUESTIONS FOR REFLECTION

1. Why does Markeisha not speak with her teacher about her reading problem?
2. What do you think might be the cause of this problem?
3. What could the teacher do to become more aware of reading problems in her classroom?

STRATEGIES FOR
IMPLEMENTING APPROACHES TO READING

IMPLEMENT AND ADAPT BASAL TEXTBOOK APPROACHES The most traditional approach to reading instruction involves the use of **basal textbooks**, with a different text assigned for each grade level from kindergarten through middle school (Durkin, 1987). These textbooks contain short stories and comprehension questions designed to meet certain grade-level criteria. Some basal textbooks emphasize phonics; others highlight literature-based stories.

Most basal reading series include workbooks and worksheets that provide supplemental practice on comprehension and specific skills. In addition, the development of literacy is often supported by language arts classes, typically distinct from reading classes, whereby students are provided separate spelling and grammar textbooks.

Most students with reading difficulties have problems attending to the sounds in words and learning to decode (Pressley, 2006). If you have students with reading difficulties who are not making adequate progress in a particular basal series, determine whether your basal series offers a clear sequence of skills and sufficient review of these skills as they are learned. Consult with the special education teacher to determine whether a more structured phonetic approach might be more helpful, as a supplement or an alternative to the classroom materials. Some basal series provide a more balanced approach to literature and phonics instruction (Carnine, Silbert, Kaméenui, & Tarver, 2004).

IMPLEMENT AND ADAPT WHOLE-LANGUAGE APPROACHES The **whole-language** approach to reading emphasizes meaning and integrates all literacy tasks within reading instruction (Routman, 1991). A basic tenet of the approach is that the immersion of children in a literature-enriched environment promotes literacy. Many traditional skills such as phonics, sounding out words, spelling, grammar, and comprehension strategies are not directly taught (these are often addressed within the reading context), and there is an increased emphasis on meaning construction and use of context clues to figure out unknown words.

During whole-language instruction, students engage in reading **authentic literature** (e.g., trade books, real literature books) independently and maintain journals documenting their progress and comprehension of reading materials. Overall, the emphasis is placed on engaging students in literacy acts and promoting meaning (Goodman, 2005).

Unfortunately, as many as 25% of students do not discover sound–symbol relationships independently and without explicit instruction (Snider, 1997). Students with serious reading difficulties frequently have deficits in **phonemic awareness,** and need special training to learn that words are composed of smaller, individual speech sounds (phonemes). For example, the word "pin" has three phonemes: /p/, /i/, and /n/, and phonemes can be added, subtracted, or rearranged to make new words (Pressley, 2006; Shaywitz, 2003).

Using children's literature is one methodology for teaching literacy.

Most students with reading problems benefit from explicit training in phonological awareness, letter recognition and formation, sound–symbol relationships, decoding practice using controlled texts, comprehension strategies, and motivational techniques (Pressley, 2006; Shaywitz, 2003). Because whole-language approaches typically do not include such components, they may be less beneficial for students with serious reading difficulties, without additional instructional support (Gersten & Dimino, 1993; Pressley & Rankin, 1994). Some commercially available literature programs, such as *Learning Through Literature* (Dodds & Goodfellow, 1990–1991), have been designed for students with reading problems and may be useful in some cases. It may be difficult, however, to find appropriate authentic literature for students who are reading at very low levels.

If you are using a whole-language approach to reading, collect reading performance data using curriculum-based measurement, and audiotapes of students' oral reading, to ensure students are progressing satisfactorily. Fountas and Pinnell (2005) provided listings of thousands of trade books by graded reading level that can be used to support whole-language approaches to reading instruction. Some students with severe reading deficits may benefit from whole-language instruction if they are also receiving specialized reading instruction from special educators (Rudenga, 1992). Finally, if you have the opportunity as a teacher to examine literature programs to make recommendations for adoption, review what considerations have been made to meet the reading needs of all students.

IMPLEMENT READING RECOVERY FOR STRUGGLING READERS   Reading Recovery is a program that has been widely adopted in some states and school districts to help promote the early reading success of students at risk for reading failure (Slavin, 2005). Reading Recovery identifies primary-age students who are not learning to read and provides them with one-to-one tutorial instruction for 30 minutes daily. Sessions emphasize reading from familiar books, instruction in letter-identification strategies, writing and reading sentences and stories, assembling cut-up stories, and introducing the process of reading a new book. Teachers maintain daily records of students' reading progress, analyze children's problems, and devise appropriate instruction and feedback.

Reading Recovery has been considered effective for many young, struggling readers (D'Agostino & Murphy, 2004; Slavin, 2005). However, some findings suggest that the program may be less successful with students who have moderate to severe reading difficulties (Denton & Mathes, 2002; Hiebert, 1994; Reynolds & Wheldall, 2007). If Reading Recovery is used in your school with students with severe reading problems, be certain that their progress is carefully documented, and determine the steps that will be taken if acceptable progress is not being made.

IMPLEMENT AND ADAPT DIRECT INSTRUCTION AND CODE-EMPHASIS APPROACHES   **Direct instruction** is an instructional method that has proved successful with students with disabilities and those at risk for school failure (Adams & Carnine, 2003). Direct instruction involves a systematic, teacher-led approach using materials that contain a controlled vocabulary and emphasize a **code-emphasis approach** to reading instruction. For example, students are taught the sound–symbol relationships among letters and are provided sufficient practice decoding specific word patterns in reading passages before being presented with reading selections containing unfamiliar words (Carnine et al., 2004). Individual sounds and words are introduced systematically and practiced in isolation and in word lists, sentences, paragraphs, short stories, and accompanying workbook activities. Frequently, students with serious reading difficulties benefit greatly from structured, code-emphasis approaches (Shaywitz, 2003).

Curriculum materials are available that contain a code-emphasis approach to reading instruction. These materials include, for example, *Reading Mastery* (SRA/McGraw-Hill), a basal series intended for the entire general education classroom, and *Corrective Reading: Decoding Series* (SRA/McGraw-Hill), a series for students with reading problems. Both of these reading series use an effective instruction model of delivery (see Chapter 6), including teacher modeling and demonstration, frequent student responding and feedback, and practice using controlled vocabulary materials to teach reading. Because students with reading disabilities frequently rely too much on context cues (Johnson, 1992; Pressley, 2006), the materials encourage use of word-attack skills, by, for example, not providing pictures, or providing pictures that can be seen only after turning the page. Figure 13.1 contains a sample page from the *Corrective Reading Series.* The accompanying passage tells the story of "Chee, the Dog," who often speaks nonsense phrases. These phrases are included to compel students to focus on their word-attack skills to read the words.

Other commercially available structured reading programs include the *Merrill Reading Program* (SRA/McGraw-Hill) and *Read Well* (Sopris West) for early reading. The *Edmark Reading Program* (published by Riverdeep) is a sight-word program designed for students with few or no reading skills, and who have not benefited from an explicit phonics approach or other reading approaches.

Considerations and Adaptations   Three commonly asked questions are whether students who are taught using a code-emphasis approach can transfer these reading skills to other, less-structured reading materials, whether they will lose motivation from all the structure, and whether they will learn comprehension skills. In fact, students with reading disabilities can transfer skills acquired from code-emphasis instruction to more literature-based programs (Snider, 1997). In addition, students can maintain their motivation if teachers use enthusiasm and the other strategies discussed in Chapter 9. Finally, teachers should ensure that any reading program is balanced, and includes engaging text and sufficient comprehension instruction once students learn needed decoding skills (Adams, 1990; Pressley, 2006; Pressley & Rankin, 1994). Ensure that your reading program provides all the elements necessary for students to become skilled and motivated readers.

MAKE ADAPTATIONS TO PROMOTE ACCESS TO TEXT   For some students, physical and motor constraints can inhibit learning to read (Heller, 2005). Regardless to approach to reading, students must be able to stabilize reading materials and position themselves to assure efficient attending to the text. Ensure that students are positioned properly, with proper posture, in midline position, using supports when needed. Check to be sure the table and chair are at the right height, and the table slanted when needed. Provide color contrasts, with, for example, colored construction paper, for students with visual impairments. See Chapter 4 for additional suggestions.

For students who have difficulty turning pages, provide rubber finger tabs (Swingline), or place notebook tabs on the outside of pages. For significant physical disabilities, a GEWA Page Turner (Zygo Industries) turns pages with rubber rollers that can be controlled by minimal movement of a joystick.

For students who lose their place on the line, prepare a clear transparency with multicolored lines, composed of 1-inch strips of different colors. Place this transparency over pages as the student reads, and fade the use of the colored lines over time. Some students may become fatigued while reading, and the length of reading sessions may have to be adjusted (Heller, 2005).

LESSON 23

1 cold store that read back
  soon job beans helped
  ham better things much

2 name like came
  note bone home

3 Gretta Chee let's day
  pay played stay someone
  saying door bigger said
  I've cook other some
  don't can't folks didn't
  another their became one

4
CHEE, THE DOG

Gretta got a little dog. She named the dog Chee. Chee got bigger and bigger each day.

On a very cold day, Gretta said, "Chee, I must go to the store. You stay home. I will be back."

Chee said, "Store, lots, of, for, no."

Then Gretta said, "Did I hear that dog say things?"

Chee said, "Say things can I do."

Gretta said, "Dogs don't say things. So I must not hear things well."

But Chee did say things. Gretta left the dog at home. When Gretta came back, Chee was sitting near the door.
[1]

Gretta said, "That dog is bigger than she was."

Then the dog said, "Read, read for me of left."

Gretta said, "Is that dog saying that she can read?" Gretta got a pad and made a note for the dog. The note said, "Dear Chee, if you can read this note I will hand you a bag of bones."

Gretta said, "Let's see if you can read.

Chee said, "Dear Chee, if you can read this note, I will ham you a bag for beans."
[1]

Gretta said, "She can read, but she can't read well. Ho, ho."

Chee became very mad. She said "For note don't read ho ho."

Gretta said, "Chee gets mad when I say ho, ho."

Chee said, "Yes, no go ho ho."

Then Gretta felt sad. She said, "I didn't mean to make you mad. I don't like you to be sad. I will help you say things well."

Then Chee said, "Yes, well, of say for things."

So every day, Gretta helped Chee say things. She helped Chee read, too.
[1]

Chee got better and better at saying things. And she got better at reading. And she got bigger and bigger. When she was one year old, she was bigger than Gretta.

On a hot day Gretta left Chee at home, but when she got back, Chee met her at the door. "Did you have fun at the your job?" Chee asked.

"Yes, I did," Gretta said.

"I don't have much fun at home," Chee said. "I think I will get a job. I don't like to stay home."

"Dogs can't have jobs," Gretta said.

Chee said, "You have a job. So I will get a job, too."
[1]

Figure 13.1 Part of a Corrective Reading Lesson
Note: From *Corrective Reading: Decoding Strategies* (p. 26), by S. Engelmann, G. Johnson, D. Carmine, L. Meyer, W. Becker, & J. Eisele, 1988, Chicago: Science Research Associates. Copyright 1988 by SRA/McGraw Hill. Reprinted by permission.

Some additional adaptations to promote access include modification of printed materials with braille or large print; use of magnifying devices; use of optical character recognition (OCR) systems, such as the Cicero Text Reader (Dolphin Computer Access), that convert text to speech or braille, and the Kurzweil Reader (Kurzweil). Other adaptations involve the use of audiotape formats, including tape-recorded text, variable-speed cassettes and speech compressors, and listening centers. Effective use of technology for students who are deaf includes use of hypertext to provide sign versions of printed text, and word-processing software to integrate reading and writing (Schirmer & McGough, 2005).

Teaching Reading Skills

Beyond the application of particular methods and materials reflecting different approaches to reading instruction, it is important for teachers to carefully attend to all aspects of the reading process, to ensure that all students are receiving the instruction they need. It is also important that reading instruction be of high quality and research-based, because in many cases it will represent the first tier of a school's response-to-intervention (RTI) approach to reading, as described later in this chapter.

STRATEGIES FOR
PROMOTING WORD IDENTIFICATION

Most students with reading difficulties require additional instruction and practice in identifying words. Readers need to become automatic and fluent at word reading so they will be able to devote sufficient cognitive energy to comprehending what they read. However, before readers can acquire this automaticity, they must be able to read individual words. In order to do this, they must learn that words are composed of individual sounds, or phonemes.

PROVIDE PHONEMIC AWARENESS TRAINING Phonemes are the smallest sound units that have meaning, such as /t/ and /l/. Some students do not develop an understanding that words are composed of individual sounds as quickly as others, and therefore may find phonics instruction confusing. **Phonemic awareness** training includes activities to provide instruction and practice in listening and using sounds in isolation initially, followed by the use of words in context and in a reading passage. The purpose of phonemic awareness training is for students to learn that words are composed of individual sounds that can be combined and separated to create new words. Later, when they study phonics, they learn how these individual phonemes are represented by letters and letter combinations (Troia, 2004b). Sample phonemic awareness activities include the following:

- Discriminating sounds, for example: "Tell me if these two words have the same, or different, first sound: *cap—cat.*"

- Sound blending or making individual sounds into words, for example: "What word am I saying?: /c/—/a/—/t/?"

- Segmenting words into individual phonemes, for example: "How many sounds are in the word *fan?* What are the sounds?"

- Rhyming sounds, for example: "Tell me some words that rhyme with *fall.* Now, tell me some 'make-believe' words that rhyme with *fall.*"

Gamelike activities are available that emphasize phonological awareness training. For example, Torgesen and Bryant (1994) developed *Phonological Awareness Training for Reading,* which includes a board game. In one game, Rocky the Robot "speaks" only in phonemes or **onset-rime** constructions, that is, the sounds that precede the first vowel in a syllable, followed by the remaining sounds. Students must create the words Rocky is trying to say. For example, a teacher could say, "Rocky says, 'p-an.' What is he trying to say?" These materials provide instruction and practice with phonemic awareness skills over a 12- to 14-week period.

Phonemic awareness training may benefit your entire primary-grade classroom (Ehri et al., 2001). For other grade levels, consult with special education teachers and speech and language specialists. These specialists can recommend specific practice activities to promote better phonemic awareness.

PROVIDE PHONICS INSTRUCTION Training in *phonics* follows phonemic awareness and refers to providing instruction in the sound–symbol associations among letters and symbols. Children who learn to read without any difficulties—and many do—may figure out this system independently. However, students without good phonics skills have to rely on visual memory, context clues, or picture clues to guess what the unfamiliar word is. Unfortunately, reliance on such clues is not always effective, especially when the many letter–sound relationships are unknown (Pressley, 2006).

Pocket charts help students practice sorting letters, words, and sounds. Pocket charts can be made for individual or whole-class use.

These students can benefit from explicit phonics instruction (Pullen & Lloyd, 2008). The National Reading Panel (2000) concluded that synthetic phonics—in which students are taught to convert letters into sounds or phonemes, and blend the sounds to form words—was associated with the largest overall positive effects in decoding, comprehension, and collateral skills such as spelling (Pullen & Lloyd, 2008).

According to Stahl (1992; see also Stahl, Duffy-Hester, & Dougherty-Stahl, 2006), an exemplary phonics program:

- builds on students' knowledge about how print works.
- builds on a phonemic awareness foundation.
- is explicit, clear, and direct.
- is integrated within a reading and language arts program.
- emphasizes reading words rather than memorizing rules.
- includes learning onsets and rimes.
- emphasizes development of independent word-recognition strategies.
- emphasizes development of fluency-building word-recognition skills.

Go to MyEducationLab, select the topic *Reading Instruction*, and go to the Activities and Applications section. As you watch the video entitled "Phonics" (in the Phonics subsection), reflect on how the teacher contextualizes her phonics instruction.

Instruction in phonics proceeds systematically; practice is provided using familiar words before new words are introduced. Usually, regular words are introduced before irregular words, and sufficient practice in reading and spelling is provided before introducing new vocabulary. In phonics-based programs, instruction follows a specific sequence of skills. Although variation exists, a possible sequence could include the following (see, for example, Polloway, Smith, & Miller, 2003):

1. Individual consonant and short vowel sounds
2. Simple patterns such as *vc* (vowel–consonant, e.g., "at," "it") and *cvc* (consonant–vowel–consonant, e.g., "bat," "hit")
3. Consonant digraphs (e.g., *ch, sh, th*) and consonant blends (e.g., *bl, st, br*)
4. Long vowels, including final *e* (such as "hope," "tape"), and double vowels or vowel digraphs (such as "keep," "tail")
5. *R*- and *l*-controlled vowels, such as "car" and "call"
6. Diphthongs, such as *ow, oi, aw*

Once these skills are mastered, students can learn higher-level word analysis skills, such as compound words, prefixes and suffixes, contractions, and syllabication. These skills should be integrated into the context of reading as they are acquired. As Stahl et al. (2006) emphasized, "Good phonics instruction should not teach rules, need not use worksheets, should not dominate instruction, and does not have to be boring" (p. 132).

Students with severe to profound hearing loss are typically far less proficient than other students in phonological skills. Reading skills of students with hearing impairments appear to be associated with language and vocabulary development (Marschark & Harris, 1996). During the elementary years, they appear to rely more on visual than acoustic cues of letters and words. In secondary school, and later in college, they may rely more on phonological information. Strategies recommended for teaching reading to students with severe hearing impairments include early access to language by means of signing, and simultaneous exposure to written texts. Unfortunately, there is little research to demonstrate the effectiveness (or lack of effectiveness) of such techniques as phonemic awareness or phonics instruction, guided oral reading, or comprehension-monitoring strategies. Instead, amount of time spent reading, greater background knowledge, language and vocabulary development, and word-recognition activities are associated with reading achievement (Schirmer & McGough, 2005). Most programs employ basal readers; however, consideration of a variety of alternatives is recommended (Stewart & Kluwin, 2001).

TEACH STRUCTURAL ANALYSIS AS STUDENTS ACQUIRE PHONICS SKILLS

Older students begin to confront more complex words. **Structural analysis** refers to the ability to examine the structures of such words and break them into pronounceable syllables. Structural analysis involves examining a word by familiar word parts, such as the prefix, suffix, syllables, or smaller word parts. Teach basic syllabication rules to help students. The *Rewards* reading program (Sopris West) provides an approach to teaching multisyllabic word decoding that may be useful for upper elementary or secondary students.

The **DISSECT strategy** uses structural analysis as well as some other steps. The DISSECT strategy provides a multiple-step procedure for figuring out unfamiliar words (Ellis, 1996; Lenz, Schumaker, Deshler, & Beals, 1984). Each letter in DISSECT stands for one of the steps in the procedure. The steps of the strategy are:

- **D**iscover the context of the word.
- **I**solate the word's prefix.
- **S**eparate the word's suffix.
- **S**ay the word's stem.
- **E**xamine the word's stem using rules of 3s and 2s and segment into pronounceable parts.
  3s rule: underline 3 letters if stem begins with a consonant (example: re<u>new</u>al).
  2s rule: underline 2 letters if stem begins with a vowel (example: un<u>op</u>ened).

  Repeat for all letters in stem.
- **C**heck with another person to see if you are correct.
- **T**ry finding the word in the dictionary.

Teaching students this strategy provides them with tools they can use independently when they encounter unfamiliar words.

Teach students other problem-solving strategies so they will become more independent readers. For example, show them how to use context clues to guess what the word might be, based on the rest of the sentence or paragraph, the title, subheadings, charts, graphs, and accompanying illustrations (Deshler & Schumaker, 2005).

Software phonics programs are also available commercially. For example, *Reader Rabbit Reading* (Riverdeep—The Learning Company), *Lexia Software* (Lexia Learning Systems), and *Fast ForWord* (Scientific Learning Corporation) are other approaches that emphasize phonemic awareness, phonics, and auditory discrimination. Troia (2004a) reported that *Fast ForWord* provided gains in sight-word reading, decoding, and expressive language for a sample of migrant students with limited English proficiency. For more information on software for promoting reading, see the *Technology Highlight* feature on page 309.

USE STRATEGIES FOR PROMOTING BASIC SIGHT VOCABULARY Many words are used frequently at various grade levels and are often referred to as basic **sight words.** These irregular words cannot be easily decoded using phonics skills, and include words such as: *the, a, is, to,* and *one.* Many word lists are available that contain graded sight-word lists (e.g., Dolch word lists). Students with reading difficulties may require additional practice at identifying and saying these words automatically. Figure 13.2 provides a list of commonly seen words referred to as sight words.

One suggestion for providing practice developing basic sight vocabulary is to have students make and use flashcards containing their sight words. Some time each day can be devoted to saying the sight words with a partner. Cards containing words pronounced correctly and quickly can be stacked together, cards containing words said correctly but slowly in another stack, and cards containing words unknown in a third stack. Maintain records of the number of words in each stack. Gradually add new words as sight words are mastered.

Some teachers prepare checklists that contain new words or difficult words for students to learn, at school and at home with their families. The checklists are practiced daily at school and at home, and teachers and parents simply put a checkmark next to words read correctly under the date.

Finally, some teachers prepare large wall charts and prominently display listings of words they want students to master. Figure 13.3 has an example of a word wall chart. Charts can be changed as students master words.

Students with moderate and severe disabilities may benefit from teaching specific sight words (using, for example the *Edmark* program) to enhance their classroom experience, daily living, and job skills (Browder & Xin, 1998). These could include words for shopping, cook-

a	came	her	look	people	too
after	can	here	looked	play	two
all	come	him	long	put	up
an	could	his	make	ran	us
and	day	house	man	run	very
are	did	how	mother	said	was
am	do	I	me	saw	we
as	don't	I'm	my	see	went
asked	down	if	no	she	were
at	for	in	not	so	what
away	from	into	now	some	when
back	get	is	of	that	where
be	go	it	old	the	will
because	going	just	on	then	with
before	good	keep	one	there	would
big	had	kind	or	they	you
boy	has	know	our	this	your
but	have	like	out	three	
by	he	little	over	to	

Figure 13.2 Sample Sight Words

Note: From *Guided Reading: Good First Teaching for All Children,* by Irene Fountas & Gay Su Pinnell. Copyright © 1996 by Irene Fountas and Gay Su Pinnell. Published by Heinemann, a division of Reed Elsevier Inc., Portsmouth, NH. Reprinted with permission.

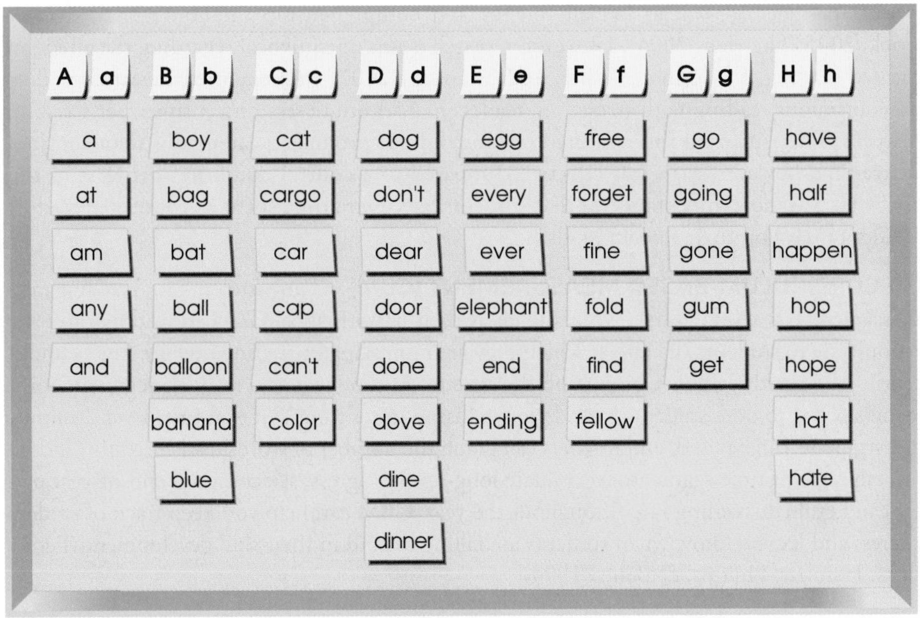

Figure 13.3 Wall Chart Containing Sight Words

ing, reading warning labels, and reading signs for community recreation, and could be enhanced with pictures from *Boardmaker* (Mayer-Johnson) to create a readable text (Fossett, Smith, & Mirenda, 2003).

Fletcher and Abood (1988) found that students with mild mental retardation who could read at nearly the fourth-grade level could not read the words on many warning labels, such as "inhale," "flammable," and "inaccessible." Sight words have been taught using a variety of methods, including modeling, prompting, error correction, and feedback (Browder & Xin, 1998). Students' comprehension can be promoted by having them find the words in pictures or real settings, or by having them give definitions. Try using classroom peers and sight-word cards to help promote sight-word recognition.

PROMOTING READING FLUENCY

Reading fluency reflects not just accuracy, but also rate. The Life Span Institute at the University of Kansas (2002) estimates that students should reach the following levels of fluency at each grade level, measured in correct words per minute (CWM): 1st: 60, 2nd: 70, 3rd: 90, 4th: 120, 5th: 150. Behavioral Research and Teaching (2005), at the University of Oregon, published very similar norms: 1st: 59, 2nd: 89, 3rd: 107, 4th: 125, 5th: 138, 6th: 150, 8th: 150.

Most students with reading difficulties require additional practice activities designed to help them read more fluently, even after they have mastered decoding skills. Several procedures are available to promote fluency (Chard, Vaughn, & Tyler, 2002; Kubina & Hughes, 2007).

USE REPEATED READINGS   No one would expect students to learn to play the piano by continuously sight-reading new passages. Rather, students are expected to practice new pieces until they have become skilled and automatic, before they move on to new and more difficult pieces (Anderson, Hiebert, Scott, & Wilkinson, 1985). Similarly, students who have struggled to learn to read a new passage should have the opportunity to reread the passage until fluent, effortless reading is achieved (Mercer, Campbell, Miller, Mercer, & Lane, 2000). As their familiarity of the passage increases, their fluency and comprehension should also increase. Record reading rates on a graph, and indicate which passages are "repeated readings" and which are first-time readings. Set target rates (e.g., 140 words per minute), and reward students for reaching these targets. Provide extra practice on difficult words or phrases that slow students' rate. Research has suggested that repeated readings can improve fluency for individual passages as well as overall fluency and comprehension (Staubitz, Cartledge, & Yurick, 2005; Therrien, 2004). However, research is not unequivocal regarding the effects of repeated reading. O'Connor, White, and Swanson (2007) implemented repeated reading and continuous reading with struggling readers in 15-minute sessions, 3 times per week for 14 weeks. They reported that repeated reading did not produce greater gains than continuous reading; however, each was effective compared to a control condition. At least in this case, what was most important was that students have extra time spent in connected reading in order to develop their fluency skills.

USE CURRICULUM-BASED MEASUREMENT (CBM)   Time students' oral reading rates on assigned texts several days a week and chart their performance. Graphed reading rates will demonstrate to students the rate at which they are improving in reading fluency. For example, identify 100-word segments, and graph the amount of time taken to read the segment. Some teachers prefer to time students for a designated amount of time. For example, 1- or 2-minute time segments can be used, and teachers can graph the number of words read correctly (and incorrectly) in this time segment. To evaluate long-term progress, select several end-of-year passages and evaluate reading rate throughout the year. CBM can help you keep track of student progress and let you know when students are falling behind in their skill development (Fuchs, Fuchs, Hamlett, Phillips, & Bentz, 1994).

USE CLASSWIDE PEER TUTORING   More time spent in oral reading can help develop fluency over time. Classwide peer tutoring, in which pairs of students take turns reading to each other, is one good way of dramatically increasing the amount of time students spend reading in class. In classwide peer tutoring configurations, students can develop fluency using such other components as sustained or repeated readings, 1- or 2-minute timings, extra practice with difficult parts, and curriculum-based measurement (see Chapter 8).

USE SOFTWARE PROGRAMS   Software designed for computers can provide an alternative means of practicing reading, decoding, and fluency-building activities. Students are usually highly motivated to use computers, and many programs contain gamelike formats to entice students to put forth extra effort. Computer software, for example, *Charlesbridge Reading Fluency* (Charlesbridge) is available to help promote reading fluency and promote reading comprehension.

Technology for Enhancing Literacy Instruction

Technological advances have provided numerous opportunities to assist with teaching literacy for students with disabilities. Many of the devices are referred to as assistive technologies, in that students' access to the curriculum is enhanced either by enhancing the input or the output procedures, while others are referred to as software, as they are materials designed to enhance literacy. Both hardware and software devices are available that can be used to enhance literacy for students with disabilities.

Intellikeys, an alternative to the traditional keyboard, is a device used to assist with keyboarding skills. *Intellikeys* contains overlays consisting of large letters and numbers that are more accessible for some students with disabilities. *Intellikeys* keyboards come in standard forms but are also programmable, using the *Overlay Maker* software program, to meet individual needs. Keyboards plug into USB ports. (Available from IntelliTools, Inc., Synapse Adaptive, 14 Lynn Court, San Rafael, CA 94901, phone: 800-

317-9611 [USA and Canada]; or the Website: http://www.synapseadaptive.com/intellitools/IntelliKeys.html.)

Software is available that provides speech-to-computerized text. For example, *Aspire Reader 4.0* developed by www.CAST.org is a tool that, when used with any computerized text, adds the speech component. Text from word-processing programs, other computerized programs, the Internet, scanned-in materials from classrooms, or any electronic text can be read orally to students once *Aspire Reader 4.0* is installed on a computer. Users can select the volume, speed, and pitch of the program and can alter the fonts and color of the text once text is imported into the program.

IntelliTalk (IntelliTools) provides speech components to word-processing texts in male or female voices. *IntelliTalk*'s read-aloud feature can read each letter as it is typed into the program and can read back what has been written. It is also available in a Spanish version. These "talking" word-processor programs that provide speech output for highlighted words in

word-processing programs are assistive technologies that enable struggling readers and writers to have more access to literacy tasks.

Write: Outloud (Don Johnston Incorporated) is another word-processing program that contains text-to-speech functions along with the typical word-processing functions such as spell checkers and search functions. This program was developed for children and is easy to learn to use. *Co: Writer* (Don Johnston Incorporated) contains word prediction components that predict words based on the initial few letters that are typed. Students select the desired word from the word choices that are supplied. Finally, *Draft Builder* (Don Johnston Incorporated), another computerized program, provides students with visual support for organization, note taking, planning, writing drafts, and writing final products through the provision of templates and assistance. Numerous software programs are available to provide assistance with literacy instruction. Examine the software to determine whether it meets the needs of your students.

Reading Comprehension

CLASSROOM SCENARIO

Carmen

Carmen can read the words in the stories, but when someone asks him what the story is about, he can't remember. Ms. Simpson, his third-grade teacher, always has him read orally during class and consistently gives him praise for his word reading. However, whenever Ms. Simpson says, "Now tell me what the story is about in your own words," Carmen is lost. He is beginning to dislike reading class because more and more time is being devoted to questioning about the stories rather than just reading out loud.

QUESTIONS FOR REFLECTION

1. If a student can read the words, why might that student have difficulty comprehending what was read?
2. When is a good time to begin comprehension activities?
3. How can comprehension be encouraged across subject areas?

Reading comprehension is the ultimate goal of reading; yet for many students, comprehension is a major problem. Fortunately, reading comprehension research has uncovered some effective strategies for improving reading comprehension for students with disabilities and other special needs (Berkeley, Scruggs, & Mastropieri, 2007; Mastropieri & Scruggs, 1997; Pressley, 2006). Students with reading comprehension difficulties often benefit from explicit instruction and practice using strategies that promote reading comprehension.

STRATEGIES FOR
TEACHING READING COMPREHENSION

Specific reading comprehension strategies can be taught for use before, during, and after reading passages. These include basic skills approaches, text enhancements, and teaching self-questioning strategies.

USE BASIC SKILLS AND REINFORCEMENT STRATEGIES **Reinforcement** refers to providing rewards or positive comments to students to encourage and motivate them as they work and answer comprehension questions successfully. **Vocabulary instruction** refers to providing students with practice learning specific vocabulary words that will be encountered in the readings (e.g., Coyne, Simmons, Kaméenui, & Stoolmiller, 2004). **Corrective feedback** refers to providing students with immediate feedback when oral reading errors are committed. The idea is that students' comprehension will improve when they are given immediate feedback on decoding errors. These strategies are often helpful; however, they may be more effective when combined with text enhancement or self-questioning strategies.

Repeated reading may also help increase comprehension of the material (Mercer et al., 2000; O'Shea, Sindelar, & O'Shea, 1987). However, use caution when assigning more than several repeated readings of the same passage because, as the number of readings increase, students' motivation may decrease.

Direct instruction refers to the use of published curriculum materials such as *Corrective Reading* and *Reading Mastery* (SRA/McGraw Hill). Research has indicated that this structured phonetic approach is effective at increasing comprehension, as students become more skilled and fluent readers (Polloway et al., 1986).

CREATE TEXT ENHANCEMENTS **Text enhancements** can include illustrations, maps, diagrams, visual spatial displays, semantic feature analysis charts, mnemonic pictures, and other adjunct aids developed to accompany text materials to increase comprehension. Although publishers of curriculum materials frequently use text enhancements, they also may be developed by teachers or students.

Illustrations drawn to represent characters, events, places, and action in texts reinforce the sequence of events in the stories. Information can be organized into concept maps or spatially organized maps that show relationships among all events, people, and places. Mnemonic text enhancements (see Chapter 10) can also be designed to promote memory of important concepts and features from reading materials.

Imagery, the process of visualizing content from readings, may be a useful substitute when illustrations are unavailable. To assist students in using this strategy, model and demonstrate the imagery process. Break the strategy into three steps. First, tell students to read a passage. Second, have them think of a picture in their mind that represents important content in the story. Third, have students describe their "mental pictures" to you or a peer. Provide feedback on the quality of the image by adding any important features that may have been missing from their images. Although imagery has not yielded as powerful comprehension effects as some self-questioning strategies, actively picturing text content may be beneficial for some of your students.

Adjunct aids, including study guides, outlines, guided notes, partial outlines, and highlighting and underlining, are also examples of useful text enhancements. Adjunct aids are discussed in more detail in Chapter 15.

TEACH SPECIFIC QUESTIONING STRATEGIES Asking students questions, and teaching them to ask themselves questions about readings, helps promote reading comprehension (Graham & Bellert, 2004). Overall guidelines for teaching reading comprehension strategies

- Set clear objectives that are logically related to the use of each strategy for reading comprehension.
- Follow a specific instructional sequence:
    1. State the purpose of instruction.
    2. Provide instruction.
    3. Model use of the strategy.
    4. Prompt students to use the strategy following your model.
    5. Give corrective feedback.
    6. Provide guided practice of the strategy.
    7. Provide independent practice of the strategy.
- Inform students about the importance of the strategy.
- Monitor student performance.
- Encourage questioning that requires students to think about the strategies in relationship to the text.
- Encourage positive attributions.
- Teach for generalized use of the strategy.

Figure 13.4 Guidelines for Teaching Reading Comprehension

are given in Figure 13.4. Several questioning and self-questioning strategies that are particularly effective are listed in Figure 13.5. Most of these strategies were validated as being effective for students with learning disabilities (Brigham, Berkeley, Simpkins, & Brigham, 2007). However, they may also be effective for other students with reading comprehension difficulties (Babyak, Koorland, & Mathes, 2000).

Activate Prior Knowledge Several strategies help students activate their prior knowledge on topics before they begin reading. One strategy for **activating prior knowledge** is the **TELLS** fact or fiction strategy (Idol-Maestas, 1985). TELLS fact or fiction is an acronym for:

- studying story **T**itles
- **E**xamining pages for clue words
- **L**ooking for important words
- **L**ooking for hard words
- describing the **S**etting of the story
- answering whether the story was **fact** or **fiction**

Before starting to read, students attempt to answer the steps in TELLS and then check their answers after reading the passage.

Brainstorming with students is another strategy for activating prior knowledge. Before a lesson, present students with the major topic that will be introduced, and ask them to generate as many ideas as possible that are related or similar to that topic. Encourage participation from all students. Brainstorming can be a component of most questioning strategies, including those intended to activate prior knowledge.

K-W-L is another strategy used to access prior knowledge before reading (Ogle, 1986). During implementation of this strategy, students ask and answer three questions:

- "What do I **K**now about this topic?"
- "What do I **W**ant to know?"
- "What did I **L**earn?"

For the first question, teachers and students brainstorm ideas of related topics of which they have prior knowledge and categorize their ideas. For the second question, teachers and students discuss what they want to know from reading the information. For the final step, students write down information they learned after reading the passage. You can create worksheets containing columns for answering each of the K-W-L steps.

Go to MyEducationLab, select the topic *Reading Instruction*, and go to the Activities and Applications section. As you watch the video entitled "Context Clues" (in the Comprehension subsection), reflect on how this teacher uses prior knowledge and context clues to give her students the tools to unlock comprehension.

Activating Prior Knowledge Features:

- Teacher asks questions relevant to forthcoming readings
- Teacher teaches relevant vocabulary
- Teacher teaches using graphic organizers containing main ideas of forthcoming topic
- Students are taught to ask questions related to forthcoming topics
- Students complete activities containing relevant questions before reading

Summarization, Main Idea, Self-Monitoring, and Attribution Features:

- Students taught to ask questions about the reading material, such as "Who or what is the passage about?" "What is happening?"
- Students answer the questions they asked and summarize or paraphrase readings in their own words
- Students state what the whole passage is about in their own words
- Students initially use self-monitoring cards while learning strategy steps
- Teacher encourages independent monitoring of strategy use
- Teacher encourages appropriate strategy attributions
- Teacher encourages independent use of strategy

Text-Structure-Based:

- Teaches passage-specific strategies for different types of text structures, including main idea, list, order, compare–contrast, problem-solving passages, as well as narrative story grammar passages

Multicomponent Packages:*

- Incorporate all or many of the above features; students are taught to ask and answer questions about the reading materials
- Questioning typically includes summarizing, predicting, and clarifying
- Teacher has direct role in instruction first and students assume more independence gradually in most models

*In some models, students assume a more active role during initial phases of instruction

Figure 13.5   Features of Self-Questioning Research

Promote Self-Generated Questions   Many reading comprehension strategies require students to self-question before, during, and after reading. As such, these strategies promote **metacognition,** the awareness of one's own cognitive processes and how they can be enhanced (Montague, 1998). While good readers may develop these skills independently, students with special needs (and many other students) can benefit from metacognitive training. Asking questions about reading material (e.g., "Why am I studying this passage?" "What is the main idea?" "What is a question about the main idea?") helps promote thinking about the information, which in turn facilitates recall and comprehension (Graham & Bellert, 2004).

Summarize and Paraphrase   Several researchers have developed steps for teaching students to summarize and paraphrase reading materials (see Gersten, Fuchs, Williams, & Baker, 2001, for a review). Although each study varied somewhat, similar components included the following:

1. Read a passage or short segment from a book.
2. Ask yourself who or what the passage is about.
3. Ask yourself what was happening in the passage.
4. Make up a summary sentence in your own words using the answers to the questions asked.

For example, Ellis (1996) described the **RAP** strategy for paraphrasing reading passages. The letters of the acronym stand for:

- **R**ead a paragraph.
- **A**sk yourself what the paragraph was about.
- **P**ut the main idea and two details in your own words. (p. 73)

Strategy instruction can help promote comprehension.

Teach students that the main idea tells what the whole story (or paragraph) is about in a short summary sentence (Wong, Wong, Perry, & Sawatsky, 1986).

Similarly, reading comprehension strategies used in classwide peer tutoring interventions (e.g., Lane, Little, & Redding-Rhodes, 2007; McMaster, Fuchs, & Fuchs, 2006, see Chapter 8) include the following questioning steps:

- What is the most important who or what in the text?
- What is the most important thing about the who or what?
- Write a summary sentence. (e.g., Mastropieri et al., 2001, p. 21)

Teach students to create concise summary sentences and to use their own words. Include self-monitoring instructions that list the above procedures on cards or charts, and display them prominently during reading to help students master the strategy steps. In the early phases of instruction, ask students to answer the questions either verbally or in writing to verify whether all strategy steps have been implemented correctly.

Teach students to examine text structure as they study textbooks, including theme and main-idea identification (Williams, 2003). In expository text, some paragraphs contain a main idea—such as wind erosion—with supporting statements or examples. Some paragraphs present a list of information, such as chief exports of Guatemala. Others contain information presented as an ordered series, such as steps in the digestive process. Still others present cause–effect relations. Students trained to identify the text structure and create appropriate outlines have significantly outperformed other students on tests of recall and comprehension (Bakken, Mastropieri, & Scruggs, 1997).

Story Maps Story-mapping strategies demonstrate for students that most stories follow a particular pattern, or story grammar, including setting, problem, goals, action, and outcomes, as shown in Figure 13.6. Teaching students to use that pattern can promote comprehension (Boulineau, Fore, Hagan-Burke, & Burke, 2004). For example, Idol and Croll (1987) taught students to complete story-mapping worksheets while reading, and found that these worksheets improved recall and comprehension.

Story grammar training cards can be designed similar to those provided in Figure 13.6. Provide instruction and practice using the sheets during reading activities. Encourage students to complete similar worksheets during independent reading. The *Research Highlight* describes a reading strategy that was implemented in ninth-grade literature classes.

Reciprocal Teaching **Reciprocal teaching** is a reading comprehension strategy that contains four comprehension-fostering strategies: (1) summarizing, (2) predicting, (3) questioning, and (4) clarifying (Palincsar & Brown, 1984). In addition, during reciprocal teaching, students assume the role of teacher during instruction and take the lead on asking questions. Teachers can prompt students to create good comprehension questions, as in the following dialogue:

TEACHER: What do you think, Nell?

NELL: How can a doctor know that a person is dreaming?

TEACHER: Excellent question, Nell! That is perfect; that is an amazing, great question. What do you think, Andy?

ANDY: Why did the doctors need to learn about dreaming?

TEACHER: That is another excellent question! (Speece, MacDonald, Kilsheimer, & Krist, 1997, p. 183)

The setting:

The characters:

The time:

The place:

The problem in the story:

The goals in the story:

The action in the story:

The outcomes of the story:

Figure 13.6 Story Grammar Training Card

Reciprocal teaching incorporates the following elements:

- Teacher and students silently read the reading selection.
- The teacher explains and demonstrates the four strategies, using "talk-alouds," or talking aloud about thought processes used. For example, a teacher might say, "To *summarize,* I might think to myself, 'What is this entire passage about? What is the overall topic, and what is being said about it?'" The talk-aloud may then describe a summary of the passage being considered, and why it is a good summary.
- Students then read another passage, and demonstrate out loud their strategy use for other students, while the teacher provides guidance and support (also known as "scaffolding"). Students construct their own comprehension questions.

Embedded Learning Strategy Instruction

Secondary literature teachers are finding more students in their classes with significant reading disabilities. Although general education classrooms at the secondary level do not directly teach reading skills, there is nevertheless a need for students to be taught appropriate reading strategies. Faggella-Luby, Schumaker, and Deshler (2007) assigned 79 ninth-grade students, including 14 with learning disabilities, to an experimental or control condition. Experimental condition students were provided with training on the Embedded Story-Structure (ESS) routine, in general education literature classes, over a 9-day period. ESS instruction focused primarily on three specific reading strategies: self-questioning (used during prereading), story-structure analysis (used during reading), and summary writing (used after reading). A graphic "ESS Organizer" device was provided to facilitate learning and integrate the three strategies.

The self-questioning strategy involved a set of seven questions provided by the teacher that corresponded to eight components of story structure (e.g., character, initiating event, location, central conflict). These questions (e.g., "What is the central conflict?", p. 136) were provided on the ESS Organizer, where students recorded their answers. For the second strategy, students filled in a Story-Structure Diagram on the back of the ESS Organizer by labeling specific events from a short story. For the third, summary writing, strategy, students provided a written statement in four sentences, including each element of story structure, on the reverse of the ESS Organizer, using their answers to the self-questions. In the comparison condition, students answered questions, used a vocabulary strategy, and created visual maps of the stories. Analysis of posttest scores indicated that students in the ESS condition significantly outperformed comparison condition students in recall of the eight stories read by both groups during the course of instruction. It was also found that both general education and special education students benefited similarly from the strategy. These results suggested that the ESS strategy can be effectively implemented in inclusive classrooms, for the benefit of all students.

QUESTIONS FOR REFLECTION

1. Why did general education students benefit as much from this strategy as the students with learning disabilities?
2. Which of the three strategies would be the most difficult for students to use?
3. Can you think of some other ways to use this strategy, for example, with peers or as an independent study strategy? How would you implement it?

- After practice, each student is expected to exhibit competence in the four strategies: summarizing, predicting, questioning, and clarifying (Palincsar & Brown, 1984; see also Lerner & Kline, 2006).

Rosenshine and Meister (1994) concluded that reciprocal teaching is more effective when direct skills-based teaching (on, for example, summarizing or predicting) occurs before the model is implemented.

As with all reading comprehension instruction, provide students with sufficient modeling, support, and guidance during the early learning phases. Later, students can be more independent in their use of the strategies (Stone, 1998).

Klingner, Vaughn, Arguelles, Hughes, and Leftwich (2004) implemented a model of "Collaborative Strategic Reading" (CSR), which incorporated elements of reciprocal teaching, in inclusive fourth-grade classrooms that contained also a substantial proportion of students limited in English proficiency. Students were taught brainstorming and predicting, monitoring understanding, generating questions, and reviewing key ideas, and implemented these strategies in cooperative groups. After a year's implementation, Klingner et al. concluded that CSR had had a positive impact on students' reading skills.

ADAPT FORMATS OF READING COMPREHENSION INSTRUCTION When needed, adapt the format of instructional materials. These adaptations may be required if students cannot read the materials, have limited writing abilities, or need more time to complete assignments. Possible adaptations are listed in Figure 13.7 and the following *In the Classroom* feature.

In the CLASSROOM

Alternative Teaching Suggestions

- Supplement texts with advance organizers

illustrations	audiovisual aids
graphic organizers	computer programs
visual spatial displays	descriptive video
concrete manipulatives	study guides
summary charts	guided notes

- Preteach
  difficult vocabulary
  new concepts
  organizational structure of text
  reading comprehension strategies

- Provide sufficient practice activities
- Use teacher effectiveness variables
- Use peers and cooperative groups
- Modify assignments
  Reduce reading or writing requirements
  Permit oral formats (e.g., tape-recorded
    answers)
  Supply alternative materials such as audiovisual
    or computer formats

- Highlight text
- Alter font, spacing, and colors of text
- Magnify text
- Tape-record text
- Use language masters for practice with difficult words
- Use talking computerized programs (scan texts)
- Use braille formats
- Rewrite text supplements using more familiar vocabulary
- Rewrite text supplements at a lower reading level
- Supplement with high-interest, low-vocabulary texts

Figure 13.7 Adapting Text Formats

In addition, promote culturally responsive literacy instruction to enhance the reading experience for all students. Suggestions are provided in the *Diversity in the Classroom* feature.

ADAPT INSTRUCTION FOR SECONDARY STUDENTS Many students with special needs advance to secondary grade levels without completely mastering important reading skills. This is a particular problem, because formal reading instruction ceases to be a part of the general education curriculum at secondary levels (Mastropieri, Scruggs, & Graetz, 2003). Nevertheless, there are actions that secondary-level teachers can take to promote reading skill development in their classes. First, they can support intensive reading instruction in resource rooms, study periods, or Tier 2 RTI (see p. 318) programs, by working with the special education teacher and emphasizing newly learned skills in the general education classroom context. Secondary teachers can also teach and promote use of word-recognition strategies, such as the DISSECT strategy described previously (Ellis, 1996), to assist with independent reading skills, understanding the text structure, and other strategies described previously to assist with text comprehension (Bakken & Whedon, 2002; Mastropieri et al., 2003). Additionally, secondary teachers can provide opportunities to practice reading skills in content-area instruction through classwide peer tutoring interventions.

For example, Mastropieri et al. (2001) implemented classwide peer tutoring in middle-school English classes, which contained students with learning and behavior problems. Stu-

Culturally Responsive Literacy Instruction

Literacy instruction is important for all students, but it is especially important to craft highly effective literacy instruction that is responsive to students representing all cultures. Many of these features are part of the effective teaching methods described in Chapter 6. Callins (2005) describes a variety of additional teaching techniques that can be helpful for working with individuals from diverse cultural backgrounds. She reports that culturally responsive pedagogy has the following elements:

- high student expectations;
- active learning activities to facilitate student learning;
- responsiveness to cultural diversity;
- inclusion of more culturally diverse readings into classes;
- cooperative learning and small-group instruction;
- culturally mediated instruction.

Multicultural literature emphasizes individuals of color, disability, religion, or ethnicity, whereas multi-ethnic literature emphasizes the cultural diversity represented within the United States (Callins, 2005). Many authors have written children's literature relevant to specific racial and ethnic groups as shown in the table below.

Students can benefit from reading about their own cultures, as well as about the cultures of others. Seek out culturally responsive literacy materials for use with your students.

Children's Literature: Racial/Ethnic Group	Sample Authors
Native American	Te Ata, Sharon CreechJean, Jamke Highwater
African American	Emily Moore, Rosa Guy, Angela Johnson
Asian American	Me Li, Paul Yee, Taro Yashima
Latino American	Carmen Lomas Gaza, Gary Soto, Ann Nolan Clark

dents worked in pairs, with the stronger reader reading first, for 5 minutes, followed by the second reader reading the same passage for 5 minutes. At the end of each reading turn, the tutoring partner would ask the reader story restatements or summarization strategies. Story restatements included, "What is the first thing you learned?", followed by, "What was the next thing you learned?", as often as needed to restate the story. Summarization strategies included, "What is the most important who or what in the text?", followed by, "What is the most important thing about the who or what in the text?", and, "What is the summary sentence?" (see also Mathes et al., 1994; Chapter 8). After 5 weeks of the program, students who had participated in tutoring scored much higher than control students on a reading comprehension test. Similar tutoring programs have helped improve reading skills as well as achievement in such secondary content areas as history, civics, and chemistry (Mastropieri et al., 2003; Spencer, Scruggs, & Mastropieri, 2003). These programs may be useful because they provide all students with additional practice on academic content, and provide additional supervised reading practice for students with special needs.

USE ASSISTIVE TECHNOLOGY TO SUPPORT SECONDARY READING Dieker and Little (2005) listed a number of assistive technology suggestions to support struggling readers at the secondary level, each classified as "high-tech" or "low-tech." Among the high-tech suggestions were *Write: Outloud* (Don Johnston publishers), one version of which includes a portable talking word processor to assist with reading and writing; and Book Share, a Website that will scan in textbooks that can then be entered into *Write: Outloud* or Microsoft Word applications. Students can also use the AutoSummarize feature on the Tools menu of Microsoft Word to create a condensed version of text representing whatever percent of total text you specify (e.g., 10%, 25%). Finally, the Scan pen (C-pen, C Technologies) allows you to scan in sentences that can be put into word-recognition software.

Under low-tech suggestions for assistive technology, Dieker and Little recommended sticky notes for posting summaries over longer text; erasable highlighters that students can use to highlight or erase highlights as sentences are read and understood; magnetic printer paper or tape for categorizing or reviewing key vocabulary; and dry-erase boards and markers for

Bookshare.org
duel voice

outlining or summarizing points. These and similar adaptations can provide needed support for struggling readers.

STRATEGIES FOR

IMPLEMENTING MULTI-TIERED READING INSTRUCTION WITH RTI

myeducationlab

Go to MyEducationLab, select the topic *Reading Instruction*, and go to the Activities and Applications section. As you complete the simulation entitled "RTI (Part 3): Reading Instruction," consider how RTI can succeed in situations where other interventions have not.

STRATEGIES FOR

IMPLEMENTING MULTI-TIERED READING INSTRUCTION WITH RTI

Response-to-intervention (RTI) programs have been designed to prevent and treat academic failure, particularly in the area of reading (Division for Learning Disabilities, 2007). An RTI program employs multiple "tiers" of intervention—usually three or four—to monitor and adjust instruction to the specific needs of students (Fuchs & Deshler, 2007).

STRATEGIES FOR IMPLEMENTING PRIMARY (TIER 1) INTERVENTIONS Tier 1 programs are usually considered evidence-based (or research-supported) instruction in the general education classroom (Foorman, 2007). Evidence-based approaches would include systematic instruction in reading skills and subskills when appropriate, lots of practice in building reading fluency, instruction in relevant reading vocabulary, use of a variety of texts, and effective comprehension-enhancing activities (Pressley, 2006). In addition, screening measures would be implemented to identify any students demonstrating problems in reading acquisition.

STRATEGIES FOR IMPLEMENTING SECONDARY (TIER 2) INTERVENTIONS Secondary (Tier 2) interventions are "directed at students who are at risk for academic problems and for whom additional, more targeted instruction is provided to close the gap between their current performance and expected performance" (Vaughn & Roberts, 2007, p. 41). These interventions can take place with small groups of students who have not responded well to Tier 1 interventions. Tier 2 interventions should be more intensive and focused than those provided in Tier 1, and may include, for example, 20 to 30 minutes of homogeneous small-group (four or six students) instruction, in addition to Tier 1 activities. During Tier 2 instruction, additional intensive instruction can be focused on phonemic awareness, phonics, spelling and writing, fluency development, vocabulary instruction, and comprehension enhancement, using many of the strategies described later in this chapter. This can be implemented as a "standard protocol" approach (in which most students receive the same intervention) or a "problem-solving" approach (in which school personnel decide upon appropriate individualized interventions; Fuchs & Fuchs, 2007). Either way, the goal is to help students "catch up" with their classmates, in a directed period of time (e.g., 10 to 20 weeks; Vaughn & Roberts, 2007). If, after a specified time period, students still do not make acceptable progress (according to, for example, school benchmarks or adequate progress on curriculum-based measures), these data may be used, according to IDEA, in support of special education identification and placement decisions.

STRATEGIES FOR IMPLEMENTING TERTIARY (TIER 3) INTERVENTIONS If students are still responding poorly to instruction after Tier 1 and Tier 2 interventions, students may be referred to special education treatments. Tier 3 intervention "is considered to be the most intensive and is focused on individual student need" (Stecker, 2007, p. 51), and uses many of the strategies described in this chapter. In addition to individualized instruction, these services would include (a) developing measurable annual goals, (b) using formative data to monitor progress and inform instruction, and (c) having special educators serve as intervention agents, who have been trained to work effectively with students with disabilities (Stecker, 2007).

Written Expression

Written language refers to handwriting, spelling, and composition. One or all of these may be especially problematic for students at risk for school failure. However, adaptations can be made in each area to promote success in inclusive classrooms.

STRATEGIES FOR
IMPROVING HANDWRITING

Competent handwriting is a functional necessity for students at all grade levels in school. However, the inability to write well can often be attributed to more than a lack of fine motor skills. For example, some students with learning disabilities may exhibit what has been referred to as **dysgraphia**, or extreme difficulty with writing. Other students experience difficulty copying from the chalkboard or overhead projector, or what is referred to as "far-point copying." Still others have difficulty copying from models on or near their desks, or "near-point copying." Finally, forming letters from memory can present handwriting problems for some students (Hallahan, Lloyd, Kauffman, Weiss, & Martinez, 2005).

No matter what the difficulty, students need to acquire fluency with the mechanical aspects of handwriting or they will experience difficulties composing written work. Illegible, dysfluent, and laborious handwriting interferes with students' abilities to complete written assignments in a timely fashion, take notes in classes, read and study materials they have written, and to undertake writing tasks such as essay writing (Berninger & Amtmann, 2003; Gregg, Coleman, Davis, & Chalk, 2007). Some have suggested that illegibly written assignments receive lower grades and less careful consideration by teachers. Graham and Weintraub (1996) provided a thorough analysis of research on handwriting, and concluded the following:

1. Handwriting problems are greatest among students who have academic difficulties.

2. Students develop their own style of writing regardless of script style taught.

3. Successful handwriting instruction for students with handwriting difficulties emphasizes the following:
   - Use paper with more space between lines.
   - Provide models of the order, number, and direction of strokes.
   - Provide sufficient practice tracing, copying, and writing from memory.
   - Use behavioral techniques such as cueing, shaping, and positive practice.
   - Teach self-regulation behaviors such as self-verbalizations during tracing, copying, and writing from memory activities.
   - Use self-assessment as part of the handwriting instruction.
   - Use self-instruction and self-correction as part of the handwriting instruction (see also Schlagal, 2007).

Berninger and Amtmann (2003) reported that studying visual cues (numbered arrow cues that show students how to write letters) and writing from memory improved both quality of handwriting and the amount written.

INCORPORATE SELF-REGULATION AND SELF-INSTRUCTION STRATEGIES It is important to model all the steps of the procedures and to provide practice opportunities for students in using self-regulation and self-instruction procedures. For example, a teacher might say while demonstrating:

> I place my pen on a line of the paper and move up to the top of the "q." Without taking my pen off the paper, I make a *circle* around to the top again. Then, I go *down* below the line, then *loop* back to the top again. Finally, I *finish* on an upswing. Remember [repeats model], "Up, circle, down, loop, finish."

Some basic self-instructions include defining tasks to be undertaken ("I must write this sentence"), focusing attention on tasks, reviewing necessary strategic steps ("For a 't,' I go up and then down the same way and later I come back to cross the 't.'"), self-evaluating and self-correcting ("Did I write a 't' correctly?"), self-control, and self-reinforcement ("My writing was correct and legible."; see Graham & Harris, 2005, for some examples).

USE MATERIALS TO DEVELOP MANUSCRIPT AND CURSIVE WRITING Debate exists over whether manuscript (printing) or cursive (handwriting) both need to be taught, or which system for teaching each should be used (Graham & Harris, 2005; Graves, 2003). Some claim that manuscript resembles print more closely, is easier to learn, and that students with learning difficulties need to learn only one system. Others assert that children can write faster,

- Regular pencil or pen
- Pencil or pen with special grip, or larger size
- Pencil or pen with special grip and special paper
- Typewriter/word processor/computer to keyboard instead of writing
- Word processor/computer with spell checker to improve spelling
- Computer with keyguard, support for arm, and so on, to improve accuracy
- Computer with word-prediction software to decrease needed keystrokes
- Single switch or other way of accessing keyboards
- Voice-recognition software to operate computer

Figure 13.8 Alternatives for Students Who Experience Handwriting Difficulties
Note: Information developed by Dr. Penny Reed. From *Has Technology Been Considered? A Guide for IEP Teams* (p. 30), by A. C. Chambers, 1997, Albuquerque, NM: CASE/TAM Assistive Technology Policy and Practice Group. Reprinted with permission.

and are more motivated to learn to write, using a cursive system. Unfortunately, since little convincing evidence supports one side over the other, you will need to decide what works best for your own individual students.

Some handwriting programs have been developed to teach handwriting skills efficiently and systematically. The *D'Nealian Handwriting* system (Thurber, 1999) teaches students a manuscript style that leads more naturally into cursive writing. The *Cursive Writing Program* (SRA) provides a systematic introduction of handwriting letters, words, and then sentences. Zaner-Bloser's *Handwriting* series provides materials for handwriting instruction from kindergarten through eighth grade.

Although many script styles exist, the quality of handwriting can be evaluated according to legibility, shape, size, spacing, alignment, line quality, speed and ease of writing, slant, uppercase and lowercase letter formations, and manuscript and cursive script styles. Set criteria for what your students should focus on first, and find an instructional system that will support students' efforts.

MAKE TECHNOLOGICAL ADAPTATIONS   Computers and typewriters are effective alternatives for students who have great difficulties with handwriting. Keyboarding and typing skills need to be mastered and can be taught using one of several computerized programs, including *StickyBear Typing* (Optimum Resource), *Type to Learn* (Sunburst), *SpongeBob SquarePants Typing* (The Learning Company), and *Mavis Beacon Teaches Typing* (Broderbund).

Advantages of using word processors include neatness, ease, increased fluency, availability of spelling and grammar checks, and increased motivation. However, because students may not always have access to computers, supplement these programs with at least some basic handwriting skills for those with sufficient fine motor ability. For students who lack fine motor skills, voice-input devices can be added to computers, enabling the students to enter information orally and receive typed output. If technological adaptations are unavailable, assign scribes for students who cannot write independently. Figure 13.8 provides additional suggestions for students experiencing handwriting difficulties.

CLASSROOM SCENARIO

Mario

Mario, a fourth-grader with learning disabilities, is included in Ms. Wills's general education class for all subjects. Ms. Wills has weekly spelling tests every Friday. On Mondays new spelling lists containing 20 words are distributed, and time is allocated throughout the week to study independently to prepare for Friday's test. But Mario is failing spelling. His recent weekly test scores are: 50%, 45%, 30%, 40%, and 35% correct. He tries hard to learn the words, but he can't pronounce some of the words on the list. Both he and Ms. Wills are becoming frustrated with his spelling.

QUESTIONS FOR REFLECTION

1. What might be the cause of Mario's spelling problems?
2. What is happening in the classroom that may contribute to Mario's problem?
3. What changes can be made in the classroom routine to help Mario spell better?

STRATEGIES FOR
TEACHING SPELLING

Spelling can be a complex and difficult task for students with reading and writing difficulties. Efficient spellers rely on good memory, phonological awareness, phonemic awareness, orthographic skills, phonics skills, and self-checking skills, all of which are often deficit areas for many students with disabilities. Research has identified a number of effective spelling strategies that can be implemented in inclusive settings (Graham, 1999; Schlagal, 2001).

First, ensure that all students can read all the words on their spelling lists. If students are unable to read spelling words, they will surely encounter difficulties learning how to spell them.

You can also improve spelling performance by shortening the list length for students with spelling problems (Bryant, Drabin, & Gettinger, 1981). This means asking students to learn 10 rather than 20 words, or 5 rather than 10, in a week. Introduce a small number of words daily, rather than providing a large list all at once. Introduce and practice three or four words on Monday, then on Tuesday review those words and introduce a few more words. However, shortening the list will not help if the words themselves are beyond the current abilities of the students.

SELECT WORDS FROM READING AND WRITING ACTIVITIES   Spelling words that are relevant to students' reading and writing activities can be easier to learn, and students may be more likely to see the importance of learning to spell these words. Additionally, students can apply their decoding skills in reading to the spelling lists.

PROVIDE DISTRIBUTED PRACTICE SESSIONS Distributed practice—providing shorter, more frequent periods for studying, rather than fewer, longer periods—may be beneficial for students with disabilities (Gettinger, Bryant, & Fayne, 1982). For example, several 15-minute spelling activity sessions scheduled throughout the school day could reinforce learning better than one 45-minute block.

USE PEER TUTORING   Peer tutoring sessions also can help students with special needs. Provide students with extra opportunities to practice spelling their new words (Delquadri, Greenwood, Stretton, & Hall, 1983) after they have been trained in peer tutoring procedures. Peer spelling sessions can be scheduled regularly. Flashcards can be used and students can record their daily performance by stacking cards spelled correctly together. Keeping the stack of misspelled words to review several times within a single tutoring session or in multiple sessions can help students be more successful on tests. Alternatively, simple word lists can also be used as tutoring materials. Tutors can check off words spelled correctly. Students can be matched in almost any way for spelling tutoring sessions, because the tutors can view the correct spellings on the word lists. Using tutoring for spelling can increase time-on-task, including increasing opportunities for responding and increasing feedback on spelling performance. Burks (2004) implemented classwide peer tutoring in spelling, and reported that spelling performance improved for three fifth-grade students with disabilities, from an average of 73% to 91% correct, over scores after more traditional methods, such as independent seatwork.

MODIFY INSTRUCTION BASED UPON ANALYSIS OF SPELLING ERRORS
Analyze the type of mistakes students are making in order to make instructional decisions. For example, if phonemes are deleted (*pince* rather than prince) or inserted (*subptract* rather than subtract), students may need phonemic awareness instruction. If spellings do not reflect conventional orthography (wi*ch* instead of wish or *hidn* instead of hiding), teach appropriate sound–spelling correspondences. If spelling errors reflect lack of knowledge of spelling rules (e.g., doubling a consonant before adding a suffix), teach these rules. Directing instruction to individual error patterns is an efficient way of promoting good spelling (Berninger & Amtmann, 2003). For errors in parts of words that are not governed by conventional rules, teach mnemonic strategies.

TEACH MNEMONIC STRATEGIES FOR SPELLING   Show students mnemonic strategies to remember the difficult or unpredictable parts of words, for example, the "s" in "island" or the "d" in Wednesday. Create a sentence that contains the difficult word and another smaller word that includes the most difficult part of the word (Mastropieri & Scruggs, 1991). Focus on those parts and create strategies to promote learning the correct way to spell them. Shefter (1974) identified mnemonic strategies for some difficult words, for example:

- It is **VILE** to allow special pri**VILE**ge.
- Don't **MAR** your writing with bad gram**MAR.**
- You **GAIN** when you buy a bar**GAIN.**
- Draw **ALL** the lines par**ALL**el. (p. 19)

Notice in each of these cases there is no particular rule that governs the spelling of the word, so spelling mnemonics are appropriate. Similarly, teach the distinction between homonyms by making up sentences using the same procedures. For example:

- A princi**PAL** is your **PAL;** a princip**LE** is a ru**LE.**
- A lett**ER** is written on station**ER**y; the j**AR** is station**AR**y.

Sometimes an interactive illustration can be shown to help students remember the correct spelling, as in the mnemonic, "She screamed **E-E-E** as she walked by the **ce**me**te**ry," to help remember the three e's in cemetery (Figure 13.9). Dowling (1995) and Suid (1981) provide books of mnemonic spellings for difficult words.

TEACH SELF-INSTRUCTIONAL AND SELF-MONITORING STRATEGIES   Strategies are often taught so students can use them independently. Self-monitoring strategies teach students to self-monitor their attention to task, their use of particular studying strategies, and their spelling performance (Schlagal, 2007). Listed on a "self-monitoring" card, these strategies teach students to:

- say the spelling word.
- write and say the spelling word.
- check the spelling.
- trace and say the word.
- write the word without looking.
- check the spelling.

Repeat the above steps as necessary (adapted from Harris, Graham, & Freeman, 1988).

Figure 13.9   Mnemonic Spelling Strategy
Note: From Teaching Students Ways to Remember: Strategies for Learning Mnemonically (p. 84), by M. A. Mastropieri & T. E. Scruggs, 1991, Cambridge, MA: Brookline Books. Reprinted with permission.

TEACH THE COVER—COPY—COMPARE STRATEGY Teach students to say the word, look at the model, and study the spelling. Then *cover* the model and try to *copy* the word from memory. Finally, look at the model and *compare* their spelling with that model. Repeat the steps until the spelling of the word is mastered. Finally, many spelling strategies include attributional and motivational components to help promote better spelling and overall studying habits (Fulk, 1997).

USE SPECIALIZED SOFTWARE AND CURRICULUM MATERIALS Computers can help improve spelling performance (MacArthur, 2000). For example, Blischak and Schlosser (2003) used a speech-generating device known as a LightWRITER™ (Zygo Industries) to support the cover—copy—compare strategy with students with autism.

Some computer software contains drill-and-practice formats in which students practice spelling new words. Other software resembles computer games, and students practice spelling words in more gamelike formats. *StickyBear Spellgrabber* (Optimum Resource) contains first- through fourth-grade high-frequency words. Various interactive gamelike features provide practice spelling the words. *The Spelling Rules* (Optimum Resource) teaches spelling using 21 rules (grades 3–9) using a variety of exercises.

Many curriculum materials also are available commercially to teach spelling, including SRA/McGraw-Hill's *Spelling Mastery* and *Spelling Through Morphographs* for older students. These programs emphasize systematic approaches using a direct instruction format and spelling patterns. Both programs recommend daily lessons of 15 to 20 minutes and have supplemental activities to provide practice with the new words. *Spell It-Write* (Zaner-Bloser) is intended to teach spelling words in a way that will promote transition and application to student writing.

The *Directed Spelling List* (first through third grade) and the *Spelling for Writing List* (including word listings for students with disabilities; Graham, Harris, & Loynachan, 1994, 1996) are word lists based on analyses of commonly used words that are problematic for students. Using the Directed Spelling Thinking Activity (DSTA; Graham et al., 1996), students actively compare and contrast words that fit different, but related, patterns.

In a study by Graham, Harris, and Chorzempa (2002), pairs of second-grade poor spellers were tutored for three 20-minute sessions per week for 12 weeks. Students were presented with word categories, each represented by a master word card; for example, "m**ade,**" "m**aid,**" and "m**ay,**" represented three patterns for the long /a/ sound. Students sorted word cards into the categories, while the tutor corrected and explained as needed. The tutor also helped students state relevant rules and generate words of their own. Students then studied new spelling words they had previously misspelled, that matched the word patterns. They also practiced sound–letter associations with flashcards, and engaged in word-building spelling activities based on word patterns and spelling rules for consonants, blends, and digraphs. Students who participated in the training dramatically increased their spelling skills, and transferred these skills to reading and writing.

ADAPT SPELLING OBJECTIVES Spelling may not be as important during some written activities as it is during other activities, so you need to prioritize spelling objectives for your class. For example, during written essay exams, knowledge of the content, rather than spelling, is probably the major objective, so consider focusing the weight of the evaluation on content knowledge.

Teach students compensation skills for spelling in their written work. Model how to use dictionaries to look up unknown words and how to use spell checkers on word-processing programs. *Children's Talking Dictionary & Spell Corrector* and *Speaking Language Master*™ (Franklin Electronic Publishers) can correct phonetic spellings of 130,000 words, and also include a number of spelling-related word games such as Speaking Spelling Bee. Encourage students to check their work for spelling, or proofread in peer partner groups.

STRATEGIES FOR
TEACHING WRITTEN COMMUNICATION

Written expression is a high level of communication that involves integration of language, spelling, and reading skills. Students with special needs frequently experience problems with writing assignments due to their deficits in reading, spelling, or language. Research has demonstrated

PEARSON
myeducationlab

Go to MyEducationLab, select the topic *Content Area Teaching*, and go to the Building Teaching Skills and Dispositions section. As you complete the activity "Scaffolding in Literacy," focus on how these teachers use scaffolding to encourage successful writing practice.

the effectiveness of planning, revising, and rewriting strategies designed to promote better writing (Graham & Harris, 2005; Graham, Harris, & MacArthur, 2004). Involve students more actively in the writing process by having them write daily, choose their own topics, and revise their papers—often in collaboration with peers. Have students share their stories with classmates, and answer questions from them. Such activities can help enforce the idea that writing is communication to an audience, and that peers can be helpful in expanding and improving that communication (Englert & Mariage, 1996). Peer groups can also be used in editing and revising activities (Englert & Mariage, 1996). Ask students to review and provide positive feedback and suggestions for each others' written work, and to collaborate in the revision process.

TEACH STUDENTS TO PLAN FOR WRITING   According to Graham and Harris (2007), planning is an important component of skilled writing. However, students with writing difficulties often plan infrequently or ineffectively, writing the first thoughts that come to mind in order to finish the task. Efforts to enhance planning for writing, particularly for struggling writers, can have a positive impact. Before students undertake any writing task, be sure they understand the purpose of the writing assignment. They should then develop a plan that reflects careful thinking about the purpose, including the topic, how it will be developed, what information will be employed, and how the written product will be structured. Discuss student plans and provide feedback before they begin writing.

PROMOTE THINKING ABOUT WRITING   Students can be taught to use action words (verbs: ran, drove, slept), action helper words (adverbs: ran *fast,* drove *slowly,* slept *soundly*), and describing words (adjectives: *beautiful* scene, *delicious* meal, *enthusiastic* teacher) as they write (Graham & Harris, 2005). You can use pictures and have students describe the action they see taking place in the pictures. For example, brainstorm lists of words relevant to students' age and backgrounds and post them in the room.

IMPLEMENT SELF-REGULATION AND SELF-INSTRUCTIONAL WRITING STRATEGIES   The importance of teaching students effective strategies combined with self-regulation and self-instruction is emphasized generally in this text, and extends to teaching writing skills. As with all strategic instruction, model the self-instruction and strategy before asking students to implement it.

Six basic types of self-instruction exist, which are presented with examples in Figure 13.10 (see also Harris, Graham, Mason, & Friedlander, 2008). Provide students with explanations of these types of self-instruction, and discuss how they can be helpful in completing writing tasks. With this background understanding, they may be more able to appreciate the value and purpose of more specific strategy instruction.

CHOOSE EFFECTIVE COMPOSITION STRATEGIES   Several strategies have been developed to help organize writing procedures. Story grammar strategies were described in the reading comprehension section of this chapter (see Figure 13.6), but can also be applied effectively as composition strategies (De La Paz, 2007; Graham & Harris, 2005). Model all steps of the story grammar strategy, making smaller individual charts containing steps for students. For example, Graham and Harris (2005) described the **3-W, 2-What, 2-How** strategy for story writing:

- **W**ho is in the story?
- **W**hen does the story take place?
- **W**here does the story take place?
- **What** happens in the story?
- **What** do the characters in the story do?
- **How** do the characters feel?
- **How** does the story end?

Discuss when the strategy is useful and how to use all the steps involved, and provide examples of how the strategy will benefit students in a variety of situations.

After modeling all the steps for self-regulation, have students practice the steps in the strategy with partners. Furnish practice sessions during which students complete the self-talk

Problem Definition

Sizing up the nature and demands of the task:

"What is it I have to do here?"

"What am I up to?"

"What is my first step?"

"I want to write a convincing essay."

Focusing of Attention and Planning

Focusing on the task at hand and generating a plan:

"I have to concentrate, be careful . . . think of the steps."

"To do this right I have to make a plan."

"First I need to . . . then . . . "

Strategy

Engaging and implementing writing or self-regulating strategies:

"First I will write down my essay writing reminder."

"The first step in writing an essay is . . . "

"My goals for this essay are . . . ; I will self-record on . . . "

Self-Evaluating and Error Correcting

Evaluating performance, catching and correcting errors:

"Have I used all of my story parts—let me check."

"Oops, I missed one; that's okay, I can revise."

"Am I following my plan?"

Coping and Self-Control

Subsuming difficulties or failures and dealing with forms of arousal:

"Don't worry, worry doesn't help."

"It's okay to feel a little anxious; a little anxiety can help."

"I'm not going to get mad; mad makes me do bad."

"I can handle this."

"I need to go slow and take my time."

Self-Reinforcement

Providing reward:

"I'm getting better at this."

"I like this ending."

"Wait 'til my teacher reads this!"

"Hurray—I'm done!"

Figure 13.10 The Six Basic Types of Self-Instruction

Note: From *Helping Young Writers Master the Craft: Strategy Instruction and Self-Regulation in the Writing Process* (p. 85), by K. R. Harris & S. Graham, 1992, Cambridge, MA: Brookline Books. Reprinted with permission.

of the regulation and self-instruction phases while completing the story grammar. Such practice sessions enable students to master both the strategy and the self-regulatory components.

The **SPACE** strategy is designed to help students think about more details that need to be included in their narrative stories.

- Note **S**ETTING
- Note **P**URPOSE
- Note **A**CTION
- Note **C**ONCLUSION
- Note **E**MOTIONS (Harris & Graham, 1992, p. 49)

Graham et al. (2004) described a three-step strategy (**THINK—STOP—DARE**) for writing persuasive essays (De La Paz, 2007; De La Paz & Graham, 1997; see also Graham & Harris, 2005):

1. THINK—Who will read this? Why am I writing this?
2. STOP—**S**uspend judgment, **T**ake a side or position, **O**rganize ideas, **P**lan more as you write.
3. DARE—**D**evelop your topic sentence, **A**dd supporting ideas, **R**eject opposing arguments, and **E**nd with a conclusion.

Modeling the writing process with students, in a variety of contexts, can help them see how the process works before they begin to put it into practice.

When teaching students these strategies, use the model of effective instruction and include models, demonstrations, and guided practice to promote independent and fluent strategy usage.

TEACH SELF-REGULATED STRATEGY DEVELOPMENT (SRSD)

SRSD is a model for promoting higher-level cognitive skills and self-regulated use of cognitive strategies (Graham et al., 2004), and has provided some of the highest effects of all writing interventions (Graham & Perin, 2007). The framework of SRSD consists of several instructional stages.

The first stage (Develop Background Knowledge) provides the pre-skills needed to acquire and use relevant writing strategies. In the second stage (Discuss It), students discuss their current writing performance and the strategies they use. In the third stage (Model It), the teacher models using the writing strategies using think-alouds of:

- problem definition (e.g., "I need to write a compare-contrast essay"),
- planning ("How will I plan out the steps?"),
- strategy use ("Which strategies shall I use?"),
- self-evaluation ("How am I doing?"),
- error correction ("This part doesn't fit."), and
- self-reinforcement ("I did a good job on this!").

Students learn and use mnemonics to remember and practice the steps of strategies (e.g., THINK—STOP—DARE) in the fourth stage (Memorize It). In the fifth stage (Support It), teachers and students collaborate to use strategies and self-instructions to complete writing assignments. Graham and Perin (2007) summarized SRSD research and concluded it led to improved writing performance across a variety of strategic writing tasks (for more information on these and other writing strategies, see Harris et al., 2008).

PROVIDE SUPPORT FOR WRITTEN RESEARCH REPORTS   Teachers frequently assign research reports as longer-term homework assignments. Such projects are often overwhelming for students with special needs, but teaching students specific strategies helps students successfully complete the assignments. Several important skills are required for writing a research report, including the following:

- Brainstorming topics
- Selecting a topic
- Finding relevant sources
- Reading and note taking
- Organizing the paper's outline
- Filling in details in the outline
- Writing a rough draft
- Proofing and correcting the draft version
- Completing a final version

Determine which of these skills need to be taught to your students. For example, you may have covered brainstorming in previous classes and can simply review the procedures with students. Once you determine which skill areas need instruction, prepare explicit instruction and provide plenty of opportunities for practice. For example, many students with disabilities require extensive instruction on "finding relevant sources." Determine the types of search procedures students need to learn, and design appropriate instructional strategies to promote the acquisition of the procedures and provide ample practice opportunities. Encourage students to meet in pairs or small groups and proofread each other's work.

USE TECHNOLOGY TO HELP WITH THE WRITING PROCESS Computer technology is available to support writers on a number of writing tasks. Keyboarding, voice-recognition, and word-prediction programs can accommodate students with slow or labored handwriting, or physical disabilities. Spell checkers and grammar checkers can assist with proofreading if students are provided with instruction in their use. Software is available to assist with the steps in the writing process and provide prompts (Berninger & Amtmann, 2003).

Story webs can help the writing process.

ADAPT INSTRUCTION TO OVERCOME MECHANICAL OBSTACLES TO WRITING Many students become frustrated with writing assignments because they are overwhelmed with the mechanical obstacles of handwriting, spelling, and punctuation. Isaacson and Gleason (1997) proposed eight methods for helping students overcome those obstacles:

1. *Allow dictation instead of writing.* Provide students the flexibility of thinking without any writing impediments; however, someone must be available to act as the scribe.

2. *Precue spelling of difficult words.* Write difficult words on the board or prominently displayed chart cards.

3. *Teach a word book strategy.* Have students maintain word books containing their own dictionaries of hard words, which they can refer to anytime to check their spelling.

4. *Ask for help.* Encourage students to ask others (teachers, aides, other students) for assistance, and ensure that someone is available to help them.

5. *Encourage invented spelling.* Sometimes students are reluctant to use interesting words, simply because they do not know how to spell them. Encourage students to write their "best guess" of a word's spelling, to encourage creativity and writing fluency. However, at some point students must learn to identify and correct any misspellings. Invented spelling can facilitate writing by helping students focus on their ideas, but it is unlikely to improve their spelling.

6. *Encourage peer collaboration.* This approach establishes a cooperative approach to writing and may be beneficial during brainstorming, preplanning, and revising stages.

7. *Encourage self-checking.* Teach students specific self-checking strategies. Some strategies include rereading to make sure sentences make logical sense, that capital letters are used appropriately, and that punctuation and spelling are accurate.

8. *Use technology.* Computers have become more available and more versatile for classroom use. Computer-assisted writing may prove to be a positive alternative for students with writing difficulties.

USE SPECIALIZED CURRICULUM MATERIALS AND SOFTWARE Some materials are commercially available to promote writing competencies for students with disabilities. *Reasoning and Writing* (SRA/McGraw-Hill) uses a direct instruction format to provide practice in learning how to think and write from beginning levels to more advanced levels. *Expressive Writing* (SRA/McGraw-Hill) is another resource using a direct instruction approach that contains approximately 50 lessons for students who can read at the third-grade level or above and teaches writing and editing skills. *Basic Writing Skills* (SRA/McGraw-Hill) addresses common writing problems for students in grades 6 through 12.

Many computerized programs also are commercially available. *ACHIEVE!*™ *Writing & Language Arts* (Broderbund) promotes grammar, spelling, and creative writing with gamelike activities. *WordQ Writing Software* (Quillsoft) uses word prediction, spoken feedback, and proofreading assistance. *Paragraph Punch* (Merit Software) is intended to help older students with learning disabilities (grades 5–10) develop their paragraph writing skills, and includes prewriting, writing, organizing, revising, rewriting, and publishing steps. *Storybook Weaver Deluxe* (Riverdeep), a multimedia program, contains story-starters, story ideas, and multicultural images to help improve students' writing skills. *StoryCraftPro*, story development software from Writers Supercenter, walks older writers through the steps of the story-writing process. Carefully examine whether the programs' features are appropriate, and to determine whether your students have the necessary skills to benefit from the software. Some programs also teach keyboarding skills (see discussion in the handwriting section) so that students can make optimal use of computerized programs designed to improve written composition.

13 Summary

- Many approaches exist for teaching students to read. Many students with reading disabilities lack phonemic awareness and phonics skills and overuse context cues when trying to read. Teachers should select reading programs that consider these areas of need.

- Phonemic awareness is the understanding that words are composed of smaller speech sounds (phonemes). Systematic instruction in phonemic awareness can be beneficial for students who lack this understanding.

- Sequenced phonics instruction is also usually helpful for students with reading problems. Phonics instruction is most helpful when it is used in conjunction with other reading and language arts activities, when it focuses on reading words rather than learning rules, and when it includes learning onsets and rimes.

- Reading comprehension strategies can be employed before, during, or after reading. These strategies include basic skills instruction and text enhancements. Self-monitoring and self-questioning strategies are among the most effective reading comprehension strategies.

- Handwriting problems can be addressed by providing models and sufficient practice, using behavioral techniques, and teaching self-regulation and self-instruction strategies.

- Various strategies have been described for improving problems with spelling performance. These include using the appropriate difficulty level and providing additional practice,

mnemonic strategies, studying word patterns, and self-instructional and self-monitoring strategies.

- Written communication problems can be addressed by using collaborative peer groups, teaching self-regulation and self-instruction strategies, and using story grammar and effective specific composition strategies. Adapting instruction for students' special needs can promote more inclusive classroom environments.

PROFESSIONAL STANDARDS LINK:
Literacy

Information in this chapter links most directly to:

- CEC Standards: 3 (Individual Learning Differences), 4 (Instructional Strategies), 5 (Learning Environments and Social Interactions), 6 (Language), 7 (Instructional Planning)

- INTASC Standards: Principles 1 (understands central concepts of the discipline), 2 (provides appropriate learning opportunities), 3 (understands learning differences, adapts instructional opportunities), 4 (instructional strategies), 5 (creates learning environments), 6 (fosters inquiry, collaboration, interaction), 7 (plans instruction)

- PRAXIS II™ Content Categories (Knowledge): 3 (Delivery of Services)

- PRAXIS II™ Content Categories (Application): 1 (Curriculum), 2 (Instruction)

LITERACY

If any of your students are having difficulty in literacy, have you done the following? If not, see the pages listed below.

STRATEGIES FOR IMPLEMENTING APPROACHES TO READING ————
- ☐ Implement and adapt basal textbook approaches, 300
- ☐ Implement and adapt whole-language approaches, 300–301
- ☐ Implement Reading Recovery for struggling readers, 301
- ☐ Implement and adapt direct instruction and code-emphasis approaches, 302
- ☐ Make adaptations to promote access to text, 302–303

STRATEGIES FOR PROMOTING WORD IDENTIFICATION ————
- ☐ Provide phonemic awareness training, 304
- ☐ Provide phonics instruction, 304–305
- ☐ Teach structural analysis as students acquire phonics skills, 305–306
- ☐ Use strategies for promoting basic sight vocabulary, 306–307

STRATEGIES FOR PROMOTING READING FLUENCY ————
- ☐ Use repeated readings, 308
- ☐ Use curriculum-based measurement (CBM), 308
- ☐ Use classwide peer tutoring, 308
- ☐ Use software programs, 308

STRATEGIES FOR TEACHING READING COMPREHENSION ————
- ☐ Use basic skills and reinforcement strategies, 310
- ☐ Create text enhancements, 310
- ☐ Teach specific questioning strategies, 310–315
- ☐ Adapt formats of reading comprehension instruction, 315–316
- ☐ Adapt instruction for secondary students, 316–317
- ☐ Use assistive technology to support secondary reading, 317–318

STRATEGIES FOR IMPLEMENTING MULTI-TIERED READING ————

INSTRUCTION WITH RTI
- ☐ Strategies for implementing primary (Tier 1) interventions, 318
- ☐ Strategies for implementing secondary (Tier 2) interventions, 318
- ☐ Strategies for implementing tertiary (Tier 3) interventions, 318

STRATEGIES FOR IMPROVING HANDWRITING ————
- ☐ Incorporate self-regulation and self-instruction strategies, 319
- ☐ Use materials to develop manuscript and cursive writing, 319–320
- ☐ Make technological adaptations, 320

STRATEGIES FOR TEACHING SPELLING ————
- ☐ Select words from reading and writing activities, 321
- ☐ Provide distributed practice sessions, 321
- ☐ Use peer tutoring, 321
- ☐ Modify instruction based upon analysis of spelling errors, 321
- ☐ Teach mnemonic strategies for spelling, 322
- ☐ Teach self-instructional and self-monitoring strategies, 322
- ☐ Teach the cover—copy—compare strategy, 323
- ☐ Use specialized software and curriculum materials, 323
- ☐ Adapt spelling objectives, 323

STRATEGIES FOR TEACHING WRITTEN COMMUNICATION ————
- ☐ Teach students to plan for writing, 324
- ☐ Promote thinking about writing, 324
- ☐ Implement self-regulation and self-instructional writing strategies, 324
- ☐ Choose effective composition strategies, 324–326
- ☐ Teach Self-Regulated Strategy Development (SRSD), 326
- ☐ Provide support for written research reports, 326
- ☐ Use technology to help with the writing process, 327
- ☐ Adapt instruction to overcome mechanical obstacles to writing, 327
- ☐ Use specialized curriculum materials and software, 327–328

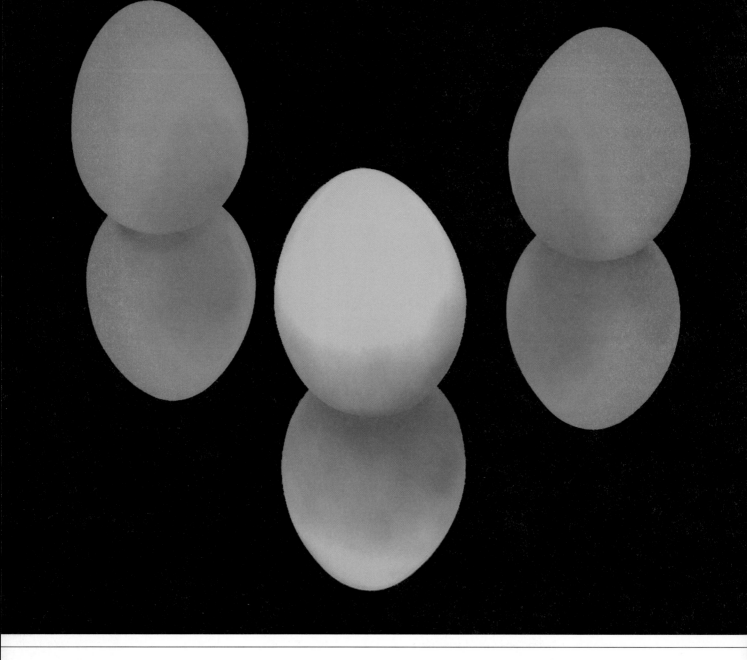

Eggs

Information about the photographer appears on page 298.

14

Mathematics

OBJECTIVES

After studying this chapter, you should be able to:

- Describe, evaluate, and implement various strategies for teaching mathematics, from early number concepts to more advanced computations such as quadratic equations.

- Provide instructional strategies for such concepts as counting, one-to-one correspondence, numeration, geometry, number lines, writing numbers, and understanding symbols.

- Describe and implement strategies for remembering addition and subtraction facts.

- List early addition and subtraction problem-solving strategies and multiplication and division concepts, such as count-bys and count-ons, and describe how they can be implemented with students with special needs.

- Identify teaching strategies for incorporating calculators and introducing new vocabulary for multiplication and division facts, and describe when these strategies are appropriate.

- Understand and implement multiplication and division algorithm strategies such as priority of operations, Demonstration Plus Permanent Model, and modeling of long division.

- Describe and implement strategies in mathematics for operations on money, time, and fractions.

- Explain the use of manipulative materials and strategies for computation, solving quadratic equations, and problem solving in algebra.

- Describe and evaluate strategies for mathematical reasoning such as graduated coaching, providing support for inventing concepts and procedures, and teaching functional math.

M athematics is the academic discipline concerned with the solution of problems that involve quantity or number. Mathematics includes such branches as arithmetic, algebra, geometry, trigonometry, and calculus. Always an important field of study in education, mathematics has taken on increasing importance in modern society (National Council of Teachers of Mathematics, 2000).

Students with disabilities will also need to gain proficiency in mathematics to fully participate in society. For this to occur, teachers must be fluent in a variety of teaching techniques that will allow students with diverse learning needs to meet their greatest potential in math.

Mathematics Education

Through much of U.S. history, mathematics was taught as a set of facts, rules, and procedures for dealing with numbers and quantitative concepts. Reform in mathematics education initiated by the National Council of Teachers of Mathematics (NCTM) resulted in the

Mathematics has been described as the key to opportunity.

Principles and Standards for School Mathematics (NCTM, 2000, 2007). In it, six overarching principles are provided to describe features of high-quality mathematics education. These principles include equity, curriculum, teaching, learning, assessment, and technology.

NCTM suggested that students with disabilities and other special needs may need accommodations in the form of language support, increased time, oral rather than written assignments, peer mentoring, and cross-age tutoring (NCTM, 2000). This chapter presents a number of strategies that may be useful in teaching mathematics to students with special needs in inclusive settings. The *Diversity in the Classroom* feature presents information on the study of mathematics in other cultures.

Mathematics and Students with Disabilities

Some students with disabilities exhibit little difficulty in learning mathematics. For most others, however, math is an extremely challenging subject area. Many students with learning disabilities may exhibit difficulties in the areas of memory and general strategy use, literacy and communication, specific processes and strategies associated with math problems, and low motivation and affect (Bryant & Bryant, 2008; Montague & Jitendra, 2006).

Students with intellectual disabilities may exhibit many of these difficulties, as well as problems with acquiring math concepts, remembering and executing math facts and procedures, and mathematical reasoning (Butler, Miller, Lee, & Pierce, 2001). Students with emotional or behavioral disorders often score below grade level on tests of mathematics achievement (Reid, Gonzalez, Nordness, Trout, & Epstein, 2004), and students with attention problems may exhibit difficulties organizing information in problem-solving tasks (Marzocchi, Lucangeli, De Meo, Fini, & Cornoldi, 2002).

For students with hearing impairments and communication disorders (as well as those for whom English is a second language), math may be an area of relative strength. Nevertheless, many students may have difficulty with the English language and communication aspects of mathematics (Lang & Pagliaro, 2007). Like many students with special needs, students with hearing impairments may benefit from authentic mathematic experiences, integrating vocabulary development, and classroom discourse about mathematics (Stewart & Kluwin, 2001). Students with visual impairments may also generally perform well on mathematics tasks, if appropriate adaptations are made (Rosenblum & Amato, 2004). Finally, some students with physical disabilities may need specific assistance if concrete manipulative materials are used (Heller, 2005).

Teaching Math in Inclusive Settings

Carnine (1998) recommends five major components that can be useful in designing effective mathematics instruction. These include the following:

- Focus on "big ideas"—that is, generalizable concepts rather than individual details.
- Teach "conspicuous" strategies (neither too broad nor too specific) for conducting math operations and solving problems.
- Make efficient use of time on prioritized objectives.
- Communicate strategies in a clear, explicit manner.
- Provide practice and review to promote retention.

For all students, and particularly for those with cognitive or intellectual disabilities, development of mathematical understandings can be facilitated by progressing from concrete rep-

Multicultural Mathematics

Many people assume that mathematics, as a subject area and a discipline, is universal and constant throughout the world. However, this is not the case. The study of the multicultural contributions to mathematics can help students understand the way different cultures throughout history have viewed mathematics, and can lead to a deeper understanding of mathematics as a subject area.

For example, some African cultures use base-20 systems for counting. Learning these systems could contribute to a greater depth of understanding of Western base-10 systems. Babylonians created tables of reciprocals, and used these tables to

divide by multiplying by the reciprocals. Mathematics and music of different cultures can be combined in the study of polyrhythms, dividing beats in a measure in two or more ways at the same time. This is relevant to the study of fractions and least common multiples.

Other examples of multicultural math include other African numeration and counting systems, the Arabic contribution to mathematics, Mayan calendars and numbering systems, Ancient Chinese mathematics, and Egyptian and Babylonian mathematics. All of these topics are likely to be of interest to students, and can help broaden their understanding of how different people have used mathematics. Samples and links to

culturally relevant activities including webquest activities for African American inventors and multicultural math fair activities are available on the Internet (Math Department, Frisbee Middle School, n.d.; McCoy, n.d.).

Several relevant books on multicultural math are available, and may be useful in including multicultural considerations in math class. These books include *Africa Counts: Number and Pattern in African Cultures* (Zaslavsky, 1999); *The Crest of the Peacock: Non-European Roots of Mathematics* (Joseph, 2000); *Multicultural Mathematics: Teaching Mathematics from a Global Perspective* (Nelson, Joseph, & Williams, 1993); and *The Multicultural Math Classroom: Bringing in the World* (Zaslavsky, 1995).

resentations of quantity (e.g., beads or blocks), to semiconcrete (e.g., pictorial) representations, and finally abstract (graphic) representations (Fuchs, Fuchs, & Courey, 2005; Mercer & Mercer, 2005). Mathematics functioning also has been improved by direct instruction, reinforcement, mnemonics, and cognitive strategy training (Mastropieri, Scruggs, Davidson, & Rana, 2004; Stein, Kinder, Silbert, & Carnine, 2006). Effective teaching strategies for different subject and skill areas are discussed in the following sections.

STRATEGIES FOR
TEACHING BEGINNING MATH

TEACH EARLY NUMBER CONCEPTS   Most children begin school already familiar with many elementary number concepts. These concepts are represented by words like *more, less, any, none, none left, together, how many,* and *each.* These concepts are necessary for the development of more complex understandings. It may become clear, however, from student responses to teacher questions (e.g., "Do you want more?" "Which container holds fewer pencils?") or by a student's statements that such concepts have not been mastered. Understanding of these concepts can be promoted by applying the strategies for teaching language concepts. For example, during snack period, after a student eats one cracker the teacher could say, "Do you want more?" When the student begins to reply correctly, the teacher could ask, "What do you want?" prompting the student to reply, "More crackers." Later, the teacher could hold two crackers in one hand and three in the other, and ask, "Which hand has more crackers?"

TEACH STRATEGIES FOR COUNTING   Learning to count is a type of factual (serial list) learning, and is best acquired with practice. Counting seems to be a very simple skill, but can appear very complicated to those who have not mastered it. Be sure to address all the components of counting in early numeracy. *Acoustic counting* refers to saying numbers in sequence ("Everybody say with me, One, two, three . . ."). *Point counting* refers to pointing to objects as

Lots of practice in counting objects can help young students with special needs learn early number concepts.

each number name is said ("Let's count all the desks in the classroom. Point and count together . . ."). Done correctly, pointing and counting are *synchronized. Resultative counting* refers to the understanding that the order in which items are counted is irrelevant to obtaining the correct total ("Now let's count them in the other direction . . ."). *Counting on* is the ability to begin counting with a number other than 1 (and is a good way to introduce adding: "I've got five pencils in my hand; let's count how many there are altogether: "Five, six, seven . . ."). *Skip counting* or "count-bys" is counting by groups of numbers, such as 2s and 5s. Finally, *subitizing* means totaling small numbers of objects (e.g., 4 pennies) without directly counting (Van Luit & Schopman, 2000).

Begin with just a few numbers, such as "One, two, three," and have students clap their hands each time they count. Students who are having more difficulty may benefit from practicing with a larger group of students. As number sequences are mastered, add a few numbers at a time. For additional time-on-task, ask peers to count with students who are still learning. Use of rhythms or regular emphasis may also help develop counting skills. Although group practice is helpful, it is also important to determine that individual students have mastered counting skills by asking them to count independently.

As the series of names of numbers is mastered, students should be introduced to the concept of counting *things.* Counting the students in the class, or the pencils in a jar, are early means of demonstrating how similar objects can be counted. Again, practice, additional time-on-task, and use of peer assistance can help enforce the concept of numeration.

REINFORCE ONE-TO-ONE CORRESPONDENCE *One-to-one correspondence* is the concept that sets of different objects (beads, blocks, and so on) can be matched according to quantity (Tucker, Singleton, & Weaver, 2006). That is, even though blocks are not the same as beads, a set of three blocks is equivalent to a set of three beads with respect to quantity. You can reinforce this correspondence by exhibiting two sets of objects, and asking students to match them item for item, as shown in Figure 14.1. Before later concepts can be mastered effectively, it is important that students understand the concept of numerical equivalence.

INTRODUCE GEOMETRY IN EARLY YEARS It may be helpful to introduce the concept of shapes during the acquisition of early math concepts. Although precise rules that define particular geometric shapes can be provided later, you can teach students to identify simple shapes such as circle, square, and triangle by the presentation of many examples and through teacher questioning.

Use different types of circles to enforce the relevant attributes of a circle—that shape is what matters, and not other attributes such as color and size. Presenting noninstances also enforces the concept of circle ("Is this a circle?" [exhibiting a square]). Also, give students different shapes, and ask that they hold up the shape that matches the teacher's shape.

STRATEGIES FOR
TEACHING ADDITION AND SUBTRACTION

USE MANIPULATIVES FOR TEACHING ADDITION AND SUBTRACTION CONCEPTS

Using such materials as beads, buttons, dried beans, or commercially available base-10 blocks (distributed by companies such as Delta Education), you can help students learn concepts of addition and subtraction by counting. For example, show students 5 beans, and ask them to add 4 more. Demonstrate how to select 4 beans to add, and employ a "counting on"

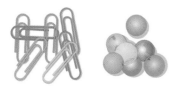

Figure 14.1 Understanding the Concept of Numerical Equivalence

As One-to-One correspondence

strategy, where they start at 5 and add the 4 beans, counting up to 9. You can also teach students to "take away," by starting with 9 beans and taking away 4, to leave the difference of 5.

USE NUMBER LINES TO PROMOTE OPERATIONS   A helpful intermediate step between counting actual objects and operating with numbers is the use of a **number line.** Number lines are lines with marks to represent quantity. Here is an example:

| | | | | | | | | | |
0 1 2 3 4 5 6 7 8 9

marks rePquantities

To add, have students place their pencils on the first addend on the number line, and count forward using the second addend. For example, to add 2 + 3, students place their pencil on the 2, and then count forward: 1(3), 2(4), 3(5). Conversely, the subtraction problem 5 − 2 is solved by placing the pencil on the 5, counting two steps to the left: 1(4), 2(3), and noting the difference, 3. The relationship between operations with number lines and adding and subtracting beans and buttons should be made explicit. Also, number lines are useful when practicing "count-ons" and "count-backs," as precursors of learning addition and subtraction facts.

Provide physical assistance, enlarge or darken the number line, or use three-dimensional number lines to provide for special needs. Later, number lines that include negative numbers can be substituted to help students understand concepts of negative numbers:

| | | | | | | | | | |
−5 −4 −3 −2 −1 0 +1 +2 +3 +4 +5

USE STRATEGIES FOR NUMBER WRITING   Some students have difficulty learning to write numbers and may benefit from the use of models, stencils, copying over dashed-line numbers, or from additional practice. Some students may reverse numbers when they write. Although many reversals may be obvious (e.g., 3), other reversals may not. A reversed 2, for example, may look like a 6, and suggest a problem with number facts, when the true problem is writing, as shown in the following illustration:

$$\begin{array}{r} 3 \\ + 6 \\ \hline 5 \end{array}$$

PEARSON
myeducationlab

Go to MyEducationLab, select the topic *Content Area Teaching,* and go to the Activities and Applications section. As you watch the video entitled "Tablet Computers in First Grade Math" (under the Math subsection), compare and contrast this lesson with the strategies presented here.

Bley and Thornton (2001) suggested a strategy for remembering the spatial orientation of 3, 5, 7, and 9. That is, the curved part of 3 and 5 can be represented with the right hand; the 7 and 9 can be represented with the right hand and right forearm. That is, if 3, 5, 7, or 9 are written correctly, they can be imitated with the right hand.

Some number writing reversals involve two digits. For example, 18 can be written as 81. Again, practice, feedback, and self-correction can be helpful in eliminating these reversals.

USE QUESTIONING TO PROMOTE UNDERSTANDING OF SYMBOLS   Ginsburg (1998a, 1998b) described the case of a first-grader who could answer problems such as 3 + 4 = ?, but could not explain what was meant by the "plus" and "equal" symbols:

TOBY:	. . . it tells you three plus four, three plus four, so it's telling you, that, um, I think, the, um, the end is coming up—the end.
INTERVIEWER:	The end is coming up—what do you mean, the end is coming up?
TOBY:	Like, if you have equals, and so you have seven, then. [She is gesturing to the problem on the table.] So if you do three plus four equals seven, that would be right. (Ginsburg, 1998a, p. 42)

Other children may state that = means "makes," as in "6 + 3 *makes* 9" (Ginsburg, 1998a). As students acquire skill in mathematics, question them to determine that they also understand concepts represented by mathematical symbols. If not, reemphasize previous concept-building activities, such as equivalence.

USE *TOUCH MATH* TO PROMOTE ADDITION AND SUBTRACTION COMPUTATION   Even when students have mastered relevant concepts of addition and subtraction, they may not necessarily be able to calculate problems quickly and accurately. A strategy for assisting with calculating arithmetic problems quickly is **Touch Math** materials (Innovative Learning Concepts). These materials represent quantity by dots on each of the numbers 1–9, as shown in Figure 14.2.

Students learn that each number is associated with a certain number of dots ("touch points"), which can be counted forward or backward to compute sums and differences. Note that the numbers 1–5 have solid dots, the total representing the quantity of the number. After 5, *Touch Math* uses circled dots, or "double touch points," each of which represents the quantity 2. Students learn to touch each of the touch points once, and to touch each double touch point twice, with their pencil when counting. For example, to compute the quantity

students are taught to start with the larger number, 7, and count forward, touching each of the double touch points in the 6 twice. So students start with 7 and count "8–9, 10–11, 12–13," to arrive at the answer. To subtract, students are taught to start with the minuend and count backward on the subtrahend, using the touch points. A complete set of *Touch Math* materials

Figure 14.2   Touch Math Numbers
Note: Reprinted with permission of Innovative Learning Concepts.

has been developed, along with worksheets and teacher materials, and is available from Innovative Learning Concepts.

Individual students can be taught to use *Touch Math* methods if they are having particular difficulty remembering addition and subtraction facts, and you want them to engage in computation problems with the rest of the class. In some cases, particularly in the primary grades, teachers use *Touch Math* with the whole class. However, if remembering math facts is a classroom standard, it may be important to continue to teach these facts.

USE PRACTICE AND SPECIFIC STRATEGIES FOR ADDITION AND SUBTRACTION FACTS   Many students, including those without disabilities, have difficulty remembering addition and subtraction facts (Geary, 2003). One way to ensure that math facts are learned is to spend enough time teaching them. Students can respond orally as a class to teacher questions ("Class, what is 4 plus 7?"), or hold up numbers at their desks ("Class, hold up the answer to 6 plus 3"). Additionally, pairs of students can drill each other using flashcards. Assigning facts to be mastered at home with the help of parents or other family members can also provide additional time-on-task.

Students who appear to be learning at a slower rate may be able to practice difficult facts with a partner. You can provide opportunities for students to practice using flashcards independently. Additionally, students can also use calculator-type machines and computer software, such as *Math Blaster* (Knowledge Adventure) to practice math facts.

When teaching facts, it is important to stress commutativity, that is, $2 + 3 = 3 + 2$. Students who understand commutativity must master only half as many facts. Bley and Thornton (2001) suggested that reversible cards be used to demonstrate the equivalence of, for example, $2 + 3$ and $3 + 2$. Use a card similar to the following, embedded with tags or paper clips:

Teachers can reverse the card ($3 + 2$) to show that both sides represent the same fact. Bley and Thornton (2001) described several strategies to assist students with math facts. Looking at the matrix of 100 addition facts, they were able to demonstrate that most can be mastered with the following specific strategies:

1. Nineteen facts involve addition with zero (e.g., $3 + 0 = 3$), and are easy to master.

2. Forty-five facts involve "count-ons," that is, addition with 1, 2, or 3 that can be "counted on" verbally to the other addend, for example, $8 + 2$ or $6 + 3$. Altogether, 64 of the 100 addition facts involve "zero facts" or "count-ons."

3. Of the remaining 36 facts (not covered by zero or count-ons), six facts involve "doubles," and can be represented by images or pictures of doubles (Figure 14.3). For example, $4 + 4$ is the "spider" fact, where the spider has four legs on each side. Double facts also exist for $2 + 2$ and $3 + 3$, but these are also covered by "count-ons."

4. In addition to the zero, count-on, and doubles facts, eight additional facts represent "doubles plus one," which means their sum is one more than the double. For example, $4 + 5$ is the same as the doubles fact (spider) $4 + 4 = 8$ plus one, or 9. The doubles and doubles-plus-one facts, together with the previously described facts, account for 78 facts in all.

5. Of the remaining 22 facts, 10 are referred to as "pattern 9" facts, and can be learned by the following rule: the sum of a +9 fact can be obtained by subtracting one from the other addend and adding 10. For example, to add $9 + 5$, subtract 1 from the 5 ($= 4$) and add 10 to make 14.

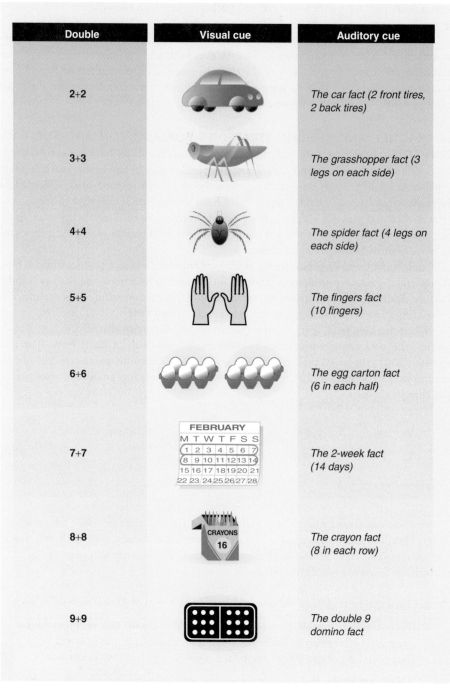

Double	Visual cue	Auditory cue
2+2		The car fact (2 front tires, 2 back tires)
3+3		The grasshopper fact (3 legs on each side)
4+4		The spider fact (4 legs on each side)
5+5		The fingers fact (10 fingers)
6+6		The egg carton fact (6 in each half)
7+7		The 2-week fact (14 days)
8+8		The crayon fact (8 in each row)
9+9		The double 9 domino fact

Figure 14.3 Doubles Facts

Note: From Teaching Mathematics to the Learning Disabled (4th ed., p. 384), by N. S. Bley & C. A. Thornton, 2001, Austin, TX: Pro-Ed. Reprinted with permission.

6. Two additional facts (6 + 4 and 4 + 6) are "other 10 sums," or other sums to 10, and two others (7 + 4 and 4 + 7) are "10 plus 1" sums. Altogether, zero, count-ons, doubles, doubles plus one, pattern nine, other 10 sums, and other 10 plus one sums, account for 92 facts of the 100 addition facts, leaving only eight.

7. There is no specific rule for learning the remaining eight facts; however, commutativity reveals that these are actually only four facts, each of which can be expressed two ways: 5 + 7 (7 + 5); 8 + 4 (4 + 8); 8 + 5 (5 + 8); and 8 + 6 (6 + 8). Use of the Bley and Thornton strategies is likely to prove helpful in assisting students who have difficulty recalling math facts.

Subtraction Facts Most students find it more difficult to learn subtraction facts than addition facts. One advantage, however, is that all subtraction facts are the inverse of particular addition facts and can be easily checked. That is, $9 - 5 = 4$ is the inverse fact of $4 + 5 = 9$. Use of base-10 blocks or other manipulatives can help enforce this concept. Some instructional materials (e.g., *Connecting Math Concepts,* published by SRA/McGraw-Hill) teach these facts together, as number families. In this case, the number family would include $4 + 5 = 9$; $5 + 4 = 9$; $9 - 5 = 4$; and $9 - 4 = 5$.

Bley and Thornton (2001) provided several strategies to assist with subtraction facts. Of the 100 total subtraction facts, these include 27 "count-backs" when subtracting 1, 2, or 3 (e.g., for $11 - 2$, "10, **9**").

There are also 19 "zero" facts, which involve subtracting zero from a number (e.g., $9 - 0$) or subtracting two identical numbers whose difference equals zero (e.g., $4 - 4$). An additional 15 facts are referred to as "count-ups," when the difference can be counted up by 1, 2, or 3. For example, for $12 - 9$, start at the subtrahend, 9, and count up to the minuend, 12, holding up fingers as you count, if needed: "9 - 10, 11, **12**," (counting 3).

Bley and Thornton (2001) also list seven "10-frame" facts, where the student imagines a "frame" of two rows of five, and calculates from these.

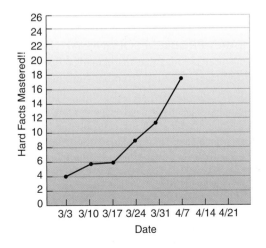

For example, for the fact $10 - 7$, subtracting 7 from the 10-frame removes all the top row and two of the bottom row, leaving 3. Bley and Thornton (2001) also include $9 - 5$ and $9 - 4$ in this series, beginning with a frame of 9 (5 on top, 4 on the bottom).

Finally, Bley and Thornton list six facts as "new doubles," which means when subtracted, doubles are revealed in the difference and subtrahend (e.g., $8 - 4 = 4$). Altogether, these strategies account for 74 subtraction facts, leaving 26 "harder facts" that must be learned through drill and practice, and application of addition rules. These harder facts include the following:

- $(17, 16, 15, 14, 13) - 9$;
- $(17, 15, 14, 13, 12) - 8$;
- $(16, 15, 13, 12, 11) - 7$;
- $(15, 14, 13, 11) - 6$;
- $(14, 13, 12, 11) - 5$; and
- $(13, 12, 11) - 4$. (Bley & Thornton, 2001)

Use of tutoring pairs, computer software, and homework can help promote mastery of these facts. Charts, such as the following, that demonstrate students' progress toward completion can help promote motivation and persistence of effort.

USE STRATEGIES FOR PLACE VALUE AND REGROUPING   Place value is a concept that is linked to our base-10 system, and students must learn this concept as they use numbers of more than one digit. Use of **base-10 blocks** can be helpful in establishing this concept. First, students learn to count individual base-10 units. They next learn that units are combined as groups of 10, and that groups of 10 are combined as groups of 100. Therefore, the quantity 111 can be represented as follows:

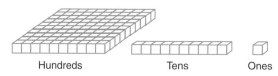

Hundreds   Tens   Ones

When students understand the concept of place value, they will be able to explain that the 1 in the quantity 123 represents 1 hundred, the 2 represents 2 tens, or twenty, and the 3 represents three units. You can practice place value by having students build, count, and record numbers from different values of 1s, 10s, and 100s.

Students can also learn to add and subtract with base-10 blocks. Making certain the appropriate values are lined up, they add or subtract within each column, as shown in Figure 14.4.

Regrouping in addition occurs when the unit values of any column exceed 10. These units must then be combined and placed in the next higher value, as shown in Figure 14.5. It is also important for students to see how numbers are used to represent these concepts, by recording number values when the building and counting have been completed.

For regrouping in subtraction, students must learn to "trade up" for 10 of a particular value in the higher column. For example, for the problem 14 − 6, students learn that the one 10 must be traded for 10 units and added to the 4 units in the units column. Subtracting 6 from the 14 units, then, leaves 8, the difference.

Uberti, Mastropieri, and Scruggs (2004) described the use of a self-monitoring checklist to improve performance on regrouping algorithms. The teacher developed self-monitoring checklists for third-grade students with learning disabilities and some students for whom English was a second language, who were having difficulties with regrouping. The checklists, based on an error analysis for each student, included steps for problem solution, including writing down the unit value in the sum and carrying the 10s value above the tens columns. Students checked off each step when they completed it. After several practice tests, students with special needs performed the calculation at the level of the mean of the whole class.

Manipulative materials can help teach and reinforce important math concepts.

USE STRATEGIES FOR TEACHING EARLY PROBLEM SOLVING WITH ADDITION AND SUBTRACTION   You can help promote the idea that mathematical operations have meaning by using manipulatives at the early stages of learning number concepts. As students move into the area of problem solving, these concepts can be enforced. Miller and Mercer (1993) demonstrated the effectiveness of a graduated word problem sequence strategy for teaching math problem solving, using concrete, semiconcrete, and abstract problem representations.

The word used in the word problems matched the manipulative objects in the concrete and semiconcrete levels. For example, if students were learning to subtract using cubes (concrete level), the word *cubes* was used in the problem (semiconcrete level):

$$\begin{array}{r} 4 \text{ cubes} \\ -2 \text{ cubes} \\ \hline \text{cubes} \end{array}$$

A. No trading

Procedure and materials:

Base-10 Blocks and a Place Value Board.

Example:

$$\begin{array}{r} 24 \\ + 35 \\ \hline \end{array}$$

Build each number on the Place Value Board.

Questions to ask.
- How many units? (9)
- Can you trade? (No)
- How many longs? (5) Record.

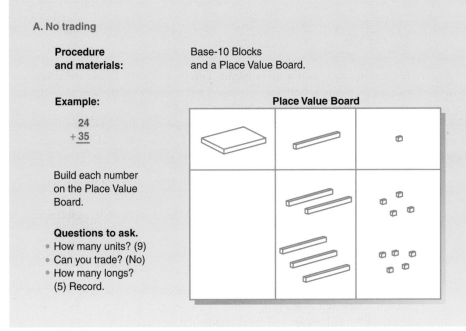

Place Value Board

Figure 14.4   Base-10 Representation of 24 + 35

Note: From Building Understanding with Base Ten Blocks (p. 21), by P. McLean, M. Laycock, & M. A. Smart, 1990, Hayward, CA: Activity Resources. Copyright 1990 by Activity Resources. Reprinted with permission.

B. Trading

Example:

$$\begin{array}{r} 35 \\ + 28 \\ \hline \end{array}$$

- How many units? Can you trade? (Yes)
- How many units left? (3) Record.
- Carry the longs to the tens place. Record.
- How many longs altogether? (6) Record.

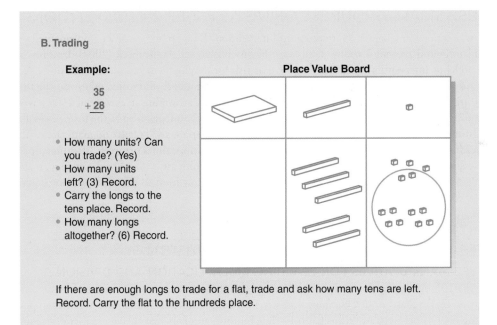

Place Value Board

If there are enough longs to trade for a flat, trade and ask how many tens are left. Record. Carry the flat to the hundreds place.

Figure 14.5   Representation of 35 + 28

Note: From Building Understanding with Base Ten Blocks (p. 21), by P. McLean, M. Laycock, & M. A. Smart, 1990, Hayward; CA: Activity Resources. Copyright 1990 by Activity Resources. Reprinted with permission.

During the abstract level of instruction, the difficulty of word problems is increased gradually from simple words, phrases, and sentences, such as:

$$\begin{array}{l} 8 \text{ pieces of candy} \\ -\underline{8 \text{ pieces of candy sold}} \\ \text{are left} \end{array}$$

to more elaborate sentences:

> Jennie had 4 pens.
> <u>She lost 2 of them.</u>
> She has _____ pens left.

Finally, students created their own word problems. This investigation demonstrated how students with learning problems in mathematics could learn to solve word problems by introducing increasing levels of complexity (see also Fuchs et al., 2005).

Students who have difficulty determining the operation for solving problems (e.g., addition, subtraction) can construct problems like this on their own. Bley and Thornton (2001) suggested several steps, summarized as follows:

1. Present a short problem that gives only the essential information (e.g., 3 apples, bought 2 more apples).

2. Tell what is missing. What is missing should be the solution of the problem (together there are _____ apples).

3. Write in numerals (3) for number words (three).

4. Compute two-step problems separately. Color code each step.

5. Use picture choices, for example, show two picture representations of the problem—such as 3 apples being added to 3 more or 2 apples being removed from a group of 3—and ask the student to choose the correct one.

Response-to-Intervention Strategies for Early Prevention and Identification

USE SMALL-GROUP TUTORING AS A TIER 2 INTERVENTION

As described in Chapter 13, response-to-intervention (RTI) strategies can be implemented to identify and prevent learning disabilities. Fuchs, Fuchs, and Hollenbeck (2007) described a model of intervention to identify students at risk for development of mathematics difficulty and a tier system for providing intervention. First-grade students who scored poorly during the third through fifth weeks of the school year (i.e., correctly answering an average of 11 or fewer of 25 problems on weekly tests) were provided with Tier 2 remedial help in the form of small-group tutoring using concrete, pictorial, and graphic materials; and practice on math facts with a software program. After 16 weeks of instruction, two or three times per week, 30 minutes per session, the proportion of students at-risk for math difficulties was sharply reduced (e.g., from 9.75% to 5.14%). Students who failed to respond profitably from the Tier 2 instruction could be considered for special education.

STRATEGIES FOR TEACHING MULTIPLICATION AND DIVISION

USE MANIPULATIVES FOR TEACHING MULTIPLICATION AND DIVISION CONCEPTS   Multiplication and division concepts can be enforced through the use of manipulatives, such as base-10 blocks. Show students, for example, a set of 3 units, and ask them to put together 4 such sets. After this has been done, inform students that they have a set of 3, four *times*. By counting total units, it can be seen that 3 taken four times, or 4 times 3, is 12.

Students should come to understand that division is "the separation of a quantity into equal sized parts" (Tucker et al., 2006, p. 167). To enforce division concepts, show students a set of 12 units, and ask them how many separate groups of 3 they can make. It can then be shown that they can *divide* 12 units into 4 sets of 3. Therefore, 12 divided by 4 is 3. These concepts may not be acquired rapidly by all students, but repeated practice activities, such as those found in *Building Understanding with Base Ten Blocks* (Activity Resources), can be helpful. It

may also be important to extend the activities beyond base-10 blocks to enhance generalization of the concept, to, for example, beans, beads, or buttons.

TEACH "COUNT-BYS" A useful bridge between learning multiplication concepts and learning multiplication facts is the use of count-bys. Students who have learned to count by 2 (2, 4, 6, 8, and so on) can use their fingers or pencil tallies to count up to 2 × 6 (2, 4, 6, 8, 10, *12*). Students also easily learn to count by 5s, because all numbers end in 5 or 0.

It may be helpful to learn to count by other numbers as an introduction to fact learning with those numbers. *Touch Math* uses strategies involving count-bys to compute multiplication and division facts. In multiplication, students count by one number while touching the points on the other number. For example, for 5 × 4, students count by fives while touching the points on the 4: "5, 10, 15, *20*." Show students that it works the same if they count by fours while touching the points on the 5: "4, 8, 12, 16, *20*." Such procedures also enforce the concept of multiplication (e.g., "5, 4 times = *4*, 5 times"). For division, students make tally marks (|) while counting up to the divisor by units of the dividend. The number of tallies is the quotient. For example, for 12 ÷ 4, students count up by 4s while tallying, 4, 8, *12* (marking, / / /, or 3).

USE SPECIFIC STRATEGIES FOR TEACHING MULTIPLICATION AND DIVISION FACTS Remember that the learning of multiplication and division facts is more of a verbal learning task than a mathematical reasoning task. That is, while understanding concepts relevant to multiplication and division (e.g., 6 groups of 4) involves mathematical reasoning, immediate recall of the fact ("What is 6 times 4?") requires verbal memory. Because that is the case, strategies for increasing verbal memory are appropriate. Use drill and practice with flashcards, computer activities, such as *Math Blaster* (Knowledge Adventure), peer tutoring, and homework assignments. The *Research Highlight* feature describes an investigation of classwide peer tutoring using peer-assisted learning strategies (PALS) in math.

Target the Essential Facts First, identify exactly how many multiplication facts students actually need to learn, so that students will not feel overwhelmed—they may already know more than they think they do. That is, students who understand relevant concepts already know the ×0 and ×1 facts (that is, any number multiplied by zero is zero; and any number multiplied by one is that same number). Students who know addition facts and understand relevant concepts already know the remaining ×2 facts (3 × 2 = 3 + 3). (Some students may also benefit from a ×4 strategy; that is, a number times four is that number doubled, twice: 3 × 4 = [3 × 2] + [3 × 2] = 12.) Students who know how to count by 5s know or can easily determine the ×5 facts.

Finally, students can use the **bent finger strategy** for calculating the ×9 facts. Using this strategy, students hold their two hands, palms down, in front of them. They then count from left to right on their fingers by the number of the fact, and bend down the relevant finger. That is, for 9 × 5, students count to 5 starting with their left little finger to their left thumb, and bend down that thumb. Then, the fingers to the left of the bent finger represent the 10s and the fingers to the right of the bent finger represent the 1s of the product. In the case of 9 × 5, there are 4 fingers to the left and 5 fingers to the right of the bent finger, so the answer is 45.

So, if students already know, or can cope with, the ×0, ×1, ×2, ×5, and ×9 facts, and if they understand the principle of commutativity (e.g., 6 × 4 = 4 × 6), you can show them that they only have 15 facts left to learn (and only 11 if they can use the ×4 strategy)! Use charts and game formats to monitor their progress toward remembering all 100 facts.

Math Tutoring with PALS

Peer-Assisted Learning Strategies (PALS) has positively influenced academic gains for students with and without disabilities in math (See Baker, Gersten, Dimino, & Griffiths, 2004; Fuchs et al., 2005). During PALS tutoring, dyads work together coaching and practicing targeted math skills. Students reverse roles of coach and player during each tutoring session, with the stronger partner assuming the role of coach first. During the coaching component, the player is coached through math problem-solving steps aloud. Coaches have question sheets that provide guidance and clarification during the problem-solving process. Students have subsequent independent math practice followed by the awarding of points by the teacher. Students take weekly computerized curriculum-based measurement (CBM) timed math tests that are intended to provide review for students and guidance on students'

learning to teachers. Graphed performance data are available to both teachers and students for evaluating math progress from the CBMs. In this research, teachers implemented PALS twice weekly in their general education classes.

Baker et al. (2004) followed eight teachers in an elementary school who had been trained to use PALS previously to determine whether these teachers continued to use PALS after the original project was completed. Teachers were interviewed and observed to find out whether and how well the research-based practices were sustained over time. All eight teachers reported that 4 years after the project was completed they continued to use PALS during math twice weekly. Observations of classes confirmed the accuracy of teacher reports, but also detected differences in the quality of implementation. For example, some teachers were described as having a higher level of understanding of the

principles underlying PALS than others. These teachers appeared to implement some of the components of PALS within their teaching during non-PALS periods as well. The ongoing support from professional development activities and the alignment of the goals of PALS with state and local standards were also cited as major reasons for the sustained use of PALS during math.

For additional information, see Fuchs et al. (2005).

QUESTIONS FOR REFLECTION

1. Why do you think teachers would either continue or discontinue using the PALS tutoring program in math after the original research was completed?

2. Why might there be differences in the level of implementation among teachers?

3. How could you assist all teachers in becoming high implementers of an evidenced-based practice?

Division facts can be taught using similar versions of the same strategies used for teaching math facts. Division by 0 is impossible (or "undefined"), but the $\div 1$, $\div 2$, and $\div 5$ facts may be similarly derived, using relevant concepts. A version of the bent finger strategy can also be applied to $\div 9$ facts: for example, for $45 \div 9 = ?$, first recognize it is a $\div 9$ fact, then make the 45 with both palms down, and 4 fingers on the left side, a bent finger (left thumb), and 5 fingers on the right side. The numbered finger bent down is the quotient, in this case the fifth finger from the left (the left thumb), or 5. For $27 \div 9 = ?$, make the 27 with your fingers; the bent finger is the third (or 3), the quotient.

Introduce students to three-number "fact families" to reinforce similarity with acquired multiplication facts (e.g., Stein et al., 2006). For example, consider the three-number fact family 3, 4, and 12. Within this family are the multiplication facts $3 \times 4 = 12$ and $4 \times 3 = 12$, as well the division facts $12 \div 4 = 3$ and $12 \div 3 = 4$. Students should refer to relevant fact families, and relevant facts they already know when mastering division facts.

Use Mnemonic Strategies   The remaining 15 multiplication facts still may not be easy for all students to learn, and many students may not automatically recognize the reverse (commutativity) of each fact. However, there is a mnemonic strategy that might be helpful in some cases (see Chapter 10). Using the pegword strategy, rhyming words are developed for all numbers (e.g., *1* is *bun*, *2* is *shoe*, *3* is *tree*, *4* is *door*, *6* is *sticks*, *7* is *heaven*, *8* is *gate*, *9* is *line* or *vine*). Pegwords for relevant numbers higher than 10 include: *12* is *elf*; *16* is *sitting*; and *18* is *aiding*. *Twenty* is represented as *twin-ty*, so *21* is *twin buns*. *Thirty* is *dirty* or *thirsty*; *40* is *party*; *50* is *gifty* (i.e., *gift-wrapped*); and *60* is *witchy*. Using these pegwords, sentences can be developed for each of the 15 remaining facts (see Mastropieri & Scruggs, 1991):

Fact	Pegword strategy
Three times three is nine.	**Tree**-to-**tree vine.**
Three times four is twelve.	**Tree** in **door** is **elf.**
Three times six is eighteen.	**Tree** losing **sticks** needs **aiding.**
Three times seven is twenty-one.	**Tree** in **heaven** has **twin buns.**
Three times eight is twenty-four.	**Tree** at a **gate** has **twin doors.**
Four times four is sixteen.	**Door**-by-**door sitting.**
Four times six is twenty-four.	**Door** with **sticks** has **twin doors.**
Four times seven is twenty-eight.	**Door** in **heaven** has **twin gates.**
Four times eight is thirty-two.	**Door** in **gate** has **dirty shoe.**
Six times six is thirty-six.	**Sticks, sticks,** and **dirty sticks.**
Six times seven is forty-two.	**Sticks** in **heaven** for **party shoe.**
Six times eight is forty-eight.	**Sticks** in **gate** is a **party gate.**
Seven times seven is forty-nine.	**Heaven** to **heaven** has **party line.**
Seven times eight is fifty-six.	**Heaven's gate** has **gifty sticks.**
Eight times eight is sixty-four.	**Gate** to **gate** is **witchy door.**

Some of these facts are easy to imagine; for example, *tree-to-tree vine* is simply a vine between two different (not twin) trees. Others, however, may be more difficult for students to imagine automatically. In these cases, a picture of the mnemonic may be helpful, such as the pictures for $4 \times 4 = 16$ and $6 \times 6 = 36$, shown in Figure 14.6.

Guide students to learn to say the paired mnemonics together, such as "Heaven's gate has gifty sticks; seven times eight is fifty-six." Reserve these strategies for the facts students appear to be having the most difficulty with, rather than teaching all 15.

USE CALCULATORS WHEN APPROPRIATE It is sometimes recommended that computers and calculators be used to replace memorization of math facts and computation exercises. Nevertheless, most schools remain committed to mastery of facts and computation procedures as important mathematics objectives. Of course, if students are not required to

Figure 14.6 Mnemonic Pictures of $6 \times 6 = 36$ and $4 \times 4 = 16$

Note: From *Mnemonic Math Facts*, by M. A. Mastropieri & T. E. Scruggs, 1990, Fairfax, VA: Graduate School of Education, George Mason University.

memorize math facts, then it is not necessary that time be spent on these objectives. However, in some cases, it may become evident that students are simply not succeeding at memorizing facts and are beginning to lose valuable instructional time in other areas of math because of this problem. In such cases, it may be prudent to allow individual students to use calculators for help with computation, while proceeding to other math objectives. If such a decision is made, however, make sure those students have a documented failure to learn facts over time, all known strategies and procedures have been attempted, and the students are beginning to lose valuable instructional time in other areas of math.

If these conditions have been met, it may be prudent to allow students to use calculators. For example, Horton, Lovitt, and White (1992) found that junior high school students with mild intellectual disabilities performed similarly to nondisabled students in computation problems when they used calculators. Without calculators, however, their performance was lower. However, do not assume all students will be able to use calculators without any training. Provide modeling, prompting, and evaluation to ensure students are independent at calculator use.

Students should be retested periodically for their capacity to learn facts. It could be that with increasing age and cognitive development, or more familiarity with other aspects of math, fact learning can be attained at a future date.

REINFORCE ARITHMETIC VOCABULARY In addition to number concepts, algorithms, and procedures, students in math classes are generally required to learn and apply many vocabulary words such as *addend, sum, minuend, subtrahend, difference, product,* and *divisor.* For some students, this vocabulary can be confusing and difficult to learn. Prioritize your objectives so that you spend time teaching the most important vocabulary words.

To teach math vocabulary, provide additional time-on-task, use flashcards and peer tutors, and monitor progress toward mastery. Also consider using verbal elaboration strategies—for example, demonstrate to students how 3 is really the *difference* between 8 and 5; therefore, the term *difference* has some meaning. To help students remember that the *multiplier* is the number on the bottom of the multiplication problem, next to the multiplication sign (when presented vertically), draw the multiplication sign to represent a pair of *pliers*. The *pliers* show which number is the multi*plier*. For another example, on a division problem, place *quotation marks* on the *quotient*.

$$8 \overline{)\ \ 24}^{\ \ ``3"}$$

USE SPECIFIC STRATEGIES FOR TEACHING MULTIPLICATION AND DIVISION ALGORITHMS Students must learn the order or sequence of arithmetic operations in more complex problems.

$$5 + 4 \times 3 - 2 =$$

To successfully solve this problem, students must know that the multiplication of the terms 4 and 3 must be done first, followed by the addition of 5 and subtraction of 2. A commonly used mnemonic to remember the order for math operations is: "*My Dear Aunt Sally*, who says, '*M*ultiply and *d*ivide before you *a*dd and *s*ubtract.'" In this case,

$$5 + (4 \times 3) - 2 =$$

where (4×3) is calculated first, followed by the addition and subtraction. An alternative strategy is "*Please excuse my dear Aunt Sally*," where *p* and *e* stand for *p*arenthetical expression and *e*xponents, respectively, and are completed first. In this case,

$$5 + (4 + 3)^2 + 12 \times 6$$

where the parenthetical expression $(4 + 3)$ is calculated first, followed by the exponent $(7)^2$, which is followed by multiplication, 12×6, followed by addition, $5 + 49 + 72$.

Another math procedure students need to learn is the sequence to follow when multiplying numbers of two or more digits. Learning how to do this kind of problem is often complicated because handwritten figures are not placed in proper relationship to one another. Try having students use graph paper, as shown in the illustration. Pro-Ed publishes *Guideline Math Paper,* specifically designed to assist students who have difficulty completing basic mathematics algorithms.

```
          1   3   1
      x   1   2
          2   6   2
      1   3   1
      1   5   7   2
```

Demonstration Plus Permanent Model   For addressing problems in computational arithmetic skills, use **Demonstration Plus Permanent Model** (Rivera & Smith, 1987); demonstrate how to complete a particular type of problem, for example, subtraction with regrouping or long division, and provide a model written on the student's page or somewhere easily accessible for future reference. The model can be written on a 3- $\times$ 5-inch index card for use when needed.

Modified Long Division   Some students exhibit extreme difficulty with long division (Montague, 2003a). If other attempts have not been successful, it may be helpful to employ a simpler procedure for long division. This procedure lacks some of the precision of traditional long division, but it employs a simpler format that some students may find beneficial (see also Reisman, 1977).

To use modified long division, construct the problem as usual, but draw a line straight down vertically from the end of the problem:

```
23) 4859 |
         |
         |
```

Now, ask students to guess the solution to the entire problem, "How many 23s are there in 4,859?" Even if students have difficulty estimating the answer closely, a good first guess might be 100. So, tell students to write the 100 to the right of the vertical line and multiply 23 by 100 and subtract from the dividend, like this:

```
23) 4859 | 100
    2300 |
    2559
```

Then, ask students the same question again, with respect to the difference, "How many 23s are there in 2,559?" Since 100 times 23 is 2,300, it makes sense to try 100 again. So, you write 100 again below the first 100, multiply 23 again by 100, and subtract from 2,559:

```
23)  4859 | 100
    -2300 | 100
     2559
    -2300 |
      259
```

The remainder is now 259, so a good next guess would be 10:

```
23)  4859 | 100
    -2300 | 100
     2559 |  10
    -2300
      259
     -230 |
       29
```

Subtracting 230 from 259 leaves 29, so we subtract one more 23, and compute a remainder of 6. This number is smaller than the divisor, 23, so we cannot go any farther. Adding all estimates yields a sum of 211 with a remainder of 6 (or 6/23), the correct solution.

```
23) 4859 | 100
   -2300 | 100
    2559 |  10
   -2300 | + 1
     259 | 211 , r. 6
    -230
      29
      23
       6
```

One advantage of modified long division is that it allows students to view the entire problem at once. Because of this, they may be more able to focus on the problem and less likely to become entangled in a maze of algorithmic procedures. Nevertheless, students may still need much practice learning and applying the steps of the modified long division procedure.

Use Error Analysis to Inform Instruction   When correcting student products, it is important to determine the *type* of error students consistently make, and what type of remedial instruction is indicated by these error patterns. Figure 14.7 lists common error types in arithmetic computation, and possible explanations for them. Remember, before a firm conclusion can be drawn about a particular error type, it is best to obtain evidence that such errors occur repeatedly in a given student's work.

STRATEGIES FOR
TEACHING PROBLEM SOLVING

PROMOTE USE OF WORD MEANINGS   Implied mathematical operations (e.g., add, multiply) are represented by the language of word problems. One problem that some students wrestle with is understanding how words are used in word problems, and what specific operations are implied by these words. Many mathematics educators have criticized a strategy known as the *clue word* or *key word* approach (not the same as the mnemonic keyword method) to solving word problems. In this approach, students are provided with key operation words and relevant operations, such as the following:

in all, together, total = add or multiply
left, remaining = subtract
each = divide

Error Examples	Possible Explanations	Suggested Interventions
$2 + 2 = 8$	1. Inadequate fact mastery. 2. Failure to apply learned strategies (e.g., "count-ons"). 3. Reversal (2 = 6).	1. Reteach facts. 2. Reteach strategies. 3. Teach strategies for writing orientation.
$22 - 9 = 27$	1. Inadequate fact mastery. 2. Regrouping error. 3. Reversed subtraction (9 − 2 = 7).	1. Reteach facts. 2. Reteach regrouping. 3. Reteach procedures.
$22 \times 12 = 66$	1. Place value error: $22 (1 \times 22) + 44 (2 \times 22) = 66$ 2. Algorithmic error (incorrect alignment of addends in problem solution): $$\begin{array}{r} 22 \\ \times 12 \\ \hline 44 \\ 22 \\ \hline 66 \end{array}$$	1. Reteach place value concepts. 2. Reteach algorithms, using Demonstration plus Permanent Model, graph paper.

Figure 14.7   Sample Error Analysis Procedures

Students are encouraged to look in the problem for one of these words, and then apply the associated operation. The concern is that students may use the method mindlessly, without carefully reasoning through problems (Kilpatrick, 1985).

However, words convey meanings, and to the extent that these meanings aid in problem solution, a careful analysis of words is appropriate. "In all" does in fact convey the idea of combining quantities (and thus, perhaps, addition or multiplication); "remaining" does suggest diminishing quantity (and thus, perhaps, subtraction). For students who have language learning disabilities or language delays, it may be important to enforce the understanding of word meanings to solve word problems.

It is true that the mindless substitution of "each" for "divide," for example, may not be an appropriate strategy in most cases (it may be appropriate for a last-ditch effort during a timed math test). However, a problem that states a particular overall quantity and requests unstated information regarding "each," or "for one," certainly seems to be implying some type of division operation, and students should attend to the relevance of such cues.

In fact, the **ask for one, tell for one** strategy may be useful in helping students determine implied operations. That is, if a larger quantity and another quantity are given (10 cookies, 5 children), and the problem "asks for one (or each)" (e.g., "How many cookies does 1 child get?"), the operation is probably division. If a quantity associated with an individual unit ("tells for one") is given (2 cookies for one or each child), and a larger number is requested (how many cookies do 5 children get?), the operation is probably multiplication. Encourage students to consider such information in addition to information gained from visualizing, using manipulatives, or drawing pictures of the problem.

TEACH COGNITIVE STRATEGIES FOR PROBLEM SOLVING Montague (1992, 2008) successfully trained students to use a seven-step strategy to solve word problems: (1) *read* the problem, (2) *paraphrase* the problem, (3) *visualize* (picture or diagram), (4) *hypothesize* (a plan to solve the problem), (5) *estimate* the answer, (6) *compute*, and (7) *check* your answer. Students were also given self-instructional training in implementing these cognitive processes, using SAY, ASK, and CHECK for each step. For example, for the *paraphrase* step, SAY indicates: "Underline the important information. Put the problem in my own words." ASK indicates: "Have I underlined the important information? What is the question?" CHECK indicates: Check "that the information goes with the question" (Montague, 2008, p. 41; see also Montague, 2003a). Teachers provide think-alouds where they model the thinking process in solving problems as they employ the seven steps.

Similarly, Shiah, Mastropieri, Scruggs, and Fulk (1994–1995) trained students with mathematics learning disabilities to use a computer program that included the following steps:

1. *Read* about the problem.
2. *Think* about the problem.
3. *Decide* the operation.
4. *Write* the math sentence.
5. *Do* the problem.
6. *Label* the answer.
7. *Check* every step.

Use of steps like these can help your students solve word problems of the following type:

There are 8 bookshelves in a library. Each bookshelf holds 26 books. How many books are in the library altogether?

Begin by providing students with a list similar to Shiah et al. (1994–1995), so that they can check off the steps as they are completed. Be sure to train students on how to undertake each of the steps. For example, for step 2, "Think about the problem," students should be told to use visualization (Montague, 2008), and draw pictures and identify and circle cue words or phrases (Case, Harris, & Graham, 1992). For the current example, students could visualize or draw a library with 8 bookshelves. Each one of the bookshelves holds 26 books. Alternately, to guide thinking, cue words such as *each* ("tells for one"), *bookshelf, books,* and *altogether* could be circled. Thinking about the problem should lead to the operation decision, and writing the

PEARSON
myeducationlab

Go to MyEducationLab, select the topic *Content Area Teaching*, and go to the Activities and Applications section. As you watch the video entitled "Elementary Math: Heads Together" (in the Math subsection), reflect on the strategies these students and teachers use in solving word problems.

Students can benefit from collaboration in problem solving.

math sentence (i.e., $8 \times 26 = $ _____). After this step, students compute the answer, label the answer, and check every step. To enforce use of the systematic procedures, you could supply students with a self-monitoring sheet, in which they can check off each step as they complete it.

USE TIER 2 PROBLEM-SOLVING INTERVENTIONS Problem-solving strategies can also be provided in Tier 2 RTI interventions. Fuchs, Fuchs, and Hollenbeck (2007) implemented small-group tutoring in specific problem-solving learning strategies combined with training in recognizing different problem types and transferring their skills to novel problem formats. After 16 weeks of tutoring sessions, two to three times per week, the proportion of nonresponsiveness to instruction (below the 16th percentile) dropped substantially.

STRATEGIES FOR
TEACHING ABOUT MONEY AND TIME

PRACTICE COIN RECOGNITION AND COUNTING MONEY WITH APPROPRIATE MATERIALS One of the primary uses of mathematics in adult life involves calculations involving money, and it is important to involve students in this area as soon as possible after basic counting skills have been mastered. An early concept students could learn is to identify coins of different values. This can be done through providing drill and practice and demonstrating instances and noninstances of coin values (simulated coins and bills or bill and coin stamps are available from Delta Education).

Once students have learned to name coins, they need to learn the value of each coin. Again, direct teaching and drill and practice, perhaps using flashcards with the coin on one side and the value on the other, will help enforce these values. When values are mastered, students will be ready to learn to count change as shown in the following *In the Classroom* feature. Additionally, the software programs *Make Change* and *Count Money* from *Math Skill Builders* (S & S Software) and *Money Challenge* (GAMCO Educational Software) can provide useful practice.

USE APPROPRIATE METHODS AND MATERIALS FOR TEACHING ABOUT TIME Another important skill for all students is telling time. Materials, such as student clocks that can be set to specific times, are available from suppliers such as Delta Education and Harcourt Achieve. Generally, students are best taught by employing a specific set of subskills, as shown in the *In the Classroom* feature.

Teachers can model times or specific features of a clock on their own model, and ask students to repeat the time on their own clock models. For example, for subskill No. 2, "Recognize the hour hand," teachers can demonstrate 4 o'clock on their own clock, and prompt students to set the hour hand on their own clock to 4 o'clock.

Peer partners, who are fluent in telling time, can be assigned to students who need more practice. Use of the time-telling checklist may be helpful in targeting the exact skills students need to practice. Peers can also be helpful in promoting other students' knowledge of time throughout the day.

Finally, students who can recognize numbers but have difficulty learning to tell time may benefit from digital clocks and watches that display time in numerical formats that may be more easily recognizable. Use of digital timepieces can help students' knowledge of time while they are learning to tell time.

STRATEGIES FOR
TEACHING FRACTIONS AND DECIMALS

USE APPROPRIATE METHODS AND MATERIALS FOR TEACHING FRACTIONS
Initial teaching of fractions should involve as much as possible the students' own experiences. Most children know about sharing things, such as cookies, by breaking them into halves or

1. *Count numbers of the same coins.* Start with different numbers of pennies, and have students count by 1s (e.g., 7 pennies = 7 cents). Then move to higher values, and count by the relevant numbers. For example, count by 5s to calculate the value of 4 nickels = 20 cents; count by 10s to calculate the value of 6 dimes = 60 cents; and 25s to calculate the value of 3 quarters = 75 cents.

2. *Teach count-on strategies with same coin values plus pennies.* That is, for 3 dimes and 3 pennies, count: "10, 20, 30 cents, 31, 32, 33 cents." For two quarters and four pennies, count: "25, 50 cents, 51, 52, 53, 54 cents."

3. *For more complex combinations of coins, teach students to first sort coins into groups containing multiples of 10.* That is, two dimes is one group, one quarter and one nickel is one group. So, for these groups, count: "10, 20 cents: (on fingers) 30, 40, 50 cents."

4. *For making change, teach students to count up from the given value, counting first to a 10s or 25s value, and then counting up to the dollar value.* For example, for making change for one dollar for a 27-cent purchase, count up: "[in pennies] 28, 29, 30; [in dimes] 40, 50; [in quarters] 75, 1 dollar."

other parts. Children are also usually aware that pizzas and pies are sliced into pieces. Use this knowledge to develop more advanced concepts of fractions. One helpful material to use is the "Fraction Burger" (Delta Education), in which the equally proportioned layers of a hamburger (e.g., meat, tomato, bun) are each made of different fractions (e.g., 3/3, 5/5) that total the same size circle. Demonstrate the different ways of creating a circle with different fraction pieces, and have students demonstrate their conceptual knowledge by posing simple problems, such as, "Show the whole burger in two halves," or "Show me a whole circle made of one half (burger) and two fourths (cheese)."

Another educational material, *Fraction Flip Charts* (Delta Education), employs laminated fraction overlays to demonstrate the equivalence of different fractions (e.g., 2/8 = 1/4).

When students have learned relevant concepts, they must also learn how to represent fraction concepts in writing, and to perform computations on fractions. One problem many students may have with fractions is in reducing them to their lowest values. For students who have less of a mathematical "sense," fractions that need to be reduced may not appear as obvious as they may for other students. To help students determine whether a fraction may be reduced, a self-monitoring sheet may be helpful.

USE APPROPRIATE METHODS AND MATERIALS FOR TEACHING DECIMALS   If students have exhibited proficiency in aspects of arithmetic, procedures for using decimals should not be an overwhelming challenge. Procedures for adding and subtracting numbers with decimals involve keeping the decimal points aligned; again, graph paper may be useful for this purpose. For multiplication and division of decimals, additional practice and permanent models may be helpful.

Even if students learn to calculate with decimals, they may be less certain what decimal numbers mean. To enforce decimal concepts, *Decimal Squares* (24 Hours 7 Days) may be helpful. Decimal squares represent decimal values on cards that have been divided into 100 or 1,000 smaller components. For example, to demonstrate a decimal value of .32, a card can be shown that represents a square divided into 100 equal parts, for which 32 squares are shaded. Students can also be shown that this proportion is equivalent to a square divided into 1,000 parts, for which 320 squares are shaded; therefore, .320 = .32. When 32 of 1,000 squares are shaded, this represents not .32, but .032 (see also Figure 14.8).

□ 1. Identify the numbers on the clock face.

□ 2. Recognize the hour hand.

□ 3. Identify the hour indicated by hour hand position.

□ 4. Identify the minute hand.

□ 5. Identify the "o'clock" position with the minute hand on the 12 and hour hand pointing to a specific hour.

□ 6. Identify position of minute hand on quarter-hours as 15-minute segments (e.g., 15, 30).

□ 7. Identify position of 5-minute intervals on the clock face (e.g., 5, 10, 15, 20).

□ 8. Recognize the minute hand and identify the minute indicated by minute hand position, by counting by 1s past the previous 5-minute interval (e.g., for 23: "5, 10, 15, 20, 21, 22, 23").

□ 9. Identify the minute indicated by minute hand position, by counting by 15s, then 5s, then 1s (e.g., for 43: "15, 30, 35, 40, 41, 42, 43").

□ 10. Tell a specific time of day given positions of hour and minute hands, by first identifying the hour, then the minute.

□ 11. Identify time of day as A.M. or P.M.

Figure 14.8 Base-10 Blocks Demonstrate Decimal Values (.36 and .360)

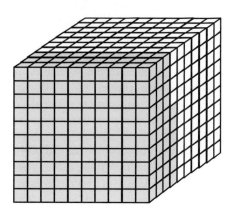

STRATEGIES FOR
TEACHING AREA AND VOLUME CONCEPTS

PROVIDE VISUAL AND THREE-DIMENSIONAL REPRESENTATIONS Concepts of area and volume can be enhanced with visual depictions. A book of overhead transparencies, *Clear View™: Area and Volume Formulas* (Delta Education), may be helpful in promoting understanding of area and volume. In this material, moveable transparency representations help clarify the formulas in computing area of trapezoids or triangles, and in estimating the area of a circle. Some transparencies demonstrate how a triangle represents half of a trapezoid or rectangle, and why the equation 1/2bh (where b = base and h = height), for determining area, is logical. Other transparencies promote the concepts of volume of three-dimensional figures. Three-dimensional representations of solids are also available from Delta Education. These figures are matched for height so that comparisons can be more easily made. Additionally, they can be filled with water, to demonstrate relative volume measures.

TEACH "BIG IDEAS" Kaméenui, Chard, and Carnine (1996; see also Stein et al., 2006) emphasized the importance of teaching "big ideas" in mathematics, so that students would have a more general idea of themes, rather than a large number of unrelated formulas and problem solutions. For example, they demonstrated that volume formulas should all proceed from the "big idea" that all represent the product of the area of the base and a multiple of the height. Then, rather than teaching separate formulas for rectangular prism, rectangular wedge, rectangular cylinder, triangular pyramid, rectangular pyramid, conic pyramid, and sphere, they can all be demonstrated to be functions of the products of base area and height. That is, for figures in which the sides go straight up, such as rectangular prism (box) or cylinder, the volume is the area of the base times the height (B × h). For figures that come to a point, such as pyramids and cones, the formula is the area of the base times 1/3 of the height (B × 1/3h) (see also Carnine, 1998). Teaching students that different procedures can stem from a common principle can help enforce understanding of the relevant concept as well as memory for specific formulae.

STRATEGIES FOR
TEACHING ALGEBRA

CLASSROOM SCENARIO

Brenda

Ever since Brenda started in algebra, she has exhibited problems with her attitude. Previously a hardworking, sincere student, she becomes angry and frustrated whenever she is confronted with an algebra problem. "This is stupid!" Brenda exclaims. "Why should I have to learn this? What difference does it make? I hate algebra!" She doesn't seem to want to make the attempt to learn. Her ninth-grade teacher, Ms. Moon, is considering placing her in a remedial math class.

QUESTIONS FOR REFLECTION

1. Why does Brenda single out algebra when other subjects also pose difficulties?
2. Do you think improving Brenda's skills or improving her attitude is of greater importance?
3. Based upon your answer to question 2, what strategies would you recommend to Ms. Moon?

Algebra is an important branch of mathematics, required for more advanced problem solving. Algebra involves the use of letters, such as x and y, to represent unknown quantities in the solution of problems. Many students with disabilities and other special needs have problems with algebra (Maccini, McNaughton, & Ruhl, 1999), in part because of basic skill deficits, students' perception of self-efficacy, and the abstract nature of the content. General strategies for addressing achievement problems in secondary-level mathematics include organized, explicit teaching of important concepts, providing many examples of new concepts that address the overall range of the concept, direct teaching of relevant cognitive routines, and systematically teaching to prioritized, general objectives (Montague & Jitendra, 2006).

USE MANIPULATIVES TO TEACH NEGATIVE NUMBERS   Many students with disabilities or other special needs have difficulty acquiring the concept of negative numbers, as in $-3 + 4 = 1$. One way of enhancing this concept is by the use of number lines, as described earlier. Another way of promoting the concept of negative numbers is by using the example of financial debt. One who owes $5, for example, must earn $5 before having 0 dollars (no surplus but no debt).

A third way of teaching about negative numbers is through the use of **algebra tiles** (Math in a Nutshell Algebra: Delta Education, or make your own). These manipulatives use dark-colored pieces to represent positive integers and lighter-colored pieces to represent negative numbers. The positive and negative tiles can be placed together to represent an equation, such as the following:

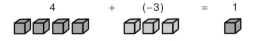

The three lighter-colored pieces "cancel out" three of the darker pieces, leaving only one positive integer, or 1. An alternative is to go to the Website of the National Library of Virtual

Go to MyEducationLab, select the topic *Content Area Teaching,* and go to the Activities and Applications section. As you read and analyze the case entitled "Applying Learning Strategies to Beginning Algebra," reflect on the best ways to help struggling students with these difficult concepts.

Manipulatives (nlvm.usu.edu), where you can find virtual representations of algebra tiles that can be manipulated online, as well as virtual manipulatives for number and operations, algebra, geometry, and measurement. (see *Technology Highlight;* for additional software for help with algebra, consider *Algebrator* [Softmath] or *Mighty Math™ Astro Algebra™* [Riverdeep].)

TEACH ALGEBRAIC REPRESENTATIONS EARLY You can begin to teach algebraic representations at an early level of problem solving. For example, students can learn to solve a problem represented as $2 + 3 = $ _____; or, $2 + 3 = ?$; or, $2 + 3 = x$. When students learn that x stands for an unknown quantity, they can also begin to solve equations such as $2 + x = 5$. Again, the concept of equivalence should be helpful in targeting the idea that both sides of the equation must represent the same quantity (Ginsburg, 1997). Using algebra tiles, a rectangular-shaped piece is used for the x value, so $2 + 3 = x$ is represented as follows:

The sets of two and three pieces can easily be combined to reveal the answer, $5 = x$; or, $x = 5$.

TEACH STRATEGIES FOR COMPUTATION Some algebraic notation and conventions must be learned in order to compute algebraic equations. For example, the rule that like quantities, such as $2x + 3x$, can be summed to equal $5x$ can be practiced and conceptualized using algebra tiles. Manipulatives can also be employed to demonstrate that unlike quantities, such as $2a + 3b$, cannot be added.

Mnemonic strategies may be helpful for learning and remembering some of these algorithms. For example, consider the problem:

$$(x + 4)(x + 2) = x^2 + 6x + 8$$

Students should recognize that the parentheses mean that each "symbol and digit" in parentheses must be multiplied by one another. To expand the left side of the equation into the values of the right side, it is necessary to multiply in a specific order. The first step is to multiply the *first* terms, $(x)(x) = x^2$. The second steps are to sum the products of the *outer* $(x)(2)$ and the *inner* $(x)(4)$ terms, $2x + 4x = 6x$. The final step is to multiply the *last* terms, $(2)(4) = 8$. Added together, they provide the answer, $x^2 + 6x + 8$. To remember the sequence of this operation, it may be helpful to remember the mnemonic acronym **FOIL**, which stands for **F**irst terms, **O**uter terms + **I**nner terms, and **L**ast terms (Kilpatrick, 1985).

TEACH STRATEGIES FOR SOLVING QUADRATIC EQUATIONS In a quadratic equation, the unknown variable is squared, and the equation can be written in the form:

$$ax^2 + bx + c = 0.$$

There are three ways to solve quadratic equations, two of which are factoring the equation and completing the square. Algebra tiles again can be helpful in developing understanding of these concepts, by using the square version of the x variable to represent x^2. A third method involves the use of an equation developed by mathematicians:

$$x = \frac{-b \pm \sqrt{b^2 - 4ac}}{2a}$$

If the numbers in the quadratic equation are used to replace a, b, and c, the equation is relatively simple to solve. For example, if the quadratic equation is $x^2 + 8x + 15 = 0$, then a = 1, b = 8, and c = 15. Replacing these values in the formula results in the value

$$\frac{-8 \pm \sqrt{8^2 - 4(1 \cdot 15)}}{2 \cdot 1}$$

One problem with this method is remembering the equation. One way to promote memory is to use a mnemonic strategy, using a bee with a minus sign for a stinger for $-b$, a "square" bee for b^2, four aces for $4ac$, and a TWA airplane for $2a$ (TWoA):

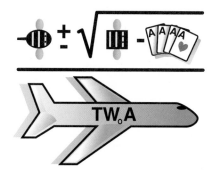

Such a strategy, of course, should be practiced many times, and particular attention must be paid to the elements that are *not* represented mnemonically (+/−, and square root). Finally, students should have many opportunities practicing the application of this equation in the solution of problems. Remember, as with any academic strategy, students must be taught to *identify* the situation in which a particular strategy is called for, *remember* the steps of the strategy, and then correctly *apply* the strategy in the appropriate context.

TEACH PROBLEM-SOLVING STRATEGIES   Students can benefit from self-questioning strategies for solving algebra word problems. Maccini and Hughes (2000) taught introductory algebra (e.g., operations with negative numbers) to secondary students with learning disabilities using concrete, semiconcrete, and abstract presentations discussed earlier. Again the strategy considered problem representation and problem solution, and employed the **STAR** strategy:

1. **S**earch the word problem (read carefully, ask questions, look for facts).
2. **T**ranslate the problem into a pictured equation (choose a variable, identify the operation, and represent the problem in a concrete [manipulative, such as algebra tiles], semiconcrete [picture], or abstract [equation] application). (Students began with concrete representations and progressed to abstract representations.)
3. **A**nswer the problem, attending to relevant signs.
4. **R**eview the solution, by reading the problem again and checking whether the answer is reasonable.

All students trained using this strategy improved in introductory algebra problem solving.

Hutchinson (1993) developed a strategy-based model that considered two separate phases: problem representation and problem solution (Janvier, 1987). Problem representation refers to an internal representation of the words of the problem. Problem solution refers to the solution planning and solution execution of the problem to obtain the answer. Hutchinson employed different problem types: relational problems, proportion problems, problems that employed two variables, and problems that employed two equations. For example, for relational problems, students were required to identify the relational statement that provided information about one unknown quantity in terms of its relationship to another unknown quantity. Then, the solution focused on procedures and order of operations. One relational problem was:

> A man walks 6 km farther than his son. If the total distance walked by both is 32 km, how far did each walk? (p. 38)

Students were then directed to use self-questioning for solving algebra problems, as shown in the worksheet in Figure 14.9.

In this instance, you would prompt students to think through the fact that the man's son walked x km, and the man, who walked 6 km farther, walked $x + 6$ km. Using the worksheet questions, then, students could identify the goal, the unknowns, the knowns, the type of problem, and the equation. These two distances, x km and $x + 6$ km, totaled 32 km. Using the problem-solution strategy, students were able to obtain the correct answer, 13 km.

$$x + (x + 6) = 32$$

or,

$$2x + 6 = 32$$
$$(2x + 6) - 6 = 32 - 6$$
$$2x = 26$$
$$x = 13$$

Goal: _____

What I don't know: _____

What I know: _____

Kind of problem: _____

Equation: _____

Solving the equation: _____

Solution: _____

Compare with goal.

Check.

Figure 14.9 Structured Worksheet

Note: From "Effects of Cognitive Strategy Instruction on Algebra Problem Solving of Adolescents with Learning Disabilities," by N. L. Hutchinson, 1993, *Learning Disability Quarterly, 16,* p. 40. Copyright 1993 by Council for Learning Disabilities. Reprinted with permission.

so,

$$\text{man walked } x + 6 = 19 \text{ km}$$
$$\text{son walked } x = 13 \text{ km}$$

Students then compare their solution to the stated goal, and check by replacing obtained values in the original problem.

Similarly, Lang, Mastropieri, Scruggs, and Porter (2004) taught an algebra problem-solving strategy to students considered at risk for math failure. The following strategy steps were used in each example problem:

 a. If I use this strategy, I will be successful.
 b. What do we know?
 c. What don't we know?
 d. How can we represent the unknowns?
 e. How can we represent the knowns?
 f. Do we need more than one equation?
 g. What is the equation(s)?
 h. Substitute the knowns into the equation(s).
 i. Solve the equation(s).
 j. Have I checked my answer?

Students went through each step of the strategy as they solved algebra problems, and greatly increased their strategy use as they went through the training.

STRATEGIES FOR TEACHING FUNCTIONAL MATH

USE APPROPRIATE METHODS AND MATERIALS FOR TEACHING FUNCTIONAL MATH Many students do not go into advanced math classes, but instead place more emphasis on basic skills and what is called **functional math** (Heller, 2005). Functional math includes aspects of mathematics that serve individuals in their daily living. These topics include using the calendar, writing checks and keeping checking and savings bank accounts, calculating household expenses, filling out income tax forms, and paying bills. These skills are important for all students to acquire, regardless of the program they are in (it is often assumed—perhaps incorrectly—that students already have these skills; Patton, Cronin, Bassett, & Koppel, 1998). A useful textbook reference on this subject is *The Pacemaker Curriculum: Practical Mathematics for Consumers* (Globe Fearon; read-

Virtual Manipulatives for Mathematics

Many mathematics skills and concepts are more concrete for students when manipulatives are used during instruction. Manipulatives provide students experience with concrete representations of underlying concepts, which helps comprehension and understanding. Teachers, however, may have a limited supply of manipulatives. An inexpensive alternative to concrete manipulatives are virtual manipulatives that are available on the Internet. The National Library of Virtual Manipulatives (*http://nlvm.usu.edu/en/nav/vlibrary.html*) provides interactive online math lessons using virtual manipulatives in the areas of numbers and operations, algebra, geometry, measurement, data analysis, and probability. Within each general math category, the site contains multiple activities and problems using the virtual manipulatives. Problems can be reset to compute again and again using different variations to provide additional practice as necessary of a general concept. In addition, all math areas are linked to grade-level standards and benchmarks and teacher and parent information on how to teach the concepts. For example, in the activity "Fractions—Parts of a Whole" for grades 3–5, practice on parts of a whole unit to a written description and numeric fraction is provided. In this activity, a picture is provided that can be divided into any number of parts. Students are taught that any whole can be divided into an equal number of parts and are asked to divide the whole picture into parts. They are then asked to highlight parts of the whole. When various fractions (parts) of the picture are highlighted, a corresponding fraction changes to reflect new values. Questions such as "How many ways can you describe parts of a unit?" are asked and students are asked to describe answers with partners.

Mathematics activities are available on many other Websites. The National Council of Teachers of Mathematics (NCTM) provides math activities, math standards, and web links on the site *http://illuminations.nctm.org/*, which includes a virtual manipulatives link and online, interactive math activities designed to match NCTM principles and standards. In addition, several indices of available virtual manipulatives web links provide links to a wealth of Websites.

ing level 3–4; Staudacher & Turner, 1994). A list of topics from the table of contents is provided in Figure 14.10. Some materials from *Essential Mathematics for Life* (McGraw-Hill) also provide activities for functional math. Pro-Ed publishes *Real Life Math* and *Real Life Math: Living on a Paycheck.* Because many of these topics may not be on the curriculum for other students, you many need to arrange some time for small-group teaching of these topics. The *Technology Highlight* feature above presents ideas using multimedia math.

Instead of advanced math classes, some students need more emphasis on functional math, including learning how to write a check, balance a checkbook, or budget household expenses.

1. Covering Expenses	10. Healthful Eating
2. Making and Changing Budgets	11. Buying Personal Items
3. Salary	12. Getting the Best Value
4. Take-Home Pay	13. Buying a Vehicle
5. Banking	14. Maintaining a Vehicle
6. Using a Checking Account	15. Credit Card Math
7. Finding a Place to Live	16. Loans and Interest
8. Furnishing an Apartment	17. Budgeting for Recreation
9. Choosing and Buying Groceries	18. Planning a Trip

Figure 14.10 Functional Math Topics

Note: From *Practical Mathematics for Consumers,* by C. Staudacher & S. Turner, 1994, Paramus, NJ: Globe Fearon. Adapted with permission.

14 Summary

- Mathematics has been considered the "key to opportunity" in society. However, many students with disabilities and other special needs exhibit problems learning mathematics. Appropriate curriculum, effective teaching, and specific strategy instruction can help alleviate many of these problems.

- Basic number and operation concepts (e.g., addition, subtraction) can be enforced by direct teaching, number lines, and manipulatives such as base-10 blocks. Learning of vocabulary concepts can be promoted by direct teaching, manipulatives, and verbal elaboration including mnemonic strategies.

- Learning of basic math facts can become a significant obstacle to many students with disabilities and other special needs. When possible, promote memory of basic facts through direct teaching, increased learning time, peer tutoring, specialized software, and independent study strategies. Additionally, use specific strategies for promoting recall of specific facts. If basic fact learning seems unproductive and frustrating, consider using calculators to continue progressing in other areas of mathematics functioning. Return to fact learning when it appears it may be profitable.

- Math word problem solving can be facilitated by using a concrete to semiconcrete to abstract sequence of instruction. In addition, use specific problem-solving strategies including a seven-step self-monitoring strategy, judicious use of clue words, highlighting, imagery, pictures, and other problem-solving strategies.

- Important money and time concepts can be enforced by direct teaching, increased practice, manipulatives, models, and providing a careful sequence of skills.

- Specific manipulative materials (commercially available or teacher-made) can be helpful in promoting learning of fractions and decimals. Specific self-monitoring and other strategies can also be useful in promoting these concepts.

- Promote concepts in algebra by providing early concept development, computation strategies, manipulatives such as algebra tiles, mnemonics, and self-monitoring strategies.

- Ensure that students are acquiring sufficient "practical" mathematics skills for use in transition to community life and future employment. Curriculum materials are available that provide for instruction in these practical areas.

PROFESSIONAL STANDARDS LINK: MATHEMATICS

Information in this chapter links most directly to:

- CEC Standards: 3 (Individual Learning Differences), 4 (Instructional Strategies), 5 (Learning Environments and Social Interactions), 6 (Language), 7 (Instructional Planning), 8 (Assessment)

- INTASC Standards: Principles 1 (understands central concepts of the discipline), 2 (provides appropriate learning opportunities), 3 (understands learning differences, adapts instructional opportunities), 4 (instructional strategies), 5 (creates learning environments), 6 (fosters inquiry, collaboration, interaction), 7 (plans instruction), 8 (assessment strategies)

- PRAXIS II™ Content Categories (Knowledge): 3 (Delivery of Services)

- PRAXIS II™ Content Categories (Application): 1 (Curriculum), 2 (Instruction), 3 (Assessment)

MATHEMATICS

If the student is having difficulty in mathematics, have you tried the following strategies? If not, see the pages listed below.

STRATEGIES FOR TEACHING BEGINNING MATH

- [ ] Teach early number concepts, 333
- [ ] Teach strategies for counting, 333–334
- [ ] Reinforce one-to-one correspondence, 334
- [ ] Introduce geometry concepts in early years, 334

STRATEGIES FOR TEACHING ADDITION AND SUBTRACTION

- [ ] Use manipulatives for teaching addition and subtraction concepts, 334–335
- [ ] Use number lines to promote operations, 335
- [ ] Use strategies for number writing, 335–336
- [ ] Use questioning to promote understanding of symbols, 336
- [ ] Use *Touch Math* to promote addition and subtraction computation, 336–337
- [ ] Use practice and specific strategies for addition and subtraction facts, 337–339
- [ ] Use strategies for place value and regrouping, 390
- [ ] Use strategies for teaching early problem solving with addition and subtraction, 340–342

STRATEGIES FOR TEACHING MULTIPLICATION AND DIVISION

- [ ] Use manipulatives for teaching multiplication and division concepts, 342–343
- [ ] Teach "count-bys," 343
- [ ] Use specific strategies for teaching multiplication and division facts, 343–345
- [ ] Use calculators when appropriate, 345–346
- [ ] Reinforce arithmetic vocabulary, 346
- [ ] Use specific strategies for teaching multiplication and division algorithms, 346–348

STRATEGIES FOR TEACHING PROBLEM SOLVING

- [ ] Promote use of word meanings, 348–349
- [ ] Teach cognitive strategies for problem solving, 349–350
- [ ] Use Tier 2 problem-solving interventions, 350

STRATEGIES FOR TEACHING ABOUT MONEY AND TIME

- [ ] Practice coin recognition and counting money with appropriate materials, 350
- [ ] Use appropriate methods and materials for teaching about time, 350

STRATEGIES FOR TEACHING FRACTIONS AND DECIMALS

- [ ] Use appropriate methods and materials for teaching fractions, 350–351
- [ ] Use appropriate methods and materials for teaching decimals, 351

STRATEGIES FOR TEACHING AREA AND VOLUME CONCEPTS

- [ ] Provide visual and three-dimensional representations, 352
- [ ] Teach "big ideas," 352–353

STRATEGIES FOR TEACHING ALGEBRA

- [ ] Use manipulatives to teach negative numbers, 353–354
- [ ] Teach algebraic representations early, 354
- [ ] Teach strategies for computation, 354
- [ ] Teach strategies for solving quadratic equations, 354–355
- [ ] Teach problem-solving strategies, 355–356

STRATEGIES FOR TEACHING FUNCTIONAL MATH

- [ ] Use appropriate methods and materials for teaching functional math, 356–357

Tenerife Turtle

COLIN BRITTAIN   Colin Brittain has temporal lobe epilepsy and severe right-sided diplopia, but that has not curbed his passion for photography. "I sometimes don't get on with my disability, or at least when it impairs what I want to do. However, like all people with disabilities, I have adapted to overcome my limitations, and my scooter now does a grand job of taking the load from my camera equipment."

15

Science and Social Studies

OBJECTIVES

After studying this chapter, you should be able to:

- Describe and apply strategies for adapting textbook/content-oriented approaches in science and social studies, such as content enhancements, semantic feature analysis, and mnemonic strategies.

- Identify criteria for selecting and adopting textbooks for your class or school district.

- Evaluate and implement strategy instruction for using content-area textbooks, such as text organization, text structure, and essential information in content textbooks.

- Describe and evaluate methods for adapting textbook materials to accommodate diverse learners in the classroom.

- Discuss considerations and adaptations to science activities and ways to make appropriate adaptations for teaching process skills.

- Provide methods and strategies for adapting activities in specific science content areas, including life science, earth science, and physical science activities, for diverse learners.

- Describe and apply methods for adapting social studies instruction for students with special needs.

- Discuss ways for adapting inquiry-oriented approaches in science and social studies.

Science and social studies are academic disciplines concerned with concepts and knowledge of the physical and social world around us (Parker, 2008; Trowbridge, Bybee, & Carlson-Powell, 2004), and as such are important subject areas for all students. Both subjects, however, present unique challenges to teachers who must adapt their instruction, materials, and procedures to accommodate students with special needs.

Adaptations for students with special needs must reflect the approach to instruction being used in the class (Scruggs & Mastropieri, 2007). That is, many schools employ a **textbook-oriented** (or content-oriented) **approach** in which students are taught and learn content information from textbooks about science and social studies. With this approach, adaptations may focus on teacher presentations and student independent learning from textbooks. Other schools may embrace an **activities-oriented approach** to learning, in which students undertake specific projects, experiments, or other activities to enhance their understanding of the subject. With this approach, adaptations may focus on physical activities as well as reading and writing requirements. In many schools, teachers may use features of both approaches.

Using either approach, teachers may emphasize an **inquiry-based model** of learning, in which students use their knowledge or experiences to invent, discover, or construct new knowledge.

Adaptations for inquiry-based learning may focus on supports or enhancements to promote the thinking and reasoning process in students with special needs.

Adapting Textbook-Oriented Approaches in Science and Social Studies

CLASSROOM SCENARIO

Jeffrey

As Mr. Norland's sixth-grade science class enters the room on Monday of the second week of school, Mr. Norland booms, "Pick up your science lab materials on your way to your seat. Open up your textbooks to Activity 2–1 in Chapter 2 on page 26 and follow the instructions. If you have any problems with the steps see me." After most of the class appears to have begun working, Mr. Norland notices that Jeffrey hasn't even started the activity. Mr. Norland speaks with Jeffrey and realizes Jeffrey can't follow through with the activity because he can't read what to do. Although embarrassed, Jeffrey agrees to work through the activity with one of his peers. At the end of the day, Mr. Norland approaches Jeffrey's special education teacher. "I know Jeffrey has a learning disability, but doing well in science this year is partly dependent on Jeffrey being able to read. We will do many of the activities in cooperative groups, but how will Jeffrey get the content background he needs unless he can read the text?"

QUESTIONS FOR REFLECTION

1. How do Mr. Norland's classroom routines affect Jeffrey's achievement in science?
2. Why doesn't Jeffrey ask for help?
3. What strategies might Mr. Norland use to help Jeffrey succeed?

Much instruction in social studies and science involves teaching and learning of content based on relevant textbook materials. Effective teacher presentations and specific strategies for studying textbooks can address a variety of special learning needs, and enhance learning for all students.

STRATEGIES FOR
EFFECTIVE TEACHING IN SCIENCE AND SOCIAL STUDIES

You can enhance learning of science and social studies in inclusive classrooms by using the teacher effectiveness variables (Good & Brophy, 2007), including the SCREAM variables described in Chapter 6.

USE EFFECTIVE TEACHING STRATEGIES   Organizing your science or social studies content around "big ideas" will make subordinate concepts easier to understand (Simmons & Kameénui, 1999; Slocum, 2004). For example, the model of convection, once clearly understood, can explain the behavior of water in a boiling pot, the movement of material in the Earth's mantle, and the movement of air masses including atmospheric convection. Emphasize the organization of your presentations with outlines and important information highlighted on the board or projector, and refer frequently to this outline. Speak in a clear, direct manner, and avoid ambiguous language. Actively model excitement and enthusiasm about the content being covered. Repeat new or unfamiliar vocabulary or concepts, and provide multiple instances of new concepts (e.g., *saprophytic, nullification, hegemony*) to strengthen comprehension. Use mnemonics or other elaborations to promote recall of new vocabulary (see Chapter 10). Question students frequently, and adjust your instruction as needed.

PROVIDE CONTENT-ENHANCEMENT STRATEGIES   Teachers can use **content-enhancement** strategies to further increase science and social studies learning. Content enhancements incorporate effective instructional design and make use of graphic organizers, including study guides, charts, diagrams, outlines, visual-spatial displays, mnemonics, and imagery, to promote learning and comprehension (Bulgren, 2004). Research has indicated that students with disabilities in inclusive classrooms have improved their performance when science and social studies teachers apply content-enhancement strategies in their teaching (Bulgren, 2004).

Go to MyEducationLab, select the topic *Content Area Teaching*, and go to the Activities and Applications section. As you read and analyze the lesson plan entitled "Demonstrating Scientific Processes," consider how this lesson addresses the concept of "big ideas" discussed here.

SMARTER Teachers can plan for instruction using the strategy cued by the acronym **SMARTER**. This includes **s**electing important content, **m**apping the organization of the content, **a**nalyzing learning problems, **r**eaching decisions about enhancement, **t**eaching according to decisions, **e**valuating, and **r**eteaching based upon the evaluation (Lenz, Bulgren, Kissam, & Taymans, 2004).

Lesson Organizer and Concept Mastery Routines Two helpful content-enhancement strategies are the lesson organizer routine and the concept mastery routine. The *lesson organizer routine* is a visual advanced organizer frame to organize a lesson so students can see the main ideas, as well as how the main ideas relate to each other and to prior knowledge (Albert & Ammer, 2004). The organizer does the following:

- Introduces the topic
- Changes difficult vocabulary to familiar vocabulary
- Teaches students relationships among concepts
- Identifies appropriate strategies for learning
- Graphically demonstrates relationships of lessons to an entire unit
- Graphically displays organization of the content
- Provides self-testing questions

As teachers present the visual displays and share information with students, they help show how the information is related to previously learned content. The organizer also functions as a teacher-planning device in that the sequences of content, concepts, and vocabulary are identified before instruction to ensure a developmentally appropriate lesson.

The *concept mastery routine* addresses the teaching of difficult concepts (King-Sears & Mooney, 2004). This content enhancement is designed around a concept diagram, a visual device that includes the following components:

- Concept name
- Class or category of concept
- Important information associated with concept
- Instances and noninstances of the concept
- Blank space for additions to the diagram
- Concept definition (Bulgren, Deshler, & Schumaker, 1993)

Specific instructional steps are provided for teachers to use when implementing the concept mastery routine. Figure 15.1 contains a sample concept diagram.

Bulgren (2004) emphasized that the graphic itself is not presented to students in its completed form; rather, the teacher may develop a graphic organizer before instruction begins, but the actual graphic organizer is developed interactively with students, as they share their own ideas, knowledge, and questions.

PROVIDE SEMANTIC FEATURE ANALYSIS **Semantic feature analysis** is an activity intended to help students learn the vocabulary and major concepts from a science or social studies chapter (Bos & Anders, 1990; Bos, Anders, Filip, & Jaffe, 1989). To use semantic feature analysis, first, analyze the content within a chapter and develop a relationship chart (see Figure 15.2). The chart contains all the vocabulary in a hierarchy of main ideas to lesser ideas. The main ideas are placed along separate columns on the top of the chart, and the related vocabulary terms are listed in separate rows along the left side of the chart. Several blank spaces can remain to add new ideas that result from class discussions. During instruction, present the information on the chart and have students participate in the discussion of the vocabulary and related concepts. After discussion, students complete the relationship chart by marking whether or not words in the rows and columns are positively or negatively related or unrelated (Bos & Anders, 1987).

USE MNEMONIC STRATEGIES Keyword, pegword, and letter strategies can be extremely useful for helping students remember vocabulary, terminology, and factual information involving science and social studies. Much information in science (e.g., *deciduous, thermic,*

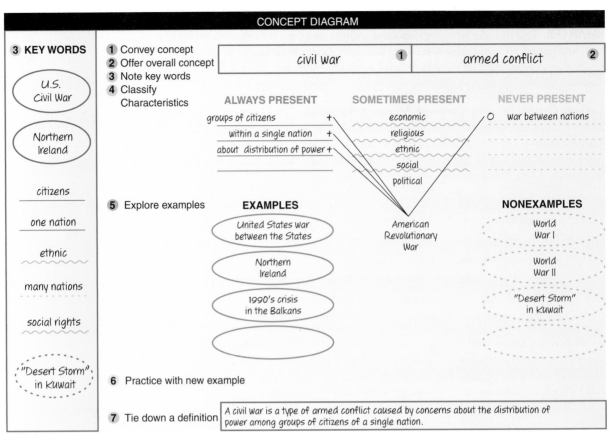

CONCEPT DIAGRAM

3 KEY WORDS

- U.S. Civil War
- Northern Ireland
- citizens
- one nation
- ethnic
- many nations
- social rights
- "Desert Storm" in Kuwait

① Convey concept
② Offer overall concept
③ Note key words
④ Classify Characteristics

| civil war ① | armed conflict ② |

| ALWAYS PRESENT | SOMETIMES PRESENT | NEVER PRESENT |

groups of citizens +
within a single nation +
about distribution of power +

economic
religious
ethnic
social
political

O war between nations

⑤ Explore examples

EXAMPLES

- United States war between the States
- Northern Ireland
- 1990's crisis in the Balkans

American Revolutionary War

NONEXAMPLES

- World War I
- World War II
- "Desert Storm" in Kuwait

⑥ Practice with new example

⑦ Tie down a definition — A civil war is a type of armed conflict caused by concerns about the distribution of power among groups of citizens of a single nation.

Figure 15.1 Sample Concept Diagram

Note: From *Teaching Adolescents with Learning Disabilities: Strategies and Methods* (2nd ed., p. 453), by D. D. Deshler, E. S. Ellis, & B. K. Lenz (Eds.), 1996, Denver, CO: Love Publishing. Reprinted with permission.

trichina) and social studies (e.g., *hegemony, anarchy, Dred Scott*) is appropriate for mnemonic elaboration. These mnemonic strategies are described in detail in Chapter 10, and should be used whenever students exhibit difficulty remembering important content. For example, Mastropieri, Sweda, and Scruggs (2000) developed mnemonics to help fourth-grade students remember important information in a social studies unit (e.g., *Europe, charter*). Although the strategies helped the entire class, students with disabilities benefited the most. Marshak (2008) employed classroom peer tutoring with mnemonic strategies in middle-school social studies classes, and found that students significantly outperformed students in a traditional instruction condition (see *Research Highlight*).

Create strategies for class presentations and ask students to develop their own strategies in group activities. For example, after information has been organized in a graphic organizer or relationship chart, ask students which important information seems most difficult to remember, and have them create effective mnemonic strategies using techniques described in Chapter 10.

MODIFY WORKSHEET ACTIVITIES   Some students with special needs are able to address the content required in worksheet activities, but may have difficulty with the mechanical aspects of writing necessary to complete the activity in the allotted time. Figure 15.3 includes a modified version of a science assignment for students with special needs. The modified assignment reduces the amount of reading and writing, but covers the same major concepts. This is an example of the concept of differentiated instruction (Tomlinson, 2005) applied to worksheet activities.

In addition to effective instruction and use of content enhancements to promote comprehension, another important area to consider is teaching students to learn independently from content-area textbooks.

Important Ideas

Important Words	Type of Life		Location			Extinct?	
	Plant	Animal	Sea	Land	Lakes	Not Extinct	Extinct
Trilobites							
Crinoids							
Giant cats							
Coral							
Bryozoans							
Guide fossils							
Dinosaurs							
Freshwater fish							
Brachiopods							
Small horses							
Ferns							
Enormous winged bugs							
Trees							

Key: + = positive relationship; – = negative relationship; 0 = no relationship; ? = uncertain.

Figure 15.2 Sample Semantic Feature Relationship Chart

Note: From "Semantic Feature Analysis: An Interactive Teaching Strategy for Facilitating Learning from Text," by C. S. Bos & P. L. Anders, 1987, *Learning Disabilities Focus, 3*(1), p. 57. Copyright 1987 Erlbaum. Reprinted with permission.

Name: Jennifer N.

The ___Water___ Cycle

1. ___Condensation___ : the change of state from gas to a liquid.

2. ___Precipitation___ : any form of water that falls to the ground.

4. ___Evaporation___: the change of state from liquid to a gas.

3. ___Water___ is ___stored___ or it is taken in by ___animals___ and ___plants___.

Figure 15.3 Worksheet Assignment and Modified Worksheet Assignment

STRATEGIES FOR
PROMOTING INDEPENDENT LEARNING FROM TEXTBOOKS

A large proportion of learning that takes place in science and social studies comes from independent studying of textbooks. For assignments, students are often required to read chapters and answer questions. Teachers often move rapidly from chapter to chapter because of pressures to cover a great deal of content. Science and social studies textbooks are often complex, contain high readability levels and many formats, and introduce a significant number of new vocabulary words and concepts (Best, Rowe, Ozuru, & McNamara, 2005; Fontana, 2004; Paxton, 1999). Jitendra et al. (2001) evaluated middle-school geography textbooks, and found them to be generally inconsiderate of poor readers and dense with factual information.

Given these analyses, it is not surprising that studying from textbooks can be frustrating for many students with disabilities and those at risk for school failure. When possible, select textbooks that effectively promote comprehension. Volunteer to be a member of your school district's textbook adoption committees. Carefully consider such features as readability, language, organization, and use of illustrations and diagrams. Your input on the selection of appropriate textbooks will benefit all students, but especially those with special learning needs. One readability measure is provided in Figure 15.4.

TEACH STUDY SKILLS STRATEGIES FOR CONTENT-AREA TEXTBOOKS
Successful students develop their own effective study skills and strategies to use when studying textbooks independently. However, students with special needs may require explicit instruction in the use of these strategies. Learning how to predict text structures, how to highlight or outline essential information, and how to use text enhancements such as lesson organizers, graphic organizers, illustrations, charts, graphs, and diagrams are strategies for effectively using textbooks.

Many related strategies for studying from textbook materials (such as organizational and study skills, and reading comprehension strategies) are described in Chapters 11 and 13. Many of these strategies are appropriate for all expository text materials and therefore would be helpful for many other secondary-level classes, such as business education, foreign languages, home economics, and physical education.

TEACH STUDENTS TO IDENTIFY TEXT ORGANIZATION
Textbooks contain organizational features intended to help students learn academic content. Unfortunately, however, many students with special needs may not figure out text organization independently. Taking time to teach students how the features of their textbooks are organized can help students learn more easily and make the use of textbooks more valuable. Point out to students how to use design features such as:

- The overall parts of the text (e.g., table of contents, index)
- The organizational system (sections, chapters)
- Specific features within chapters (objectives, outlines, boldface, vocabulary, illustrations, charts)
- Features associated with supplemental materials (workbooks, lab books, activity sheets)

Understanding the organization of a textbook can enhance students' comprehension of the content-area information presented. Use the effective instruction principles when designing lessons to teach students about text features.

Train Students to Identify Text Structures Expository science and social studies textbooks use several distinct types of structures (Cook & Mayer, 1988; Williams, 2003). These text structures include, for example, main idea, time–order, cause–effect, enumeration, and sequence.

All types of text structures may appear throughout a single science or social studies textbook. Therefore, students are likely to encounter many structures not only within a single textbook, but also within a single chapter. Students must understand these structures to be able to realize what information is important for them to learn and remember (Cook & Mayer, 1988).

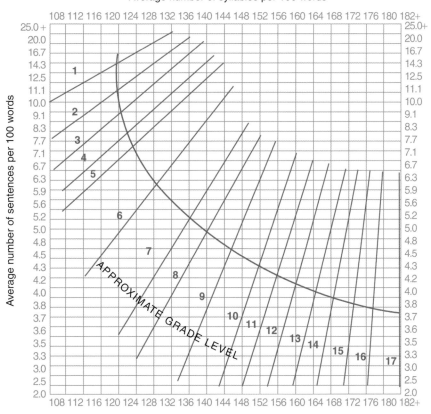

Average number of syllables per 100 words

1. Randomly select three text samples of exactly 100 words, beginning with the beginning of a sentence. Count proper nouns, numerals, and initializations as words.

2. Count the number of sentences in each 100-word sample, estimating the length of the last sentence to the nearest one-tenth.

3. Count the total number of syllables in each 100-word sample. Count one syllable for each numeral or initial or symbol; for example, 1990 is one word and four syllables, LD is one word and two syllables, and "&" is one word and one syllable.

4. Average the number of sentences and number of syllables across the three samples.

5. Enter the average sentence length and average number of syllables on the graph. Put a dot where the two lines intersect. The area in which the dot is plotted will give you an approximate estimated readability.

6. If there is a great deal of variability in the syllable or sentence count across the three samples, more samples can be added.

Figure 15.4 Fry's Readability Graph and Formula

Note: From "Fry's Readability Graph: Clarifications, Validity, and Extension to Level 17," by E. Fry, 1977, *Journal of Reading, 21*, pp. 242–252.

Once passage structures are identified, structure-specific reading comprehension strategies can be used to improve understanding and recall. Bakken, Mastropieri, and Scruggs (1997) successfully taught students with learning disabilities to recognize *main idea, list,* and *order* passage types and to apply structure-specific reading comprehension strategies. For example, when studying main idea passages, students were taught to write down the main idea, and then write supporting statements. For list passages (e.g., of a country's natural resources), students were taught to note items in the list. For order passages (e.g., ordered steps in the digestive process), they were taught to write down the items in the appropriate sequence presented. These students greatly outperformed students who were given more general training, either to paraphrase information or to answer questions about the passages.

TEACH HIGHLIGHTING AND OUTLINING STRATEGIES   Highlighting and outlining are used to increase learning and memory of text by identifying the critical information in text or notes. Both of these techniques have been adapted to increase learning of students with special needs (e.g., Horton & Lovitt, 1989; Horton, Boone, & Lovitt, 1990). Information highlighted with bright colors, such as fluorescent yellow, stands out dramatically from the text, and can be used to quickly find important information. Underlining is usually done in pencil or pen, but brightly colored highlighting pens can also be used. Brightly colored sticky notes can be used when students are not allowed to write in their textbooks.

The most difficult aspect of highlighting or underlining for students is choosing which information is most important. Without training, many students may be unable to discern what is important to highlight or underline and may highlight or underline everything on a page. Obviously, this defeats the purpose of highlighting.

When using actual science or social studies text materials, proceed through a highlighting activity in which you describe to students why you are selecting certain sections to highlight, using a think-aloud protocol. Say, for example:

- "This looks like a new science concept, therefore I will highlight it. This next section just provides more information on the same concept, so I won't highlight it."
- "This looks like an important person in this history chapter so I will highlight her, but this next paragraph just describes her background, so I won't highlight that."
- "This looks like an important vocabulary word so I'll highlight it, but I already know what the next word means, so I won't highlight that."

Show students how to examine the features associated with their textbook. For example, organizational subheadings sometimes provide clues as to whether something is essential, and valuable information is often presented in maps, figures, charts, and diagrams within the text.

Finally, provide guided practice in which students work with partners or in small groups and practice identifying important information for highlighting. Stop occasionally and ask students whether they think some of the points meet the criteria for highlighting. Have students share with each other their rationale for the selections they highlighted.

Teach Outlining   Outlining is another study strategy that students can use while studying science and social studies textbooks independently. Before expecting students to outline, be sure they can identify different text structures. Point out how textbooks are organized under various levels of subheads, which often can be used as levels in outlines. Then be sure to teach or review how to develop outlines. Demonstrate to students how determining the main idea is a first step, followed by selecting supporting ideas and details for each major idea. Before requiring students to create outlines independently, provide them with partially completed outlines in which they complete missing information as they study independently. Outlines set up like this are called **framed outlines**, and have been used to promote textbook learning of students with and without disabilities (Kim, Vaughn, Wanzek, & Wei, 2004). Figure 15.5 displays an example of a framed outline that can be used for your teaching.

INTRODUCE STUDY GUIDES   Study guides take on a variety of forms and can be developed by teachers, students, or by both teachers and students using partially completed study guides similar to partially completed outlines. Lovitt and Horton and their colleagues studied the effects of various study guides on textbook comprehension of students with and without disabilities (e.g., Horton, Boone, & Lovitt, 1990). Students used information in the science and social studies textbooks to complete short-answer questions on the study guide form. Students who used the study guides consistently outperformed students who did not have instruction using study guides. To create a study guide for your students, include critical features such as the formulation of questions, the use of vocabulary, the amount of content coverage, and a predictable format for the guide. Consider such features as the amount of content covered, the type of study guide (question–answer, framed outline, schematic graph, graphic organizer), the difficulty level of the language, and the format of the questions (fill-in-the-blank, open-ended, or multiple-choice).

Try developing a few study guides annually to accompany your text. Save them or share them with another teacher who may also develop a few to share with you. Do not pres-

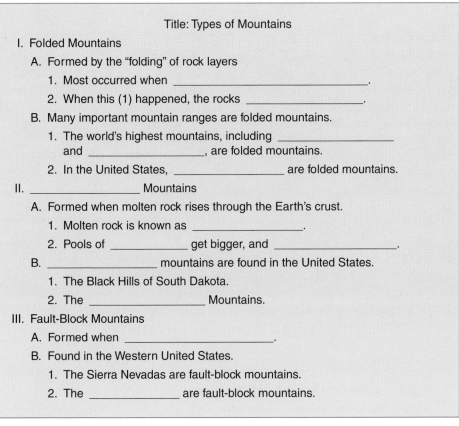

Title: Types of Mountains

I. Folded Mountains
    A. Formed by the "folding" of rock layers
        1. Most occurred when _____.
        2. When this (1) happened, the rocks _____.
    B. Many important mountain ranges are folded mountains.
        1. The world's highest mountains, including _____
           and _____, are folded mountains.
        2. In the United States, _____ are folded mountains.
II. _____ Mountains
    A. Formed when molten rock rises through the Earth's crust.
        1. Molten rock is known as _____.
        2. Pools of _____ get bigger, and _____.
    B. _____ mountains are found in the United States.
        1. The Black Hills of South Dakota.
        2. The _____ Mountains.
III. Fault-Block Mountains
    A. Formed when _____.
    B. Found in the Western United States.
        1. The Sierra Nevadas are fault-block mountains.
        2. The _____ are fault-block mountains.

Figure 15.5   Sample Framed Outline

sure yourself to complete the entire text at one time or you may become overwhelmed. Over time, you will have accompanying study guides developed for entire textbooks in science and social studies.

TEACH LEARNING STRATEGIES   Deshler and Schumaker and their colleagues at the University of Kansas Institute for Research in Learning Disabilities developed some excellent learning strategies, including an instructional model for optimal delivery of these strategies (see Deshler & Schumaker, 2006; Lenz, Deshler, & Kissam, 2004; Schumaker & Deshler, 2003). Learning strategies should be implemented slowly over time to ensure that all students master all steps involved in learning and generalizing strategies. Key elements in the learning strategies model are listed in the following *In the Classroom* feature. The intent of instruction in the learning strategies is for students to become independent at implementing the strategies in their own studying.

MultiPass   A useful learning strategy for reading science and social studies textbooks is **MultiPass** (Schumaker, Deshler, Alley, Warner, & Denton, 1982). The steps in MultiPass are similar to the SQ3R strategy—survey, question, read, recite, and review (McCormick & Cooper, 1991). With MultiPass, students are taught to review textbook reading materials three times, first to "survey," second to "size up," and third to "sort out."

During the *survey* pass, students familiarize themselves with the organization of the text chapter, including the title, beginning paragraphs, subheadings, summary paragraphs, and the major ideas. Teach students to make associations with the information in this chapter and previously read chapters. Finally, teach students to summarize the information in the chapter in their own words.

For the *size-up* pass, teach students more study techniques to use when reviewing the chapter:

- Identify highlighted information.
- Read the questions at the end of the chapter.

PEARSON
myeducationlab

Go to MyEducationLab, select the topic *Instructional Practices and Learning Strategies*, and go to the Activities and Applications section. As you complete the simulation entitled "Using Learning Strategies," compare and contrast the strategy presented in the simulation with those discussed here in the text.

Steps in Learning Strategy Model

Step 1: Pretest learners and have students make a commitment to learning.

Step 2: Present and describe the learning strategy.

Step 3: Model strategy usage using think-alouds and provide initial student practice with the strategy.

Step 4: Provide additional rehearsal and verbal elaboration practice with the strategy.

Step 5: Provide controlled practice and feedback with the strategy (guided practice).

Step 6: Provide advanced practice and feedback with the strategy (independent practice).

Step 7: Provide positive feedback for learning strategy and enlist support for generalization of self-use of strategy.

Step 8: Provide generalization and maintenance training, support, and feedback.

Note: From "An Instructional Model for Teaching Students How to Learn," by D. D. Deshler & J. B. Schumaker, 1988, in J. L. Graden, J. E. Zins, & M. J. Curtis (Eds.), *Alternative Instructional Delivery Systems: Enhancing Instructional Options for All Students*, Washington, DC: National Association of School Psychologists.

- Make up questions from statements.
- Skim text to find answers to questions.
- Paraphrase answers without looking back at the chapter.

Finally, for the *sort-out* phase, teach students to test themselves on the information in the chapter. In addition, throughout all three phases of instruction, students can use self-monitoring procedures to ensure they have completed all necessary steps, including appropriate attribution. An example attribution statement to teach students is: "Using MultiPass should help me do better on the next test."

IT FITS   IT FITS was developed to help students with learning difficulties remember important information from science textbooks (King-Sears, Mercer, & Sindelar, 1992). IT FITS is an acronym for steps in creating mnemonic keyword strategies. King-Sears et al. taught students with learning disabilities to use the IT FITS strategy:

Identify the term (example: "*ptero-*" as in "pterosaur" or "pteranodon").

Tell the definition of the term ("winged").

Find a key word ("tire").

Imagine the definition doing something with the key word ("a tire with wings attached").

Think about the definition doing something with the key word.

Study what you imagined until you know the definition (*ptero-* → tire → tire with wings → "winged") (King-Sears et al., 1992; see also King-Sears & Mooney, 2004).

One student reported using the strategy to learn the meaning of *acoustic*. After *identifying* the term, he *told* the definition of the term ("having to do with hearing"), then *found* a key word ("stick"). Next, he *imagined* the definition doing something with the key word, by considering the stick that his bandleader used, which made a noise when it was tapped. He then *thought* about this definition, and *studied* what he imagined until he remembered the key word. Results indicated that students learned more science vocabulary when they used and implemented the IT FITS strategy.

TRAVEL   Boyle and Weishaar (1997) taught students with learning disabilities to use the **TRAVEL** strategy for developing their own cognitive organizers to improve their comprehension and recall of text content:

Topic: Write down the topic and circle it.

Read: Read a paragraph.

Ask: Ask what the main idea and three details are and write them down.

Verify: Verify the main idea by circling it and linking its details.

Examine: Examine the next paragraph and Ask and Verify again.

Link: When finished with the story, link all circles. (p. 230)

Students who used the TRAVEL strategy outperformed control-condition students—as well as students who had studied an expert-generated cognitive organizer—on tests of literal and inferential recall.

Self-Monitoring Strategies   You can also train students to use a self-monitoring strategy as they encounter headings and subheadings in content textbooks. For example, train students to turn the heading, "The Election of 1976," into a question, such as, "Who won the election of 1976?" After reading the section, students should ask themselves, "Can I answer the question?" and then circle "yes" or "no" on a self-monitoring worksheet. If they circled "no," train students to find the answer by, for example, (a) rereading the text, (b) checking their vocabulary understanding, (c) examining illustrations, tables, or figures, or (d) writing down questions to ask the teacher. Berkeley, Marshak, Mastropieri, and Scruggs (2008) trained middle-school students to use this strategy in inclusive history classes, and reported that students trained in this self-monitoring strategy scored much higher on content tests than students who were simply told to read the passages and remember as much as possible.

STRATEGIES FOR
ADAPTING TEXTBOOK MATERIALS

Because textbooks are adopted for entire school districts, it is inevitable that the reading level of some books may be too difficult, and thus inaccessible, for some students. Some suggestions to help promote learning in these cases are presented in Figure 15.6.

Other students may have difficulties because they are learning to speak English at the same time they are learning academic content. Echevarria and Graves (2003) described a model of sheltered instruction to support content learning of students for English language learners. This model is described in the *Diversity in the Classroom* feature.

PROMOTE PREREADING AND POSTREADING STRATEGIES
Before assigning independent textbook reading, explain the purpose of the assignment. For example, you could say, "When you finish reading the section of your U.S. History text tonight, you will all be able to tell me the causes of the Civil War tomorrow at the beginning of class."

Provide organizers as overviews of the text structures and the content they will be studying. Figure 15.7 provides an example spatially organized template from Inspiration Software that allows you or your students to create visual displays of historical events. Information from the visual display can be converted and printed in an outline format.

Timelines can be constructed to demonstrate graphically the sequence of important events, for example, the events leading up to the Civil War. Timelines may or may not include pictures or symbols, but do contain a chronological sequence in a graphic format. Design, develop, and show timelines that present detailed events that will be covered in the next social studies chapter.

Students who are not reading at grade level can benefit from listening to textbooks on tapes, which are often available from the textbook publisher.

Provide alternative text formats.
- Use published audiotapes of texts or develop your own.
- Use computerized text with audio components.
- Acquire enlarged-type versions of materials.
- As appropriate, use braille versions of materials.
- Assign peers to read text.

Develop or plan for use of alternative curricular materials.
- Revise or rewrite text, deleting higher-level concepts and vocabulary; insert guided questions to use with simplified text.
- Prepare and distribute study guides, outlines, or guided notes.
- Prepare and distribute mnemonic illustrations.
- Supplement with software focused on simpler presentation of concepts.
- Use high-interest, low-vocabulary materials.
- Use activities-based materials (see next section).
- Shorten reading and writing assignments.
- Develop pictorial versions of text materials.

Modify teaching presentations.
- Preteach difficult concepts and vocabulary.
- Provide concrete examples.
- Activate prior knowledge.
- Reduce amount of new information.
- Provide illustrative aids and spatial organizers.
- Use study guides.
- Encourage active participation.
- Schedule regular meetings with special needs students.
- Require frequent verbal responses to check for understanding.
- Provide additional review sessions.
- Use trade books as supplements.
- Use audiovisual supplements.
- Use flashcards for studying.
- Have students maintain journals containing new concepts and vocabulary.

Use peers (or parent volunteers) as assistants.
- To read or listen to reading.
- As study partners.
- To assist with writing tasks.

Figure 15.6 Suggestions for Adapting and Using Textbooks

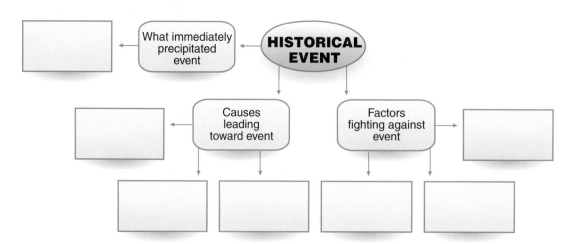

Figure 15.7 Template for Creating Visual Display for Historical Event
Note: Reprinted with permission from Inspiration Software, Portland, OR.

Content-Area Instruction for Diverse Learners

 English language learners require additional supports in content-area classes, referred to as *sheltered instruction* (Echevarria & Graves, 2003). Sheltered instruction involves assisting with learning English while teaching content areas including the concepts and vocabulary of science, social studies, or math. It is important to have language objectives in addition to the content-area objectives. Echevarria and Graves (2003) indicate that sheltered instruction shares components of effective instruction (see Chapter 6) but in addition adds the following:

☐ identifying language proficiency levels;
☐ adapting speech, language, and vocabulary to proficiency levels;
☐ adapting content to students' language proficiency;
☐ providing sufficient response wait time;
☐ providing supplemental materials;
☐ providing examples relevant to students' cultural and linguistic backgrounds.

Other features that share elements of effective instruction include using clear language, providing consistent review, and using concrete, meaningful lessons with practice and multiple interaction opportunities.

Present difficult concepts or vocabulary words to students with disabilities in class before having them read about the information independently. Use some of the suggestions described in the MultiPass, semantic feature analysis, or mnemonic strategies sections to introduce and teach these concepts first. Demonstrate how students can use context clues, glossaries, and dictionaries to figure out new words they will encounter in the text. Have students practice these words at home and school to become familiar with the new words before hearing them for the first time in class. Figure 15.8 contains a partial vocabulary checklist.

Vocabulary and Phrases

<u>Direction:</u> Place a checkmark in the box if the student reads and defines the word correctly.

Chapter 4: Ecosystems   S = At School   H = At Home

	S	H	S	H	S	H	S	H	S	H
Vocabulary Words & Phrases	Mon	Mon	Tues	Tues	Wed	Wed	Thur	Thur	Fri	Fri
ecosystem										
producer										
consumer										
decomposer										
community										
predator										
prey										
parasite										
host										

Figure 15.8 Sample Vocabulary Checklist
Note: From unpublished materials by M. A. Mastropieri & T. E. Scruggs, 1996, Fairfax, VA: Graduate School of Education, George Mason University. Reprinted with permission.

Use Postreading Strategies   When textbook reading assignments have been completed, provide additional assistance to ensure content mastery, including reviewing major points in class, providing additional practice with peer tutors, providing extra help sessions, reviewing study guides, directing students to tell or write summaries, and providing practice tests. This additional review on the most important content can lead to greater academic success.

MAKE ADAPTATIONS FOR STUDENTS WITH VISUAL IMPAIRMENTS OR SEVERE READING PROBLEMS

As Mr. Norland discovered of Jeffrey in the scenario at the beginning of this chapter, reading problems can significantly inhibit science learning. Students with visual impairments or severe reading problems will need to have written text available to them in alternative formats. Alternative formats include taped versions, computerized versions containing audio components, larger-print versions, or braille formats for students with very limited vision (see also Chapter 13). The Kurzweil Reader is also useful for reading and interacting with text. Services are available to assist with completing braille versions of materials. Some special educators can make copies of class materials accessible in braille and raised formats.

PROMOTE LEARNING WITH CLASSWIDE PEER TUTORING

Classwide peer tutoring can be an excellent way for all students to gain extra practice on the most important content of science and social studies units. For example, Maheady, Sacca, and Harper (1988) employed classwide peer tutoring in inclusive 10th-grade social studies classrooms. Maheady et al. developed 30-item weekly study guides for the most important content of each chapter. Students tutored each other in pairs for about 30 minutes per day, 2 days per week, using items from the study guides (e.g., "What does imperialism mean?", "What is the governmental structure of the Communist Party?"). When participating in the peer tutoring condition, students scored over 21 percentage points higher than they scored before the intervention began. More recently, Mastropieri, Scruggs, Spencer, and Fontana (2003) implemented classwide peer tutoring using reading comprehension strategies described in Chapter 8 ("Who or what is the section about?" "What is happening to the who or what?" "Write a summary sentence") and summary sheets in 10th-grade World History classes, in units on the world wars. Students who had participated in tutoring outperformed students who had studied with guided notes, on chapter tests, unit tests, and end-of-year tests.

Spencer, Scruggs, and Mastropieri (2003) implemented a similar reading comprehension strategy using classwide peer tutoring with middle-school students with emotional or behavioral disabilities studying social studies content (history and civics). Students read textbooks to each other in pairs and questioned each other about factual text content ("What was the Teapot Dome scandal?"). Results revealed that students scored about 15 percentage points higher on weekly quizzes and chapter tests in the tutoring condition, and were observed to have higher rates of academic on-task behavior. One teacher expressed surprise that the tutoring pairs generally interacted well, but noted the value of careful student pairings.

Mastropieri, Scruggs, and Marshak (2008) implemented classwide peer tutoring in inclusive seventh-grade U.S. History classes. Teachers developed "fact sheets" of the most important textbook content to be remembered (e.g., "What was the position of the United States at the beginning of World War I?"; "What was the *Lusitania* and why was it important?"). Partners questioned each other on critical information using materials aligned with the high-stakes testing content and took practice tests covering the information. All parents were trained to use the Web-based *BlackBoard* program to access and use the same tutoring materials at home. Findings indicated that students scored higher in peer tutoring than in control conditions and the parents learned to use *BlackBoard* and the tutoring materials effectively. Although the materials were the same for all students, instruction can be differentiated in that all students can practice until they reach mastery.

Classwide peer tutoring has also been used in inclusive high school chemistry classes (Mastropieri, Scruggs, & Graetz, 2005). Students were assigned to tutoring pairs and provided with materials containing relevant information (e.g., exothermic and endothermic reactions, enthalpy, the periodic table of elements, alkali metals, halogens, molarity, Avogadro's number). Students questioned each other on the information (e.g., "What is molarity"). If the question was answered correctly, the tutor asked for further elaborations on the content to promote comprehension (e.g., "What else is important about molarity?"). If the question was incorrectly answered, strategies such as the keyword method (see Chapter 10) were provided, as shown in

What is molarity?

Concentration of a solute in a solution; moles per liter.

If your partner is correct, go to $\Rightarrow$
If your partner doesn't know the answer, review the strategy.

Strategy: Think of the word "moles" for mole, and remember the picture of a number of moles in solution, to remember molarity is the concentration of a solute in a solution, in moles per liter.

Then ask: *What is the strategy to remember molarity?*

Then ask again: *What does molarity mean?*

$\Rightarrow$ Then ask:
What else is important about molarity?

[Answers include: molarity is a ratio, moles of solute divided by liters of solution]

Figure 15.9 What Is Molarity?

Note: From "Teaching Tutorial: Mnemonic Instruction," by T. Scruggs & M. A. Mastropieri, 2002, *TeachingLD.org*, p. 19. Copyright 2002 by the Division for Learning Disabilities. Reprinted with permission.

Figure 15.9. When the item was answered correctly, further elaboration was prompted. Results indicated that students in the tutoring condition outperformed comparison students in both recall and comprehension of chemistry content. In this case, instruction was differentiated in that students used elaborative strategies only when they were needed, although materials overall were the same for all students. For a similar example with social studies content, see the *Research Highlight*.

Differentiated Curriculum Enhancements You can implement differentiated instruction through creation of activities of different difficulty levels, implemented by tutoring pairs. Mastropieri et al. (2006) developed materials for the "Scientific Method" unit for inclusive middle-school science classes. For example, for the "Experimental Design" activity, students read research scenarios (e.g., an experiment of plant growth) and matched independent (e.g., fertilizer) with dependent variables (e.g., plant height) (Level 1); independently produced the variables and hypotheses, with prompting when needed (Level 2); and finally, produced variables and hypotheses without prompting (Level 3). Since all students moved through all levels of all activities, there was no stigma associated with the lower-level materials. Students in classes

Peer Tutoring in Inclusive Social Studies Classes

 Secondary social studies courses contain a remarkable amount of factual information that students must assimilate in order to succeed in school and to pass state high-stakes tests. Many students with disabilities have great difficulty mastering this content. Since many students with disabilities today receive social studies instruction in inclusive classes, strategies must be employed that accommodate all learners. Marshak (2008) implemented a peer tutoring intervention designed to deliver appropriate instruction to all students in inclusive history classes, and to maximize student engagement. Eight seventh-grade classrooms, containing 202 students without disabilities and 42 students with disabilities, were assigned at random to experimental and comparison conditions. The comparison classrooms received high-quality instruction in American history, with methods and materials including PowerPoint presentations, lecture, mapping activities, study guides for tests, graphic organizers, primary source documents, video clips, simulations, and fill-in-the-blank worksheets. The experimental

classrooms included, in addition, classwide peer tutoring methods. Instructional time was equated for both conditions.

Teachers determined the most important content for the three units being taught (industrialization, progressive era, imperialism), and tutoring materials were developed for students to question each other on the content. Each item was associated with a mnemonic picture (see Chapter 10) to help students remember, but these were only employed when students failed to recall the target content. When a student answered correctly, the tutor was instructed to provide positive feedback and move on to the next item. If an item was answered incorrectly, or there was no response in 3 seconds, the tutor showed the mnemonic picture and prompted the student to use the picture as a memory aid. For example, to remember that John D. Rockefeller controlled much of the oil business, a mnemonic picture was shown of oil being poured on a *rock* (key word for Rockefeller). Tutees were taught, when asked about Rockefeller, to think of the picture of the rock, remember the oil being poured on rock, and respond with the correct answer. This procedure

was implemented about 2 days per week for about 20 minutes each day.

All students were pre- and posttested on the content of the three units. Results indicated that experimental-condition classrooms retained substantially more social studies content than comparison condition classrooms. Students with and without disabilities both gained similarly from the intervention. Survey data suggested that students and teachers alike enjoyed the intervention and felt it promoted learning for all students. This study demonstrated that classwide peer tutoring with differentiated mnemonic materials can significantly improve learning in middle-school social studies classes.

QUESTIONS FOR REFLECTION

1. Why do you think students would enjoy classwide peer tutoring more than whole-class activities?
2. Do you think students should be allowed to choose their own tutoring partners? Why or why not?
3. Why do you think, in this investigation, that students with and without disabilities learned the same amount in the tutoring condition?

employing these differentiated curriculum enhancements significantly outperformed students in comparison conditions. Simpkins, Mastropieri, and Scruggs (in press) found that similar materials using game-like formats (e.g., Jeopardy, Concentration, Sorry) on two levels (Level 1: identification; Level 2: production) significantly increased learning of Earth/Space and Light and Sound units in inclusive fifth-grade classes.

Adapting Activities-Oriented Approaches in Science and Social Studies

Rather than relying primarily on textbooks, you can develop conceptual understanding of science and social studies with an activities-oriented approach to teaching. Research has indicated that activities-oriented approaches frequently produce superior learning in general education science and social studies classes (Chiappetta & Koballa, 2006; Parker, 2008). Some research indicates that activities-oriented approaches may be beneficial for students with disabilities when sufficient support is provided (Mastropieri et al., 1998; Scruggs, Mastropieri, Bakken, & Brigham, 1993). Some of the advantages of activities-oriented approaches to science and social studies education is that they de-emphasize vocabulary learning and learning dependent on the reading of textbooks (areas of relative difficulty for many students with special needs). In addition, activities provide direct interaction with concrete, meaningful materials (areas of relative strength for many students with special needs). Two potential disadvantages to an activities approach are difficulty adjusting to the less-structured atmosphere of activities-oriented instruction and the fact that some students may exhibit difficulty with the inductive thinking often associated with such instruction (Mastropieri, Scruggs, Boon, & Carter, 2001).

Students with special needs may require adaptations and support when undertaking activities-oriented approaches to science and social studies learning (Heller, 2005). However, there are many different types of activities, and these different activities may require different adaptations. The following sections describe adaptations that may help you more effectively include your students with disabilities in science and social studies activities.

STRATEGIES FOR
ADAPTING SCIENCE ACTIVITIES

Students with disabilities can benefit greatly from the authentic learning experiences afforded by science activities, and many science activities can be adapted to accommodate special learning needs (Scruggs & Mastropieri, 2007). When planning activities-oriented instruction in science, consider both general accommodations as well as adaptations targeted to the specific disability area and the specific science activity. Both general and specific adaptations are described in the sections that follow. Many of these suggestions are described in more detail in Heller (2005), Kumar, Ramasamy, and Stefanich (2001); Mastropieri and Scruggs (1993); McGinnis and Stefanich (2007); Pence, Workman, and Riecke (2003); and Scruggs and Mastropieri (1994, 1995a, 1995b).

DEVELOP GENERAL LABORATORY PROCEDURES AND PRECAUTIONS Many adaptations can be implemented that enable students with all types of disabilities to be more active participants in science. As you think through the activity process, review the PASS variables (see Chapter 6): *P*rioritize all objectives and determine whether all objectives are necessary (for example, are lab activities such as slide-staining important objectives, or is observing cellular structure the most important objective?). Then, *a*dapt materials, the environment, or instructional procedures as needed to ensure success for all students. Use the *S*CREAM variables (e.g., structure, clarity, redundancy) to maximize the effectiveness of your teaching. Finally, *s*ystematically evaluate whether your instruction has been successful. After considering these PASS variables, consider a number of general procedures to address diverse learning needs.

List Rules Explain, post, and strictly enforce laboratory rules. Speak privately with students when necessary. Have a "cooling-off" place in the room designated for any students who lose control of their behavior. Generously use praise to reinforce following of the science lab rules.

Ensure Safety Because safety is a major concern when using scientific equipment and materials, stabilize all scientific equipment and materials to avoid unnecessary spills. Velcro can be used to attach lighter objects to tables or trays, while string and trays can be used to hold larger and heavier objects. Use large, clear labels on all equipment and materials, including braille labels when needed for students with visual impairments. Be sure there is sufficient space for easy mobility and access to materials around the room and lab tables for all students, including those with physical and visual disabilities.

Science instruction is more meaningful when students can explore science concepts using hands-on materials.

Give Clear Directions Be sure directions are clearly communicated, are parallel in construction, and follow a step-by-step process. List directions on the board or overhead projector so students can refer to them easily. Color code tasks by order of importance. For instance, tasks written in red must be completed by all students, while tasks written in other colors may be less important. Provide adapted lab booklets that contain extra lines or spaces for writing or drawing examples of specimens. Make braille and textured versions of lab booklets when necessary. Furnish checklists of what needs to be accomplished in lab to assist students who have difficulties completing longer tasks. Frequently check on student progress during lab activities. If students are working in cooperative groups, verify that students with disabilities are active participants rather than observers while their peers complete all activities.

Enhance Stimulus Value Implement closed-circuit television (CCTV) to ensure that students with vision problems can see all phenomena being observed in labs. CCTV can show enlarged versions of anything being studied. Acquire extra lighting and magnifying lenses to help visibility when needed during lab activities. For example, a "Big Eye Lamp" (Big Eye Lamp, Inc.) is available that consists of a high-intensity light with a large magnifying lens attached. Use of such a device can enhance viewing of small objects for all students, but may be especially beneficial for students with low vision. It may also be helpful for students with less-well-developed fine motor skills, for example, when they remove small animal bones from an owl pellet. Use videotapes and videodisks to enforce relevant concepts and provide redundancy; use or create descriptive video presentations for students who cannot see a television monitor clearly. Acquire extra microphones, stethoscopes, or tuning forks that can help students with hearing impairments hear or feel vibrations of various activities. For example, tuning forks can be placed in water and students with hearing impairments can observe the sound waves in the water.

Prepare for Spills Prepare areas for spills by having plenty of clean-up materials handy. Place tarps on the floor before engaging in activities that may result in spills. This will save the floor or carpets and help keep custodians on your side. Have students bring in extra large shirts that can be worn as "lab coats" that will protect their clothing in case of spills. Put felt on desk surfaces that are particularly slippery to help stabilize materials. Use trays, slatted trays, or small tubs to hold smaller items on students' desks. Anchor these trays or receptacles with bags of sand or marbles to reinforce and stabilize their positions. Then trays and tubs will reduce the area of any potential spills.

MAKE ADAPTATIONS FOR TEACHING LAB SKILLS All students, including those with disabilities, benefit greatly from participating in lab activities. To ensure successful participation, prepare activities with tailor-made adaptations, as discussed next.

Measuring and Pouring Obtain adaptive equipment for measuring and pouring activities. The Lawrence Hall of Science at the University of California at Berkeley has many materials available to help students with visual and physical disabilities. Some of these materials were developed for the curriculum materials Science Activities for the Visually Impaired/Science Enrichment for the Physically Handicapped (SAVI/SELPH) and Full Option Science System (FOSS; available through Delta Education). All of their adapted materials include enlarged labels in print and braille formats. Some specific adapted materials include enlarged type and braille on enlarged rulers and number lines, enlarged syringe-like devices for measuring, enlarged graduated cylinders for measuring and pouring activities, and larger balance-scales containing a plastic guide that students with visual or cognitive impairments can touch to determine whether the sides of the scale are equivalent. Have students use "scooper" devices, for example, a plastic quart bottle with the bottom removed, for obtaining water from larger receptacles, rather than obtaining it directly from the tap.

Balancing and Weighing Obtain simpler and larger scales and balances for weighing materials. A spring scale that is suitable for students with visual impairments is made available by the American Printing House for the Blind. Other measuring devices such as measuring wheels that click at each rotation to assist with measuring larger areas are available from the American Foundation for the Blind. Devise your own measuring adaptations to suit the activities in your class. For example, when repeatedly using a specific measure on rulers, place a piece of tape or rubber band on the exact measure required to help students with motor or cognitive difficulties be more precise with measuring. Substitute three-dimensional articles made of different textures so students with visual impairments can feel objects that others are able to see to explore weight, texture, and simple measurements.

Charting/Graphing and Recording Data　Most activities in science and many in social studies require students to record their observations on some type of chart, graph, pictorial, or in narrative format. Students with disabilities may require some preinstruction with the specific charting or recording procedures for your class. Prefamiliarize students with various types of charts and graphs, such as graph paper, bar charts, frequency charts, and histograms, using very concrete examples. Some of the STC (Science and Technology for Children, available from Carolina Biological Supply Company) and the AIMS curriculum materials (Activities for Integrating Math and Science) contain some excellent lessons for teachers to use to teach preskills in graphing, charting, and recording data. Try using some very familiar topics and construct class graphs, such as students' favorite television programs.

Use larger graph paper for students with motor or visual difficulties. Label charts and graphs or use paper that has guidelines for students with reading and writing difficulties. Replace pencil or pen markings on charts or graphs with felt circles or squares, or some other textured materials, such as Velcro, stickers, guide strips from computer paper, braille dots, or tactile dots, so students with visual and cognitive disabilities can feel the differences in the types of items charted and the quantities associated with each item. Make three-dimensional graphs using clay, tiles, golf tees, pushpins, yarn, chicken wire, and other materials to help students' comprehension. Three-dimensional graphs in larger formats can be more easily made by students with fine motor difficulties. Students with visual impairments may record observations by drawing on a screen board (crayon on paper over a screen), using clay models, or using braille numbers and raised lines.

Some computer programs, such as Microsoft Word™, make charts and graphs and may be especially helpful for students with disabilities. In addition, many computer programs collect, record, and graph data, as do graphing calculators. Finally, consider grouping students with and without disabilities to record and graph data cooperatively. Peers may be able to assist with some of the more difficult components of the task. However, verify that all students are completing their share of the recording activities and are comprehending relevant concepts.

STRATEGIES FOR
ADAPTING LIFE SCIENCE ACTIVITIES

Life science strands include living things, ecology, cells, genetics, and evolution. By considering the following adaptations, students with special needs may become more actively involved during science.

ADAPT PLANT GROWTH AND DEVELOPMENT ACTIVITIES

- Because most household plants die from overwatering, and small fish are frequently overfed, set up a strict schedule for watering and feeding, using specific amounts of water or fish food. Water syringes may help students deliver the precise amount of water needed by the plant, and food portions can be prepared ahead of time.

- After planting seeds, plan other science activities to do while plants are growing. Since some students may have difficulty sustaining interest or attention over longer time periods, consider using plants that grow and develop quickly. For example, beans normally grow faster and flower sooner than peas. Further, consider acquiring Wisconsin Fast Plants (Wisconsin Fast Plants Program), which develop much faster than most plants.

- To help students plant seeds at a standard depth, wrap a rubber band around a dowel or pencil for use as a depth gauge.

- To help students directly observe root structure, grow plants in clear plastic baggies, or in hydroponic (all-water) containers. Students with visual impairments can also be encouraged to feel the sunlight in relation to a plant, and feel the effect of the sunlight on the development of the plant.

ADAPT ACTIVITIES INVOLVING ANIMALS

- Carefully consider the purpose of acquiring classroom animals. Many schools have specific restrictions regarding animals, so it is important to first check out these policies before acquiring any animals.

- Any animals' characteristics or peculiarities need to be noted. For example, hamsters are largely nocturnal, and may be less active during school hours. Reptiles must be kept warm (e.g., with special heaters), or they will not eat, and may catch "colds" and die. Newts' water must be kept clean, or they may not be able to detect the presence of food placed in their tank. Crayfish are prone to diseases that may spread rapidly to other crayfish. Isolate crayfish for 5 days, check for any sign of red tinge to the underside, and quarantine affected crawfish.

- When ordering animals from supply houses, make sure the outdoor climate is appropriate for the animal being shipped, and be certain it will arrive at a time when it can be immediately attended to by an adult. For example, ordering a butterfly kit in the winter may mean releasing them when the weather is too cold for survival.

- Some animals (e.g., reptiles) require live food, so consider the effect this may have on students in your class. Some students with emotional handicaps may react strongly to some animals, or to the behaviors of some animals. Finally, some students may be disposed to abuse animals in captivity, so be certain to promote an attitude of respect toward living things, and ensure that captive animals will be kept safe.

ADAPT ANATOMY ACTIVITIES

- A variety of three-dimensional models is available from supply companies, such as the Carolina Biological Supply Company. The *Visible Man/Visible Woman* also provides concrete information on anatomy. However, be careful that too much valuable instructional time is not lost on assembling models versus learning anatomy concepts.

- Students with hearing impairments who cannot use a stethoscope may be able to feel a pulse at the carotid or brachial arteries. Students with physical disabilities who cannot run in place can substitute another activity (such as raising or lowering the body from the arms of a wheelchair) to increase heartbeat.

- For students who do not have a good sense of their own bodies (e.g., younger students, students with cognitive or intellectual disabilities, or some students with emotional disturbance), use photographs, videotapes, and mirrors to reinforce body image.

ADAPT MICROSCOPE ACTIVITIES When acquiring microscopes, consider the Brock Magiscope® (Brock Optical). This sturdy microscope is simple to use and maintains sufficient light even when it is moved around (see also the Wolfe® Wonderscope™, available from Carolina Biological Supply). The Big Screen Microscope (available from Carolina Biological Supply) offers 20× and 40× magnification on a 7-inch screen. Digital microscope images can also be displayed on large monitors for students with visual or physical impairments, or can be printed from the screen and made into a three-dimensional image. When microscopes are not available, or their use is not practical, acquire large color pictures or three-dimensional models of the microscopic objects being studied (see Scruggs & Mastropieri, 1994). For example, Carolina Biological Supply Company supplies

Video presentations of microscopic specimens can be a valuable experience for all students.

three-dimentional plant and animal cells that present cross-sectional layers of cell structure. Many sites on the Internet provide relevant photographs and video presentations of microscopic organisms.

CONSIDER HEALTH ISSUES   Students who have asthma or serious allergies may react negatively to dander in animal fur, or to molds or pollens in plants. Consider the health needs of all students before including specific animals or plants in the classroom.

STRATEGIES FOR
ADAPTING EARTH SCIENCE ACTIVITIES

Earth science covers meteorology, astronomy, geology, and oceanography. Many relevant activities can be conducted in the classroom to enhance comprehension in these areas. Unlike life sciences, students may be unfamiliar with many of the concepts and terms used, so be sure that relevant vocabulary is being learned.

ADAPT WEATHER ACTIVITIES

- Some concepts, such as humidity or air pressure, may be more difficult for younger students or students with intellectual impairments. Use students' prior knowledge of, for example, hot showers versus dry oven heat, and traveling in an airplane or a fast elevator, to make the concepts more meaningful.
- Place a barometer in a glass container with a rubber top to demonstrate changes as a function of pressure generated by pushing or pulling on the rubber top.
- Available from the Lawrence Hall of Science are adapted thermometers, adapted graduated cylinders and beakers, and tactile floating scales (for measuring rainfall) to assist students with visual impairments.

ADAPT ROCKS AND MINERALS ACTIVITIES

- The FOSS materials feature an activity titled "Mock Rocks." The teacher creates "rocks" composed of such ingredients as water, flour, aquarium gravel, crushed oyster shells, and food coloring. Students disassemble these rocks into component parts, enforcing the concept that rocks are composed of many other components. Activities such as this may be helpful for students with cognitive or intellectual impairments.
- Models of sedimentary rock can be created from differently colored layers of sand or gravel, in white glue and water, or plaster of Paris. Use of alternate layers can represent the layers of rock built up over time.
- Many specimens and models of rocks and minerals are available from supply companies. Generally, larger, loose specimens are preferable to smaller examples glued on a card. Students with visual impairments should be able to feel many properties of minerals, including heft, cleavage (see, especially, mica), fracture, and crystal faces. If students feel a specific place on a mineral before a scratch test, it may be possible to feel the scratch. It may be more difficult for students with visual impairments to detect color, luster, and streak, but students with some vision may detect these properties with illumination or magnification.

STRATEGIES FOR
ADAPTING PHYSICAL SCIENCE ACTIVITIES

Physical science activities can include sound, magnetism and electricity, force and motion, light, and powders, mixtures, and solutions.

ADAPT PHYSICS OF SOUND ACTIVITIES

- Students can observe and compare sounds made by different objects, and conduct experiments on variations in tension, thickness, and length of strings, cords, and rubber bands. Students may also examine the effect of sound-producing devices in vacuum chambers.

- Students with hearing impairments may have specific difficulties with this content area. For students with some hearing, amplification may be helpful. It may also be helpful to ensure that no other sound is detectable in the classroom other than the one being observed.

- Students with severe hearing loss may in many cases be able to feel the vibrations in different sound-producing objects. Carefully place tuning forks in water after being struck to demonstrate the vibrations in water. When using "waterphone bottle" (bottles filled with different levels of water) activities, indicate the level of the water with rubber bands placed around the bottles for students with visual impairments.

ADAPT MAGNETISM AND ELECTRICITY ACTIVITIES

- Students can make simple connections from batteries to small motors and lightbulbs, identify conductors and insulators, and create series and parallel circuits, electromagnets, and telegraphs. Some science activities encourage students to find insulators and conductors by connecting circuits. Monitor these activities carefully and be certain that classroom wiring and outlets are inaccessible.

- The SAVI/SELPH science materials include electricity boards that are made to be easy to work with, including alligator clips and battery holders. These boards may be beneficial for students with visual and physical disabilities, as well as any students who lack well-developed fine motor skills. For students with more severe physical disabilities, wires can be permanently attached to most connections.

- For students who cannot see whether lightbulbs are lighted, substitute small electric motors, which can be heard when they are connected to a battery. When using electric motors with students with hearing impairments, attach a small paper flag to the rotor, so the movement can be observed when the power is connected.

- When constructing telegraphs, connect a lightbulb to flash, so that the message can be observed by students with hearing impairments.

- Students with intellectual disabilities and younger students may have less-well-developed preconceptions about electricity—for example, the battery as a power source, the current that travels through a conductor, and the concept of a "circuit." Pretraining on some of these concepts may be helpful.

ADAPT FORCE AND MOTION ACTIVITIES

- Force and motion activities include investigations with simple machines (such as levers and pulleys), pendulum motion, and rubber-band-propelled airplanes. The concepts presented in force and motion activities are more abstract than they are in some other subjects; therefore, some concept-enhancement activities may be helpful for students with lower cognitive or intellectual functioning. Provide and practice many examples from students' experiences of new concepts as they are investigated.

- See-saws, hammers, rakes, and crowbars are good examples of levers; ramps and slides are good examples of inclined planes; playground swings and pendulum clocks are good examples of pendulums. Demonstrate how the principles learned in class generally apply to these more familiar objects.

ADAPT POWDERS, MIXTURES, AND SOLUTIONS ACTIVITIES

- An important first consideration for creating mixtures and solutions—and examining chemical properties and observing chemical changes such as saturation, concentration, and separation—is safety. Make certain that all students, including students with disabilities or other special needs, are familiar with specific rules about handling relevant materials. Such rules may include the following: never taste anything, clean up spilled substances immediately, avoid direct contact with the substances unless supervised, avoid blowing (or sneezing) into the powders, and use heat sources only with teacher supervision.

- Mixing substances together often produces some sound, such as fizzing. Encourage students to employ their hearing when making observations. Stethoscopes or microphones can be used to amplify the sound.

- Students with visual impairments can be encouraged to feel powders and substances that are not harmful to touch. Additionally, students can feel paper or other filters before and after mixtures and solutions have passed through them.

- For students with physical disabilities and fine or gross motor difficulties, determine whether measuring and pouring is an essential part of that particular activity. If not, perhaps these students can concentrate more on the more central aspects of the activity and rely on peers for measuring and pouring liquids. If measuring and pouring liquid is important and spilling is a concern, pour inside a sink or in a larger container. Practice with smaller quantities first.

STRATEGIES FOR
ADAPTING SOCIAL STUDIES ACTIVITIES

Social studies activities can address motivational problems and negative reactions to independent textbook-based assignments for students who have problems with reading or writing. These activities might include producing plays, reenacting historical events, creating maps, preparing foods from other cultures and historical periods, making historical or cultural dioramas, and interacting with experts on cultural events or historical periods. Students can also engage in discussion or debate about current issues or historical events. Finally, students can participate in field trips to museums or historical sites. Overall, social studies activities ordinarily may not involve such a wide range of different materials and equipment as activities in science, and therefore fewer overall specific adaptations may be considered. General recommendations are noted in the following section, and are also found in Fontana (2004), O'Brien (2000), and Parker (2008).

SUPPLEMENT TEXTBOOK-BASED INSTRUCTION As suggested throughout this book, whole-class teaching devoted solely to textbooks and worksheets is not an optimal way of addressing the diverse needs of students. Instead, use concrete activities, video presentations, student projects, and technological applications whenever possible. For a description of software that can supplement textbooks in science and social studies, see the *Technology Highlight* feature.

Because disability awareness is very much a social issue, plan disability awareness issues as a component of the social studies curriculum. Many significant historical characters either had disabilities themselves or were very concerned with promoting rights of individuals with disabilities, for example, Alexander Graham Bell, Franklin Roosevelt, Dorothy Dix, and Julia Ward Howe (see, for example, the Website of the Disability Social History Project).

MAKE ADAPTATIONS FOR SPECIFIC SOCIAL STUDIES ACTIVITIES
- When planning meals from other cultures or historical periods, consider whether any of your students have specific food allergies.

- Role-play and reenactment activities can be supplemented with videotape presentations of the events being role-played, to enhance understanding of the activity. Keep in mind students' special needs when assigning roles; for example, in reenactments, plan or adapt appropriate roles for students with mobility impairments.

- In geography, relief maps may be helpful not only for students with low vision, but for other students who may need assistance understanding the representative function of maps. Braille maps, raised globes, and illuminated globes are also available to assist students with visual impairments.

Technology Highlight

Inspiration and Kidspiration Software

Spatial organizers help make content more concrete and more familiar to students when studying science and social studies. Graphic organizers can be used in almost any content area. Organizers can be used to teach sequence of events and cause-and-effect relationships, to compare and contrast ideas or concepts, or to illustrate hierarchies. Organizers can be used as story webs during the brainstorming phase of writing papers. Graphic organizers can be developed as story maps that include specific details to facilitate comprehension and learning about historical figures, major events, and historical themes. Organizers can be used to develop hierarchies of important-to-least-important content in science and social studies. Graphic organizers can also be used to design study guides to accompany content-area textbooks.

Organizers can take many forms. Inspiration and Kidspiration software provide assistance in developing graphic organizers, webs, brainstorming, diagramming, outlining, and prewriting strategies. Both programs contain numerous templates that can be adapted to suit needs, but also offer the flexibility to allow users to create custom-made templates and designs. Directions for developing organizers appear fairly clear, and students who have some facility with computer use and various software programs typically experience little difficulty in developing organizers independently.

Both Inspiration and Kidspiration have extensive libraries of graphics that can be integrated within diagrams to help make the information even more concrete and meaningful to students. Libraries of content areas, such as animals, foods, shapes, or plants, organize colored graphics. Users can also import graphics of their own from personal photos or from the Internet into Inspiration documents. The technology also offers a wide range of fonts and colors that can be changed during production of an organizer. Various fonts and colors can be used to highlight specific organized details within a single graphic organizer. Both programs have features that enable users to switch from diagrams to outlines and vice versa very easily and are printable in either format. Kidspiration has the unique feature of adding sound to the program such that words entered into the organizers can be "read aloud" for students. Both also have features that allow the versions to be saved into text documents or have applets that can be used with AlphaSmarts and then combined with the full-scale programs on computers.

Inspiration is listed as being appropriate from grades 6 through 12, while Kidspiration is appropriate for K–5. However, both may be adaptable up or down in grade levels depending on the individual ability levels of your students. Sample organizers from each are provided. Contact http://www.inspiration.com for additional information. A 30-day free trial version is available to be downloaded from the Website.

- Prepare students for visitors who come into the classroom to demonstrate, for example, instruments, clothing, lifestyles, and habits from different countries. Some students may need additional preparation in appropriate attending skills, and appropriate questions to ask.

MAKE ADAPTATIONS FOR SPECIAL NEEDS FOR FIELD TRIPS   Field trips can often allow students to obtain first-hand exposure to people and things that they may not be able to experience in the classroom. In addition to museums and zoos, field trips can include visits to historical sites, living farms, archeological sites, weather stations, observatories, and public parks, to name only a few possibilities. Many students with special needs may benefit at least as much as other students, particularly if they have had fewer relevant background experiences, or when they can benefit particularly from the enhanced stimulus value and added concreteness of the experience. Planning and supervision can ensure the field trip is a positive experience.

- Call the facility in advance and inform the staff that you will be attending, and inform them of any special needs your students may have. Advance visitation and planning will help you provide the needed supports for students' needs.

- Set learning objectives before the trip and discuss them with your students.
- Preview the field trip with students, including the procedures that will be involved and the behaviors they will be expected to exhibit. Obtain handouts of the facility, and preview them with the class.
- Practice any difficult or unusual vocabulary that students will encounter on the field trip, to maximize comprehension.
- Discuss the behavioral objectives for the trip, and describe your behavior management plan.
- Assign peer partners, buddies, or helpers when appropriate.
- During the trip, encourage active participation of all students.
- Use familiar and descriptive language whenever possible. Summarize information from the field trip to the students as they participate, and ask them to summarize what they have done.
- When it is not possible to touch or manipulate exhibits, describe sounds, odors, shapes, colors, and textures as much as possible.
- Emphasize multisensory presentations or examples whenever possible.
- Record the field trip, using photographs, videotape, or audiotape. Edit the recordings, and review them with the students after the field trip, emphasizing important objectives.
- Make a book of the field trip for the class, or create a book as a class activity, and review it with students.

Figure 15.10 Teacher Guidelines for Field Trips

- Students with visual impairments may require modifications or adaptations in lighting, printed materials, videotape presentations, seating arrangements, and in any visually presented information.

- Considerations for students with hearing impairments may include the amount of background noise, seating, distance from speaker, interpreters, rate of speaker presentation, effective visual aids, and multisensory experiences, depending on the level of the hearing disability.

- Students with cognitive or intellectual impairments may need preparation or on-site support of teachers, aides, or peers to promote understanding of the information being presented.

- Students with attentional disorders may need assistance focusing attention on relevant exhibits, and efficiently sequencing their visit.

Additional guidelines for teachers to consider on field trips are given in Figure 15.10.

When it is not possible to visit specific locations, consider taking students on "virtual" field trips. Use Internet search engines to identify virtual field trip sites, or consult Cooper and Cooper (2001) for suggestions.

Inquiry Learning in Science and Social Studies

Many advocates of science and social studies instruction strongly endorse inquiry and problem-solving approaches to teaching. Inquiry approaches involve the presentation of questions and problems to students with less direct guidance during the problem-solution stages, and can be a significant component of both activities-oriented and textbook-based learning. Inquiry approaches promote critical thinking skills in addition to increasing content knowledge.

PROMOTE ACTIVE THINKING WITH INQUIRY AND DEBATE   Ferretti, MacArthur, and Okolo (2001) directed an 8-week, project-based unit in American westward expansion. Fifth-grade students were formed into groups of learners with diverse skills and prior knowledge. In these groups, students collected information and analyzed primary and secondary sources to create multimedia presentations. All of the group activities involved oral reading of the evidence and group discussion. Students were taught about perspectives and asked to provide supported answers for questions such as, "What is bias in evidence?", "How do you know a piece of evidence is biased?", and "Why do historians have different opinions about things that happened in the past?". All students gained in content knowledge as well as in their understanding of historical inquiry.

MacArthur, Ferretti, and Okolo (2002) formed cooperative groups of students in inclusive sixth-grade social studies classes, and asked them to represent the historical views of immigrant groups versus nativists (anti-immigration groups) in class debates. Students collected information on these topics and used this information in debates. Results revealed that students with and without disabilities and boys and girls participated equally in the debates, and that all students gained similarly in tests of content knowledge. However, MacArthur et al. reported that at times debates seemed more like arguments, and that guidance and modeling were necessary to shape the level of debate.

PROMOTE REASONING WITH GUIDED QUESTIONING   Students with disabilities comprehend more and understand better when they actively reason through new information (e.g., Sullivan, Mastropieri, & Scruggs, 1995). For example, in a lesson about penguins, ask students to explain—rather than simply tell them—the fact that some penguins carry their eggs on top of their feet. If they cannot explain immediately, prompt them with directed questions, such as "Where do penguins live?" "What is it like there?" and "Why would that explain why penguins carry their eggs on top of their feet?" (see also Chapter 10).

In this case, students can be prompted to use information from their prior knowledge. In other cases ("Why do stars twinkle?"), relevant information may need to be provided.

Guided questioning can promote thinking in science classes containing students with cognitive or intellectual disabilities, as seen in this example of a discussion of the effects of capillary action when white flowers were placed in colored water:

TEACHER:	What do you think happened? I have a flower in blue water and a flower in green water, a white flower, right? How did I get the colors there?
KEN:	...Oh, you watered it with food coloring.
TEACHER:	But I didn't put any up here [the flower], did I?
KEN:	You put it in the dirt.
TEACHER:	But there's no dirt.
KEN:	Oh.
TEACHER:	How did it get from there to here?
JIMMY:	It went all the way up to here.
TEACHER:	Went all the way through water? The what, Mary?
MARY:	A stem.
TEACHER:	The stem. It went all the way through the stem, you're right. (Scruggs & Mastropieri, 1995b, p. 264)

In social studies subjects, teachers can describe the nature and characteristics of harbors, and ask students why it makes sense that many cities are located on or near natural harbors. Or, describe the "fall line" where rivers near the coast are still navigable but move swiftly enough to power industry. Then, show students a physical map and ask them to predict where major cities probably would be located. They can then test their predictions on a political map.

ADAPT INSTRUCTION FOR DEVELOPMENTAL DIFFERENCES Some students, especially those with intellectual disabilities, may have more difficulty with inductive reasoning tasks (Caffrey & Fuchs, 2007). For example, when a fourth-grader with intellectual disabilities was questioned about the nature of air, he said it is cold, windy, and found outdoors (Scruggs, Mastropieri, & Wolfe, 1995, p. 228), a view commonly held by preschoolers (Driver, Asoko, Leach, Mortimer, & Scott, 1994). Consider these possible differences in "preconceptions," or prior understandings, when planning inquiry-oriented instruction, and provide additional instruction when needed.

While many normally achieving students can answer higher-level questions with only subtle coaching, students with disabilities may require extensive levels of coaching to draw the same inference, or to construct or discover scientific principles (e.g., buoyancy or pendulum movement; Scruggs & Mastropieri, 2007). However, more structured coaching can lead students to draw relevant inferences. For example, show students a number of pendulums with different weights attached, and ask them if they swing at different rates (they do not). Then show students a number of pendulums of different length, and ask them the same question (the longer pendulums swing more slowly). Then ask them to construct a general rule. Be sure all students have enough time to construct answers for themselves.

Promote deductive reasoning as well as inductive reasoning in students with special needs (see Woodward & Noell, 1992). For example, rather than asking students to draw inductive conclusions about pendulum motion, directly provide the "rule" about pendulum motion (e.g., "The longer the string, the slower the swing"). Next, demonstrate different pendulums, and ask students to make predictions ("Which one do you think will swing faster, the short one or the long one?"). Finally, provide more divergent examples to further promote generalized knowledge of the concept ("What can I do to the bob of the pendulum [point to the bob] to make it run faster?").

Although inductive thinking activities have been widely promoted in education for many years, deductive thinking activities also are important, and in some cases may provide more realistic thinking activities for some students with special learning needs.

15 Summary

- Much learning in science and social studies takes place in the context of textbook learning. To address the needs of diverse classrooms, teachers should evaluate their texts for "considerateness."

- Content-enhancement devices are means for increasing recall and comprehension of content information, and include use of graphic organizers, study guides, diagrams, visual-spatial displays, and mnemonics.

- Familiarization with text organization and structure can help students understand text content. Students can be taught to incorporate analysis of text structure into their study strategies. Highlighting, outlining, and study guides are also helpful.

- Textbooks can be adapted for students with reading problems with such methods as audiotaped texts, braille or enlarged-print versions, simplified texts, or modified presentations.

- Before assigned readings, students can be familiarized with new vocabulary and provided with advance organizers such as visual-spatial displays, timelines, or concept maps.

- After assigned readings, students can be provided with reviews and summaries of the readings, practice with peers, and extra help sessions.

- Activities-oriented instruction can be helpful for students who have reading problems, or who benefit from the enhanced concreteness and meaningfulness afforded by such instruction.

- Many adaptations are available for accommodating special needs in such science activity areas as balancing and weighing, activities with plants and animals, anatomy, microscope activities, weather, rocks and minerals, and activities involving sound and light. These adaptations address specific needs areas, and also can enhance comprehension of the associated concepts.

- Adaptations can also be incorporated into social studies areas, including role-play, simulation activities, and field trips.

- Inquiry-oriented approaches to science and social studies, found in both textbook and activities approaches, can also be adapted for students with special needs. These adaptations include use of hands-on materials, carefully structured questioning, redirecting attention, and reinforcing divergent, independent thinking.

PROFESSIONAL STANDARDS LINK:
Science and Social Studies

Information in this chapter links most directly to:

- CEC Standards: 3 (Individual Learning Differences), 4 (Instructional Strategies), 5 (Learning Environments and Social Interactions), 6 (Language), 7 (Instructional Planning)

- INTASC Standards: Principles 1 (understands central concepts of the discipline), 2 (provides appropriate learning opportunities), 3 (understands learning differences, adapts instructional opportunities), 4 (instructional strategies), 5 (creates learning environments), 6 (fosters inquiry, collaboration, interaction), 7 (plans instruction)

- PRAXIS II™ Content Categories (Knowledge): 3 (Delivery of Services)

- PRAXIS II™ Content Categories (Application): 1 (Curriculum), 2 (Instruction)

SCIENCE AND SOCIAL STUDIES

If students are having difficulty learning from textbooks, have you tried the following?
If not, see the pages listed below.

STRATEGIES FOR EFFECTIVE TEACHING IN SCIENCE AND SOCIAL STUDIES

STRATEGIES FOR PROMOTING INDEPENDENT LEARNING FROM TEXTBOOKS

STRATEGIES FOR ADAPTING TEXTBOOK MATERIALS

STRATEGIES FOR ADAPTING SCIENCE ACTIVITIES

STRATEGIES FOR ADAPTING LIFE SCIENCE ACTIVITIES

STRATEGIES FOR ADAPTING EARTH SCIENCE ACTIVITIES

STRATEGIES FOR ADAPTING PHYSICAL SCIENCE ACTIVITIES

STRATEGIES FOR ADAPTING SOCIAL STUDIES ACTIVITIES

STRATEGIES FOR ADAPTING INQUIRY LEARNING ACTIVITIES

E on 3

GEOFF BURBRIDGE   Geoff Burbridge has challenges with depression, phonophobia, and severe muscle dystrophy. He explains his connection to photography: "Photography has given me the incentive to venture out more and focus my attention away from my problems. This has been especially frustrating and difficult for me after being a competitive sportsman who was involved in many outdoor activities and conservation work. Being a member of the DPS helps me feel connected and gives me an outlet for my competitive spirit."

16

Career and Technical Education, and Transitions

OBJECTIVES

After studying this chapter, you should be able to:

- Understand the importance of setting realistic career and technical education goals and objectives as well as environmental, curriculum, and instructional strategies and modifications.

- Identify the meaning of transition and the purpose of planning and designing transition programs for students with disabilities.

- Gain understanding of the significance of teaching self-advocacy and self-determination skills toward promoting assertiveness and advocacy.

- Understand the importance of planning and transitioning for graduation, future education, job opportunities, and independent living.

Career and technical education is of critical importance for many students with disabilities, who may benefit greatly from education and training in job skills necessary for employment and for living a productive, fulfilling life. All of these significant areas of education are discussed in this chapter.

Transitions are natural passages in life that happen continually as we move to new schools, new jobs, and join new recreational organizations. Students with special needs typically have more difficulties than do students without disabilities adjusting to new transitions. Planning for those transitions by making instructional accommodations can promote smoother and more successful transitions for students with disabilities (Bakken & Obiakor, 2008). Planning, designing, and adapting appropriate programs for students with disabilities will allow many individuals to have successful careers and become self-sufficient.

Career and Technical Education

Career and technical education is an extensive and varied field that includes both secondary and postsecondary education. Career and technical education is a most important content area, and may be particularly important in the education of individuals with special needs, many of whom may go directly to paid employment after leaving high school, and many of whom drop out of high school (Dunn, Chambers, & Rabren, 2004; Sarkees-Wircenski & Scott, 2003).

OVERVIEW OF CAREER AND TECHNICAL EDUCATION

Career and technical education (previously referred to as industrial education or vocational education) includes a variety of educational programs intended to prepare students for employment and for life after high school (Gordon, 2007). Career and technical education is generally considered to comprise several areas associated with different labor markets, including agriculture, business, family and consumer sciences, marketing, health, trade and industry, and technical/communications. An overview of these is provided in Table 16.1. Familiarity with these areas can help you understand why the Carl D. Perkins Vocational Act can make a difference in the lives of students with disabilities and students at risk for school failure.

THE CARL D. PERKINS VOCATIONAL EDUCATION ACT

Career and technical education has a long and varied history in the United States, and has been growing in importance in recent years. One of the most significant events in the history of career and technical education was the passage of PL 98-524, or the Carl D. Perkins Vocational Education Act of 1984, reauthorized as the Carl D. Perkins Career and Technical Education Act of 2006 (U.S. Department of Education, 2006). Since passage of the Vocational Education Act of 1963, federal and state legislation has continued to encourage educational programs to provide services for students at risk because of disability or economic disadvantage. Under the Perkins Act, each state was obliged to provide educational programs and other activities designed to increase the participation of, and meet any special needs of, previously underserved groups of individuals, including the following:

1. Individuals with disabilities

2. Individuals from positions of economic disadvantage

3. Adults who need training and/or retraining

4. Single parents or homemakers

5. Individuals who would participate in programs designed to eliminate sex bias or stereotyping in career and technical education

6. Criminal offenders who are serving time in a correctional institution

Table 16.1 Career and Technical Education Areas

Career or Technical Area	Area of Study
Agricultural education promotes an understanding of the field of agriculture and identifies the role it plays in society ("agricultural literacy").	Caring for and production of agricultural plants and animals, forestry, agribusiness, agricultural economics, agronomy, crop science, dairy science, plant pathology, and veterinary technology.
Business education not only prepares students for occupations in business but also teaches students how to conduct their own business.	Skill development in the use of high-speed copiers, laser printers, fax machines, and computers including word processing; office management, accounting, economics, keyboarding, spreadsheets, computer graphics, networking, computer programming, paralegal secretarial, information and office technology.
Family and consumer science helps prepare students for family life, work life, and careers in family and consumer sciences.	Knowledge in nutrition, physical wellness, balancing family, home, personal, and work activities, travel services, textile and clothing, food science, interior decorating, and child and elder care.
Marketing education prepares students for marketing and management careers.	Learning about recruiting, training, financing, researching, communicating, and selling goods, ideas, and services.
Health occupations education provides information on careers in health services.	Introduces knowledge on dental hygienists and assistants, medical secretaries and receptionists, registered and licensed practical nurses, physicians, and dentists.
Trade and industrial education prepares students for multiple-level careers, from operatives to semiskilled to skilled craftspersons, such as in carpentry, masonry, plumbing, and electricity.	Knowledge in a wide range of careers including electronics, auto and marine mechanics, culinary arts, collision repair, welding, heavy equipment mechanics, and barbering.
Technology education helps prepare students in technological literacy and for careers in technology-related areas.	Learning about technology and its effects on daily life including communications, broadcasting, robotics, photography, and use of recent technological advances.

The Perkins Act also provides the Criteria for Services and Activities for the Handicapped and for the Disadvantaged (Title II, Part A). These require state boards providing vocational services and activities for individuals with disabilities or disadvantage to provide specific assurances—for example, that equal access will be provided to individuals with disabilities or disadvantages in recruitment, enrollment, placement, and that equal access will be provided for the full range of career and technical programs. It also requires that individuals with disabilities or disadvantages will receive instruction in the least restrictive environment, and will receive career and technical education services when appropriate as a component of the IEP, developed jointly by special educators and career and technical educators (U.S. Department of Education, 2006).

As a result of federal and state legislation, states have established support programs intended to assist students with special needs in career and technical programs. Students with disabilities and students considered at risk for dropping out of school have been provided with counseling, special coursework, and collaborative assistance from teacher teams to help them acquire entry-level job skills (Kochnar, 1998).

STRATEGIES FOR
ADAPTING CAREER AND TECHNICAL EDUCATION

To make any modification to the curriculum to initiate career and technical education, start by prioritizing objectives. For each instructional area of content, ask whether each particular objective is necessary. Establish the most important objectives, and address these most intensively. Next, adapt environments, curriculum, and instruction to meet the needs of individual learners. Use effective teaching strategies, as presented in the teacher presentation variables: structure, clarity, redundancy, enthusiasm, appropriate pace, maximized engagement, questioning, and feedback. Finally, systematically evaluate whether acceptable progress toward prespecified objectives is being made.

PRIORITIZE GOALS AND OBJECTIVES Goals and objectives specified for students with special needs in career and technical programs should be, above all, realistic. Reviewing and prioritizing goals and objectives can be achieved by having career and technical educators communicate with special educators about the entry-level expectations of the program, the objectives addressed in the program, and the exit expectations for students in the program. Such information can be useful in developing specific IEPs, and can help identify necessary teaching strategies and support services. Of course, it is necessary to prioritize all course or program objectives to determine which are absolutely necessary and which are most important. It can also be helpful to identify the many "exit points" for specific job descriptions for which students are training. Figure 16.1 provides examples of multiple exit points and entry-level competencies in masonry.

MODIFY THE ENVIRONMENT As with all school environments, career and technical training areas can contain physical barriers to accessibility for all students. Barriers such as curbs, stairs, and doors can hinder access to the training area. Other barriers can be found in the training area itself (ramps, aisles, restrooms, and workstations). Examine all potential barriers to accessibility for career and technical training areas, and modify environments as needed, using considerations discussed in Chapter 4.

MODIFY CURRICULUM Curriculum modifications for career and technical education parallel those for other content areas previously discussed. Some particularly important areas to address are student

Hands-on practice is critical for the development of vocational skills.

MULTIPLE EXIT POINTS AND ENTRY-LEVEL COMPETENCIES IN MASONRY

TASK LISTING BY DOT CODE

MASONRY

TASK NO.	TASK NAME	POSSIBLE EXIT POINTS — DOT* DESCRIPTIONS (DOT NO.)	Cement Mason Helper 869.687-026	Bricklayer Helper 861.687-010	Stone Mason Helper 869.687-026	Cement Mason 844.364-010	Stone Mason 861.381-038	Bricklayer Construction 001.301-010
01	Spreading mortar		X	X	X	X	X	X
02	Laying brick to a line			X				X
03	Building a brick corner							X
04	Cutting brick and block			X	X		X	X
05	Determining spacing for standard-size brick							X
06	Laying out courses to sill and cornice height							X
07	Interpreting and using a line modular rule			X	X		X	X
08	Dimensioning and scaling a working drawing							X
09	Identifying names and uses of lines and symbols on a working drawing							X
10	Identifying different views and their uses on a working drawing							X
11	Setting batter boards		X	X		X		X
12	Inspecting grading at building site					X	X	X
13	Finishing grading at building site		X	X	X	X	X	X

Figure 16.1 Multiple Exit Points and Entry-Level Competencies in Masonry
Note: From *Vocational Special Needs* (p. 338), by M. Sarkees-Wircenski & J. L. Scott, 1995, Homewood, IL: American Technical Publishers. Reprinted with permission. (*DOT is the *Dictionary of Occupational Titles,* produced by the U.S. Department of Commerce, Bureau of the Census.)

affect, motivation, and positive peer relations. Figure 16.2 presents some sample problem-solving questions and suggested curriculum modifications for questions that can be encountered in career and technical training areas. Following are some specific considerations for career and technical education programs.

Plan for Safety   The most important consideration in any career and technical program is safety. All students must be provided with basic safety instruction before undertaking activities in that area. Even if some students require more time and practice acquiring safety techniques, additional time allocations can pay dividends, as a primary cause of accidents in laboratory settings is lack of understanding of safety rules and procedures.

One helpful way to address safety considerations is by developing a "safety profile" for individual students. An example of a safety profile is provided in the *In the Classroom* feature on pages 397–399. This profile, designed for a machine shop, provides specific competencies

POSSIBLE PROBLEMS AND POSSIBLE MODIFICATIONS FOR CAREER AND TECHNICAL EDUCATION

Problem	Possible Modifications
Safety	Use peer assistance; teach safety skills; reduce danger (e.g., holders for hot materials); use student safety profile.
Measuring	Preset measures, using tactual (e.g., rubber bands), or visual (e.g., color) guides.
Reading	Provide modified reading passages; use audiotapes; use peer assistance (see Chapter 13).
Physical manipulation	Enhance grips with rubber bands; provide larger materials; use holders or hoists (see Chapter 4).
Comprehension	Use multiple examples; use more concrete examples; provide additional practice; use summarization/restatement strategies (see Chapter 13).
Memory	Provide repetition; enhance stimulus value; increase questioning; provide enactments; use organizational or mnemonic strategies (see Chapter 10).
Feeling	Use sandpaper or other material to enhance tactual stimulus value.
Motivation	Increase student decision making; use goal-setting; use peer mediation; teach enthusiastically; use praise and rewards; create task-oriented classrooms (see Chapter 9).
Fatigue	Provide frequent breaks; use supports to reduce effort requirements; use peer assistance.
Mobility	Provide sufficient aisle space; replace doorknobs with levers; use ramps where needed; plan ahead for emergencies; prepare work surfaces at appropriate height (see Chapter 4).
Vision	Provide safety precautions; use closed-circuit television; enhance lighting; provide physical models; use peer assistance (see chapter 4).
Hearing	Plan for emergencies; use peer assistance; reduce reading requirements; provide visual cues and models (see Chapter 4).
Attention	Use teacher proximity, direct appeal, peer assistance, and self-monitoring; change activities frequently (see Chapters 5 and 10).

Figure 16.2 Possible Problems and Possible Modifications for Career and Technical Education

for safety in this setting, and the dates these competencies have been demonstrated. Although safety considerations are of great importance for all students, it is also important to consider carefully the characteristics of individual students with special needs, and how these specific characteristics may interact with safety concerns of particular instructional areas.

Modify Instructional Materials   Many students with special needs enrolled in career and technical programs have limited reading skills. Teachers must ensure that appropriate adaptations are made for students with reading difficulties.

In many cases, students learn career and technical procedures from printed material such as lab manuals and textbooks. These materials can be modified for students with reading difficulties by using some of the following strategies:

- Rewrite the most important parts of the text in simpler language, highlighting the most important points. This modified text then can be used for other students with similar reading difficulties.

- Tape-record readings of the text, so students can listen independently or use the tape recordings to assist their own reading. Be certain to include in the recordings references to figures, tables, and illustrations, and page numbers. Also include summaries of the information read.

- Create videotape presentations of procedures in specific career and technical areas, such as masonry, carpentry, or electrical wiring. Present the same information as in the text versions, but also include demonstrations of the procedures. All students may benefit from this type of modification.
- Teach unfamiliar vocabulary separately, using direct instruction, demonstrations and examples, and verbal elaborations such as the keyword method (see Chapter 10). Some students can read adequately once they have become fluent with specialized vocabulary.

Since technical terms are of such importance in many career and technical areas, it may be helpful to use a technical terms tabulation sheet, such as the one shown in Figure 16.3. This tabulation allows the instructor to identify each significant term to be encountered in a unit, how each is applied in the text materials, and appropriate teaching strategies to be considered.

TECHNICAL TERMS TABULATION SHEET

Name _____ Text/Reference _____
Date _____ Chapter/Section _____ Pages _____

	Application in Text					Teaching Strategies						
Vocabulary Terms	Defined in text content	Illustrated	Included in index	Included in glossary	Included in review questions	Teacher lecture	Teacher demonstration	Word lists	Puzzle or game	Written assignment	Computer exercise	Comments
Wheel alignment						X	X					Demonstrate
Stability	X					X		X				Illustrate with transparencies
Ball joint	X	X				X	X	X				Show actual ball joints
Spindle						X	X	X				Show actual spindle
Toe-in	X	X	X		X	X	X	X				Show with transparencies
Toe-out	X	X	X		X	X	X	X				Show with transparencies
Caster	X	X	X		X	X	X	X				Show with transparencies
Camber	X	X	X		X	X	X	X				Show with transparencies
Steering axis inclination angle	X	X	X		X	X	X	X				Chalkboard drawing
Steering knuckle	X		X			X	X	X				Show actual knuckle
Elongated holes	X					X	X					Chalkboard illustration
Control arms	X	X	X			X	X	X				Show actual control arms
Shims	X	X	X			X	X	X				Show shims
Visualiner	X	X	X			X	X					Audiovisual presentation
Lite-a-line	X	X	X			X	X					Audiovisual presentation
Tie-rods	X		X			X	X	X				

Figure 16.3 Technical Terms Tabulation Sheet

Note: From *Special Populations in Career and Technical Education* (3rd ed., p. 432), by M. Sarkees-Wircenski & J. L. Scott, 2003, Homewood, IL: American Technical Publishers. Reprinted by permission.

Student Safety Profile

General Laboratory

Student: _____   Date: _____

Trade and Industrial

Program: _____   Date of Entry: _____

Date of Safety

Instructor: _____   Orientation: _____

Date Student Completes Specific Objectives of Safety Orientation:

	Date Accomplished
Specific Objectives	
Develops awareness of hazards and becomes more safety conscious	_____
Develops a serious attitude toward safety	_____
Prepares for safety before entering work area	_____
Prepares for safety at workstations	_____
Understands color coding	_____
Practices safety procedures	_____
Prepares for safety on leaving shop	_____

	Date Competence Demonstrated
Successfully responds to the following:	
1. Why provide safety for yourself and others?	_____
2. How does shop safety help production?	_____
3. What laws and agencies regulate shop safety?	_____
4. What are the causes of shop accidents?	_____
Develops a serious attitude toward safety	
1. Gives serious thought to work safety	_____
2. Remains alert in the shop area	_____
3. Works carefully	_____
4. Remains calm and holds temper	_____
5. Focuses attention on what is being done	_____
6. Assumes responsibility for own safety and safety of others	_____
Prepares for safety before entering shop	
1. What are the characteristics of a training program?	_____
a. Determines what tools, machines, and materials are required	_____
b. Determines what hazards are involved	_____
c. Determines what skills are needed	_____

(continued)

In the CLASSROOM

Student Safety Profile—*continued*

2. What clothing and safety equipment to wear?

    a. Recognizes types of clothing suitable for the shop area   _____

    b. Recognizes types of foot and leg covering   _____

    c. Recognizes types of head covering   _____

    d. Recognizes types of eye and face protection   _____

    e. Recognizes types of hearing protection   _____

    f. Recognizes types of hand and arm protection   _____

    g. Recognizes types of lung and breathing protection   _____

Prepares for safety on entering the shop

1. What safety provision to locate?

    a. Locates exit   _____

    b. Locates emergency fire equipment   _____

    c. Locates emergency aids   _____

    d. Locates main power disconnect area   _____

    e. Locates safety zones and lanes   _____

2. What potential hazards to keep in mind?

    a. Identifies flammable materials   _____

    b. Identifies mobile equipment   _____

    c. Identifies activities of others   _____

Prepares for safety at workstation

1. Obtaining tools and materials

    a. Remembers where tool was obtained   _____

    b. Follows established procedures for obtaining tools   _____

    c. Checks condition of tool upon receipt   _____

    d. Uses care in handling tools   _____

2. What safety precautions to observe?

    a. Checks for the condition of floor openings and storage areas   _____

    b. Checks for proper lighting   _____

    c. Checks for proper ventilation   _____

    d. Checks for caution areas and protective signs   _____

    e. Checks for guardrails   _____

3. What power is available?

    a. Uses electrical power safely   _____

    b. Uses air power safely   _____

    c. Uses hydraulic power safely   _____

(continued)

Student Safety Profile—*continued*

4. What solvents and chemicals are present?

    a. Checks the parts cleaning area   _____

    b. Checks the dispensing containers   _____

Practicing shop safety skills

1. Recognizes how to prevent bodily injuries

    a. Understands how to prevent slipping or falling   _____

    b. Understands how to avoid injuries from lifting   _____

    c. Understands how to avoid crushing injuries   _____

    d. Understands how to avoid hand and arm injuries   _____

2. Develops tool and machine safety skills

    a. Demonstrates hand tool safety skills   _____

    b. Demonstrates power tool safety skills on the following machines:

        (1) Milling machines   _____

        (2) Lathes   _____

        (3) Shapers   _____

        (4) Drill presses   _____

        (5) Power hacksaws   _____

        (6) Band saws   _____

        (7) Electrical discharge machines   _____

Understands color coding

1. Recognizes safety color codes for shop machines and equipment   _____

Prepares to leave the school shop

1. Stores tools, machines, and materials

    a. Stores hand and portable power tools   _____

    b. Secures stationary power tools   _____

    c. Stores usable materials and supplies   _____

2. Disposes of waste materials

    a. Disposes of scrap metal, filings, and chips   _____

    b. Disposes of hot metal   _____

    c. Disposes of waste liquids   _____

    d. Disposes of sawdust and absorbent compounds   _____

3. Cleans the workbench and floor   _____

4. Stores safety equipment   _____

5. Cleans hands and other parts of body   _____

6. Performs final check of shop area   _____

Note: From *Vocational Special Needs* (pp. 344–345), by M. Sarkees-Wircenski & J. L. Scott, 1995, Homewood, IL: American Technical Publishers. Reprinted with permission.

Select Computer Software   Career and technical programs have seen the increased use of computer-assisted learning techniques, which can be helpful in promoting learning. For example, software applications can be helpful in learning important content in the fields of health or business applications. When selecting software for career and technical training programs that include students with special needs, several important questions should be answered:

1. Is the content presented in the software directly relevant to the objectives of the unit?
2. Can the software be operated independently by students, or are adaptations or supervision required?
3. Is the information presented current and technically correct?
4. Is the pace of presentation of information compatible with special learning needs?
5. Do students consider the software more interesting and motivating than alternative approaches to learning the same information?
6. Will students have enough opportunities to practice using the software to make the activities worthwhile?
7. Is the particular software application an improvement over the instruction that is currently provided?

As with other instructional strategies, formative evaluation can help determine whether particular software applications are effective. Some possible adaptations for students with special needs using computer software include increased time-on-task, direct supervision, using peers as tutors or "buddies," or working on computer assignments in pairs.

MODIFY INSTRUCTIONAL STRATEGIES   Appropriate instructional strategies for teaching students with special needs in career and technical education are similar to instructional strategies appropriate for other classes. Overall, the "effective instruction" strategies described in Chapter 6 are useful for career and technical areas. Important variables to consider in effectively teaching all students include maximizing engaged time-on-task, appropriate content coverage, and pace of instruction. Further, teachers should maximize the effectiveness of instructional variables such as providing information, direct questioning, and feedback in response to teacher questions.

Teach Procedures for Career and Technical Tasks   Much learning in career and technical classes is procedural. That is, students learn the procedures for undertaking specific tasks, such as displaying or stocking merchandise, using an office software program, or installing a light-dimming system. As such, careful demonstrations and modeling, with a substantial amount of practice and feedback, can be particularly helpful. Simulations and role-playing can also be helpful when direct access to real situations is not available. Formative evaluation including task analysis can determine the rate of progress for individual students, and whether instruction should be modified or intensified. Task analysis can be particularly useful in determining the specific subtasks or subroutines that need additional practice or in developing a more refined sequence of skills and competencies that needs to be mastered to execute any subtasks.

Increase Time-on-Task   As with many other areas of learning, increased time-on-task can be helpful in developing career and technical skills. This can be accomplished by additional supervised time with the teacher or aide (when time is available), additional work with peers, or work with tutors. Choosing students who have recently mastered a specific skill to act as tutors can be particularly helpful, as the tutee can gain important skill development and the tutor can consolidate and reinforce previous learning.

Individualize Instruction   One teaching method that can be helpful in many career and technical areas is individualizing instruction (Sarkees-Wircenski & Scott, 2003). Figure 16.4 provides an example of an individualized instruction assignment sheet for the task "Cleaning or replacing spark plugs" in the major block "Basic Engine Tune-Up." Using this procedure, the objectives for the task are clearly specified, and the activities to accomplish this task are identified. Three activities are specified: written assignments, audiovisual presentations, and laboratory assignments. In addition, instructor checkpoints are identified. On the assignment sheet, the sequence of activities and checkpoints is clearly provided. Individualized instruction can be helpful in providing relevant activities that meet the needs of individual learners. However, many individualized instruction practices lean heavily on independent learning from pro-

INDIVIDUALIZED INSTRUCTION ASSIGNMENT SHEET

MAJOR BLOCK   Basic Engine Tune-up   NAME _____

TASK   Cleaning or replacing spark plugs _____

UNIT   223-9 _____ TIME (est.)   2 hrs. _____ (act) _____

OBJECTIVE(S)

To remove and diagnose condition of spark plugs, analyze spark plug deposits, clean plugs, file electrodes, and set plug gap to specifications; plug gap to be within .001 of recommended setting. Ground electrode must be at right angle to center electrode. Install and torque to specifications. Correctly answer 16 of 20 test questions on spark plug types, application, and service procedures.

START ⟶ W-1 ⟩ W-2 ⟩ A-1 ⟩ L-1 ⟩ C-1 ⟩ L-2 ⟩ L-3 ⟩

C-2 ⟩ L-4 ⟩ C-3 ⟩ ⟩ ⟩ ⟩ ⟩ ⟩

⟩ ⟩ ⟩ ⟩ ⟩ ⟩ ⟩ ⟩

WRITTEN		AUDIO VISUALS	
W–1	Assignment Sheet 223-9	A–1	Slide set 223-9
W–2	Assignment 223-9-1	A–2	
W–3		A–3	
W–4		A–4	
W–5		A–5	
W–6		A–6	
W–7		A–7	

LABORATORY		CHECK POINT	
L–1	Assignment 223-9-2	C–1	Instructor check
L–2	Install spark plugs	C–2	Instructor check
L–3	Performance test plugs	C–3	Give test, evaluate, and
L–4	Secure work station	C–4	make next assignment
L–5		C–5	
L–6		C–6	
L–7		C–7	
L–7		C–7	
L–7		C–7	

Figure 16.4 Individualized Instruction Assignment Sheet

Note: From *Special Populations in Career and Technical Education* (3rd ed., p. 463), by M. Sarkees-Wircenski & J. L. Scott, 2003, Homewood, IL: American Technical Publishers. Reprinted by permission.

vided practice activities. When implementing individualized procedures such as these, determine the level of independent learning that can reasonably be expected of individual students, and provide guided practice and supervision when needed.

TEACH GENERALIZABLE SKILLS An important area of career and technical education is the area of generalizable skills. These are skills that are necessary across many different areas of career and technical training, and appear to be closely related to success in a number of different fields. Four areas of generalizable skills have been identified (see also Sarkees-Wircenski & Scott, 2003):

1. Mathematics (e.g., measurements and calculations, fractions, decimals)
2. Communications (e.g., words and meanings, reading, writing)
3. Interpersonal relations (e.g., work behaviors, instructional and supervisory relations)
4. Reasoning skills (e.g., verbal reasoning, problem solving)

In mathematics, generalizable skills are found in such areas as whole numbers, percentages, measurement and calculation, and estimation. In communications, generalizable skills include words and their meanings, reading, writing, speaking, and listening. In interpersonal relations, generalizable skills include work-related behaviors, instructional and supervisory conversations, and social conversations. Finally, generalizable skills in reasoning include self-determination, listening and problem solving, verbal reasoning, and planning (see also Glago, Mastropieri, & Scruggs, in press; Sarkees-Wircenski & Scott, 2003). Instruction in these generalizable skill areas can lead to improvement in a number of different career and technical domains (Wu & Greenan, 2003).

Students with disabilities and other special learning needs may lack the important generalizable skills necessary to succeed in a variety of career and technical training areas, and may not be aware that they lack these skills. In planning curriculum, it is important for career and technical education teachers to work closely with academic teachers to identify important generalizable skill areas and ensure that these skills are taught and reinforced in all relevant classes (Loeding & Greenan, 1999).

Planning for Transition

WHAT DOES TRANSITION MEAN?

Transition is the process of planning for changes throughout a student's life. Most frequently, transition is referred to as the planning for a student's life after high school; however, planning for changes throughout life is a more accurate definition. **Transition programs** help prepare students for changes from one grade level to another, from preschool to elementary school, elementary to middle school, middle school to high school, and high school to life after high school. Preparing students for transitions after high school may include career and technical education, and directions to manage employment, supported living, or independent living arrangements.

CLASSROOM SCENARIO

Quinetra

Quinetra is a 5-year-old with cerebral palsy who has gross and fine motor difficulties in addition to speech and language challenges. She has been enrolled in a half-day preschool program near her home. During preschool she receives physical therapy, occupational therapy, and speech and language therapy daily. Quinetra also participates in the activities that take place as part of the regular preschool program. Quinetra feels comfortable in this program, as she has been enrolled there for 4 years, and she has had the same teachers for the entire time. Beginning next fall, Quinetra will begin a regular education kindergarten program. This transition will involve moving to another building, the neighborhood public school, which is farther from her home, and is quite large in comparison to her preschool. This transition also means having a new general education kindergarten teacher, being included with many more students without disabilities, changing to new special education teachers and therapists, riding a bus to school, and having a much longer day away from home.

QUESTIONS FOR REFLECTION

1. What do you think will be the greatest challenges for Quinetra as she moves to the kindergarten program?
2. How can you help prepare Quinetra, her family, her teachers, her new school, and all of her support personnel for this important transition?
3. What things could be done after the transition to help Quinetra?

Transitions, while exciting and challenging, can be traumatic events. Planning for transitions and preparing students with disabilities for those transitions can eliminate some of the difficult aspects of adjustment. Examples of transitions include the following:

- Attending preschool for the first time and separating from Mom and Dad and home life
- Changing from half-day to full-day school programs

- Moving to first grade from kindergarten
- Moving to any new grade level
- Changing from elementary school to middle school
- Changing from middle school to high school
- Moving to new school buildings
- Attending college for the first time
- Returning to school after a summer vacation
- Changing school placement from special education settings to general education settings
- Changing to postsecondary school training and education
- Obtaining a job
- Joining recreational activities
- Moving to independent living arrangements
- Moving to a new community

IDEA defines transition services as coordinating services for students that promote the change from school to post-school. This means IDEA emphasizes only planning for transitions from high school to vocational education, postsecondary education, adult services, independent living, and community participation (Bakken & Obiakor, 2008). The coordination of transition services is based on student preferences, interests, and abilities, and includes instruction, experiences in the community, and development of employment, postsecondary, daily living, and vocational objectives (Asselin, Todd-Allen, & DeFur, 1998). However, it has been seen that planning for transitions at all ages promotes social and emotional well-being of students with disabilities (Wehman, 2006).

CLASSROOM SCENARIO

Jamal

Jamal is a 16-year-old with severe disabilities who has recently begun a part-time job in a supported work environment. He lives with his parents and has assistance getting to and from his work environment, where he gets along well with others. At age 22, he will graduate from his high school and, it is hoped, will engage in some meaningful adult activity. Jamal's teachers and supervisors are concerned about preparing Jamal for the transition from public school to adult life.

QUESTIONS FOR REFLECTION

1. What services need to be coordinated?
2. How can Jamal develop self-advocacy skills and how can he be helped to understand the differences between ADA and IDEA?
3. How can he be prepared for transition to new community services and vocational rehabilitation services?
4. How can Jamal be prepared to be more independent in his life?

Planning for transitions helps prepare students for the expected changes that take place in their lives. The amount of planning for transitions and adaptations necessary varies depending upon the type of transition and the severity level of disability. Planning includes involving all individuals who will be affected by the transition, including the following:

- the student
- the parents
- teachers
- special education teachers
- transition coordinators
- specialists (e.g., speech and language, physical therapists, occupational therapists)

- counselors
- community representatives
- advocates
- support personnel (e.g., bus drivers, cafeteria workers, custodians, school secretary)
- employers

Effective transition planning begins early, includes everyone who may be involved, provides an initial timeline, and involves continuous evaluation.

STRATEGIES FOR PROMOTING TRANSITIONS

MAKE PREPARATIONS WITH STUDENTS TO PLAN FOR TRANSITIONS Many students have a difficult time going to school from home for the first time. Many young children with disabilities may not have been exposed to many different situations and people. It can also be frightening to move to a new school, teachers, and peers. The new school may be farther from home, which means leaving home earlier in the morning, riding a new school bus, and having a longer school day. Students may become more tired, frightened, and anxious until they feel accepted in the new environment. Preparatory actions can be undertaken to ease transitions where everything is so different, otherwise students with disabilities may experience difficulties transitioning to the new site. Such actions include the following:

- Deciding on a time for optimal placement
- Establishing a transition timeline
- Preparing all individuals involved
- Establishing communication procedures
- Sharing information with all individuals
- Collecting data on student performance
- Visiting the new school with the student
- Arranging a meeting with new teachers and support personnel
- Allowing time to explore the new setting
- Planning activities to simulate the new environment to prepare the student
- Reviewing new procedures and explaining what the student can expect in the new environment
- Showing the student that you are supportive and will still be supportive even when the student is attending the new school
- Preparing new teachers and students for the new student with disabilities
- Attending the first day of the new school with the student
- Arranging a communication plan
- Scheduling follow-up evaluation times

For example, Carter, Clark, Cushing, and Kennedy (2005) described a program for smoothing transitions from elementary to middle school for students with severe disabilities. They emphasized the importance of early planning and collaboration across schools, and recommended encouraging family involvement; addressing organizational issues such as lockers, books, schedules, assignments, and restrooms (see also Chapter 11); developing programs of peer support that extend to unstructured times such as lunch and in the hallways; promoting school involvement; and fostering more independence through, for example, self-management strategies.

The ultimate goal of education for individuals with special needs is to enable them to live and work as independently as possible.

PLAN TRANSITIONS TO ADULTHOOD   Planning transitions for adulthood is vitally important for students with disabilities. All students with disabilities who have IEPs are required to have individual transition plans (ITPs) when they reach the age of 14. Planning and instruction includes teaching students self-advocacy and self-determination skills; planning for future education, such as college or other postsecondary training; planning for future employment opportunities; and preparing students for independent living situations (Asselin et al., 1998; Beakley & Yoder, 1998; Pierangelo & Giuliani, 2004).

CLASSROOM SCENARIO

Ricardo

Ricardo, an 18-year-old with learning disabilities, is preparing to move to the local university beginning the next fall semester. Ricardo has had special education services for his learning disabilities since third grade. He has particular difficulties with basic literacy tasks, especially reading and writing activities, which tend to require a great deal of time to complete. He has never lived away from home, and his parents have always been very supportive of anything he has tried to do. However, his parents have also had a tendency to help him with everything, including organizing his schoolwork and his homework schedule.

QUESTIONS FOR REFLECTION

1. How can you help prepare Ricardo for the transition to college, in all the areas of anticipated changes?
2. How can you help Ricardo develop self-advocacy and self-determination skills?
3. How can you prepare him for the changes from IDEA to ADA and describe what those changes will mean in terms of responsibilities that he will have to assume?
4. What is a reasonable timeline for meeting the transition needs?

PROMOTE SELF-ADVOCACY AND SELF-DETERMINATION   Many students with special needs are overly dependent on others and are passive with respect to decision making. Although making decisions is difficult, students with disabilities will eventually be required to participate more actively in that process for themselves. Therefore, it is vital that opportunities, instruction, and practice in becoming more independent and in decision making are a part of a student's curriculum. Thus, training in **self-advocacy** and **self-determination** skills is a must. This means that students may need assistance, instruction, and practice in learning how to become knowledgeable about themselves with respect to learning strengths, needs, preferences, interests, and rights and responsibilities. This knowledge can be used to request accommodations that promote more success at jobs, independent living, and postsecondary education. Sample self-advocacy skills include the following:

- Awareness of legal rights and responsibilities
- Requesting adaptations and accommodations (e.g., ADA requires that college students with disabilities go to professors, self-identify themselves as having disabilities, and request that specific adaptations be made.)
- Meeting with vocational rehabilitation personnel
- Requesting assistance from social security offices
- Meeting with medical personnel and asking relevant questions
- Possessing appropriate social skills, such as requesting assistance, seeking clarification
- Having job-related skills and job-related social skills
- Thinking about and planning for the future with realistic goals
- Making informed choices
- Seeking assistance when necessary

Students with strong self-determination skills generally have better post-school outcomes. Nevertheless, self-determination skills are not always taught to students with disabilities, and in fact overprotection in some cases by teachers, advocates, and parents may negatively affect the

Training Students in Self-Determination and Self-Advocacy

 Training students to use self-determination and self-advocacy skills independently facilitates independence, and may help promote motivation to succeed. Self-determination is defined as identifying and achieving goals independently (Field & Hoffman, 2002). A great deal of the research on self-determination has been conducted with secondary students at the point of making transitions. However, educators have indicated a need to start to train students with disabilities in self-determination skills at younger ages, so by the time they need to transition to the workplace, they have had numerous opportunities for practicing and developing such skills. Glago et al. (in press) taught fourth- and fifth-grade elementary students with learning and emotional disabilities a problem-solving strategy for assisting with self-determination and self-advocacy.

Students were randomly assigned to treatment or control conditions, and treatment-condition students participated in 9 weeks of training using problem-solving strategy instruction. The steps were as follows: (1) Identify the problem, (2) Think of solutions, (3) Pick the best one, (4) Try it out, (5) Decide if it worked.

Students were taught the problem-solving steps and practiced them on real-life scenarios designed to teach them to: (a) identify classroom problems that required self-determination, (b) produce solutions to problems, (c) select optimal solutions, and (d) request assistance and accommodations required. Initially, students were provided with scenarios and asked to select optimal solutions from a list. Later, training required students to generate solutions independently. A sample scenario for which students were asked to generate three solutions is, "Jennifer has to get her planner signed every night by her mom or dad so she can earn class points. Her mom and dad work late and she goes to bed before they get home." Continuous feedback occurred during training, and all student-genrated solutions were discussed. Findings indicated that trained students outperformed control students on learning the problem-solving steps, applying the strategy to real-life scenarios, and generalizing use of the problem-solving strategy.

QUESTIONS FOR REFLECTION

1. What might you do to help students learn and generalize the self-determination behaviors?
2. Can you adapt these procedures for middle-school and secondary-level students with disabilities?
3. What strategies similar to the ones just described would be appropriate for you to share with the parents of your students?

PEARSON myeducationlab

Go to MyEducationLab, select the topic *Transition Planning*, and go to the Activities and Applications section. As you watch the video entitled "Beyond School: Rachel," reflect on the skills and training Rachel received as part of her transition planning.

autonomy of students with disabilities (Test, Fowler, Wood, Brewer, & Eddy, 2005). To be successful and independent in their lives after formal schooling, students need to learn about their learning strengths and needs, to articulate those abilities and needs, and to participate actively in the IEP process. For an investigation of the effects of self-determination training on younger students, see the *Research Highlight* feature. For information pertaining to how different cultural groups might perceive self-determination, see the *Diversity in the Classroom* feature.

Test et al. (2005) developed a conceptual framework for self-advocacy, which included four components:

1. Knowledge of self (e.g., strengths, support needs, goals)
2. Knowledge of rights (e.g., personal rights, educational rights, steps to advocate for change)
3. Communication (e.g., assertiveness, negotiation, compromise)
4. Leadership (e.g., knowledge of group's rights, political action)

All of these components contribute to an overall sense of self-advocacy.

TEACH STRATEGIES FOR TRANSITIONS   The I PLAN self-advocacy strategy includes several steps to assist students in acquiring skills for transition (Test & Neale, 2004; Van Reusen, Bos, Schumaker, & Deshler, 1994). Students evaluate and plan for the following transition areas:

- independent living skills
- consumer and financial skills
- legal and citizenship skills

Culture and Self-Determination

Self-determination helps promote independence in students with disabilities and is an important component of transition programs. Components of self-determination training related to transition planning include self-regulation of behavior, problem solving, and self-evaluation. Perceived this way, students are encouraged to think, solve problems, and plan for themselves. However, self-determination may represent different entities to individuals from various cultures. If self-determination training is going to be successful, then an awareness of how various cultures define and perceive self-determination skills is critical. Although it is never wise to generalize how an entire cultural group would respond to anything, especially one definition of self-determination, insights can be gained from exploring what has been written about specific cultural groups. For example, Frankland, Turnbull, Wehmeyer, and Blackmountain (2004) described how individuals from a Navajo culture might perceive self-determination differently from individuals from an Anglo-European culture. With respect to self-regulation and making decisions for oneself, Frankland et al. reported that Navajo students may put their families' needs above their own. For example, rather than setting a goal for themselves, they may be more likely to select the goal that is appropriate for their clan or extended family. Navajos may be more likely to prioritize goals that emphasize harmony in life with their clan or extended family over individualistic goals. Talking with families from different cultures will help provide an important context for designing instruction that is relevant and important for students.

- community involvement skills
- career and employment skills
- family-living and social skills
- recreational and leisure skills

The analysis also includes identifying strengths such as math computation and social skills, and needs such as reading, reading comprehension, and written expression. Specific goals are identified, such as independent living and career employment goals. Choices for student learning preferences are also included on the inventory. For example, student preferences for certain activities and listings of helpful materials and testing procedures are identified. Finally, accommodations that are necessary to help students succeed are listed. After the inventory is completed, students are taught to use communication skills more effectively by using **PLAN** and **SHARE** strategy prompts (Test & Neale, 2004).

Plan

Provide the inventory to teachers.

Listen and respond to the comments.

Ask relevant questions.

Name your goals.

Share

Sit up straight.

Have a nice tone of voice.

Activate your thinking.

Relax and remain calm.

Engage in eye contact (Van Reusen et al., 1994).

TEACH ASSERTIVENESS SKILLS   Many students require explicit social skills instruction in assertiveness, such as requesting assistance, asking for clarification, and negotiating changes.

Provide instruction and role-play situations during which students can practice developing and refining these skills in a safe environment. Finally, provide opportunities to practice generalizing the skills in a variety of situations with a number of different adults. During

myeducationlab

Go to MyEducationLab, select the topic *Transition Planning*, and go to the Activities and Applications section. As you watch the video entitled "Pursuing Interests in the Community," reflect on the skills this man has used to accomplish his goals in community and work settings.

high school, teachers assume major responsibilities for ensuring that students with disabilities are given a free and appropriate education (FAPE) as required by IDEA. Remember that teachers are part of the IEP team and are legally bound to implement IEP objectives and classroom modifications. However, once students leave high schools and enroll in colleges, they are no longer covered by IDEA. They do have rights and responsibilities identified in the Americans with Disabilities Act (ADA) and Section 504 of the Rehabilitation Act. Students, however, must meet any new classification criteria established at their respective institutions. Once student services are identified, usually with the assistance of personnel at a dean of students office, extended testing times, test administrations in a distraction-free environment, and provision of notes or copies of overhead materials may be made available. However, according to ADA, students have to be more assertive and identify themselves as having disabilities to their professors before they are guaranteed modifications to their educational programs. Then they need to notify professors of their learning needs. One method devised by some college students with disabilities is to compose a brief statement containing learning strengths and needs. Figure 16.5 contains a sample letter written by a college student, Toni, who has learning disabilities. Toni distributes the letter to all of her professors each semester during the first week of classes and then meets individually with them during the next week to discuss any follow-up questions or concerns.

Toni has received positive feedback on her letter from her professors. Most professors report that the letter provided them with helpful background information and insights into Toni's learning strengths and needs. They also kept the letter on file for later referral. This letter documents the type of self-advocacy skills that will be necessary for students with disabilities.

Dear Professor:

I am Toni, a student enrolled in your class this semester. I have a learning disability. I learn best by seeing and hearing information rather than by reading. I can sit through lectures and not take any notes and do fairly well on exams. When I sit in lectures and try to take notes at the same time I usually do poorly on exams. I do not seem to be able to take notes and listen at the same time very well at all. When I have had the opportunity to have my textbooks provided on cassette audiotapes I can perform even better.

I have also noticed that I have a very keen sense of hearing but have the inability to filter out unwanted noises. This causes a problem for me in some lectures. To cope with this I usually sit near the front of the room so I can see the lecturer's face and try to lip read. Lecture outlines are also very helpful for me to be able to keep up with the information being presented in class. I tape record all of my lectures so that I am able to listen more carefully later on when studying for exams. I use the tapes and the lecture outlines as review. At that time I usually insert additional important points into the outline to help with studying and remembering important information.

I also do better on exams if I can take them in a private, very quiet room. I know that the Dean of Students Office has testing facilities that can be used to take my exams, and I would prefer to be able to take all of my exams for this class there.

I work very hard in school and am willing to try to work as hard as possible in your class. I am looking forward to learning in your class this semester. I can be reached by phone or by e-mail, but e-mail seems to be a more reliable method of communicating since my roommates and I are usually unavailable during the day.

Sincerely,

Toni Sanchez

Phone: 993-7346
E-mail: *toni@gmu.edu*

Figure 16.5   Self-Advocacy Letter to a College Professor from Toni, a Student with Learning Disabilities

Consider assisting students with disabilities while they are enrolled in middle and high school in developing statements similar to the one used by Toni. This activity familiarizes students with their learning needs, helps them communicate these needs whenever necessary, and provides them with practice for doing this when they no longer have the protective services of IDEA and must be independent.

PROMOTE TRANSITIONS WITH ASSESSMENT Assessment for transition consists of collecting information on students from all available sources (Wehman, 2006). This includes the current IEPs, the school permanent records, school guidance counselors, formal and informal interviews with students and their families, and the answers to formal and informal transition planning and **occupational surveys.** The collected information is compiled and evaluated by members of the transition team, who then make recommendations for the ITP.

One transition survey addresses the four domains of instruction, community experiences, employment, and post-school goals required by IDEA. The *Transition Planning Inventory—Updated Version* (Clark & Patton, 2006) contains 46 transition planning statements organized around the four IDEA domains on four main forms and are supplemental: the student form, the home form, the school form, the profile and further assessment recommendations form, and a supplemental parent preferences and interest form. Raters indicate their level of agreement on a 5-point scale from strongly disagree to strongly agree with statements such as "Recognizes and accepts own strengths and limitations." Particular areas addressed and a sample item for each are shown below:

- Employment: knows how to get a job
- Further education/training: knows how to gain entry into a college or university
- Daily living: manages own money
- Leisure activities: uses settings that offer entertainment
- Community participation: knows basic legal rights
- Self-determination: sets personal goals
- Communication: has needed speaking skills
- Interpersonal relationships: displays appropriate social behavior in a variety of settings*

The profile and further recommendations form presents a summary of responses across the individual forms and can be used to make generalizations regarding strengths and individual needs. This information assists in determining whether or not additional information should be collected prior to designing ITPs.

Occupational surveys are also commercially available. For example, the *Occupational Aptitude Survey and Interest Schedule* (OASIS-3) (Parker, 2002) assesses whether students like, dislike, or have neutral feelings toward occupations and job activities from a pool of 240 items ranging across 12 vocational domains, including: artistic, scientific, nature, protective, mechanical, industrial, business detail, selling, accommodating, humanitarian, leading-influencing, and physical performing. Findings from this survey help develop a more comprehensive transition plan in the post-secondary vocational and educational areas. Figure 16.6 presents a listing of commercially available tests that may also prove beneficial in assessing for transition. The *Technology Highlight* feature provides suggestions for using alternative formats for accessing career information.

IMPLEMENT TRANSITION CURRICULUM Commercially prepared curriculum resources are available that provide examples of life skills and **life-centered career objectives** and materials (Cronin, Patton, & Wood, 2007). Most curriculums are designed around basic competencies that are subdivided according to the needs of targeted students. One curriculum, "Life Centered Career Education" (Council for Exceptional Children), for example, contains the following major areas: Daily Living Skills, Personal-Social Skills, and Occupational Guidance and Preparation. Each area is then subdivided into more specific level competencies and objectives that also contain teaching suggestions to develop skills for successful living in maintaining a home and accepting responsibility for community living. Other suggestions for integrating a life skills curriculum within the general curriculum are provided by Cronin et al. (2007). Finally, Wehman (2006) recommended that teachers identify as many community-based sites as possible and integrate those sites into their

*Note: From *Transition Planning Inventory: Administration and Scoring Guide,* by G. M. Clark & J. R. Patton, 1997, Austin, TX: Pro-Ed. Reprinted with permission.

	Employment	Further Educational Training	Leisure Activities	Daily Living	Community Participation	Health	Self-Determination	Communication	Interpersonal Relationships
Achievement									
Adult Basic Learning Examination		X						X	
Brigance Inventory of Essential Skills		X						X	
Iowa Test of Basic Skills		X						X	
Peabody Individual Achievement Test		X						X	
Woodcock-Johnson Psycho-Educational Battery		X						X	
Adaptive Behavior									
AAMR Adaptive Behavior Scales	X			X	X			X	X
Adaptive Behavior Inventory	X	X		X	X			X	X
Normative Adaptive Behavior Checklist	X		X	X	X			X	X
Scales of Independent Behavior	X		X	X	X			X	X
Street Survival Skills Questionnaire				X	X	X			
Vineland Adaptive Behavior Scale	X			X	X			X	X
Aptitude									
APTICOM Program	X	X							
Armed Services Vocational Aptitude Battery	X	X							
Differential Aptitude Test	X	X							
General Aptitude Test Battery (GATB)	X	X							
JEVS Work Sample System	X								
McCarron-Dial Evaluation System	X								
MESA	X								
Micro-TOWER System	X								
Occupational Aptitude and Interest Scale-2	X	X							
Talent Assessment Program	X								
TOWER System	X								

Figure 16.6 Commercially Available Assessment Measures

Note: From "Transitional Planning Assessment for Secondary-Level Students with Learning Disabilities," by G. M. Clark, 1996, *Journal of Learning Disabilities,* *29*(1), pp. 91–92. Reprinted with permission.

curriculum for students with disabilities, especially individuals with moderate to severe disabilities. Integrating community-based sites will increase awareness of what is available in the community for later access by students.

STRATEGIES FOR TRANSITIONING FOR THE FUTURE

PLAN FOR GRADUATION   In many states, more demanding coursework (in, for example, algebra, geometry, or foreign languages) and passing state competency exams are being required for graduation (see, for example, the *Science Standards of Learning for Virginia Public Schools* in English, math, science, history, and social studies, 2003). At the same time, some more basic and career-oriented courses are being phased out to free teachers for the more demanding courses. Some students with disabilities may find it extremely difficult, be-

	Employment	Further Educational Training	Leisure Activities	Daily Living	Community Participation	Health	Self-Determination	Communication	Interpersonal Relationships
Communication									
Communicative Abilities in Daily Living								X	
Individual Reading Placement Inventory								X	
Test of Written Language								X	
Woodcock Reading Mastery Test								X	
Functional Capacity									
Functional Assessment Profile	X			X			X	X	X
General Health Questionnaire						X			
Independent Living Behavior Checklist				X	X				
Life Functioning Index	X	X		X				X	
Personal Capacities Questionnaire	X			X			X	X	X
Learning Styles									
Learning Style Inventory	X							X	
Learning Styles and Strategies	X							X	
Manual Dexterity									
Crawford Small Part Dexterity Test	X								
Minnesota Rate of Manipulation Test	X								
Pennsylvania Bi-Manual Worksample	X								
Purdue Pegboard	X								

Figure 16.6 Continued

cause of their disability, to pass one or more of these classes, even if modifications are made (Katsiyannis, Zhang, & Ryan, 2007). If a student's apparent inability to pass one or more particularly demanding courses appears to stand in the way of graduation, determine whether a substitute course could be included on the student's IEP that would be accepted toward the diploma.

States have variable policies toward awarding diplomas. Some states award what is known as differentiated or tiered diplomas, which may include certificates of attendance, standard diplomas, or advanced diplomas (Lang, 2006). For example, students meeting all requirements and who pass the state high-stakes tests can be awarded an appropriate diploma; students who meet all requirements except passing the state high-stakes test could be awarded a general diploma. For individuals who have not been able to meet all the requirements for a standard diploma, an attendance certificate can be awarded for those who nonetheless have stayed in school and satisfactorily met attendance requirements throughout their school career. For students who have gone significantly beyond graduation requirements, advanced diplomas can be awarded to acknowledge this level of achievement. Any differentiated or tiered diploma may be associated with specific course and competence requirements. In your own school, find out what factors determine the type of diploma individual students will receive, and how students' postsecondary futures (employment, vocational training, college entrance) will be affected by the type of diploma received.

Other states, attempting to ensure uniformly high standards, have begun to eliminate differentiated diplomas in favor of one more advanced diploma. Consultation with career counselors, vocational schools, parents, and community resources can help provide relevant information on how to best meet the needs of students with disabilities under these circumstances. Because IDEA

Career Information Using Technology

Students with reading difficulties need access to career information. However, the traditional formats that rely on reading independently may be inappropriate for many of these students. Several alternatives exist for adapting this information for students. One alternative format is to provide the text material in audio formats. Recordings for the Blind and Dyslexic will make audio recordings of text materials for individuals with visual disabilities, including those who are blind and those with low vision, and for individuals with learning disabilities and dyslexia.

Another alternative is to obtain one of the electronic text readers, such as *Aspire Reader 4.0* by CAST, that will provide speech output for any electronic text. This software will be particularly useful for materials that are available electronically. Since many career surveys are now widely available on CDs, they can be combined with a program such as *Aspire Reader 4.0* to provide the speech output necessary for students. For example, the *Career IO and Interest Survey* electronically assesses broad interest areas of students, including aptitudes of general ability, verbal ability, numbers, perception, and space.

College information is also widely available on the Internet. By using a text-to-speech program, students with reading difficulties can access the information. For example, every university has a Website that contains its admission procedures. Catalogues and course descriptions are generally available on the Internet. In addition, the Advocacy Institute provides on its Website a wealth of information about the transition from high school to college for students with learning disabilities—information on selecting colleges that have services for students with disabilities, applying to colleges, and for making a successful transition to college, including suggestions on getting help once there.

---

allows students with disabilities to continue to attend school until age 22, some students with disabilities may be able to meet the higher requirements with additional years of schooling.

PLAN FOR FUTURE EDUCATION   Applying for colleges is an arduous task for all students, but may be particularly overwhelming for students with disabilities. Provide additional assistance to those students to encourage them to pursue further education. Many resources are available commercially to help students learn more about colleges' and universities' programs and their services for students with disabilities. The Learning Disabilities Association of America provides one such listing. Another helpful resource is *The Complete Learning Disabilities Directory* (Grey House Publishing, Millerton, New York) that contains information on products, resources, books, and services that are available to help individuals with learning disabilities. For example, names, addresses, and phone numbers are provided for government agencies and professional organizations, as well as listings of books for parents of and individuals with disabilities, major catalogues, pamphlets, and instructional materials including videos, computer software, and study guides. Interested students and parents should contact their local state chapter of the Council for Exceptional Children for additional information on services provided within their region at the higher education level. Much of this information also may be available on the World Wide Web. Many of these resource guides are also available at your local library or local bookstore.

Provide information on the standards necessary for admission to the college that students wish to attend. For example, some colleges require courses in foreign languages, others require specific units (high school credits) in math, science, and English, and most require submission of the Scholastic Assessment Test (SAT) or American College Testing (ACT) scores with the completed applications by prespecified dates. This information can help students select the courses for their last few years in high school. Additionally, they can prepare for taking the SAT or ACT by studying pamphlets, commercially available books, computer programs, or enrolling in classes designed to improve performance on the tests. Some students may qualify for adapted testing procedures on the SAT. For example, some may be allowed extended time to take the SAT, others may be given the SAT in a larger-print format. Seek assistance from your local high school counselor to determine whether or not students qualify for testing adaptations and help them obtain and submit the appropriate application forms.

Most colleges now have Web pages and application forms that can be submitted via e-mail. Provide opportunities for students to access this information via the Internet so they will be able to peruse the information independently. They can also practice writing their application forms on computers and decide whether or not they would like to submit their forms via e-mail or regular mail.

PLAN FOR FUTURE EMPLOYMENT OPPORTUNITIES   Planning for future employment can include internships, adult education, trade and technical schools, competitive employment, supported employment, sheltered workshops, and methods for searching for employment (Pierangelo & Giuliani, 2004). Provide opportunities to discuss future job options. Relate your class content to employment options and opportunities. Invite professionals from the community to discuss how their educational backgrounds assisted them in their vocations. Discuss what types of educational backgrounds are required for various professions. Plan field trips to community-based organizations so students can see firsthand the types of employment opportunities available. Use the expertise of your school guidance counselors to assist in disseminating job-related information. Integrate whenever possible relevant job-related information with your regular curriculum. Use published curriculum materials for assessing and teaching employment-related skills. Check out the monster.com website for employment suggestions for individuals with disabilities (Lipow, n.d.; Woog, n.d.).

The *In the Classroom* feature provides an employment planning checklist. For additional information on employment planning, see Bakken and Obiakor (2008) and Flexer, Simmons, Luft, and Baer (2005).

PLAN FOR INDEPENDENT LIVING SITUATIONS   Many students require information on preparing for future independent living situations. One important issue is selecting, managing, and maintaining a home. Questions to consider include the following:

- What are your residential options?
- Where would you like to live?
  - With family?
  - With friends?
  - Independently?
  - In a residential group home?
  - In a supported living situation?
  - In a semi-independent living program?
  - In independent living arrangements?

Provide information on the types of resources that will be required to go with each type of living arrangement. For example, if students select an independent living arrangement as their first choice, then they need to realize what financial resources will be necessary to accomplish this goal. Many teachers have included units on planning for independent living within their regular curriculum and have reported that students have enjoyed the opportunities to gain familiarity with what is required to own a car and live in an apartment. Preparing budgets allows students to examine expenses they will incur and help them examine employment opportunities that will enable them to realize their goals. Efforts to increase awareness of future needs helps students to be more planful and successful later in life.

Other important living skills include caring for personal needs, getting around in the community, buying and preparing food, buying and maintaining clothing, engaging in community and civic activities, and selecting meaningful recreation and leisure activities (Loyd & Brolin, 1997). Individuals preparing for independent living also need to know about credit and how it can be used effectively.

Finally, vocational, personal, and social skills are important in independent living. Information provided by Cronin et al. (2007) can be helpful in planning and implementing programs to facilitate independent living, in school settings and beyond. It is important that support for students with disabilities and other special needs not stop at the end of schooling, but that all individuals receive needed preparation and necessary support to ensure quality and fulfillment in all of their life's activities.

Employment Planning Checklist

In planning for post-secondary employment opportunities for students with disabilities, have you considered the following?

___1. Adult education programs, to facilitate entry to employment

___2. Technical or trade schools

___3. Sheltered employment through community or social agencies, particularly with the goal of facilitating competitive employment in the future

___4. Supported employment, through affiliates of the International Association for Persons in Supported Employment

___5. Customized employment, which individualizes the relation between the employee and employer, and that addresses the needs of both

___6. Job clubs, which are formed to provide support and improve employment prospects

___7. Placement efforts through Business Advisory Councils

___8. Assistance through state agencies, such as vocational rehabilitation agencies, developmental disabilities agencies, mental health agencies, visual impairment rehabilitation programs, or the Bureau of Employment Services

___9. Supported self-employment or entrepreneurship, with assistance from community, state, or federal agencies

16 Summary

- Career and technical education includes a wide variety of educational programs that are intended to prepare students for employment and for living. Career and technical education may be particularly important for students with disabilities or other special needs who become employed immediately after high school.

- Career and technical education areas include agriculture, business, family and consumer sciences, marketing, health, trade and industry, and technical/communications.

- The Carl D. Perkins Vocational Act of 1984/2005 was of significant importance in promoting access to career and technical education for students with disabilities or other special needs.

- Special considerations for adapting instruction for students with special needs include modifying the physical environment, choosing goals and objectives carefully, adapting curriculum materials, and adapting instructional procedures.

- Transitions in life are important, and transition planning is critical for students with disabilities. All students with IEPs must have individual transition plans by the age of 16.

- Prepare students of all ages for transitions, including transitions from home to preschool, to new schools, to new teachers, and, most important, for life after high school. Involve students, parents, teachers, counselors, transition coordinators, and community-based personnel as members of the transition team.

- Students with disabilities require instruction in self-advocacy and self-determination skills to provide them with skills to be more successful during and after high school. Provide ample practice in safe environments for the development of these skills.

- Prepare students for life after high school by using appropriate transition assessment measures, carefully evaluating the results, and designing and implementing life skills programs.

- Help prepare students for the appropriate high school graduation requirements necessary for their transition plans.

- Provide educational opportunities that prepare students with disabilities for future education, jobs, and independent or supported living arrangements.

PROFESSIONAL STANDARDS LINK:
Career and Technical Education, and Transitions

Information in this chapter links most directly to:

- CEC Standards: 3 (Individual Learning Differences), 4 (Instructional Strategies), 5 (Learning Environments and Social Interactions), 6 (Language), 7 (Instructional Planning), 8 (Assessment), 9 (Professional and Ethical Practice), 10 (Collaboration)

- INTASC Standards: Principles 1 (understands central concepts of the discipline), 2 (provides appropriate learning opportunities), 3 (understands learning differences, adapts instructional opportunities), 4 (instructional strategies), 5 (creates learning environments), 6 (fosters inquiry, collaboration, interaction), 7 (plans instruction), 8 (assessment strategies), 9 (relationships with school personnel, families, agencies), 10 (reflects on practice)

- PRAXIS II™ Content Categories (Knowledge): 2 (Issues), 3 (Delivery of Services)

- PRAXIS II™ Content Categories (Application): 1 (Curriculum), 2 (Instruction), 3 (Assessment), 5 (Professional Roles)

CAREER AND TECHNICAL EDUCATION, AND TRANSITION

If you are teaching career and technical education, or promoting transitions, have you considered the following? If not, see the pages listed below.

STRATEGIES FOR ADAPTING CAREER AND TECHNICAL EDUCATION

STRATEGIES FOR PROMOTING TRANSITIONS

STRATEGIES FOR TRANSITIONING FOR THE FUTURE

Chapter 1

Alaska Statutes, Title 14, Chapter 30, 1971.

Beattie v. Board of Education of City of Antigo, 172 N.W. 153, 154 (1919).

Blaska, J. (1993). The power of language: Speak and write using "person first." In M. Nagler (Ed.), *Perspectives on disability* (2nd ed., pp. 25–32). Palo Alto, CA: Health Markets Research.

Brown v. Board of Education, 347 U.S. 483 (1954).

Code of Virginia, Section, 22.275.3 (1973).

Cook, B. G., Tankersley, M., Cook, L., & Landrum, T. J. (2000). Teachers' attitudes toward their included students with disabilities. *Exceptional Children, 67,* 115–135.

Council for Exceptional Children. (2002). No Child Left Behind has major implications for special education. *CEC Today, 9*(4), 4.

Davis, G. A., & Rimm, S. B. (2004). *Education of the gifted and talented* (5th ed.). Boston: Allyn & Bacon.

deBettencourt, L. U. (2002). Understanding the differences between IDEA and Section 504. *Teaching Exceptional Children, 34*(3), 16–23.

Dettmer, P., Thurston, L., & Dyck, N. (2005). *Consultation, collaboration, and teamwork for students with special needs.* Boston: Allyn & Bacon.

Diana v. State Board of Education, Civ. No. C-70-37 RFP (N.D. Cal. 1970, 1973).

Downing, J. A. (2004). Related services for students with disabilities: Introduction to the special issue. *Intervention in School and Clinic, 39,* 195–208.

Educational Testing Service. (2002). *Special education: Core knowledge study guide.* Princeton, NJ: Author.

Frieman, B. B. (2001). *What teachers need to know about children at-risk.* New York: Allyn & Bacon.

Fuchs, D., & Fuchs, L. S. (1994). Inclusive schools movement and the radicalization of special education reform. *Exceptional Children, 60,* 294–309.

Gollnick, D. M., & Chinn, P. C. (2009). *Multicultural education in a pluralistic society* (8th ed.). Upper Saddle River, NJ: Merrill/Pearson.

Hayden, D., Takemoto, C., Anderson, W., & Chitwood, S. (2008). *Negotiating the special education maze: A guide for parents and teachers.* Bethesda, MD: Woodbine House.

Honig v. Doe, 484 U.S. 305 S.Ct. 592, 98 L.Ed.2d 686, 43 Ed. Law Rep. 857 (1988).

Individuals with Disabilities Education Improvement Act of 2004. Public Law 108-446. (2007). Washington, DC: U.S. Government Printing Office.

Johnson, T. P. (1986). *The principal's guide to the educational rights of handicapped students.* Reston, VA: National Association of Secondary School Principals.

Kauffman, J. M. (1995). Why we must celebrate a diversity of restrictive environments. *Learning Disabilities Research & Practice, 10,* 225–232.

Kauffman, J. M., & Hallahan, D. P. (Eds.). (1995). *The illusion of full inclusion: A comprehensive critique of a current special education bandwagon.* Austin, TX: Pro-Ed.

Knowlton, E. (2004). Special education policies and procedures. In B. K. Lenz & D. D. Deshler (Eds.), *Teaching content to all: Evidence-based inclusive practices in middle and secondary schools* (pp. 279–300). Boston: Pearson Education.

Lane, H. (1995). The education of deaf children: Drowning in the mainstream and the sidestream. In J. M. Kauffman & D. P. Hallahan (Eds.), *The illusion of full inclusion* (pp. 275–287). Austin, TX: Pro-Ed.

Larry P. v. Riles, 343 F. Supp. 1306 (N. D. Cal. 1972, *aff'd* 502 F.2d 963 (9th Cir. 1974), *further action* 495 F. Supp. 926 N. D. Cal. 1979), *aff'd* 793 F. 2d 969 (9th Cir. 1984).

Lipsky, D. K., & Gartner, A. (1997). *Inclusion and school reform: Transforming America's classrooms.* Baltimore, MD: Paul H. Brookes.

Mandlawitz, M. (2006). *What every teacher should know about IDEA 2004.* Boston: Pearson Education.

Mills v. Board of Education, 348 F. Supp. 866 (D.D.C. 1972).

Murdick, N. L., Gartin, B. C., & Crabtree, T. L. (2006). *Special education law* (2nd ed.) Upper Saddle River, NJ: Merrill/Prentice Hall.

Nevada Revised Statutes, Section 39.050 (1963).

Nougaret, A., Scruggs, T. E., & Mastropieri, M. A. (2004). The effects of teacher licensure on teachers' pedagogical competence: Implications for elementary and secondary teachers of students with learning and behavioral disabilities. In T. E. Scruggs & M. A. Mastropieri (Eds.), *Research in secondary settings: Advances in learning and behavioral disabilities* (Vol. 17, pp. 301–318). Oxford, UK: Elsevier Science.

Oberti v. Board of Education of the Borough of Clementon School District, 995 F. 2d 1204 (3rd Cir. 1993).

Palmer, D. S., Fuller, K., Arora, T., & Nelson, M. (2001). Taking sides: Parent views on inclusion for their children with severe disabilities. *Exceptional Children, 67,* 467–484.

Pennsylvania Association for Retarded Children v. Commonwealth of Pennsylvania (PARC), 334 F. Supp. 1257 (E.D. Pa. 1972).

Rimland, B. (1993). Inclusive education: Right for some. *Autism Research Review International, 7,* 3.

Rothstein, L. F. (1999). *Special education law* (3rd ed.). New York: Longman.

Scruggs, T. E., & Mastropieri, M. A. (1996a). Teacher perceptions of mainstreaming/inclusion, 1958–1995: A research synthesis. *Exceptional Children, 63,* 59–74.

Scruggs, T. E., & Mastropieri, M. A. (1996b). Quantitative synthesis of survey research: Methodology and validation. In T. E. Scruggs & M. A. Mastropieri (Eds.), *Advances in learning and behavioral disabilities* (Vol. 10, pp. 209–223). Greenwich, CT: JAI Press.

Scruggs, T. E., & Mastropieri, M. A. (Eds.). (2005). *Cognition and learning in diverse settings: Advances in learning and behavioral disabilities* (Vol. 18). Oxford, UK: Elsevier Science.

Simpson, R. L., LaCava, P. G., & Graner, P. S. (2004). The No Child Left Behind Act: Challenges and implications for educators. *Intervention in School and Clinic, 40,* 67–75.

Sindelar, P. T., McCray, E. D., Kiely, M. T., & Kamman, M. (2008). The impact of No Child Left Behind on special education teacher supply and the preparation of the workforce. In T. E. Scruggs & M. A. Mastropieri (Eds.), *Personnel preparation: Advances in learning and behavioral disabilities* (Vol. 21, pp. 89–123). Bingley, UK: Emerald.

Smith, T. E. C. (2001). Section 504, the ADA, and public schools: What educators need to know. *Remedial and Special Education, 22,* 335–343.

Stainback, W., & Stainback, S. (Eds.). (1996). *Controversial issues confronting special education: Divergent perspectives* (2nd ed.). Boston: Allyn & Bacon.

U.S. Department of Education. (2006). *Carl D. Perkins Career and Technical Education Act of 2006: Reauthorization of Perkins.* Washington, DC: Author. Retrieved April 10, 2008, from http://www.ed.gov/policy/sectech/leg/perkins/index.html.

U.S. Department of Education, Office of Special Education and Rehabilitative Services. (2006a). *Assistance to states for the education of children with disabilities and preschool grants for children with disabilities.* Final Regulations. 71 Fed. Reg. 46540 (30 C.F.R. Parts 300 and 301). Washington, DC: Author.

U.S. Department of Education. (2007). *To assure the free appropriate public education of all children with disabilities: Twenty-seventh annual report to Congress on the implementation of the Individuals with Disabilities Education Act.* Washington, DC: Author.

Watson v. City of Cambridge, 32 N.E. 864, 864 (1893).

Will, M. (1986). Educating students with learning problems: A shared responsibility. *Exceptional Children, 52,* 411–415.

Wright, P. W. D., & Wright, P. D. (2005). *Wright's law IDEA 2004: Parts A & B.* Hartfield, VA: Harbor House Law Press.

Wright, P. W. D., & Wright, P. D. (2007). *Wrightslaw: Special education law* (2nd ed.). Hartfield, VA: Harbor House Law Press.

Wright, P. W. D., Wright, P. D., & Heath, S. W. (2004). *Wright's law: No child left behind.* Hartfield, VA: Harbor House Law Press.

Yell, M. (2006). *The law and special education* (2nd ed.). Upper Saddle River, NJ: Merrill/Prentice-Hall.

Chapter 2

Buck, G. H., Polloway, E. A., Smith-Thomas, A., & Cook, K. W. (2003). Prereferral intervention processes: A survey of state practices. *Exceptional Children, 69,* 349–360.

Burns, M. K., & Symington, T. (2002). A meta-analysis of prereferral intervention teams: Student and systematic outcomes. *Journal of School Psychology, 40,* 437–447.

Castro, V. E. (2007). *The effect of co-teaching on academic achievement of k–2 students with and without disabilities in inclusive and noninclusive classrooms.* Unpublished doctoral dissertation, Fordham University, New York.

Conners, N. A. (2008). *An in-depth study of expert middle school special educators.* Unpublished doctoral dissertation. Fairfax, VA: George Mason University.

Correa, V., Jones, H. A., Thomas, C. C., & Morsink, C. V. (2005). *Interactive teaming: Enhancing programs for students with special needs.* Upper Saddle River, NJ: Merrill/Prentice Hall.

Davern, L. (2004). School-to-home notebooks: What parents have to say. *Teaching Exceptional Children, 36*(5), 22–27.

Division for Learning Disabilities. (2007). *Thinking about response to instruction and learning disabilities: A teacher's guide.* Arlington, VA: Author.

Friend, M., & Cook, L. (2007). *Interactions: Collaboration skills for school professionals* (5th ed.). Boston: Allyn & Bacon.

Frisk, C. A. (2004). Teacher collaboration: Learning from inclusion dyad dialogues. Unpublished doctoral dissertation, University of Rhode Island, Kingston. *Dissertation Abstracts International, 65*(6), 2158A. (UMI No. AAI3135903)

Giangreco, M. F., & Broer, S. M. (2007). School-based screening to determine overreliance on paraprofessionals. *Focus on Autism and Other Developmental Disabilities, 22,* 149–158.

Giangreco, M. F., Edelman, S. W., Broer, S. M., & Doyle, M. B. (2001). Paraprofessional support of students with disabilities: Literature from the past decade. *Exceptional Children, 68,* 45–63.

Ginott, H. (1995). *Teacher and child.* New York: Collier.

Ginott, H. G., Ginott, A., & Goddard, H. W. (2003). *Between parent and child.* New York: Three Rivers.

Gordon, T. (2003). *T.E.T.: Teacher effectiveness training.* New York: Three Rivers.

Kamps, D., Abbott, M., Greenwood, C., Wills, H., Veerkamp, M., & Kaufman, J. (2008). Effects of small-group reading instruction and curriculum differences for students most at risk in kindergarten. *Journal of Learning Disabilities, 41,* 101–114.

Kampwirth, T. J. (2006). *Collaborative consultation in the schools* (3rd ed.). Upper Saddle River, NJ: Prentice Hall.

Luckner, J. L., (1999). An examination of two co-teaching classrooms. *American Annals of the Deaf, 144,* 24–34.

Marks, S. U., Schrader, C., & Levine, M. (1999). Paraeducator experiences in inclusive settings: Helping, hovering, or holding their own? *Exceptional Children, 65,* 315–328.

Mastropieri, M. A., & Scruggs, T. E. (2001). Promoting inclusion in secondary classrooms. *Learning Disability Quarterly, 24,* 265–274.

McCann, B. (2008). *An examination of teachers' attitudes toward inclusion and co-teaching.* Unpublished doctoral dissertation, George Mason University, Fairfax, VA.

McDuffie, M. A., Mastropieri, M. A., & Scruggs, T. E. (in press). Differential effects of co-teaching and peer-mediated instruction: Results for content learning and student–teacher interactions. *Exceptional Children.*

McLaughlin, M. J. (2002). Examining special and general education collaborative practices in exemplary schools. *Journal of Educational & Psychological Consultation, 13,* 279–283.

Murawski, W. W. (2006). Student outcomes in co-taught secondary English classes: How can we improve? *Reading & Writing Quarterly: Overcoming Learning Difficulties, 22,* 227–247.

Murawski, W. W., & Dieker, L. (2004). Tips and strategies for co-teaching at the secondary level. *Teaching Exceptional Children, 36,* 52–58.

Murawski, W. W., & Swanson, H. L. (2001). A meta-analysis of co-teaching research: Where are the data? *Remedial and Special Education, 22,* 258–267.

Murdick, N. L., Gartin, B. C., & Crabtree, T. L. (2002). *Special education law.* Upper Saddle River, NJ: Merrill/Prentice Hall.

Murray, C. (2004). Clarifying collaborative roles in urban high schools: General educators' perspectives. *Teaching Exceptional Children, 36*(5), 44–51.

Overton, S. (2005). *Collaborating with families.* Upper Saddle River, NJ: Merrill/Prentice Hall.

Pierangelo, R., & Giuliani, G. A. (2004). *Transition services in special education: A practical approach.* Boston: Allyn & Bacon.

Pickett, A. L., & Gerlach, K. (Eds.). (2003). *Supervising paraeducators in educational settings: A team approach* (2nd ed.). Austin: Pro-Ed.

Polloway, E. A., Patton, J. R., & Serna, L. (2001). *Strategies for teaching learners with special needs* (7th ed.). Upper Saddle River, NJ: Merrill/Prentice Hall.

Riggs, C. G. (2004). To teachers: What paraeducators want you to know. *Teaching Exceptional Children, 36*(5), 8–13.

Rock, M. L., & Zigmond, N. (2001). Intervention assistance: Is it substance or symbolism? *Preventing School Failure, 45,* 153–159.

Scruggs, T. E., Mastropieri, M. A., & McDuffie, K. A. (2007). Co-teaching in inclusive classrooms: A meta-synthesis of qualitative research. *Exceptional Children, 73,* 392–416.

Trautman, M. L. (2004). Preparing and managing paraprofessionals. *Intervention in School and Clinic, 39,* 131–138.

Vaughn, S., & Roberts, G. (2007). Secondary interventions in reading: Providing additional instruction for students at risk. *Teaching Exceptional Children, 39*(5), 40–46.

Walther-Thomas, C. S. (1997). Co-teaching experiences: The benefits and problems that teachers and principals report over time. *Journal of Learning Disabilities, 30,* 395–408.

Weiss, M. P., & Brigham, F. J. (2000). Co-teaching and the model of shared responsibility: What does the research support? In T. E. Scruggs & M. A. Mastropieri (Eds.), *Advances in learning and behavioral disabilities* (Vol. 14, pp. 217–245). Oxford, UK: JAI/Elsevier Science.

Weiss, M. P., & Lloyd, J. W. (2003). Conditions for co-teaching: Lessons from a case study. *Teacher Education and Special Education, 26,* 27–41.

Chapter 3

American Association on Intellectual and Developmental Disabilities (AAIDD). (2008). *Frequently asked questions on intellectual disability and the AAIDD Definition.* Washington, DC: Author. Retrieved April 17, 2008, from http://www.aamr.org/Policies/faq_mental_retardation.shtml.

American Association on Mental Retardation. (2002). *Mental retardation: Definition, classification, and systems of support* (10th ed.). Washington, DC: Author.

American Psychiatric Association. (2000). *Diagnostic and statistical manual of mental disorders: DSM–IV–TR* (4th ed., text revision). Washington, DC: American Psychiatric Association.

Astrom, R. L., Wadsworth, S. J., & DeFries, J. C. (2007). Etiology of the stability of reading difficulties: The longitudinal twin study of reading disabilities. *Twin Research and Human Genetics, 10,* 434–439.

Austin, V. L. (2003). Pharmacological interventions for students with ADD. *Intervention in School and Clinic, 38,* 289–296.

Barkley, R. A. (1990). *Attention deficit hyperactivity disorder: A handbook for diagnosis and treatment.* New York: Guilford Press.

Barkley, R. A. (1998). *Attention deficit hyperactivity disorder: A handbook for diagnosis and treatment* (2nd ed.). New York: Guilford Press.

Barkley, R. A. (2000). *Taking charge of ADHD: The complete, authoritative guide for parents.* New York: Guilford Press.

Beirne-Smith, M., Patton, J., & Kim, S. (2006). *Mental retardation* (7th ed.). Upper Saddle River, NJ: Merrill/Prentice Hall.

Bender, W. N. (1997). *Understanding ADHD: A practical guide for teachers and parents.* Upper Saddle River, NJ: Merrill/Prentice Hall.

Berkeley, S., Bender, W. N., Peaster, L., & Saunders, L. (in press). Implementation of responsiveness to intervention: A snapshot of progress. *Remedial and Special Education.*

Beukelman, D. R., & Mirenda, P. (2006). *Augmentative and alternative communication: Supporting children and adults with complex communication needs.* Baltimore: Brookes.

Biederman, J., Faranone, S. V., Keenan, K., Benjamin, J., Krifcher, B., Moore, C., et al. (1992). Further evidence for family-genetic risk factors in attention deficit hyperactivity disorder. *Archives of General Psychiatry, 48,* 633–642.

Blue-Blanning, M., Turnbull, A., & Pereira, L. (2000). Group action planning as a support strategy for Hispanic families: Parent and professional perspectives. *Mental Retardation, 38,* 262–275.

Brigham, F. J., & Cole, J. E. (1999). Selective mutism: Developments in definition, etiology, assessment and treatment. In T. E. Scruggs & M. A. Mastropieri (Eds.), *Advances in learning and behavioral disabilities* (Vol. 13, pp. 183–216). Greenwich, CT: JAI Press.

Brown, T. E. (2005). *Attention deficit disorder: The unfocused mind in children and adults.* New Haven, CT: Yale University Press.

Bui, Y. N., & Turnbull, A. (2003). East meets west: Analysis of person-centered planning in the context of Asian American values. *Education and Training in Developmental Disabilities, 38,* 18–31.

Cascella, P. W. (2004). Receptive communication abilities among adults with significant intellectual disability. *Journal of Intellectual & Developmental Disability, 29,* 70–78.

Cohen, D. E. (2000). Health promotion and disability prevention: The case for personal responsibility and independence. In M. L. Wehmeyer & J. R. Patton (Eds.), *Mental retardation in the 21st century* (pp. 251–264). Austin, TX: Pro-Ed.

Connor, P. D., Sampson, P. D., Bookstein, F. L., Barr, H. M., & Streissguth, A. P. (2001). Direct and indirect effects of prenatal alcohol damage on executive function. *Developmental Neuropsychology, 18,* 331–354.

Conture, E. G. (1989). Why does my child stutter? In *Stuttering and your child: Questions and answers* (pp. 13–22). Memphis: Stuttering Foundation of America.

Council for Exceptional Children (CEC). (1992). *Children with ADD: A shared responsibility.* Reston, VA: Council for Exceptional Children.

Cronin, M. E., Patton, J. R., & Wood, S. J. (2007). *Life skills instruction* (2nd ed.). Austin, TX: Pro-Ed.

Cullinan, D. (2004). Classification and definition of emotional and behavioral disorders. In R. B. Rutherford, M. M. Quinn, & S. R. Mathur (Eds.), *Handbook of research in emotional and behavioral disorders* (pp. 32–53). New York: Guilford.

Curlee, R. F. (1989). Does my child stutter? In *Stuttering and your child: Questions and answers* (pp. 7–12). Memphis: Stuttering Foundation of America.

Cutting, L. E., & Denckla, M. B. (2003). Attention: Relationships between attention-deficit hyperactivity disorder and learning disabilities. In H. L. Swanson, K. R. Harris, & S. Graham (Eds.), *Handbook of learning disabilities* (pp. 125–139). New York: Guilford.

Division for Learning Disabilities (2007). *Thinking about response to instruction and learning disabilities: A teacher's guide.* Arlington, VA: Author.

Drew, C. J., & Hardman, M. L. (2007). *Mental retardation: A lifespan approach to people with intellectual disabilities* (9th ed.). Upper Saddle River, NJ: Merrill/Prentice Hall.

Duhaney, L. M. G. (2003). A practical approach to managing the behaviors of students with ADD. *Intervention in School and Clinic, 38,* 267–279.

Elbaum, B., & Vaughn, S. (2003). Self-concept and students with learning disabilities. In H. L. Swanson, K. R. Harris, & S. Graham (Eds.), *Handbook of learning disabilities* (pp. 229–241). New York: Guilford.

Ezell, D., & Klein, C. (2003). Impact of portfolio assessment on locus of control of students with and without disabilities. *Education and Training in Developmental Disabilities, 38,* 220–228.

Faust, M., Dimitrovsky, L., & Shacht, T. (2003). Naming difficulties in children with dyslexia: Application of the tip-of-the-tongue paradigm. *Journal of Learning Disabilities, 36,* 203–215.

Federal Register. (1977, December 29). Procedures for evaluating specific learning disabilities. Washington, DC: Department of Health, Education, and Welfare.

Feingold, B. (1975). *Why your child is hyperactive.* New York: Random House.

Fletcher, J. M., Lyon, G. R., Barnes, M., Stuebing, K. K., Francis, D. J., Olson, R. K., et al. (2002). Classification of learning disabilities: An evidence-based evaluation. In R. Bradley, L. Danielson, & D. P. Hallahan (Eds.), *Identification of learning disabilities: Research to practice* (pp. 185–250). Mahwah, NJ: Lawrence Erlbaum Associates.

Fletcher, J. M., Lyon, G. R., Fuchs, L. S., & Barnes, M. (2007). *Learning disabilities: From identification to intervention.* New York: Guilford.

Fuchs, D., & Fuchs, L. (2006). Introduction to response to intervention: What, why, and how valid is it? *Reading Research Quarterly, 41,* 93–99.

Fuchs, D., Fuchs, L., Mathes, P. G., Lipsey, M. W., & Roberts, P. H. (2002). Is "learning disabilities" just a fancy term for low achievement? A meta-analysis of reading differences between low achievers with and without the label. In R. Bradley, L. Danielson, & D. P. Hallahan (Eds.), *Identification of learning disabilities: Research to practice* (pp. 737–762). Mahwah, NJ: Lawrence Erlbaum.

Fuchs, D., Mock, D., Morgan, P. L., & Young, C. L. (2003). Responsiveness-to-intervention: Definitions, evidence, and implications for the learning disabilities construct. *Learning Disabilities Research & Practice, 18,* 157–171.

Fuchs, L. S., & Fuchs, D. (2003). Enhancing the mathematical problem solving of students with mathematics disabilities. In H. L. Swanson, K. R. Harris, & S. Graham (Eds.), *Handbook of learning disabilities* (pp. 323–344). New York: Guilford.

Furlong, M. J., Morrison, G. M., & Jimerson, S. (2004). Externalizing behaviors of aggression and violence. In R. B. Rutherford, M. M. Quinn, & S. R. Mathur (Eds.), *Handbook of research in emotional and behavioral disorders* (pp. 243–261). New York: Guilford.

Gaskins, I., & Pressley, M. (2007). Teaching metacognitive strategies that address executive function processes within a schoolwide curriculum. In L. Meltzer (Ed.), *Executive function in education: From theory to practice* (pp. 261–286). New York: Guilford.

Geary, D. C. (2003). Learning disabilities in arithmetic: Problem-solving differences and cognitive deficits. In H. L. Swanson, K. R. Harris, & S. Graham (Eds.), *Handbook of learning disabilities* (pp. 199–212). New York: Guilford.

Gerber, M. M. (2005). Teachers are still the test: Limitations of response to instruction strategies for identifying children with learning disabilities. *Journal of Learning Disabilities, 38,* 516–524.

Graham, S. (2004). Writing instruction. In B. Y. L. Wong (Ed.), *Learning about learning disabilities* (3rd ed., pp. 281–314). San Diego, CA: Elsevier Academic Press.

Gregg, N., & Mather, N. (2002). School is fun at recess: Informal analyses of written language for students with learning disabilities. *Journal of Learning Disabilities, 35,* 7–22.

Gresham, F. M. (2002). Responsiveness to intervention: An alternative approach to the identification of learning disabilities. In R. Bradley, L. Danielson, & D. P. Hallahan (Eds.), *Identification of learning disabilities* (pp. 467–519). Mahwah, NJ: Lawrence Erlbaum.

Gresham, F. M., & Kern, L. (2004). Internalizing behavior problems in children and adolescents. In R. B. Rutherford, M. M. Quinn, & S. R. Mathur (Eds.), *Handbook of research in emotional and behavioral disorders* (pp. 262–281). New York: Guilford.

Hallahan, D. P., & Mock, D. (2003). A brief history of the field of learning disabilities. In H. L. Swanson, K. R. Harris, & S. Graham (Eds.), *Handbook of learning disabilities* (pp. 16–29). New York: Guilford.

Harris, K. R., Reid, R. R., & Graham, S. (2004). Self-regulation among students with LD and ADHD. In B. Y. L. Wong (Ed.), *Learning about learning disabilities* (3rd ed., pp. 167–194). San Diego, CA: Elsevier Academic Press.

Hutchinson, N. L., Freemen, J. G., & Berg, D. H. (2004). Social competence of adolescents with learning disabilities: Interventions and issues. In B. Y. L. Wong (Ed.), *Learning about learning disabilities* (3rd ed., pp. 415–448). San Diego, CA: Elsevier Academic Press.

Jacobson, J. W., & Mulick, J. A. (1996). *Manual on diagnosis and professional practice in mental retardation.* Washington, DC: American Psychological Association.

Kauffman, J. M., & Landrum, T. (2009). *Characteristics of emotional and behavioral disorders of children and youth* (9th ed.). Upper Saddle River, NJ: Merrill/Pearson.

Kavale, K., Mathur, S. R., & Mostert, M. (2004). Social skills training and teaching social behavior. In R. B. Rutherford, M. M. Quinn, & S. R. Mathur (Eds.), *Handbook of research in emotional and behavioral disorders* (pp. 446–461). New York: Guilford.

Lane, K. L. (2004). Academic instruction and tutoring interventions for students with emotional/behavioral disorders 1990 to present. In R. B. Rutherford, M. M. Quinn, & S. R. Mathur (Eds.), *Handbook of research in emotional and behavioral disorders* (pp. 462–486). New York: Guilford.

Lloyd, L. L., Fuller, D. R., & Arvidson, H. H. (1997). *Augmentative and alternative communication: A handbook of principles and practices.* Boston: Allyn & Bacon.

Lyon, G. R., Fletcher, J. M., Shaywitz, S. E., Shaywitz, B. A., Torgesen, J. K., Wood, F. B., Schulte, A., & Olson, R. (2001). Rethinking learning disabilities. In C. E. Finn, Jr., A. J. Rotherham, & C. R. Hokanson, Jr. (Eds.), *Rethinking special education for a new century* (pp. 259–287). Washington, DC: Thomas B. Fordham Foundation.

Macmillan, D. L., & Siperstein, G. N. (2002). Learning disabilities as operationally defined by schools. In R. Bradley, L. Danielson, & D. P. Hallahan (Eds.), *Identification of learning disabilities* (pp. 287–333). Mahwah, NJ: Lawrence Erlbaum.

Mann, V. A. (2003). Language processes: Keys to reading disability. In H. L. Swanson, K. R. Harris, & S. Graham (Eds.), *Handbook of learning disabilities* (pp. 213–228). New York: Guilford.

Markel, G., & Greenbaum, J. (1996). *Performance breakthroughs for adolescents with learning disabilities or ADD: How to help students succeed in the regular education classroom.* Champaign, IL: Research Press.

Mastropieri, M. A., & Scruggs, T. E. (2002a). *Effective instruction for special education* (3rd ed.). Austin, TX: Pro-Ed.

Mastropieri, M. A., & Scruggs, T. E. (2002b). Discrepancy models in the identification of learning disabilities. In R. Bradley, L. Danielson, & D. P. Hallahan (Eds.), *Identification of learning disabilities* (pp. 449–466). Mahwah, NJ: Lawrence Erlbaum.

Mastropieri, M. A., & Scruggs, T. E. (2005). Feasibility and consequences of response to intervention (RTI): Examination of the issues and scientific evidence as a model for the identification of individuals with learning disabilities. *Journal of Learning Disabilities, 38,* 525–531.

Mastropieri, M. A., Scruggs, T. E., Boon, R., & Carter, K. B. (2001). Correlates of inquiry learning in science: Constructing concepts of density and buoyancy. *Remedial and Special Education, 22,* 130–138.

Mastropieri, M. A., Scruggs, T. E., & Carter, K. B. (1997). How effective is inquiry learning for students with mild disabilities? *Journal of Special Education, 31,* 199–211.

Mastropieri, M. A., Scruggs, T. E., Davidson, T., & Rana, R. (2004). Instructional interventions in mathematics for students with learning disabilities. In B. Y. L. Wong (Ed.), *Learning about learning disabilities* (3rd ed., pp. 315–340). San Diego, CA: Elsevier Academic Press.

Mercer, C. D., & Pullen, P. C. (2009). *Students with learning disabilities* (7th ed.). Upper Saddle River, NJ: Merrill/Pearson.

Mohan, A., Singh, A. P., & Mandal, M. K. (2001). Transfer and interference of motor skills in people with intellectual disability. *Journal of Intellectual Disability Research, 45,* 361–369.

Osborn, R. G., & Meador, D. M. (1990). The memory performance of selected depressed and nondepressed nine- to eleven-year-old male children. *Behavioral Disorders, 16,* 32–38.

Oswald, D. P., Best, A. M., Coutinho, M. J., & Nagle, H. A. L. (2003). Trends in the special education identification rates of boys and girls: A call for research and change. *Exceptionality, 11,* 223–237.

Owens, R. E., Metz, D. E., & Haas, A. (2006). *Introduction to communication disorders: A life span perspective* (3rd ed.). Boston: Allyn & Bacon.

Palson, K. (1986). *Essence of Kirstin.* Medfield, MA: Author.

Polsgrove, L., & Smith, S. W. (2004). Informed practice in teaching self-control to children with emotional and behavioral disorders. In R. B. Rutherford, M. M. Quinn, & S. R. Mathur (Eds.), *Handbook of research in emotional and behavioral disorders* (pp. 399–425). New York: Guilford.

Reid, R., Gonzalez, J. E., Nordness, P. D., Trout, A., & Epstein, M. H. (2004). A meta-analysis of the academic status of students with emotional/behavioral disturbance. *Journal of Special Education, 38,* 130–143.

Riccio, C. A., Hynd, G. W., & Cohen, M. J. (1997). Etiology and neurobiology of ADHD. In W. N. Bender (Ed.), *Understanding ADHD: A practical guide for teachers and parents* (pp. 23–44). Upper Saddle River, NJ: Merrill/Prentice Hall.

Schalock, R. L., Luckasson, R. A., Shogren, K. A., Borthwick-Duffie, S., Bradley, V., Buntinx, W. H. E., et al. (2007). The renaming of mental retardation: Understanding the change to the term intellectual disability. *Intellectual and Developmental Disabilities, 45,* 116–124.

Schwanz, K. A., & Kamphaus, R. W. (1997). Assessment and diagnosis of ADHD. In W. N. Bender (Ed.), *Understanding ADHD: A practical guide for teachers and parents* (pp. 81–106). Upper Saddle River, NJ: Merrill/Prentice Hall.

Scruggs, T. E., & Marsing, L. (1988). Teaching test-taking skills to behaviorally disordered students. *Behavioral Disorders, 13,* 240–244.

Scruggs, T. E., & Mastropieri, M. A. (2002). On babies and bathwater: Addressing the problems of assessment and identification of learning disabilities. *Learning Disability Quarterly, 25,* 155–168.

Shriner J. G., & Wehby, J. H. (2004). Accountability and assessment for students with emotional and behavioral disorders. In R. B. Rutherford, M. M. Quinn, & S. R. Mathur (Eds.), *Handbook of research in emotional and behavioral disorders* (pp. 216–234). New York: Guilford.

Smith, L. (1975). *Your child's behavior chemistry.* New York: Random House.

Steele, R. G., Forehand, R., Armistead, L., & Brody, G. (1995). Predicting alcohol and drug use in early adulthood: The role of internalizing and externalizing behavior problems in early adolescence. *American Journal of Orthopsychiatry, 65,* 380, 388.

Stuttering Foundation of America. (2007). *The child who stutters at school: Notes to the teacher.* Memphis: Author. Retrieved April 12, 2008, from http://www.stutteringhelp.org/Portals/english/0042NT.pdf.

Swanson, H. L., Cooney, J. B., & McNamara, J. K. (2004). Learning disabilities and memory. In B. Y. L. Wong (Ed.), *Learning about learning disabilities* (3rd ed., pp. 315–339). San Diego, CA: Elsevier Academic Press.

Thomson, J. B., & Raskind, W. H. (2003). Genetic influences on reading and writing disabilities. In H. L. Swanson, K. R. Harris, & S. Graham (Eds.), *Handbook of learning disabilities* (pp. 256–270). New York: Guilford.

U.S. Department of Education. (2007). *Twenty-seventh annual report to Congress on the implementation of the Individuals with Disabilities Education Act.* Washington, DC: Author.

Vaughn, S., Sinagub, J., & Kim, A. (2004). Social competence/social skills of students with learning disabilities: Interventions and issues. In B. Y. L. Wong (Ed.), *Learning about learning disabilities* (3rd ed., pp. 341–373). San Diego, CA: Elsevier Academic Press.

Vicari, S., Caselli, M. C., Gagliardi, C., Tonucci, F., & Volterra, V. (2002). Language acquisition in special populations: A comparison between Down and Williams syndrome. *Neuropsychologia, 40,* 2461–2470.

Wolraich, M., Milich, R., Stumbo, P., & Schultz, F. (1985). The effects of sucrose ingestion on the behavior of hyperactive boys. *Pediatrics, 106,* 742–747.

Woodward, J. (1994). Effects of curriculum discourse style on eighth graders' recall and problem solving in earth science. *Elementary School Journal, 94,* 299–314.

Wright, P. W. D., & Wright, P. D. (2005). *Wrightslaw: IDEA 2004.* Hartfield, VA: Harbor House Law Press.

Young, L., Moni, K. B., Jobling, A., & van Kraayenoord, C. E. (2004). Literacy skills of adults with intellectual disabilities in two community-based day programs. *International Journal of Disability, Development & Education, 51,* 83–97.

Zigler, E., Bennett-Gates, D., Hodapp, R., & Henrich, C. C. (2002). Assessing personality traits of individuals with mental retardation. *American Journal on Mental Retardation, 107,* 181–193.

Chapter 4

American Association on Mental Retardation. (2002). *Mental retardation: Definition, classification, and systems of support* (10th ed.). Washington, DC: Author.

American Medical Association. (2004). *The American Medical Association family medical guide.* Hoboken, NJ: Wiley.

American Psychiatric Association. (2000). *Diagnostic and statistical manual of mental disorders: DSM–IV–TR* (4th ed., text revision). Washington, DC: American Psychiatric Association.

Austin, V. L. (2003). Pharmacological interventions for students with ADD. *Intervention in School and Clinic, 38,* 289–296.

Barry, L. M., & Burlew, S. B. (2004). Using social stories to teach choice and play skills to children with autism. *Focus on Autism and Developmental Disabilities, 19,* 45–51.

Beirne-Smith, M., Patton, J., & Kim, S. (2006). *Mental retardation* (7th ed.). Upper Saddle River, NJ: Merrill/Prentice Hall.

Berla, E. P. (1981). Tactile scanning and memory for a spatial display by blind students. *Journal of Special Education, 15,* 341–350.

Best, S. J. (2005a). Definitions, supports, issues, and services in schools and communities. In S. J. Best, K. W. Heller, & J. L. Bigge (Eds.), *Teaching individuals with physical or multiple disabilities* (5th ed., pp. 31–58). Upper Saddle River, NJ: Merrill/Prentice Hall.

Best, S. J. (2005b). Health impairments and infectious diseases. In S. J. Best, K. W. Heller, & J. L. Bigge (Eds.), *Teaching individuals with physical or multiple disabilities* (5th ed., pp. 59–85). Upper Saddle River, NJ: Merrill/Prentice Hall.

Best, S. J. (2005c). Physical disabilities. In S. J. Best, K. W. Heller, & J. L. Bigge (Eds.), *Teaching individuals with physical or multiple disabilities* (5th ed., pp. 31–58). Upper Saddle River, NJ: Merrill/Prentice Hall.

Best, S. J., & Bigge, J. L. (2005). Cerebral palsy. In S. J. Best, K. W. Heller, & J. L. Bigge (Eds.), *Teaching individuals with physical or multiple disabilities* (5th ed., pp. 87–109). Upper Saddle River, NJ: Merrill/Prentice Hall.

Best, S. J., & Heller, K. W. (2008). Acquired infections and AIDS. In K. W. Heller, P. E. Forney, P. A. Alberto, S. J. Best, & M. N. Schwartzman (Eds.), *Understanding physical, health, and multiple disabilities* (pp. 368–386). Upper Saddle River, NJ: Merrill/Prentice Hall.

Best, S. J., Heller, K. W., & Bigge, J. L. (2005). *Teaching individuals with physical or multiple disabilities* (5th ed.). Upper Saddle River, NJ: Merrill/Prentice Hall.

Best, S. J., Reed, P., & Bigge, J. L. (2005). Assistive technology. In S. J. Best, K. W. Heller, & J. L. Bigge (Eds.), *Teaching individuals with physical or multiple disabilities* (5th ed., pp. 179–226). Upper Saddle River, NJ: Merrill/Prentice Hall.

Bigelow, A. (1991). Spatial mapping of familiar locations in blind children. *Journal of Visual Impairments and Blindness, 85*(3), 113–117.

Bishop, D. V. M., Whitehouse, A. J. O., Watt, H. J., & Line, E. A. (2008). Autism and diagnostic substitution: Evidence from a study of adults with a history of developmental language disorder. *Developmental Medicine and Child Neurology, 50,* 341–345.

Blasco, P. A., & Blasco, P. M. (2004). Cerebral palsy and associated dysfunctions. In R. H. A. Haslam & P. J. Valletutti (Eds.), *Medical problems in the classroom: The teacher's role in diagnosis and management* (4th ed., pp. 395–425). Austin, TX: Pro-Ed.

Bondy, A., & Frost, L. (2002). *A picture's worth: PECS and other visual communication strategies in autism.* Bethesda, MD: Woodbine House.

Briggs, G. (2001). *Drugs in pregnancy and lactation* (6th ed.). Baltimore: Williams and Wilkins.

Byrom, E., & Katz, G. (Eds.). (1991). *HIV prevention and aids education: Resources for special educators.* Reston, VA: Council for Exceptional Children.

Carroll, D. (2001). Considering paraeducator training, roles, and responsibilities. *Teaching Exceptional Children, 34,* 60–64.

Cronin, B. J., & King, S. R. (1990). The development of the Descriptive Video Service. *Journal of Visual Impairment and Blindness, 86*(12), 503–506.

Daneman, D., & Frank, M. (2004). The student with diabetes mellitus. In R. H. A. Haslam & P. J. Valletutti (Eds.), *Medical problems in the classroom: The teacher's role in diagnosis and management* (4th ed., pp. 109–129). Austin, TX: Pro-Ed.

Davis, P. (2003). *Including children with visual impairment in mainstream schools: A practical guide.* London, UK: David Fulton.

Downing, J. E., Ryndak, D. L., & Clark, D. (2000). Paraeducators in inclusive classrooms: Their own perceptions. *Remedial and Special Education, 21,* 171–181.

Flower, A., Burns, M. K., & Bottesford-Miller, N. A. (2007). Meta-analysis of disability simulation research. *Remedial and Special Education, 28,* 72–79.

Giangreco, M. F., & Broer, S. M. (2007). School-based screening to determine overreliance on paraprofessionals. *Focus on Autism and Other Developmental Disabilities, 22,* 149–158.

Giangreco, M. F., Broer, S. M., & Edelman, S. W. (1999). The tip of the iceberg: Determining whether paraprofessional support is needed for students with disabilities in general education settings. *The Journal of the Association for Persons with Severe Handicaps, 24,* 281–291.

Graetz, J. S., Mastropieri, M. A., & Scruggs, T. E. (in press). Promoting social behavior for adolescents with autism with social stories. *Education and Training in Developmental Disabilities.*

Grandinette, S., & Best, S. J. (2008). Traumatic brain injury. In K. W. Heller, P. E. Forney, P. A. Alberto, S. J. Best, & M. N. Schwartzman (Eds.), *Understanding physical, health, and multiple disabilities* (pp. 118–138). Upper Saddle River, NJ: Merrill/Prentice Hall.

Gray, C. (1994). *The new social story book.* Arlington, TX: Future Horizons, Inc.

Gray, C., & Garand, J. (1993). Social stories: Improving responses of students with autism with accurate social information. *Focus on Autistic Behavior, 8,* 1–10.

Griffin, H. C., & Gerber, P. J. (1982). Tactile development and its implication for the development of blind children. *Education of the Visually Handicapped, 13,* 116–123.

Hall, L. J. (2009). *Autism spectrum disorders: From theory to practice.* Upper Saddle River, NJ: Merrill/Pearson.

Hallahan, D. P., Kauffman, J. M., & Pullen, P. (2009). *Exceptional learners: An introduction to special education* (11th ed.). Boston: Allyn & Bacon.

Hallenbeck, M. J., & McMaster, D. (1991). Disability simulation. *TEACHING Exceptional Children, 23*(3), 12–15.

Haslam, R. H. A. (2004). Common neurologic disorders in children. In R. H. A. Haslam & P. J. Valletutti (Eds.), *Medical problems in the classroom: The teacher's role in diagnosis and management* (4th ed., pp. 351–393). Austin, TX: Pro-Ed.

Haslam, R. H. A., & Valletutti, P. J. (2004). *Medical problems in the classroom: The teacher's role in diagnosis and management* (4th ed.). Austin, TX: Pro-Ed.

Heller, K. W. (2008). Traumatic spinal cord injury and spina bifida. In K. W. Heller, P. E. Forney, P. A. Alberto, S. J. Best, & M. N. Schwartzman (Eds.), *Understanding physical, health, and multiple disabilities* (pp. 94–117). Upper Saddle River, NJ: Merrill/Prentice Hall.

Heller, K. W., & Avant, M. J. T. (2008). Juvenile rheumatoid arthritis, arthrogryposis, and osteogenesis imperfecta. In K. W. Heller, P. E. Forney, P. A. Alberto, S. J. Best, & M. N. Schwartzman (Eds.), *Understanding physical, health, and multiple disabilities* (pp. 172–191). Upper Saddle River, NJ: Merrill/Prentice Hall.

Heller, K. W., Bigge, J. L., & Allgood, P. (2005). Adaptations for personal independence. In S. J. Best, K. W. Heller, & J. L. Bigge (Eds.), *Teaching individuals with physical or multiple disabilities* (5th ed., pp. 309–335). Upper Saddle River, NJ: Merrill/Prentice Hall.

Heller, K. W., & Cohen, E. T. (2008). Seizures and epilepsy. In K. W. Heller, P. E. Forney, P. A. Alberto, S. J. Best, & M. N. Schwartzman (Eds.), *Understanding physical, health, and multiple disabilities* (pp. 294–315). Upper Saddle River, NJ: Merrill/Prentice Hall.

Heller, K. W., & Garrett, J. T. (2008). Cerebral palsy. In K. W. Heller, P. E. Forney, P. A. Alberto, S. J. Best, & M. N. Schwartzman (Eds.), *Understanding physical, health, and multiple disabilities* (pp. 72–93). Upper Saddle River, NJ: Merrill/Prentice Hall.

Heward, W. L. (2009). *Exceptional children: An introduction to special education* (9th ed.). Upper Saddle River, NJ: Merrill/Pearson.

Hull, J. M. (1990). *Touching the rock.* New York: Pantheon Books.

Jacobson, J. W., & Mulick, J. A. (1996). *Manual of diagnosis and professional practice in mental retardation.* Washington, DC: American Psychological Association.

Jones, K. L., Smith, D. W., Ulleland, C. N., & Streissguth, A. P. (1973). Patterns of malformation in offspring of chronic alcoholic mothers. *The Lancet, 1*(1267), 1271.

Kamps, D. M., Leonard, B., Potucek, J., & Garrison-Harrell, L. (1995). Cooperative learning groups in reading: An integration strategy for students with autism and general classroom peers. *Behavioral Disorders, 21*(1), 89–109.

Kelly, T. E. (2004). The role of genetic mechanisms in childhood disabilities. In R. H. A. Haslam & P. J. Valletutti (Eds.), *Medical problems in the classroom: The teacher's role in diagnosis and management* (4th ed., pp. 147–186). Austin, TX: Pro-Ed.

Martin, G., & Pear, J. (2003). *Behavior modification: What it is and how to do it* (7th ed.). Upper Saddle River, NJ: Merrill/Prentice Hall.

Mathews, J. (2008, March 31). New microphones are bringing crystal-clear changes. *Washington Post,* p. B2.

Meadow-Orlans, K. P. (1990). Research on developmental aspects of deafness. In D. F. Moores & K. P. Meadow-Orlans (Eds.), *Educational and developmental aspects of deafness* (pp. 283–298). Washington, DC: Gallaudet University Press.

Michael, R. J. (1992). Seizures: Teacher observations and record keeping. *Intervention in School and Clinic, 27,* 212.

Michaud, L., Duhaime, A., & Lazar, M. F. (1997). Traumatic brain injury. In M. L. Batshaw (Ed.), *Children with disabilities* (4th ed., pp. 595–617). Baltimore: Paul Brookes.

Obiakor, F. E., Mehring, T. A., & Schwenn, J. O. (1997). *Disruption, disaster, and death: Helping students deal with crises.* Reston, VA: Council for Exceptional Children.

Obiakor, F. E., Utley, C. A., Smith, R., & Harris-Obiakor, P. (2002). The Comprehensive Support Model for culturally diverse exceptional learners: Intervention in an age of change. *Intervention in School and Clinic, 38,* 14–27.

Owens, R. E., Metz, D. E., & Haas, A. (2006). *Introduction to communication disorders: A life span perspective* (3rd ed.). Boston: Allyn & Bacon.

Pakulski, L. A., & Kaderavek, J. N. (2002). Children with minimal hearing loss: Interventions in the classroom. *Intervention in School and Clinic, 38,* 96–103.

Petersen, S., & Straub, R. L. (1992). *School crisis survival guide.* West Nyack, NY: Center for Applied Research in Education.

Plumb, I. J., & Brown, D. C. (1990). SPAN: Special peer action network. *Teaching Exceptional Children, 56,* 291–304.

Polloway, E. A., Miller, L., & Smith, T. E. C. (2004). *Language instruction for students with disabilities* (3rd ed.). Denver: Love.

Reagan, T. (1990). Cultural considerations in the education of deaf children. In D. F. Moores & K. P. Meadow-Orlans (Eds.), *Educational and developmental aspects of deafness* (pp. 73–84). Washington, DC: Gallaudet University Press.

Ross, D. B., & Koening, A. J. (1991). A cognitive approach to reducing stereotypic head rocking. *Journal of Visual Impairment & Blindness, 85*(1), 17–19.

Ruble, L. A., & Dalrymple, N. J. (1996). An alternative view of outcome in autism. *Focus on Autism and Other Developmental Disabilities, 11*(1), 3–14.

Salend, S. J., & Longo, M. (1994). The roles of the education interpreter in mainstream settings. *Teaching Exceptional Children, 26*(4), 22–28.

Sapon-Shevin, M. (1992). Celebrating diversity, creating community: Curriculum that honors and builds on differences. In S. Stainback & W. Stainback (Eds.), *Curriculum considerations in inclusive classrooms: Facilitating learning for all students.* Baltimore: Paul Brookes.

Schoenbrodt, L. (2001). *Children with traumatic brain injury: A parent's guide.* Bethesda, MD: Woodbine House.

Scott, J., Clark, C., & Brady, M. (2000). *Students with autism: Characteristics and instructional programming for special educators.* San Diego: Singular Press.

Shouldice, M. (2004). Chronic illness in children. In R. H. A. Haslam & P. J. Valletutti (Eds.), *Medical problems in the classroom: The teacher's role in diagnosis and management* (4th ed., pp. 131–146). Austin, TX: Pro-Ed.

Simpson, R. L., & Zionts, P. (2000). *Autism: Information and resources for professionals and parents* (2nd ed.). Austin, TX: Pro-Ed.

Smith, T. E. C. (2002). Section 504: What teachers need to know. *Intervention in School and Clinic, 37,* 259–266.

Snell, M. E., & Brown, F. (2005). *Instruction of students with severe disabilities* (6th ed.). Upper Saddle River, NJ: Merrill/Prentice Hall.

Spiegel, G. L., Cutler, S. K., & Yetter, C. E. (1996). What every teacher should know about epilepsy. *Intervention in School and Clinic, 32*(1), 34–38.

Stewart, D. A., & Kluwin, T. N. (2001). *Teaching deaf and hard of hearing students: Content, strategies, and curriculum.* Boston: Allyn & Bacon.

Streissguth, A. (1997). *Fetal alchohol syndrome: A guide for families and communities.* Baltimore: Brookes.

U.S. Department of Education. (2006). *The Individuals with Disabilities Act Amendments of 2004.* Final regulations. Washington, DC: Author. Retrieved May 1, 2008, from http://idea.ed.gov/explore/view/p/,root,regs,300,A,300%252E8.

U.S. Department of Education. (2007). *Twenty-seventh annual report to Congress on the implementation of the Individuals with Disabilities Education Act.* Washington, DC: Author.

Valletutti, P. J. (2004). The crucial role of the teacher. In R. H. A. Haslam & P. J. Valletutti (Eds.), *Medical problems in the classroom: The teacher's role in diagnosis and management* (4th ed., pp. 1–28). Austin, TX: Pro-Ed.

Warren, D. H. (1984). *Blindness and early childhood development* (2nd ed.). New York: American Foundation for the Blind.

Westling, D. L., & Fox, L. (2004). *Teaching students with severe disabilities* (3rd ed.). Upper Saddle River, NJ: Merrill/Prentice Hall.

Ylvisaker, M., & Feeney, T. J. (1998). School reentry after traumatic brain injury. In M. Ylvisaker (Ed.), *Traumatic brain injury rehabilitation: Children and adolescents* (2nd ed., pp. 369–387). Boston: Butterworth-Heinemann.

Chapter 5

Anderson, M. G., & Webb-Johnson, G. (1995). Cultural contexts, the seriously emotionally disturbed classification, and African American learners. In B. A. Ford, F. E. Obiakor, & J. M. Patton (Eds.), *Effective education of African American exceptional learners: New perspectives* (pp. 151–188). Austin, TX: Pro-Ed.

Antunez, B. (2003). *English language learners in the great city schools: Survey results on students, languages, and programs.* Washington, DC: Council of the Great City Schools. Retrieved February 13, 2005, from http://www.cgcs.org.

Artiles, A. J., & Zamora-Durán, G. (1997). *Reducing disproportionate representation of culturally diverse students in special and gifted education.* Reston, VA: Council for Exceptional Children.

Baca, L. M., & Almanza, E. (1991). *Language minority students with disabilities.* Reston, VA: Council for Exceptional Children.

Baca L. M., Baca, E., & de Valenzuela, J. S. (2004a). Background and rationale for bilingual special education. In L. M. Baca & H. T. Cervantes (Eds.), *The bilingual special education interface* (4th ed., pp. 1–23). Upper Saddle River, NJ: Merrill/Prentice Hall.

Baca, L. M., Baca, E., & de Valenzuela, J. S. (2004b). Development of the bilingual special education interface. In L. M. Baca & H. T. Cervantes (Eds.), *The bilingual special education interface* (4th ed., pp. 101–123). Upper Saddle River, NJ: Merrill/Prentice Hall.

Baca, L. M., & Cervantes, H. T. (2004). *The bilingual special education interface* (4th ed.). Upper Saddle River, NJ: Merrill/Prentice Hall.

Bassuk, F., & Rubin, L. (1987). Homeless children: A neglected population. *American Journal of Orthopsychiatry, 57,* 279–286.

Bireley, M. (1995). Identifying high ability/high achievement giftedness. In J. L. Genshaft, M. Bireley, & C. L. Hollinger (Eds.), *Serving gifted and talented students: A resource for school personnel* (pp. 49–65). Austin, TX: Pro-Ed.

Brice, A. (2002). *The Hispanic child: Speech, language, culture, and education.* Boston: Allyn & Bacon.

Burstahler, S. (2005). Universal design of instruction, definition, principles, and examples. Retrieved June 4, 2008 from University of Washinton, DO-IT: Disabilities, opportunities, internetworking, and technology Website, http://www.washington.edu/doit/Brochures/Programs/ud.html.

Caplan, P., & Dinardo, L. (1986). Is there a relationship between child abuse and learning disability? *Canadian Journal of Behavioral Science, 18,* 367–380.

Castellano, J. A. (Ed.). (2003). *Special populations in gifted education: Working with diverse gifted learners.* Boston: Allyn & Bacon.

Children's Defense Fund. (2005). *The state of America's children: 2005.* Washington, DC: Author. Retrieved May 6, 2008, from http://www.childrensdefense.org/site/DocServer/Greenbook_2005.pdf?docID=1741

Chinn, P. C., & Hughes, S. (1987). Representation of minority students in special education classes. *Remedial and Special Education, 8*(4), 41–46.

Clark, B. (2008). *Growing up gifted* (8th ed.). Upper Saddle River, NJ: Merrill/Prentice Hall.

Crosson-Tower, C. (2007). *Understanding child abuse and neglect* (7th ed.). Boston: Allyn & Bacon.

Culturally responsive instruction addressing the needs of minority and international students and students with disabilities: Universal design strategies. Retrieved June 4, 2008 from Gonzaga University, Culturally Responsive Instruction Website, http://www.gonzaga.edu/Academics/Diversity/Academics/CulturallyResponsiveInstruction.asp.

Davis, G. A. (1995). Identifying the creatively gifted. In J. L. Genshaft, M. Bireley, & C. L. Hollinger (Eds.), *Serving gifted and talented students: A resource for school personnel* (pp. 67–82). Austin, TX: Pro-Ed.

Davis, G. A., & Rimm, S. B. (2004). *Education of the gifted and talented* (5th ed.). Boston: Allyn & Bacon.

de Melendez, W. R., & Ostertag, V. (1997). *Teaching young children in multicultural classrooms: Issues, concepts, and strategies.* Clifton Park, NY: Thomson Delmar Learning.

de Valenzuela, J. S., & Baca, L. (2004). Procedures and techniques for assessing the bilingual exceptional child. In L. M. Baca & H. T. Cervantes (Eds.), *The bilingual special education interface* (4th ed., pp. 184–203). Upper Saddle River, NJ: Merrill/Prentice Hall.

de Valenzuela, J. S., Baca, L., & Baca, E. (2004). Family involvement in bilingual special education: Challenging the norm. In L. M. Baca & H. T. Cervantes (Eds.), *The bilingual special education interface* (4th ed., pp. 336–359). Upper Saddle River, NJ: Merrill/Prentice Hall.

Diamond, L. J., & Jaudes, P. K. (1983). Child abuse in a cerebral-palsied population. *Developmental Medicine and Child Neurology, 25,* 169–174.

Donovan, S., & Cross, C. (Eds.). (2002). *Minority students in special and gifted education.* Washington, DC: National Research Council.

East, K., & Thomas, R. L. (2007). *Across cultures: A guide to multicultural literature for children.* Portsmouth, NH: Libraries Unlimited.

Education Commission of the States. (2004). *State gifted and talented definitions.* Denver, CO: Author. Retrieved May 2, 2008, from http://www.ecs.org/clearinghouse/52/28/5228.htm

Feldhusen, J. F., & Moon, S. (1995). The educational continuum and delivery of services. In J. L. Genshaft, M. Bireley, & C. L. Hollinger (Eds.), *Serving gifted and talented students: A resource for school personnel* (pp. 103–121). Austin, TX: Pro-Ed.

Frieman, B. B. (2001). *What teachers need to know about children at risk.* Boston: Allyn & Bacon.

Garbarino, J., Brookhouser, P. E., & Authier, K. J. (Eds.). (1987). *Special children special risks: The maltreatment of children with disabilities.* Hawthorn, NY: Aldine de Gruyter.

Garcia, S. B., & Ortiz, A. B. (2005). Preventing disproportionate representation: Culturally and linquistically responsive prereferral interventions. *Practitioner Brief Series: National Center for Culturally Responsive Educational Systems.* Retrieved April 20, 2005, from http://www.nccrest.org/publications/display.asp?filename=Briefs/Pre-referral_Brief.pdf&type=pdf

Gardner, D. P. (1983). *A nation at risk: The imperative for education reform.* Washington, DC: U.S. Department of Education.

Gardner, H. (2006). *Multiple intelligences: New horizons.* New York: Basic Books.

Gerber, M. M., Jimenez, T., Leafstedt, J., Villaruz, J., Richards, C., & English, J. (2004). English reading effects of small-group intensive intervention in Spanish for English learners. *Learning Disabilities Research & Practice, 19,* 239–251.

Gollnick, D. M., & Chinn, P. C. (2009). *Multicultural education in a pluralistic society* (8th ed.). Upper Saddle River, NJ: Merrill/Pearson.

Gregory, D. A., Starnes, W. T., & Blaylock, A. W. (1988). Finding and nurturing potential giftedness among Black and Hispanic students. In A. A. Ortiz & B. A. Ramirez (Eds.), *Schools and the culturally diverse exceptional student: Promising practices and future directions* (pp. 76–85). Reston, VA: Council for Exceptional Children.

Grossman, R. (1997, July 6). What is an American? *Chicago Tribune Magazine,* pp. 11–16, 21. Sunday July 6, 1997, *Chicago Tribune.*

Guetzloe, E. C. (1991). *Depression and suicide: Special education students at risk.* Reston, VA: Council for Exceptional Children.

Hallahan, D. P., & Kauffman, J. M. (2009). *Exceptional learners: Introduction to special education* (11th ed.). Boston: Allyn & Bacon.

Harry, B. (1992). *Cultural diversity, families, and the special education system.* New York: Teachers College Press.

Harry, B. (1994). *The disproportionate representation of minority students in special education.* Alexandria, VA: National Association of State Directors of Special Education.

Harry, B. (1995). African American families. In B. A. Ford, F. E. Obiakor, & J. M. Patton (Eds.), *Effective education of African American exceptional learners* (pp. 211–234). Austin, TX: Pro-Ed.

Harry, B., Arnaiz, P., Klingner, J., & Sturges, K. (2008). Schooling and the construction of identify in Spain and the United States. *Journal of Special Education, 42,* 15–25.

Harry, B., & Klingner, J. (2006). *Why are so many minority students in special education? Understanding race and disability in schools.* New York: Teachers College Press.

Harry, B., Klingner, J., & Hart, J. (2005). African American families under fire: Ethnographic views of family strengths. *Remedial and Special Education, 26,* 101–112.

Heflin, L. J., & Rudy, K. (1991). *Homeless and in need of special education.* Reston, VA: Council for Exceptional Children.

Heward, W. L. (2009). *Exceptional children* (9th ed.). Upper Saddle River, NJ: Merrill/Pearson.

Hosp, J. L., & Reschly, D. J. (2002). Predictors of restrictiveness of placement for African American and Caucasian students. *Exceptional Children, 68*(2), 225–239.

Johnston, L. D., O'Malley, P. M., Bachman, J. G., & Schulenberg, J. E. (2004). *Overall teen drug use continues gradual decline; but use of inhalants rises.* University of Michigan News and Information Services: Ann Arbor, MI. [On-line]. Retrieved March 2, 2005, from http://www.monitoringthefuture.org

Jones, N. A., & Smith, A. S. (2001). *The two or more races population: 2000. U.S. Census Bureau Brief.* Washington, DC: U.S. Census Bureau. Retrieved May 6, 2008, from http://www.census.gov/prod/2001pubs/c2kbr01-6.pdf

Kalyanpur, M. (2008). The paradox of majority underrepresentation in special education in India: Constructions of difference in a developing country. *Journal of Special Education, 42,* 55–64.

Kauffman, J. M., & Landrum, T. (2009). *Characteristics of emotional and behavioral disorders of children and youth* (9th ed.). Upper Saddle River, NJ: Merrill/Pearson.

Kerr, M. M., & Nelson, C. M. (2006). *Strategies for managing behavior problems in the classroom* (5th ed.). Upper Saddle River, NJ: Merrill/Prentice Hall.

Klein, M., & Stern, L. (1971). Low birth weight and the battered child syndrome. *American Journal of Disabled Children, 122,* 15–18.

Klingner, J., K., & Edwards, P. A. (2006). Cultural considerations with response to intervention models. *Reading Research Quarterly, 41,* 108–117.

Lynch, E. W. (1992). Developing cross-cultural competence. In E. W. Lynch & M. J. Hanson (Eds.), *Developing cross-cultural competence* (pp. 35–59). Baltimore: Brookes Publishing.

MacMillan, D. L., & Reschly, D. J. (1998). Overrepresentation of minority students: The case for greater specificity or reconsideration of the variables examined. *Journal of Special Education, 32,* 15–24.

Miksic, S. (1987). Drug abuse management in adolescent special education. In M. M. Kerr, C. M. Nelson, & D. L. Lambert (Eds.), *Helping adolescents with learning and behavior problems* (pp. 226–253). Upper Saddle River, NJ: Merrill/Prentice Hall.

Muccigrosso, L., Scavarda, M., Simpson-Brown, R., & Thalacker, B. E. (1991). *Double jeopardy: Pregnant and parenting youth in special education.* Reston, VA: Council for Exceptional Children.

National Association for Gifted Children. (2008). *Critical issues and practices in gifted education.* Waco, TX: Prufrock Press.

National Coalition for the Homeless. (2007). *Education of homeless children and youth.* Washington, DC: Author. Retrieved May 6, 2008, from http://www.nationalhomeless.org/publications/facts/education.pdf.

National Education Association. (2005). *50 multicultural books every child should read.* Washington, DC: Author. Retrieved June 10, 2008, from http://www.nea.org/readacross/resources/50multibooks.html

Navan, J. (2008). *Nurturing the gifted female: A guide for educators and parents.* Thousand Oaks, CA: Corwin Press.

Norton, D. E. (2008). *Multicultural children's literature: Through the eyes of many children* (3rd ed.). Upper Saddle River, NJ: Merrill/Prentice Hall.

Obiakor, F. E., & Ford, B. A. (Eds.). (2003). *Creating successful learning environments for African-American learners with exceptionalities.* Thousand Oaks, CA: Corwin.

Ovando, C. J., & Collier, V. P. (1998). *Bilingual and ESL classroom: Teaching in multicultural contexts* (2nd ed.). Boston: McGraw-Hill.

Patton, J. M. (1997). Disproportionate representation in gifted programs: Best practices for meeting this challenge. In A. J. Artiles & G. Zamora-Durán (Eds.), *Reducing disproportionate representation of culturally diverse students in special and gifted education* (pp. 59–86). Reston, VA: Council for Exceptional Children.

Patton, J. M. (1998). The disproportionate representation of African Americans in special education: Looking behind the curtain for understanding and solutions. *Journal of Special Education, 32,* 25–31.

Public Law 100-297, Sec. 4103. *Definitions (gifted).*

Renzulli, J. S. (1978). *The enrichment triad model: A guide for developing defensible programs for gifted and talented.* Weathersfield, CT: Creative Learning Press.

Renzulli, J. S., & Reiss, S. M. (1991). The school-wide enrichment model: A comprehensive plan for the development of creative productivity. In N. Colangelo & G. A. Davis (Eds.), *Handbook of gifted education* (pp. 111–141). Boston: Allyn & Bacon.

Salend, S. J., & Duhaney, L. M. G. (2005). Understanding and addressing the disproportionate representation of students of color in special education. *Intervention in School and Clinic, 40,* 213–221.

Shin, H. B., & Bruno, R. (2003). *Language use and English-speaking ability: 2000. Census brief.* Washington, DC: U.S. Census Bureau. Retrieved May 6, 2008, from http://www.census.gov/prod/2003pubs/c2kbr-29.pdf

Silverman, L. K. (1995). Highly gifted children. In J. L. Genshaft, M. Bireley, & C. L. Hollingsworth (Eds.), *Serving gifted and talented students: A resource for school personnel.* Austin, TX: Pro-Ed.

Sternberg, R. J. (2005). The triarchic theory of successful intelligence. In D. P. Flanagan & P. L. Harrison (Eds.), *Contemporary intellectual assessment: Theories, tests, and issues* (pp. 103–119). New York: Guilford.

Stronge, J. H., & Tenhouse, C. (1990). *Educating homeless children: Issues and answers.* Bloomington, IN: Phi Delta Kappa Educational Foundation.

Taylor, L. S., & Whittaker, C. R. (2008). *Bridging multiple worlds: Case studies of diverse educational communities* (2nd ed.). Boston: Allyn & Bacon.

Tornquist, E.H., Mastropieri, M. A., Scruggs, T.E., Berry, H.G., & Halloran, W.D. (in press). The impact of poverty on special education. In T.E. Scruggs & M.A. Mastropieri (Eds.), *Policy and practice: Advances in learning and behavioral disabilities* (Vol. 22). Bingley, UK: Emerald.

U.S. Department of Education. (2003). *Education for homeless children and youth program.* Report to Congress Fiscal Year 2000. Washington, DC: Author.

U.S. Department of Education. (2007). *To assure the free appropriate public education of all children with disabilities: Twenty-seventh annual report to Congress on the implementation of the Individuals with Disabilities Education Act.* Washington, DC: Author.

Vaughn, S., & Fuchs, L. S. (2003). Redefining LD as inadequate response to instruction: The promise and potential problems. *Learning Disabilities Research & Practice, 18,* 137–146.

Vincent, L. J., Poulsen, M. K., Cole, C. K., Woodruff, G., & Griffith, D. R. (1991). *Born substance exposed, educationally vulnerable.* Reston, VA: Council for Exceptional Children.

Wagner, M., Marder, C., Blackorby, J., & Cardosa, D. (2004). Special education longitudinal study. Unpublished raw data retrieved from http://www.seels.net.

Warger, C. L., Tewey, S., & Megivern, M. (1991). *Abuse and neglect of exceptional children.* Reston, VA: Council for Exceptional Children.

Yates, J. R., & Ortiz, A. A. (2004). Developing individualized education programs for exceptional language minority students. In L. M. Baca & H. T. Cervantes (Eds.), *The bilingual special education interface* (4th ed., pp. 204–229). Upper Saddle River, NJ: Merrill/Prentice Hall.

Chapter 6

Alberto, P. A., & Troutman, A. C. (2009). *Applied behavior analysis for teachers* (8th ed.). Upper Saddle River, NJ: Merrill/Prentice Hall.

American Association of University Women. (1998). *Gender gaps: Where schools still fail our children.* New York: Marlowe & Company.

Brigham, F. J., Scruggs, T. E., & Mastropieri, M. A. (1992). The effect of teacher enthusiasm on the learning and behavior of learning disabled students. *Learning Disabilities Research & Practice, 7,* 68–73.

Burnett, P. C. (2003). The impact of teacher feedback on student self-talk and self-concept in reading and mathematics. *Journal of Classroom Interaction, 38,* 11–16.

Burstahler, S. (2005). *Universal design of instruction, definition, principles, and examples.* Retrieved June 4, 2008 from University of Washington, DO-IT: Disabilities, Opportunities, Internetworking, and Technology Website, http://www.washington.edu/doit/Brochures/Programs/ud.html

Carnine, D. (1976). Effects of two teacher presentation rates on off-task behavior, answering correctly, and participation. *Journal of Applied Behavior Analysis, 9,* 199–206.

Center for Applied Special Education Technology (CAST). (2008). *Universal design guidelines* (version 1). Retrieved June 5, 2008 from the CAST Website, http://www.cast.org/publications/UDLguidelines/version1.html

Clare, S. K., Jenson, W. R., Kehle, T. J., & Bray, M. A. (2000). Self-modeling as a treatment for increasing on task behavior. *Psychology in the School, 37,* 517–523.

Gartin, B. C., Murdick, N. L., Imbeau, M., & Perner, D. E. (2002). *How to use differentiated instruction with students with developmental disabilities in the general education classroom.* Reston, VA: Council for Exceptional Children.

Gleason, M., Carnine, D., & Vala, N. (1991). Cumulative versus rapid introduction of new information. *Exceptional Children, 57,* 353–358.

Good, T. L., & Brophy, J. E. (2007). *Looking in classrooms* (10th ed.). Boston: Allyn & Bacon.

Greenwood, C.R., Horton, B.T., & Utley, C.A. (2002). Academic engagement: Current perspectives on research and practice. *School Psychology Review, 31,* 328-349.

Groisser, P. (1964). *How to use the fine art of questioning.* Valley Stream, NY: Teachers Practical Press. [distributed by Prentice-Hall, Upper Saddle River, NJ]

Jakulski, J., & Mastropieri, M. A. (2004). Homework for students with disabilities. In T. E. Scruggs & M. A. Mastropieri (Eds.), *Advances in learning and behavioral disabilities: Research in secondary settings* (Vol. 18, pp. 77–122).

Larrivee, B. (1985). *Effective teaching for successful mainstreaming.* New York: Longman.

Madigan, J. C. (2003). Female students of color in special education: Classroom behaviors and perceptions in single-gender and coeducational classrooms. *E-journal of Teaching and Learning in Diverse Settings, 1,* 75–93.

Mastropieri, M. A. (1995). L' instruzione mnemonica e l' interrogazione elaborativa: Strategie per ricordarsi e per pensare. In C. Cornoldi & R. Vianello (Eds.), *Handicap e apprendimento: Ricerche e proposte di intervento* (pp. 117–124). Bergamo, Italy: Juvenilia.

Mastropieri, M. A., & Scruggs, T. E. (2002). *Effective instruction for special education* (3rd ed.). Austin, TX: Pro-Ed.

Mastropieri, M. A., & Scruggs, T. E. (2004). Effective classroom instruction. In C. Spielberger (Ed.), *Encyclopedia of applied psychology* (pp. 687–691). Oxford, UK: Elsevier.

Mastropieri, M. A., Scruggs, T. E., & Cicciarelli, D. (2007, April). Overcoming a significant challenge: Motivating students to learn! Paper presented at the annual meeting of the Council for Exceptional Children, Louisville, KY.

Mastropieri, M. A., Scruggs, T. E., Mantzicopoulos, P. Y., Sturgeon, A., Goodwin, L., & Chung, S. (1998). "A place where living things affect and depend on each other": Qualitative and quantitative outcomes associated with inclusive science teaching. *Science Education, 82,* 163–179.

Principles of Universal Design. (n.d.). Retrieved June 5, 2008, from North Carolina State University, Center for Universal Design Website, http://www.design.ncsu.edu/cud/about_ud/about_ud.htm

Rosenshine, B., & Stevens, R. (1986). Teaching functions. In M. C. Wittrock (Ed.), *Handbook of research on teaching* (3rd ed., pp. 376–391). New York: MacMillan.

Sabornie, E. J., & deBettencourt, L. U. (2004). *Teaching students with mild and high-incidence disabilities at the secondary level* (2nd ed.). Upper Saddle River, NJ: Merrill/Prentice Hall.

Scruggs, T. E., & Mastropieri, M. A. (1994a). The effectiveness of generalization training: A quantitative synthesis of single subject research. In T. E. Scruggs & M. A. Mastropieri (Eds.), *Advances in learning and behavioral disabilities* (Vol. 8, pp. 259–280). Greenwich, CT: JAI Press.

Scruggs, T. E., & Mastropieri, M. A. (1994b). Successful mainstreaming in elementary science classes: A qualitative investigation of three reputational cases. *American Educational Research Journal, 31,* 785–811.

Scruggs, T. E., & Mastropieri, M. A. (1995). What makes special education special? An analysis of the PASS variables in inclusion settings. *Journal of Special Education, 29,* 224–233.

Scruggs, T. E., Mastropieri, M. A., & Sullivan, G. S. (1994). Promoting relational thinking skills: Elaborative interrogation for mildly handicapped students. *Exceptional Children, 60,* 450–457.

Seo, S., Brownell, M. T., Bishop, A. G., & Dingle, M. (2008). An examination of beginning special education teachers' classroom practices that engage elementary students with learning disabilities in reading instruction. *Exceptional Children, 75,* 97–122.

Skinner, E., & Belmont, M. (1993). Motivation in the classroom: Reciprocal effects of teacher behavior and student engagement across the school year. *Journal of Educational Psychology, 85,* 571-581.

Smith, L. (1977). Aspects of teacher discourse and student achievement in mathematics. *Journal for Research in Mathematics Education, 8,* 195–204.

Smith, L., & Land, M. (1981). Low-inference verbal behaviors related to teacher clarity. *Journal of Classroom Interaction, 17,* 37–42.

Sullivan, G. S., Mastropieri, M. A., & Scruggs, T. E. (1995). Reasoning and remembering: Coaching thinking with students with learning disabilities. *Journal of Special Education, 29,* 310–322.

Wittrock, M. C. (Ed.). (1986). *Handbook on research on teaching* (3rd ed.). New York: Macmillan.

Chapter 7

Alberto, P. A., & Troutman, A. C. (2009). *Applied behavior analysis for teachers* (8th ed.). Upper Saddle River, NJ: Merrill/Pearson.

Baker, J. (2006). *The social skills picture book for high school and beyond.* Arlington, TX: Future Horizons.

Barnhill, G. P. (2005). Functional behavioral assessment in schools. *Intervention in School and Clinic, 40,* 131–143.

Beck, M. A., Roblee, K., & Johns, C. (1982). The psychoeducational management of disturbed children. *Education, 102,* 232–235.

Becker, W. C., Madsen, C. H., & Arnold, C. R. (1967). The contingent use of teacher praise in reducing behavior problems. *The Journal of Special Education, 1,* 287–307.

Bellini, S., Peters, J. K., Benner, L., & Hopf, A. (2007). A meta-analysis of school-based social skills interventions for children with autism spectrum disorders. *Remedial and Special Education, 28,* 153–162.

Bijou, S. W., Peterson, R. F., & Ault, M. H. (1968). A method to integrate descriptive and experimental field studies at the level of data and empirical concepts. *Journal of Applied Behavior Analysis, 1,* 175–191.

Brigham, F. J., Bakken, J., Scruggs, T. E., & Mastropieri, M. A. (1992). Cooperative behavior management: A technique for improving classroom behavior. *Education and Training of the Mentally Retarded, 27,* 3–12.

Brigham, F. J., Scruggs, T. E., & Mastropieri, M. A. (1992). The effect of teacher enthusiasm on the learning and behavior of learning disabled students. *Learning Disabilities Research & Practice, 7,* 68–73.

Buchard, J. D., & Barrera, F. (1972). An analysis of time out and response cost in a programmed environment. *Journal of Applied Behavior Analysis, 5,* 271–282.

Canter, L., & Canter, M. (1993). *Succeeding with difficult students: New strategies for reaching your most challenging students.* Santa Monica, CA: Lee Canter & Associates.

Carey, T. A., & Bourbon, W. T. (2004). Countercontrol: A new look at some old problems. *Intervention in School and Clinic, 40,* 3–9.

Center for Effective Discipline. (2008). *Discipline at school.* Retrieved February 10, 2008, from http://www.stophitting.com/disatschool/

Conroy, M. A., Asmus, J. M., Ladwig, C. N., Sellers, J. A., & Valcante, G. (2004). The effects of proximity on the classroom behaviors of students with autism in general education settings. *Behavioral Disorders, 29,* 119–129.

Council for Children with Behavioral Disorders. (1990). Position paper on behavior reduction strategies with children with behavioral disorders. *Behavioral Disorders, 15,* 243–260.

Cowan, R. J. (2004). Enhancing the utilization and generalization of positive social skills in students who demonstrate serious emotional disturbance. Unpublished doctoral dissertation, University of Nebraska, Lincoln.

Crone, C. A., & Horner, R. (2003). *Building positive behavior support systems in schools: Functional behavioral assessment.* New York: Guilford.

Davis, S., & Davis, J. (2007). *Schools where everyone belongs: Practical strategies for reducing bullying* (2nd ed.). Champaign, IL: Research Press.

Fairbanks, S., Sugai, G., Guardino, D., & Lathrop, M. (2007). Response to intervention: Examining classroom behavior support in second grade. *Exceptional Children, 73*, 288–310.

Finch, A. J., Jr., Spirito, A., Imm, P. S., & Ott, E. S. (1993). Cognitive self-instruction for impulse control in children. In A. J. Finch, W. M. Nelson, & E. S. Ott (Eds.), *Cognitive-behavioral procedures with children and adolescents: A practical guide* (pp. 233–256). Boston: Allyn & Bacon.

Freeman, K. A., & Dexter-Mazza, E. T. (2004). Using self-monitoring with an adolescent with disruptive classroom behavior: Preliminary analysis of the role of adult feedback. *Behavior Modification, 28*, 402–419.

Graetz, J. S., Mastropieri, M. A., & Scruggs, T. E. (in press). Promoting social behavior for adolescents with autism with social stories. *Education and Training in Developmental Disabilities.*

Harris, V. W., & Sherman, J. A. (1973). Use and analysis of the "Good Behavior Game" to reduce disruptive classroom behavior. *Journal of Applied Behavior Analysis, 6*, 405–417.

Harry, B., Klingner, J. K., & Hart, J. (2005). African American families under fire: Ethnographic views of family strengths. *Remedial and Special Education, 26*, 101–112.

Heinrichs, R. R. (2003). A whole-school approach to bullying: Special considerations for children with exceptionalities. *Intervention in School and Clinic, 38*, 195–204.

Horner, R. H., & Sugai, G. (1999). Developing positive behavioral support systems. In G. Sugai & T. Lewis (Eds.), *Developing positive behavioral support for students with challenging behaviors* (pp. 15–23). Arlington, VA: Council for Exceptional Children. (ERIC Document Reproduction Service No. 435155)

Hughes, C. A., Ruhl, K. L., & Misra, A. (1989). Self-management with behaviorally disordered students in school settings: A promise unfulfilled? *Behavioral Disorders, 14*, 250–262.

Jackson, D. A., Jackson, N. F., & Bennett, M. L. (1998). *Teaching social competence to youth and adults with developmental disabilities.* Austin, TX: Pro-Ed.

Jackson, N. F., Jackson, D. A., & Monroe, C. (1983). *Getting along with others.* Champaign, IL: Research Press.

Jenkins, J. R., & Gorrafa, S. (1974). Academic performance of mentally handicapped children as a function of token economies and contingency contracts. *Education and Training of the Mentally Retarded, 9*, 183–186.

Jones, D. B., & Van Houten, R. (1985). The use of daily quizzes and public posting to decrease the disruptive behavior of secondary school students. *Education and Treatment of Children, 8*, 91–106.

Kavale, K. A., Mathur, S. R., & Mostert, M. P. (2004). Social skills training and teaching social behavior to students with emotional and behavioral disorders. In R. B. Rutherford, M. M. Quinn, & S. R. Mathur (Eds.), *Handbook of research in emotional and behavioral disorders* (pp. 446–461). New York: Guilford.

Kavale, K. A., & Mostert, M. P. (2004). Social skills interventions for individuals with learning disabilities. *Learning Disability Quarterly, 27*, 31–43.

Kerr, M. M., & Nelson, C. M. (2006). *Strategies for managing behavior problems in the classroom* (5th ed.). Upper Saddle River, NJ: Merrill/Prentice Hall.

Leber, N. J. (2002). *Easy activities for building social skills.* New York: Scholastic.

Lewis-Palmer, T., & Barrett, S. (2007). Establishing and sustaining statewide positive behavior supports implementation: A description of Maryland's model. *Journal of Evidence-Based Practices for Schools, 8*, 45–62.

Maag, J. (2001). Rewarded by punishment: Reflections on the disuse of positive reinforcement in schools. *Exceptional Children, 67*, 173–186.

Maag, J. (2004). *Behavior management: From theoretical implications to practical applications* (2nd ed.). Florence, KY: Thompson/Wadsworth.

Madsen, C. H., Becker, W. C., & Thomas, D. R. (1968). Rules, praise, and ignoring: Elements of elementary classroom control. *Journal of Applied Behavior Analysis, 1*, 139–150.

Martin, G., & Pear, J. (2007). *Behavior modification: What it is and how to do it* (8th ed.). Upper Saddle River, NJ: Merrill/Prentice Hall.

Mason, K. (2008). Cyberbullying: A preliminary assessment for school personnel. *Psychology in the Schools, 45*, 323–348.

Mastropieri, M. A., & Scruggs, T. E. (2002). *Effective instruction for special education* (3rd ed.). Austin, TX: Pro-Ed.

Matson, J. L., Matson, M. L., & Rivet, T. T. (2007). Social-skills treatments for children with autism spectrum disorders: An overview. *Behavior Modification, 31*, 682–707.

Mayer, G. R., Nafpaktitis, M., Butterworth, T., & Hollingsworth, P. (1987). A search for the elusive setting events of school vandalism: A correlational study. *Education and Treatment of Children, 10*, 259–270.

McLaughlin, T. F., & Malaby, J. E. (1976). An analysis of assignment completion and accuracy across time under fixed, variable, and extended token exchange periods in a classroom token economy. *Contemporary Educational Psychology, 1*, 346–355.

Montague, M., & Lund, K. A. (1991). *Job-related social skills: A curriculum for adolescents with special needs.* Ann Arbor, MI: Exceptional Innovations.

Moore, R. J., Cartledge, G., & Heckaman, K. (1994). The effects of social skill instruction and self-monitoring on game-related behaviors of adolescents with emotional or behavioral disorders. *Behavioral Disorders, 20*, 253–266.

National Technical Assistance Center on Positive Behavioral Interventions and Supports. (2007). Schoolwide PBS. Retrieved February 9, 2008, from http://www.pbis.org/schoolwide.htm.

Nelson, J. R., & Sugai, G. (1999). School-wide application of positive behavioral supports. In G. Sugai & T. Lewis (Eds.), *Developing positive behavioral support for students with challenging behaviors* (pp. 25–34). Arlington, VA: Council for Exceptional Children. (ERIC Document Reproduction Service No. 435155)

Rosenberg, M. S., & Jackman, L. A. (2003). Development, implementation, and sustainability of comprehensive schoolwide behavior management systems. *Intervention in School and Clinic, 39*, 10–21.

Safran, S. P., & Oswald, K. (2003). Positive behavior supports: Can schools reshape disciplinary practices? *Exceptional Children, 69*, 362–373.

Scruggs, T. E., & Mastropieri, M. A. (1984). Issues in generalization: Implications for special education. *Psychology in the Schools, 21*, 397–403.

Scruggs, T. E., & Mastropieri, M. A. (1994). The effectiveness of generalization training: A quantitative synthesis of single subject research. In T. E. Scruggs & M. A. Mastropieri (Eds.), *Advances in learning and behavioral disabilities* (Vol. 8, pp. 259–280). Greenwich, CT: JAI Press.

Smith, S. W., & Gilles, D. L. (2003). Using key instructional elements to systematically promote social skill generalization for students with challenging behavior. *Intervention in School and Clinic, 39,* 30–37.

Snapshots 2: Video for Special Education. Videotape to accompany Hallahan, D. P., & Kauffman, J. M. (1997). *Exceptional learners: Introduction to special education.* Boston: Allyn & Bacon.

Stokes, T. F., & Baer, D. M. (1977). An implicit technology of generalization. *Journal of Applied Behavior Analysis, 10,* 349–367.

Twyman, J. S., Johnson, H., Buie, J. D., & Nelson, C. M. (1994). The use of a warning procedure to signal a more intrusive timeout contingency. *Behavioral Disorders, 19,* 243–253.

Walker, H. M., McConnell, S., Holmes, D., Todis, B., Walker, J., & Golden, N. (1988). *The Walker social skills curriculum: The ACCEPTS program.* Austin, TX: Pro-Ed.

Watling, R., & Schwartz, I. S. (2004). Understanding and implementing positive reinforcement as an intervention strategy for children with disabilities. *American Journal of Occupational Therapy, 58,* 113–116.

Chapter 8

Calhoon, M. B., & Fuchs, L. S. (2003). The effects of peer-assisted learning strategies and curriculum-based measurement on the mathematics performance of secondary students with disabilities. *Remedial and Special Education, 24,* 235–245.

Cole, D. A., Vandercook, T., & Rynders, J. (1988). Comparison of two peer interaction programs: Children with and without severe disabilities. *American Educational Research Journal, 25,* 415–439.

Cushing, L. S., & Kennedy, C. H. (2003). Facilitating social relationships in general education settings. In D. L. Ryndak & S. Alper (Eds.), *Curriculum and instruction for students with significant disabilities in inclusive settings* (pp. 206–216). Boston: Allyn & Bacon.

Favazza, P. C., Phillipsen, L., & Kumar, P. (2000). Measuring and promoting acceptance of young children with disabilities. *Exceptional Children, 66,* 491–508.

Ferretti, R. P., MacArthur, C. D., & Okolo, C. M. (2001). Teaching for historical understanding in inclusive classrooms. *Learning Disability Quarterly, 24,* 59–71.

Ferretti, R. P., MacArthur, C. D., & Okolo, C. M. (2005). Misconceptions about history: Reflections on teaching for historical understanding in a fifth grade inclusive classroom. In T. E. Scruggs & M. A. Mastropieri (Eds.), *Cognition and learning in diverse settings: Advances in learning and behavioral disabilities* (pp. 275–313). Oxford, UK: Elsevier.

Forest, M., & Lusthaus, E. (1989). Promoting educational equity for all students. In S. Stainback, W. Stainback, & M. Forest (Eds.), *Educating all students in the mainstream of regular education* (pp. 47–49). Baltimore: Paul Brookes.

Frederickson, N. L., & Furnham, A. F. (2004). Peer-assessed behavioural characteristics and sociometric rejection: Differences between pupils who have moderate learning difficulties and their mainstream peers. *British Journal of Educational Psychology, 74,* 391–410.

Frederickson, N. L., & Turner, J. (2002). Utilizing the classroom peer group to address children's social needs: An evaluation of the Circle of Friends intervention approach. *Journal of Special Education, 36,* 234–245.

Frederickson, N. L., & Turner, J.(2005). "Circle of Friends": An exploration of impact over time. *Educational Psychology in Practice, 21,* 197–217.

Fuchs, D., & Fuchs, L. S. (2005). Peer-assisted learning strategies: Promoting word recognition, fluency, and reading comprehension in young children. *Journal of Special Education, 39,* 34–44.

Fuchs, D., Fuchs, L. S., & Burish, P. (2000). Peer-Assisted Learning strategies: An evidence-based practice to promote reading achievement. *Learning Disabilities Research & Practice, 15,* 85–91.

Fuchs, D., Fuchs, L., Mathes, P. G., & Martinez, E. A. (2002). Preliminary evidence on the social standing of students with learning disabilities in PALS and No-PALS classrooms. *Learning Disabilities Research & Practice, 17,* 205–215.

Fuchs, D., Fuchs, L., Thompson, A., Svenson, E., Yen, L., Al-Otaiba, S., Yang, N., McMaster, K. N., Prentice, K., Kazdan, S., & Saenz, L. (2001). Peer-assisted learning strategies in reading: Extensions for kindergarten, first grade, and high school. *Remedial and Special Education, 20,* 309–318.

Fuchs, L. S., Fuchs, D., Hamlett, C. L., & Appleton, A. C. (2002). Explicitly teaching for transfer: Effects on the mathematical problem-solving performance of students with mathematics disabilities. *Learning Disabilities Research & Practice, 17,* 90–106.

Gillies, R. M., & Ashman, A. F. (Eds.). (2003). *Co-operative learning: The social and intellectual outcomes of learning in groups.* New York: Routledge Falmer.

Greenwood, C. R., Arreaga-Mayer, C., Utley, C. A., Gavin, K. M., & Terry, J. (2001). Classwide peer tutoring learning management system: Applications with elementary-level English language learners. *Remedial and Special Education, 22,* 34–47.

Higgins, T. S. (1982). A comparison of two methods of practice on the spelling performance of learning disabled adolescents. Unpublished doctoral dissertation, Georgia State University, Atlanta.

Jenkins, J. R., & Jenkins, L. M. (1981). *Cross age and peer tutoring: Help for students with learning problems.* Reston, VA: Council for Exceptional Children.

Jenkins, J. R., & O'Connor, R. E. (2003). Cooperative learning for students with learning disabilities: Evidence from experiments, observations, and interviews. In H. L. Swanson, K. Harris, & S. Graham (Eds.), *Handbook of learning disabilities* (pp. 417–430). New York: Guilford.

Johnson, D. W., Johnson, R., Dudley, B., Ward, M., & Magnuson, D. (1995). The impact of peer mediation training on the management of school and home conflicts. *American Educational Research Journal, 32,* 829–844.

Johnson, D. W., & Johnson, R. T. (1986). Mainstreaming and cooperative learning strategies. *Exceptional Children, 52,* 553–561.

Johnson, D. W., Johnson, R. T., & Holubec, E. J. (1991). *Cooperation in the classroom.* Edina, MN: Interaction Book Company.

Johnson, D. W., Maruyama, G., Johnson, R., Nelson, D., & Skon, L. (1981). The effects of cooperative, competitive, and individualistic goal structures on achievement: A meta-analysis. *Psychological Bulletin, 89,* 47–62.

Kamps, D., Royer, J., Degan, E., Kravits, T., Gonzalez-Lopez, A., Garcia, J., Carnazzo, K., Morrison, L., & Kane, L. G. (2002). Peer training to facilitate social interaction for elementary students with autism and their peers. *Exceptional Children, 68,* 173–187.

Kerr, M. M., & Nelson, C. M. (2006). *Strategies for addressing behavior problems in the classroom* (5th ed.). Upper Saddle River, NJ: Merrill/Prentice Hall.

Licciardello, C. C., Harchik, A. E., & Luiselli, J. K. (2008). Social skills intervention for children with autism during interactive play at a public elementary school. *Education and Treatment of Children, 31,* 27–37.

Maheady, L., Mallette, B., & Harper, G. F. (2006). Four classwide peer tutoring models: Similarities, differences, and implications for research and practice. *Reading & Writing Quarterly: Overcoming Learning Difficulties, 22,* 65–89.

Maheady, L., Sacca, M. K., & Harper, G. F. (1988). Class-wide peer tutoring with mildly handicapped high school students. *Exceptional Children, 55,* 52–59.

Manetti, M., Schneider, B. H., & Siperstein, G. (2001). Social acceptance of children with mental retardation: Testing the contact hypothesis with an Italian sample. *International Journal of Behavioral Development, 25,* 279–286.

Mastropieri, M. A., & Scruggs, T. E. (1993). *A practical guide for teaching science to students with special needs in inclusive settings.* Austin, TX: Pro-Ed.

Mastropieri, M. A., Scruggs, T. E., & Graetz, J. (2005). Cognition and learning in inclusive high school chemistry classes. In T. E. Scruggs & M. A. Mastropieri (Eds.), *Cognition and learning in diverse settings: Advances in learning and behavioral disabilities* (Vol. 18, pp. 107–118). Oxford, UK: Elsevier.

Mastropieri, M. A., Scruggs, T. E., Mantzicopoulos, P. Y., Sturgeon, A., Goodwin, L., & Chung, S. (1998). "A place where living things affect and depend upon each other": Qualitative and quantitative outcomes associated with inclusive science teaching. *Science Education, 82,* 163–179.

Mastropieri, M. A., Scruggs, T. E., & Marshak, L. (2008). Training teachers, parents, and peers to implement effective teaching strategies for content area learning. In T. E. Scruggs & M. A. Mastropieri (Eds.), *Advances in learning and behavioral disabilities: Vol. 21. Personnel preparation.* Bingley, UK: Emerald.

Mastropieri, M. A., Scruggs, T. E., Mohler, L. J., Beranek, M. L., Spencer, V., Boon, R. T., & Talbott, E. (2001). Can middle school students with serious reading difficulties help each other and learn anything? *Learning Disabilities Research & Practice, 16,* 18–27.

Mastropieri, M. A., Scruggs, T. E., Spencer, V., & Fontana, J. (2003). Promoting success in high school world history: Peer tutoring versus guided notes. *Learning Disabilities Research & Practice, 18,* 52–65.

Mathes, P. G., Fuchs, D., Fuchs, L. S., Henley, A. M., & Sanders, A. (1994). Increasing strategic reading practice with Peabody Classwide Peer Tutoring. *Learning Disabilities Research & Practice, 9,* 44–48.

McMaster, K. L., Fuchs, D., & Fuchs, L. S. (2006). Research on peer-assisted learning strategies: The promise and limitations of peer-mediated instruction. *Reading & Writing Quarterly: Overcoming Learning Difficulties, 22,* 5–25.

McMaster, K. L., Kung, S., Han, I., & Cao, M. (2008). Peer-assisted learning strategies: A "Tier 1" approach to promoting English learners' response to intervention. *Exceptional Children, 74,* 194–214.

McMaster, K. N., & Fuchs, D. (2002). Effects of cooperative learning on the academic achievement of students with learning disabilities: An update of Tateyama-Sniezek's review. *Learning Disabilities Research & Practice, 17,* 107–117.

McMaster, K. N., & Fuchs, D. (2005). *Cooperative learning: Use caution.* Reston, VA: Current practice alerts, Division for Research and Division for Learning Disabilities, Council for Exceptional Children, Issue 11.

Myles, B. (2007). *Priming.* Arlington, VA: Council for Exceptional Children Blog. Retrieved February, 19, 2008, from http://cecblog.typepad.com/cec/

Norland, J. J. (2005). *English language learners' interactions with various science curriculum features.* Unpublished doctoral dissertation, George Mason University, Fairfax, VA.

O'Connor, R. E., & Jenkins, J. R. (1996). Cooperative learning as an inclusion strategy: A closer look. *Exceptionality, 6,* 29–51.

Odom, S. L., Brown, W. H., Frey, T., Karasu, N., Smith-Canter, L. L., & Strain, P. S. (2003). Evidence-based practices for young children with autism: Contributions for single-subject design research. *Focus on Autism and Other Developmental Disabilities, 18,* 166–175.

Oortwijn, M. B., Boekaerts, M., & Vedder, P. (2008). The impact of a cooperative learning experience on pupils' popularity, non-cooperativeness, and interethnic bias in multiethnic elementary schools. *Educational Psychology, 28*(2), 1–11.

Saddler, B., & Graham, S. (2005). The effects of peer-assisted sentence-combining instruction on the writing performance of more and less skilled young writers. *Journal of Educational Psychology, 97,* 43–54.

Sáenz, L. M., Fuchs, L. S., & Fuchs, D. (2005). Peer-assisted learning strategies for English language learners with learning disabilities. *Exceptional Children, 71,* 231–247.

Scruggs, T. E., & Mastropieri, M. A. (1998). Peer tutoring and students with special needs. In K. Topping & S. Ehly (Eds.), *Peer-assisted learning* (pp. 165–182). Mahwah, NJ: Lawrence Erlbaum.

Scruggs, T. E., & Mastropieri, M. A. (2004). Recent research in secondary content areas for students with learning and behavioral disabilities. In T. E. Scruggs & M. A. Mastropieri (Eds.), *Advances in learning and behavioral disabilities: Research in secondary schools* (Vol. 17, pp. 243–263). Oxford, UK: Elsevier.

Shabani, D. B., Katz, R. C., & Wilder, D. A. (2002). Increasing social initiations in children with autism: Effects of a tactile prompt. *Journal of Applied Behavior Analysis, 35,* 79–83.

Sindelar, P. T. (1982). The effects of cross-age tutoring on the comprehension skills of remedial reading students. *Journal of Special Education, 16,* 199–206.

Slavin, R. E. (1991). Synthesis of research on cooperative learning. *Educational Leadership, 48*(5), 71–82.

Slavin, R. E., & Karweit, N. L. (1985). Effects of whole class, ability grouped, and individualized instruction on mathematics achievement. *American Educational Research Journal, 22,* 351–367.

Souvignier, E., & Kronenberger, J. (2007). Cooperative learning in third graders' jigsaw groups for mathematics and science with and without questioning training. *British Journal of Educational Psychology, 77,* 755–771.

Spencer, V. G. (2006). Peer tutoring and students with emotional or behavioral disorders: A review of the literature. *Behavioral Disorders, 31,* 204–222.

Spencer, V. G., Scruggs, T. E., & Mastropieri, M. A. (2003). Content area learning in middle school social studies classrooms and students with emotional or behavioral disorders: A comparison of strategies. *Behavioral Disorders, 28,* 77–93.

Stainback, W., & Stainback, S. (1990). Facilitating peer supports and friendships. In W. Stainback & S. Stainback (Eds.), *Support networks for inclusive schooling* (pp. 51–63). Baltimore: Paul Brookes.

Stenhoff, D. M., & Lignugaris/Kraft, B. (2007). A review of the effects of peer tutoring on students with mild disabilities in secondary settings. *Exceptional Children, 74,* 8–30.

Stevahn, L., Johnson, D. W., Johnson, R. T., & Schultz, R. (2002). Effects of conflict resolution training integrated into a high school social studies curriculum. *Journal of Social Psychology, 142,* 305–331.

Stevens, R. J., & Slavin, R. E. (1991). When cooperative learning improves the achievement of students with mild disabilities: A response to Tateyama-Sniezek. *Exceptional Children, 57,* 276–280.

Tateyama-Sniezek, K. M. (1990). Cooperative learning: Does it improve the academic achievement of students with handicaps? *Exceptional Children, 56,* 426–437.

Chapter 9

Berkeley, S., Mastropieri, M. A., & Scruggs, T. E. (2007). *Reading comprehension strategy instruction and attribution retraining for secondary students with disabilities.* Athens, GA: University of Georgia, Department of Special Education.

Bettencourt, E. M., Gillett, M. H., Gall, M. D., & Hull, R. E. (1983). Effects of teacher enthusiasm training on student on-task behavior and achievement. *American Educational Research Journal, 20,* 435–450.

Borkowski, J. G., Weyhing, R. S., & Carr, M. (1988). Effects of attributional retraining on strategy-based reading comprehension in learning disabled students. *Journal of Educational Psychology, 80,* 46–53.

Brigham, F. J., Scruggs, T. E., & Mastropieri, M. A. (1992). The effect of teacher enthusiasm on the learning and behavior of learning disabled students. *Learning Disabilities Research & Practice, 7,* 68–73.

Brophy, J. (1981). Teacher praise: A functional analysis. *Review of Educational Research, 51,* 5–32.

Brophy, J. (1987). Synthesis of research on strategies for motivating students to learn. *Educational Leadership, 45,* 40–48.

Carlson, C. L., Booth, J. E., Shin, M., & Canu, W. H. (2002). Parent-, teacher-, and self-rated motivational styles in ADHD subtypes. *Journal of Learning Disabilities, 35,* 104–113.

Dev, P. (1997). Intrinsic motivation and academic achievement: What does their relationship imply for the classroom teacher? *Remedial and Special Education, 18,* 12–19.

Dunn, N. A., & Baker, S. B. (2002). Readiness to serve students with disabilities: A survey of elementary school counselors. *Professional School Counseling, 5,* 275–284.

Ford, M. E. (1995). Motivation and competence development in special and remedial education. *Intervention in School and Clinic, 31,* 70–83.

Fuchs, L. S., Fuchs, D., & Deno, S. (1985). Importance of goal ambitiousness and goal mastery to student achievement. *Exceptional Children, 52,* 63–71.

Fuchs, L. S., Fuchs, D., Prentice, K., Burch, M., Hamlett, C. L., Owen, R., & Schroeter, K. (2003). Enhancing third-grade students' mathematical problem solving with self-regulated learning strategies. *Journal of Educational Psychology, 95,* 306–315.

Fulk, B. M., & Montgomery-Grimes, D. J. (1994). Strategies to improve student motivation. *Intervention in School and Clinic, 30,* 28–33.

Gable D. (2003). Enhancing the conceptual understanding of science. *Educational Horizons, 81,* 70–76.

Ginsberg, M. B. (2005). *King Middle School: A composite of successful multicultural schools committed to diminishing the achievement gap through comprehensive, motivationally-anchored school renewal.* Retrieved May 6, 2005, from http://www.newhorizons.org/strategies/multicultural/ginsberg.htm

Gollnick, D. M., & Chinn, P. C. (2009). *Multicultural education in a pluralistic society* (8th ed.). Upper Saddle River, NJ: Merrill/Prentice Hall.

Harter, S. (2001). *The construction of the self: A developmental perspective.* New York: Guilford.

Harter, S., Whitesell, N. R., & Junkin, L. J. (1998). Similarities and differences in domain-specific and global self-evaluations of learning-disabled, behaviorally disordered, and normally achieving adolescents. *American Educational Research Journal, 35,* 653–680.

Henderlong, J., & Lepper, M. R. (2002). The effects of praise on children's intrinsic motivation: A review and synthesis. *Psychological Bulletin, 128,* 774–795.

Konrad, M., Fowler, C., & Walker, A. R. (2007). Effects of self-determination interventions on the academic skills of students with learning disabilities. *Learning Disability Quarterly, 30,* 89–113.

Lavoie, R. (1996). *How difficult can this be? Understanding learning disabilities: Frustration, anxiety, tension, the FAT city workshop.* Alexandria, VA: PBS Video.

Lavoie, R. (2007). *The motivation breakthrough: Six secrets to turning on the tuned-out child.* New York: Simon and Schuster.

Lepper, M. R., & Hodell, M. (1989). Intrinsic motivation in the classroom. In C. Ames & R. Ames (Eds.), *Research on motivation in education: Goals and cognitions* (Vol. 3, pp. 73–105). San Diego: Academic Press.

Licht, B. (1992). Achievement-related beliefs in children with learning disabilities. In L. J. Meltzer (Ed.), *Strategy assessment and instruction for students with learning disabilities: From theory to practice* (pp. 195–220). Austin, TX: Pro-Ed.

Maag, J. W. (2001). Rewarded by punishment: Reflections on the disuse of positive reinforcement in schools. *Exceptional Children, 67,* 173–186.

Mamlin, N., Harris, K. R., & Case, L. P. (2001). A methodological analysis of research on locus of control and learning disabilities: Rethinking a common assumption. *Journal of Special Education, 34,* 214–225.

Martin, G., & Pear, J. (1978). *Behavior modification: What it is and how to do it.* Upper Saddle River, NJ: Merrill/Prentice Hall.

Mastropieri, M. A., Scruggs, T. E., & Bohs, K. (1994). Mainstreaming an emotionally handicapped student in science: A qualitative investigation. In T. E. Scruggs & M. A. Mastropieri (Eds.), *Advances in learning and behavioral disabilities* (Vol. 8, pp. 131–146). Greenwich, CT: JAI.

Mastropieri, M. A., Scruggs, T. E., & Butcher, K. (1997). Counseling individuals with learning disabilities: Research, practice, and future issues. In T. E. Scruggs & M. A. Mastropieri (Eds.), *Advances in learning and behavioral disabilities* (Vol. 8, pp. 131–146). Oxford, UK: Elsevier/JAI.

McMaster, K. N., & Fuchs, D. (2002). Effects of cooperative learning on the academic achievement of students with learning disabilities: An update of Tateyama-Sniezek's review. *Learning Disabilities Research & Practice, 17,* 107–117.

Milsom, A., & Akos, P. (2003). Counselor preparation: Preparing school counselors to work with students with disabilities. *Counselor Education and Supervision, 43,* 86–95.

Milsom, A. S., & Hartley, M. T. (2005). Assisting students with learning disabilities transitioning to college: What school counselors should know. *Professional School Counseling, 8,* 436–441.

Milsom, A. S. (2002). Students with disabilities: School counselor involvement and preparation. *Professional School Counseling, 5,* 331–338.

Mishna, F. (1996). Finding their voice: Group therapy for adolescents with learning disabilities. *Learning Disabilities Research & Practice, 11,* 249–258.

Nicholls, J. G. (1989). *The competitive ethos and democratic education.* Cambridge, MA: Harvard University Press.

Omizo, M. M., & Omizo, S. A. (1987). The effects of group counseling on classroom behavior and self-concept among elementary school children. *The Exceptional Child, 34,* 57–61.

Patrick, B. C., Hisley, J., & Kempler, T. (2000). "What's everybody so excited about?": The effects of teacher enthusiasm on student intrinsic motivation and vitality. *Journal of Experimental Education, 68,* 217–236.

Scruggs, T. E., & Mastropieri, M. A. (1983). Self-esteem differences by sex and ethnicity: Native American, handicapped Native American, and Anglo children. *Journal of Instructional Psychology, 10,* 177–179.

Scruggs, T. E., & Mastropieri, M. A. (1994). Successful mainstreaming in elementary science classes: A qualitative investigation of three reputational cases. *American Educational Research Journal, 31,* 785–811.

Sideridis, G. D. (2007). Why are students with LD depressed? A goal orientation model of depression vulnerability. *Journal of Learning Disabilities, 40,* 526–539.

Sideridis, G. D., Morgan, P. L., Botsas, G., Padeliadu, S., & Fuchs, D. (2006). Predicting LD on the basis of motivation, metacognition, and psychopathology: An ROC analysis. *Journal of Learning Disabilities, 39,* 215–229.

Thurneck, D. A., Warner, P. J., & Cobb H. C. (2007). Children and adolescents with disabilities and health care needs: Implications for intervention. In H. T. Prout & D. T. Brown (Eds.), *Counseling and psychotherapy with children and adolescents: Theory and practice for school and clinical settings* (4th ed., pp. 419–453). Hoboken, NJ: Wiley.

Winkler, H. (2008, April). Keynote address. Presented at the annual meeting of the Council for Exceptional Children, Boston.

Wright, E. L., & Govindarajan, G. (1995). Discrepant event demonstrations. *Science Teacher, 62*(1), 25–28.

Zimmerman, B., & Kitsantas, A. (2007). Reliability and validity of Self-Efficacy for Learning Form (SELF) scores of college students. *Journal of Psychology, 215,* 157–163.

Chapter 10

Abramowitz, A. J., O'Leary, S. G., & Futtersak, M. W. (1988). The relative impact of long and short reprimands on children's off-task behavior in the classroom. *Behavior Therapy, 19,* 243–247.

Abramowitz, A. J., O'Leary, S. G., & Rosen, L. S. (1987). Reducing off-task behavior in the classroom: A comparison of encouragement and reprimands. *Journal of Abnormal Child Psychology, 15,* 155–163.

Austin, V. L. (2003). Pharmacological interventions for students with ADD. *Intervention in School and Clinic, 38,* 289–296.

Baddeley, A. (2004). *Your memory: A user's guide.* Buffalo, NY: Firefly.

Barkley, R. A. (2005). *Attention deficit hyperactivity disorder: A handbook for diagnosis and treatment* (3rd ed.). New York: Guilford Press.

Beck, M. A., Roblee, K., & Johns, C. (1982). Psychoeducational management of disturbed children. *Education, 102,* 232–235.

Beirne-Smith, M., Patton, J., & Kim, S. (2006). *Mental retardation* (7th ed.). Upper Saddle River, NJ: Merrill/Prentice Hall.

Brown, A. L. (1978). Knowing when, where, and how to remember: A problem of metacognition. In R. Glaser (Ed.), *Advances in instructional psychology* (pp. 77–157). Hillsdale, NJ: Lawrence Erlbaum.

Browning, W. G. (1983). *Memory power for exams.* Lincoln, NE: Cliff Notes.

Burchers, S., Burchers, M., & Burchers, B. (1997). *Vocabulary cartoons: Building an educated vocabulary with visual mnemonics.* Punta Gorda, FL: New Monic Books.

Burchers, S., Burchers, M., & Burchers, B. (2000). *Vocabulary cartoons II: Building an educated vocabulary with sight and sound memory aids.* Punta Gorda, FL: New Monic Books.

Burns, M. K. (2005). Using incremental rehearsal to increase fluency of single-digit multiplication facts with children identified as learning disabled in mathematics computation. *Education & Treatment of Children, 28,* 237–249.

Cohen, R. L. (1989). Memory for action events: The power of enactment. *Educational Psychology Review, 1,* 57–80.

Conroy, M. A., Asmus, J. M., Ladwig, C. N., Sellers, J. A., & Valcante, G. (2004). The effects of proximity on the classroom behaviors of students with autism in general education settings. *Behavioral Disorders, 29,* 119–129.

Craik, F. I. M., & Lockhart, R. S. (1972). Levels of processing: A framework for memory research. *Journal of Verbal Learning and Verbal Behavior, 11,* 671–684.

Crossairt, A., Hall, R. V., & Hopkins, B. L. (1973). The effects of experimenter's instructions, feedback, and praise on teacher praise and student attending behavior. *Journal of Applied Behavior Analysis, 6,* 89–100.

Duhaney, L. M. G. (2003). A practical approach to managing the behaviors of students with ADD. *Intervention in School and Clinic, 38,* 267–279.

Ferguson, H., Myles, B. S., & Hagiwara, T. (2005). Using a personal digital assistant to enhance independence for an adolescent with autism. *Education and Training in Developmental Disabilities, 40,* 60–67.

Flood, W. A., Wilder, D. A., & Flood, A. L. (2005). Peer-mediated reinforcement plus prompting as treatment for off-task behavior in children with attention deficit hyperactivity disorder. *Journal of Applied Behavior Analysis, 35,* 199–204.

Fontana, J., Mastropieri, M. A., & Scruggs, T. E. (2007). Mnemonic strategy instruction in inclusive secondary social studies classes. *Remedial and Special Education, 28,* 345–355.

Frase-Blunt, M. (2000). High-stakes testing a mixed blessing for special students. *CEC Today, 7*(2), 1, 5, 7, 15.

Greene, G. (1999). Mnemonic multiplication fact instruction for students with learning disabilities. *Learning Disabilities Research & Practice, 14,* 141–148.

Greenspan, S. I., Wieder, S., & Simons, R. (1998). *The child with special needs: Encouraging intellectual and emotional growth.* New York: Perseus Books.

Gustashaw, W. E., & Brigham, F. J. (2006). Instructional support employing spatial abilities: Using complimentary cognitive pathways to support learning in students with achievement deficits. In T. E. Scruggs & M. A. Mastropieri (Eds.), *Cognition and learning in diverse settings: Advances in learning and behavioral disabilities* (Vol. 18, pp. 51–76). Oxford, UK: Elsevier.

Hallahan, D. P., & Cottone, E. A. (1997). Attention deficit hyperactivity disorder. In T. E. Scruggs & M. A. Mastropieri (Eds.), *Advances in learning and behavioral disabilities* (Vol. 11, pp. 27–68). Oxford, UK: Elsevier/JAI.

Harris, K., Friedlander, B. D., & Saddler, B. (2005). Self-monitoring of attention versus self-monitoring of academic performance: Effects among students with ADHD in the general education classroom. *Journal of Special Education, 39,* 145–156.

Harris, K., Graham, S., Reid, R., McElroy, K., & Hamby, R. S. (1994). Self-monitoring of attention versus self-monitoring of performance: Replication and cross-task comparison studies. *Learning Disability Quarterly, 17,* 121–139.

Heward, W. L. (2009). *Exceptional children* (9th ed.). Upper Saddle River, NJ: Merrill/Prentice Hall.

James, W. (1890/1990). *Principles of psychology.* Chicago: Encyclopedia Britannica.

Kerr, M. M., & Nelson, C. M. (2006). *Strategies for addressing behavior problems in the classroom* (5th ed.). Upper Saddle River, NJ: Merrill/Prentice Hall.

King-Sears, M. E., Mercer, C. D., & Sindelar, P. T. (1992). Toward independence with keyword mnemonic: A strategy for science vocabulary instruction. *Remedial and Special Education, 13,* 22–33.

Lerner, J., & Kline, F. (2006). *Learning disabilities and related disorders: Characteristics and teaching strategies* (10th ed.). Boston: Houghton-Mifflin.

Lucangeli, D., Galderisi, D., & Cornoldi, C. (1995). Specific and general transfer effects following metamemory training. *Learning Disabilities Research & Practice, 10,* 11–21.

Mastropieri, M. A., & Scruggs, T. E. (1991). *Teaching students ways to remember: Strategies for learning mnemonically.* Cambridge, MA: Brookline Books.

Mastropieri, M. A., Scruggs, T. E., & Graetz, J. (2005). Cognition and learning in inclusive high school chemistry classes. In T. E. Scruggs & M. A. Mastropieri (Eds.), *Cognition and learning in diverse settings: Advances in learning and behavioral disabilities* (Vol. 18, pp. 107–118). Oxford, UK: Elsevier.

Mastropieri, M. A., Scruggs, T. E., Mantzicopoulos, P., Sturgeon, A., Goodwin, L., & Chung, S. (1998). "A place where living things affect and depend on each other": Qualitative and quantitative outcomes associated with inclusive science teaching. *Science Education, 82,* 163–179.

Mastropieri, M. A., Scruggs, T. E., & Whedon, C. (1997). Using mnemonic strategies to teach information about U.S. presidents: A classroom-based investigation. *Learning Disability Quarterly, 20,* 13–21.

Montague, M., Fiore, T., Hocutt, A., McKinney, J. D., & Harris, J. (1996). Interventions for students with attention deficit hyperactivity disorder: A review of the literature. In T. E. Scruggs & M. A. Mastropieri (Eds.), *Advances in learning and behavioral disabilities: Intervention research* (Vol. 10, Part B, pp. 23–50). Greenwich, CT: JAI.

Nelson, L. G. L., Summers, J. A., & Turnbull, A. P. (2004). Boundaries in family-professional relationships: Implications for special education. *Remedial and Special Education, 25,* 153–165.

Paivio, A., & Okovita, H. W. (1971). Word imagery modalities and associative learning in blind and sighted subjects. *Journal of Verbal Learning and Verbal Behavior, 101,* 506–510.

Plumber, P. J., & Stoner, G. (2005). The relative effects of classwide peer tutoring and peer coaching on the positive social behaviors of children with ADHD. *Journal of Attention Disorders, 9,* 290–300.

Purdie, N., Hattie, J., & Carroll, A. (2002). A review of the research on interventions for attention deficit hyperactivity disorder: What works best? *Review of Educational Research, 72,* 61–99.

Putnam, M. L. (1992). Characteristics of questions on tests administered by mainstream secondary classroom teachers. *Learning Disabilities Research & Practice, 7,* 129–136.

Redl, F. (1952). *Controls from within: Techniques for the treatment of the aggressive child.* Glencoe, IL: Free Press.

Rocha, M. L., Schreibman, L., & Stahmer, A. C. (2007). Effectiveness of training parents to teach joint attention in children with autism. *Journal of Early Intervention, 29,* 154–172.

Rohwer, W. D., Raines, J. M., Eoff, J., & Wagner, M. (1977). The development of elaborative propensity in adolescence. *Journal of Experimental Child Psychology, 23,* 472–492.

Rooney, K. J., Hallahan, D. P., & Lloyd, J. W. (1984). Self-recording of attention by learning disabled students in the regular classroom. *Journal of Learning Disabilities, 17,* 360–364.

Salend, S. J., Elhoweris, H., & Van Garderen, D. (2003). Educational interventions for students with ADD. *Intervention in School and Clinic, 38,* 280–288.

Scott, J., Clark, C., & Brady, M. (2000). *Students with autism: Characteristics and instructional programming for special educators.* San Diego: Singular Press.

Scruggs, T. E., & Mastropieri, M. A. (1989). Reconstructive elaborations: A model for content area learning. *American Educational Research Journal, 26,* 311–327.

Scruggs, T. E., & Mastropieri, M. A. (1992). Classroom applications of mnemonic instruction: Acquisition, maintenance, and generalization. *Exceptional Children, 58,* 219–229.

Scruggs, T. E., & Mastropieri, M. A. (2003). Science and social studies. In H. L. Swanson, K. Harris, & S. Graham (Eds.), *Handbook of learning disabilities* (pp. 364–379). New York: Guilford.

Scruggs, T. E., & Mastropieri, M. A. (2005, March). *Mnemonic strategy instruction for students with learning disabilities: Lessons learned from 20 years of experimental research.* Paper presented at the Pervasive Developmental and Learning Disabilities Conference, Miami.

Scruggs, T. E., Mastropieri, M. A., Levin, J. R., & Gaffney, J. S. (1985). Facilitating the acquisition of science facts in learning disabled students. *American Educational Research Journal, 22,* 575–586.

Simpson, R. L., & Zionts, P. (2000). *Autism: Information and resources for professionals and parents* (2nd ed.). Austin, TX: Pro-Ed.

Snider, V. E., Busch, T., & Arrowood, L. (2003). Teacher knowledge of stimulant medication and ADHD. *Remedial and Special Education, 24,* 47–57.

Sullivan, G. S., Mastropieri, M. A., & Scruggs, T. E. (1995). Reasoning and remembering: Coaching thinking with students with learning disabilities. *Journal of Special Education, 29,* 310–322.

Terrill, C., Scruggs, T. E., & Mastropieri, M. A. (2004). SAT vocabulary instruction for high school students with learning disabilities. *Intervention in School and Clinic, 39,* 288–294.

Uberti, H. Z., Scruggs, T. E., & Mastropieri, M. A. (2003). Keywords make the difference! Mnemonic instruction in inclusive classrooms. A classroom application. *Teaching Exceptional Children, 35*(3), 56–61.

Underwood, B. J. (1983). *Attributes of memory.* Glenview, IL: Scott, Foresman.

van Daal, J., Verhoeven, L., & Van Leeuwe, J. (2008). Working memory limitations in children with severe language impairment. *Journal of Communication Disorders, 41,* 85–107.

Van der Molen, M. J., Van Luit, J. E. H., & Jongmans, M. J. (2007). Verbal working memory in children with mild intellectual disabilities. *Journal of Intellectual Disability Research, 51,* 162–169.

Veit, D. T., Scruggs, T. E., & Mastropieri, M. A. (1986). Extended mnemonic instruction with learning disabled students. *Journal of Educational Psychology, 78,* 300–308.

Walker, J. M., & Buckley, N. K. (1968). The use of positive reinforcement in conditioning attending behavior. *Journal of Applied Behavior Analysis, 1,* 245–250.

Willott, P. C. (1982). *The use of imagery as a mnemonic to teach basic multiplication facts to students with learning disabilities.* Unpublished doctoral dissertation, West Virginia University, Morgantown.

Wolgemuth, J. R., Cobb, R. B., & Alwell, M. (2008). The effects of mnemonic interventions on academic outcomes for youth with disabilities: A systematic review. *Learning Disabilities Research & Practice, 23,* 1–10.

Chapter 11

Alley, G., & Deshler, D. D. (1979). *Teaching the learning disabled adolescent: Strategies and methods.* Denver: Love Publishing.

Berry, G., Hall, D., & Gildroy, P. G. (2004). Teaching learning strategies. In B. K. Lenz, D. D. Deshler, & B. R. Kissam (Eds.), *Teaching content to all: Evidence-based inclusive practices in middle and secondary schools* (pp. 258–278). Boston: Allyn & Bacon.

Carter, C., Bishop, J., Block, J., & Kravits, S. L. (2005). *Keys to effective learning* (4th ed.). Upper Saddle River, NJ: Merrill/Prentice Hall.

Deshler, D. D., & Schumaker, J. B. (2005). *Teaching adolescents with disabilities: Accessing the general education curriculum.* Thousand Oaks, CA: Corwin.

Deshler, D. D., Schumaker, J. B., Alley, G. R., Clark, F. L., & Warner, M. M. (1981). *LINKS: A listening/notetaking strategy.* Unpublished manuscript, University of Kansas Institute for Research in Learning Disabilities, Lawrence.

Devine, T. G. (1987). *Teaching study skills* (2nd ed.). Boston: Allyn & Bacon.

Fitzgerald, G., & Koury, K. (2001–2002). *The KidTools support system* (Project #H327A000005). Washington, DC: United States Department of Education, Office of Special Education Programs.

Fitzgerald, G., & Koury, K. (2004–2005). *The Strategy Tools support system* (Project #H327A000005). Washington, DC: United States Department of Education, Office of Special Education Programs.

Gall, M. D., Gall, J. P., Jacobsen, D. R., & Bullock, T. L. (1990). *Tools for learning: A guide for teaching study skills.* Alexandria, VA: Association for Supervision and Curriculum Development.

Garcia, S. B., & Ortiz, A. B. (2005). Preventing disproportionate representation: Culturally and linguistically responsive prereferral interventions. *Practitioner Brief Series: National Center for Culturally Responsive Educational Systems.* Retrieved April 20, 2005, from http://www.nccrest.org/publications/display.asp?filename=Briefs/Pre-referral_Brief.pdf.&type=pdf

Greene, L. J. (2004). *Study max: Improving study skills in grades 9–12.* Thousand Oaks, CA: Corwin.

Guerin, G., & Male, M. C. (2006). Strategies to improve learning skills. In G. Guerin & M. Male (Eds.), *Addressing learning disabilities and difficulties: How to reach and teach every student* (pp. 15–40). Thousand Oaks, CA: Corwin Press.

Hoover, J. J. (1993). *Teaching study skills to students with learning problems.* Boulder, CO: Hamilton.

Horton, S. V., Lovitt, T. C., & Christensen, C. C. (1991). Notetaking from textbooks: Effects of a columnar format on three categories of secondary students. *Exceptionality, 2*(1), 19–40.

Hughes, C. A., Ruhl, K. L., Schumaker, J. B., & Deshler, D. D. (2002). Effects of instruction in an assignment completion strategy on the homework performance of students with learning disabilities in general education classes. *Learning Disabilities Research & Practice, 17,* 1–18.

Jakulski, J., & Mastropieri, M. A. (2004). Homework for students with disabilities. In T. E. Scruggs & M. A. Mastropieri (Eds.), *Research in secondary schools: Advances in learning and behavioral disabilities* (pp. 77–122). Oxford, UK: Elsevier.

Lynch, A. (2006). *Comparison of group contingencies with mystery motivators and randomized criteria: A homework investigation.* Unpublished doctoral dissertation, Hofstra University, Hempstead, NY.

Mastropieri, M. A., & Scruggs, T. E. (2002). *Effective instruction for special education* (3rd ed.). Austin, TX: Pro-Ed.

Meltzer, L. J., Roditi, B. N., Haynes, D. P., Biddle, K. R., Paster, M., & Taber, S. E. (1996). *Strategies for success: Classroom teaching techniques for students with learning problems.* Austin, TX: Pro-Ed.

Miller, L. (2003). Developing listening skills with authentic materials. *ESL Magazine, 6*(2), 16–18.

Mitchem, K., Kight, J., Fitzgerald, G., Koury, K., & Boonseng, T. (2007). Electronic performance support systems: An assistive technology tool for secondary students with mild disabilities. *Journal of Special Education Technology, 22*(2), 1–14.

Myles, B. S., Ferguson, H., & Hagiwara, T. (2007). Using a personal digital assistant to improve the recording homework assignments by an adolescent with Asperger syndrome. *Focus on Autism and Other Developmental Disabilities, 22,* 96–99.

Norland, J. J. (2005). *English language learners' interactions with various science curriculum features.* Unpublished doctoral dissertation, George Mason University, Fairfax, VA.

O'Melia, M. C., & Rosenberg, M. S. (1994). Effects of cooperative homework teams on the acquisition of mathematics skills by secondary students with mild disabilities. *Exceptional Children, 60,* 538–548.

Patterson, K. B. (2005). Increasing positive outcomes for African American males in special education with the use of guided notes. *Journal of Negro Education, 74,* 311–320.

Pauk, W. (1987). *Study skills for junior and community colleges.* Clearwater, FL: Reston-Stuart.

Polloway, E. A., Epstein, M. H., Bursuck, W. D., Jayanthi, M., & Cumblad, C. (1994). A national survey of homework practices of general education teachers. *Journal of Learning Disabilities, 27,* 500–509.

Polloway, E. A., Foley, R. M., & Epstein, M. H. (1992). Homework problems of students with learning disabilities and nonhandicapped students. *Learning Disabilities Research & Practice, 7,* 203–209.

Rafoth, M. A., Leal, L., & DeFabo, L. (1993). *Strategies for learning and remembering: Study skills across the curriculum.* Washington, DC: NEA Professional Library.

Suritsky, S. K., & Hughes, C. A. (1993). *Notetaking strategy training for college students with learning disabilities.* Unpublished manuscript. College Park: Pennsylvania State University.

Suritsky, S. K., & Hughes, C. A. (1996). Notetaking strategy instruction. In D. D. Deshler, E. S. Ellis, & B. K. Lenz (Eds.), *Teaching adolescents with learning disabilities: Strategies and methods* (2nd ed., pp. 267–312). Denver: Love Publishing.

Wood, E., Woloshyn, V. E., & Willoughby, T. (Eds.). (1995). *Cognitive strategy instruction for middle and high schools.* Cambridge, MA: Brookline Books.

Chapter 12

Artiles, A. J., & Zamora-Durán, G. (1997). *Reducing disproportionate representation of culturally diverse students in special and gifted education.* Reston, VA: Council for Exceptional Children.

Baca, L. M., & Cervantes, H. T. (2004). *The bilingual special education interface.* Upper Saddle River, NJ: Merrill/Prentice Hall.

Baron, J. B. (1990). Performance assessment: Blurring the edges among assessment, curriculum, and instruction. In A. B. Champaign, B. E. Lovitts, & B. J. Callinger (Eds.), *Assessment in the service of instruction* (pp. 127–148). Washington, DC: American Association for the Advancement of Science.

Bolt, S. E., & Thurlow, M. L. (2004). Five of the most frequently allowed testing accommodations in state policy. *Remedial and Special Education, 25,* 141–152.

Bradley, D. F., & Calvin, M. B. (1998). Grading modified assignments. *Teaching Exceptional Children, 31*(2), 24–29.

Brookhart, S. M. (2004). *Grading.* Upper Saddle River, NJ: Merrill/Prentice Hall.

Bursuck, W. D., Polloway, E. A., Plante, L., Epstein, M. H., Jayanthi, M., & McConeghy, J. (1996). Report card grading and adaptations: A national survey of classroom practices. *Exceptional Children, 62,* 301–318.

Carman, R. A., & Adams, W. R. (1972). *Study skills: A student's guide for survival.* New York: Wiley.

Cawthon, S. W. (2008). Accommodations use for statewide standardized assessments: Prevalence and recommendations for students who are deaf or hard of hearing. *Journal of Deaf Studies and Deaf Education, 13,* 55–76.

Christiansen, J., & Vogel, J. R. (1998). A decision model for grading students with disabilities. *Teaching Exceptional Children, 31*(2), 30–35.

Crawford, L., Helwig, R., & Tindal, G. (2004). Writing performance assessments: How important is extended time? *Journal of Learning Disabilities, 37,* 132–142.

Deshler, D. D., & Schumaker, J. B. (2006). *Teaching adolescents with disabilities: Accessing the general education curriculum.* Thousand Oaks, CA: Corwin.

Eliott, S. N., & Fuchs, L. S. (1997). The utility of curriculum-based measurement and performance assessment as alternatives to traditional intelligence and achievement tests. *School Psychology Review, 26,* 224–233.

Elliott, S. N., Kratochwill, T. R., & Schulte, A. A. G. (1998). The assessment accommodation checklist: Who, what, where, when, why, and how? *Teaching Exceptional Children, 31*(2), 10–14.

Elliott, S. N., & Marquart, A. M. (2004). Extended time as a testing accommodation: Its effects and perceived consequences. *Exceptional Children, 70*, pp. 349–367.

Erickson, R., Ysseldyke, J., Thurlow, M., & Elliott, J. (1998). Inclusive assessments and accountability systems: Tools of the trade in educational reform. *Teaching Exceptional Children, 31*(2), 4–9.

Erwin, B., & Dunwiddie, E. T. (1983). *Test without trauma.* New York: Grosset and Dunlap.

Ford, B. A., Obiakor, F. E., & Patton, J. M. (Eds.). (1995). *Effective education of African American exceptional learners: New perspectives.* Austin, TX: Pro-Ed.

Fuchs, L. (2008). *Progress monitoring within a multi-level prevention system.* Retrieved from the Response to Intervention Network Action Website on June 2, 2008, from http://www.rtinetwork.org/ Essential/Assessment/Progress/ar/MutlilevelPrevention

Fuchs, D., & Fuchs, L. S. (1989). Effects of examiner familiarity on Black, Caucasian, and Hispanic children: A meta-analysis. *Exceptional Children, 55,* 303–308.

Fuchs, D., Fuchs, L. S., Benowitz, S., & Barringer, K. (1987). Norm-referenced tests: Are they valid for use with handicapped students? *Exceptional Children, 54,* 263–271.

Fuchs, D., Fuchs, L. S., & Power, M. H. (1987). Effects of examiner familiarity of LD and MR students' language performance. *Remedial and Special Education, 8*(4), 47–52.

Fuchs, L. S. (1994). *Connecting performance assessment to instruction.* Reston, VA: Council for Exceptional Children.

Fuchs, L. S., & Fuchs, D. (1994). Academic assessment and instrumentation. In S. Vaughn & C. Bos (Eds.), *Research issues in learning disabilities: Theory, methodology, assessment, and ethics* (pp. 233–245). New York: Springer-Verlag.

Fuchs, L. S., Fuchs, D., Allinder, R. M., & Hamlett, C. L. (1992). Diagnostic spelling analysis within curriculum-based measurement: Implications for students with learning disabilities. In T. E. Scruggs & M. A. Mastropieri (Eds.), *Advances in learning and behavioral disabilities* (Vol. 7, pp. 35–55). Oxford, UK: Elsevier/JAI.

Fuchs, L. S., Fuchs, D., Hamlett, C. L., Phillips, N. B., & Bentz, J. (1994). Classwide curriculum-based measurement: Helping general educators meet the challenge of student diversity. *Exceptional Children, 60,* 518–537.

Gajria, M., Salend, S. J., & Hemrick, M. A. (1994). Teacher acceptability of testing modifications for mainstreamed students. *Learning Disabilities Research & Practice, 9,* 236–243.

Gollnick, D. M., & Chinn, P. C. (2009). *Multicultural education in a pluralistic society* (8th ed.). Upper Saddle River, NJ: Merrill/Pearson.

Gomez, E. (2001). Assessment portfolios: Including English language learners in large-scale assessments. *ERIC Digest.* Washington, DC: ERIC Clearinghouse on Languages and Linguistics. (ERIC Document Reproduction Service No. ED447725)

Hammill, D. D., & Larsen, S. C. (1996). *Test of written language.* Austin, TX: Pro-Ed.

Harry, B., & Klingner, J. K. (2006). *Why are so many minority students in special education?: Understanding race and disability in schools.* New York: Teachers College Press.

Hosp, M. K., Hosp, J. L. & Howell, K. W. (2007). *The ABCs of CBM: A practical guide to curriculum-based measurement.* New York: Guilford.

Howell, K. W., & Nolet, V. (2000). *Curriculum-based evaluation: Teaching and decision making* (3rd ed.). Florence, KY: Thomson Learning/Wadsworth.

Hughes, C. (1996). Memory and test-taking strategies. In D. D. Deshler, E. S. Ellis, & B. K. Lenz (Eds.), *Teaching adolescents with learning disabilities: Strategies and methods* (2nd ed., pp. 209–266). Denver: Love Publishing.

Hughes, C. A., Rule, K. L., Deshler, D., & Schumaker, J. B. (1993). Test-taking strategy instruction for adolescents with emotional and behavioral disorders. *Journal of Emotional and Behavioral Disorders, 1,* 189–198.

Hughes, C. A., & Schumaker, J. B. (1991). Test-taking strategy for adolescents with learning disabilities. *Exceptionality, 2,* 205–221.

Hughes, C. A., Schumaker, J. B., Deshler, D. D., & Mercer, C. D. (1988). *The test-taking strategy.* Lawrence, KS: Edge Enterprises.

Jayanthi, M., Epstein, M. H., Polloway, E. A., & Bursuck, W. D. (1996). A national survey of general education teachers' perceptions of testing adaptations. *Journal of Special Education, 30,* 99–115.

Johnson, E., Kimball, K., Brown, S. O., & Anderson, D. (2001). A statewide review of the use of accommodations in large-scale, high-stakes assessments. *Exceptional Children, 67,* 251–264.

Kaufman, A., & Kaufman, N. (2006). *The Kaufman assessment battery for children—II.* Circle Pines, MN: American Guidance Service.

Kaufman, A. S., & Kaufman, N. L. (2004). *Kaufman test of educational achievement* (2nd ed.). Circle Pines, MN: American Guidance Service.

Kearns, J., Burdge, M. D., & Clayton, J. (2006). How students demonstrate academic performance in portfolio assessment. In D. M. Browder & F. Spooner (Eds.), *Teaching language arts, math, & science to students with significant cognitive disabilities* (pp. 277–293). Baltimore: Paul H Brookes.

Kesselman-Turkel, J., & Peterson, F. (2004). *Test-taking strategies.* Madison, WI: University of Wisconsin Press.

Learning Disabilities Association. (1994). *Fact sheet: Entrance tests for postsecondary programs.* Pittsburgh: Author.

Learning Disabilities Association. (1995). *Fact sheet: Learning disabilities and educational standards.* Pittsburgh: Author.

Learning Disabilities Association. (2004). *Graduation Equivalency Diploma: The GED. Accommodations for the GED.* Pittsburgh: Author. Retrieved April 19, 2005, from http://www.ldanatl.org/ aboutld/adults/assessment/print_accomodations.asp

Lewandowski, L. J., Lovett, B. J., Parolin, R., Gordon, M., & Codding, R. S. (2007). Extended time accommodations and the mathematics performance of students with and without ADHD. *Journal of Psychoeducational Assessment, 25,* 17–28.

Lucangeli, D., & Scruggs, T. E. (2003). Test anxiety, perceived competence, and academic achievement in secondary school students. In T. E. Scruggs & M. A. Mastropieri (Eds.), *Identification and assessment: Advances in learning and behavioral disabilities* (pp. 223–230). Oxford, UK: Elsevier Science.

MacArthur, C. A., & Cavalier, A. R. (2004). Dictation and speech recognition technology as test accommodations. *Exceptional Children, 71,* 43–58.

Markwardt, F. C. (1997). *Peabody individual achievement test—normative update.* Upper Saddle River, NJ: Pearson.

Massachusetts Department of Education. (2004). *Requirements for the participation of students with disabilities in MCAS including test accommodations and alternate assessment.* Boston, MA: Massachusetts Department of Education. Retrieved April 15, 2005, from http:// www.donjohnston.com/pdf/massacc.pdf#search='massachusetts%20 department %20of%20education%20test%20accommodations'

Mastropieri, M. A., Scruggs, T. E., Mantzicopoulos, P. Y., Sturgeon, A., Goodwin, L., & Chung, S. (1998). "A place where living things affect and depend on each other": Qualitative and quantitative outcomes associated with inclusive science teaching. *Science Education, 82,* 163–179.

McLoughlin, J. A., & Lewis, R. B. (2008). *Assessing students with special needs* (7th ed.). Upper Saddle River, NJ: Merrill/Prentice Hall.

Millman, J., & Pauk, W. (1969). *How to take tests.* New York: McGraw-Hill.

Munk, D., & Bursuck, W. D. (1998). Report card adaptations for students with disabilities: Types and acceptability. *Intervention in School and Clinic, 33,* 306–308.

Munk, D., & Bursuck, W. D.(2001). Preliminary findings on personalized grading plans for middle school students with learning disabilities. *Exceptional Children, 67,* 211–234.

Pauk, W. (1987). *Study skills for junior and community colleges.* Clearwater, FL: Reston-Stuart.

Phillips, S. E. (1995). *All students, same test, same standards: What the new Title I legislation will mean for the educational assessment of special education students.* Oak Brook, IL: North Central Regional Educational Lab. (ERIC Document Reproduction Service No. ED394269)

Polloway, E. A., Epstein, M. H., Bursuck, W. D., Roderique, T. W., McConeky, J. L., & Jayanthi, M. (1994). Classroom grading: A national survey of policies. *Remedial and Special Education, 15*(3), 162–170.

Putnam, M. L. (1992). The testing practices of mainstream secondary classroom teachers. *Remedial and Special Education, 13*(5), 11–21.

Ritter, S., & Idol-Maestas, L. (1986). Teaching middle school students to use a test-taking strategy. *Journal of Educational Research, 79,* 350–357.

Roid, G. H. (2003). *Stanford-Binet intelligence scale* (5th ed.). Itasca, IL: Riverside.

Rojewski, J. W., Pollard, R. R., & Meers, G. D. (1992). Grading secondary vocational education students with disabilities: A national perspective. *Exceptional Children, 59,* 68–76.

Salend, S. (1995). Modifying tests for diverse learners. *Intervention in School and Clinic, 31,* 84–90.

Salend, S. (1998). Using portfolios to assess student performance. *Teaching Exceptional Children, 31*(2), 36–43.

Salend, S. (2008). Determining appropriate testing accommodations: Complying with NCLB and IDEA. *Teaching Exceptional Children, 40*(4), 14–22.

Salvia, J., & Ysseldyke, J. E. (2007). *Assessment in special and inclusive education* (10th ed.). Boston: Houghton Mifflin.

Schirmer, B. R., & Bailey, J. (2000). Writing assessment rubric: An instructional approach with struggling writers. *Teaching Exceptional Children, 33,* 52–58.

Scruggs, T. E., & Mastropieri, M. A. (1988). Are learning disabled students "test-wise"?: A review of recent research. *Learning Disabilities Focus, 3,* 87–97.

Scruggs, T. E., & Mastropieri, M. A. (1992). *Teaching test-taking skills: Helping students show what they know.* Cambridge, MA: Brookline Books.

Scruggs, T. E., Mastropieri, M. A., Bakken, J. P., & Brigham, F. J. (1993). Reading vs. doing: The relative effectiveness of textbook-based and inquiry-oriented approaches to science education. *Journal of Special Education, 27,* 1–15.

Shriner, J. G., & Ganguly, R. (2007). Assessment and accommodation issues under the No Child Left Behind Act and the Individuals with Disabilities Education Improvement Act: Information for IEP teams. *Assessment for Effective Intervention, 32,* 231–243.

Songlee, D. H. (2007). *Effects of test-taking strategy instruction on high-functioning adolescents with autism spectrum disorder.* Unpublished doctoral dissertation, University of Nevada, Las Vegas.

Stecker, P. M., Fuchs, L. S., & Fuchs, D. (2005). Using curriculum-based measurement to improve student achievement: Review of research. *Psychology in the Schools, 42,* 795–819.

Swicegood, P. (1994). Portfolio-based assessment practices. *Intervention in School and Clinic, 30*(1), 6–15.

Thurlow, M. L., Lazarus, S. S., Thompson, S. J., & Morse, A. B. (2005). State policies on assessment participation and accommodations for students with disabilities. *Journal of Special Education, 38,* 232–240.

Training and Technical Assistance Center at the College of William and Mary. (2005). *Virginia's alternate assessment program.* Williamsburg, VA: Author.

Vavrus, L. (1990). Put portfolios to the test. *Instructor, 100*(1), 48–53.

Virginia Department of Education. (2007). *Virginia alternative and alternate assessments administrator's manual.* Richmond, VA: Author. Retrieved March 12, 2008, from http://www.doe.virginia.gov/VDOE/Assessment/2007-2008_VProgram_Adm_Manual.pdf

Wechsler, D. (2003). *Wechsler intelligence scale for children* (4th ed.). San Antonio, TX: Psychological Corporation.

Wesson, C. L., & King, R. P. (1996). Portfolio assessment and special education students. *Teaching Exceptional Children, 28*(2), 44–48.

Wilkenson, G. S., & Robertson, G. J. (2006). *Wide range achievement test—4.* Los Angeles: Western Psychological Services.

Wood, W., & Willoughby, T. (1995). Cognitive strategies for test-taking. In E. Wood, V. E. Woloshyn, & T. Willoughby (Eds.), *Cognitive strategy instruction for middle and high schools* (pp. 245–258). Cambridge, MA: Brookline Books.

Woodcock, R. W. (1998). *Woodcock reading mastery tests—revised—normative update.* Circle Pines, MN: American Guidance Service.

Woodcock, R. W., Johnson, M. B., & Mather, N. (2001). *Woodcock–Johnson III, Tests of achievement.* Circle Pines, MN: American Guidance Service.

Chapter 13

Adams, G., & Carnine, D. (2003). Direct instruction. In H. L. Swanson, K. Harris, & S. Graham (Eds.), *Handbook of learning disabilities* (pp. 403–416). New York: Guilford.

Adams, M. J. (1990). *Beginning to read.* Cambridge, MA: MIT Press.

Anderson, R. C., Hiebert, E. H., Scott, J. A., & Wilkinson, I. A. G. (1985). *Becoming a nation of readers: The report of the commission on reading.* Washington, DC: National Academy of Education, Commission on Education and Public Policy.

Babyak, A. E., Koorland, M., & Mathes, P. G. (2000). The effects of story mapping instruction on the reading comprehension of students with behavioral disorders. *Behavioral Disorders, 25,* 239–258.

Bakken, J. P., Mastropieri, M. A., & Scruggs, T. E. (1997). Reading comprehension of expository science material and students with learning disabilities: A comparison of strategies. *Journal of Special Education, 31,* 300–324.

Bakken, J. P., & Whedon, C. K. (2002). Teaching text structure to improve reading comprehension. *Intervention in School and Clinic, 37,* 229–33.

Behavioral Research and Teaching. (2005). *Oral reading fluency: 90 years of measurement.* Eugene, OR: Author.

Berkeley, S. L., Scruggs, T. E., & Mastropieri, M. A. (2007, April). *An updated synthesis of intervention research on reading comprehension for students with learning disabilities (1995–2005).* Paper presented at the annual meeting of the American Education Research Association, Chicago.

Berninger, V., & Amtmann, D. (2003). Preventing written expression disabilities through early and continuing assessment and intervention for handwriting and/or spelling problems: Research into practice. In H. L. Swanson, K. Harris, & S. Graham (Eds.), *Handbook of learning disabilities* (pp. 345–363). New York: Guilford.

Best, S. J., Heller, K. W., & Bigge, J. L. (2005). *Teaching individuals with physical or multiple disabilities.* (5th ed.). Upper Saddle River, NJ: Merrill/Prentice Hall.

Blischak, D. M., & Schlosser, R. W. (2003). Use of technology to support independent spelling by students with autism. *Topics in Language Disorders, 23,* 293–304.

Boulineau, T., Fore, C., Hagan-Burke, S., & Burke, M. D. (2004). Use of story-mapping to increase the story-grammar text comprehension of elementary students with learning disabilities. *Learning Disability Quarterly, 27,* 105–121.

Brigham, F. J., Berkeley, S. A., Simpkins, P., & Brigham, M. (2007). Reading comprehension instruction. *DLD-DR Current Practice Alerts, Alert 12.* Arlington, VA: Council for Exceptional Children, Division for Learning Disabilities.

Browder, D. M., & Xin, Y. P. (1998). A meta-analysis and review of sight word research and its implications for teaching functional reading to individuals with moderate and severe disabilities. *Journal of Special Education, 32,* 130–153.

Bryant, N. D., Drabin, I. R., & Gettinger, M. (1981). Effects of varying unit size on spelling achievement of learning disabled children. *Journal of Learning Disabilities, 14,* 200–203.

Burks, M. (2004). Effects of classwide peer tutoring on the number of words spelled correctly by students with LD. *Intervention in School and Clinic, 39,* 301–304.

Callins, T. (2005). Culturally responsive literacy instruction. *Practitioner Brief Series: National Center for Culturally Responsive Educational Systems.* Retrieved April 20, 2005, from http://www.nccrest.org/publications/display.asp?filename=Briefs/Literacy_final.pdf&type=pdf

Carnine, D., Silbert, J., Kameénui, E. J., & Tarver, S. G. (2004). *Direct instruction reading* (4th ed.). Upper Saddle River, NJ: Merrill/Prentice Hall.

Chall, J. (1987). Reading development in adults. *Annals of Dyslexia, 37,* 240–251.

Chamberlain, J., & Leal, D. J. (1999). Caldecott Medal books and readability levels: Not just picture books. *The Reading Teacher, 52,* 898–902.

Chard, D. J., Vaughn, S., & Tyler, B. (2002). A synthesis of research on effective interventions for building reading fluency with elementary students with learning disabilities. *Journal of Learning Disabilities, 35,* 386–406.

Coyne, M. D., Simmons, D. C., Kameénui, E. J., & Stoolmiller, M. (2004). Teaching vocabulary during shared storybook readings: An examination of differential effects. *Exceptionality, 12,* 145–162.

D'Agostino, J. V., & Murphy, J. A. (2004). A meta-analysis of reading recovery in United States schools. *Educational Evaluation & Policy Analysis, 26,* 23–38.

De La Paz, S. (2007). Best practices in teaching writing to students with special needs. In S. Graham, C. MacArthur, & J. Fitzgerald (Eds.), *Best practices in writing instruction* (pp. 163–178). New York: Guilford.

De La Paz, S., & Graham, S. (1997). Effects of dictation and advanced planning instruction on the composing of students with writing and learning problems. *Journal of Educational Psychology, 89,* 203–222.

Delquadri, J. C., Greenwood, C. R., Stretton, K., & Hall, R. V. (1983). The peer tutoring spelling game: A classroom procedure for increasing opportunity to respond and spelling performance. *Education and Treatment of Children, 6,* 225–239.

Denton, C. A., & Mathes, P. G. (2002). Reading recovery: *DLD-DR Current Practice Alerts,* Alert 7. Arlington, VA: Council for Exceptional Children, Division for Learning Disabilities.

Deshler, D. D., & Schumaker, J. (2005). *Teaching adolescents with disabilities: Accessing the general education curriculum.* Thousand Oaks, CA: Corwin.

Dieker, L. A., & Little, M. (2005). Secondary reading: Not just for reading teachers anymore. *Intervention in School and Clinic, 40,* 276–283.

Division for Learning Disabilities. (2007). *Thinking about response to intervention and learning disabilities: A teacher's guide.* Arlington, VA: Author.

Dodds, T., & Goodfellow, F. (1990–1991). *Learning through literature.* Desoto, TX: SRA McGraw-Hill.

Dowling, D. (1995). *303 dumb spelling mistakes . . . and what you can do about them.* Lincolnwood, IL: National Textbook Company.

Durkin, D. (1987). Influences on basal reader programs. *The Elementary School Journal, 87,* 331–341.

Ehri, L. C., Nunes, S. R., Willows, D. M., Schuster, B. V., Yaghoub-Zadeh, Z., & Shanahan, T. (2001). Phonemic awareness instruction helps children learn to read: Evidence from the National Reading Panel's meta-analysis. *Reading Research Quarterly, 36,* 250–287.

Ellis, E. (1996). Reading strategy instruction. In D. Deshler, E. S. Ellis, & B. Lenz (Eds.), *Teaching adolescents with learning disabilities: Strategies and methods* (2nd ed., pp. 61–125). Denver: Love Publishing.

Engelmann, S., Carnine, L., Johnson, G., Meyer, L., Becker, W., & Eisele, J. (2008). *Corrective reading: Decoding strategies.* Columbus, OH: McGraw Hill.

Englert, C. S., & Mariage, T. V. (1996). A sociocultural perspective: Teaching ways-of-thinking and ways-of-talking in a literacy community. *Learning Disabilities Research & Practice, 11,* 157–167.

Faggella-Luby, M., Schumaker, J., & Deshler, D. D. (2007). Embedded learning strategy instruction: Story-structure pedagogy in heterogeneous secondary literature classes. *Learning Disability Quarterly, 30,* 131–147.

Fletcher, D., & Abood, D. (1988). An analysis of the readability of product warning labels: Implications for curriculum development for persons with moderate and severe mental retardation. *Education and Training in Mental Retardation, 23,* 224–227.

Foorman, B. R. (2007). Primary prevention in classroom reading instruction. *Teaching Exceptional Children, 39*(5), 24–30.

Fossett, B., Smith, V., & Mirenda, P. (2003). Facilitating oral language and literacy development during general education activities. In D. L. Ryndak & S. Alper (Eds.), *Curriculum and instruction for students with significant disabilities in inclusive settings* (2nd ed., pp. 173–205). Boston: Allyn & Bacon.

Fountas, I. C., & Pinnell, G. S. (2005). *The Fountas & Pinnell leveled book list, K–8, 2006–2008 Edition.* Portsmouth, NH: Heinemann.

Fuchs, D., & Deshler, D. D. (2007). What we need to know about the responsiveness to intervention (and shouldn't be afraid to ask). *Learning Disabilities Research & Practice, 22,* 129–136.

Fuchs, L.S., Fuchs, D. (2007). The role of assessment in the three-tier approach to reading instruction. In D. Haager, J. Klingner, & S. Vaughn (Eds.), *Evidence-based reading practices for response to intervention* (pp. 29-42).Baltimore, MD: Paul H Brookes.

Fuchs, L.S., Fuchs, D., Hamlett, C.L., Phillips, N.B., & Bentz, J. (1994). Classwide curriculum-based measurement: Helping general educators meet the challenge of student diversity. *Exceptional Children, 60,* 518-537.

Fulk, B. M. (1997). Think while you spell: A cognitive motivational approach to spelling instruction. *Teaching Exceptional Children, 29*(4), 70–71.

Gersten, R., & Dimino, J. (1993). Visions and revisions: A special education perspective on the whole language controversy. *Remedial and Special Education, 14*(4), 5–13.

Gersten, R., Fuchs, L. S., Williams, J., & Baker, S. (2001). Teaching reading comprehension strategies to students with learning disabilities: A review of research. *Review of Educational Research, 71,* 279–320.

Gettinger, M., Bryant, N. D., & Fayne, H. R. (1982). Designing spelling instruction for learning disabled children: An emphasis on unit size, distributed practice, and training for transfer. *Journal of Special Education, 16,* 339–448.

Goodman, K. (2005). *What's whole in whole language?* Muskegon, MI: RDR Books.

Graham, L., & Bellert, A. (2004). Difficulties in reading comprehension for students with learning disabilities. In B. Y. L. Wong (Ed.), *Learning about learning disabilities* (pp. 251–279). San Diego, CA: Elsevier Academic Press.

Graham, S. (1999). Handwriting and spelling instruction for students with learning disabilities: A review. *Learning Disability Quarterly, 22,* 78–98.

Graham, S., & Harris, K. R. (2005). *Writing better: Effective strategies for teaching students with learning difficulties.* Baltimore: Brookes.

Graham, S., & Harris, K. (2007). Best practices in teaching planning. In S. Graham, C. MacArthur, & J. Fitzgerald (Eds.), *Best practices in writing instruction* (pp. 119–140). New York: Guilford.

Graham, S., Harris, K. R., & Chorzempa, B. F. (2002). Contribution of spelling instruction to the spelling, writing, and reading of poor spellers. *Journal of Educational Psychology, 94,* 669–686.

Graham, S., Harris, K. R., & Loynachan, C. (1994). The spelling for writing list. *Journal of Learning Disabilities, 27,* 210–214.

Graham, S., Harris, K. R., & Loynachan, C. (1996). The directed spelling thinking activity: Application with high-frequency words. *Learning Disabilities Research & Practice, 11,* 34–40.

Graham, S., Harris, K. R., & MacArthur, C. (2004). Writing instruction. In B. Y. L. Wong (Ed.), *Learning about learning disabilities* (3rd ed., pp. 281–313). San Diego, CA: Elsevier Academic Press.

Graham, S., & Perin, D. (2007). A meta-analysis of writing instruction for adolescent students. *Journal of Educational Psychology, 99,* 445–476.

Graham, S., & Weintraub, N. (1996). A review of handwriting research: Progress and prospects from 1980 to 1994. *Educational Psychology Review, 8,* 7–87.

Graves, D. H. (2003). *Writing: Teachers and children at work.* Portsmouth, NH: Heinemann.

Gregg, N. C., & Coleman, C., Davis, M., & Chalk, J. C. (2007). Timed essay writing: Implications for high-stakes tests. *Journal of Learning Disabilities, 40,* 306–318.

Gregg, N. C., Chris, D. M. (2007). Timed essay writing: Implications for high-stakes tests. *Journal of Learning Disabilities, 40,* 306–318.

Hallahan, D. P., Lloyd, J. W., Kauffman, J. M., Weiss, M. P., & Martinez, E. A. (2005). *Learning disabilities: Foundations, characteristics, and effective teaching* (3rd ed.). Boston: Allyn & Bacon.

Harris, K. K., Graham, S., & Freeman, S. (1988). Effects of strategy training on metamemory among learning disabled students. *Exceptional Children, 54,* 332–338.

Harris, K. K., Graham, S., Mason, L. H., & Friedlander, B. (2008). *Powerful writing strategies for all students.* Baltimore: Brookes.

Heller, K. W. (2005). Adaptations and instruction in literacy and language arts. In S. J. Best, K. W. Heller, & J. L. Bigge (Eds.), *Teaching individuals with physical or multiple disabilities* (5th ed., pp. 401–439). Upper Saddle River, NJ: Merrill/Prentice Hall.

Hiebert, E. H. (1994). Reading recovery in the United States: What difference does it make to an age cohort? *Educational Researcher, 23*(9), 15–25.

Idol, L., & Croll, V. J. (1987). Story-mapping training as a means of improving reading comprehension. *Learning Disability Quarterly, 10,* 214–229.

Idol-Maestas, L. (1985). Getting ready to read: Guided probing for poor comprehenders. *Learning Disability Quarterly, 8,* 243–254.

Isaacson, S., & Gleason, M. M. (1997). Mechanical obstacles to writing: What can teachers do to help students with learning problems? *Learning Disabilities Research & Practice, 12,* 188–194.

Johnson, P. H. (1992). Understanding reading disability: A case study approach. In T. Heir & T. Latus (Eds.), *Special education at century's end: Evolution of theory and practice since 1970* (pp. 275–304). Reprint series No. 23, Harvard Educational Review. Cambridge, MA: President and Fellows of Harvard College.

Klingner, J. K., Vaughn, S., Arguelles, M. E., Hughes, M. T., & Leftwich, S. A. (2004). Collaborative strategic reading: "Real world" lessons from classroom teachers. *Remedial and Special Education, 25,* 291–302.

Kubina, R. & Hughes, C. A. (2007). Fluency instruction: *DLD-DR Current Practice Alerts, Alert 15.* Arlington, VA: Council for Exceptional Children, Division for Learning Disabilities.

Lane, K. L., Little, M. A., & Redding-Rhodes, J. (2007). Outcomes of a teacher-led reading intervention for elementary students at risk for behavioral disorders. *Exceptional Children, 74,* 47–70.

Lenz, B. K., Schumaker, J. B., Deshler, D. D., & Beals, V. L. (1984). *The word identification strategy.* Lawrence: University of Kansas.

Lerner, J., & Kline, F. (2006). *Learning disabilities and related disorders: Characteristics and teaching strategies* (10th ed.). Boston: Houghton-Mifflin.

Liang, L. A. (2002). On the shelves of the local library: High-interest, easy reading trade books for struggling middle and high school readers. *Preventing School Failure, 46,* 183–188.

Life Span Institute. (2002). *Reading fluency tables.* Lawrence, KS: University of Kansas. Retrieved April 25, 2005, from http://www.lsi.ku.edu/jgprojects/cwptlms/html2002/ProjectManagement/reading_fluency_table.htm.

MacArthur, C. A. (2000). New tools for writing: Assistive technology for students with writing difficulties. *Topics in Language Disorders, 20*(4), 85–100.

Marschark, M., & Harris, M. (1996). Success and failure in learning to read: The special case (?) of deaf children. In C. Cornoldi & J. Oakhill (Eds.), *Reading comprehension difficulties: Processes and intervention* (pp. 279–300). Mahwah, NJ: Lawrence Erlbaum.

Mastropieri, M. A., & Scruggs, T. E. (1991). *Teaching students ways to remember: Strategies for learning mnemonically.* Cambridge, MA: Brookline Books.

Mastropieri, M. A., & Scruggs, T. E. (1997). Best practices in promoting reading comprehension in students with learning disabilities: 1976 to 1996. *Remedial and Special Education, 18,* 197–213.

Mastropieri, M. A., Scruggs, T. E., & Graetz, J. (2003). Reading comprehension for secondary students. *Learning Disability Quarterly, 26,* 103–116.

Mastropieri, M. A., Scruggs, T. E., Mohler, L. J., Beranek, M. L., Spencer, V., Boon, R. T., & Talbott, E. (2001). Can middle school students with serious reading difficulties help each other and learn anything? *Learning Disabilities Research & Practice, 16,* 18–27.

Mathes, P. G., Fuchs, D., Fuchs, L. S., Henley, A. M., & Sanders, A. (1994). Increasing strategic reading practice with Peabody Classwide Peer Tutoring. *Learning Disabilities Research & Practice, 9,* 44–48.

McMaster, K. L., Fuchs, D., & Fuchs, L. S. (2006). Research on peer-assisted learning strategies: The promise and limitations of peer-mediated instruction. *Reading & Writing Quarterly: Overcoming Learning Difficulties, 22,* 5–25.

Mercer, C. D., Campbell, K. U., Miller, M. D., Mercer, K. D., & Lane, H. B. (2000). Effects of a reading fluency intervention for middle schoolers with specific learning disabilities. *Learning Disabilities Research & Practice, 15,* 179–189.

Montague, M. (1998). Research on metacognition in special education. In T. E. Scruggs & M. A. Mastropieri (Eds.), *Advances in learning and behavioral disabilities* (Vol. 12, pp. 151–184). Greenwich, CT: JAI.

National Reading Panel. (2000). *Report of the National Reading Panel. Teaching children to read: An evidence-based assessment of the scientific research literature on reading and its implications for reading instruction.* Washington, DC: U.S. Department of Health and Human Services.

O'Connor, R. E., White, A., & Swanson, H. L. (2007). Repeated reading versus continuous reading: Influences on reading fluency and comprehension. *Exceptional Children, 74,* 31–46.

Ogle, D. M. (1986). K-W-L: A teaching model that develops active reading of expository text. *The Reading Teacher, 39,* 564–570.

O'Shea, L. J., Sindelar, P. T., & O'Shea, D. (1987). The effects of repeated readings and attentional cues on the reading fluency and comprehension of learning disabled readers. *Learning Disabilities Research, 2,* 103–109.

Palincsar, A. S., & Brown, A. L. (1984). Reciprocal teaching of comprehension fostering and comprehension monitoring activities. *Cognition and Instruction, 1,* 117–175.

Polloway, E. A., Epstein, M. H., Epstein, M. H., Polloway, C. H., Patton, J. R., & Ball, D. W. (1986). Corrective reading program: Its effectiveness with learning disabled and mentally retarded students. *Remedial and Special Education, 7*(4), 41–47.

Polloway, E. A., Smith, T. E. C., & Miller, L. (2003). *Language instruction for students with disabilities* (3rd ed.). Denver: Love Publishing.

Pressley, M. (2006). *Reading instruction that works: The case for balanced teaching* (3rd ed.). New York: Guilford.

Pressley, M., & Rankin, J. (1994). More about whole language methods of reading instruction for students at-risk for early reading failure. *Learning Disabilities Research & Practice, 9,* 156–168.

Pullen, P., & Lloyd, J. (2008). Phonics instruction. *DLD-DR Current Practice Alerts, Alert 12.* Arlington, VA: Council for Exceptional Children, Division for Learning Disabilities.

Reid, R., Gonzalez, J. E., Nordness, P. D., Trout, A., & Epstein, M. H. (2004). A meta-analysis of the academic status of students with emotional/behavioral disturbance. *Journal of Special Education, 38,* 130–143.

Reynolds, M., & Wheldall, K. (2007). Reading recovery 20 years down the track: Looking forward, looking back. *International Journal of Disability, Development and Education, 54,* 199–223.

Rosenshine, B., & Meister, C. (1994). Reciprocal teaching: A review of the research. *Review of Educational Research, 64,* 479–530.

Routman, R. (1991). *Invitations: Changing as teachers and learners K–12.* Portsmouth, NH: Heinemann.

Rudenga, E. A. V. (1992). *Incompatibility? Ethnographic case studies of learning disabled students in a whole language classroom.* Unpublished doctoral dissertation, Purdue University, West Lafayette, IN.

Schirmer, B. R., & McGough, S. M. (2005). Reaching reading to children who are deaf: Do the conclusions of the National Reading Panel apply? *Review of Educational Research, 75,* 83–117.

Schlagal, B. (2001). Traditional, developmental, and structured language approaches to spelling: Review and recommendations. *Annals of Dyslexia, 51,* 147–176.

Scruggs, T. E., Mastropieri, M. A., & Sullivan, G. S. (1994). Promoting relational thinking skills: Elaborative interrogation for mildly handicapped students. *Exceptional Children, 60,* 450–457.

Shaywitz, S. (2003). *Overcoming dyslexia.* New York: Knopf.

Shefter, H. (1974). *6 minutes a day to perfect spelling.* New York: Pocket Books.

Slavin, R. (2005). *Evidence-based reform: Advancing the education of students at risk.* Washington, DC: Center for American Progress.

Snider, V. E. (1997). Transfer of decoding skills to a literature basal. *Learning Disabilities Research & Practice, 12,* 54–62.

Snow, C. E., Burns, M. S., & Griffin, P. (Eds.). (1998). *Preventing reading difficulties in young children.* Washington, DC: National Academy Press.

Speece, D. L., MacDonald, V., Kilsheimer, L., & Krist, J. (1997). Research to practice: Preservice teachers reflect on reciprocal teaching. *Learning Disabilities Research & Practice, 12,* 177–187.

Spencer, V. G., Scruggs, T. E., & Mastropieri, M. A. (2003). Content area learning in middle school social studies classrooms and stu-

dents with emotional or behavioral disorders: A comparison of strategies. *Behavioral Disorders, 28,* 77–93.

Stahl, S. A. (1992). Saying the "p" word: Nine guidelines for exemplary phonics instruction. *The Reading Teacher, 45,* 618–625.

Stahl, S. A., Duffy-Hester, A. M., & Dougherty-Stahl, K. A. (2006). Everything you wanted to know about phonics (and were afraid to ask). In L. M. Morrow, K. A. Dougherty-Stahl, & M. C. McKenna (Eds.), *Reading research at work: Foundations of effective practice* (pp. 126–156). New York: Guilford.

Staubitz, J. E., Cartledge, G., & Yurick, A. L. (2005). Repeated reading for students with emotional or behavioral disorders: Peer- and trainer-mediated instruction. *Behavioral Disorders, 31,* 51–64.

Stecker, P. M. (2007). Tertiary intervention: Using progress monitoring with intensive services. *Teaching Exceptional Children, 39*(5), 50–57.

Stewart, D. A., & Kluwin, T. N. (2001). *Teaching deaf and hard of hearing students: Content, strategies, and curriculum.* Boston: Allyn & Bacon.

Stone, C. A. (1998). The metaphor of scaffolding: Its utility for the field of learning disabilities. *Journal of Learning Disabilities, 31,* 344–364.

Stone, C. A., Silliman, E. R., Ehren, B. J. & Apel, K. (Eds.). (2004). *Handbook of language and literacy: Development and disorders.* New York: Guilford.

Suid, M. (1981). *Demonic mnemonics.* New York: Dell Publishing.

Therrien, W. J. (2004). Fluency and comprehension gains as a result of repeated reading: A meta-analysis. *Remedial and Special Education, 25,* 252–261.

Thurber, D. N. (1999). *D'Nealian handwriting.* Upper Saddle River, NJ: Pearson Education.

Torgesen, J. K., & Bryant, B. R. (1994). *Phonological awareness training for reading.* Austin, TX: Pro-Ed.

Troia, G. A. (2004a). Migrant students with limited English proficiency: Can Fast ForWord Language™ make a difference in their language skills and academic achievement? *Remedial and Special Education, 25,* 353–366.

Troia, G. A. (2004b). *Phonological awareness acquisition and intervention: Current practice alerts, issue 10.* Arlington, VA: Council for Exceptional Children, Division for Learning Disabilities.

Vaughn, S., & Roberts, G. (2007). Secondary interventions in reading: Providing additional instruction for students at risk. *Teaching Exceptional Children, 39*(5), 40–46.

Williams, J. (2003). Teaching text structure to improve reading comprehension. In H. L. Swanson, K. Harris, & S. Graham (Eds.), *Handbook of learning disabilities* (pp. 293–305). New York: Guilford.

Wong, B. Y. L., Wong, R., Perry, N., & Sawatsky, D. (1986). The efficacy of a self-questioning summarization strategy for use by underachievers and learning disabled adolescents in social studies. *Learning Disabilities Focus, 2*(2), 20–35.

Zaner-Bloser handwriting. (2003). Columbus, OH: Zaner-Bloser.

Chapter 14

Baker, S., Gersten, R., Dimino, J. A., & Griffiths, R. (2004). The sustained use of research based instructional practice: A case study of peer-assisted learning strategies in math. *Remedial and Special Education, 25,* 5–24.

Bley, N. S., & Thornton, C. A. (2001). *Teaching mathematics to students with learning disabilities* (4th ed.). Austin, TX: Pro-Ed.

Bryant, B. R., & Bryant, D. P. (2008). Introduction to the special series: Mathematics and learning disabilities. *Learning Disability Quarterly, 31,* 3–10.

Butler, F. M., Miller, S. P., Lee, K., & Pierce, T. (2001). Teaching mathematics to students with mild-to-moderate mental retardation: A review of the literature. *Mental Retardation, 39,* 20–31.

Carnine, D. (1998). Instructional design in mathematics for students with learning disabilities. In D. Rivera (Ed.), *Mathematics education for students with learning disabilities* (pp. 119–138). Austin, TX: Pro-Ed.

Case, L. P., Harris, K. R., & Graham, S. (1992). Improving the mathematical problem-solving skills of students with learning disabilities: Self-regulated strategy development. *Journal of Special Education, 26,* 1–19.

Fuchs, L., Fuchs, D., & Courey, S. (2005). Curriculum-based measurement of mathematics competence: From computation to concepts and applications to real-life problem solving. *Assessment for Effective Intervention, 30*(2), 33–46.

Fuchs, L. S., Fuchs, D. (2008). Mathematics disabilities in the primary grades: Seven principles of effective practice. *New Times for DLD, 26*(1), 1–2.

Fuchs, L. S., Fuchs, D., & Hollenbeck, K. N. (2007). Extending responsiveness to intervention to mathematics at first and third grades. *Learning Disabilities Research & Practice, 22,* 13–24.

Geary, D. C. (2003). Learning disabilities in arithmetic: Problem-solving differences and cognitive deficits. In H. L. Swanson, K. Harris, & S. Graham (Eds.), *Handbook of learning disabilities* (pp. 199–212). New York: Guilford.

Ginsburg, H. P. (1997). Mathematics learning disabilities: A view from developmental psychology. *Journal of Learning Disabilities, 30,* 20–33.

Ginsburg, H. P. (1998a). Mathematics learning disabilities: A view from developmental psychology. In D. Rivera (Ed.), *Mathematics education for students with learning disabilities* (pp. 22–58). Austin, TX: Pro-Ed.

Ginsburg, H. P. (1998b). Toby's math. In R. J. Sternberg & T. Ben-Zeev (Eds.), *The nature of mathematical thinking* (pp. 175–202). Hillsdale, NJ: Lawrence Erlbaum.

Heller, K. W. (2005). Adaptations and instruction in mathematics. In S. J. Best, K. W. Heller, & J. L. Bigge (Eds.), *Teaching individuals with physical or multiple disabilities* (5th ed., pp. 501–543). Upper Saddle River, NJ: Merrill/Prentice Hall.

Horton, S. V., Lovitt, T. C., & White, O. R. (1992). Teaching mathematics to adolescents classified as educable mentally handicapped: Using calculators to remove the computational onus. *Remedial and Special Education, 13*(3), 36–60.

Hutchinson, N. L. (1993). Effects of cognitive strategy instruction on algebra problem solving of adolescents with learning disabilities. *Learning Disability Quarterly, 16,* 34–63.

Janvier, C. (1987). *Problems of representation in the teaching and learning of mathematics.* Mahwah, NJ: Lawrence Erlbaum.

Joseph, G. G. (2000). *The crest of the peacock: Non-European roots of mathematics* (2nd ed.). Princeton, NJ: Princeton University Press.

Kaméenui, E. J., Chard, D. J., & Carnine, D. W. (1996). The new school mathematics and the age-old dilemma of diversity: Cutting or untying the Gordian knot. In M. C. Pugach & C. L. Warger (Eds.), *Curriculum trends, special education, and reform: Refocusing the conversation* (pp. 94–105). New York: Teachers College Press.

Kilpatrick, J. (1985). Doing mathematics without understanding it: A commentary on Higbee and Kunihira. *Educational Psychologist, 20*(2), 65–68.

Lang, C., Mastropieri, M. A., Scruggs, T. E., & Porter, M. (2004). The effects of self-instructional strategies on problem solving in algebra for students with special needs. In T. E. Scruggs & M. A. Mastropieri (Eds.), *Research in secondary schools: Advances in learning and behavioral disabilities* (Vol. 17, pp. 27–54). Oxford, UK: Elsevier.

Lang, H., & Pagliaro, C. (2007). Factors predicting recall of mathematics terms by deaf students: Implications for teaching. *Journal of Deaf Studies and Deaf Education, 12,* 449–460.

Maccini, P., & Hughes, C. (2000). Effects of a problem-solving strategy on the introductory algebra performance of secondary students with learning disabilities. *Learning Disabilities Research & Practice, 15,* 10–21.

Maccini, P., McNaughton, D., & Ruhl, K. (1999). Algebra instruction for students with learning disabilities: Implications from a research review. *Learning Disability Quarterly, 22,* 113–126.

Marzocchi, G. M., Lucangeli, D., De Meo, T., Fini, F., & Cornoldi, C. (2002). The disturbing effect of irrelevant information on arithmetic problem solving in inattentive children. *Developmental Neuropsychology, 21,* 73–92.

Mastropieri, M. A., & Scruggs, T. E. (1991). *Teaching students ways to remember: Strategies for learning mnemonically.* Cambridge, MA: Brookline Books.

Mastropieri, M. A., Scruggs, T. E., Davidson, T., & Rana, R. (2004). Instructional interventions for students with mathematics learning disabilities. In B. Y. L. Wong (Ed.), *Learning about learning disabilities* (3rd ed., pp. 311–329). New York: Elsevier Science.

Math Department, Frisbee Middle School. (n.d.). *Multicultural math fair.* Retrieved June 4, 2008, from Drexel University, Multicultural Math Fair Website, http://mathforum.org/alejandre/mathfair/.

McCoy, L. P. (n.d.). *Multicultural mathematics.* Retrieved June 4, 2008, from Wake Forest University Multicultural Math Website, http://www.wfu.edu/~mccoy/multmath.html

Mercer, C. D., & Mercer, A. R. (2005). *Teaching students with learning problems* (7th ed.). Upper Saddle River, NJ: Merrill/Prentice Hall.

Miller, S. P., & Mercer, C. D. (1993). Using a graduated word problem sequence to promote problem-solving skills. *Learning Disabilities Research & Practice, 8,* 169–174.

Montague, M. (1992). The effects of cognitive and metacognitive strategy instruction on the mathematical problem solving of middle school students with learning disabilities. *Journal of Learning Disabilities, 25,* 230–248.

Montague, M. (2003a). *Solve it! A practical approach to teaching mathematical problem solving skills.* Reston, VA: Exceptional Innovations.

Montague, M. (2003b). Teaching division to students with learning disabilities: A constructivist aproach. *Exceptionality, 11,* 165–176.

Montague, M. (2008). Self-regulation strategies to improve mathematical problem solving for students with learning disabilities. *Learning Disability Quarterly, 31,* 37–44.

Montague, M., & Jitendra, A. (Eds.) (2006). *Teaching mathematics to middle school students with learning difficulties.* New York: Guilford.

National Council of Teachers of Mathematics. (2000). *Principles and standards for school mathematics.* Reston, VA: Author.

National Council of Teachers of Mathematics. (2007). *Mathematics teaching today: Professional standards for teaching mathematics.* Reston, VA: Author

Nelson, D., Joseph, G. G., & Williams, J. (1993). *Multicultural mathematics: Teaching mathematics from a global perspective.* Oxford, UK: Oxford University Press.

Patton, J.R., Cronin, M.E., Bassett, D.S., & Koppel, A.E. (1998). A life skills approach to mathematics instruction: Preparing students with learning disabilities for the real-life math demands of adulthood. In D. Rivera (Ed.), *Mathematics education for students with learning disabilities* (pp. 201-218). Austin, TX: Pro-Ed.

Reid, R., Gonzalez, J. E., Nordness, P. D., Trout, A., & Epstein, M. H. (2004). A meta-analysis of the academic status of students with emotional/behavioral disturbance. *Journal of Special Education, 38,* 130–143.

Reisman, F. K. (1977). *Diagnostic teaching of elementary school mathematics: Methods and content.* Chicago: Rand McNally.

Rivera, D. P., & Smith, D. D. (1987). Influence of modeling on acquisition and generalization of computational skills: A summary of research findings from three sites. *Learning Disability Quarterly, 10,* 69–80.

Rosenblum, L. P., & Amato, S. (2004). Preparation in and use of the Nemeth Braille Code for Mathematics by teachers of students with visual impairments. *Journal of Visual Impairment & Blindness, 98,* 484–495.

Sherman, H. J., Richardson, L. I., & Yard, G. J. (2009). *Teaching learners who struggle with mathematics* (2nd ed.). Upper Saddle River, NJ: Merrill/Pearson.

Shiah, R. L., Mastropieri, M. A., Scruggs, T. E., & Fulk, B. J. M. (1994–1995). The effects of computer assisted instruction on the mathematical problem solving of students with learning disabilities. *Exceptionality, 5,* 131–161.

Stein, M., Kinder, D., Silbert, J., & Carnine, D. (2006). *Designing effective mathematics instruction* (4th ed.). Upper Saddle River, NJ: Merrill/Prentice Hall.

Stewart, D. A., & Kluwin, T. N. (2001). *Teaching deaf and hard of hearing students: Content, strategies, and curriculum.* Boston: Allyn & Bacon.

Tucker, B. F., Singleton, A. H., & Weaver, T. L. (2006). *Teaching mathematics to all children: Designing and adapting instruction to meet the needs of diverse learners* (2nd ed.). Upper Saddle River, NJ: Merrill/Prentice Hall.

Uberti, H., Mastropieri, M. A., & Scruggs, T. E. (2004). Check it off: Individualizing a math algorithm for students with disabilities via self-monitoring checklists. *Intervention in School and Clinic, 39,* 269–275.

Van Luit, J. E. H., & Schopman, E. A. M. (2000). Improving early numeracy of young children with special educational needs. *Remedial and Special Education, 21,* 27–40.

Zaslavsky, C. (1995). *The multicultural math classroom: Bringing in the world.* Portsmouth, NH: Heinemann.

Zaslavsky, C. (1999). *Africa counts: Number and pattern in African cultures* (3rd ed.). Chicago: Lawrence Hill.

Chapter 15

Albert, L. R., & Ammer, J. J. (2004). Lesson planning and delivery. In B. K. Lenz, D. D. Deshler, & B. R. Kissam (Eds.), *Teaching content to all: Evidence-based inclusive practices in middle and secondary schools* (pp. 195–220). Boston: Allyn & Bacon.

Bakken, J. P., Mastropieri, M. A., & Scruggs, T. E. (1997). Reading comprehension of expository science material and students with learning disabilities: A comparison of strategies. *Journal of Special Education, 31,* 300–324.

Berkeley, S. L., Marshak, L., Mastropieri, M. A., & Scruggs, T. E. (2008, April). *Improving student comprehension of social studies text: A self-questioning strategy for inclusive middle school classes.* Paper presented at the annual meeting of the American Educational Research Association, New York.

Best, R. M., Rowe, M., Ozuru, Y., & McNamara, D. S. (2005). Deep-level comprehension of science texts: The role of the reader and the text. *Topics in Language Disorders, 25,* 65–83.

Bos, C. S., & Anders, P. L. (1987). Semantic feature analysis: An interactive teaching strategy for facilitating learning from text. *Learning Disabilities Focus, 3*(1), 55–59.

Bos, C. S., & Anders, P. L. (1990). Effects of interactive vocabulary instruction on the vocabulary learning and reading comprehension of junior high learning disabled students. *Learning Disability Quarterly, 13,* 31–42.

Bos, C. S., Anders, P. L., Filip, D., & Jaffe, L. E. (1989). The effects of an interactive instructional strategy for enhancing reading comprehension and content area learning for students with learning disabilities. *Journal of Learning Disabilities, 22*(6), 384–390.

Boyle, J. R., & Weishaar, M. (1997). The effects of expert-generated versus student-generated cognitive organizers on the reading comprehension of students with learning disabilities. *Learning Disabilities Research & Practice, 12,* 228–251.

Bulgren, J. A. (2004). Effective content area instruction for all students. In T. E. Scruggs & M. A. Mastropieri (Eds.), *Research in secondary schools: Advances in learning and behavioral disabilities* (Vol. 17, pp. 147–174). Oxford, UK: Elsevier.

Bulgren, J. A., Deshler, D. D., & Schumaker, J. B. (1993). *The content enhancement series: The concept mastery routine.* Lawrence, KS: Edge Enterprises.

Chiappetta, E. L., & Koballa, T. R. (2006). *Science instruction in the middle and secondary schools: Developing fundamental knowledge and skills for teachers* (6th ed.). Upper Saddle River, NJ: Merrill/Prentice Hall.

Caffrey, E., & Fuchs, D. (2007). Differences in performance between students with learning disabilities and mild mental retardation: Implications for categorical instruction. *Learning Disabilities Research & Practice, 22,* 119–128.

Cook, L. K., & Mayer, R. E. (1988). Teaching readers about the structure of scientific text. *Journal of Educational Psychology, 80,* 448–456.

Cooper, G., & Cooper. G. (2001). *New virtual field trips.* Westport, CT: Libraries Unlimited.

Deshler, D. D., & Schumaker, J. B. (2006). *Teaching adolescents with disabilities: Accessing the general education curriculum.* Thousand Oaks, CA: Corwin.

Driver, R., Asoko, H., Leach, J., Mortimer, E., & Scott, P. (1994). Constructing scientific knowledge in the classroom. *Educational Researcher, 23*(7), 5–12.

Echevarria, J., & Graves, A. (2003). *Sheltered content instruction: Teaching English Language Learners with diverse abilities* (2nd ed.). Boston: Allyn & Bacon.

Ferretti, R. P., MacArthur, C. D., & Okolo, C. M. (2001). Teaching for historical understanding in inclusive classrooms. *Learning Disability Quarterly, 24,* 59–71.

Ferretti, R. P., & Okolo, C. M. (1996). Authenticity in learning: Multimedia design projects in the social studies for students with disabilities. *Journal of Learning Disabilities, 29,* 450–460.

Fontana, J. L. (2004). Social studies and students with disabilities. Current status of instruction and a review of intervention research with middle and high school students. In T. E. Scruggs & M. A. Mastropieri (Eds.), *Research in secondary schools: Advances in learning and behavioral disabilities* (Vol. 17, pp. 175–205). Oxford, UK: Elsevier.

Good, T. L., & Brophy, J. E. (2007). *Looking in classrooms* (10th ed.). Boston: Allyn & Bacon.

Heller, K. W. (2005). Adaptations and instruction in science and social studies. In S. J. Best, K. W. Heller, & J. L. Bigge (Eds.), *Teaching individuals with physical or multiple disabilities* (5th ed., pp. 471–499). Upper Saddle River, NJ: Merrill/Prentice Hall.

Horton, S. V., Boone, R. A., & Lovitt, T. C. (1990). Teaching social studies to learning disabled high school students: Effects of a hypertext study guide. *British Journal of Educational Technology, 21,* 118–131.

Horton, S. V., & Lovitt, T. C. (1989). Using study guides with three classifications of secondary students. *Journal of Special Education, 22,* 447–462.

Jitendra, A., Nolet, V., Xin, Y. P., Gomez, O., Renouf, K., Iskold, L., & DaCosta, J. (2001). An analysis of middle school geography textbooks: Implications for students with learning problems. *Reading & Writing Quarterly: Overcoming Learning Difficulties, 17,* 151–173.

Kim, A., Vaughn, S., Wanzek, J., & Wei, S. (2004). Graphic organizers and their effects on the reading comprehension of students with LD: A synthesis of research. *Journal of Learning Disabilities, 37,* 105–118.

King-Sears, M. E., Mercer, C. D., & Sindelar, P. T. (1992). Toward independence with keyword mnemonics: A strategy for science vocabulary instruction. *Remedial and Special Education, 13,* 22–33.

King-Sears, M. E., & Mooney, J. F. (2004). Teaching content in an academically diverse class. In B. K. Lenz, D. D. Deshler, & B. R. Kissam (Eds.), *Teaching content to all: Evidence-based inclusive practices in middle and secondary schools* (pp. 221–257). Boston: Allyn & Bacon.

Kumar, D. D., Ramasamy, R., & Stefanich, G. P. (2001). *Science instruction for students with visual impairments.* ERIC Digest. ERIC Clearinghouse for Science, Mathematics, and Environmental Education. (ERIC Document Reproduction Service Number ED464805)

Lenz, B. K., Bulgren, J., Kissam, B. R., & Taymans, J. (2004). SMARTER planning for academic diversity. In B. K. Lenz, D. D. Deshler, & B. R. Kissam (Eds.), *Teaching content to all: Evidence-based inclusive practices in middle and secondary schools* (pp. 47–77). Boston: Allyn & Bacon.

Lenz, B. K., Deshler, D. D., & Kissam, B. R. (Eds.). (2004). *Teaching content to all: Evidence-based inclusive practices in middle and secondary schools.* Boston: Allyn & Bacon.

MacArthur, C. A., Ferretti, R. P., & Okolo, C. M. (2002). On defending controversial viewpoints: Debates of sixth graders about the desirability of early 20th century American immigration. *Learning Disabilities Research & Practice, 17,* 160–172.

Maheady, L., Sacca, M. K., & Harper, G. F. (1988). Classwide peer tutoring with mildly handicapped high school students. *Exceptional Children, 55,* 52–59.

Marshak, L. (2008). *Curriculum enhancements in inclusive social studies classrooms: Effects on students with and without disabilities.* Unpublished doctoral dissertation, George Mason University, Fairfax, VA.

Mastropieri, M. A., & Scruggs, T. E. (1993). *A practical guide for teaching science to students with special needs in inclusive settings.* Austin, TX: Pro-Ed.

Mastropieri, M. A., & Scruggs, T. E. (2002). *Effective instruction for special education* (3rd ed.). Austin, TX: Pro-Ed.

Mastropieri, M. A., Scruggs, T. E., Boon, R., & Carter, K. B. (2001). Correlates of inquiry learning in science: Constructing concepts of density and buoyancy. *Remedial and Special Education, 22,* 130–137.

Mastropieri, M. A., Scruggs, T. E., & Graetz, J. (2005). Cognition and learning in inclusive high school chemistry classes. In T. E. Scruggs & M. A. Mastropieri (Eds.), *Cognition and learning in diverse settings: Advances in learning and behavioral disabilities* (Vol. 18, pp. 107–118). Oxford, UK: Elsevier Science.

Mastropieri, M. A., Scruggs, T. E., Mantzicopoulos, P. Y., Sturgeon, A., Goodwin, L., & Chung, S. (1998). "A place where living things affect and depend on each other": Qualitative and quantitative outcomes associated with inclusive science teaching. *Science Education, 82,* 163–179.

Mastropieri, M. A., Scruggs, T. E., & Marshak, L. (2008). Training teachers, parents, and peers to implement effective teaching strategies for content area learning. In T. E. Scruggs & M. A. Mastropieri (Eds.), *Personal Preparation: Advances in learning and behavioral disabilities* (Vol. 21, pp. 311–329). Bingley, UK: Emerald.

Mastropieri, M. A., Scruggs, T. E., Norland, J., Berkeley, S., McDuffie, K., Tornquist, E. H., & Conners, N. (2006). Differentiated curriculum enhancement in inclusive middle school science: Effects on classroom and high-stakes tests. *Journal of Special Education, 40,* 130–137.

Mastropieri, M. A., Scruggs, T. E., Spencer, V., & Fontana, J. (2003). Promoting success in high school world history: Peer tutoring versus guided notes. *Learning Disabilities Research & Practice, 18,* 52–65.

Mastropieri, M. A., Sweda, J., & Scruggs, T. E. (2000). Putting mnemonic strategies to work in an inclusive classroom. *Learning Disabilities Research & Practice, 15,* 69–74.

McGinnis, J. R., & Stefanich, G. P. (2007). Special needs and talents in science learning. In S. K. Abell & N. G. Lederman (Eds.), *Handbook of research in science education* (pp. 287–317). Mahwah, NJ: Erlbaum.

McCormick, S., & Cooper, J. O. (1991). Can SQ3R facilitate learning disabled students' literal comprehension of expository test? Three experiments. *Reading Psychology, 12,* 239–271.

O'Brien, J. (2000). Enabling all students to learn in the laboratory of democracy. *Intervention in School and Clinic, 35,* 195–206.

Parker, W. C. (2008). *Social studies in elementary education* (13th ed.). Upper Saddle River, NJ: Merrill/Prentice Hall.

Paxton, R. J. (1999). A deafening silence: History textbooks and the students who read them. *Review of Educational Research, 69,* 315–339.

Pence, L. E., Workman, H. J., & Riecke, P. (2003). Effective laboratory experiences for students with disabilities: The role of a student laboratory assistant. *Journal of Chemical Education, 80,* 295–298.

Schumaker, J., & Deshler, D. (2003). Can students with LD become competent writers? *Learning Disability Quarterly, 26,* 129–141.

Schumaker, J. B., Deshler, D. D., Alley, G. R., Warner, M. M., & Denton, P. H. (1982). Multipass: A learning strategy for improving reading comprehension. *Learning Disability Quarterly, 5,* 295–304.

Scruggs, T. E., & Mastropieri, M. A. (1994). Refocusing microscope activities for special students. *Science Scope, 17,* 74–78.

Scruggs, T. E., & Mastropieri, M. A. (1995a). Science education for students with behavior disorders. *Education and Treatment of Children, 3,* 322–334.

Scruggs, T. E., & Mastropieri, M. A. (1995b). Science and mental retardation: An analysis of curriculum features and learner characteristics. *Science Education, 79,* 251–271.

Scruggs, T. E., & Mastropieri, M. A. (2007). Science learning in special education: The case for constructed vs. instructed learning. *Exceptionality, 15,* 57–74.

Scruggs, T. E., Mastropieri, M. A., Bakken, J. P., & Brigham, F. J. (1993). Reading vs. doing. The relative effectiveness of textbook-based and inquiry-oriented approaches to science education. *Journal of Special Education, 27,* 1–15.

Scruggs, T. E., Mastropieri, M. A., & Wolfe, S. (1995). Scientific reasoning of students with mental retardation: Investigating preconceptions and conceptual change. *Exceptionality, 5,* 223–244.

Simmons, D., & Kaméenui, E. J. (1999). *Toward successful inclusion of students with disabilities: The architecture of instruction.* Reston, VA: Council for Exceptional Children.

Simpkins, P. M., Mastropieri, M. A., & Scruggs, T. E. (in press). Differentiated curriculum enhancements in inclusive 5th grade science classes. *Remedial and Special Education.*

Slocum, T. A. (2004). Direct instruction: The big ideas. In D. J. Moran & R. W. Malott (Eds.), *Evidence-based educational methods* (pp. 81–94). San Diego, CA: Elsevier Academic Press.

Spencer, V. G., Scruggs, T. E., & Mastropieri, M. A. (2003). Content area learning in middle school social studies classrooms and students with emotional or behavioral disorders: A comparison of strategies. *Behavioral Disorders, 28,* 77–93.

Sullivan, G. S., Mastropieri, M. A., & Scruggs, T. E. (1995). Reasoning and remembering: Coaching thinking with students with learning disabilities. *Journal of Special Education, 29,* 310–322.

Tomlinson, C. A. (2005). *How to differentiate instruction in mixed ability classrooms.* Upper Saddle River, NJ: Merrill/Prentice Hall.

Trowbridge, L. W., Bybee, R. W., & Carlson-Powell, J. (2004). *Teaching secondary school science: Strategies for developing scientific literacy* (8th ed.). Upper Saddle River, NJ: Merrill/Prentice Hall.

Williams, J. P. (2003). Teaching text structure to improve reading comprehension. In H. L. Swanson, K. R. Harris, & S. Graham (Eds.), *Handbook of learning disabilities* (pp. 293–305). New York: Guilford Press.

Woodward, J., & Noell, J. (1992). Science instruction at the secondary level: Implications for students with learning disabilities. In D. Carnine & E. J. Kameénui (Eds.), *Higher order thinking: Designing curriculum for mainstreamed students* (pp. 39–58). Austin, TX: Pro-Ed.

Chapter 16

Asselin, S. B., Todd-Allen, M., & deFur, S. (1998). Transition coordinators: Define yourselves. *Teaching Exceptional Children, 30,* 11–15.

Bakken, J. P., & Obiokor, F. E. (2008). *Transition planning for students with disabilities: What educators and service providers can do.* Springfield, IL: Charles C. Thomas.

Beakley, B. A., & Yoder, S. L. (1998). Middle schoolers learn community skills. *Teaching Exceptional Children, 30*(3), 16–21.

Carter, E. W., Clark, N. M., Cushing, L. S., & Kennedy, C. H. (2005). Moving from elementary to middle school: Supporting a smooth transition for students with severe disabilities. *Teaching Exceptional Children, 37*(3), 8–19.

Clark, G. M., & Patton, J. R. (2006). *TPI-UV: Transition planning inventory: Updated version.* Austin, TX: Pro-Ed.

Cronin, M. E., Patton, J. R., & Wood, S. J. (2007). *Life skills instruction for all students with special needs* (2nd ed.). Austin, TX: Pro-Ed.

Dunn, C., Chambers, D., & Rabren, K. (2004). Variables affecting students' decisions to drop out of school. *Remedial and Special Education, 25,* 314–323.

Field, S., & Hoffman, A. (2002). Lessons learned from implementing the steps to self-determination curriculum. *Remedial and Special Education, 23,* 90–99.

Flexer, R. W., Simmons, T. J., Luft, P., & Baer, R. M. (2005). *Transition planning for secondary students with disabilities* (2nd ed.). Upper Saddle River, NJ: Merrill/Prentice Hall.

Frankland, H. C., Turnbull, A. P., Wehmeyer, M. L., & Blackmountain, L. (2004). An exploration of the self determination construct and disability as it relates to the Dine (Navajo) culture. *Education and Training in Developmental Disabilities, 39,* 191–205.

Glago, K., Mastropieri, M. A., & Scruggs, T. E. (in press). Improving problem solving of elementary students with mild disabilities. *Remedial and Special Education.*

Gordon, H. R. D. (2007). *The history and growth of career and technical education in America* (3rd ed.). Long Grove, IL: Waveland.

Katsiyannis, A., Zhang, D., & Ryan, J. B. (2007). High-stakes testing and students with disabilities: Challenges and promises. *Journal of Disability Policy Studies, 18,* 160–167.

Kochnar, C. (1998). Analysis of the special populations provisions in the 1998 Carl D. Perkins Vocational Technical Education Act Amendments. *Journal for Vocational Special Needs Education, 21,* 3–20.

Lanford, A. G., & Cary, L. G. (2000). Graduation requirements for students with disabilities. *Remedial and Special Education, 21,* 152–160.

Lang, S. (2006, May 16). Two-tiered diploma system is fair to all. *Boston Globe.* Retrieved April 1, 2008, from http://www.boston.com/news/globe/editorial_opinion/oped/artcles/2006/05/16/two_tiered_diploma_system_is_fair_to_all/

Lipow, V. (n.d.). *Don't let disabilities get in the way of getting the job.* Retrieved June 8, 2008, from the monster.com Website, http://career-advice.monster.com/workers-with-disabilities/workers-with-disabilities/Dont-Let-Disabilities-Get-in-the-Wa/home.aspx

Loeding, B. L., & Greenan, J. P. (1999). Relationship between self-ratings by sensory impaired students and teachers' ratings of generalizable skills. *Journal of Visual Impairment & Blindness, 93,* 716–727.

Loyd, R. J., & Brolin, D. E. (1997). *Life centered education: Modified curriculum for individuals with moderate and special needs.* Arlington, VA: Council for Exceptional Children.

Parker, R. M. (2002). *OASIS-3: Occupational aptitude survey and interest schedule* (3rd ed.). Austin, TX: Pro-Ed.

Pierangelo, R., & Giuliani, G. A. (2004). *Transition services in special education: A practical approach.* Boston: Allyn & Bacon.

Sarkees-Wircenski, M., & Scott, J. L. (2003). *Special populations in career and technical education.* Homewood, IL: American Technical Publishers.

Science standards of learning for Virginia public schools. (2003). Commonwealth of Virginia: Richmond, VA: Board of Education.

Test, D. W., Fowler, C. H., Wood, W. M., Brewer, D. M., & Eddy, S. (2005). A conceptual framework of self-advocacy for students with disabilities. *Remedial and Special Education, 26,* 43–54.

Test, D. W., & Neale, M. (2004). Using the self-advocacy strategy to increase middle graders' IEP participation. *Journal of Behavioral Education, 13,* 135–145.

U.S. Department of Education. (2006). *Carl D. Perkins Career and Technical Education Act of 2006: Reauthorization of Perkins.* Washington, DC: Author. Retrieved April 1, 2008, from http://www.ed.gov/policy/sectech/leg/perkins/index.html

Van Reusen, A. K., Bos, C. A., Schumaker, J. B., & Deshler, D. D. (1994). *The self-advocacy strategy for education and transition planning.* Lawrence, KS: Edge Enterprises.

Wehman, P. (2006). *Life beyond the classroom: Transition strategies for young people with disabilities* (4th ed.). Baltimore: Brookes.

Woog, D. (n.d.). *How workers with disabilities can assess job fit.* Retrieved June 8, 2008, from the monster.com Website, http://career-advice.monster.com/workers-with-disabilities/workers-with-disabilities/How-Workers-with-Disabilities-Can-A/home.aspx

Wu, M., & Greenan, J. P. (2003). The effects of a generalizable mathematics skills instructional intervention on the mathematics achievement of learners in secondary CTE programs. *Journal of Industrial Teacher Education, 40*(2), 23–50.

Mather, N., 58
Mathes, P. G., 56, 186, 188, 301, 311, 317
Mathews, J., 98
Mathur, S. R., 67, 173
Matson, J. L., 171
Matson, M. L., 171
Mayer, G. R., 166
Mayer, R. E., 366
McCann, B., 42
McConnell, S., 171
McCormick, S., 369
McCray, E. D., 16
McDuffie, K. A., 42
McDuffie, M. A., 44
McElroy, K., 228
McGinnis, J. R., 377
McGough, S. M., 303, 305
McKinney, J. D., 228
McLaughlin, T. F., 158
McLean, P., 341
McLoughlin, J. A., 274, 276, 277
McMaster, D., 83
McMaster, K. L., 186–187, 187, 313
McMaster, K. N., 195, 214
McNamara, D. S., 366
McNamara, J. K., 58
McNaughton, D., 353
Meador, D. M., 67
Meadow-Orlans, K. P., 97
Meers, G. D., 292
Megivern, M., 114
Mehring, T. A., 85
Meister, C., 315
Meltzer, L. J., 264
Mercer, A. R., 333
Mercer, C. D., 56, 58, 59, 288, 308, 310, 333, 340, 370
Mercer, K. D., 308
Metz, D. E., 52, 97
Meyer, L., 303
Michael, R. J., 84
Michaud, L., 81
Miksic, S., 117
Milich, R., 72
Miller, L., 88, 258, 300, 305
Miller, M. D., 308
Miller, S. P., 332, 340
Milsom, A. S., 209
Milson, A., 209
Mirenda, P., 52, 307
Mishna, F., 209
Misra, A., 162
Mitchem, K., 269
Mock, D., 56, 57
Mohan, A., 62
Mohler, L. J., 189
Moni, K. B., 63
Monroe, C., 171
Montague, M., 170, 228, 229, 312, 332, 347, 349, 353
Montgomery-Grimes, D. J., 208
Moon, S., 104
Mooney, J. F., 363, 370
Moore, R. J., 173

Morgan, P. L., 57, 211
Moritimer, E., 387
Morrison, G. M., 66
Morse, A. B., 278
Morsink, C. V., 43
Mostert, M. P., 67, 173
Muccigrosso, L., 118
Mulick, J. A., 61, 62, 91
Munk, D., 293
Murawski, W. W., 43, 44
Murdick, N. L., 10, 13, 41, 127
Murphy, J. A., 301
Murray, C., 43, 44
Myles, B. S., 178, 232, 253
Nafpaktitis, M., 166
Nagle, H. A. L., 55
Navon, J., 104
Neale, M., 406, 407
Nelson, C. M., 118, 151, 152, 156, 157, 158, 160, 161, 165, 166, 167, 181, 225, 229
Nelson, D., 189, 333
Nelson, J. R., 167
Nelson, L. G. L., 235
Nelson, M., 20
Nicholls, J. G., 204
Noell, J., 387
Nolet, V., 272
Nordness, P. D., 67, 300, 332
Norland, J. J., 195, 196, 258
Norton, D. E., 112
Nougaret, A., 16
Obiakor, F. E., 85, 92, 111, 276, 403, 413
O'Brien, J., 383
O'Connor, R. E., 192, 193, 195, 308
Odom, S. L., 181
Ogle, D. M., 311
Okolo, C. M., 191, 386
Okovita, H. W., 236
O'Leary, S. G., 228
O'Malley, P. M., 117
O'Melia, M. C., 256
Omizo, M. M., 209
Omizo, S. A., 209
Oortwijn, M. B., 189
Ortiz, A. A., 110, 111
Ortiz, A. B., 112, 258
Osborn, R. G., 67
O'Shea, D., 310
O'Shea, L. J., 310
Ostertag, V., 111, 112, 117
Oswald, D. P., 55, 65
Oswald, K., 167
Ott, E. S., 162
Ovando, C. J., 110
Overton, S., 46
Owens, R. E., 52, 53, 97
Ozuru, Y., 366
Padeliadu, S., 211
Pagliaro, C., 332
Paivio, A., 236
Pakulski, L. S., 98
Palincsar, A. S., 313, 315
Palmer, D. S., 20, 22

Parker, R. M., 409
Parker, W. C., 361, 376, 383
Parolin, R., 280
Patrick, B. C., 214
Patterson, K. B., 263
Patton, 356
Patton, J. M., 91, 104, 108, 224, 276
Patton, J. R., 40, 60, 64, 356, 409
Pauk, W., 265, 289
Paxton, R. J., 366
Pear, J., 90, 152, 154, 217
Peaster, L., 57
Pence, L. E., 377
Pereira, L., 65
Perin, D., 326
Perner, D. E., 127
Perry, N., 313
Petersen, S., 85
Peterson, F., 288
Peterson, R. F., 152
Phillips, N. B., 282, 308
Phillips, S. E., 277
Phillipsen, L., 178
Pickett, A. L., 45
Pierangelo, R., 40, 405, 413
Pierce, T., 332
Pinnell, G. S., 301, 307
Plumb, I. J., 93
Plumber, P. J., 226
Pollard, R. R., 292
Polloway, E. A., 32, 40, 88, 253, 280, 292, 300, 305, 310
Polsgrove, L., 69
Porter, M., 356
Potucek, J., 89
Poulsen, M. K., 118
Power, M. H., 277
Pressley, M., 58, 299, 300, 301, 302, 304, 310, 318
Pullen, P. C., 56, 58, 59, 87, 97, 305
Purdie, N., 227
Putnam, M. L., 230, 279
Rabren, K., 391
Rafoth, M. A., 252
Raines, J. M., 236
Ramasamy, R., 377
Rana, R., 58, 333
Rankin, J., 301, 302
Raskind, W. H., 56
Reagan, T., 97
Redding-Rhodes, J., 313
Redl, F., 225
Reed, P., 85, 96, 320
Reid, R. R., 58, 67, 68, 228, 300, 332
Reisman, F. K., 347
Reiss, S. M., 105
Renzulli, J. S., 104, 105
Reschly, D. J., 108, 112, 119
Reynolds, M., 301
Riccio, C. A., 72
Richards, C., 112
Riecke, P., 377
Riggs, C. G., 45
Rimland, B., 20

Rimm, S. B., 10, 104, 105, 106
Ritter, S., 291
Rivera, D. P., 347
Rivet, T. T., 171
Roberts, G., 33, 318
Roberts, P. H., 56
Roblee, K., 156, 225
Rocha, M. L., 230
Rock, M. L., 32
Rohwer, W. D., 236
Rojewski, J. W., 292, 293
Rooney, K. J., 228
Rosen, L. S., 228
Rosenberg, M. S., 166, 256
Rosenblum, L. P., 332
Rosenshine, B., 145, 315
Ross, D. B., 95
Rothstein, L. F., 10
Routman, R., 300
Rowe, M., 366
Rubin, L., 115
Ruble, L. A., 88
Rudenga, E. A. V., 301
Rudy, K., 115, 120
Ruhl, K. L., 162, 256, 291, 353
Ryan, J. B., 411
Ryndak, D. L., 92
Rynders, J., 178, 179
Sabornie, E. J., 131
Sacca, M. K., 188, 374
Saddler, B., 185, 228
Sáenz, L. M., 186
Safran, S. P., 167
Salend, S. J., 99, 108, 224, 225, 278, 279, 280, 281, 285
Sampson, P. D., 61
Sapon-Shevin, M., 93
Sarkees-Wircenski, M., 391, 394, 396, 399, 400, 401, 402
Saunders, L., 57
Sawatsky, D., 313
Scavarda, M., 118
Schalock, R. L., 61
Schirmer, B. R., 285, 303, 305
Schlagal, B., 319, 321, 322
Schlosser, R. W., 323
Schneider, B. H., 178
Schoenbrodt, L., 79
Schopman, E. A. M., 334
Schreibman, L., 230
Schulenberg, J. E., 117
Schulte, A. A. G., 276
Schultz, F., 72
Schultz, R., 194
Schumaker, J. B., 250, 256, 257, 261, 264, 268, 288, 291, 306, 315, 363, 369, 370, 406
Schwanz, K. A., 72
Schwartz, I. S., 158
Schwenn, J. O., 85
Scott, J., 87, 230
Scott, J. A., 308
Scott, J. L., 391, 394, 396, 399, 400, 401, 402
Scott, P., 387

personal digital assistants (PDAs), 232
recordkeeping software, 281
self-monitoring systems, 163
study skills, software for, 269
time management tools, 142
working with computers and peers, 191
Television captioning, 98
TELLS fact or fiction strategy, 311
Terminal illness, 85
Testing
    competency-based, 277–279
    criterion-referenced, 279–282
    curriculum-based measurements, 282–283
    diversity and, 13–14, 108
    formative tests, 144–147, 274
    grading, 292–293
    norm-referenced, 274–277
    performance assessments, 283–285
    portfolio assessments, 285–288
    statewide, 277–279
    teacher-made, 279–282
    test-taking skills, 288–292
    types of test, 273–275
Test-taking skills, 276–277
Textbook-oriented approach, teaching, 361, 366–376, 383
Text enhancements, 310
Text-to-speech software, 309, 412
Three R's strategy, 265. *See also* Note taking
Time, math skills, 350
Timelines, interventions, 31–32
Timelines, social studies, 371–372
Time management, teachers, 141–144
Timeouts, 160–161
Toddlers, 14
Token systems (economies), 158, 218
Total communication, hearing impaired, 97
Touch Math materials, 336–337, 343
Touch, sense of, 95
Tourette syndrome, 66

Trade education, 392
Transitional activities, 141–142
Transition Planning Inventory, 409
Transitions
    assessments, 409
    graduation, 410–412
    overview, 402–404
    promoting, 404–410
    services, 14, 40–41
Translators, multilingual, 110
Transportation, 19
Traumatic brain injury, 9, 79, 81
TRAVEL, 371
Treatment-resisters, 57
TTY (adapted telephone equipment), 98
Tuberculosis, 78
Tutoring, peers, 182–189
U.S. Department of Education, 16
Universal design (UD), 132–133
Validity, tests, 274
Verbal associations, 237–239
Video presentations, 232–233, 378
Violence, 118
Visual impairments, 77, 94–96
    career information software, 412
    IDEA disability category, 9
    laboratory activities, 378
    math skills, 332
    peer assistance, 180
    reading adaptations, 302–303
    textbook adaptations, 374
Vocabulary
    arithmetic, 346
    career and technical education, 396
    listening, 258
    mnemonics, 239
    presentations, 135
    reading comprehension, 310
    response-to-intervention (RTI), 318
    semantic feature analysis, 363

sight words, 306–307
    textbook strategies, 373
Vocational education, 391–393, 402–410
Vocational Rehabilitation Act (1973), 11–12, 72, 78
Voice disorders, 52–55
Volume, 352–353
Watches, self-monitoring systems, 163
Web sites
    Boardmaker, 80
    career information, 412
    federal government updates, 16
    graphic organizers, 384
    literacy instruction, 309
    manipulatives, math, 353–354
    News-2-You, 80
    podcasts, 212
    recordkeeping software, 281
    self-monitoring systems, 163
    using, 266–268
Whole language, 300–301
Word problems, 340–342, 348–350
Word-recognition software, 317
Word wall chart, 306–307
Working memory, 231. *See also* Memory
Worksheet activities, modifying, 364–365
Write: Outloud, 309, 317
Writing
    handwriting skills, 319–321
    numbers, 335–336
    reports and projects, 268–270
    response-to-intervention (RTI), 318
    software for, 309
    spelling, 321–323
    technologies/software for, 327–328
    written communication, teaching, 323–328
    written tests, 291
Zaner-Bloser handwriting system, 320
Zero reject principle, 13